Practicing Therapeutic Jurisprudence

Assignments: Chapter 15 ✓
Chapter 2 ✓

Practicing Therapeutic Jurisprudence

Law as a Helping Profession

Edited by

Dennis P. Stolle

David B. Wexler

Bruce J. Winick

Carolina Academic Press
Durham, North Carolina

ISBN 0-89089-941-X
LCCN 00-107065

Cover design by Eileen Russell

Carolina Academic Press
700 Kent Street
Durham, North Carolina 27701
Telephone (919) 489-7486
Fax (919) 493-5668
E-mail: cap@cap-press.com
www.cap-press.com

Printed in the United States of America

For my father
D.P.S.

For Rhoda
D.B.W.

*For Soia Mentschikoff, mother of legal realism, who brought
me from law practice into legal education, was my mentor, friend,
and on one occasion, lawyer, and who would have liked therapeutic
jurisprudence and its contribution to the craft of lawyering;
and for my new granddaughter, Beatrix Pearl Kinney Winick,
born June 26, 2000, who one day will read this book and
I hope will apply its principles in whatever she decides to do.*
B.J.W.

Contents

Acknowledgments   xi

Foreword, by Edward A. Dauer   xiii

Introduction, by Dennis P. Stolle   xv

PART I — INTEGRATING THERAPEUTIC JURISPRUDENCE
AND PREVENTIVE LAW

Chapter 1   Integrating Preventive Law and Therapeutic
Jurisprudence: A Law and Psychology Based
Approach to Lawyering
Dennis P. Stolle, David B. Wexler,
Bruce J. Winick, and Edward A. Dauer   5

Chapter 2   Practicing Therapeutic Jurisprudence:
Psycholegal Soft Spots and Strategies
David B. Wexler   45

Chapter 3   Better Legal Counseling Through Empirical
Research: Identifying Psycholegal Soft Spots
and Strategies
Marc W. Patry, David B. Wexler,
Dennis P. Stolle, and Alan J. Tomkins   69

PART II — CIVIL PRACTICE

Chapter 4   Advance Directives, AIDS, and Mental Health:
TJ Preventive Law for the HIV-Positive Client
Dennis P. Stolle   83

Chapter 5   Legal Planning for Unmarried Committed
Partners: Empirical Lessons for a Preventive
and Therapeutic Approach
Jennifer K. Robbennolt and
Monica Kirkpatrick Johnson   113

Chapter 6   Preventive Lawyering Strategies to Mitigate
the Detrimental Effects of Clients' Divorces
on Their Children
Kathryn E. Maxwell   161

Chapter 7   Collaborative Law: What it is and Why
Lawyers Need to Know About It
Pauline H. Tesler   187

Chapter 8   A Therapeutic Jurisprudence and Preventive
Law Approach to Family Law
Stephen J. Anderer and David J. Glass   207

PART III — CRIMINAL PRACTICE

Chapter 9   Relapse Prevention Planning Principles for
Criminal Law Practice
David B. Wexler   237

Chapter 10   Redefining the Role of the Criminal Defense Lawyer
at Plea Bargaining and Sentencing: A Therapeutic
Jurisprudence/Preventive Law Model
Bruce J. Winick   245

PART IV — LITIGATION

Chapter 11   Therapeutic Jurisprudence and the Role of
Counsel in Litigation
Bruce J. Winick   309

PART V — ATTORNEY/CLIENT COMMUNICATIONS

Chapter 12   Client Denial and Resistance in the Advance
Directive Context: Reflections on How Attorneys
Can Identify and Deal With A Psycholegal Soft Spot
Bruce J. Winick   327

Chapter 13   Love, Hate, and Other Emotional Interference
in the Lawyer/Client Relationship
Marjorie A. Silver   357

Chapter 14   Affective Lawyering: The Emotional Dimensions
of the Lawyer-Client Relation
Linda G. Mills   419

VI — Therapeutic Jurisprudence and Legal Culture

Chapter 15   Therapeutic Jurisprudence and the Culture
of Critique
David B. Wexler   449

Afterword   The Role of Therapeutic Jurisprudence within
the Comprehensive Law Movement
Susan Daicoff   465

Appendix   Identification of Psycholegal Soft Spots
and Strategies   493

About the Contributors   499

About the Editors   503

Index   505

Acknowledgments

Bruce Winick thanks Dean Dennis O. Lynch for his and the law school's support, and his secretary Eileen Russell and work study/assistant Jaymy Bengio for their secretarial assistance. He also thanks research assistants Cheryl Potter, Tricia Shakelford, and Frank Anzalone. David Wexler thanks Deans Toni Massaro (University of Arizona) and Antonio Garcia Padilla (University of Puerto Rico) for their encouragement and support, Jessica Cousineau for her research assistance, and Norma Kelly for her secretarial and administrative services. Dennis Stolle gratefully acknowledges the support of the University of Nebraska Law/Psychology Program during a portion of the preparation of this volume and thanks many of his colleagues at Barnes & Thornburg for their encouragement. We also thank Carolina Academic Press, especially its President Keith Sipe, and also Tim Colton and Kathy Kay.

Special thanks goes to Ed Dauer and Susan Daicoff for contributing the Foreword and Afterword, respectively. Finally, we are most grateful to the authors who contributed to this volume and their publishers. In their order of appearance, they are:

Chapter 1 (Dennis P. Stolle, David B. Wexler, Bruce J. Winick, & Edward A. Dauer) "Integrating Preventive Law and Therapeutic Jurisprudence: A Law and Psychology Based Approach to Lawyering," 34 California Western Law Review 15 (1997). Reprinted with permission.

Chapter 2 (David B. Wexler) "Practicing Therapeutic Jurisprudence: Psycholegal Soft Spots and Strategies," 67 Revista Juridica Universidad de Puerto Rico 317 (1998). Reprinted with permission.

Chapter 3 (Marc W. Patry, David B. Wexler, Dennis P. Stolle, & Alan J. Tomkins) "Better Legal Counseling Through Empirical Research," 34 California Western Law Review 440 (1998). Reprinted with permission.

Chapter 4 (Dennis P. Stolle) "Advance Directives, AIDS, and Mental Health: TJ Preventive Law for the HIV-Positive Client," 4 Psychology, Public Policy & Law 954 (1998). Copyright 1998 by the American Psychological Association. Reprinted with permission.

Chapter 5 (Jennifer K. Robbennolt & Monica Kirkpatrick Johnson) "Legal Planning for Unmarried Committed Partners: Empirical Lessons for a Preventive and Therapeutic Approach," 41 Arizona Law Review 417 (1999). Copyright 1999 by the Arizona Board of Regents. Reprinted by permission.

Chapter 6 (Kathryn E. Maxwell) "Preventive Lawyering Strategies to Mitigate the Detrimental Effects of Client's Divorces on Their Children," 67 Revista Juridica Universidad de Puerto Rico 137 (1998). Reprinted with permission.

Chapter 7 (Pauline H. Tesler) "Collaborative Law: What it is and Why Lawyers Need to Know About It," 13 American Journal of Family Law 215 (1999). Reprinted with permission.

Chapter 8 (Stephen J. Anderer & David J. Glass) "A Therapeutic Jurisprudence and Preventive Law Approach to Family Law." Prepared specifically for this volume.

Chapter 9 (David B. Wexler) "Relapse Prevention Planning Principles for Criminal Law Practice." 5 Psychology, Public Policy & Law (1999, in press). Copyright 1999 by the American Psychological Association. Reprinted with permission.

Chapter 10 (Bruce J. Winick) "Redefining the Role of the Criminal Defense Lawyer at Plea Bargaining and Sentencing: A Therapeutic Jurisprudence/Preventive Law Model." 5 Psychology, Public Policy & Law (1999, in press). Copyright 1999 by the American Psychological Association. Reprinted with permission.

Chapter 11 (Bruce J. Winick) "Therapeutic Jurisprudence and the Role of Counsel in Litigation." 37 California Western Law Review (2000, in press). Reprinted with permission.

Chapter 12 (Bruce J. Winick) "Client Denial and Resistance in the Advance Directive Context: Reflections on How Attorneys Can Identify and Deal With A Psycholegal Soft Spot," 4 Psychology, Public Policy & Law 901 (1998). Copyright 1998 by the American Psychological Association. Reprinted with permission.

Chapter 13 (Marjorie A. Silver) "Love, Hate, and Other Emotional Interference in the Lawyer/Client Relationship," 6 Clinical Law Review 259 (1999). Reprinted with permission.

Chapter 14 (Linda G. Mills) "Affective Lawyering: The Emotional Dimensions of the Lawyer-Client Relation." Prepared specifically for this volume.

Chapter 15 (David B. Wexler) "Therapeutic Jurisprudence and the Culture of Critique," 10 The Journal of Contemporary Legal Issues 263 (1999). Copyright 1999 Journal of Contemporary Legal Issues. Reprinted with the permission of the Journal of Contemporary Legal Issues.

Foreword

Few things have captured the tide of the times so well. In the scant five years since Wexler and Winick first described the wide angle lens of Therapeutic Jurisprudence in their book "Law in a Therapeutic Key," TJ has become a managing partner in the enterprise of fashioning the 21st century's lawyer; and Wexler, Winick and Stolle are—though they might disclaim the role—the managers of TJ. It was their vision that uncovered the benefits of a liaison among TJ and Preventive Law and ADR and Creative Problem Solving, and the crises of purpose with which the profession and many of its members are grappling today: How might the humane objectives of law and lawyering be returned, from being the platitudes and abstractions that drive public policy to become the daily rewards of lawyers and their clients? Their energy continues to integrate the seemingly diverse ideas (and their proponents) that together offer promise for a new legal reality. This book is the latest product of that effort, and one of the most immediately useful.

This is no small or unimportant task. When the legal history of the twentieth century is written, it will in all likelihood tell of an unparalleled explosion of legal protections for those members of society perceived to be disadvantaged in a world otherwise red in tooth and claw. The resulting character was, perhaps, inevitable, for America has had two driving traditions. The first is cultural diversity.

In monocultural societies, norms are born in history, embedded in expectation and tradition, learned almost since weaning, seldom debated. The common denominators are the fabric of everyday life. In authoritarian societies, norms are simply dictated, even less often debated. In America—by hope and definition a non-authoritarian and poly-cultural place—there is little unanimity about norms, and much of our Constitutional structure is designed precisely to prevent the views of a majority from becoming inescapable common denominators. Lacking confidence in the universality of substance, we have invested heavily in the construction of process.

The second tradition has been, throughout our legal history, the adversarial nature of legal process. For better or worse, dialectical advocacy (with all of its effects and extremes) has been legal truth's primary source of nutrition. No wonder, then, that as American society matured to recognize the imperative of inclusiveness and the protection of the less advantaged, it would do so by erecting vast systems of rights, implemented through elaborate procedures, drawn with the colors of advocacy.

We are beginning now to understand the cost of all of this. Somehow, in the churning of the legal protections, we have lost important parts of the humanity of the people for whom the law is supposed to work. And so we have lost some part of the humanity of the law too—and no less, of those who practice it.

The many threads that weave in and out of Therapeutic Jurisprudence have this in common—a concern to recapture and reassert these missing meanings. Separately, they are significant threads. Together, they form a fabric—a sensitive and sensible new paradigm for what law and lawyering could be. TJ and its proponents are weaving that fabric. Few things show promise of changing the tide so well.

Edward A. Dauer
August 2000

Introduction

How can mental-health law maximize therapeutic outcomes? This was the fundamental question presented by my co-editors, David Wexler and Bruce Winick, when they formally introduced therapeutic jurisprudence as a distinct legal theory, about a decade ago. The subsequent impact of this question on mental-health law scholarship, and legal scholarship in general, has been nothing short of phenomenal. Therapeutic jurisprudence offered a fresh and creative new perspective, which served as a catalyst for a cooperative and truly interdisciplinary approach to legal scholarship. The result has been scores of authors writing hundreds of articles addressing this fundamental question in legal contexts ranging from traditional areas of mental-health law, such as involuntary commitment, to areas far beyond traditional mental-health law, such as commercial law and contracts.[1]

Much of the success of therapeutic jurisprudence stems from its refusal to displace other values or priorities. Like law and economics, which often asks "how can the law maximize economic utility?," therapeutic jurisprudence takes a quasi-utilitarian approach to jurisprudence, asking "how can the law maximize therapeutic outcomes?" However, therapeutic jurisprudence does not attempt to displace the maximization of economic utility with the maximization of therapeutic outcomes, nor does it attempt to trump individual rights, or other values or priorities, in the name of avoiding anti-therapeutic consequences. Rather, therapeutic jurisprudence places the psychological and emotional health of persons affected by the law and by legal actors as one important consideration among many.

The question of how to maximize therapeutic outcomes has most often been approached from a systemic, or "top-down," perspective. This systemic approach tends to focus on law reform and its methodology tends to identify anti-therapeutic (or potentially anti-therapeutic) aspects of existing laws, legal institutions, or legal procedures and then advocate specific legal reforms, often at the legislative level, with the intention of maximizing therapeutic outcomes. By the mid 1990's, though, my co-editors were also thinking about "bottom-up" approaches to therapeutic jurisprudence. That is, they were thinking not only about how laws could be *changed* to

---

1. *See e.g.*, David B. Wexler & Bruce J. Winick, Law in a Therapeutic Key (1996). *See also*, Therapeutic Jurisprudence Bibliography available at www.law.arizona.edu/uprintj.

be more therapeutic, but also about how *existing* laws could be more therapeutic *in application*. This approach of applying the law therapeutically, it was thought, would compliment the systemic approach and, perhaps, provide an important, and previously lacking, connection between therapeutic jurisprudence and the day-to-day work of legal practitioners.

At about the same time that my co-editors were considering an approach of applying the law therapeutically (though before I knew them), I was immersing myself in the literature of therapeutic jurisprudence as a graduate student in the University of Nebraska's Law and Psychology Program. Independent of my readings on therapeutic jurisprudence, at least initially, I was also studying articles and books on preventive law, mainly the work of Louis Brown and Edward Dauer. In contemporaneously studying these seemingly disparate literatures, I recognized many parallels in the underlying principles of these two theories as well as many potential synergies between them. It seemed that preventive law could lend to therapeutic jurisprudence practical procedures and client-counseling techniques that would both compliment the goals of therapeutic jurisprudence and provide a structure for applying the law therapeutically. In turn, therapeutic jurisprudence could enhance preventive law's interdisciplinary perspective and lend to preventive law a stronger empirical and theoretical grounding in the social sciences. Neither school, of course, needed the other, but both, it seemed, would profit from collaborative efforts.

I first began working through an integration of therapeutic jurisprudence and preventive law in the context of elder law and I submitted the resulting manuscript to *Behavioral Sciences and the Law* for publication.[2] Fortuitously, the manuscript's peer reviewers included David Wexler. David was intrigued by the strong parallels between the integration of therapeutic jurisprudence and preventive law and some of his recent thinking and writing, such as "Applying the Law Therapeutically,"[3] which, coincidentally, was in press at the time I was working on the elder-law manuscript. As a result of David's review of the elder-law manuscript, David and I met, began discussing therapeutic jurisprudence and preventive law, and quickly began working together on additional manuscripts.

Soon thereafter, I traveled to Denver to meet with Edward Dauer, Professor and Dean Emeritus at Denver University and then President of the National Center for Preventive Law. We discussed the projects that David and I had begun and, more generally, discussed the relationship between preventive law and therapeutic jurisprudence. Within a few months, David,

---

2. Dennis P. Stolle, *Professional Responsibility in Elder Law: A Synthesis of Preventive Law and Therapeutic Jurisprudence*, 14 BEHAV. SCI. & L. 257 (1996).

3. David B. Wexler, *Applying the Law Therapeutically*, 5 APPLIED & PREVENTIVE PSYCHOL. 179 (1996).

Bruce, Ed, myself, and others met in Los Angeles to begin planning a program of scholarship focused on integrating therapeutic jurisprudence and preventive law. The first step, it seemed, would be the preparation of a fully-integrated theory, to which we each would contribute. We first presented that theory at the May 1997 meeting of the Law and Society Association in St. Louis, Missouri. The Law and Society presentation elicited insightful comments from the audience, leading to a spirited and constructive discussion that continued over dinner and into the evening. That discussion formed the basis for, and essentially became, chapter one of this book—"Integrating Preventive Law and Therapeutic Jurisprudence: A Law and Psychology Based Approach to Lawyering." Together, Chapters One, Two, and Three present the fundamentals of therapeutic jurisprudence, preventive law, and the integrated theory, with particular emphasis on the practice, unique to the integrated theory, of identifying "psycholegal soft spots."

This book, however, is not intended to merely present a theory, but, rather, to present potential and actual applications of the principles underlying that theory, regardless of whether the application of those principles expressly proceeds under the name "therapeutic jurisprudence," "preventive law," or neither. To that end, Chapters Four through Fourteen present applications of the integrated theory as well as related theories, such as collaborative law and affective lawyering, in the contexts of civil practice, criminal practice, litigation, and client counseling. However, I believe that the scope of the potential applications of the principles underlying these theories is much broader than the few topic areas presented in this volume. My hope is that this book will encourage practitioners, scholars, teachers, and students of the law to take the application of these principles beyond the contexts presented in this volume and to more fully develop and apply them in such contexts as juvenile law, health law, commercial law, and tort law.

If the principles espoused in this book, regardless of whether or not they are advanced under the names "therapeutic jurisprudence" or "preventive law," are to have an impact on legal practice, the principles need to become part of law school education and, ultimately, the broader legal (and social) culture in which modern practitioners must function. Together, Chapter Fifteen and Susan Daicoff's Afterword consider the place of therapeutic jurisprudence in our "culture of critique," including the context in which that culture is perhaps most palpable, law school education. My hope, and that of my co-editors, is that the principles embodied in this book will become a part of law school education and that therapeutic concerns, a preventive orientation, and creative problem solving might, thereby, become as much the hallmarks of legal culture as argument, debate, and critique.

Dennis P. Stolle
August 2000

Practicing Therapeutic Jurisprudence

I.

Integrating Therapeutic Jurisprudence and Preventive Law

Integrating Preventive Law and Therapeutic Jurisprudence: A Law and Psychology Based Approach to Lawyering

Dennis P. Stolle
David B. Wexler
Bruce J. Winick
Edward A. Dauer

I. Introduction

This article grows out of a panel presentation and discussion held at the 1997 Annual Meeting of the Law & Society Association.[1] The presentation brought together proponents of both preventive law and therapeutic jurisprudence ("TJ") to consider the potential for an integration of these two fields. At the time of the presentation, two of the authors (Stolle & Wexler) had recently published a series of initial efforts at introducing an integrated TJ/preventive perspective on lawyering,[2] which served loosely as a springboard for the remarks of the panelists. The present article provides introductions to preventive law, therapeutic jurisprudence, and the integrated TJ Preventive Law perspective. Several examples of TJ preventive lawyering are provided, followed by a detailed discussion of future directions and novel issues explored by us at the session or in its aftermath.

---

1. Preventive Law and Therapeutic Jurisprudence: A Psychology and Law Based Approach to Everyday Lawyering, Address Before the Annual Meeting of the Law and Society Association (May 30, 1997).

2. Dennis P. Stolle & David B. Wexler, *Therapeutic Jurisprudence and Preventive Law: A Combined Concentration to Invigorate the Everyday Practice of Law*, 39 ARIZ. L. REV. 25 (1997) [hereinafter *Therapeutic Jurisprudence*]; Dennis P. Stolle, *Professional Responsibility in Elder Law: A Synthesis of Preventive Law and Therapeutic Jurisprudence*, 14 BEHAV. SCI. & L. (1996) [hereinafter *Professional Responsibility*]; Dennis P. Stolle & David B. Wexler, *Preventive Law and Therapeutic Jurisprudence: A Symbiotic Relationship*, 16 PREVENTIVE L. REP. 4 (1997) [hereinafter *Preventive Law*].

A. Preventive Law

Preventive law has been defined as "a branch of law that endeavors to minimize the risk of litigation or to secure more certainty as to legal rights and duties."[3] Preventive law provides a frame work in which the practicing lawyer may conduct professional activities in a manner that both minimizes his or her clients' potential legal liability and enhances their legal opportunities. In essence, preventive law is a proactive approach to lawyering.[4] It emphasizes the lawyer's role as a planner[5] and proposes the careful private ordering of affairs as a method of avoiding the high costs of litigation and ensuring desired outcomes and opportunities.[6]

An analogy is often drawn between preventive law and preventive medicine.[7] Just as preventive medicine works from the premise that keeping people healthy constitutes a better allocation of resources than treating people who become sick, preventive law works from the premise that preventing legal disputes is less costly than litigation.[8] Furthermore, preventive law promotes a client-centered approach, just as preventive medicine promotes a patient-centered approach.[9] In preventive law, the lawyer and client engage in a joint decision making process regarding legal strategies. The decision making is not limited to a particular dispute, but rather the decision making contemplates the client's long term goals and interests and how best to achieve them while minimizing exposure to the risk of legal difficulties. "By receiving updates on a client's life events (not limited to disputes), the lawyer can then assist the client to improve decision making and planning to prevent problems, reduce conflict, and increase life opportunities."[10] Such "legal check-ups"[11] are in many ways analogous to a medical check-up with a primary care physician.[12]

---

3. Honorable Edward D. Re, *The Lawyer as Counselor and the Prevention of Litigation,* 31 CATH. U. L. REV. 685, 692 (1995) (citing WEBSTER'S THIRD NEW INTERNATIONAL DICTIONARY 1798 (1961)). This definition provides a starting point for understanding preventive law. However, like most definitions of preventive law to date, this definition falls short of an accurate description of both the breadth and detail of the preventive law enterprise. *See* discussion *infra* part III.

4. *See* ROBERT M. HARDAWAY, PREVENTIVE LAW: MATERIALS ON A NON ADVERSARIAL LEGAL PROCESS (1997).

5. *See generally id.;* LOUIS M. BROWN & EDWARD A. DAUER, PERSPECTIVES ON THE LAWYER AS PLANNER (1978).

6. *See* HARDAWAY, supra note 4, at xxxvii-xli.

7. *See* HARDAWAY, *supra* note 4, at xxxvii.

8. *See* HARDAWAY, *supra* note 4, at xxxvii.

9. *See* BROWN & DAUER, *supra* note 5, at xix.

10. Forrest S. Mosten, *Unbundling of Legal Services and the Family Lawyer,* 28 FAM. L. Q. 421, 440 (1994).

Preventive law has generated considerable interest, scholarly and practice-oriented legal publications, and a dedicated corps of preventive law practitioners.[13] Yet the movement has its critics, and it has failed to convert large numbers of lawyers.[14] A frequently heard (but ironically contradictory) criticism among lawyers is that the practice of preventive law is "impossible,... and I already do it anyway." Furthermore, some lawyers worry that their clients will complain if they seek legal advice for one subject, and wind up paying a preventive lawyer more than was anticipated to deal with problems that they didn't know they had.[15] It has also been suggested that the proactive orientation of preventive law may come dangerously close to improper solicitations of legal business.[16] Thus, although some preventive law ideas have caught on, many lawyers remain resistant.

B. Therapeutic Jurisprudence

Therapeutic jurisprudence is an interdisciplinary approach to law that builds on the basic insight that law is a social force that has inevitable (if unintended) consequences for the mental health and psychological functioning of those it affects. Therapeutic jurisprudence suggests that these positive and negative consequences be studied with the tools of the behavioral sciences, and that, consistent with considerations of justice and other relevant normative values, law be reformed to minimize anti-therapeutic consequences and to facilitate achievement of therapeutic ones.[17]

---

11. HARDAWAY, *supra* note 4, at 180-222; *See* Mosten *supra* note 10, at 445.

12. *See* Mosten *supra* note 10, at 447.

13. The interest in preventive law is exemplified by the success of the National Center for Preventive Law, the recent publication of HARDAWAY, *supra* note 4, and the continued success of the PREVENTIVE LAW REPORTER.

14. Interestingly, many good lawyers practice preventive law instinctively; however, far fewer explicitly refer to their work as involving preventive law. *See* HARDAWAY, *supra* note 4, at xxxvii; *See also* Scott E. Isaacson, *Preventive Law: A Personal Essay*, 9 UTAH B.J., Oct. 1996, at 14, 16 (discussing potential reasons why preventive law is not more often explicitly recognized and advocated).

15. *See infra* note 79 and accompanying text.

16. This argument is most often incorrect. Preventive law, practiced as it was intended by its founders to be practiced, creates no potential for improper solicitations of business. *See* Louis M. Brown, *The Law Office-A Preventive Law Laboratory*, 104 U. PA. L. REV. 940, 948 (1956); Louis M. Brown, *The Scheme: Maximize Opportunities, Minimize Future Legal Trouble*, 6 PREVENTIVE L. REP. 17, 19 (1987) [hereinafter *The Scheme*] (noting that "the law of professional responsibility has always permitted lawyers to initiate legal discussions with existing clients. That process is not a process of solicitation in the traditional definition of that word. Solicitation that was not permitted was solicitation to obtain a client."); *see generally* HARDAWAY, *supra* note 4.

Although the approach originated in the area of mental health law, it has quickly expanded beyond that context, and has become a mental health law approach to law generally. As Wexler and Winick's 1996 book Law in a Therapeutic Key[18] illustrates, the therapeutic jurisprudence perspective has recently been applied in the contexts of criminal law, family law, juvenile law, disability law, discrimination law, health law, evidence law, tort law, contracts and commercial law, labor arbitration, workers' compensation law, probate law, and legal profession. The approach has provoked an entire field of original interdisciplinary work by law professors, psychologists, sociologists, criminologists, philosophers, lawyers, and judges.[19] And, most recently, there is growing interest in a dimension of therapeutic jurisprudence that takes the law as given and explores ways in which existing law might be most therapeutically applied.[20]

However, like preventive law, therapeutic jurisprudence is not without its critics. Therapeutic jurisprudence has been accused of being paternalistic, in some respects as a result of a confusion provoked by the title itself, which for some sounds like a call for a return to the therapeutic state. Its proponents have been careful to point out that although the law's therapeutic consequences should be studied, law often serves other normative values that often will dictate the existence of a rule of law or a legal practice even if anti-therapeutic.[21] Therapeutic jurisprudence serves to sharpen the public policy debate about law and law reform, but does not purport to resolve it when therapeutic considerations conflict with other normative values. Therapeutic jurisprudence, like preventive law, also has been subjected to the ironic critique that law's therapeutic consequences

---

17. *See generally* David B. Wexler, *An Introduction to Therapeutic Jurisprudence, in* DAVID B. WEXLER, THERAPEUTIC JURISPRUDENCE: THE LAW AS A THERAPEUTIC AGENT 3 (1990) [hereinafter THERAPEUTIC AGENT].

18. DAVID B. WEXLER & BRUCE J. WINICK, LAW IN A THERAPEUTIC KEY: DEVELOPMENTS IN THERAPEUTIC JURISPRUDENCE (1996) [hereinafter THERAPEUTIC KEY]; *See also* DAVID B. WEXLER & BRUCE J. WINICK, ESSAYS IN THERAPEUTIC JURISPRUDENCE (1991) [hereinafter ESSAYS]; Wexler, *supra* note 17; BRUCE J. WINICK, THERAPEUTIC JURISPRUDENCE APPLIED: ESSAYS ON MENTAL HEALTH LAW (1997) [hereinafter MENTAL HEALTH].

19. *See generally* WEXLER & WINICK, THERAPEUTIC KEY, *supra* note 18.

20. *See generally* David B. Wexler, *Applying the Law Therapeutically*, 5 APPLIED & PREVENTIVE PSYCHOL. 179 (1996); Stolle, *Professional Responsibility, supra* note 2; David Finkelman & Thomas Grisso, *Therapeutic Jurisprudence: From Idea to Application*, 20 NEW ENG. J. ON CRIM. & CIV. CONFINEMENT 243 (1994); Bruce J. Winick, *The Jurisprudence of Therapeutic Jurisprudence*, 3 PSYCHOL. PUB. POL'Y. & L. 184, 201-03 (1997).

21. *See generally* Wexler, *supra* note 17.

ought not be considered, or that they are too difficult to ascertain, but also that they are already taken into account.

C. Integrating Preventive Law and Therapeutic Jurisprudence

One of us (Stolle) has recently attempted a synthesis of preventive law and therapeutic jurisprudence.[22] Writing in the context of elder law, Stolle suggests that a preventive lawyer should be sensitive to the therapeutic and psychological consequences of attorney-client interactions. Stolle argues that TJ has much to offer preventive law and that it can help to reconceptualize and broaden the approach to encompass an important but frequently overlooked dimension of legal practice.[23] Likewise, recent scholarship by Stolle & Wexler has suggested that "preventive law, and the legal check-up in particular, at least when used by a lawyer keenly attuned to how the law may affect a client's psychological well-being, can provide the very legal context or mechanism needed for lawyers to work with clients to apply the law therapeutically."[24]

The integration of these two approaches can greatly enhance the potential of each to achieve its objectives. Therapeutic jurisprudence alone lacks the practical procedures for law office application. Preventive law alone lacks an analytical framework for justifying emotional well-being as one priority in legal planning. Bringing the two fields together can remedy these difficulties. Through a synthesis of preventive law and therapeutic jurisprudence, preventive law can "provide a framework for the practice of therapeutic jurisprudence. And therapeutic jurisprudence, in turn, can provide a rich and rewarding 'human aspect' and interdisciplinary orientation for a preventive lawyer to use in everyday law practice."[25]

This integrated framework, like preventive law and therapeutic jurisprudence in general, is not substantively restricted to any particular field of law. Of course, application of the integrated framework may be more sensible in some legal contexts than in others.[26] Furthermore, the combined framework is likely to be of most immediate interest to lawyers providing prepaid legal services, legal-aid lawyers, lawyers and students in law school legal clinics, or lawyers working with special populations such as children, the

---

22. *See* Stolle, *Professional Responsibility, supra* note 2.
23. *See* Stolle, *Professional Responsibility, supra* note 2.
24. Stolle & Wexler, *Therapeutic Jurisprudence, supra* note 2, at 27.
25. *Id.* at 28.
26. *See* discussion *infra* Part IV, particularly the Venn diagram; Stolle & Wexler, *Therapeutic Jurisprudence, supra* note 2, at 28.

elderly, or the disabled.[27] Indeed, many such lawyers already blend elements of preventive law with concerns for a client's emotional well-being.[28] The integrated frame work merely seeks to explicate the point and perhaps sharpen the focus. The combined framework is intended to generate thinking that otherwise would not occur and to create a community of lawyers sharing the same perspective and systematically and expressly applying the principles of both therapeutic jurisprudence and preventive law in their daily practice.[29]

The potential offered by an integration of these two approaches is per haps best illustrated through examples. This Article therefore presents several examples of TJ preventive lawyering, which serve as catalysts for further discussion of the integration. Part II offers examples of the integrated framework drawn from the contexts of elder law, HIV/AIDS law, family law, and business planning law. Part III provides a critical examination of the potential utility of the integration from the established analytic perspectives of preventive law and therapeutic jurisprudence. Part IV then discusses appropriate channels for future research and scholarship on the combined framework. Finally, Part V concludes with a call for a transformation of legal practice in a direction consistent with the principles of TJ Preventive Law.

II. Examples of the Integration in Practice

A. Elder Law[30]

The TJ Preventive Law framework may lend itself particularly well to working with older clients. In a recent article appearing in Behavioral Sciences and the Law, Stolle applied a TJ Preventive Law perspective in ana-

---

27. *See* Stolle & Wexler, *Therapeutic Jurisprudence, supra* note 2, at 28 ("After all, such lawyers can be involved in a client-centered practice that seeks to negotiate the legal arena with maximum attention to the psychological well-being of clients. Such practitioners—in essence, primary care counselors-at-law—are truly helping professionals....").

28. *See* Peter Margulies, *Access, Connection and Voice: A Contextual Approach to Representing Senior Citizens of Questionable Capacity*, 62 FORDHAM L. REV. 1073 (1994); Mosten, *supra* note 10; Gerald R. Williams, *Negotiation as a Healing Process*, 1996 J. DISP. RESOL. 1 (1996); Peter Margulies, *Representation of Domestic Violence Survivors as a New Paradigm of Poverty law: In Search of Access, Connection, and Voice*, 63 GEO. WASH. L. REV. 1071 (1995).

29. *See* Stolle & Wexler, *Therapeutic Jurisprudence,* supra note 2; *See also* Stolle & Wexler, *Preventive Law, supra* note 2.

30. This example has been adapted from Stolle, *Professional Responsibility, supra* note 2.

lyzing an elder law example adapted from Frolik & Brown's treatise on elder law.[31] Imagine Frank and Eleanor Burke, both age sixty-five and married for forty years, who enter a lawyer's office wishing to "have a simple will drafted." Neither Frank nor Eleanor has ever consulted with a lawyer before. It might appear that such a client consultation would likely be relatively straightforward, mostly involving well established legal principles related to estate planning. Indeed, in many law offices, the Burkes would walk in with this agenda and would walk out with a simple will and nothing more.

However, Stolle suggested that a lawyer working with elderly clients ought to stay abreast of social science literature relevant to older clients, as well as legal developments relevant to the elderly.[32] Such information could then be applied during client consultations to achieve a sophisticated preventive/therapeutic approach to elder law. In Stolle's framework, the first step for a TJ preventive lawyer confronted with clients such as the Burkes is to determine whether emotional or psychological well-being will be in any way relevant in this client consultation.

The Burkes have entered the lawyer's office with narrow economic concerns in mind — the drafting of a simple will. However, the preventive lawyer should be able to use client counseling skills to quickly bring out information regarding the Burkes' age, health conditions, family structure, vocations, and avocations, all of which may prove to be critical information in drafting a document to distribute their assets in accord with their intent. Furthermore, this information can be used to alert the preventive lawyer to any potential therapeutic concerns.

An initial conversation might reveal that the Burkes have recently become concerned with setting their affairs in order as they approach their later years of life. The Burkes have three children, two of whom are married and each have children of their own. The Burkes' third child, Tom, now age twenty-eight, has been divorced twice. Unfortunately, over the last few years Tom has also been through a series of drug and alcohol abuse treatment centers. Of particular concern for the Burkes is treating their children fairly and avoiding future dependency on their children. The

31. Lawrence A. Frolik & Melissa C. Brown, Advising the Elderly or Disabled Client: Legal, Health Care, Financial, and Estate Planning (1992).

32. For example, a subscription to one or more of the following journals may go a long way toward keeping a lawyer on top of the social scientific literature relevant to older clients: Journal of Gerontology, Psychology and Aging, Developmental Psychology, Abstracts in Social Gerontology, Age and Ageing, Ageing and Society, Aging and Mental Health, Journal of Aging and Health, Journal of Aging and Social Policy, Journal of Applied Gerontology, Research on Aging.

Burkes appear to be in good physical and mental health; however, Frank did take an early retirement because of recurring problems with arthritis. Frank spends his free time with woodworking projects when his arthritis is in remission. He sells some of his projects for a profit and donates the remainder to his church for sale at auctions and craft shows. For the past thirty years Eleanor has been a homemaker. Frank's parents both passed away a number of years ago. Eleanor's father also died several years ago. Her mother is eighty-six and in poor health. She is suffering from Alzheimer's disease, and has been living in a nearby nursing home for the past several months. The primary sources of the Burkes' income are Social Security, Frank's fixed pension, dividends from a number of investments, and a small amount from the sale of Frank's carvings.

Upon considering this information, a TJ preventive lawyer should recognize that, beyond the economic and legal concerns normally associated with drafting a will, many therapeutic concerns may also confront the Burkes in the future.

First, the Burkes' age should serve as an indicator that therapeutic goals may become important. Reaching age sixty-five often has psychological implications beyond the readily apparent legal and economic benefits. In addition to meeting or approaching the threshold age requirements for Medicare, private pensions, Social Security, and private benefits such as retail and service discounts, approaching age sixty-five may also bring the label of "elderly."[33] The therapeutically insightful lawyer should be cognizant that being labeled elderly may have adverse consequences on an individual's self-image.[34] However, the lawyer should also not overlook the reality that, as a matter of actuarial science, growing older is associated with an increasing potential for mental and physical health problems.[35] Therefore, although the Burkes currently appear to be in relatively good mental and physical health, health maintenance might properly become a priority in their life.

Second, the Burkes' concern about directing the distribution of their assets might itself raise therapeutic concerns. As evidenced by the Burkes' very presence in the lawyer's office, the Burkes have been contemplating the future, including the possibility of their own death or incapacity. Such con-

---

33. *See* Lawrence A. Frolik & Alison P. Barnes, *An Aging Population: A Challenge to the Law*, 42 HASTINGS L. J. 683, 684-87 (1991) (discussing "who really is elderly?").

34. *See generally id.*

35. At the same time, it is critical that a lawyer not buy into stereotypes of the aged and avoid the "temptation to substitute decisions made by him or her for decisions that should properly be made by the client." JOAN M. KRAUSKOPF, ADVOCACY FOR THE AGING 24 (1983).

cerns are common among older persons;[36] however, the topic of one's own death remains sensitive, and may often be accompanied by feelings of anxiety, uncertainty, or depression. The fact that the Burkes have never before consulted with a lawyer may also contribute to feelings of anxiety in discussing these private and emotionally charged issues.

Third, the fact that Eleanor's mother is suffering from Alzheimer's disease should raise serious therapeutic concerns. Because Eleanor's mother is eighty-six years old and suffering from a severe neurological disease, she may have a very limited life expectancy. This raises the issue of the impact on Eleanor and Frank of witnessing Eleanor's mother's mental deterioration and coping with her eventual death. In addition to the difficult emotional and psychological circumstances the Burkes are facing, the continuation of adequate care for Eleanor's mother may have the potential to place an additional financial burden on the Burkes. Indeed, struggling with financing Eleanor's mother's care may place yet another psychological stressor on the Burkes. Finally, some evidence suggests that Alzheimer's disease may have a hereditary component.[37] Eleanor's mother's condition thus ought to serve as a warning sign that Eleanor too may be at increased risk of developing Alzheimer's disease in later life.[38]

Fourth, Frank's arthritis should raise therapeutic concerns in the mind of the preventive lawyer. Arthritis is a chronic disease that often contributes to future disability among older persons[39] and is a characteristic impairment of "consistently high users" of medical services.[40] Furthermore, the severity of an arthritic condition is related to a decline on some measures of psychological well-being.[41] In Frank's case, an increase in the severity of his

---

36. *See* Judith W. McCue et al., *Disability Planning for the Senior Citizen*, C126 ALI-ABA 339, 343 (1995) ("Increasingly, clients are concerned about the possibility of their own incapacity and wish to take steps to assure, should they become disabled in the future, that their assets will be protected and that health care decisions will be made on their behalf without court intervention or other delays.")

37. *See generally* Ge Li et al., *Age at Onset and Familial Risk in Alzheimer's Disease*, 152 Am. J. Psychiatry 424 (1995). This is especially true of early onset Alzheimer's disease. *Id.*

38. *See generally id.*

39. *See generally* Susan L. Hughes et al., *Impact of Joint Impairment on Longitudinal Disability in Elderly Persons*, 49 J. Gerontology S291 (1994).

40. Donald K. Freeborn et al., *Consistently High Users of Medical Care Among the Elderly*, 28 Med. Care 527 (1990).

41. *See* Barbara L. Downe-Wamboldt & Patricia M. Melanson, *Emotions, Coping, and Psychological Well-Being in Elderly People with Arthritis*, 17 W. J. Nursing Res. 250 (1995); Baqar A. Husaini & Stephen T. Moore, *Arthritis Disability, Depression, and Life Satisfaction Among Black Elderly People*, 15 Health & Soc. Work 253 (1990).

arthritic condition may infringe on his woodworking hobby and, consequently, have a particularly detrimental impact on his psychological well-being.

Stolle suggested that, by keeping abreast of social scientific literature on geriatric issues, a preventive lawyer, as a first step, can identify therapeutic concerns such as those listed above.[42] The presence of such therapeutic issues should suggest to the TJ preventive lawyer that planning for the possibility of future incapacity or disability should be important in working with the Burkes. Thus, the lawyer should discuss therapeutic goals openly with the Burkes as one potential consideration in their planning. This conversation must, of course, be conducted in a sensitive and respectful manner. However, the client should be involved from the beginning in the identification of therapeutic concerns.

On one hand, the lawyer should encourage the Burkes to consider the real possibility of future incapacity. A detailed client interview and a discussion of the clients' plans can provide an opportunity for the Burkes to take a realistic look at their own health and the possibility of declining health in upcoming years. On the other hand, the lawyer should also encourage the Burkes to value their current healthy condition, and might even use this opportunity to encourage the Burkes to make health maintenance a priority.

Here, the lawyer is clearly stepping outside of his role of legal counselor, and should make that absolutely clear to the client.[43] The lawyer might say, "Look, I'm not a doctor, but I see a lot of older clients. I always say to them that I hope the documents that I draft won't be used for a long, long time; and, I mean that. But, over the years, I can really see the difference between my clients who make an effort to take care of themselves, and those who don't. So keep checking in with your doctor and living a healthy life-style. You guys are in great shape and I want you to stay that way. After all, I would like to be your lawyer for a long time." Thus, by using the law office as a forum for encouraging the Burkes to both plan for the worst and attempt to maintain their health so that the worst never comes

---

42. *See* Stolle, *Professional Responsibility, supra* note 2.

43. This point represents a refinement of the analysis presented in Stolle, *Professional Responsibility, supra* note 2. Although TJ preventive lawyering involves an expansion of the role of the lawyer as counselor, the TJ preventive lawyer's expertise has clear limits. When the lawyer chooses to give advice or suggestions falling outside of that area of expertise, the lawyer must make clear that his role in giving that advice is as a friend or acquaintance, not an expert. Furthermore, any such advice should be restricted to general and innocuous statements.

about, the lawyer can maximize the probability of therapeutic outcomes and minimize the probability of anti-therapeutic outcomes.

The lawyer's task is, however, primarily legal. Given this, the lawyer must use the appropriate legal tools to ensure that the Burkes' intent is achieved, or if their intent cannot be achieved, inform the Burkes of this and discuss alternative strategies. However, if more than one legal tool is available to achieve the Burkes' intent, the role of the integrated framework is to choose the most therapeutic, or, at minimum, the least anti-therapeutic alternative, all other things being equal, or nearly so. Even where only one legal solution is available, that solution may, in some cases, be tailored to enhance its therapeutic effect without jeopardizing its legal enforceability.

In the present situation, the lawyer might first consider the Burkes' relationship to one another. The Burkes have had a long and successful marriage and appear to care deeply for one another. In such circumstances, the death of one spouse may have a substantial negative psychological impact on the surviving spouse, rendering the surviving spouse temporarily unable to manage his or her own affairs. Consequently, a complementary set of revocable trusts may be appropriate. Such a set of mirror-image documents would prevent financial disaster if the surviving spouse is unable to make financial decisions, yet retains a level of autonomy that may be critical to a person's self-esteem.[44]

The preventive lawyer should also carefully consider the nature of the Burkes' relationship with their children. The Burkes appear to want to leave most of their assets to their children. However, the Burkes' comments should suggest that they may expect that their two happily married children will spend any inheritance more wisely than their third child, who apparently has a serious drug and alcohol problem. Although the Burkes said that they want to treat their children fairly, they may have reservations about leaving assets to a child who currently has a serious substance abuse problem. If further discussion reveals that this is the case, the lawyer might suggest alternative legal solutions, such as leaving their third child's inheritance to him in trust.

In many law offices, the lawyer may suggest leaving Tom's inheritance in a trust, the Burkes would agree, and there would be no further discussion of the matter. However, the goal of the TJ Preventive Law enterprise is to take the legal consultation a step further by considering not only the legal or economic ramifications of implementing a particular legal tool, but to also consider the psychological or emotional ramifications. A deci-

---

44. See generally FROLIK & BROWN, supra note 31, for an introduction to revocable trusts.

sion to leave an inheritance in a trust for one child and not for the other children could provoke family quarrels, or alienate Tom from other family members.[45] Thus, before drafting such documents, the TJ preventive lawyer should discuss openly with the Burkes the potential psychological impact of their decisions. The lawyer might also ask for the Burkes' views on whether they would like to discuss the matter with Tom or with the other children before finalizing the document. The decisions, of course, remain the Burkes' to make, but only after a discussion of both the legal and psychological effects of leaving Tom's inheritance in a trust can the Burkes make a truly informed decision regarding which legal strategies to elect.

The lawyer might also suggest that the Burkes consider advance directives regarding health care.[46] The lawyer should emphasize that having such legal directives might have the benefit of providing the Burkes with additional psychological comfort and security regarding their future. Furthermore, if either Frank or Eleanor became incapacitated, such documents can reduce the stress on family members who otherwise might be faced with difficult surrogate health care decisions.[47] Similarly, the lawyer should inquire as to whether the Burkes have adequate long-term care insurance and whether the insurance plan adequately covers special care needed in cases of mental illness.[48] Given that the Burkes are involved in organized religion, the lawyer might also suggest that the Burkes consider the advance directive options for health care in relation to their religious beliefs, or perhaps even suggest consulting with one of their church leaders before the document is drafted.

Ultimately, a TJ preventive lawyer can ensure therapeutic outcomes through the careful use of preventive law tools. By considering not only economic and legal priorities, but also personal goals, values, and relationships, a lawyer can create a superior package of preventive legal documents that may include a complementary set of wills or revocable trusts, and a complementary set of living wills or health care proxies. In doing so, a lawyer can both reduce the potential for anti-therapeutic outcomes down the road and maximize the older client's present sense of security and autonomy.

---

45. Furthermore, the selection of a trustee might create family tension, if not chosen wisely.

46. It is important to note that such suggestions are not improper solicitations of business. *See* Brown, *The Scheme, supra* note 16.

47. *See generally* THOMAS L. HAFEMEISTER & PAULA L. HANNAFORD, RESOLVING DISPUTES OVER LIFE-SUSTAINING TREATMENT 10, 16-20 (1996).

48. This may become of particular importance for Eleanor given the possibly hereditary nature of Alzheimer's disease. *See supra* note 37.

⚹ A final and critical step for a TJ preventive lawyer confronted with the Burkes' situation is the establishment of a legal check-up system.[49] The preventive lawyer should explain to the client that the legal documents he or she has drafted on their behalf may be amended, and that such amendments may be desirable in the face of any major life changes or any statutory changes. The lawyer should encourage the client to provide him or her with information any time a major illness, crisis, conflict, or change of financial circumstances arises. Likewise, the lawyer should agree to keep the client informed of any legal developments affecting the client's documents. Additionally, the lawyer should encourage the client to periodically return to the office for a short legal check-up, perhaps once a year. At the legal check-up the lawyer and client can discuss both negative events such as conflicts or illnesses, as well as positive goals or opportunities that may have arisen in the client's life.

When the Burkes return in a year, the topics of conversation might include any important financial changes, Tom's addiction recovery progress, Eleanor's mother's condition, or any other significant life events that may have arisen during the year. This meeting will give the lawyer and the Burkes an opportunity to evaluate whether the Burkes' goals have changed and whether their current advance directives and any other legal instruments remain adequate.

Such a legal check-up itself can serve a therapeutic function. The legal check-up is a structured opportunity for the client to reevaluate his or her current life situation relative to his or her goals, and to think about and plan for the immediate and distant future. The check-up also serves as an opportunity for the client to ask the lawyer questions about issues that the client might be reluctant to schedule a separate appointment to discuss. For example, many older individuals have anxiety about and questions regarding medical and insurance paperwork that is sent to their homes.[50] There-

---

49. Legal check-ups have been within the preventive law armamentarium for some time. One of us (Dauer) has been conducting field trials of a periodic legal check-up particularly for the elderly, thus far with useful results. Samples of the check-up materials are on file at the National Center for Preventive Law in Denver and available to qualified individuals and groups.

50. *See* Wayne Moore, *Improving the Delivery of Legal Services for the Elderly: A Comprehensive Approach*, 41 Emory L. J. 805, 810 & 811 n.44 (1992) (*citing* The Spangeberg Group, Wisconsin Elder Legal Needs Study, 1 The Final Report of the ABA Commission on Legal Problems of the Elderly 42 (Apr. 1991)) (on file with the Emory Law Journal), which found that one area of quasi-legal nature of great concern to older people was finding assistance with medical paper work related to Medicare and Medigap reimbursement; *See also* Thomas D. Overcast, The Development and Evaluation of Handbooks Providing Law Related Information for the Elderly (1980) (unpublished Ph.D. dissertation, University of Nebraska) (on file with the University of Nebraska-Lin-

fore, a <u>lawyer's reminder letter,</u> sent out shortly before the check-up, might also remind clients to keep a list of questions they may have and perhaps to bring along any related correspondence, confusing documents that have come in the mail, etcetera. In this way, the legal check-up can provide a chance for older clients to discuss such matters with a knowledgeable and trustworthy professional.

Thus, a regularly scheduled legal check-up conducted by a therapeutically insightful preventive lawyer may provide the client with an increased sense of security. Indeed, the legal check-up can perhaps ultimately become a therapeutic part of the client's experience of growing older.

B. HIV/AIDS Law

Elder law, therefore, provides fertile ground for the development of the TJ Preventive Law framework. The framework is not, however, restricted to working with elderly clients. Consider also the example of HIV/AIDS law. Although a new sense of optimism has arisen from recent successes with protease inhibitors and "cocktail" treatments,[51] a person who learns that he or she is HIV-positive continues to face not only the overwhelming health care issues related to living with AIDS, but also a myriad of legal and social issues. These issues can include, for example, concerns over estate planning, employment discrimination, child custody, health care costs, disability insurance, life insurance, and government aid.[52] Given the number

---

coln library) (empirically exploring the impact of providing legal information packets to elderly individuals).

51. The term "cocktail" refers to a mixture of several drugs. Such mixtures have shown better results than monotherapies in fighting HIV. *See* Joan Stephenson, *New Anti-HIV Drugs and Treatment Strategies Buoy AIDS Researchers*, 275 JAMA 579 (1996); *See also* Lawrence Corey & King K. Homes, *Therapy for Human Immunodeficiency Virus Infection—What Have We Learned?*, 335 NEW ENG. J. MED. 1143 (1996).

52. *See, e.g.*, James Monroe Smith, *Legal Issues Confronting Fami lies Affected by HIV*, 24 J. MARSHALL L. REV. 543 (1991); MARK S. SENAK, HIV, AIDS AND THE LAW: A GUIDE TO OUR RIGHTS AND CHALLENGES (1996); Emily Berendt & Laura Lynn Michaels, *Your HIV Positive Client: Easing the Burden on the Family Through Estate Planning*, 24 J. MARSHALL L. REV. 509 (1991); W.E. Scott Hoot, *Introduction* to Symposium, *Estate Planning for Artists: Will Your Art Survive?*, 21 COLUM-VLA J.L. & ARTS 15 (1996); Charles J. Groppe & Eileen E. Hudson, *Estate Planning for the Client with AIDS*, 64 N.Y. ST. B.J. 20 (1992); Georgiana K. Roussos, *Protections Against HIV-Based Employment Discrimination in the United States and Australia*, 13 HASTINGS INT'L & COMP. L. REV. 609 (1990). John Douglas, Note, *HIV Disease and Disparate Impact Under the Americans With Disabili ties Act: A Federal Prohibition of Discrimination on the Basis of Sexual Orientation?* 16 BERKELEY J. EMP. & LAB. L. 288 (1995); Tracy Jackson Smith, Comment, *AIDS and the Law: Protecting the HIV-Infected Employee from*

and complexity of the legal issues associated with AIDS, most HIV-positive persons will need some specialized legal planning.[53] Furthermore, many of the legal issues that an HIV-positive client will potentially face, such as child custody disputes, employment disputes, and health care decision making, are issues of both legal and psychological significance.[54]

Consider health care decision-making. There is a growing consensus among lawyers and medical professionals that HIV-positive persons should execute some type of advance directive instrument. Furthermore, much recent commentary has suggested that such advance directive instruments may be a good idea from a legal and medical standpoint, as well as from a psychological or emotional standpoint.[55] Planning for death and exerting some level of control over the process, it is hypothesized, may have inherent therapeutic value.[56]

A TJ preventive lawyer, especially one experienced in working with HIV-positive clients, should recognize that some HIV-positive clients are likely to be alienated from their families as a result of past or present behaviors that their family condemns.[57] This raises the issue of who the client ought to name as a surrogate decision-maker. In some cases the client may prefer that a domestic partner be named as the decision-maker. However, if this partner is also HIV-positive, the partner may be grieving and may himself be gravely ill at the time of critical decision-making. As a result, a secondary and even tertiary surrogate decision-maker should be named.[58]

In some cases, this dilemma may provide an opportunity for the client to have some reconciliation with alienated family members and to even-

---

Discrimination, 57 TENN. L. REV. 539 (1990); Jody B. Gabel, *Release from Terminal Suffering? The Impact of Aids on Medically Assisted Suicide Legislation*, 22 FLA. ST. U. L. REV. 369 (1994); Sana Loue, *Living Wills, Durable Powers of Attorney for Health Care, and HIV Infection: The Need for Statutory Reform*, 16 J. LEGAL MED. 461 (1995).

53. *See* SENAK, *supra* note 52 (discussing the need for advance legal planning for HIV-positive persons).

54. *See generally* SENAK, *supra* note 52.

55. *See* Bruce J. Winick, *Advance Directive Instruments for those with Mental Illness*, 51 U. MIAMI L. REV. 57, 83 (1996) (suggesting in the context of advance directive instruments for those with mental illness that "having the opportunity to engage in advance planning concerning hospitalization and treatment may have significant therapeutic benefits. The ability to be self-determining—to plan for the future, to envision future contingencies and bring about those that are desired and avoid those that are undesired, to set goals and see them achieved—is an important aspect of mental health and self-esteem").

56. *See generally* SENAK, *supra* note 52.

57. *See generally* SENAK, *supra* note 52.

58. *See* Stolle & Wexler, *Therapeutic Jurisprudence*, *supra* note 2, at 31; *See also Uniform Health-Care Decisions Act*, 9 U.L.A. 239, §4 (1993) (explaining the Act's optional form provides a signature line for a primary, secondary, and tertiary decision-maker).

tually name a parent or sibling as a secondary or tertiary decision-maker. This reconciliation may also have significant therapeutic effects on the client and the client's family. In other cases, there may be no hope of reconciliation. The client-centered approach of TJ preventive lawyering allows for the lawyer and client, who best knows his family situation, to jointly engage in decision-making regarding whether approaching family members would be useful.

Just as the establishment of a legal check-up system was a critical component of ongoing success in the elder law example above, so too in the context of HIV/AIDS law. The TJ legal check-up would allow for the ongoing development of the advance directive documents. Indeed, the therapeutic value need not end when the document is signed. At an annual legal check-up, the HIV-positive client could update the lawyer concerning developments in family relationships and friendships that may influence who ought to be named as a surrogate decision-maker.

A dedicated TJ preventive lawyer, who often works with HIV-positive clients, ought to keep up with current AIDS literature, both literature directly pertaining to legal implications and literature dealing with social or medical aspects of AIDS.[59] Under those circumstances, the lawyer and client could also discuss any recent advancements in medical technology or therapy that may influence the client's election or rejection of certain medicines or treatments. Furthermore, the legal check-up would provide the lawyer with an opportunity to update the client on any recent legal developments that may affect the client's advance directives or any other issues that the client may be facing.[60]

We have now presented two examples of client counseling situations in which the approach of TJ Preventive Law seems particularly useful. Each example involved working with a special population of clients, defined more by physical or social characteristics than by legal relationships or

---

59. Such literature need not always be journal articles or technical books and reports, which might consume much of a lawyer's free-time. Rather, as Stolle & Wexler have suggested, much information regarding questions that clients may be reluctant to ask or the emotional difficulties underlying legal problems that clients may hesitate to discuss can be gleaned from consumer oriented law books. *See* Stolle & Wexler, *Therapeutic Jurisprudence, supra* note 2, at 30-31.

60. Again, it is important to note that this type of legal consultation with an existing client does not amount to improper solicitation of business. *See* Brown, *The Scheme, supra* note 16. The difficulty with proactive legal planning, however, is getting the individual who is in need of legal planning to seek out a lawyer's advice in the first instance. In the case of populations such as HIV-positive persons, who are widely recognized as being in need of general legal counsel, HIV clinics or support groups might compile listings of local lawyers who emphasize AIDS related issues in their legal practice and make those listings available to HIV-positive persons.

legal status. However, the TJ Preventive Law framework, as will be illustrated by the following two examples drawn from family law and business planning law, is not limited to such contexts.

C. Family Law

✴ The TJ Preventive Law framework also lends itself particularly well to family law, which, perhaps, is an area likely to be encountered by more lawyers at some point in their legal career than elder law or HIV/AIDS law. In a recent article, Kathryn Maxwell examines preventive and therapeutic strategies that lawyers might implement in an attempt to minimize the anti-therapeutic effects of divorce on their clients' children.[61]

Maxwell suggests that in many law offices matrimonial lawyers are unlikely to give significant consideration to the psychological and emotional effects that their clients' divorces will have on the children involved.[62] Furthermore, some lawyers may even unnecessarily heighten the negative psychological effects of divorce on children by magnifying the acrimony between the divorcing parents, and by implicitly or even explicitly using the children as bargaining chips in the divorce negotiations.[63] In contrast, Maxwell proposes that divorce lawyers adopt a preventive/therapeutic approach, giving explicit consideration to the emotional or psychological well-being of the children as one important factor in divorce proceedings.[64]

Maxwell provides practical lawyering strategies for mitigating the negative effects of divorce on children. Lawyers concerned with the effects of divorce on children might, as a first step, choose like-minded clients. Maxwell suggests that these lawyers simply refuse to represent clients who, in an initial client interview, display some propensity toward disregarding the best interests of the children in order to achieve financial gain or some sort of vindication against their spouse.[65] Such lawyers might even adver-

---

61. Kathryn E. Maxwell, *Preventive Lawyering Strategies to Mitigate the Detrimental Effects of Client's Divorces on Their Children*, 66 REVISTA JURIDICA U.P.R. (forthcoming 1997). The focus on the interest of the client's child or children rather than the interests of the client raises the issue of whose psychological well-being ought to be the focus of the TJ preventive lawyer's focus. For more on the issue of "therapeutic for whom?", see David B. Wexler, *Reflections on the Scope of Therapeutic Jurisprudence*, in WEXLER & WINICK, THERAUPEUTIC KEY, *supra* note 18, at 811.

62. *See* Maxwell, *supra* note 61.

63. *See id.*

64. *See id.*

65. *See id.*

tise a "preference for child-friendly divorce, in order to attract like-minded clients and avoid future conflicts with contrary clients."[66]

Maxwell further suggests that once the lawyer has agreed to represent the client, the lawyer should educate the client regarding the potential detrimental effects of divorce on children, and plan a specific preventive/therapeutic strategy to mitigate any such negative effects in this client's case.[67] Maxwell provides, as an addendum to her article, a sample packet of materials that might be used in educating the client and developing the preventive/therapeutic plan.[68] The materials include a TJ Preventive Law checklist for the divorce agreement and an information packet for divorcing parents.[69]

Maxwell's article thus provides an example of another context to which the TJ preventive lawyering approach lends itself well. Indeed, the approach of TJ Preventive Law seems to fit nicely within the context of family law as a whole, not simply divorce law.[70] A TJ Preventive Law approach may also be appropriate for lawyers serving as a guardian ad litem for a troubled youth, lawyers involved in paternity actions, adoption cases, or cases of abuse and neglect, and even lawyers drafting prenuptial agreements.[71]

D. Corporate and Business Planning Law

Consider next the close corporation. A closely held corporation typically involves a small, tightly knit group of shareholders. Often many of the shareholders are family members or close friends. Many, though perhaps not all, shareholders may depend upon the corporation for their livelihood, either through a salary or through dividends. Furthermore, the initial capital contribution of individual shareholders often varies dramatically.

Imagine Bob and Jane, a husband and wife who enter a lawyer's office and explain that they are "interested in opening a small, family run cafe."

---

66. *Id.*

67. *See id.*

68. *See id.*

69. *See id.*

70. *See generally* Barbara A. Babb, *An Interdisciplinary Approach to Family Law Jurisprudence: Application of an Ecological and Therapeutic Perspective*, 72 IND. L.J. 775, 802 (1997) (providing an interesting application of the TJ framework within the context of family law, although not an explicitly TJ Preventive Law approach).

71. *See generally* Melvin Aron Eisenberg, *The Limits of Cognition and Limits of Contract*, 47 STAN. L. REV. 211, 254-58 (1995) (discussing the application of social cognitive psychology in the context of prenuptial agreements as a way to understand both why parties might choose to enter into certain agreements and why courts might choose to enforce or not enforce those same agreements).

They are consulting a lawyer because they would like the cafe to be incorporated. They have heard that incorporation is a good method of limiting business liabilities. From their explanation, it appears that the cafe would have four potential shareholders.

Two of the potential shareholders are Bob and Jane. They have only $5,000 in initial capital to contribute, but both have experience in the restaurant business and plan to manage the day-to-day operations. Both Bob and Jane would be dependent upon the success of the cafe for their livelihood. Jack, Bob's brother, is a third potential shareholder. Jack wants nothing to do with the day-to-day operations, but is a wealthy investor. Jack is willing to contribute $30,000 in initial capital, believing the cafe will be a highly profitable investment. Jack is, however, very concerned about limiting his liability to only his $30,000 investment. Sally is the fourth potential shareholder. Sally is Jane's best friend. Sally is willing to contribute $5,000 in initial capital and she plans to be a full-time hostess and waitress at the cafe.

An enterprise such as this cafe, in which there exist differing expectations and differing levels of capital contribution against the backdrop of family and social relationships, provides a classic example of a situation in which advance legal planning will be critical to the continued success of the business. By taking the approach of TJ preventive lawyering seriously in a context like this, the lawyer may be able, through skillful client counseling, to elicit information about the relationships and expectations of the parties that might not otherwise be revealed. This information can be used, through the client-centered approach of TJ preventive lawyering, to develop a structure of corporate control and internal dispute resolution that satisfies the needs and expectations of each of the shareholders.

Again, the establishment of a legal check-up system will be a critical component of the TJ Preventive Law approach. One cannot expect that the relationships in such a business will remain static, nor will the business itself. As relationships change and the business grows and prospers, changes in the corporate structure may become appropriate.[72] Likewise, changes in the legal regulatory environment may necessitate some change in corporate structure or operations. Absent some continuing dialogue between the attorney and the corporate client, developments giving rise to the need for an adjustment of legal relationships may go unnoticed. However, by engaging in regular legal check-ups, not confined solely to legal information, the TJ-oriented preventive lawyer may anticipate necessary changes, thereby smoothing the bumps on what otherwise might be a jolting entrepreneurial ride.

---

72. *See* discussion *infra* Part III for another example of changing personal relationships and their potential impact on corporate structure.

Ultimately, a well drafted corporate agreement that takes into consideration not only the financial investment of the shareholders, but also their social and emotional investment, could avoid future disputes, which have the potential to tear apart the corporation, friendships, and family relationships. Furthermore, the certainty created by working through expectations and contingencies with the shareholders in advance might reduce the stress that will inevitably accompany any attempt to start a new business. Thus, just as psychological or emotional well-being ought to be one priority in legal planning for the elderly, for HIV-positive clients, or divorcing parents with children, emotional well-being ought to be one priority in some aspects of corporate law. [73]

III. Looking Across the Aisle:
How Each Discipline Views the Other

Although hypothetical scenarios such as those described above allow the luxury of creating ideal circumstances that may not always exist under the situational constraints of actual practice, the hypotheticals provide an important starting point for exploring the potential integration of preventive law and therapeutic jurisprudence. That potential can be viewed both from the perspective of a preventive lawyer evaluating the contribution of therapeutic jurisprudence, and from the perspective of a proponent of therapeutic jurisprudence evaluating the contribution of preventive law.

A. The View from the Preventive Law Side of the Aisle

The literature of therapeutic jurisprudence can be thought of as describing a four-fold program. One substantial half of the enterprise is addressed to law reform in the sense of advocating attention to the substance and the process of law itself with the objective that law should advance, and in any event not retard, the therapeutic or psychological well-being of those whom it affects. The complementary half of the therapeutic jurisprudence program lies in the realm of private counseling. Here it focuses on the ways in which consultations with members of the legal profession can similarly affect a client's mental health or psychological well-being.

---

73. *See* LOUIS M. BROWN & EDWARD A. DAUER, PLANNING BY LAWYERS: MATERIALS ON A NONADVERSARIAL LEGAL PROCESS 564-65 (1977) (describing a business organization as a "small society").

Each of these two halves may then be divided again into what might be called the "weak" sense and the "strong" sense of the therapeutic jurisprudence claim. Here, the words weak and strong are meant not as comparative or evaluative terms, but as ways of describing the reach or the ambition of the subject.

As it applies to counseling by private attorneys, therapeutic jurisprudence in its strong sense seeks to alert lawyers to the need to recognize clinically identifiable psychological implications of their counseling and other lawyering activities. Therapeutic jurisprudence is in this regard most closely related to mental health law: and to what was known, some decades ago, as "law and psychiatry." If there is a claim that TJ makes here, it is that lawyers both can and ought to conduct their lawyering in this way.

What might be termed the weaker claim suggests that a significant aspect of lawyering is client well-being—broadly defined as meaning a condition of acceptable or enhanced personal satisfaction and the absence of untoward psychological disturbance.

Between the strong and weak senses there is a continuum, which may be observed from the perspective of preventive law. At the weak end of that continuum, therapeutic jurisprudence appears to be virtually identical with the counseling ambitions of preventive law. At the outer margin of the strong end of the continuum, however, the TJ program appears to be beyond what can be achieved by most preventive lawyers practicing under most everyday circumstances. The question is where on the continuum should legal education aim and where should we place our expectations of practicing lawyers.

Consider the observation that the weak therapeutic jurisprudence claim is not just compatible with preventive law, but is integral to it and possibly inevitable within it. There is no single definition of preventive law that satisfies all preventive law scholars and preventive lawyers. We can for this purpose, however, summarize it by suggesting that the objective of the lawyer practicing preventive law on behalf of a client is to work with that client in arranging his or her affairs, through the use of legal techniques and documents, in such a way as to maximize the probability of achieving the client's objectives and, in doing so, to minimize legal risks and costs associated with those objectives.

Consider this concrete case, which returns us to the context of a close corporation. A client whom a lawyer has seen once or twice before enters the law office and puts this question: "Is it possible for my small, closely- held corporation to have a class of common stock that carries with it the right to participate in the corporation's financial successes, but that does not carry with it the right to vote or otherwise participate in control of the company?"

At the most basic level that is a question about the law to which there is an answer. In most jurisdictions the answer is yes and the techniques by which such a class of stock can be created are easily within the reach of even the least experienced lawyer. To respond to that client's stated request is therefore a relatively simple matter.

If we take the matter to level two, we can visualize a lawyer saying, "Why would you like to do this?" And we can envision the client responding, "Because I want to reward an employee for the fruits of his efforts by giving him a stake in the company." Now we are one layer deeper and the opportunities for helping the client have expanded considerably. There are many routes by which employees can be provided with incentives that match their income with the success of the organization—stock options plans, profit-linked bonuses, and a variety of other things that are equally not terribly arcane.

Now the third level: The lawyer asks, "Any particular employee?" To which the client responds, "My son." Ah. Things are becoming interesting. It would still be possible to provide a purely technical answer to the client's question, but the lawyer might probe further: "Tell me about the relationship of your son to your corporation and your business?"

The client then delivers a long story about a son who has gone down a lifestyle route of which the father does not approve—living in Boulder or Madison or Berkeley and eating but sprouts and tofu. The father, in any case, thinks that all of these problems can be straightened out if the son simply comes into the business with the appropriate incentives in place, and that in no time at all their relationship will be humming and the son's direction will be the right one. At this fourth level the options widen even more broadly. And creating a class of non-voting shares is hardly the best of them.

One of us (Dauer) has used this illustration in teaching preventive law to both law students and to young lawyers, because it creates the opportunity to derive a number of important observations. First, there is in legal counseling a strictly analytical dimension. Clients come to lawyers not with questions, but very often with answers. What it is fascinating to note is how the solution possibilities broaden as the consultation goes deeper into underlying layers of the client's "purpose." Taking the client's request at face value may leave only one or two options. Digging a bit into what the client is really trying to accomplish typically opens up many more, and so even the most basic good lawyering requires good counseling.

The second point is a bit of modesty about the importance of legal solutions to clients' problems. One often hears lawyers or law students say things such as, "The best test of a good contract is its ability to withstand challenges in litigation." Nonsense. Clients don't care about winning lawsuits, just as they really don't care about classes of stock. What they do care about is achieving their objectives.[74] All the rest of it is simply instru-

---

74. *See* Stewart Macaulay, *Non-contractual Relations in Business: A Preliminary Study*, 28 Am. Soc. Rev. 55 (1963) (providing empirical evidence that, in entering into

mental. The best test of a good contract is whether it leads to those kinds of arrangements that achieve a client's objective with the minimum of cost and risk. Thus preventive law requires that lawyers help people achieve their objectives, not that they simply create technically perfect legal documents. Students, and lawyers, often simply fail to understand this point.

The third point is an expansion of the second. Abraham Maslow once said, "If the only thing you have is a hammer, then everything looks like a nail." Sometimes legal solutions are counter-productive. Occasionally clients' problems call for a kind of ministration that has nothing to do with those things that are generally handled by law, lawyers, or any other part of the legal apparatus. As lawyers, we need to know when we are the wrong person. Or at a minimum, we need to know when to associate the case with someone who is the right person. But, the objector will say, the client has decided that a lawyer is what he or she wants.

Again, nonsense. That argument requires that we accept the client's diagnosis to the complete exclusion of our own. It is as if a physician were to allow a patient to enter the examining room and direct the course of the examination by saying, "Palpate my pancreas and do nothing else. I know that the problem lies there." No self-respecting physician would do such a thing. Clients come to lawyers after having engaged in self-diagnosis that is in many if not most cases uninformed by the kind of knowledge about the potential of the law that we hold. While we must respect client autonomy, we must also not abandon the opportunity to offer professional guidance even when it might lead the client out of our office. Indeed, that may well be our duty.

Finally, and this is related to the preceding points as well, incipient legal problems—as opposed to existing litigation—are very often non-symptomatic. Litigation is like a broken arm. By contrast, a legal risk that a client does not recognize is like high blood pressure. It is our job to help clients identify the symptoms of legal risks in time to deal with them. Because clients come to us when they feel they should come to us, part of the preventive law program is the challenge of delivery of legal services to those people who may need it but who have not manifested any demand for it. This, in fact, is very likely the largest single challenge the preventive law program faces—how to help people recognize the occasions for the appropriate use of professional legal help.

---

contractual relations, most businessmen are more concerned with the objective of relationship building and creating good-will than with legal enforceability or anticipating litigation); Stewart Macaulay, *Organic Transactions: Contract, Frank Lloyd Wright and the Johnson Building*, 1996 WIS. L. REV. 75 (1996) (providing a case study illustrating the dominance of important personal/business relationships over legal concerns, even in high-dollar transactions).

To return to the point of departure, this example illustrates why therapeutic jurisprudence taken in its weak sense is an indispensable component of preventive law, taken at its most fundamental level. Because we are concerned in practicing preventive law with achieving our client's objectives and therefore with maximizing our client's individual welfare, we should not be satisfied with measuring the outcomes of our activities simply by testing their legal sufficiency. Our test must ultimately be the impact of what we do on the client's total welfare. The word "welfare" overlaps with well-being and includes psychological well-being, in its non-clinical sense. It would therefore be difficult if not impossible to practice preventive law well without heeding the lessons and concerns of therapeutic jurisprudence.

B. The View from the Therapeutic Jurisprudence Side of the Aisle

At the outset, the integration reveals certain limits in the way the two approaches have traditionally been conceptualized. Preventive law traditionally has focused on estate and business planning,[75] yet the recognition that attorney-client interactions have inevitable therapeutic consequences extends beyond these contexts to encompass as well attorneys performing traditional litigation roles. For example, a motion to exclude the public from a civil commitment hearing when embarrassing information is about to be presented may serve a TJ-preventive function by reducing the chances of further undermining the client's self-image.[76] Likewise, though perhaps at the weaker end of the TJ continuum, lawyers defending clients against tort suits or other civil litigation may, through their conduct, help to reduce the risk of exposure to future litigation. This can avoid both future legal risk and psychological difficulties, thereby plainly serving an important TJ preventive function.

Therapeutic jurisprudence thus has the potential to expand considerably the preventive law paradigm. This expansion may even come in areas in which the lawyer's intervention is primarily psychological in its effects, but incidentally also may produce legal advantages or prevent legal disadvantages. For example, Winick has suggested that, in view of the neg-

---

75. However, preventive law, like therapeutic jurisprudence, has expanded its scope in recent years, extending to such areas "as environmental law, sex discrimination, and computer law. In addition new applications have been found in the more traditional areas of estate planning, corporate compliance, business planning, and property transactions." HARDAWAY, *supra* note 4, at xxv.

76. *See* WEXLER, THERAPEUTIC AGENT, *supra* note 17, at 18.

ative psychological effects of incompetency labeling, criminal attorneys representing defendants in the incompetency to stand trial context who are found incompetent can help the client to interpret that legal label in a way that minimizes the risk of adverse psychological consequences.[77] Thus, the lawyer can tell his or her client that the incompetency determination is merely an opportunity for the client to secure needed treatment and a delay in the proceedings that will enable the client to function more effectively in the attorney-client relationship when the criminal proceedings are resumed.[78]

By helping the client to reframe the legal label as a form of treatment continuance, the attorney thus can help the client to avoid what might otherwise be negative self-attributional effects triggered by application of the incompetency label. If successful, attorney efforts in this regard can help to improve the client's legal situation. As a result, these efforts can properly be understood to be a form of preventive law. ✶

The preventive law paradigm can also help attorneys in their everyday practice of law to better realize the full potential of therapeutic jurisprudence. Although much of the early therapeutic jurisprudence scholarship centered on the impact of legal rules or procedures on the mental health and psychological functioning of those affected, more recent work has suggested that the way various legal actors—judges, lawyers, police officers and some times state-employed clinicians—apply the law also can have important therapeutic effects.[79] Preventive law provides a concrete context in which the therapeutic impact of attorney conduct can be identified and studied.

While preventive law and therapeutic jurisprudence may sometimes be mutually exclusive categories, there is undeniably an area in which the two overlap. Figure 1 illustrates this point.

Figure 1

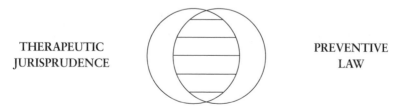

THERAPEUTIC
JURISPRUDENCE   PREVENTIVE
                                                        LAW

Some legal advice might prevent future legal dilemmas but have only slight if any consequences on the mental health or psychological func-

---

77. *See* Winick, Mental Health, *supra* note 18, at 63-65.
78. *Id.*
79. *See* Wexler, *supra* note 17.

tioning of the client. Some legal advice might be related to positive therapeutic consequences, but largely unrelated to avoiding future legal problems. One rather clear example of therapeutic jurisprudence that is not preventive law is the use of therapeutic jurisprudence arguments in test case litigation designed to change a rule of law.[80] An example of preventive law that is not obviously therapeutic jurisprudence is helping a client copyright an innovation in computer software. In the area of intersection, however, legal actions can have both preventive law and therapeutic consequences.

The above examples—from the areas of elder law, HIV/AIDS law, matrimonial law, and business planning—are illustrative of contexts in which preventive law and therapeutic jurisprudence may have a substantial overlap. In these areas of overlap, sensitizing the preventive lawyer to the potential psychological impact of various problems and methods of dealing with them can both enhance the preventive law mission and also minimize psychological difficulties or even mental health problems. Lawyers performing a preventive law check-up who have developed a sensitivity to psychological issues will be better equipped to conduct the attorney-client interview and to provide effective counseling. This psychological sensitivity will allow the attorney to put the client at ease, to engender trust and confidence, to obtain information from the client more effectively, and to better understand the client's needs, desires, and capacities.[81] Such an attorney will be better able to deal with the emotional dimensions of particular problems, to help the client understand such situations more clearly and to design and implement preventive law solutions more effectively.[82]

Having this psychological orientation can allow the attorney more effectively to perform the preventive law function. In addition, a therapeutically-oriented preventive lawyer can also encounter many opportunities to avoid and relieve psychological stress in clients, to avoid law-created psychological dysfunctional effects, and otherwise to act in ways that will increase the client's psychological well-being. The practice of preventive law thus provides many therapeutic jurisprudence opportunities. And, an integration of these two fields can provide considerably expanded opportunities for both.[83]

---

80. *See* Michael L. Perlin et al., *Therapeutic Jurisprudence and the Civil Rights of Institutionalized Mentally Disabled Persons: Hopeless Oxymoron or Path to Redemption?, in* Wexler & Winick, Therapeutic Key, *supra* note 18, at 739.

81. *See generally* Linda G. Mills, *Affective Lawyering: The Emotional Structure of the Lawyer-Client Relation* (forthcoming 1997).

82. *See id.*

83. *See* Stolle & Wexler, *Preventive Law, supra* note 2.

IV. Promise, Prospects, and Proposed Paths

The proposition that therapeutic jurisprudence and preventive law are interrelated and overlapping is clearly a welcome one from both the preventive law and therapeutic jurisprudence sides of the aisle. To put it perhaps more crisply than might be justified, it has been suggested that therapeutic jurisprudence (in its private counseling sense) is a body of substance in need of a method of application.[84] If that is so, then preventive law has been a method of application with an incomplete body of substance. The advantages of coordination between the two schools of thought and of the interaction between them are therefore obvious.

Inasmuch as there is agreement concerning the advantages of an integration of the two fields, the question becomes, "What's next?" The areas that may demand our attention are: (a) In practice, how far on the continuum from the weak claim to the strong claim should we strive to go? (b) What should the research and scholarship component of TJ Preventive Law look like?[85] and (c) how might the educational or teaching component of TJ Preventive Law proceed?

A. Practice

Attorney-client counseling will often reveal circumstances in which the client's psychological well-being may be directly affected by the situation under discussion. The examples drawn from the context of elder law and matrimonial law, as well as the HIV/AIDS and business planning examples discussed above, are illustrative. Some lawyers will have an intuitive sensitivity to the psychological dilemmas presented and may have developed sensible strategies for communicating to clients about these dilemmas and alternative strategies for dealing with them. Many attorneys, however, will not. Many will simply lack a knowledge base concerning psychology and how to identify and deal with the psychological issues that may arise in practice contexts, and will feel uncomfortable offering counseling on these matters as a result.

---

84. Therapeutic jurisprudence is actually not so much a body of substance as it is an approach (through careful analysis and empirical research) to creating a body of substance. To date, therapeutic jurisprudence has been required to draw on social science literature that is related to law but often not explicitly an investigation of law-related psychological distress. The body of explicit therapeutic jurisprudence substance is growing; however, much more empirical research is needed.

85. As will become evident in the discussion that follows, these in quiries are intimately related. The more our research and educational components prosper, the easier it is to move, in practice, from the weaker to the stronger side of the continuum.

Some lawyers will say, "I'm not a psychologist. If the client feels the need for psychological counseling, he or she can seek the services of a counselor." But, is it psychology when you discuss with a terminally ill parent the importance of talking to the kids about a standby guardian,[86] or with an HIV-positive client the desirability of talking to his partner about being named — or not being named — executor?[87] These illustrations show just how interdisciplinary the enterprise is, for if a psychologist were to advise such steps, wouldn't he or she similarly be subject to the turf-related accusation of practicing law? And wouldn't a psychologist likely be even more in the dark about standby guardians and executors than would a lawyer about psychologically-sensitive points relating to legal situations?

Many with the view that they are strictly a lawyer and not a counselor may ignore the psychological dimensions of a client's problem and become insensitive to them. This approach is problematic. Clients may resent their lawyers if they display such an emotional insensitivity and may feel misunderstood. A sense that a lawyer lacks empathy may diminish client trust and confidence, with possibly negative effects on the attorney-client relationship and its ability to achieve positive client outcomes.[88] Lawyers with a preventive law orientation in particular should reject this attitude and adopt the posture of sensitivity and openness to their client's psychological responses. They should understand that in their relationships with clients, they are inevitably psychological and even therapeutic agents. They should, in short, embrace the teachings and insights of therapeutic jurisprudence.[89]

However, in embracing a TJ Preventive Law approach to legal practice, it is important to bear in mind that, individually, therapeutic jurisprudence and preventive law each have their own baggage, and the integration of the two means that each perspective will now inherit the baggage of its

---

86. *See* Stolle & Wexler, *Therapeutic Jurisprudence, supra* note 2; *see also* discussion *supra* Part II.

87. *See generally* Stolle & Wexler, *Therapeutic Jurisprudence, supra* note 2; *see also* discussion *supra* Part II.

88. *See generally* Mills, *supra* note 81 (providing an insightful discussion of the importance of attorney/client rapport).

89. The approach of TJ Preventive Law may also have the potential to enhance the well-being of the lawyer. Indeed, one lawyer recently described the practice of preventive law as "life-affirming." *See* Isaacson, *supra* note 14, at 33; *see also* Robert B. Hughes, *If Anybody Should be Immune from Lawyer-Bashing, It's Us!*, 1990 PREVENTIVE L. REP. 14 (1990) (suggesting that "if there is any real justification for lawyer bashing, I think we can state unequivocally that the segment of our legal profession (possibly a small segment) which is working actively toward preventive law certainly does not fit into that mold").

new partner. For example, preventive law is sometimes (improperly) accused of promoting solicitation,[90] and clients or prospective clients sometimes fear that a lawyer is creating work that is not truly needed.[91] When the preventive work also takes on a TJ dimension—alerting the client to foreseeable psychological/emotional fallout of certain courses of legal action—there is the additional potential concern among lawyers that, unless skillfully communicated, this additional advice may unnerve the client and kill the deal.[92]

In a related way, some lawyers have raised objections to preventive law checklists on the grounds that checklists, once promulgated, will potentially set a new—and higher—standard of care in legal malpractice matters. Therapeutic jurisprudence has confronted a similar issue regarding the reluctance of organizations of mental health professionals to promulgate crystallized standards for professional practice, fearing that they will be creating "duties that their members are then held liable for transgressing."[93] With the addition of therapeutic jurisprudence, the preventive law malpractice concerns may be magnified.[94]

Who are lawyers, it may be asked, to anticipate and advise clients on avoiding psychological pressures, stresses, reactions—even if those psycho logical states are intricately related to legal advice and proposed legal courses of action? And what sort of standard of care (and malpractice coverage) should be used if this advice backfires? What if a lawyer recommends a marital or family discussion about an especially sensitive situation, and that discussion results in a permanently breached familial relationship

---

90. *See* discussion and accompanying footnotes *supra* note 16.

91. This supports the notion that it is best initially to encourage the use of the perspective in legal services offices, prepaid legal plans, and law school clinics—contexts where this concern should surely not be an issue. *See supra* note 16; *see generally* Mosten *supra* note 10, at 443 (addressing the issue of client's perceiving preventive law yering as "financially motivated"). *But cf.* Isaacson, *supra* note 14 (suggesting that "[t]here is simply not as much money in counseling and advising clients on how to avoid legal problems as there is in litigating disputes"); *see also* David S. Rowley, *Preventive Law Can Be—And Is-A Solo Practitioner's Career*, 1989 PREVENTIVE L. REP. 13 (March 1989) (arguing that "[p]reventive law is not a mechanical profit center").

92. For example, some lawyers may worry that pointing out all of the potential quarrels that could arise in opening a business with friends and family, such as the cafe described in our Corporate and Business Planning Law discussion, might discourage the client and cause the client to abandon the whole idea. *See* discussion *supra* Part II.D.

93. Robert F. Schopp & David B. Wexler, *Shooting Yourself in the Foot with Due Care: Psychotherapists and Crystallized Standards of Tort Liability*, in WEXLER & WINICK, ESSAYS, *supra* note 18, at 179 (proposing some ways of dealing with the matter).

94. *See generally* Mosten, *supra* note 10, at 430 (discussing malpractice exposure within the context of "unbundled" legal services).

or even in violence? Of course, with a touch of preventive law, the legal expo-sure of the TJ preventive lawyer can perhaps be minimized by the lawyer behaving in a non-directive fashion and simply presenting the client with an array of options.[95]

Such questions regarding the proper parameters of the TJ Preventive Law enterprise, and questions regarding its relationship to issues of pro-fessional responsibility, will inevitably arise. These questions should not be avoided, nor should they quell hopes for the full development of the integrated framework in practice contexts. Rather, such questions can become topics addressed by a new brand of psycholegal scholarship that focuses efforts on both understanding the therapeutic and anti-therapeu-tic impact of everyday lawyering, and developing practical methods for maximizing preventive and therapeutic outcomes. As answers to these and other questions materialize, TJ Preventive Law will settle into a comfort-able position on the continuum between the weak and the strong TJ claim.

B. Research and Scholarship

A major difficulty with the TJ Preventive Law approach to law yering lies in the fact that lawyers have almost no empirical base on which to pro-ceed. It is one thing to teach a young lawyer that the act of executing a durable power of attorney has an important psychological effect on many older clients. It may even be that we have some sense of what that effect is. But if there are three or four legal routes to the same personal objec-tive, there typically exists no literature that suggests empirically any link between each of those routes and the relevant features of its psychologi-cal outcomes or side effects.

While physicians share experiential information derived from specific cases in their literature, lawyers tend not to do so. Whether for reasons of confi-dentiality, competitiveness, or whatever, the fact is that there is virtually no empirical base on which we can say with any confidence that the therapeu-tic implications of one kind of document, in specified circumstances, are supe-rior to the therapeutic implications of another. The available data about the uses of these documents comes almost exclusively from case reports, and cases never mention the kinds of psychological implications in which the ther-apeutic jurisprudence and preventive law enterprise would be interested.

---

95. Therapeutic jurisprudence has seen this issue in the context of the Ramona repressed memory lawsuit, where a therapist was sued by the father of a patient who was encouraged by the therapist to confront the father regarding new memories of childhood sexual abuse; therapists have been advised to avoid possible Ramona liability by behaving in a far less directive manner than apparently occurred in Ramona. *See* David B. Wexler, *Therapeutic Jurisprudence in Clinical Practice*, 153 Am. J. Psychiatry 453 (1996).

Of course, comprehensive encyclopedias need not exist for some gains to be achieved in this area. Rather, it would suffice if there were a manageable number of general propositions that could be conveyed, tested, and validated in the field. This would provide, at least, a substantial improvement over the ignorance (or judgment or intuition) with which many lawyers now operate. Lawyers' current knowledge base of things psychological can and should be increased through additional TJ Preventive Law research and scholarship. The focus of this new breed of legal psychology should be (1) identifying "psycholegal soft spots"; (2) identifying or developing several preventive legal strategies relevant to those psycholegal soft spots; and (3) evaluating the therapeutic or anti-therapeutic effects of the available strategies.

C. Identifying Psycholegal Soft Spots

The "psycholegal soft spot" is a TJ Preventive Law concept which grows out of the preventive law concept of the "legal soft spot" advanced by Louis Brown.[96] Whereas the concept of legal soft spots refers to factors in a client's affairs that may give rise to future legal trouble, the concept of psycholegal soft spots might include the identification of social relationships or emotional issues that ought to be considered in order to avoid conflict or stress when contemplating the use of a particular legal instrument.

For example, the relationships among children might be considered before leaving an inheritance in trust for one child and outright for another, as in the elder law example above.[97] Or, the relationships between an HIV-positive client and his or her family might be considered before making decisions about naming a proxy health care decision maker.[98] In addition, the impact on the welfare of children of divorce might be considered in the determination of custody arrangements and even the mode of resolving divorce and property settlement disputes between divorcing spouses.[99] Many additional examples likely exist across numerous areas of practice. Furthermore, the psycholegal soft spot concept need not be restricted to social relations. A psycholegal soft spot may simply be recognition that a particular type of legal proceeding, such as a request to modify a child

---

96. Louis Brown, *Manual for Periodic Check-up*, CLS (1974), *ex cerpted in* HARD-AWAY, *supra* note 4, at 191-92; *see also* Mosten, *supra* note 10, at 446 (pro viding examples of legal soft spots and corresponding client actions that might be considered and pointing out that "[s]ome legal soft spots may be 'pure' legal issues—most are not").

97. *See supra* Part II.

98. *See supra* Part II.

99. *See* Maxwell, *supra* note 61.

custody arrangement, often places clients under severe psychological or emotional distress.

How might lawyers or scholars actually go about identifying and cataloguing such recurring psycholegal soft spots? For starters, attorneys encountering the psycholegal soft spots that arise in their preventive law practices can become sensitive to these situations and can share information with one another, either formally or informally.[100] Many good lawyers will already possess a degree of wisdom and insight concerning these matters. But as lawyers, we should periodically question our insights and compare notes with our colleagues, as we would on other matters—ethical dilemmas, for example, or new or newly changed areas of practice. These psychological dilemmas should become the subject of professional dialogue—in legal newspapers, bar meetings, and continuing education programs.[101]

Furthermore, TJ Preventive Law case studies that identify psycholegal soft spots could be written up in the manner in which bio-ethics case studies appear in the Hastings Center Report. That publication frequently contains case studies drawn from medical practice or research, accompanied by commentary by various experts. Legal case studies with accompanying commentary by attorneys and/or psychologists could perhaps become a recurring feature in the Preventive Law Reporter, in the newly-established Therapeutic Jurisprudence Forum of the University of Puerto Rico's law journal,[102] or in a peer-reviewed interdisciplinary journal.

Another potential type of research is the performance by teams of academic lawyers, social scientists, and their students of surveys of lawyers practicing in various areas of specialization to ascertain recurring pressure points and emotional dilemmas arising in lawyer/client counseling contexts.[103] Such a survey instrument perhaps could be administered to all Preventive Law Reporter subscribers, or other practitioner oriented publication subscribers.

---

100. One informal method might be through an automated e-mail list-serve. *See* Stolle & Wexler, *Preventive Law*, *supra* note 2.

101. *See* Stolle & Wexler, *Preventive Law*, *supra* note 2.

102. A regular Therapeutic Jurisprudence Forum of REVISTA JURIDICA U.P.R., dedicated to the publication of TJ articles and essays, is one important component of the University of Puerto Rico's newly-created International Network on Therapeutic Jurisprudence, which will serve as a clearinghouse and resource center for developments in therapeutic jurisprudence.

103. Additionally, such interdisciplinary research could include the systematic collection of the experiences of law students and of their supervising attorneys in legal clinics sensitized to the TJ preventive approach. *See* discussion *infra*.

D. Identifying and Developing Preventive Legal Strategies

Once psycholegal soft spots have been identified and catalogued, legal scholars and practitioners can publish work that identifies and discusses various legal strategies relevant to a particular psycholegal soft spot. Such scholarship might include analyses of the appropriateness of the potential legal strategies from perspectives such as the enforceability, the cost effectiveness, the level of difficulty, and the professional responsibility implications of engaging in one legal strategy over another. In those cases in which only one legal strategy appears obviously to be available, the scholarship might involve the theoretical development of new and alternative legal strategies. This may include the creative use of lawyering skills, the creative interpretation or application of existing law, or proposals for law reform.

In addition to these theoretical and analytical approaches, empirical approaches to identifying alternative legal strategies may be developed as well. For example, an empirical approach might involve the preparation of standardized case studies raising psychological trouble points in lawyer/client counseling contexts, and the submission of such case studies to samples of lawyers practicing in the relevant area. Data could be collected concerning how these attorneys would react in the situation portrayed. It could then be ascertained whether there was consensus among attorneys in certain areas of practice concerning how to handle various psychological dilemmas arising in practice. Indeed, tabulations of this data might inspire further theoretical and analytical scholarship. Areas revealing a lack of consensus could become the subjects of debate by law professors, psychologists, and attorneys in scholarly and practitioner journals. They could also become the subject of professional meetings of bar association practice area groups or of such organizations as the Inns of Court. The publication of such data and the commentary it could generate could go a long way to increasing our knowledge base concerning the psychological implications of various legal practice situations and how best to minimize or avoid psychological dilemmas.

E. Evaluating the Therapeutic or Antitherapeutic Effects of the Available Strategies

Most of the psycholegal soft spots that are identified will lack a developed psychological literature with appropriate guideposts. In such circumstances, therapeutic jurisprudence scholars can discuss psychological doctrine in analogous areas in an effort to speculate about likely therapeutic and anti-therapeutic consequences of various alternatives. This is, in fact, the conventional mode of therapeutic jurisprudence scholarship illustrated by Wexler's use of health care compliance principles to make reform proposals for the insanity acquittee release process,[104] and Winick's use of the literature on the psychology of choice to speculate about the likely therapeutic consequences of recognizing a right to refuse mental health treatment.[105] By drawing on existing areas of psychological research, therapeutic jurisprudence scholars can frame hypotheses about likely therapeutic and anti-therapeutic outcomes in lawyer/client counseling contexts.[106]

In addition, the identification of psycholegal soft spots can serve as the basis for generating empirical research on both the likely outcomes and the therapeutic value of alternative solutions. Social scientists could frame and test hypotheses concerning outcomes and alternative solutions through the use of various experimental and quasi-experimental research designs. Although such research may be difficult, it is not impossible to perform.[107] Even though social science research methods may not always be sufficient to provide clear answers, they can produce considerable additional information that can be quite helpful. The identification of recurring psychological trouble points in preventive law counseling and the subsequent evaluation of preventive/therapeutic strategies for dealing with those trouble points could provide fascinating empirical social science research opportunities. And, the results of such research would be enormously useful to preventive lawyers in their counseling efforts.

Among the possible empirical strategies, a sample of attorneys surveyed could be interviewed telephonically for further details or perhaps at periodic intervals to determine whether an anticipated psychological problem materialized or whether a particular solution worked or failed. Felsteiner

---

104. *See* WEXLER & WINICK, ESSAYS, *supra* note 18.

105. *See* WINICK, MENTAL HEALTH, *supra* note 18, at 67-91; BRUCE J. WINICK, RIGHT TO REFUSE MENTAL HEALTH TREATMENT 327-44 (1997).

106. The areas of relevant psychological research need not be limited to clinical issues. Indeed, much social-cognitive psychology—especially the areas of cognitive heuristics, stereotypes, cognitive schemas, and judgment under uncertainty—is likely to be relevant to understanding patterns of client decision-making. *See* Lynn A. Baker & Robert E. Emery, *When Every Relationship Is Above Average: Perceptions and Expecta tions of Divorce at the Time of Marriage*, 17 L. & HUM. BEHAV. 439 (1993). For an introduction to social cognition, see FISKE & TAYLOR, SOCIAL COGNITION (1991).

107. *See generally* WEXLER & WINICK, THERAUPEUTIC KEY, *supra* note 18, at 845-994 (providing numerous examples of creative empirical research related to therapeutic jurisprudence).

and Sarat performed research that is somewhat related when they record-ed conversations of attorneys and their clients involving divorce.[108] The research suggested here could go considerably further, in that it might begin with qualitative or survey methods but then move to quasi-experi-mental methods, and even true experiments. Thus, the research would move beyond being largely descriptive and would begin to actually test novel approaches and enable researchers to draw causal conclusions. By no means are we suggesting that such research would be easy to conduct. Rather, such research is likely to pose interesting, though not insur-mountable, methodological issues. Indeed, analysis of methodological problems arising in the conduct of research of this kind can itself be the sub-ject of interesting and significant scholarship. Ultimately, however, we believe that research using accepted methodologies to collect and evalu-ate this type of psycholegal data can be developed and will result in a new and highly useful form of empirical legal psychology.

In this way, the attorney-client relationship can become the subject of a new body of interdisciplinary research that can then impact the way in which the law develops in this area as well as how lawyers apply the law and con-duct their counseling function. Several analogies exist. For example, prior to the 1970's, much of antitrust law was developed based largely upon judicial intuitions about the anti-competitive impact of various business practices. In the years since then, a significant body of law and economics scholarship has examined these issues through economic modeling and, in some cases, empir-ical investigation.[109] This law and economic scholarship has proved to be of enormous use to courts and to antitrust lawyers. Moreover, the law and eco-nomics approach has spilled over to affect many other areas of the law.

A second example arises from medical practice. Physicians frequently face a variety of ethical dilemmas in dealing with patient treatment and research involving human subjects. While some physicians may have developed intuitive approaches to dealing with these dilemmas, many lacked a suffi-cient knowledge base in this area. This vacuum created an entire field that has come to be known as "bio-ethics." Philosophers applied ethical the-ory to deal with these emerging treatment and research issues, and this new body of interdisciplinary work has been of enormous use to practic-ing physicians and to institutional review boards that now exist in virtu-ally all hospitals and health care facilities.

---

108. *See* William L.F. Felstiner & Austin Sarat, *Enactments of Power: Negotiating Reality and Responsibility in Lawyer-Client Interactions*, 77 CORNELL L. REV. 1447 (1992) [hereinafter *Enactments of Power*]; Austin Sarat & William L.F. Felstiner, *Lawyers and Legal Consciousness: Law Talk in the Divorce Lawyer's Office*, 98 YALE L.J. 1663 (1989) [hereinafter *Lawyers and Legal Consciousness*].

109. *See id.*

A similar body of theoretical and empirical work can, we hope, be developed to address the various psychological dilemmas that are recurring in lawyer/client preventive law contexts. The fruits of this new work could help considerably to expand the knowledge base of preventive lawyers who seek to apply a TJ-oriented approach in their lawyering. This work may be unlikely to result in fixed algorithms that attorneys can apply in every context. The people and circumstances involved in legal counseling situations are perhaps too varied and lawyers are perhaps too often presented with novel situations for the methods of actuarial decision making to supplant the traditional legal methods of clinical decision making anytime in the foreseeable future.[110] Indeed, a healthy measure of professional discretion may be both inevitable and desirable in the attorney counseling context. However, that discretion can be informed considerably by the kind of probabilistic information that careful empirical research can provide.[111] We hope that this discussion and future discussions like it will continue to inspire such empirical psycholegal research.

F. Teaching[112]

Once this body of empirical knowledge regarding the therapeutic impact of various lawyer/client interactions begins to emerge, the information must be disseminated to a relevant audience. Law school education is the obvious starting point. Law school seminars are already being separately taught on the topics of preventive law and therapeutic jurisprudence.[113]

---

110. For an introduction to the distinction between actuarial and clinical decision-making in the context of psychology, see Marc C. Marchese, *Clinical Versus Actuarial Prediction: A Review of the Literature*, 75 PERCEPTUAL & MOTOR SKILLS 583 (1992); *see also* John Monahan, *Clinical and Actuarial Predictions of Violence, in* 1 MODERN SCIENTIFIC EVIDENCE: THE LAW AND SCIENCE OF EXPERT TESTIMONY 300 (D. Faigman et al. eds., 1997). For further discussion of the issue of standardization in legal checklists, see HARDAWAY, *supra* note 4, at 496.

111. This information is perhaps best utilized in practice in the form of preventive/therapeutic checklists. Preventive law has long touted the use of checklists. The integrated preventive/therapeutic framework provides an opportunity to develop checklists that move a step beyond the traditional preventive checklist by contemplating both legal and psychological or social concerns. Furthermore, such checklists could be based not merely upon intuition, or poorly documented experience. Rather, the checklists could be based upon sound empirical research that identifies those factors that contribute significantly to outcomes of interest and those that do not.

112. Portions of this section were adapted from Stolle & Wexler, *Preventive Law*, *supra* note 2.

113. For example, seminars on preventive law have been offered at the University of Denver School of Law and at the University of Southern California School of Law, and a

Seminars devoted jointly to preventive law and therapeutic jurisprudence could also be developed. Students could read interdisciplinary scholarship, including empirical psycholegal studies and theoretical therapeutic jurisprudence scholarship, and discuss how the ideas presented might be put into practice with a preventive orientation. Such a seminar would have a strong emphasis on the importance of client counseling and might even be integrated into a standing course on client counseling or negotiation.

Such a seminar could employ the usual features of legal education — reading and discussing appellate case reports with some form of Socratic questioning led by the professor — as well as less traditional classroom activities. For example, students could be presented with concrete examples and required to role-play the probable lawyer/client interactions in the classroom.[114] The role-play exercises could involve law students either playing the part of the lawyer or of the client, or, at some universities, could involve undergraduate students from a law and psychology course or a sociology of law course to play the parts of the clients. Following the lawyer/client role-play, students could then attempt to draft documents that resolve the legal trouble area without undermining the client's extralegal interests, which were brought out during the role-play.[115]

Students might also be required to research preventive legal resources outside of the classroom materials, and to draft checklists for client counseling. Such a checklist could focus on any substantive area of law in which the student has an interest in practicing in the future. Ideally, students would research relevant legal precedent as well as relevant social science literature, in an attempt to develop checklists that incorporate both legal

---

preventive law oriented course on transactional lawyering is offered at Whittier Law School. Likewise, courses on therapeutic jurisprudence have been offered at the following law schools or joint law/psychology programs: University of Arizona, the University of Puerto Rico, the University of Miami, New York Law School, the University of Nebraska, Capital University, Widener University, and Osgoode Hall Law School of York University. *See* David B. Wexler, *Some Thoughts and Observations on the Teaching of Therapeutic Jurisprudence*, 35 REVISTA DE DERECHO PUERTORRIQUENO 273, 273 n.2 (1996).

114. *See* HARDAWAY, *supra* note 4, at xliv (discussing role playing as a technique for teaching preventive law). An excellent book on counseling skills is DAVID A. BINDER ET AL., LAWYERS AS COUNSELORS: A CLIENT-CENTERED APPROACH (1991). The work urges lawyers to anticipate and consider the "nonlegal" consequences—including psychological ones—that invariably accompany legal measures, but note that "nonlegal consequences are often difficult to predict." *Id.* at 12. We hope that the research we propose on identifying psycholegal soft spots and strategies will enable us explicitly and systematically to focus on the law-related psychological dimension in legal counseling—and that it will make this sort of nonlegal consequence less difficult to predict.

115. *See* HARDAWAY, *supra* note 4, at xliv (discussing document drafting as a technique for teaching preventive law).

concerns as well as psychological concerns, each grounded in information gathered from appropriate sources of authority. A well-drafted checklist of this type may be one of the few written assignments completed during law school that a student will actually retain and utilize during his or her practice.[116] Likewise students might be required to choose an area of law of interest to them, to read treatises and consumer oriented books on the chosen area, interview several lawyers working in the area,[117] and finally prepare and present a paper on some important psycholegal soft spots and strategies for dealing with them.[118]

At some law schools, materials on TJ Preventive Law could also be integrated into the first year course on legal process or lawyering skills.[119] This section of the first year course, consuming perhaps only a small portion of the total semester, could be entitled "counseling and prevention" or simply "preventive law," and may pique students' interest in later taking an upper level seminar devoted exclusively to the topic. At law schools that do not require a first year course on legal process, lawyering skills, or some analogous course, some introduction to the integrated framework somewhere in the first year, perhaps in property or contracts, might set the tone for the remainder of a law student's career, legitimizing the concepts of counseling and prevention.

Ideally, some TJ Preventive Law principles might also seep into the clinically-oriented upper level courses.[120] Many upper- level courses will nat-

---

116. Some such projects might be of publishable quality. Even those that may fall short of publishable quality could be retained as unpublished manuscripts, forming the foundation for a library of TJ preventive materials. *See generally* Louis M. Brown, *Decisions in the Law Office, Like Those in Appellate Courts, Should be Available*, 1990 PREVENTIVE L. REP. 17 (1990); Louis M. Brown, *Lawyering Decisions: New Materials for Law Libraries to Collect*, 87 LAW LIBR. J. 7 (1995).

117. The interviewing component of the assignment has the potential to make the project come to life for the students. Furthermore, the interviews will likely expose students to the wide range of approaches to lawyering and to the extent to which lawyers intuitively take a preventive, or even TJ preventive, approach to working with clients.

118. Again, some of these papers will likely rise to the level of publishable quality, and even those that do not could still make a significant contribution to an ongoing collection of TJ preventive lawyering materials. *See, e.g., Felstiner & Sarat, Enactments of Power, supra* note 108; *Sarat & Felstiner, Lawyers and Legal Consciousness, supra* note 108.

119. For example, at the University of Missouri-Kansas City Law School, preventive law is being introduced in the first year course on Torts taught by Edward Richards, as well as in his upper level courses on Health Law and Products Liability. Likewise, Richard Gruner includes a preventive law component in his Corporations course at Whittier Law School.

120. *See generally* Louis M. Brown, *Experimental Preventive Law Courses*, 18 J. LEGAL EDUC. 212 (1965) (describing the plan for a course intended to teach preventive lawyering techniques to third-year law students).

urally lend themselves to a TJ Preventive Law approach, such as client counseling, wills and trusts, family law, estate planning, and negotiations. Furthermore, criminal and civil clinics might take on a preventive orientation, emphasizing psychological well-being as one important consideration in legal planning.[121] Law school clinics operated with a TJ Preventive Law orientation might benefit both the students, by preparing them to be thoughtful and careful practitioners, and the public, by providing needy citizens with psychologically sophisticated preventive legal counsel.[122]

V. Conclusion

Lawyers once described themselves as "counselors and attorneys- at-law." But the role of lawyer as counselor has seemed to diminish markedly in recent years. The proposed integration of therapeutic jurisprudence and preventive law seeks to reclaim this lost ground and to reshape the everyday practice of law in ways that emphasize this counseling function and that give this counseling function real structure and substance, rather than merely paying it lip-service or describing it in amorphous and often unhelpful ways.

In recent years, the consumers of legal services have experienced what seems to be a growing dissatisfaction with lawyers. Lawyers more frequently are seen as unethical professionals whose interest in their clients' welfare is subordinated to their own pecuniary interests. The prevalence of lawyer jokes in the popular media and the portrayal of lawyers as objects

---

121. In fact, under the direction of Professor Mariluz Jimenez, the legal clinic at the University of Puerto Rico (a law school clinic in which all third-year students are required to participate) is in the process of undertaking just such an orientation to supervised law practice.

122. In order to take on a comprehensive TJ Preventive Law orientation, legal clinics should consider offering preventive legal services and legal checkups to certain groups of prospective clients, and should even consider creating outreach programs to make such services known and available. *Cf.* Melanie B. Abbott, *Seeking Shelter Under a Deconstructed Roof: Homelessness and Critical Lawyering*, 64 TENN. L. REV. 269, 289 (1997) (analyzing the relationship between jurisprudence and social action within the context of the problem of homelessness). Abbott also notes that the impact of therapeutic jurisprudence "has so far been limited to the academic realm." *Id.* at 289. We hope, however, that the integration of TJ with preventive law will take TJ into the realm of the practicing lawyer. Likewise, TJ is beginning to attract the interest of the judiciary. For example, TJ was the theme of the Annual Conference of Women Judges, held in September 1997, Salt Lake City, Utah. *See also* William Schma, *Book Review*, 36 JUDGES JOURNAL 81 (1997) (reviewing WEXLER & WINICK, THERAPEUTIC KEY, *supra* note 18) (suggesting that TJ has much to offer the judiciary in its day-to-day business).

of ridicule evidences just how far the reputation of lawyers has fallen in recent years. Moreover, many lawyers seem increasingly dissatisfied with the practice of law, and lawyers as a professional group experience a higher incidence of mental illness and substance abuse than other professions.[123]

Reshaping the role of lawyer in the way proposed here can do much to change both public attitudes concerning lawyers and the personal and professional satisfaction of practitioners in the field. Rather than merely dealing with people's problems, and with the perhaps inevitable perception that they are part of those problems, lawyers should become problem-avoiders, counseling their clients in ways that can anticipate and prevent future difficulties. While this is the basic mission of preventive law, the sensitivity to the psychological dimensions of law practice that the integration of therapeutic jurisprudence and preventive law can bring about will permit the preventive law approach to be applied more effectively, with greater client and lawyer satisfaction. Bringing therapeutic jurisprudence and preventive law together can broaden the counseling mission, and can convert the practice of law into a helping and healing profession in ways that may make it a much more humanitarian tool.

As broadened and redefined by the integration suggested here, the practice of law can bring enormous personal satisfaction and can become a force that will enhance the mental health and psychological well-being of the client. Integrating these two fields will surely enhance the potential of each. In the process, the practice of law can be transformed into an instrument for helping people, ultimately revitalizing the professional life of the lawyer by making law practice more enriched and fulfilling.

---

123. *See generally* Amiram Elwork & G. Andrew H. Benjamin, *Lawyers in Distress*, in WEXLER & WINICK, THERAPEUTIC KEY, *supra* note 18, at 569; Susan Daicoff, *Lawyer, Know Thyself: A Review of Empirical Research on Attorney Attributes Bearing on Professionalism*, 46 AM. U.L. REV. (forthcoming 1997).

Chapter 2

Practicing Therapeutic Jurisprudence: Psycholegal Soft Spots and Strategies

David B. Wexler

I. Introduction

Therapeutic jurisprudence focuses on the law's impact on emotional life and psychological well-being. It is a perspective that views the law itself (legal rules, legal procedures, and the roles of legal actors) as a potential therapeutic agent. Recent therapeutic jurisprudence writing makes it clear that the approach is not substantively restricted to the area of mental health law, but is instead a therapeutic perspective on the law in general.[1] In addition, this interdisciplinary approach looks not only at possible law reform, but pays attention, too, to how existing law—whatever it is—may be *applied* in a manner more conducive to the psychological well-being of those it affects.[2]

Despite its robust scholarship, if therapeutic jurisprudence is to take hold as a truly meaningful development, it must *be felt by practitioners.*[3]

---

1. *See generally*, DAVID B. WEXLER & BRUCE J. WINICK, LAW IN A THERAPEUTIC KEY: DEVELOPMENTS IN THERAPEUTIC JURISPRUDENCE (1996) [hereinafter LAW IN A THERAPEUTIC KEY].

2. David B. Wexler, *Applying the Law Therapeutically*, *in* LAW IN A THERAPEUTIC KEY, *id.* at 831. *See also* David B. Wexler, *Therapeutic Jurisprudence in Clinical Practice*, 153 AM. J. PSYCHIATRY 453 (1996).

3. Melanie B. Abbott, *Seeking Shelter Under a Deconstructed Roof: Homelessness and Critical Lawyering*, 64 TENN. L. REV. 269, 289 (1997). Abbot's distinction between "progressive" and "critical" lawyering is relevant to practicing therapeutic jurisprudence. Some may see an attempt to apply existing law therapeutically as an indirect attempt to undermine the law, while others will see an approach that seeks to take some of the sting out of the law as a means of prolonging an unjust legal status quo. It seems obvious, however, that lawyers can forge an important and satisfying career assisting clients to best cope with the existing law, and that legal and psycholegal scholars can play an important role in increasing the effectiveness of practitioners engaged in this client-centered counseling function.

Fortunately, the movement from theory to practice[4] is now occurring, as therapeutic jurisprudence begins to strike a responsive chord among segments of the judiciary[5] and of the legal profession. The present article focuses on lawyering.

The actual legal *practice* of therapeutic jurisprudence will principally involve lawyers working with clients to apply existing law in a manner likely to promote psychological well-being. For that enterprise to be feasible, however, the lawyer must adopt the framework of a preventive law practitioner, where careful planning and client counseling are essential elements of the endeavor.

Writing in the context of elder law, the integration of therapeutic jurisprudence and preventive law was first proposed by Dennis Stolle.[6] The integrated approach quickly attracted the attention both of therapeutic jurisprudence and of preventive law proponents, and the integrated framework was immediately seen as an approach that could apply not only to elder law but to law practice in general,[7] and it was seen as an approach and that could work to the benefit of each of its components: Preventive law—with its office procedures of "legal check ups" and the like—can give to therapeutic jurisprudence a legal context and a real opportunity for lawyers to counsel clients to apply and invoke the law therapeutically. Therapeutic jurisprudence, in turn, can give a human, psychological dimension to preventive law, and can give true structure and substance to the notion of the lawyer as counselor,[8] a notion too often referred to merely by the use of lofty language.[9]

---

4. David Finkelman & Thomas Grisso, *Therapeutic Jurisprudence: From Idea to Application, in* LAW IN A THERAPEUTIC KEY, *supra* note 1, at 587.

5. William Schma, *Book Review*, 36 THE JUDGES' J. 81 (1997) (reviewing LAW IN A THERAPEUTIC KEY, *supra* note 1); Jack Lehman, *The Movement Toward Therapeutic Jurisprudence: As Inside Look at the Origin and Operation of America's First Drug Courts*, 10 N.J.C. ALUMNI 13 (1995); Robert J. Kane, *A Sentencing Model for the 21st Century, in* LAW IN A THERAPEUTIC KEY, *supra* note 1, at 203.

6. Dennis P. Stolle, *Professional Responsibility in Elder Law: A Synthesis of Preventive Law and Therapeutic Jurisprudence*, 14 BEHAV. SCI. & L. 459 (1996).

7. Dennis P. Stolle & David B. Wexler, *Therapeutic Jurisprudence and Preventive Law: A Combined Concentration to Invigorate the Everyday Practice of Law*, 39 ARIZ. L. REV. 25 (1997) [hereinafter Stolle & Wexler, *Combined Concentration*]; Dennis P. Stolle & David B. Wexler, *Preventive Law and Therapeutic Jurisprudence: A Symbiotic Relationship*, 16 PREV. L. REV. 4 (1997) [hereinafter Stolle & Wexler, *Symbiotic Relationship*].

8. ROBERT M. HARDAWAY, PREVENTIVE LAW: MATERIALS ON A NONADVERSARIAL LEGAL PROCESS 65 (1997). The text provides an excellent overview of the field of preventive law.

9. The absence of such structure and substance in the counseling function is evident. Express attention to the "human element" in counseling receives only the following para-

A preventive law approach seeks to uncover and to anticipate *legal soft spots*[10] in a client's situation, and then to consider strategies for best dealing with those soft spots so they might be avoided, eliminated, or minimized. The essential function is to use careful planning, drafting, and other interventions to prevent the development of legal conflicts.

When integrated with therapeutic jurisprudence, the preventive law enterprise is explicitly and systematically enlarged to consider the impact of the law and of legal strategies not only on matters of *legal conflict* but also on matters of *law-related psychological well-being* deemed relevant to the client. From training and experience, for example, a lawyer may know that certain legal arrangements—a particular disposition in a will, for instance—may create a reasonably air-tight situation with regard to susceptibility to legal challenge, but may at the same time cause hard and hurt feelings, family disruption, and psychological distress. The integrated framework would suggest that those matters be systematically raised and addressed in the counseling context.

In fact, in recent articles, Stolle and Wexler have proposed that interested lawyers develop a combined concentration in therapeutic jurisprudence (TJ) and preventive law,[11] and most recently, Stolle, Wexler, Winick and Dauer have outlined in more detail just how a lawyer might become what

---

graph in Hardaway:

> For an analysis of the human element of legal counseling, see Redmount, *Humanistic Law Through Legal Counseling*, 2 CONN L. REV. 98 (1969). Counseling a client about the legal ramifications of a potential conflict requires a broad approach that will identify collateral human issues that may significantly affect the client's decision-making process on a course of action to resolve the conflict in addition to treatment of the core issues. Social and psychological interests of the client or the client's family are examples of such collateral human issues. It is the lawyer's duty to identify and clarify any core or collateral issues that may potentially affect a client's interests.

Id. at 75.

An excellent book on legal counseling is DAVID A. BINDER ET AL., LAWYERS AS COUNSELORS: A CLIENT CENTERED APPROACH (1991). The work urges lawyers to anticipate and consider the "nonlegal" consequences—including psychological ones—that invariably accompany legal measures, but note that "nonlegal consequences are often difficult to predict." *Id.* at 12. The approach proposed in the present article should enable us to focus explicitly and systematically on the law-related psychological dimension in legal counseling, and should make this sort of nonlegal consequences less difficult to predict.

10. Hardaway, *supra* note 9, at 189-92.

11. Stolle & Wexler, *Combined Concentration*, *supra* note 7. Dennis P. Stolle & David B. Wexler, *Symbiotic Relationship*, *supra* note 7.

we have termed (for want of a better term—an occupational hazard in therapeutic jurisprudence) a *TJ preventive lawyer*.[12]

More precisely, we believe that, just as preventive lawyers can anticipate and work with recurring, predictable *legal soft spots* in certain legal situations and transactions, so too lawyers can learn to anticipate and work with recurring predictable *psycholegal soft spots*[13]—ways in which certain legal procedures (e.g. litigation or its alternatives) or legal interventions (e.g., filing for bankruptcy or making certain testamentary dispositions) may expectedly produce or reduce anxiety, anger, hurt feelings, and other dimensions of law-related psychological well-being.

Of course, as the previous articles have noted, many client-centered lawyers already practice with a real sensitivity to these concerns. Many regard themselves first and foremost as counselors, or even as *holistic* lawyers.[14]

We believe, however, that attention to the *psycholegal soft spot* concept can provide a framework for highlighting sensitivity to the law-related psychological dimension in an explicit, systematic way; that the integrated approach can create a new type of legal and interdisciplinary scholarship geared to identifying these psycholegal soft spots and discussing and investigating the strategies used for dealing with them; in other words, that an exploration of such soft spots in different substantive areas and practice settings can help us know *how, when,* and about *what* to be psychologically sensitive. We propose, in other words, a truly psychology and law-based approach to lawyering.

One method for increasing our awareness of psycholegal soft spots and strategies is to begin to describe and discuss them. When we are armed with even a tentative schema, or vocabulary, we should be able to better identify relevant soft spots (and plausible strategies) when they arise in practice situations.[15] We can then see whether the identified soft spot fits comfortably

---

12. Dennis P. Stolle, et al., *Integrating Preventive Law and Therapeutic Jurisprudence: A Law and Psychology Based Approach to Lawyering*, 34 CAL. L. REV. (forthcoming 1997).

13. *Id.* We see this counseling function of the lawyer not as lawyer as *therapist* but more as lawyer as *educator*: a lawyer sharing with the client anticipated psychological fallout of certain legal actions, and the lawyer's knowledge of strategies clients have taken to lessen that fallout.

14. There is, for example, a Holistic Justice Center and an International Alliance of Holistic Lawyers. *See* Stolle & Wexler, *Combined Concentration, supra* note 7, at 28 n. 9.

15. *See* David E. Rumelhart & Andrew Ortony, *The Representation of Knowledge in Memory, in* SCHOOLING AND THE ACQUISITION OF KNOWLEDGE 99 (Richard C. Anderson, et al. eds., 1977); Richard C. Anderson, *The Notion of Schemata and the Educational Enterprise: General Discussion of the Conference, in* SCHOOLING AND THE ACQUISITION OF KNOWLEDGE, at 415.

within the existing description or vocabulary, or whether it requires a modification or embellishment of the framework. We can also discuss and study the ethical propriety and the likely behavioral/emotional effectiveness of various strategies suggested to deal with the identified psycholegal soft spot.

The present article is a first step in developing a working description of psycholegal soft spots. In the next section, I simply summarize a number of law-related psychological situations that were used in the previous papers as examples of TJ preventive lawyering. Then, in the following section, I discuss, distinguish, compare and contrast the soft spots and strategies in the hope that the endeavor may aid the development of a TJ preventive law bar.

II. Cases Examples

A. The Burkes' Stay in Shape Example[16]

The Burkes, a couple in their mid-sixties, come to a lawyer's office principally to prepare their wills. They are in good health, although one of them suffers from arthritis and the other may be at increased risk of developing Alzheimer's disease in later life.

The presence of such therapeutic issues should suggest to the TJ preventive lawyer that planning for incapacity and developing a plan for mental and physical health maintenance should be important in working with the Burkes. As such, the lawyer should discuss therapeutic goals openly with the Burkes as one potential consideration in their planning. This conversation must, of course, be conducted in a sensitive and respectful manner. However, the client should be involved from the beginning in the identification of therapeutic concerns.

On one hand, the lawyer should encourage the Burkes to consider the real possibility of future incapacity. A detailed client interview and a discussion of the clients' plans can provide an opportunity for the Burkes to take a realistic look at their own health and the possibility of declining health in upcoming years. On the other hand, the lawyer should also encourage the Burkes to value their current healthy condition, and might even use this opportunity to encourage the Burkes to make health maintenance a priority.

Here, the lawyer is clearly stepping outside of the role of legal counselor, and should make that absolutely clear to the client. The lawyer might say, "Look, I'm not a doctor, but I see a lot of older clients. I always say

---

16. This example is adapted from Stolle et al., *supra* note 12.

to them that I hope the documents that I draft won't be used for a long, long time; and, I mean that. But, over the years, I can really see the difference between my clients who make an effort to take care of themselves, and those who don't. So keep checking in with your doctor and living a healthy life-style. You guys are in great shape and I want you to stay that way. After all, I would like to be your lawyer for a long time". Thus, by using the law office as a forum for encouraging the Burkes to both plan for the worst and to attempt to maintain their health so that the worst never comes about, the lawyer can maximize the probability of therapeutic outcomes and minimize the probability of anti-therapeutic outcomes.

B. Tom's Drug Problem/Trust Example[17]

The TJ preventive lawyer should pay particular attention to the nature of the Burkes' relationship with their children. The Burkes appear likely to want to leave most of their assets to their children. However, the Burkes' comments should suggest that they may expect that their two happily married children will spend any inheritance more wisely than their third child, Tom, who apparently has a serious drug and alcohol problem. Although the Burkes said that they want to treat their children equally, they may have reservations about leaving a portion of their inheritance to a child who currently has a serious substance abuse problem.[18] If further discussion reveals that this is the case, the lawyer might suggest alternative legal solutions to the Burkes, such as leaving their third child's inheritance to him in trust.

In many law offices, when confronted with this situation, the lawyer may suggest leaving Tom's inheritance in a trust, the Burkes would agree, and there would be no further discussion of the matter. However, the goal of the TJ preventive lawyer is to take the legal consultation a step further by considering not only the legal or economic ramifications of implementing a particular legal tool, but also to consider the psychological or emotional ramifications. A decision to leave an inheritance in a trust for one child and not for the other children could provoke family quarrels, or alienate Tom from other family members. Thus, before drafting such documents, the TJ preventive lawyer should discuss openly with the Burkes the poten-

---

17. *Id.*

18. A lump-sum payment may contribute to relapse. *See* Mark D. Herbst et al., *Treatment Outcome for Methadone Clients Receiving Lump-Sum Payments at Initiation of Disability Benefits*, 47 PSYCHIATRIC SERVICES 119 (1996).

tially sensitive matter. The lawyer might also ask for the Burkes' views on whether they would like to discuss the matter with Tom or with the other children before finalizing the document, or whether they may wish to prepare a separate explanatory letter to Tom to be delivered upon their death. The decisions, of course, remain the Burkes' to make, but only after a discussion of both the legal and psychological effects of leaving Tom's inheritance in a trust can the Burkes make a truly informed decision regarding which legal strategies to elect.

C. The Planning for Future Disability Example[19]

Prior publications have touched on the role of the TJ preventive lawyer in working with clients to prepare for possible future disability. This is true of the Burkes, who may, with age, experience declining health. It is also true with clients who have periodic bouts with mental illness and who may wish to develop appropriate advance directive instruments regarding psychiatric treatment.[20] And it is certainly true when working with clients who are HIV positive.

For instance, attorney Mark Senak notes the importance of preparing for possible future disability so as to avoid emotionally-draining bureaucratic battles if disability benefits are later sought. The advice is crisp and practical: "Find your birth certificate. A Xerox copy will get you nowhere. If you can't find your birth certificate, call the hospital where you were born..."[21] Of equal importance, Senak deals with the delicate point that "it is not an admission of getting sicker to prepare for the possibility that one day a person may need these programs."[22] Ironically, of course, it is quite possible that the more a person with HIV is able to plan for such matters, and thus lower the stress level, the better the chance that severe sickness will itself be postponed or perhaps avoided.[23]

---

19. This example is adapted from Stolle et al., *supra* note 12, and from Stolle & Wexler, *Combined Concentration, supra* note 7.

20. Bruce J. Winick, *Advance Directive Instruments for Those with Mental Illness*, 51 U. OF MIAMI L. REV. 57 (1996). *See also* Stolle & Wexler, *Combined Concentration, supra* note 7, at 32 n. 35.

21. Mark S. Senak, HIV, AIDS AND THE LAW: A GUIDE TO OUR RIGHTS AND CHALLENGES 72 (1996).

22. *Id.* at 69.

23. *Id.* at 109. In fact, there is now a growing recognition of links between psychological well-being and physical health. *See generally* WILLIAM R. LOVALLO, STRESS & HEALTH: BIOLOGICAL AND PSYCHOLOGICAL INTERACTIONS (1997). *See also* JAMES W.

D. The Tax Preparation Example[24]

How much stress—and how many family fights—are provoked by the process of tax preparation? Can a system be devised now for collecting important tax documents so that the stress and arguments will not occur next year?

E. The Bankruptcy Example[25]

Is bankruptcy the answer to one's financial situation? If so, how will one cope with the stigma and embarrassment that continues to accompany bankruptcy status? Who will one tell, and how, and when?

F. The HIV/Family Reconciliation Example[26]

A TJ preventive lawyer should recognize that some HIV-positive clients are likely to be alienated from their families as a result of engaging in behaviors that family members may condemn. Yet, the legal context of the HIV-positive family member preparing a will or executing an advance directive instrument may provide an opportunity for the client to attempt reconciliation with alienated family members, and perhaps eventually to name a family member as an executor or surrogate decision maker. The client-centered approach of TJ preventive lawyering allows for the lawyer to discuss with the client, who best knows his family situation, whether approaching a family member would be useful.

PENNEBAKER, OPENING UP: THE HEALING POWER OF CONFIDING IN OTHERS (1990) (writing about traumatic events can improve physical health); James W. Pennebaker, *Putting Stress into Words: Health, Linguistic, and Therapeutic Implications*, 31 BEHAV. RES. THERAPY 539 (1993) (same); Daniel W. Shuman, *Therapeutic Jurisprudence and Tort Law: A Limited Subjective Standard of Care, in* LAW IN A THERAPEUTIC KEY, *supra* note 1, at 385-93 (relationship between stress and accident proneness). Preventive law has, of course, often been analogized to preventive medicine. *See* Hardaway, *supra* note 8, at xxxvii. In light of the link between psychological well-being and physical health, however, TJ preventive lawyering may take us beyond analogy: preventive law, when mixed with a heavy dose of therapeutic jurisprudence, may in itself actually *constitute* a type of preventive medicine.

24. This example is adapted from Stolle et al, *supra* note 12.

25. *Id.* at 31.

26. This example is adapted from Stolle et al., *supra* note 12.

G. The Children of Divorce Example[27]

In a recent article, Maxwell provides practical lawyering strategies for mitigating the negative psychological effects of divorce on children.[28] Lawyers concerned with the effects of divorce on children might, as a first step, choose like-minded clients.[29] Maxwell suggests that these lawyers simply refuse to represent clients who, in an initial client interview, display some propensity toward disregarding the best interests of the children in order to achieve financial gain or some sort of vindication against the other spouse.[30] Such lawyers might even advertise a "preference for child-friendly divorce, in order to attract like-minded clients and avoid future conflicts with contrary clients."[31] Maxwell further suggests that once the lawyer has agreed to represent the client, the lawyer should educate the client regarding the potential detrimental effects of divorce on children, and plan a specific preventive/therapeutic strategy to mitigate any such negative effects in this client's case, such as trying to establish a convenient weekly time, outside the presence of the child, for the parents to discuss child-related matters of mutual concern.[32]

H. The Incompetence Labeling Example[33]

Winick has suggested that, in view of the negative psychological effects of incompetency labeling, criminal attorneys representing defendants who are found incompetent to stand trial can help the client to interpret that legal label in a way that minimizes the risk of adverse psychological consequences.[34] Thus, the lawyer can tell his or her client that the incompetency determination is merely an opportunity for the client to secure needed treatment and a delay in the proceedings that will enable the client to function more effectively in the attorney-client relationship when the criminal

---

27. This example, summarized in Stolle et al., *id*. originates with Kathryn E. Maxwell, *Preventive Lawyering Strategies to Mitigate the Detrimental Effects of Clients' Divorces on Their Children*, 67 Rev. Jur. UPR (forthcoming 1998).

28. *Id*.

29. *Id*.

30. *Id*.

31. *Id*.

32. *Id*.

33. This example is adapted from Stolle et al., *supra* note 12.

34. Bruce J. Winick, *The Side Effects of Incompetency Labeling and the Implications for Mental Health Law, in* Law in a Therapeutic Key, *supra* note 1, at 17.

proceedings are resumed. By helping the client to reframe the legal label as a form of treatment continuance, the attorney thus can help the client to avoid what might otherwise be negative self-attributional effects triggered by application of the incompetency label.

I. The Civil Commitment Hearing/Embarrassing Material Example[35]

At the civil commitment hearing, a lawyer may move to exclude members of the public from the hearing if it appears that testimony highly embarrassing to the respondent is about to be offered.[36]

J. The Don't Ask, Don't Tell Example[37]

A recent article critiqued the *Don't Ask, Don't Tell* military regulation on the ground that, among other things, it leads to the social isolation of gay service members.[38] Sexual orientation, the claim goes, is so intertwined with matters of daily living—with whom one spent the holidays, for example—that a legal ban on discussing one's sexual orientation will naturally chill the discussion of the other matters as well, leading to superficial social relations and marginality.[39]

With the advice of a TJ preventive lawyer, however, a gay service member may learn that, although the existing law may "naturally" chill discussion of many daily life events, the "natural" result may not be the *legally obligatory* result: it may be that if a gay service member can learn (perhaps even through role play) to be comfortable deflecting, or refusing to answer, questions relating specifically to his or her gay orientation, disclosure of where and with whom he or she spent the holidays might be perfectly permissible, and might reduce the service member's feelings of social isolation.

---

35. This example is adapted from Stolle et al., *supra* note 12.

36. THERAPEUTIC JURISPRUDENCE: THE LAW AS A THERAPEUTIC AGENT 18 (David B. Wexler ed., 1990).

37. This example is adapted from STOLLE & WEXLER, *Combined Concentration, supra* note 7, at 25-26.

38. Kay Kavanagh, *Don't Ask, Don't Tell: Deception Required, Disclosure Denied, in* LAW IN A THERAPEUTIC KEY, *supra* note 1, at 343.

39. *Id.* at 344.

K. The ADA/Confidentiality Example[40]

Under the Americans with Disabilities Act (ADA), if an employee with a disability wishes a reasonable accommodation in the workplace in order to perform his or her duties (e.g., the modification of equipment or of a work schedule), the employee can reveal the disability to the employer and request an adjustment or accommodation. Under the confidentiality provision, the disability would need to be disclosed only to the employer, the employee's supervisor, and perhaps to safety personnel—it would not be disclosed to the employee's co-workers.

It has been suggested, however, that an employee with a disability may often profit from waiving confidentiality and from voluntarily disclosing the disability to relevant co-workers.[41] Secrecy may lead to isolation and superficial social relations. Writing about the issue, Daly-Rooney provides an example of a nondisclosing employee with mild retardation who lives in a group home. If, to protect her secret, she declines a co-worker's offer of a ride home on a rainy day, she may well appear strange or unfriendly.[42]

Moreover, Daly-Rooney posits that an employee with a disability might be best integrated into the workplace if co-workers are asked by the employer to play a part in the employee's workplace integration.[43] The co-workers, who, after all, probably know more than the new employee (and perhaps even more than the employer) about the requirements of the given job, could help design reasonable accommodations for the employee with a disability. This interaction might decrease rumors about the new employee and might decrease resentment by the co-workers, who now have had a voice in the process and have some sort of stake in the success of the designed accommodation.

A legal checkup by a TJ preventive lawyer should ideally indicate that a client with a disability is in possible need of a reasonable accommodation. If so, a discussion might ensue regarding whether to request an accommodation and, if so, how and when to approach the employer. The question of confidentiality with respect to co-workers and the issue of possible co-worker involvement in designing the accommodation can also be dis-

---

40. This example is adapted from STOLLE & WEXLER, *Combined Concentration, supra* note 7, at 26.

41. Rose A. Daly-Rooney, *Designing Reasonable Accommodations through Co-Worker Participation: Therapeutic Jurisprudence and the Confidentiality Provision of the Americans with Disabilities Act, in* LAW IN A THERAPEUTIC KEY, *supra* note 1, at 365.

42. *Id.* at 375-76.

43. *Id.* at 374.

cussed — as well as the matter of how this procedure should be raised delicately with the employer, and whether the employer should be approached by the employee personally or, in rare instances, perhaps by the lawyer. If co-workers are likely to be ignorant about a particular disability and are accordingly likely to be awkward in their interactions with the employee — such as knowing when to offer assistance and when not to — the lawyer might suggest that one type of reasonable accommodation could simply be an educational session whereby co-workers learn, by commercial videotapes or by an informal discussion with the client-employee, details about the disability and its impact on the employee's performance of certain tasks.

III. Discussion and Analysis

The *Burkes Stay in Shape* example probably falls at the outer edge of the TJ preventive lawyer's role. In encouraging the Burkes to keep up the good work regarding exercise and diet, the lawyer is stepping outside his role of legal counselor, and should make that clear ("Look I'm not a doctor, but I see a lot of older clients, and...").[44] Furthermore, "any such advice should be restricted to general and innocuous statements,"[45] or should involve possible referral to another class of professional. The *Burkes Stay in Shape* example shows the limits of the TJ preventive lawyer's expertise — as counselor *at law*, not counselor *in general* — but also shows the sorts of issues that often border on the psychologically-sensitive lawyer's topics of professional discussion.

When a TJ preventive lawyer counsels a client regarding a matter, the lawyer should be asking whether the advice relates to a legal matter, or to a matter of law-related psychological well-being, or whether it is really neither of those and is more like a *Burkes Stay in Shape* case. If it is a *Burkes Stay in Shape* case, the red flag should be raised, and the lawyer should think in terms of caveats, cautions, innocuous statements, and possible referral to a different class of professional.

The *Burkes Stay in Shape* example involves a lawyer stepping a bit outside the professional legal role to advise a client to take some action. By con-

---

44. Our approach will become more and more refined as we increasingly raise and grapple with the issues. The suggestion in the text regarding clarifying the lawyer's role in the present context represents somewhat of a departure from the view originally expressed in Stolle, *supra* note 6, at 473-74, where the lawyer recommended to the clients that they engage in healthful activities.

45. Stolle et al., *supra* note 12.

trast, the *Incompetence Labeling* example, where the lawyer puts the best *therapeutic spin*[46] on an incompetency determination, seems to fall properly within the professional role of the TJ preventive lawyer. Here, the judicial determination—the imposition of an incompetency label—may itself carry with it dangerous emotional and behavioral side-effects,[47] and the lawyer's interpretation of the event can take some of the antitherapeutic sting out of the situation.

In the *Incompetence Labeling* example, the lawyer's conduct, designed to ameliorate the sting, is an end in itself. In that sense, it is slightly different from the *Planning for Future Disability* example, where the lawyer discusses future disability with the client, and delicately tries to avoid creating a self-fulfilling prophesy ("it is not an admission of getting sicker to prepare for the possibility that one day a person may need these programs"[48]). In the *Planning for Future Disability* example, the lawyer's delicate linguistic behavior is not so much an end in itself as it is an attempt to pave the way for later steps by the client—such as getting the paper work together for possible future social security benefit claims, or executing an advance directive instrument.[49] Also, if the lawyer, without addressing the psychological situation, merely forges ahead and suggests to a client the preparation of advance directive instruments and the like, the psychological matters are *not* being sidestepped; presumably, the lawyer who plunges right into the substantive legal issues may be *contributing* to psychological distress that might have been avoided by the use of preliminary remarks.

The *Incompetence Labeling* example is also interesting to compare with the *Civil Commitment Hearing/Embarrassing Material* example. Those two examples are similar insofar as both of them involve efforts to lessen litigation-related antitherapeutic consequences, the former involving a possibly destructive label, the latter involving the humiliation and trauma associated with embarrassing testimony being revealed in a public forum. The two examples also establish clearly the possible role of the TJ preventive lawyer not only in the law office setting but also in the courtroom. But the cases are different insofar as the *Incompetence Labeling* example involves the lawyer's action and behavior alone, whereas the *Civil Commitment Hearing/Embarrassing Material* example involves the lawyer,

---

46. Keri K. Gould & Michael Perlin, *Johnny's in the Basement/Mixing up His Medicine: Therapeutic Jurisprudence and Clinical Teaching* (unpublished manuscript).

47. Winick, *supra* note 34.

48. Senak, *supra* note 21, at 69.

49. This example is perhaps akin to the familiar difficulty faced by lawyers positioning a client to face the inevitability of death as a prelude to drafting a will.

presumably after consultation with the client, requesting action by the court (i.e, ordering the removal of the public from the hearing room).[50]

In that respect, the *Civil Commitment Hearing Embarrassing Material* example shares some characteristics with the non-litigation context *ADA/Confidentiality* example. In both cases, the therapeutic application of the law rests with a third party—one other than the lawyer or the client. It is the *judge* who must exclude the public from portions of the civil commitment hearing, and it is, practically speaking, the *employer* who must agree to involve co-workers in the process of designing a reasonable accommodation for a new employee with a disability. Sometimes—as in the civil commitment case—it will obviously be the lawyer who will make the request (here in the form of a motion) to the third party (e.g. the judge). Sometimes, as in the *ADA/Confidentiality* example, the question of *which* person—the lawyer or the client personally—should approach the third person (e.g., the employer) will itself be a matter of lawyer-client discussion. Ordinarily, I would think, the approach here should best be made by the employee, although situations can be imagined where it might be best for the employer to be approached by a tactful and concerned lawyer.

Both the civil commitment and the ADA examples are different, therefore, from the *Don't Ask, Don't Tell* example. There, whatever action must be initiated to try to take the sting out of the law will come, after lawyer-client consultation, from the client personally. A gay service member who would like to disclose matters of his or her sexual orientation, but who is barred by law from doing so, can be given legal advice at just how much disclosure is actually allowable ("Joe and I saw a great movie last night; Joe and I really loved Aruba") short of express statements of homosexual orientation. Ultimately, the client must decide if he wants to make such disclosures as a means of decreasing his social isolation. He must also decide if he can learn to make such disclosures and still stay clear of crossing the prohibited line. If these disclosures in fact will make his work life richer and less superficial,[51] it is he himself who, with legal advice, will act to enrich his life.

It is also the client personally—or perhaps the client and his or her spouse—who must act to improve the situation in the *Tax Preparation* example. The lawyer may suggest certain simple record-keeping measures

---

50. Even at earlier stage of the litigation, where the lawyer and client may together discuss the advisability of seeking a competency evaluation and an incompetency determination, it is the lawyer's behavior toward the client that is crucial in softening the impact of the label. Keri A. Gould, *A Therapeutic Jurisprudence Analysis of Competency Evaluation Requests: The Defense Attorney's Dilemma*, 18 Int'l J. L. & Psychiatry 83 (1995).

51. *But see* text following note 57 *infra* for the view that this strategy is not a satisfactory one.

to take some of the stress out of the tax form filing process, but it is of course the taxpayer personally who must implement the suggested system.

There is another respect in which the *Don't Ask, Don't Tell* and the *Tax Preparation* examples are similar. In both cases, the law itself seems to be the *source* of the stress, and the TJ preventive lawyer can recommend certain strategies (certain legally permissible disclosures; certain record-keeping techniques) to *relieve* the law-caused stress. That sort of psycholegal soft spot—where the law causes the stress and the lawyer recommends certain behavior to relieve the stress—seems in one conceptual sense to be different from the *Bankruptcy* example. In the latter example, it seems not to be the *law* producing the stress, but rather *non-legal* sources: bad luck, bad business decisions, a downturn of the economy. In one respect, therefore, the *Bankruptcy* example seems to represent a type of psycholegal soft spot where non-legal factors lead to stress and a possible *legal intervention* (e.g. filing for bankruptcy) is suggested as a strategy to relieve some of the stress.

The *Bankruptcy* example, however, is more interesting and complex than the above discussion indicates. For once the decision to file for bankruptcy is seriously considered, that legal intervention *itself* precipitates another psycholegal soft spot—the embarrassment and stigma of bankruptcy—and calls for the development of strategies one may use to cope with, manage, and possibly reduce that embarrassment and stigma (e.g., who to tell, how, and when). This *secondary* or *derivative* psycholegal soft spot is *caused* by the law or the legal intervention of filing for bankruptcy, and now the strategies for coping with this law-again reminiscent of the behavioral strategies recommended to relieve the law-caused stress in the *Don't Ask, Don't Tell* and the *Tax Preparation* examples.

To complicate matters even more, however, consider also the following interrelationships: the potential stigma and embarrassment of bankruptcy is not ordinarily a worry that first surfaces on the eve of one seriously contemplating filing for bankruptcy. Indeed, the stress of that feared stigma likely mixes at a much earlier stage with the stress precipitate by financial pressures. The client in desperate financial straits who visits a lawyer is, therefore, likely under stress from a combination of sources, both non-legal (bad luck) as well as legal (fear of stigma from possible future bankruptcy). The law, then, can easily be a source of stress even before it becomes technically applicable to a given situation. This is evident in the *Bankruptcy* example, but may surface also in many other settings. Thus, the *Don't Ask, Don't Tell* law may adversely affect not only one who has joined the military; the prospect of social isolation and of artificially controlled conversation may also discourage one from seriously considering a military career.

Seeking strategies for coping with the stigma of bankruptcy is in some ways not unlike the *Tom's Drug Problem/Trust* example—both involve devising strategies to best deal with the anticipated psychological fallout from pursuing a certain legal course of action.[52] In the latter, the Burkes' decision to leave money to Tom in trust, while leaving his siblings' shares to them outright, may not pose a technical legal difficulty, but is does spawn a psycholegal soft spot, perhaps straining Tom's relations with his siblings, and possibly creating hurt feelings on Tom's part. A TJ preventive lawyer would raise this matter with the Burkes, and would discuss possible ways of accomplishing their legal objective in a manner less likely to cause psychological strife (e.g., talk with Tom now, or state your reasons in a loving letter to be given to Tom upon your death). The ultimate decision about what, if any, action to take would, of course, remain with the Burkes.

Although the *Bankruptcy* example and the *Tom's Drug Problem/Trust* example are similar in trying to diminish the adverse psychological consequences of the legal mechanism (bankruptcy, trust), they differ in terms of *on whom* the adverse psychological consequences will likely be visited. In the *Bankruptcy* example, the client personally is at the center of the psychological drama, although the client's family members may also be greatly affected. In the *Tom's Drug Problem/Trust* example, it is not so much the client, the Burkes, who will feel the emotional consequences of the trust arrangement; it is instead Tom, and to some extent, indirectly, the other siblings.

Although the clients themselves are not the focal point of the emotional stress in the *Tom's Drug Problem/Trust* example, the client's loved one is, and the clients may well wish to act in a manner that softens that emotional fallout. Since the ultimate decision lies with the Burkes, the approach remains a client-centered one, with the *clients themselves* deciding issues that, in other contexts, complicate therapeutic jurisprudence projects— *what* is therapeutic, and for *whom*? [53]

---

52. This discussion underscores the importance to the TJ preventive lawyer of a thorough knowledge of alternative dispute resolution techniques. Nathalie Des Rosiers et al., *Legal Compensation for Sexual Violence: Therapeutic Consequences and Consequences for the Judicial System*, 4 PSYCHOL, PUB. POL. & L. (forthcoming 1998). The researchers note that some sexual battery victims considering action for compensation wish to confront the perpetrator, while others want desperately to avoid such a confrontation. They also note that a tort suit is far more likely to result in the perpetrator's presence at the proceeding than is a claim for compensation filed with an administrative tribunal.

53. David B. Wexler, *Reflections on the Scope of Therapeutic Jurisprudence, in* LAW IN A THERAPEUTIC KEY, *supra* note 1, at 811, 812-816; Christopher Slobogin, *Therapeutic Jurisprudence: Five Dilemmas to Ponder, in* LAW IN A THERAPEUTIC KEY, *supra* note 1, at 763.

Technically, the clients remain in charge even in the *Children of Divorce* example, where preventive law strategies are suggested to reduce trauma to the children of divorcing parents. The situation posited is one where the divorcing client in essence agrees to follow certain approaches that will place the psychological well-being of the children above other competing interests.

In the *Children of Divorce* example, however, the lawyer is encouraged to seek clients who favor this approach. To the extent that lawyers refuse to accept clients who fail to agree to the approach, the *Children of Divorce* example may be most non-controversially employed by lawyers in private practice. If practiced across the board by lawyers in legal clinics, legal services offices, and prepaid legal plans, it would raise questions of appropriate professional responsibility and the meaning and importance of client-centered representation.

The *Children of Divorce* example also differs from the *Tom's Drug Problem/Trust* example in what might be called the "shape" of the respective psycholegal soft spots. The trust issue is rather narrow and precise. The *Children of Divorce* example, however, produces a highly amorphous mass of legal forces, psychological repercussions, and possible preventive strategies.

Finally, the *HIV/Family Reconciliation* example represents still another sort of psycholegal soft spot and resulting strategy. If *Tom's Drug Problem/Trust* example can be viewed as a law-related stressor (the trust and "unequal" treatment of the children) dealt with by a non-legal strategy (e.g., the Burkes talking to Tom about the disposition), and if the *Bankruptcy* example can be looked at in large part as stress from mostly *non-legal* causes (e.g. bad luck) that can be dealt with by invoking the law (e.g., filing bankruptcy), the *HIV/Family Reconciliation* example may be regarded as a stress from *non-legal* causes (eg, life style differences precipitating a breach in family relations) that can possibly be lessened *in the course of* invoking the law (drafting a will, naming an executor or substitute decision maker). Here, the preparation of a legal instrument—an instrument that is needed and that will presumably be prepared in any event—serves as a potential *opportunity* to attempt a reconciliation with fallen away family members. The *HIV/Family Reconciliation* example, therefore, reminds us that psycholegal soft spots are not restricted to potential *trouble* spots (although they often are such). They may, at times, also be *opportunity* spots.[54]

---

54. Once again, the analogy to preventive law concepts is apt. The preventive law literature makes reference to "positive" legal problems and soft spots:

Periodic legal checkup ... seeks to identify potential legal problems before they become acute. In this context, "legal problems" are of two kinds. "Problems" of a negative sort; that unanticipated risk. The other sort of "problem" the positive

The above analysis consists of discussing in greater detail those soft spots and strategies that have already been raised in the nascent TJ preventive law literature. If the approach is helpful, as I hope it is, we should consider how we may add to our data base. That is the task of the final section of this article.

IV. Next Step

The development of a TJ preventive law bar will require efforts on many fronts, including research, education,[55] and continuing education. A crucial component of the TJ preventive lawyer's professional development should consist in the continuing collection, classification, discussion, and debate of psycholegal soft spots and strategies.[56] This article is intended as a step in that direction. In fact, preliminary writings about TJ preventive lawyering are themselves beginning to generate the kind of thinking and discussion that is essential to the growth of the field. For example, the *Burkes' Stay in Shape* example is itself a refinement and modification of an earlier example provided by Stolle, an example that did not then clearly mark the limits of the lawyer's role as lawyer.[57] Further, the strategy suggested in the *Don't Ask, Don't Tell* example for taking some of the sting

---

sort, occurs where the client has some potential right or benefit or gain of which the client is unaware.

PREVENTIVE LAW, supra note 8, at 191 (quoting L. BROWN, MANUAL FOR PERIODIC CHECK-UP).

55. See Stolle et al., *supra* note 12; Stolle & Wexler, *Combined Concentration, supra* note 7, at 31-32. This education will ideally integrate into a model of lawyering two distinct orientations: an analytic orientation and an ethic of care. *See* Susan Daicoff, *Lawyer Know Thyself: A Review of Empirical Research of Attorney Attributes Bearing on Professionalism*, 46 AMER. U. L. REV. (forthcoming 1998). In terms of education, law courses would ideally include therapeutic jurisprudence, preventive law, alternative dispute resolution, interviewing and counseling, and legal clinics with a TJ preventive law orientation or stream—as is being developed at the legal clinic of the University of Puerto Rico School of Law. Certain non-law courses, in psychology, social work, or counseling, might also be helpful. Some students may even decide to acquire a masters degree in such a field, perhaps as a joint program with the JD degree. It would be interesting, also, to develop a masters program in one of those fields with a specialty geared specifically to lawyers, as Harvard University has done in its Master of Public Health Program. Alternatively, a year-long LL. M. program could be developed—perhaps in Legal Counseling, Therapeutic Jurisprudence, and Preventive Law—to offer a combination of the critical law courses, behavioral science courses, and legal clinics.

56. Stolle et al., *supra* note 12.

57. *See* Stolle et al., supra note 12, at 473-74 (The preventive lawyer can recommend consideration of activities likely to maintain the Schmidt's physical and mental health,

out of the law has sparked some important discussion. In a personal communication reacting to the strategy, a law professor wrote:

> Your example of the "therapeutic application" to "Don't Ask; Don't Tell" did not feel realistic to me. By constantly being careful to censor one's speech (by deflecting or refusing to answer) in order to not "reveal" (i.e. tell) is exactly what the law wants and what most gay folks have had to live with for years. When I first started in law teaching, I simply did not refer to my partner at all. However, if I slipped and said "we", folks immediately asked who the other person was. "Room-mate"..oh, get a clue, I was 37. "Housemate", "woman" etc. This constant self censorship was maddening and self destructive. In reality, either one avoids any, and I mean ANY, discussion of one's outside-the-workplace life, to the point of eccentricity, especially difficult where one is supposed to be "collegial", or the self-censorship required is so difficult and so constant that either disclosure or mental illness is only a matter of time.

> My personal view is that deflecting or refusing to answer questions about one's everyday life answers the question anyway, in the majority of cases. I would not find that method very "therapeutic" if I were in the military. I had a large number of clients who had been or were military members. Almost always, I found that having practiced either deflection, silence, or in many, outright lying, had affected the ability of those folks to live a mentally healthy life. I think that atmosphere contributed to rampant alcohol-abuse, significant depression, and sexual promiscuity. I have no empirical evidence for this view.

We need now to expand our data base of situations and strategies. The law clinic at the University of Puerto Rico, under the direction of Professor Mariluz Jiménez, is beginning to introduce the students to TJ preventive lawyering. The students are beginning to keep journals of psycholegal soft spots and suggested strategies, which will be collected and discussed.[58]

---

such as exercise, hobbies, family involvement, frequent medical check-ups, and church or community involvement).

58. The UPR Legal Clinic is also assembling a small group of lawyer consultants, some of whom also have training in social work or psychology, who already seem intuitively to use a TJ preventive law approach to some extent, although not systematically. These lawyers will be available as consultants and as sounding boards for ideas about suggested strategies.

The clinic will also seek the services of a supervised social work student to assist in this enterprise. A number of law school clinics now employ social workers. A TJ preventive law approach can provide social workers with an additional role in such clinics. Indeed, to the extent that the TJ preventive law approach is implemented in

Another source of information is now coming from the judiciary. Therapeutic jurisprudence was the theme of the 1997 Annual Convention of the National Association of Women Judges, held in Salt Lake City.[59]

At the opening plenary session, conducted by Judge William Schma, Judge Peggy Hora, Professor Bruce Winick, and myself, we introduced the concept of "psychojudicial" soft spots and strategies for managing them—a direct parallel, of course, to the "psycholegal" soft spots of the TJ preventive lawyer.

At the session, Judges Schma and Hora discussed with the attendees several psychojudicial soft sports and strategies—such as how the acceptance of no contest pleas may frustrate later attempts at rehabilitation[60]—and elicited from the attendees instances where trials and hearings were managed, within legal limits, to themselves promote healing or to reduce trauma.

One situation, presented by Judge Hora, precipitated a discussion of the links between judging and TJ preventive lawyering, and led as well to the creation of an on going Therapeutic Jurisprudence Judging Project, which has great potential for increasing the data base of the TJ preventive lawyer.

In what may now be referred to as *The Will Contest* example, Judge Hora described a trial involving a brother and sister. The brother was challenging, on the grounds of undue influence by the sister, a disposition in the mother's will leaving the mother's broken down house to the sister, who had cared for the mother during the mother's later years. The brother, unlike the sister, had a decent income and a home of his own.

Judge Hora found no undue influence, and upheld the will. She sensed, however, that the case had little to do with money and had to do, instead, with the brother's hurt feelings. At the close of the hearing, she remarked to the brother that, given the different financial situations of the siblings, the disposition seemed understandable and in no way seemed to her to suggest that the mother loved him any less than she loved his sister. The brother broke down in tears.

Judge Hora's case is itself the kind of vignette that should, for purposes of judicial education, be collected, discussed, and debated.[61] But by

---

legal service offices, by prepaid legal service plans, or in private law offices, social workers may usefully serve as consultants in those settings as well. Social workers in private practice might also consult in these various settings.

59. Sheila R. Mc Cann, *Female Judges Hear Plan: Don't Just Punish—Heal,* Salt Lake Trib., September 26, 1997, at A1.

60. David B. Wexler, *Therapeutic Jurisprudence and the Criminal Courts, in* Law in a Therapeutic Key, *supra* note 1, at 157-60.

61. This, of course, is not the time for the discussion and the debate. But, for a glimpse of how such a conversation might proceed, and how it can help develop the use of the therapeutic jurisprudence perspective in judging, it may be interesting to recount some of the discussion sparked by Judge Hora's example. *See also* Daniel W. Van Ness, *New Wine*

employing a preventive law pedagogical "rewind" technique,[62] these judicial vignettes can also be of great value to TJ preventive lawyers. In law school teaching, for example, the faculty member, after discussing an appellate decision in contract law, might "rewind" the case back to the contract drafting stage, and could ask what might have been done differently to avoid the legal problem presented by the case.[63]

Judge Hora's *Will Contest* example can actually be twice rewound. First, we can rewind to the lawyer's office when the brother and his lawyer are contemplating the challenge to the will. If, after ascertaining the facts (as Judge Hora did at the hearing), the lawyer had given to the brother the same assessment—legally and emotionally—of the case that Judge Hora gave at trial ("You know undue influence is hard to prove, and I don't think we can prove it. And, besides, I've had lots of cases where parents have given property to one kid who's struggling and not to the one who's doing o.k. It usually doesn't have anything to do with them loving one kid more or less; it's their attempt to help out one who really can use a boost"), perhaps the brother would not have brought the unsuccessful case at all. Of course, this raises many questions about the lawyer's role, financial

---

and Old Wineskins: Four Challenges of Restorative Justice, 4 Crim. L. F. 251, 252 (1993) (remarks by judge to victim at close of sexual assault case that sentence of imprisonment demonstrates conclusively that "what happened was not your fault"). Most who commented believed her actions were appropiate and helpful. One judge, however, was concerned with this use of discretion and its possible misuse. Suppose the trial judge had instead said "this disposition suggests you must have been a rotten son who mistreated your mother." Others felt that while such behavior is possible, the role of a judge here should be to help, not hurt, and, instead of making such a remark, a judge should instead leave matters as they are and say nothing. In addition, the notion of being able to leave matters as they are may serve to distinguish Judge Hora's will contest case from other possible judicial situations, such as the acceptance or rejection of a no contest plea. Judge Hora's will contest case *could* have ended the "traditional" way, with the judge saying no more. In that sense, therefore, the remark to the brother might be regarded as a gratuitous exercise of judicial discretion. In the no contest case example, however, the judge is required to do *something*—either accept or reject the plea. There may be therapeutic or antitherapeutic consequences to whatever action the court takes, but the court must take some action. Judges uncomfortable about entering the therapeutic ticket, therefore, may be more uncomfortable trying to act therapeutically in the will contest situation than in the no contest plea situation. But this exercise of categorizing, classifying, and discussing "psychojudicial soft spots" and strategies is, I think, an exciting future course of interdisciplinary and practical legal scholarship. *See* Harry T. Edwards, *The Growing Disjunction Between Legal Education and the Legal Profession: A Postscript,* 91 Mich. L. Rev. 2191, 2196 n. 20 (1993) (therapeutic jurisprudence as "practical interdisciplinary scholarship").

62. Hardaway, *supra* note 8, at xlii.

63. *Id.* at xliii-xliv.

incentives, and professional responsibility—but those are all appropiate matters for discussion in shaping a TJ preventive lawyer.

The second rewind of the *Will Contest* example takes us back not to the law office of the *brother's* attorney, but rather to the law office of the *mother's* attorney, at the time of the drafting of her will. In that setting, somewhat similar to the *Tom's Drug Problem/Trust* example, a TJ preventive lawyer should recognize the proposed disposition as a *psycholegal soft spot* and might discuss with the client possible preventive strategies: perhaps talk with your son now, or state in the will, or in a separate letter, or in an audiotape or videotape, that you love your son very much, and are delighted that his financial situation is good, and are saddened at how much his sister is struggling.

The Therapeutic Jurisprudence Judging Project may be able to produce forms, to be filled out by interested judges, describing psychojudicial soft spots and *therapeutic moment*, ideally also with a *rewind* component, where the judge may give her views on what actions lawyers might have taken at an earlier stage. (As this article goes to press, Alan Tomkins and Marc Patry at the University of Nebraska are beginning a research project to collect such data. This endeavor, which uses empirical research methods to improve the humanistic functioning of the law, will likely also eventually involve other dimensions, such as lawyer and judge interviews, surveys, and focus groups). Ideally, too, a *rewind* component should also be used in the law school clinic journal entries—especially since, at the moment at least, most of the clinic cases first reach the clinic when a serious legal problem or crisis has erupted.[64]

---

64. Ideally, legal clinics fully implementing a TJ preventive law approach should have an effective outreach program. At the moment, law school clinics cater principally to law students' understandable craving for a taste of litigation. A TJ preventive law stream, however, should be available to students who opt for it, and the approach in general can nurture, rather than suppress, the "ethic of care" that some students bring with them to law school. *See* Daicoff, *supra* note 55. On outreach activities and lawyering in the area of homelessness, *see* Abbott, *supra* note 3, at 312.

With an appropriate outreach program, clinic lawyers and students might, in a non-crisis situation, conduct true preventive law legal checkups. Even under the structure of most existing law school clinics, however, where clients typically arrive with a serious problem in hand, legal checkups could be offered not at intake but rather at the close of the clinic's involvement with the matter that precipitated the client's visit.

Of course, some work by legal clinics will involve matters that are neither preventive law nor therapeutic jurisprudence. Further, although preventive law, broadly-conceived, and therapeutic jurisprudence, broadly-conceived, overlap substantialy, *see* Stolle et al., *supra* note 12, they are not co-extensive: some matters may constitute preventive law but not therapeutic jurisprudence, and vice versa. A TJ preven-

When we have many relevant vignettes, we can begin to use them to build our knowledge base, much as we traditionally make use of case law. Instead of comparing and contrasting *Mapp v. Ohio*[65] with *United States v. Leon*,[66] we may be comparing and contrasting *Tom's Drug Problem/Trust* example with the *Children of Divorce* example and with the latest case to reach the clinic.[67] These situations, and this new form of *case* analysis, will constitute the stock in trade of the TJ preventive lawyer.

---

tive lawyer will actually have a combined concentration in the two fields. *See* Stolle & Wexler, *Combined Concentration, supra* note 7. Again analogizing to the field of medicine, we may see a TJ preventive lawyer more as a counterpart to the hypothetical pediatrician/surgeon than as a pediatric surgeon.: while most of the hypothetical pediatrician/surgeon's work will involve surgery on children, some may involve non-surgical pediatric care.

An additional issue regarding the implementation of TJ preventive lawyering in jurisdictions following or heavily influenced by the European legal tradition relates to the division of lawyering functions between advocates and notaries. For an introduction to the Latin

Notary, *see* Pedro A. Malavet, *Counsel for the Situation: The Latin Notary, A Historical and Comparative Model*, 19 HASTINGS INT'L & COMP. L. REV. 389 (1996).

65. 367 U. S. 643 (1961).

66. 468 U. S. 897 (1984).

67. Stolle et al., *supra* note 12, we note that initial efforts at TJ preventive lawyering are perhaps ideally suited for legal clinics, legal services offices, and prepaid legal plans. In those settings, where lawyers are salaried, clients will not worry that a preventive law approach is "creating" remunerative legal issues for the lawyers to work on. It is interesting, however, that the *Children of Divorce* example, where the lawyer is seeking "like-minded" clients, may most non-controversially apply in private practice settings.

Chapter 3

Better Legal Counseling Through Empirical Research: Identifying Psycholegal Soft Spots and Strategies

Marc W. Patry
David B. Wexler
Dennis P. Stolle
Alan J. Tomkins

A major problem faced by the legal profession is the public perception, unfortunately apparently grounded in reality,[1] that lawyers typically do not practice with an "ethic of care."[2] For the most part, lawyers define client problems narrowly—too narrowly for our taste—and often deal with legal matters without paying careful attention to accompanying psychological fallout.

Even lawyers who recognize the importance of the law-related psychological realm have difficulty advising other lawyers just *how* such factors might be identified or taken into account. For instance, in an excellent text on preventive law, the "human element" in legal counseling is briefly recognized, but specific strategies are absent:

> For an analysis of the human element of legal counseling, see Redmount, *Humanistic Law Through Legal Counseling*, 2 CONN. L. REV. 98 (1969). Counseling a client about the legal ramifications of a potential conflict requires a broad approach that will identify collateral human issues that may significantly affect the client's decision-making process on a course of action to resolve the conflict in addition to treatment of the core issues. Social and psychological interests of the client or the client's family are examples of such col-

---

1. *See* Susan Daicoff, *Lawyer, Know Thyself: A Review of Empirical Research on Attorney Attributes Bearing on Professionalism*, 46 AM. U. L. REV. 1337 (1997).
2. *See id.* at 1401-03.

lateral human issues. It is the lawyer's duty to identify and clarify any core or collateral issues that may potentially affect a client's inter-est.[3]

And the leading work on legal counseling strongly urges lawyers to anticipate and consider the "nonlegal" consequences—including psychological ones—that invariably accompany legal measures, but notes that "nonlegal consequences are often difficult to predict."[4]

We believe that recent efforts to integrate preventive law with therapeutic jurisprudence can ease the task of predicting psychological consequences, and can give real substance and structure to the area of legal counseling.[5] The remainder of this essay explores the integration and suggests how we may develop a truly law and psychology based approach to legal counseling.

Therapeutic jurisprudence ("TJ") is concerned with the law's impact on emotional life and psychological well-being,[6] and is interested not only in law reform, but also in how existing law may be most therapeutically *applied*.[7] As such, it offers to preventive law an opportunity of an expanded focus that will embrace explicitly an ethic of care.

Preventive law involves careful client interviewing and counseling, and careful planning and drafting to avoid legal conflicts and disputes. Pre-

---

3. Robert M. Hardaway, Preventive Law: Materials on a Non Adversarial Legal Process 75 (1997).

4. David A. Binder et al., Lawyers as Counselors: A Client-Centered Approach 12 (1991).

5. The most ambitious effort at integration is Dennis P. Stolle et al., *Integrating Preventive Law and Therapeutic Jurisprudence: A Law and Psychology Based Approach to Lawyering*, 34 Cal. W. L. Rev. 15 (1997) [hereinafter *Integrating Preventive Law*]. *See also* Dennis P. Stolle, *Professional Responsibility in Elder Law: A Synthesis of Preventive Law and Therapeutic Jurisprudence*, 14 Behav. Sci. & L. 257 (1996); Dennis P. Stolle & David B. Wexler, *Therapeutic Jurisprudence and Preventive Law: A Combined Concentration to Invigorate the Everyday Practice of Law*, 29 Ariz. L. Rev. 25 (1997); Dennis P. Stolle & David B. Wexler, *Preventive Law and Therapeutic Jurisprudence: A Symbiotic Relationship*, 16 Preventive L. Rep. 4 (1997); David B. Wexler, *Practicing Therapeutic Jurisprudence: Psycholegal Soft Spots and Strategies*, 67 Revista Juridica UPR (forthcoming 1998) [hereinafter *Psycholegal Soft Spots*]; Dennis P. Stolle, *Advance Directives, AIDS, and Mental Health: TJ Preventive Law for the HIV-Positive Client*, 4 Psychol. Pub. Pol'y & L. (forthcoming 1998).

6. The most comprehensive work on therapeutic jurisprudence is Law in a Therapeutic Key: Developments in Therapeutic Jurisprudence (David B. Wexler & Bruce J. Winick eds., 1996) [hereinafter Law in a Therapeutic Key].

7. *See* David B. Wexler, *Applying the Law Therapeutically*, 5 Applied & Preventive Psychol. 179 (1996) [hereinafter *Applying the Law*], *reprinted in* Law in a Therapeutic Key, *supra* note 6, at 831.

ventive law practice emphasizes the importance of "periodic legal check-ups."[8] It also seeks to identify "legal soft spots" (potential trouble points) and to come up with strategies to avoid or minimize the anticipated legal trouble.[9]

In anticipating and preventing legal problems, preventive law encourages us to "fast forward" to an imagined future time and trouble, and then to plan to avoid that occurrence. As a pedagogical device—in law school teaching, for example—preventive law proponents also suggest a "rewind" technique.[10] For example, after discussing an appellate decision in contract law, we might "rewind" the situation back to the stage of drafting, and ask what might have been done differently to avoid the legal problem presented by the case.

If therapeutic jurisprudence offers preventive law a robust possibility of incorporating an ethic of care, preventive law reciprocates by offering therapeutic jurisprudence a set of practical, law office procedures (including periodic checkups, basic checklists, and planning instruments) whereby lawyers may counsel clients to apply or invoke the law in a therapeutic manner.[11] These methods and procedures, in other words, pave the way for therapeutic jurisprudence truly to be "felt by practitioners."[12]

When integrated with preventive law, therapeutic jurisprudence would suggest that, during legal checkups and client interviewing and counseling sessions, lawyers look not only to "legal soft spots" (areas that can lead to future legal trouble) but also to "*psycholegal* soft spots"[13] (areas where legal intervention or procedures may not lead to a lawsuit or to legal vulnerability, but may lead to anxiety, distress, depression, hard and hurt feelings, etc.).[14] The lawyer should then raise that issue with the client,

---

8. *See* HARDAWAY, *supra* note 3, at 189-92.

9. *See id.* at 92.

10. *See id.* at xlii.

11. As noted in Wexler, *Psycholegal Soft Spots*, *supra* note 5, there are certain instances where the client will be invoking the law personally, and other instances where the lawyer will be applying or invoking the law.

12. Melanie B. Abbott, *Seeking Shelter Under a Deconstructed Roof: Homelessness and Critical Lawyering*, 64 TENN. L. REV. 269, 289 (1997).

13. The concept of "psycholegal soft spots" was introduced in Stolle et al., *Integrating Preventive Law*, *supra* note 5. It is developed more fully in Wexler, *Psycholegal Soft Spots*, *supra* note 5.

14. Preventing anxiety, depression, and other negative psychological consequences has long been viewed as an important goal when dealing with psychologically vulnerable persons. *See, e.g.*, MURRAY LEVINE & DAVID W. PERKINS, PRINCIPLES OF COMMUNITY PSYCHOLOGY ch. 7 (2d ed. 1997). Preventing psychosocial problems (or, in this context, law-

and discuss possible strategies for dealing with it. For example, consider the situation of elderly parents with two adult children, one of whom functions marginally because of a history of drug and alcohol problems. If, in drafting a will, the parents leave funds outright to one child, but leave the money in a trust to the one with drug problems, the parents may be creating a situation of hurt and hard feelings—toward them and toward the sibling left funds without strings attached. A lawyer combining the perspectives of therapeutic jurisprudence and preventive law will anticipate this situation, will regard the proposed testamentary disposition as a "psycholegal soft spot" (though not necessarily as a "legal soft spot," vulnerable to legal attack), and will discuss with the clients possible strategies of dealing with—and minimizing—the law-related psychological distress. For instance, the clients might speak now with the adult children, or they might specify in the will why they are taking the indicated action, and so forth.

Despite our opening remarks about an absence, in the aggregate, of an ethic of care in contemporary lawyering, we of course know that many psychologically-sensitive lawyers already practice, albeit implicitly and unsystematically, what we preach. Moreover, others might be eager to do so if only they had a better handle on how to do so. For this reason, we are hereby launching a research project to mine the experience of practitioners in identifying and dealing with psycholegal soft spots in the various areas of law practice.

So far as we are aware, the approach of problem solving and knowledge-building through the medium of a law review publication is itself a novel technique, but we are hopeful it will be appropriate to our task. For example, we are not in this project seeking a "random sample" of attorney responses. We are not especially interested at this juncture in knowing how the "representative" attorney might handle a given situation; instead, we are interested in learning how psychologically-sensitive attorneys might deal creatively with certain situations.

Accordingly, we close this essay with a prepared form for eliciting relevant information from interested members of the legal profession. The blank form is preceded by three examples intended to serve as models for structuring responses to this invitation to share your experience. They include a Will Contest case, an Americans with Disabilities Act (ADA) case, and a Guardianship-HIV case.[15]

---

related psychological problems) can be more cost-effective than handling such problems once they erupt. *See id.* at 251.

15. The Will Contest case and the Guardianship-HIV case are adapted from actual cases. *See* Wexler, *Applying the Law, supra* note 7 (discussing the will contest case); Mark S. Senak, HIV, AIDS and the Law: A Guide to Our Rights and Challenges 41

We encourage the dissemination of the essay and forms among lawyers in practice settings and at professional meetings, and among law students practicing in supervised clinical programs or in clerking positions. While the principal focus of this essay is on lawyers as legal counselors, we also heartily welcome the participation of the judiciary. In fact, the first example in our forms, a will contest, comes from the trial bench. Judges, of course, confront psychologically difficult situations each day and some of them have employed interesting and creative strategies to deal with those situations. They should profit from the collection, analysis, and dissemination of the judicial examples. Moreover, with the preventive law "rewind" technique, judges may be able to provide much advice to attorneys on how, at an earlier time, certain strategies and techniques might have been employed to head-off the very court case described in the form.

As these examples accumulate, we can use them for discussion, debate, dissemination, and education. These cases, describing psycholegal soft spots and strategies, can be collected, categorized, critiqued, compared, and contrasted—much as appellate decisions are now.[16] They may ultimately constitute the corpus of a new form of "case" analysis that will form the stock in trade of legal counselors and TJ preventive lawyers.[17] By sharing and synthesizing our experience, we hope to make the psychological consequences of certain legal courses of action less difficult to anticipate. Thus, we invite you to "brief" some of your own such cases on the provided form. Please note that, as long as appropriate credit is given, the *California Western Law Review* hereby authorizes the reproduction of the essay and the forms.

* * *

Identification of Psycholegal
Soft Spots and Strategies

The enclosed questionnaire is designed as a format for the discussion of legal situations that may have an impact on psychological well-being. Sometimes, when such situations are encountered, the use of certain strategies

---

(1996) (discussing the guardian ship-HIV case). The ADA case was suggested by the writings of a disability advocate. *See* Rose A. Daly-Rooney, *Designing Reasonable Accommodations Through Co-Worker Participation: Therapeutic Jurisprudence and the Confidentiality Provision of the Americans with Disabilities Act*, 8 J.L. & HEALTH 89 (1994), *reprinted in* LAW IN A THERAPEUTIC KEY, *supra* note 6, at 365.

16. *See* Wexler, *Psycholegal Soft Spots, supra* note 5.

17. *See id.*

may lead to reduced negative psychological impact or even to a positive psychological impact. We call these situations "psycholegal soft spots." Three examples of psycholegal soft spots and strategies are outlined below. These examples are provided to assist you in answering the same questions on a copy of the blank form that appears in the Appendix to this volume.

A judge's experience inspired our first example:

1) Identify the area of law that this problem relates to:

Wills

2) Provide a brief description of the legal situation as it was at the time you initially became involved:

There is a will contest between a brother and sister. The sister, who cared for the Mother in her dying years, has been left the broken-down family home. Unlike his sister, the brother has a steady income and a home of his own. He seeks to overturn the will.

3) Describe the potential or actual nonlegal motivations or consequences to the parties involved:

This situation seems to have little to do with the money involved, but appears to be related to the brother's hurt feelings. There is potential for the brother to remain bitter about the will and to distance himself from his sister.

4) In your experience, how often does this type of situation occur?

I have only about five will contest cases per year, one or two of which might be motivated by hurt feelings.

5) Provide a description of the action taken and the legal and nonlegal outcomes:

Finding that there was no undue influence, I upheld the will. Because of my perspective on the situation, however, I made some remarks at the close of the hearing. I commented that the differing financial circumstances between the brother and sister made the outcome understandable, and that I didn't think that it meant that the mother loved the brother any less.

6) Explain whether or not you believe this approach resulted in successful legal and nonlegal outcomes and why:

After hearing my comments, the brother broke down in tears. In a legal sense, there is no question that justice was done. The brother simply did not have sufficient reasons or evidence for me to justify overturning the will. More importantly, in a nonlegal sense, I feel that this outcome was completely successful in that the brother would probably not remain resentful about his mother's will or alienated from his sister.

7) Describe alternate approaches that could have been taken and how the legal and nonlegal outcomes may have been more or less successful than the actual outcomes:

Quite simply, I could have called it as I saw it without any additional remarks. I feel that the outcome of such a hearing would not have resolved any negative feelings that the brother had about the will .

8) Using the "rewind" technique (e.g., "rewinding" the case to an earlier point in time), describe how this situation may have been prevented or diminished in severity by other attorneys or other judges at earlier points in time:

This situation could have been resolved long before it entered the courtroom. Looking back to the lawyer's office when the brother was contemplating legal action on the will, the lawyer might have been able to make similar observations to mine, and to a similar effect. Looking even further back to the mother's lawyer at the drafting of the will, the lawyer may have thought about the potential perceptions of the brother and sister and suggested preventive measures against future hard feelings, such as a letter to the brother explaining her reasons for leaving the house to the sister.

9) General comments:

It seems that when this type of situation arises, there may be alternative ways of handling the problem of one sibling feeling that a will is unfair. Since the mother did not, before or after her death, communicate to her children the reasons for the division of assets in her will, my courtroom may have seemed to the brother the logical place to air the family feud. It is quite possible that the brother's attorney attempted to tell him the same thing that I did, but that the brother nonetheless pushed to go to court. In cases like this, I often feel that the authority I have as a judge can result in success where others may have failed. Hearing me tell him that I didn't think the mother's division of assets meant she loved him any less may have had a much stronger impact on the brother than anyone else could have had.

Second is an example adapted from an attorney's experience:

1) Identify the area of law that this problem relates to:

Guardianship and AIDs law

2) Provide a brief description of the legal situation as it was at the time you initially became involved:

A client dying of AIDS didn't feel that her relatives would make good parents. She found someone outside the family who she wanted to raise her seven-year-old daughter.

3) Describe the potential or actual nonlegal motivations or con sequences to the parties involved:

The mother wanted to prevent her family from taking custody of her child. She wanted to leave her child in the custody of another adult that she trusted. The potential difficulties that could have resulted for the child if the family were to take custody are too numerous to list here. The anxiety that this issue caused for the mother was extreme and it would have been very traumatic for this dying woman if her family had taken custody of her daughter.

4) In your experience, how often does this type of situation occur?

I know of several similar instances in my personal legal experience. I imagine that, with the increasing prevalence of AIDS and children with AIDS-infected parents, this type of situation will occur with increasing frequency.

5) Provide a description of the action taken and the legal and nonlegal outcomes:

Fortunately, my jurisdiction allows for the appointment of a "standby guardian," and I made legal arrangements for the new caretaker to have standby guardianship of the child while the formal adoption papers were being processed and suggested that the mother, daughter, and the standby guardian begin immediately to spend time together.

6) Explain whether or not you believe this approach resulted in successful legal and nonlegal outcomes and why:

The standby guardianship arrangement was very successful from both legal and nonlegal perspectives. From a legal perspective, the new guardian had immediate custody over the child, which would have prevented the family from taking custody if the mother had unexpectedly died. From a nonlegal perspective, the standby status allowed the daughter to get to know her new mother before her maternal mother died. The three were able to spend time together and bond before the mother had to be hospitalized. This made things much easier on the daughter than it might otherwise have been. I feel that a very important nonlegal aspect of this standby guardianship arrangement was for the mother. It was an incredible comfort to her to know that her daughter would be properly cared for.

7)   Describe alternate approaches that could have been taken and how the legal and nonlegal outcomes may have been more or less successful than the actual outcomes:

We could have simply started the adoption process without arranging for a standby guardianship. This could have created a host of problems for the child if the mother had passed away unexpectedly, especially if the family had sought custody. In this way the legal outcome could have been extremely convoluted. The nonlegal consequences of such a complicated situation could have been extremely troublesome to all involved, especially for the young girl.

8)   Using the "rewind" technique (e.g., "rewinding" the case to an earlier point in time), describe how this situation may have been prevented or diminished in severity by other attorneys or other judges at earlier points in time:

I am unsure that "rewinding" this scenario shows any earlier times when this situation could have been ameliorated. It is possible, however, with a good "outreach" legal assistance program, that the mother could have consulted with an attorney when she discovered she was infected with HIV. If she did, then the lawyer could have suggested that she begin thinking about making arrangements for her child before her health began to severely decline.

9)   General comments:

This seems like it might be a good case to keep in mind for lawyers or judges who encounter individuals with HIV. A simple suggestion from someone that children will need to have legal guardianship arrangements may help to get the client thinking along those lines and eliminate a host of problems at a later point.

The third example also reflects the perspective of an attorney; it is adapted from a law journal article:

1)   Identify the area of law that this problem relates to:

Americans with Disabilities Act

2)   Provide a brief description of the legal situation as it was at the time you initially became involved:

A client with a disability came to me requesting facilitation of special working conditions. Because she is paraplegic, she wanted to have a special desk constructed for her so that she could easily reach her computer keyboard, telephone, and working surface at her new job in a telemar-

*keting firm. Her supervisor had told her that the company expected employ-
ees to make the best of the existing equipment and furniture.*

3)   Describe the potential or actual nonlegal motivations or consequences to the parties involved:

*This case is a clear-cut example of a person with a disability requesting
necessary working conditions through the ADA. The nonlegal ramifications
are much more far-reaching, however. In many similar cases, the worker with
a disability experiences social isolation in the workplace because other workers feel that there is some sort of "special treatment" being given to the
employee with a disability. This type of scenario can create a host of undesirable
consequences for the disabled person, sometimes resulting in leaving the job.*

4)   In your experience, how often does this type of situation occur?

*This type of situation is common in cases where ADA reasonable accom-
modations are being sought. Rarely, however, do clients approach me with
requests to facilitate adequate working conditions. Usually, employers are
extremely responsive to the needs of employees with disabilities. I have
handled only two similar complaints in my career.*

5)   Provide a description of the action taken and the legal and nonlegal
outcomes:

*I drafted a letter to the employer on behalf of my client. I suggested to
my client that she consider asking her employer to have an informal meeting with supervisors and co-workers so that she could explain her situation and her need for special workspace. The employer agreed to provide
the special workstation and held the requested meeting. Supervisors and
co-workers were very responsive and remain helpful and friendly toward
my client and her needs.*

6)   Explain whether or not you believe this approach resulted in successful legal and nonlegal outcomes and why:

*I believe both the legal and nonlegal consequences of this situation to
be quite successful. My client was able to get the working conditions she
was legally entitled to under the ADA. In addition, her meeting with supervisors and co-workers helped to familiarize others with her disability. It is
my belief that my client's openness about her disability resulted in much
more positive working relationships with peers and supervisors than other
courses of action may have caused.*

7)   Describe alternate approaches that could have been taken and how
the legal and nonlegal outcomes may have been more or less successful
than the actual outcomes:

I could have simply informed my client of her rights and drafted the letter citing the ADA, asking for the workstation as a reasonable accommodation under the Act. This may have been a less successful course of action in the nonlegal sense in that it may have created tension with supervisors and co-workers if my client had not personally discussed her disability and workplace needs.

8)   Using the "rewind" technique (e.g., "rewinding" the case to an earlier point in time), describe how this situation may have been prevented or diminished in severity by other attorneys or other judges at earlier points in time:

In cases such as this, it is usually ignorance on the part of the employer which results in clients coming to me and requesting what is legally theirs. Once employers become aware of their duty under the ADA, they usually comply without further hesitation. If the company were fully aware of ADA requirements, it could integrate disability requirements into its hiring and training policies. This would eliminate the problem of employees with disabilities needing to come for legal assistance to get the working conditions they need and are entitled to. This sort of preventive approach on the part of the employer might also reduce supervisor and co-worker hostility towards people with disabilities, if training could include awareness of disabilities and related workplace issues.

9)   General comments:

The blank questionnaire that appeared at the end of this article in the CALIFORNIA WESTERN LAW REVIEW appears at the Appendix to this volume. We invite you to photocopy the Appendix, complete the questionnaire, and return the completed questionnaire to the address listed in the Appendix.

II.

Civil Practice

Advance Directives, AIDS, and Mental Health: TJ Preventive Law for the HIV-Positive Client

Dennis P. Stolle

The devastating impact of AIDS on the physical and financial health of those affected, coupled with the rapid spread of the disease, quickly led to a substantial and growing body of scholarly commentary on the topic of legal planning for HIV-positive clients. Although there is a new sense of optimism arising from recent successes with protease inhibitors and "cocktail" treatments,[1] a person who learns that he or she is HIV-positive continues to face not only the overwhelming health care issues related to living with a potentially terminal disease, but also a myriad of legal and social issues. These issues can include concerns over estate planning, employment discrimination, child custody, health-care costs, disability insurance, life insurance, and government aid.[2]

---

1. The term "cocktail" refers to a mixture of several drugs. Such mixtures have shown better results than monotherapies in fighting HIV. *See New Anti-HIV Drugs and Treatment Strategies Buoy AIDS Researchers*, 275 JAMA 579 (1996). *See also* Lawrence Corey & King K. Homes, *Therapy for Human Immunodeficiency Virus Infection— What Have We Learned?*, 335 New Eng. J. Med. 1143 (1996).

2. *See, e.g.*, MARK S. SENAK, HIV, AIDS AND THE LAW (1996); Emily Berendt & Laura Lynn Michaels, *Your HIV Positive Client: Easing the Burden on the Family Through Estate Planning*, 24 J. MARSHALL L. REV. 509 (1991); Gody B. Gabel, *Release From Terminal Suffering? The Impact of Aids on Medically Assisted Suicide Legislation*, 22 FLA. ST. U. L. REV. 369 (1994); Charles J. Groppe & Eileen E. Hudson, *Estate Planning for the Client with the Risk of AIDS*, 64 N. Y. ST. B.J. 20 (1992); James Monroe Smith, *Legal Issues Confronting Families Affected by HIV*, 24 J. MARSHALL L. REV. 543 (1991); W. E. Scott Hoot (editor), *Estate Planning for Artists: Will Your Art Survive?*, 21 COLUM-VLA J.L. & ARTS 15 (1996); Sana Loue, *Living Wills, Durable Powers of Attorney for Health Care, and HIV Infection: The Need for Statutory Reform*, 16 J. LEGAL MED. 461 (1995); Benjamin Schatz, *The AIDS Insurance Crisis: Underwriting or Overreaching?*, 100 HARVARD L. REV. 1782 (1987); John Douglas, Comment, *HIV Disease and Disparate Impact*

A general consensus readily emerges from this literature that proactive planning is critical in short-circuiting the host of potential legal problems that an HIV-positive client might face. There also seems to exist a consensus that the values underlying such planning, at least the articulated values, are those of preserving financial and legal autonomy. Yet, a closer analysis reveals that much of this commentary explicitly promoting autonomy also implicitly promotes the value of psychological or emotional well-being. There typically seems to be a sense, although often unstated, that promotion of autonomy will somehow, in turn, promote psychological well-being. It has been suggested that if the client can determine important issues in advance, such as who will get his or her property or who will make health-care decisions when and if the client is unable to do so, that this will somehow ease the psychological and emotional burden of the disease, ultimately promoting both autonomy and emotional well-being.[3] Nevertheless, little legal commentary has been devoted to using legal planning to explicitly preserve or enhance the psychological or emotional well-being of HIV-positive clients.[4]

The purpose of this article is to suggest that, in legal planning for the HIV-positive client, concerns of psychological and emotional well-being ought to be explicitly recognized as one priority among many. Through an application of TJ Preventive Law, which is essentially the product of the combination of therapeutic jurisprudence (TJ) and preventive law,[5] a lawyer may be able to both enhance an HIV-positive client's autonomy by protecting his or her individual liberties and enhance the client's psychological well-being by making emotional concerns one priority in legal planning. This article focuses on the dual goal of promoting both autonomy and

---

Under the Americans With Disabilities Act: A Federal Prohibition of Discrimination on the Basis of Sexual Orientation? 16 BERKELEY J. EMP. & LAB. L. 288 (1995); Georgiana K. Roussos, *Note: Protections Against HIV-Based Employment Discrimination in the United States and Australia,* 13 HASTINGS INT'L & COMP. L. REV. 609 (1990); Jackson Smith, Comment, *AIDS and the Law: Protecting the HIV- Infected Employee from Discrimination,* 57 TENN. L. REV. 539 (1990).

3. *See, e.g.,* Senak, *supra* note 2.

4. This is, perhaps, not surprising given that protecting individual liberty, not necessarily well-being, has been the traditional province of the legal profession. There have, however, been some scholarly attempts. *See, e.g.,* Berendt & Michaels, *supra* note 2; John Parry, *Life Services Planning for Persons With AIDS-Related Mental Illnesses,* 13 MENTAL & PHYSICAL DISABILITY L. REP. 82, 84 (1989); James Monroe Smith, *When Knowing the Law is Not Enough: Confronting Denial and Considering Sociocultural Issues Affecting HIV Positive People,* 17 HAMLINE J. PUB. L. & POL'Y 1 (1995).

5. *See* Dennis P. Stolle et al., *Integrating Preventive Law and Therapeutic Jurisprudence: A Law and Psychology Based Approach to Lawyering,* 34 CAL. W. L. REV. 15 (1997).

psychological well-being by analyzing the enforceability and potential therapeutic utility of mental health-care advance directives for HIV-positive clients. Considerations of psychological well-being need not, however, be limited to the legal issues surrounding health-care, which serve as the focus of this article. The approach of TJ Preventive Law will generalize to many of the other common legal problems faced by HIV-positive clients such as estate planning, employment issues, insurance issues, or custody issues, among others.[6]

Combining Therapeutic Jurisprudence and Preventive Law

Therapeutic Jurisprudence

Therapeutic jurisprudence is a scholarly perspective that focuses on the law's impact on psychological and emotional well-being.[7] The analytic methods of TJ are eclectic,[8] combining the skills and modes of analysis traditionally associated with the disparate disciplines of law, clinical psychology, psychiatry, social and experimental psychology, and philosophy.[9] Thus, TJ is an interdisciplinary endeavor that attempts to glean appropriate analytic and empirical techniques from a variety of relevant disciplines, bringing them to bear on the psychological and emotional impact that laws and legal authorities may have on the participants in the legal system.[10]

Although TJ is an interdisciplinary endeavor with a strong focus on social science,[11] TJ has maintained a firm grounding in the law. Therapeutic jurisprudence has long rejected the advancement of the therapeutic

---

6. Indeed, the approach of TJ Preventive Law generalizes to such diverse areas of law as elder law, corporate and business planning law, and matrimonial law. *See generally* Dennis P. Stolle et al., *supra* note 5.

7. *David B. Wexler, Applying the Law Therapeutically*, 5 APPLIED & PREVENTIVE PSYCHOL. 179 (1996).

8. David B. Wexler & Bruce J. Winick, *Therapeutic Jurisprudence as a New Research Tool, in* ESSAYS IN THERAPEUTIC JURISPRUDENCE 303 (David B. Wexler & Bruce J. Winick eds., 1991).

9. David B. Wexler, *An Introduction to Therapeutic Jurisprudence, in* THERAPEUTIC JURISPRUDENCE: THE LAW AS A THERAPEUTIC AGENT 3 (David B. Wexler ed., 1990).

10. *See* Wexler, *supra* note 9, at 8.

11. For a description of the potential of TJ as a program of empirical research, see Wexler & Winick, *supra* note 8.

mission as the sole consideration in the development of legal policy.[12] Rather, TJ recognizes that the law "serves many ends."[13] Therapeutic effects are simply proposed as one consideration among many in legal decision making, though perhaps one that is too often overlooked.[14]

Therapeutic jurisprudence scholarship has developed and expanded rapidly in recent years.[15] Early TJ scholarship tended to focus on instituting changes in existing laws or legal procedures in order to enhance their therapeutic impact.[16] However, a newly emerging direction in TJ scholarship is the exploration of taking the law as given and developing methods for applying the existing law therapeutically.[17]

Practicing lawyers spend much of their time trying to guide clients through the legal process in a manner most beneficial to the client. As a lawyer faces the myriad of legal options available to a client, the lawyer typically makes choices that might maximize the client's legal rights. However, the lawyer also typically considers the impact that legal decisions will have on such extralegal matters as the client's financial assets. With these considerations in mind, good lawyers will apply existing law, to the extent possible, in a manner that will enhance both the client's legal and financial

---

12. DAVID B. WEXLER & BRUCE J. WINICK, ESSAYS IN THERAPEUTIC JURISPRUDENCE, xi, 1991.

13. *Id.*

14. *Id.* Furthermore, TJ involves a recognition that occasionally therapeutic goals may come into direct conflict with other important values such as individual liberty, and that such conflicts cannot be resolved through empirical inquiry alone. *See, e.g.,* Robert F. Schopp, *Therapeutic Jurisprudence and Conflicts Among Values in Mental Health Law,* 11 BEHAV. SCI. & THE L. 31 (1993); David B. Wexler & Robert F. Schopp, *Therapeutic Jurisprudence: A New Approach to Mental Health Law, in* THE HANDBOOK OF PSYCHOLOGY AND LAW 361 (Dorothy Kaigehero & W. F. Laufer eds., 1990).

15. TJ initially grew out of mental health law scholarship. Wexler, *supra* note 7. But, the scope of TJ scholarship has grown rapidly. David B. Wexler, *Therapeutic Jurisprudence In Clinical Practice,* 153 AM. J. PSYCHIATRY 453, 453 (1996) (noting that "the reach of therapeutic jurisprudence is by no means confined narrowly to mental health law"). *See generally* DAVID B. WEXLER & BRUCE J. WINICK, LAW IN A THERAPEUTIC KEY (1996).

16. Wexler, *supra* note 7. Dennis P. Stolle & David B. Wexler, *Therapeutic Jurisprudence and Preventive Law: A Combined Concentration to Invigorate the Everyday Practice of Law,* 39 ARIZ. L. REV. 25 (1997).

17. Wexler *supra* note 7. *See also* David Finkelman & Thomas Grisso, *Therapeutic Jurisprudence: From Idea to Application,* 20 NEW ENG. J. ON CRIM. & CIV. CONFINEMENT 243 (1994); Dennis P. Stolle, *Professional Responsibility in Elder Law: A Synthesis of Preventive Law and Therapeutic Jurisprudence,* 14 BEHAV. SCI. & L. 459 (1996); Dennis P. Stolle & David B. Wexler, *Preventive Law and Therapeutic Jurisprudence: A Symbiotic Relationship,* 16 PREVENTIVE L. REP. 4 (1997); Wexler, *supra* note 15.

goals. Just as legal process can impact financial concerns, so too can legal process impact psychological or emotional well-being.[18] Yet, unlike financial concerns, psychological and emotional well-being are often regarded as being outside of the lawyer's province or simply overlooked. This does not, however, have to be the case. To the extent that choices about legal procedures impact a client's psychological well-being, a lawyer can and ought to make psychological or emotional concerns an additional priority in client counseling.[19] By informing the client of the potential psychological or emotional impact of a particular legal procedure, the lawyer provides the client with an opportunity to choose from the available legal procedures in light of these concerns. In this way, the lawyer and client can actually apply existing law, or legal procedures, therapeutically.

This approach of applying the law therapeutically seems particularly appropriate in the context of working with HIV-positive clients. The HIV-positive client presents a special case of a client who is likely to be under extreme psychological and emotional pressures.[20] Furthermore, the nature of the client's distress is likely to change as the disease progresses. One psychological model suggests that an individual's initial reaction to learning of his or her HIV-positive status includes denial, depression, or persistent anxiety.[21] This can be followed by a transitional state involving anger, fear, or self-blame, followed by reactions to becoming symptomatic, possibly including a sense of hopelessness or a preoccupation with symptom control.[22] Finally, there is often a psychological reaction that involves preparation for dying and might include fear of death and a concern with finalizing one's affairs.[23] Unfortunately, throughout each of these stages, there can also be the lingering fear of losing one's mental capacity to AIDS Dementia Complex.[24]

---

18. *See* Stolle et al., *supra* note 5.

19. Making such decisions intelligently requires practicing lawyers to become consumers of research on the therapeutic or anti-therapeutic effects of both formal (courtroom) legal procedures and informal (law office) legal procedures. There are, of course, practical difficulties in adequately disseminating empirical research results among practicing lawyers. For a discussion of the difficulties *see* Stolle et al. *supra* note 5.

20. *See* Helena Brett-Smith & Gerald H. Frieland, *Transmission and Treatment*, in AIDS LAW TODAY: A NEW GUIDE FOR THE PUBLIC 23 (Scott Burris et al. eds. 1993). Deanna E. Grimes & Richard M. Grimes, *Psychological Reaction to HIV Infection*, in AIDS AND HIV INFECTION (Grimes & Grimes eds., 1994). Senak, *supra* note 2.

21. *See* Grimes & Grimes, *supra* note 20.

22. *See* Grimes & Grimes, *supra* note 20.

23. *See* Grimes & Grimes, *supra* note 20.

24. *See, e.g.*, LAURY McKEAN, AIDS DEMENTIA COMPLEX (ADC): A FACT SHEET FROM SEATTLE TREATMENT EDUCATION PROJECT (1992).

A TJ analysis would suggest that this psychological progression ought to be taken seriously by the legal system, both at macro levels, such as legislative decision-making, and at micro levels, such as the interactions between individual legal officials and HIV-positive persons involved in legal processes. Emphasizing the micro level, the new direction in TJ scholarship of applying the law therapeutically would suggest that a lawyer working with an HIV-positive client ought to pay particular attention to any potentially anti-therapeutic side effects of his or her legal advice. For example, advice that might discourage the client from seeking needed treatment or contribute to a client's level of depression or anxiety is to be avoided unless these negative consequences are outweighed by some legal priority.

Thus, the approach of applying the law therapeutically attempts to provide explicit justifications for the consideration of psychological and emotional health as one priority in legal planning. The psychological well-being of those persons affected by legal decisions, therefore, *can* become one important consideration among many in legal decision making. However, TJ alone does not always give the practitioner practical procedures for achieving therapeutic outcomes.[25]

In considering this approach, one might ask, "How would a lawyer know when he or she is rendering legal advice that carries potentially anti-therapeutic side effects?" Although empirical research should be the primary source of information regarding the potential psychological impact of various legal procedures, practicing lawyers clearly cannot be expected to conduct their own empirical research regarding individual client's needs. Rather, the practitioner's relationship to relevant empirical research will most often be one of consumer, not producer.[26] The most useful research for facilitating the therapeutic application of existing law is that research which empirically tests the psychological or emotional side effects of several legal procedures available to effectuate the same client objective.[27] With that information in hand, the lawyer may make informed decisions about applying the law therapeutically, rather than merely relying on guesswork or intuition. Unfortunately, such research most often simply does not exist.[28]

---

25. *See* Stolle & Wexler, *supra* note 16. *See also* Stolle & Wexler, *supra* note 17.

26. *See* Stolle & Wexler, *supra* note 17. However, *see* Stolle et al., *supra* note 5 at 42-43 (describing the identification of psycholegal soft spots as a type of empirical data collection that could be conducted by even busy practitioners who are not trained in social science). *See also*, David B. Wexler, *Practicing Therapeutic Jurisprudence: Psycholegal Soft Spots and Strategies*, 67 REVISTA JURIDICA UPR (forthcoming, 1998); Marc W. Patry, et al., *Better Legal Counseling Through Empirical Research: Identifying Psycholegal Soft Spots and Strategies*, 34 CAL. W. L. REV. (forthcoming, 1998).

27. *See* Stolle et al., *supra* note 5.

28. *See* Stolle et al., *supra* note 5.

Because on-point empirical research is seldom available, TJ scholars typically discuss psychological principles in analogous areas in an effort to speculate about likely therapeutic and anti-therapeutic consequences of various legal alternatives.[29] This approach to TJ scholarship is useful, though incomplete for the purpose of providing the legal practitioner with clear direction in applying the law therapeutically. Even when on-point empirical research is available, merely knowing that research or theory would predict that particular legal procedures are likely to have a therapeutic or anti-therapeutic effect does not necessarily provide the practitioner with the tools required to actually apply the law therapeutically. In some cases, for existing law to be applied therapeutically, it must also be applied with foresight. By the time a dispute has arisen and reached the level of urgency requiring consultation with a lawyer, emotional crises that perhaps could have been anticipated and avoided weeks earlier may have already occurred. However, recent scholarship on applying the law therapeutically has suggested that the framework of preventive law may provide the legal practitioner with the necessary bridge from TJ theory to application by lending the practical tools needed to engage in proactive lawyering.[30]

Preventive Law

Preventive law is a proactive approach to lawyering. The mission of the preventive lawyer is essentially twofold. The preventive lawyer attempts to both minimize the potential legal liability of his or her clients through legal planning and, at the same time, maximize their legal opportunities. The emphasis of preventive law, therefore, is on the lawyer's role as a planner, counselor, and negotiator.[31] In this way, preventive law differs from many traditional perspectives on lawyering, which more often focus on the lawyer's role as litigator or advocate. Preventive law thus acknowledges that much of day-to-day lawyering involves the lawyer acting as a planner or advisor, not a litigator, and *encourages* this counseling role.[32]

---

29. *See, e.g.*, David B. Wexler, *Health Care Compliance Principles and the Insanity Acquittee Conditional Release Process, in* ESSAYS IN THERAPEUTIC JURISPRUDENCE 199 (David B. Wexler & Bruce J. Winick eds., 1991).

30. *See* Stolle, *supra* note 17.

31. *See, e.g.*, ROBERT M. HARDAWAY, PREVENTIVE LAW: MATERIALS ON A NON ADVERSARIAL LEGAL PROCESS, at xix (1997).

32. *See generally* HARDAWAY, *supra* note 31.

Preventive law also promotes a client-centered approach.[33] In preventive law, the lawyer and client engage in a joint decision-making process regarding legal strategies.[34] Of course, the client should always play a role in legal decision making; however, preventive law, unlike other approaches to lawyering, positively emphasizes the importance of that role.[35] Furthermore, the decision making is not limited to a particular dispute. Rather, the decision-making process contemplates the client's long-term goals, interests, and relationships.[36] Increased involvement in joint planning activities with the client, it is suggested, will avoid legal disputes and ultimately cost the client, and perhaps society, less than resolving disputes as they arise.[37]

The preventive lawyer is able to achieve this type of lawyer/client relationship, in part, through the use of the "periodic legal check up."[38] A legal check up is an opportunity for a lawyer/client interaction that is somewhat analogous to a medical check up.[39] The legal check up provides an opportunity for the lawyer and client to visit about matters that may give rise to eventual legal trouble. Such matters are referred to within preventive law as "legal soft spots."[40] By identifying legal soft spots in a period-

---

33. See HARDAWAY, *supra* note 31. *See also* LOUIS M. BROWN & EDWARD A. DAUER, PLANNING BY LAWYERS: MATERIALS ON A NONADVERSARIAL LEGAL PROCESS (1977).

34. See HARDAWAY, *supra* note 31.

35. In its most explicit manifestation, the emphasis on the client-centered approach takes the form of "unbundling." The unbundling of legal services involves the client selecting only those services from the lawyer's full service legal package that the client is willing to purchase. The remainder is the responsibility of the client. For example, "a client may seek the advice and support of a family lawyer in negotiating a settlement, but may choose to self-represent or retain another attorney for actual court representation." *See* Forrest S. Mosten, *Unbundling of Legal Services and the Family Lawyer,* 28 FAMILY L. Q. 421, 440 (1994). *See also* Mary Helen McNeal, *Redefining Attorney-Client Roles: Unbundling and Moderate-Income Elderly Clients,* 32 WAKE FOREST L. REV. 295 (1997); Forrest S. Mosten, *Unbundling Legal Services: A Key Component in the Future of Access to Justice,* 1997 OREGON STATE B. J. 9.

36. See Louis M. Brown, *The Scheme: Maximize Opportunities, Minimize Future Legal Trouble,* 6 PREVENTIVE L. REP. 17 (1987).

37. See HARDAWAY, *supra* note 31. *See also* Forrest S. Mosten, *Unbundling of Legal Services and the Family Lawyer,* 28 FAMILY L. Q. 421, 440 (1994).

38. See HARDAWAY *supra* note 31. *See* Edward A. Dauer, *Future of the Legal Profession Lies in Utilizing Preventive Law,* 9 PREVENTIVE L. REP. 20, 25 (1990).

39. See HARDAWAY, *supra* note 31.

40. See Louis Brown, Manual for Periodic Check-up, CLS 1974, *excerpted in* HARDAWAY, *supra* note 31, at 191-192. *See also* Mosten *supra* note 37, at 446 (Mosten provides examples of legal soft spots and corresponding client actions that might be considered. Furthermore, Mosten points out that "[s]ome legal soft spots may be "pure" legal issues-most are not.").

ic check up, the lawyer can be thought of as diagnosing legal problems that are perhaps, at the time of the check up, asymptomatic.[41] This diagnosis can then be followed by the joint development, between the lawyer and client, of strategies for preventing the potential legal problems.

Preventive law also emphasizes the skillful use of client intake forms and legal checklists.[42] These practical documents, which can be used in conjunction with the periodic legal check up, assist the preventive lawyer in spotting many legal soft spots relatively quickly.[43] Through a combination of well-drafted checklists and skillful client counseling, the preventive lawyer can also spot legal opportunities. Of course, attainment of this dual goal of reducing legal troubles and increasing legal opportunities requires the lawyer to exercise foresight and to be sensitive to both the short-term and long-term needs of individual clients. Additionally, preventive law involves a solid understanding of the legal tools available to secure legal rights and responsibilities without resorting to litigation.[44] This often includes a working knowledge of relevant state and federal statutory schemes that facilitate the use of legal planning instruments such as wills, contracts, trusts, insurance, and advance directives.[45]

Preventive law is a critical component of successfully working with HIV-positive clients. Although the role of preventive lawyering is often not explicitly recognized, the spirit of preventive law has pervaded the legal commentary on counseling an HIV-positive client.[46] There has been a strong consensus among legal commentators that a person should contact a lawyer shortly after learning of his or her HIV-positive status and begin planning for the potential legal ramifications.[47] Mark Senak sums up the point nicely in his excellent consumer-oriented book on HIV/AIDS law:

"The first thing people should do when they learn they are positive is to find friends and family who will give them unconditional support and love; the second thing they should do is see a competent and knowledgeable physician; and on the third day, they should see

---

41. *See* HARDAWAY, *supra* note 31.

42. Scott E. Isaacson, *Preventive Law: A Personal Essay*, 9-Oct. UTAH B.J. 14 (1996).

43. *See* HARDAWAY *supra* note 31, at 191.

44. *See* Stolle, *supra* note 17.

45. *See* Stolle, *supra* note 17.

46. *See, e.g.*, SENAK, *supra* note 2. *See also* Berendt & Micheals, *supra* note 2; Groppe & Hudson, *supra* note 2.

47. *See, e.g.*, SENAK, *supra* note 2. This sentiment can also be found among health care professionals, *See, e.g.*, Stephan L. Buckingham & Wilfred G. Van Gorp, *HIV-Associated Dementia: A Clinician's Guide to Early Detection, Diagnosis, and Intervention*, FAMILIES IN SOC. 333 (1994); Anne Katz, *AIDS Dementia Complex*, 10 J. Palliative Care 46 (1994).

a competent and knowledgeable HIV lawyer to give them the legal version of a medical checkup."[48]

TJ Preventive Law

David Wexler and I have recently suggested that "preventive law, and the legal check-up in particular, at least when used by a lawyer keenly attuned to how the law may affect a client's psychological well-being, can provide the very legal context or mechanism needed for lawyers to work with clients to apply the law therapeutically."[49] Therapeutic jurisprudence alone lacks practical procedures for application. Conversely, preventive law alone lacks, to some extent, an explicit analytical framework for justifying psychological well-being as one factor in legal planning and clearly lacks a substantive body of psychological knowledge related to litigation prevention. However, through a synthesis of preventive law and TJ, preventive law can provide a framework for the practical application of therapeutic jurisprudence. Likewise, therapeutic jurisprudence can provide both an explicit analytic framework for the consideration of psychological and emotional well-being as one factor in legal decision making and a strong interdisciplinary orientation that directly taps relevant bodies of empirical and theoretical psychological knowledge. Thus, TJ brings to preventive law the potential to inform a preventive lawyer about surprising psychological nuances of aspects of law practice that previously may have been regarded as routine or even mundane.[50]

Recent scholarship has applied the TJ Preventive Law framework in the contexts of matrimonial law, business planning law, and elder law.[51] Consider, for example, the context of elder law. In working with an elderly client a TJ preventive lawyer[52] would engage in legal planning typical of elder law practice, but would do so with an eye toward the potential psychological or emotional consequences of legal decisions.[53] The TJ preventive lawyer might pay particular attention to the client's mental health, the

48. SENAK, *supra* note 2, at 111.

49. *See* Stolle & Wexler, *supra* note 16, at 27.

50. *See* Stolle & Wexler, *supra* note 16.

51. *See* Stolle, *supra* note 17.

52. *See* Stolle & Wexler, *supra* note 16. *See also* Stolle & Wexler, *supra* note 17.

53. *See* Stolle, *supra* note 17. It is important to note that such client counseling is within the scope of a lawyer's ethical obligations. MODEL RULE OF PROFESSIONAL CONDUCT 2.1 provides that in the lawyer's role as an advisor the "lawyer may refer not only to law but to other considerations such as moral, economic, social and political factors, that may be relevant to the client's situation."

important friendships or family relationships in the client's life, and the client's personal goals and fears.[54] With such factors in mind, the lawyer and client can engage in a joint process of developing a package of health-care advance directives and documents directing the distribution of assets that will ultimately enhance the client's sense of comfort and control as the client approaches his or her later years.[55] An application of TJ Preventive Law in the context of matrimonial law might involve the consideration of the psychological impact of divorce on a client's children as one factor in legal decision making.[56] Or, in the context of business planning law, an application of TJ Preventive Law might involve developing a mechanism of corporate governance and internal dispute resolution that is sensitive to the importance of friendships and family relationships among shareholders of a close corporation.[57]

The TJ Preventive Law enterprise adapts the tools of preventive lawyering to address the concerns of therapeutic jurisprudence. For example, TJ Preventive Law advocates the use of TJ-oriented legal check ups. In a TJ-oriented legal check up, a lawyer would attempt to identify "psycholegal soft spots" in addition to legal soft spots. Imagine a lawyer working with elderly clients who want to, upon their deaths, distribute their assets equally to each of their three children. However, their youngest child has a serious problem with drug and alcohol abuse, so the clients want to leave the inheritance for that child in trust, while leaving the inheritance for the other two children outright. A TJ preventive lawyer would likely identify this set of circumstances as being a psycholegal soft spot. Although the clients want to ensure that their youngest child does not lose his inheritance because of impaired judgment caused by drugs or alcohol, leaving an inheritance in trust for one child, but not the other children could cause serious family disputes and may actually harm their son's recovery from his addictions by undermining his self-confidence or his perception of emotional support from the family. Thus, the TJ preventive lawyer would point

---

54. Such information can be elicited through client intake forms, preventive law checklists, and skillful client counseling. *See generally* Stolle et al., *supra* note 5.

55. For a more thorough discussion of TJ preventive lawyering for older clients, *see* Stolle *supra* note 17.

56. *See* Kathryn E. Maxwell, *Preventive Lawyering Strategies to Mitigate the Detrimental Effects of Client's Divorces on Their Children*, REVISTA JURIDICA UPR (forthcoming 1997). The focus on the interest of the client's child or children rather than the interests of the client raises the issue of whose psychological well-being ought to be the focus of the TJ preventive lawyer's focus. For more on the issue of "therapeutic for whom?," see David B. Wexler, *Reflections on the Scope of Therapeutic Jurisprudence, in* LAW IN A THERAPEUTIC KEY, 811 (David B. Wexler & Bruce J. Winick Eds., 1996).

57. *See* Stolle et al., *supra* note 5.

out these possibilities to the clients and perhaps discuss alternative solutions.

It is important to emphasize that TJ Preventive Law adopts the client-centered approach of preventive law. Thus, the goal of TJ Preventive Law is not to shift power away from the client and toward the lawyer. Rather, the goal is to provide the client with complete information, including information about psychological or emotional considerations, such as the potential implications of leaving an inheritance in trust to one child and not the others, so that the client can make a truly informed decision. It is up to the client, with the lawyer's counseling, to weigh the considerations and make the final decision. Likewise, TJ Preventive Law does not propose that a lawyer should assume the role of a therapist. In many instances, a lawyer will clearly not be qualified to give substantive advice relating to psychological or emotional dysfunction. However, in other instances, lawyers will be qualified to recognize, based upon their experience, when psychological or emotional concerns may become an important factor in their clients' decision making. Under such circumstances, TJ Preventive Law suggests that the lawyer ought to make such concerns known to the client and, if the magnitude of the concerns are substantial, suggest that the client may want to consider seeking expert advice from a counselor or therapist.

By adapting the general tools and client-centered orientation of preventive law, the TJ Preventive Law program readily lends itself to a diverse set of legal counseling contexts. The enterprise can be conceived of as a Venn diagram in which the preventive law circle and the therapeutic jurisprudence circle overlap substantially.[58] However, at the margins, there will be preventive law contexts in which concerns of therapeutic jurisprudence might be inappropriate[59] and therapeutic jurisprudence contexts in which concerns of preventive law would be inappropriate.[60] Although the TJ Preventive Law framework is far-reaching, there are parameters beyond which TJ Preventive Law cannot or should not reach. The TJ Preventive Law framework is, however, a sensible approach to much of the everyday client counseling encountered by the general practitioner. Furthermore, TJ Preventive Law may be of particular interest to lawyers providing prepaid

---

58. See Stolle et al., *supra* note 5.

59. See Stolle et al., *supra* note 5, at 38 ("An example of preventive law that is not obviously therapeutic jurisprudence is helping a client copyright an innovation in computer software.").

60. See Stolle et al., *supra* note 5, at 38 ("One rather clear example of therapeutic jurisprudence that is not preventive law is the use of therapeutic jurisprudence arguments in test case litigation designed to change a rule of law.").

legal services, legal-aid lawyers, law school clinics,[61] or lawyers working with special populations such as children, the elderly, or the disabled.[62]

Indeed, TJ Preventive Law provides a particularly sensible approach to working with HIV-positive clients.[63] Most HIV-positive persons will need some specialized legal planning as a result of their HIV-positive status. Furthermore, many of the legal issues that an HIV-positive client will potentially face, such as custody disputes and employment disputes, are issues of both legal and psychological significance.[64] The need for a health-care advance directive provides a particularly poignant example of an issue faced by HIV-positive clients that carries legal as well as psychological significance. There is a growing consensus among lawyers and medical professionals that HIV-positive persons should execute some type of advance directive instrument.[65] Furthermore, some recent commentary has suggested that such advance directive instruments are a good idea not only from a legal and medical standpoint, but also from a psychological or emotional standpoint.[66] Planning for death and exerting some control over the process, it is hypothesized, may have inherent therapeutic value.

Advance Directives, AIDS, and Mental Health

An Overview of Advance Directive Instruments

Health-care advance directives typically take on one of three general forms: instruction directives, proxy directives, or hybrid directives.[67] Instruction directives, commonly referred to as living wills, are perhaps the most

---

61. The University of Puerto Rico Law School Clinic has recently adopted the TJ Preventive Law Paradigm as their approach to client counseling.

62. See Stolle & Wexler, *supra* note 16, at 28 ("After all, such lawyers can be involved in a client-centered practice that seeks to negotiate the legal arena with maximum attention to the psychological well-being of clients. Such practitioners—in essence, primary care counselors-at-law—are truly helping professionals…").

63. See Stolle et al., *supra* note 5.

64. See SENAK, *supra* note 2.

65. See articles cited *supra* note 47.

66. See SENAK, *supra* note 2. Cf. Patricia Monroe Winsom, *Note: Probate Law and Mediation: A Therapeutic Perspective*, 37 ARIZONA L. REV. 1345 (1995). See Berendt & Micheals, *supra* note 2.

67. I have here adopted the vocabulary used by Bruce Winick in Bruce J. Winick, *Advance Directive Instruments for Those with Mental Illness*, 51 U. MIAMI L. REV. 57, 80 (1996).

familiar. The traditional living will authorizes and directs the withholding, withdrawing, or continuance of medical life support equipment under particular circumstances specified within the document. The living will is created by the patient while the patient is competent to exercise his or her liberty-based right to refuse treatment.[68] Living wills function to make the patient's wishes known, thereby providing some assurance of their fruition should the patient later become unable to express those wishes or lack decision-making capacity. The decision remains that of the patient, not a surrogate. The patient is simply indicating his or her intentions in advance.

Some form of the living will is recognized in nearly every state.[69] However, a major drawback of living wills is the difficulty in anticipating future events. Any living will is unlikely to cover all of the possible contingencies that a patient may face. Furthermore, rapid changes in medical technology, such as those occurring in the context of HIV/AIDS, or other unanticipated circumstances are likely to impinge upon the present prudence of decisions made prior to new technology or changed circumstances. Indeed, some commentators have harshly criticized living wills because they largely preclude any reconsideration of earlier decisions made by a now incapacitated person, even though the earlier decision may, in hindsight, clearly not be in the best interest of the patient.[70]

The health-care proxy overcomes some of the major limitations of the instructional directive. Proxy directives differ from instructional directives in that health-care proxies authorize a named individual to make health-care decisions on behalf of a patient lacking decision-making capacity rather than enforcing the patient's own decisions that were made in advance of a loss of capacity. Because the decision is made at the time that treatment is to be rendered, rather than at some prior point in time, the decision-maker is in a position to give consideration to all current circumstances. In the context of HIV/AIDS, such considerations may include recent advancements in medical technology, the patient's apparent current level of discomfort, and the opinions of doctors currently treating the patient.

The obvious drawback of the health-care proxy is that the patient is not exercising his or her own right to refuse treatment. Rather, the patient has delegated his or her right to another, who may either not fully understand the wishes of the patient, or may understand the patient's wishes but choose to ignore those wishes either as a result of the proxy's own values or as a result of inappropriate pressures placed on the proxy by the

---

68. *See generally,* Cruzan v. Director, Missouri Dept. of Health, 497 U.S. 261 (1990).

69. Unif. Health-Care Decisions Act Prefatory Comments, 9 U.L.A. (Supp. 1996).

70. Rebecca Dresser, *Relitigating Life and Death,* 51 Ohio State L. J. 425, 433 (1990).

patient's friends or family. This raises the issues of the extent to which such a delegation ought to be enforceable and the parameters that ought to be set upon the decision maker's authority.[71] Most states have enacted durable power of attorney statutes or health-care proxy statutes that specifically recognize and empower such surrogate decision makers.[72] Generally, these statutes also require that the decision maker act in accordance with the patient's instructions or wishes, if known.[73] If the patient's wishes are unknown, the surrogate decision maker is most often required to act in accordance with the best interests of the patient.[74]

Many states have separate statutes recognizing instruction directives and proxy directives.[75] The existence of separate health-care proxy and living will documents, however, may increase the chances of a patient executing one type of document but not the other, thereby creating potential gaps in the patient's advance directive coverage.[76] Some states have therefore passed "unified" statutes.[77] Under such schemes, a single statute enables the creation of one hybrid document that encompasses aspects of both traditional living wills and health-care proxies.[78] A hybrid directive might authorize a named individual to make health-care decisions on behalf of the declarant, but will also provide the surrogate decision maker with specific and explicit directions to be followed in circumstances contemplated by the patient or with explicit limitations on the decision-making authority.[79]

Clearly, both instruction directives and proxy directives suffer from distinct disadvantages. Hybrid directives eliminate some of the shortcomings of instruction and proxy directives by combining features of each. However, all three types of health-care advance directives suffer from an addi-

---

71. *See generally* Winick, *supra* note 67, for a thoughtful discussion of the probable parameters of enforceability.

72. *See* UNIF. HEALTH-CARE DECISIONS ACT, PREFATORY NOTE, *supra* note 69.

73. *See, e.g.*, UNIF. HEALTH-CARE DECISIONS ACT §5(f), 9 U.L.A. (1993).

74. *Id.*

75. *See* Christopher R. Geary, *Note: Advance Directives for Health Care Matters: Unified Statutes Solve Many Problems*, 13 PROB. L. J. 85, 94 (1996).

76. Geary, *id.*, suggested that separate statutes might also increase the chance of conflicts between the documents or may present a more complex drafting exercise than a single document encompassing both the living will and the health care proxy.

77. The Uniform Laws Annotated Uniform Health-Care Decisions Act of 1993 provides this type of scheme. *See* UNIF. HEALTH CARE DECISIONS ACT, PREFATORY NOTE. *See also* Geary, *supra* note 75 (listing Florida, Virginia, and New Jersey).

78. *See, e.g.*, UNIF. HEALTH-CARE DECISIONS ACT, 9 U.L.A. (1993).

79. *See, e.g.*, UNIF. HEALTH-CARE DECISIONS ACT (1993). *See also*, Winick, *supra* note 67.

tional limitation. Most health-care advance directives contemplate only circumstances surrounding physical health, such as choices regarding prolonging life, providing artificial nutrition and hydration, and providing relief from pain.[80] The legal and medical commentaries on advance directives, as well as the legislative histories of advance directive enabling statutes, typically spend little or no time on issues of mental health. Yet, issues of mental health present difficult decisions that ought to be given thorough advance planning. This type of advance planning is particularly prudent for persons who are known to be at risk for future mental illness.[81] HIV-positive clients are one such group.

AIDS Dementia Complex

HIV-positive persons often experience some form of cognitive/motor impairment. Indeed, the Center for Disease Control and Prevention's (CDC) definition of AIDS includes HIV-positive persons whose only demonstrated symptomatology are neurologic impairments.[82] This malady has been referred to under differing labels, including AIDS Dementia Complex (ADC), AIDS-related neurologic impairment, HIV encephalopathy, and HIV-1-associated cognitive/motor complex.[83] The associated cluster of symptoms can include impaired mental concentration, memory problems, anxiety, social withdrawal, confusion, disorientation, slowness of hand movements, lack of energy, and difficulty in walking.[84] However, the nature and severity of the cognitive/motor and affective impairments varies widely between patients. This variability, and disputes over definitions, complicates diagnosis as well as estimations of prevalence.

It has been estimated that approximately 90% of people who die with AIDS experience some degree of neuropathologic abnormalities.[85] Although

---

80. *See, e.g.,* UNIF. HEALTH-CARE DECISIONS ACT §4, 9 U.L.A. (1993).

81. *See generally* Winick, *supra* note 67.

82. CDC, Revision of the CDC surveillance case definition for acquired immunodeficiency syndrom. 36 MMWR 1s (Supp. 1987).

83. Stuart A. Lipton & Howard E. Gendelman, *Dementia Associated with the Acquired Immunodeficiency Syndrome,* 332 NEW ENG. J. OF MED. 934, 934 (1995). For purposes of this article, I will use the term ADC to encompass any of the various definitions of HIV related cognitive, neurological, or affective impairments.

84. *Id.* at 934. Katz, *supra* note 47, at 46; Milton Rosenbaum, *Similarities of Psychiatric Disorders of AIDS and Syphilis: History Repeats Itself,* 58 BULL. MENNINGER CLINIC 375, 376 (1994); Eileen Feldman, *HIV-Dementia and Countertransference: A Case Study,* 20 ARTS IN PSYCHOTHERAPY, 317 (1993).

85. Stephan L. Buckingham & Wilfred G. Van Gorp, *HIV-Associated Dementia: A Clinician's Guide to Early Detection, Diagnosis, and Intervention,* J. OF CONTEMP. HUM. SERVICES 333, 334 (1994).

perhaps suffering from some level of detectable cognitive impairment, many of these patients retain the capacity to make decisions and remain capable of engaging in day-to-day cognitive activities.[86] Such mild cognitive impairments alone would be insufficient to support either a diagnosis of AIDS or a judgment of incompetence. Recent estimates are that 20 to 30% of HIV-positive persons eventually develop cognitive or affective impairments severe enough to support a diagnosis of AIDS dementia,[87] which would be much more likely to support a judgment of incompetence.

To date, the treatment of ADC has met with limited success. Treatments range from mild behavioral interventions to extremely invasive medical procedures. In a 1994 article, Milton Rosenbaum suggested that until a more successful treatment is developed, "it is important to treat the psychoses of AIDS with anti-AIDS drugs, neuroleptics, ECT [electroconvulsive therapy], and various psychosocial supportive therapies."[88]

It is not yet clear what effect the new protease inhibitors and cocktail medications will have on the prevalence and severity of ADC. It appears that many of the medications that exhibit effectiveness in prolonging life and enhancing physical health may be much less effective at protecting the brain and spinal cord from HIV infection.[89] This has raised concerns that "while drugs help AIDS patients live longer, they also give HIV more time to invade the brain."[90]

Fortunately, a considerable amount of research has recently been devoted to developing medications to treat or even prevent ADC.[91] Some suc-

---

86. A number of strategies are recommended to help HIV-positive persons cope with mild cognitive impairment, such as confining activities to one task at a time and increasing reliance upon calendars, appointment books, post-it notes, and lists. *See, e.g.*, Steve Buckingham, *Your Quality of Life Can Be Maintained Despite Neurological Changes*, AIDS Project Positive Living Newsletter (March 1995). *See also* JUDITH LANDAU-STANTON & COLLEEN D. CLEMENTS, AIDS HEALTH AND MENTAL HEALTH: A PRIMARY SOURCEBOOK, 209-211 (1993).

87. The percentages are higher among children. *See* Lipton & Gendelman, *supra* note 83 ("Approximately one third of adults and half of children with the acquired immunodeficienty syndrom (AIDS) eventually have neurologic complications, which are directly attributable to infection of the brain by the human immunodeficiency virus type 1"). Few of these patients present with neurologic impairments as the first or only symptom of AIDS. *See* BRETT-SMITH & FRIEDLAND, *supra* note 18.

88. *See* Rosenbaum, *supra* note 84, at 381.

89. *See* LANDAU-STANTON & CLEMENTS, *supra* note 86.

90. Roger Signor, *AIDS Dementia: The New Enemy*, ST. LOUIS POST DISPATCH, February 2, 1995 at 1A.

91. *AIDS Dementia Featured at Paris Conference*, Reuters Health Information Services, March 15, 1996; *The Neurological Effects of HIV: New Findings Described at AIDS Meeting*, Reuters Health Information Services, July 8, 1996; David Perlman, *Key*

cess has been shown with atevirdine and new compounds such as meman-tine.[92] Some researchers even hold out hope for the ability of the brain, with proper treatment, to reverse some of the damage caused by HIV infection.[93] However, ADC currently remains a much feared and somewhat poorly understood aspect of HIV disease. Until further advancements in the treatment and prevention of ADC are made, the possibility of severe cognitive impairment must remain one consideration in legal planning for an HIV-positive client.[94] It is important not to overstate the prevalence and severity of ADC, as doing so is likely to create unjustified fears and to enhance negative stereotypes of HIV-positive persons. However, it is also important not to ignore the possibility of future decision-making incapacity as well as the practical and legal implications of that possibility.

The practical implications of ADC are numerous. HIV-positive persons suffering from cognitive impairments may become unable to retain their employment.[95] Even slight cognitive deficits, unlikely to be noticed in daily interaction, could be identified as significant risks in some industries.[96] People with moderate to severe cognitive impairments may become unable to adhere to complex drug regimens, requiring dependence upon others to ensure that they are taking the proper amounts of their medications at the proper times. Severe dementia, usually manifesting itself in late stages of the disease, can even lead to the patient becoming dangerous to himself or herself or others.[97] Furthermore, lapses of severe cognitive impair-

---

Finding in Fight Against AIDS Dementia: S.F. Researchers Believe Blood Test Could Detect Onset, SAN FRANCISCO CHRONICLE, March 14, 1997; *AIDS Dementia New Clues to Cause of Dementia in AIDS Patients,* AIDS WEEKLY PLUS, March 3, 1997; *AIDS Dementia: Researchers Map Path of HIV Virus to Brain,* CHICAGO TRIBUNE, February 17, 1997.

92. B. J. Brew et al., *AIDS Dementia Complex Therapy Pilot Study of the Efficacy of Atevirdine in the Treatment of AIDS Dementia Complex,"* DISEASE WEEKLY PLUS, November 25, 1996; *Tests Start on Drug for Dementia: May Help Victims of AIDS, Strokes,* THE ARIZONA REPUBLIC, December 26, 1996.

93. Richard A Knox, *Brain Robber: As New Drugs Help Control HIV, Concern Grows an AIDS Dementia,* THE BOSTON GLOBE, October 21, 1996.

94. *See* Parry, *supra* note 4.

95. *See generally* Edward P. Richards, *The Risks Every Business Should Know About AIDS and HIV Infection,* 6 HEALTH LAWYER 11 (1992).

96. *Id.* at 11 (noting that AIDS dementia may have profound implications for physicians, pilots, and truck drivers, among other professions and occupations).

97. *See, e.g.* Jim Herron Zamora, *S.F. General AIDS Patient Wanders Off, Dies in Street,* THE SAN FRANSISCO EXAMINER at A-1 (November 15, 1996) (This article describes the story of a patient with ADC who wandered out of a San Francisco hospital and into the streets where he was apparently killed by a hit and run driver). Steve Liewer, *Fire Death Ruled Accidental: Officials Say Cigarette Ignited Man's Clothes at County*

ment are likely to raise legal questions regarding a person's competency for such legal purposes as standing trial,[98] executing a will, entering into binding contracts, and making health-care decisions.[99]

The approach of TJ Preventive Law may provide an avenue for a lawyer working with an HIV-positive client to anticipate and prevent some of these legal problems. Furthermore, by not confining the analysis to legal problems alone, the TJ preventive lawyer will be able to identify not only legal soft spots, but psycholegal soft spots as well. Thus, the approach of TJ Preventive Law provides a method for the lawyer to assist the client in avoiding not only the legal problems associated with ADC, but also some of the psychological or emotional difficulties that are inevitably intertwined with legal problems. One tool that the TJ preventive lawyer might employ to achieve this dual goal is the mental health-care advance directive.

Mental Health-Care Advance Directives for HIV-Positive Clients

Although advance legal planning for financial matters and for physical health care is common, advance legal planning for mental health care is a topic that has received less attention.[100] Early treatments of the topic tended to advocate either against or in favor of psychiatric treatment in gen-

---

Home, SUN-SENTINEL, April 24, 1995 (This article describes the story of a resident of a county-run nursing home who was found sitting on a bench with his clothing ablaze from a cigarette he had been smoking. The man's mother reportedly stated that her son suffered from ADC and should not have been smoking unsupervised.) Jefferey T. Kirchner, *AIDS and Suicide*, 41 J. FAMILY PRACTICE 493 (1995) (discussing the possibility that the presence of ADC may be one risk factor for patient suicide).

98. Christine Stapleton, *Parson Too Sick for Murder Trial, Not Too Ill for Jail*, PALM BEACH POST, February 10, 1996.

99. A patient cannot, however, be assumed to be lacking decision-making capacity simply because a person is suffering from some form of AIDS related cognitive impairment. GARY JAMES WOOD, ET AL., AIDS LAW FOR MENTAL HEALTH PROFESSIONALS: A HANDBOOK FOR JUDICIOUS PRACTICE 88 (1990).

100. One of the earliest discussions of the psychiatric advance directive can be found at Thomas S. Szasz, *The Psychiatric Will: A new Mechanism for Protecting Persons Against "Psychosis" and Psychiatry*, 37 AM. PSYCHOLOGIST 762 (1982). The most recent and most comprehensive treatment of the subject is Winick, *supra* note 67. Other contributions include Lester J. Perling, *Health Care Advance Directives: Implications for Florida Mental Health Patients*, 48 U. MIAMI L. REV. 193 (1993); Paul S. Appelbaum, *Advance Directive for Psychiatric Treatment*, 42 HOSP. AND COMMUNITY PSYCHIATRY 983 (1991).

eral. Thomas Szasz proposed that psychiatric advance directives could provide a mechanism for individuals to avoid psychiatric treatment, which Szasz believed was largely ineffective.[101] In contrast, advocates of psychiatric treatment suggested that persons with a history of recurring mental illness ought to bind themselves to treatment in advance to avoid the possibility of refusing needed treatment at a later time when their decision-making capacity may be compromised by mental illness.[102] Most recently, mental health-care advance directive instruments have been recognized as practical and important documents for those with a personal or family history of mental illness.[103] Such directives have the potential practical value of avoiding treatment disputes as well as the potential therapeutic value that might arise from facing the reality of possible future mental illness and exerting some control over one's fate if and when mental illness strikes.[104]

Form

The form of a mental health care advance directive need not differ dramatically from the form of a traditional advance directive that contemplates only physical health care. Consider the optional form for creating health-care advance directives provided by the Uniform Laws Annotated (ULA) Health Care Decisions Act of 1993 (Act).[105] The ULA form is essentially a hybrid directive, which allows for ease of drafting and reduces the potential for subsequent conflicts.[106] The ULA form provides check-boxes for traditional physical health-care decisions, such as whether or not to prolong life, to provide artificial nutrition and hydration, and to provide relief from pain.[107] However, the ULA form also provides a place for addi-

---

101. *See* Thomas Szasz, *The Psychiatric Will: A New Mechanism for Protecting Persons Against "Psychosis" and Psychiatry*, 37 AM. PSYCHOL. 762 (1982).

102. Such directives have become known as Ulysses contracts. *See* Perling, *supra* note 100. *See also* Rebecca S. Dresser, *Ulysses and the Psychiatrists: A legal and Policy Analysis of the Voluntary Commitment Contract*, 16 HARV. C.R. C. L. L. REV. 777 (1982).

103. *See generally* Winick, *supra* note 67.

104. *See generally* Winick, *supra* note 67.

105. UNIF. HEALTH-CARE DECISIONS ACT §4, 9 U.L.A. (Supp. 1996).

106. The form of an advance directive will be more complicated in states that have not adopted the ULA Act or some similar statutory scheme. However, as various states continue to revise their advance directive legislation, it is likely that statutes supporting the creation of hybrid directives will become increasingly common.

107. *See* UNIF. HEALTH-CARE DECISIONS ACT, 9 U.L.A. (1993).

tional instructions under the heading "Other Wishes."[108] The Act's prefatory note states that "an individual's instructions may extend to any and all health-care decisions that might arise and, unless limited by the principal, an agent has authority to make all health-care decisions which the individual could have made."[109] As such, there is nothing to prevent a lawyer working with an HIV-positive client from inserting instructions regarding mental health care under the "other wishes" category.[110]

An HIV-positive client may wish to expressly contemplate the possibility of ADC. A lawyer assisting a client to do this should encourage the client to consult his or her doctor or other sources for reliable information regarding the nature, prevalence, and treatment of AIDS-related neurological and psychological maladies. This approach of encouraging the client to investigate the nature of the disease and its treatments, represents the "unbundling" aspect of TJ Preventive Law, which is essentially an attempt to lower client costs and increase client involvement in decision making.[111]

Based upon the information that the client collects and information that the lawyer has, the lawyer and client can discuss whether the client wants to refuse certain antipsychotic medications[112] or other highly invasive psychiatric procedures.[113] Likewise, the client may, after consulting with his or her doctor, wish to expressly elect certain treatments. For example, the client may want to express his or her desire to be treated with psychosocial supportive therapies if the client begins to show signs of cognitive/motor

---

108. *Id.*

109. Unif. Health-Care Decisions Act Prefatory Note, 9 U.L.A. (Supp. 1996). The note goes on to state that "The Act recognizes and validates an individual's authority to define the scope of an instruction or agency as broadly or as narrowly as the individual chooses."

110. The "other wishes" category may also allow a client the opportunity to express their wishes in a more sophisticated and thoughtful manner than the mere marking of a check-box will allow.

111. *See supra* note 35 and accompanying text.

112. *See* Landau-Stanton & Clements, *supra* note 86 (stating that "antipsychotics do become necessary at times in the treatment of people with HIV disease").

113. Electroconvulsive therapy would be one example. Although published reports of the use of electroconvulsive therapy for ADC do exist, *supra* note 84, at 381, it seems highly unlikely to be a typical treatment. Furthermore, many states have statues that significantly restrict the conditions under which electorconvulsive therapy can be applied to an incompetent patient. *See* Aden v. Younger, 57 Cal. App. 3d 662 (1976) (upholding the constitutionality of a rule requiring a thorough substitute decision-making process prior to the application of electroconvulsive therapy to an incompetent patient).

deficits or other symptoms of mental illness. Such therapies can include buddy support, respite care, meal service, training in behavioral strategies,[114] and expressive therapy.[115] A lawyer working with such a client might inquire into whether the client further wishes to express that he or she would want these therapies to be conducted with the goal of facilitating the client's independent living for as long as possible.

The lawyer might also suggest that the client consider expressing preferences with regard to placement, should independent living become impossible. Issues of placement can be particularly difficult for patients with ADC.[116] In severe cases, 24-hour supervision may be required. This, combined with an extensive medication regimen and the palliative care necessary for a person living with a terminal illness, can make finding a suitable placement difficult. Given these difficulties, the client may want to carefully investigate placement options in advance, discuss those options with the lawyer, and express a preference in the mental health-care advance directive.

Enforceability

The form of mental health advance directives is unlikely to differ dramatically from that of physical health-care advance directives. Likewise, both types of instruments have the underlying purposes of protecting individual autonomy in health-care decision making and avoiding unpleasant, and perhaps unhealthy, disputes at a time when a patient has become incapacitated and unable to express his or her own wishes. Merely the specifics of the content of these two types of advance directives differ. Thus, it seems that most mental health-care advance directives, like their physical health-care counterparts, should be enforceable. However, as will be seen below, the effect on enforceability of adding mental health-care directives warrants a somewhat closer analysis. In a recent article discussing the potential enforceability of mental health-care advance directives, Bruce Winick noted three distinctions that might prove critical in analyzing the parameters of enforceability: (1) the distinction between the state's police power and its parens patriae power, (2) the distinction between advance direc-

---

114. *See supra* note 47 and accompanying text. *See also* A. Griepp et al., *The Neuropsychiatric Aspects of HIV Infection and Patient Care*, in JUDITH LANDAU-STANTON & COLLEEN D. CLEMENTS, AIDS HEALTH AND MENTAL HEALTH: A PRIMARY SOURCEBOOK (1993).

115. Eileen Feldman, *HIV-Dementia and Countertransference: A Case Study*, 20 ARTS IN PSYCHOTHERAPY, 317 (1993).

116. *See* Katz, *supra* note 47.

tives electing treatment and those rejecting it, and (3) the distinction between instruction directives and health-care proxies.[117] Consider these distinctions in the context of mental health advance directives for HIV-positive clients.

In the absence of an advance directive instrument, a state can use its *parens patriae* power to compel an incompetent person to undergo psychiatric treatment.[118] However, an advance directive instrument that refuses treatment and was executed while the individual had decision-making capacity and was legally competent should trump the state's *parens patraie* power.[119] In contrast, a state can compel a legally incompetent, or competent, person to undergo psychiatric treatment regardless of the existence of an advance directive if the state's decision is grounded in its police power.[120] In the case of physical treatments contemplated by traditional living wills, such as artificial life support or artificial nutrition, a state would ordinarily be unable to ground the decision to treat in the state police power. As a general matter, only efforts at controlling an epidemic would justify the states' exertion of police power to compel treatment for a physical health problem against the wishes of the patient.[121] In the case of mental health care, however, the state's police power may be more likely to come into play. A state has a legitimate interest in preventing a patient from harming himself or others.[122] Patients suffering from severe mental illness, including patients suffering from ADC, may pose a direct danger

---

117. *See* Winick, *supra* note 67, at 70-81.

118. Addington v. Texas, 441 U.S. 418, 426 (1979) ("the state has a legitimate interest under its parens patriae powers in providing care to its citizens who are unable to care for themselves…"). *See also*, In re Boyd, 403 A.2d 744 (1979).

119. *See* Cruzan, *supra* note 68. In re Boyd, 403 A.2d 744 (1979) ("when an individual, prior to incompetence, has objected, absolutely, to medical care on religious grounds…the court should conclude that the individual would reject medical treatment"). *See also* Winick *supra* note 67, at 73.

120. Rogers v. Okin, 634 F.2d 650 (1st cir. 1980) ("The parties agree that the state has a legitimate interest in protecting persons from physical harm at the hands of the mentally ill. They also agree that this interest can justify the forcible administration of drugs to a mentally ill person whether or not that person has been adjudicated incompetent to make his own treatment decisions."). *See also* Winick, *supra* note 67, at 74 ("Just as the state would be able to hospitalize or treat dangerous, although competent mental patients over their present objections, the state would be able to hospitalize or treat mental patients who are both dangerous and incompetent over the objections they expressed in the past.").

121. *See, e.g.*, Jacobson v. Massachusetts, 197 U.S. 11 (1905) (compulsory smallpox vaccination). Moore v. Draper, 57 So.2d 648 (1952) (commitment to sanitarium for tuberculosis). Application of Halko, 54 Cal. Rptr. 661 (1966) (tuberculosis).

122. *See* Washington v. Harper, 494 U.S. 210 (1990).

to themselves or others[123] thereby justifying imposition of treatment even in the face of an advance directive to the contrary.[124]

Just as the state may enjoy more latitude in regulating advance directives when the regulation is justified in the state's police power, the state is also likely to enjoy more latitude in regulating advance directives that elect a particular treatment than those that refuse a particular treatment.[125] Although the Supreme Court has recognized a constitutionally protected right to refuse treatment and appears willing to grant substantial deference to a patient's wishes when there is clear and convincing evidence of those wishes,[126] any right to receive treatment will likely be more limited.[127] A particular treatment elected by an ADC patient in an advance directive instrument may, at the time the treatment is to be administered, be deemed by the treating professional to be clinically inappropriate or even financially impractical. In this case, the patient will likely not get the treatment even though they expressed a preference for the treatment in an advance directive.[128] However, a mental health-care advance directive instrument that combines elements of instruction directives with a health-care proxy will create a situation in which the surrogate decision maker is able to consent to the available clinically appropriate treatments that come closest to the expressed wishes of the patient. Although the ADC patient may not get the exact care contemplated in the advance directive, with a hybrid directive the patient will likely come as close as possible to the desired treatment, given the circumstances.

Theoretically, the state may also enjoy more latitude in regulating mental health-care proxies than in regulating mental health-care advance directives.[129] With a health-care proxy, the patient is not exercising his or her own right to refuse treatment. Rather, the patient has delegated his or her

---

123. *See supra* note 97.

124. *See* Winick, *supra* note 67. For example, consider a mental health advance directive indicating that in case of mental illness the patient wishes to live with his brother, who has agreed to care for him, and not to be institutionalized. If the patient later becomes both incompetent and dangerous to himself and to his brother, the state will have an interest in protecting its citizens from harm by committing the patient to a psychiatric hospital. This interest will override the advance directive instrument, just as the state's interest in protecting its citizens would override a refusal of treatment by a dangerous but competent individual. *See* Washington v. Harper, 494 U.S. 210 (1990).

125. Winick, *supra* note 67, at 70.

126. *See* Cruzan, *supra* note 68.

127. *See* Winick, *supra* note 67, at 70.

128. *See, e.g.,* UNIF. HEALTH-CARE DECISIONS ACT § 7, 9 U.L.A. 239 (1993) (allowing a health care professional to decline to comply with an advance directive for reasons of conscience or professional judgment). *See also* Winick, *supra* note 67 .

129. Winick, *supra* note 67, at 75.

right to another, raising the issue of the enforceability of such a delegation. Most states have enacted durable power of attorney statutes or health-
care proxy statutes that specifically recognize and empower such surrogate decision makers but also limit the decision-making power to matters
of health care.[130] Generally, these statutes also require that the decision
maker act in accordance with the patient's instructions or wishes, if
known.[131] If the patient's wishes are unknown, the surrogate decision
maker is most often required to act in accordance with the best interests
of the patient.[132] Winick, however, suggests that the state may attempt to
regulate the surrogate's ability to elect experimental or highly invasive
mental health procedures.[133] Given the rapid and continuing advancements
in the treatment of ADC, this may pose difficulties for an HIV-positive
client who wishes to be treated with new or experimental medications.
However, an HIV-positive client may be able to increase his or her chances
of receiving new or experimental medications by indicating as part of the
hybrid directive that he or she wishes to be treated with such medications
and explicitly grants the surrogate the authority to elect such treatments.
As such, the directive takes on more of the character of a decision made by
the patient, but in advance, rather than a decision made on behalf of the
patient by a named surrogate.

Therapeutic Potential

Some commentators have suggested that there may be therapeutic value
in the process of creating advance directives generally, and especially for
HIV-positive clients.[134] The suggestion is that the process of exerting control over the circumstances surrounding death will restore some of the loss
of control that the client has experienced as a result of the disease. This
reclaiming of control is hypothesized to have inherent therapeutic value.
Winick has further suggested that the mental health advance directive may
have some special therapeutic value, given the particularly disempowering
and disenfranchising effects of mental illness.[135] HIV-positive persons must
cope with the dual burden of facing nearly certain physical deterioration
and potential mental deterioration. Thus, if the process of preparing an

---

130. *See, e.g.,* UNIF. HEALTH-CARE DECISIONS ACT § 5(f) (1993).

131. *See, e.g.,* UNIF. HEALTH-CARE DECISIONS ACT § 5(f) (1993).

132. *Id.*

133. *See* Winick *supra* note 67, at 79, pointing, for example, to a Florida statute that
prohibits a surrogate from consenting to electroshock therapy, unless the principal
expressly delegated this authority in writing. FLA. STAT. § 765.113(1) (1995).

134. SENAK, *supra* note 2. Smith, *supra* note 4, at 22-23.

135. Winick, *supra* note 67, at 81.

advance directive does indeed have some inherent therapeutic value, the process of preparing an advance directive for both physical and mental healthcare may hold particular therapeutic potential for HIV-positive persons.

There is, however, little or no empirical evidence directly supporting the therapeutic value of preparing an advance directive instrument. The idea, again, is that facing the possibility of future incapacity and proactively exercising one's present legal powers to ensure proper treatment is more therapeutic than simply worrying about future incapacity but taking no action to control it. This notion certainly comports with common sense. It is also consistent with theory and data from other areas of legal psychology. For example, procedural justice research suggests that an opportunity to voice preferences and the opportunity to take actions that may influence outcomes increases satisfaction with legal procedures.[136] However, there clearly remains a need for empirical data explicitly focused on the therapeutic effects of executing an advance directive, and, perhaps, data explicitly focused on the therapeutic effects for HIV-positive persons.[137] Empirical data may be able to clarify questions such as which aspects of the process of creating an advance directive are most beneficial and for whom. With reliable data in hand, the process of executing an advance directive could be tailored to realize its full therapeutic potential.

The empirical information alone, of course, would not be self-executing. Winick has suggested that "as the use of [mental health-care advance directives] becomes more widespread, lawyers and health-care professionals experienced in their use can help guide individuals through the process of planning and drafting the instrument."[138] Lawyers practicing explicitly and systematically as TJ preventive lawyers would perhaps be in a better position than other lawyers and, under some circumstances, be in a better position than mental health professionals to guide HIV-positive clients and other clients through this process. Winick has focused largely on possible therapist/patient interactions that may arise in developing a mental health-care advance directive instrument, and the thera-

---

136. *See generally* TOM R. TYLER, WHY PEOPLE OBEY THE LAW (1990). Procedural justice theories focus on perceptions of fairness and participant satisfaction with legal proceedings. Although participant satisfaction and perceptions of fairness may perhaps be related to and sometimes overlap with therapeutic outcomes, procedural justice remains a distinct construct that is distinguishable from the notion of therapeutic jurisprudence.

137. It is quite possible that the most therapeutic aspects of executing an advance directive may vary between populations. For example, the experience of elderly clients in executing an advance directive may be quite distinct from the experience of HIV-positive clients.

138. *See* Winick, *supra* note 67, at n. 126.

peutic potential of such interactions.[139] Clearly, this is an important consideration and psychologists should, to the extent possible, utilize the development of a mental health-care advance directive as a therapeutic opportunity. However, a therapist or mental health-care professional who is familiar with mental health-care directives may be unlikely to have contact with a patient until after the patient has experienced a period of incompetence.[140] In contrast, a TJ preventive lawyer might know from his initial client interview or from a client questionnaire that the client is at risk for future mental illness, perhaps because the client is HIV-positive, or perhaps because the client has a family history of mental illness. The preventive lawyer would then be in a position to work with that client toward developing an advance directive instrument for psychiatric treatment. If that same client waited until there was a mental health-care professional involved, he or she may well have waited too long.[141]

Likewise, a mental health-care professional who lacks legal training may be unlikely to deviate from the standard forms for advance directives provided by state statutes. Because most state statutes do not explicitly contemplate mental health care, some deviation from the standard form in drafting the directive will likely be necessary. A lawyer familiar with the legal arguments surrounding the probable parameters of enforceability of mental health-care advance directives, such as those outlined in the preceding section, would be in a better position than a mental health-care professional to deviate from the standard form without compromising the document's enforceability. Furthermore, such a lawyer would also be in a better position to discuss with the client the probable enforceability of various aspects of the directive or the enforceability of particular choices that the client wishes to make in the directive.

It is true that a mental health professional will be better equipped than most lawyers to truly exploit the full therapeutic potential of the process of executing an advance directive. However, the goal of TJ Preventive Law is not to suggest that lawyers are capable of replacing a therapist or psychologist, nor is it to suggest that lawyers ought to try to replace such mental health professionals. Rather, the purpose of TJ Preventive Law is to equip lawyers with at least enough knowledge or sensitivity to psychological and emotional factors that they will be able to avoid giving psychologically destructive or anti-therapeutic advice and, in the best of worlds, render advice that is more therapeutic than the advice that would be rendered absent the TJ Preventive Law perspective.

---

139. See Winick, *supra* note 67, at 82.
140. See Stolle & Wexler, *supra* note 16, at n. 35.
141. See Stolle & Wexler, *supra* note 16, at n. 35.

Ideally then, a therapeutically-oriented preventive lawyer should be able to enhance both the legal and therapeutic value of the advance directive process; [142] although, as a lawyer, the point of greatest emphasis must remain on the legal issues. A knowledge base for the additional focus on the therapeutic issues can develop as interested lawyers become consumers of psychological literature. The model of TJ preventive lawyering contemplates the lawyer's involvement in continuing legal education seminars that disseminate relevant empirical information and involvement in reading/discussion groups with psychologists, counselors, and other TJ preventive lawyers. [143] These forums could provide the TJ preventive lawyer with the information necessary to identify some psycholegal soft spots and to ultimately enhance the therapeutic potential of various legal instruments. [144] And, to some extent, TJ preventive lawyers who work exclusively or primarily with particular populations, such as HIV-positive clients, will be able to draw their own conclusions regarding therapeutic value based upon past experience.

For example, a TJ preventive lawyer experienced in working with HIV-positive clients is likely to recognize that some HIV-positive clients may be alienated from their families as a result of past or present behaviors that their family condemns. This raises the issue of who the client ought to name as a surrogate decision-maker. In some cases the client may prefer that a life partner be named as the decision-maker. However, if this partner is also HIV-positive, the partner may be unable to engage in decision making at the critical time. As such, a secondary and even tertiary surrogate decision maker should be named. [145] In some cases, this dilemma may provide an opportunity for the client to have some reconciliation with alienated family members and to eventually name a parent or sibling as a secondary or tertiary decision maker. This reconciliation may have significant therapeutic effects on the client and the client's family. In other cases, there may be no hope of reconciliation or no desire for reconciliation on the part of the client. The approach of TJ preventive lawyering, however, at least provides an opportunity for the lawyer to suggest to the client, if it seems appropriate, that reconciliation might be possible. Furthermore, the client-centered approach of TJ preventive lawyering allows for the lawyer and the client, who best knows his family situation, to joint-

---

142. This may be particularly true of lawyers with joint degree training, such as lawyers possessing both a J.D. and an M.A. in counseling or an M.S.W.

143. *See* Stolle & Wexler, *supra* note 16. *See also* Stolle & Wexler, *supra* note 17.

144. *See* Stolle & Wexler, *supra* note 16.

145. *See, e.g.,* Unif. Health-Care Decisions Act §4, 9 U.L.A. 239 (1993) (the Act's optional form provides a signature line for a primary, secondary, and tertiary decision-maker).

ly evaluate the relevant considerations, both legal and psychological, so that the client can ultimately make an informed and intelligent decision regarding whether approaching family would be useful.[146]

The TJ-oriented legal check up also allows for the ongoing development of advance directive documents. The therapeutic value, therefore, need not end when the document is signed. At an annual legal check up, the HIV-positive client can update the lawyer concerning developments in family relationships and friendships that may influence who ought to be named as a surrogate decision-maker. The lawyer and client can also discuss any recent advances in medical technology or therapy that have come to the client's attention and that may influence the client's election or rejection of certain medicines or treatments. Furthermore, the legal check up provides the TJ preventive lawyer with an opportunity to update the client on any recent legal developments that may affect the client's advance directives or any other issues that the client may be facing.[147] These issues might include confusing insurance or health-care paperwork that has been sent to the client's home. The client might be encouraged to actually bring such paperwork to the legal check up, thereby providing an opportunity for the lawyer and client to discuss these troubling issues that the client might otherwise be unlikely to contact the lawyer to discuss. This interaction has the potential both to serve a preventive law function by clearing up any insurance or health-care related difficulties before they reach the level of formal legal proceedings, and to serve a TJ function by alleviating the client's fear or confusion surrounding the paperwork.[148]

---

146. I do not mean to suggest, in this section, that there is empirical evidence supporting the conclusion that approaching alienated family members regarding health- care decision making has therapeutic value. Nor do I mean to suggest that most clinical psychologists would agree that such a strategy would have therapeutic benefits. Rather, I am suggesting the plausibility of therapeutic benefits from such a strategy. These and other such client counseling strategies are ideal candidates for discussion at TJ Preventive Law CLE workshops or TJ Preventive Law reading groups, in which both lawyers and psychologists might be present to comment on the potential implications of adopting such a strategy. *See generally* Stolle & Wexler, *supra* note 16.

147. It is important to note that this type of legal consultation with an existing client does not amount to improper solicitation of business. *See* Brown, *supra* note 36. The difficulty with proactive legal planning, however, is getting the individual who is in need of legal planning to seek out a lawyer's advice in the first instance. In the case of populations such as HIV-positive persons, who are widely recognized as being in need of general legal counsel, HIV clinics or support groups might compile listings of local lawyers who emphasize AIDS related issues in their legal practice and make those listings available to HIV-positive persons.

148. *See* Stolle et al., *supra* note 17, at 26-27 (making a similar point in the context of a TJ-oriented legal check up for an elderly client).

Conclusion

HIV-positive persons face a host of potential legal problems upon learning of their HIV-positive status. Proactive legal planning for HIV-positive persons is widely recognized as an important element in avoiding legal crises. However, traditional legal education and legal culture encourages lawyers to emphasize only autonomy and individual liberty in legal planning. Psychological and emotional well-being are typically addressed, if at all, only as side benefits of increased autonomy. Yet, in working with HIV-positive clients or other special populations, psychological and emotional well-being ought to be explicitly recognized as one priority in legal planning. The approach of TJ Preventive Law gives the practitioner both the analytic justifications and the practical tools for prioritizing psychological well-being. Because HIV-positive persons are at increased risk for future mental illness, planning for mental health care through the use of mental health-care advance directives should be one important part of this therapeutic legal planning process. In addition to ensuring proper care, the very process of executing the advance directive, if handled by a lawyer sensitive to the social and psychological context, may be inherently therapeutic.

The form, enforceability, and therapeutic potential of advance directive instruments, and psychiatric directives in particular, remain important topics that should continue to be addressed by legal and empirical research. Such research should be conducted with an eye toward disseminating the information to TJ preventive legal practitioners who can implement the research and ultimately facilitate the realization of the therapeutic potential of advance directive instruments. Such practitioners can, through a combination of therapeutic jurisprudence and preventive law, provide a higher quality of legal service to populations in need. As one insightful HIV lawyer has noted, "So many legal problems that people with HIV face...can be prevented if they are anticipated and planned for rather than reacted to after the problem arises."[149] Furthermore, "the intermixing of people's psychological needs and people's legal rights and duties is something that I think any sensitive lawyer must always be aware of."[150]

---

149. See SENAK, *supra* note 2, at 110, quoting David Schulman.
150. See SENAK, *supra* note 2, at 106, quoting David Schulman.

Chapter 5

Legal Planning for Unmarried Committed Partners: Empirical Lessons for a Preventive and Therapeutic Approach

Jennifer K. Robbennolt
Monica Kirkpatrick Johnson

I. Introduction

Increasing rates of cohabitation among unmarried couples have brought a number of contentious issues to the forefront of American political and corporate decision making. For example, whether to recognize or to prohibit same-sex marriages and whether to extend employment benefits to domestic partners have been common topics in the media in recent years.[1] Much attention has been paid to legal reforms in these areas. However, legal policy changes are likely to be slow to materialize and could either advance or hinder the interests of unmarried committed partners. An approach to the issues facing unmarried committed partners founded in therapeutic jurisprudence and preventive law[2] suggests that attorneys can help individuals in nonmarital committed relationships to privately order their affairs in a manner that is both legally effective and therapeutic. The present analysis examines the application of therapeutic jurisprudence and preventive law principles to the issues involved in the long-term property and health care planning of unmarried couples.

---

1. *See, e.g., Democrats Give Health Benefits to Gay Couples*, N.Y. TIMES, May 17, 1997, at 11; David W. Dunlap, *Gay Partners of I.B.M. Workers to Get Benefits*, N.Y. TIMES, Sept. 20, 1996, at B2; David W. Dunlap, *Fearing a Toehold for Gay Marriages, Conservatives Rush to Bar the Door*, N.Y. TIMES, Mar. 6, 1996, at A7 [hereinafter Dunlap, *Fearing a Toehold*].

2. *See* Dennis P. Stolle et al., *Integrating Preventive Law and Therapeutic Jurisprudence: A Law and Psychology Based Approach to Lawyering*, 34 CAL. W. L. REV. 15 (1997).

Part II of this paper describes, generally, the law affecting the long-term property and health care planning of unmarried committed partners. Attention is also given to some recent policy proposals and reforms that have attempted to alter the law in this area. Part III describes the synthesis of therapeutic jurisprudence and preventive law ("TJ-preventive law") as a framework for analysis of this problem. Part IV presents an empirical study intended to shed light on the long-term planning practices of unmarried committed partners. Finally, Part V applies TJ-preventive law principles to the issues involved in legal planning for unmarried committed partners and offers suggestions for practitioners.

The structure of American families and households is undergoing an important series of interrelated changes. Over the last several decades, rates of marriage among unmarried women have fallen and rates of divorce and nonmarital childbearing have risen.[3] Contemporary young men and women are delaying marriage, delaying childbearing, and having smaller families.[4] In a related trend, the rate of cohabitation among unmarried couples has been rapidly increasing. Approximately 7% of the nation's couples are in unmarried committed relationships,[5] including roughly 1.7 million gay and lesbian couples.[6] Approximately one-fourth of the adult population has cohabited at some time. Younger adults have even higher rates of cohabitation; among those in their early thirties, nearly one-half have cohabited.[7] However, these figures only include heterosexual cohabitation and, therefore, underestimate the level of cohabitation in the country. It is evident that cohabitation has emerged as an important new family form in the United States.

---

3. *See* NAT'L CTR. FOR HEALTH STATISTICS, U.S. DEPT. OF HEALTH AND HUMAN SERVICES, MONTHLY VITAL STATISTICS REPORT 3 (July 17, 1997); NAT'L CTR. FOR HEALTH STATISTICS, U.S. DEPT. OF HEALTH AND HUMAN SERVICES, MONTHLY VITAL STATISTICS REPORT 2 (July 14, 1995); Dennis A. Ahlburg & Carol J. De Vita, *New Realities of the American Family*, 47 POPULATION BULL. 1, 11-12, 14-15, 22-23 (1992). During the 1980s and early 1990s, the divorce rate leveled and dropped slightly. NAT'L CTR. FOR HEALTH STATISTICS, U.S. DEPT. OF HEALTH AND HUMAN SERVICES, MONTHLY VITAL STATISTICS REPORT 3 (July 17, 1997). *See* Larry L. Bumpass, *What's Happening to the Family? Interactions Between Demographic and Institutional Change*, 27 DEMOGRAPHY 483 (1990).

4. *See* Ahlburg & DeVita, *supra* note 3, at 12-13, 18-19.

5. *See* ARLENE F. SALUTER, U.S. DEP'T OF COMMERCE, CURRENT POPULATION REPORTS, SERIES P20-484, MARITAL STATUS AND LIVING ARRANGEMENTS: MARCH 1994 xiii (1996).

6. *One-Third of Unmarried Partners Are Gay*, NUMBER NEWS, May 1996, at 1.

7. *See* Larry L. Bumpass & James A. Sweet, *National Estimates of Cohabitation*, 26 DEMOGRAPHY 615, 617-19 (1989).

Public attitudes toward cohabitation have become more accepting in the 1980s[8] and the 1990s.[9] Such attitudes are strongly related to age. Only 20-30% of persons over age seventy find cohabitation acceptable even if the couple does not plan marriage, while three-quarters of persons ages twenty-five to twenty-nine find such an arrangement acceptable.[10] These findings suggest a continuing trend of increasing cohabitation into the future as younger cohorts continue to replace older cohorts in the population.

People live in nonmarital relationships for a variety of reasons. Because same-sex couples are prohibited from marrying, many live in long-term committed partnerships. Whether same-sex couples should have the right to marry is subject to considerable debate, both inside and outside the gay community.[11] Considering the amount of resistance to marriage rights among some gay men and lesbians,[12] it is quite reasonable to conclude that a significant number would choose to live in nonmarital relationships even if marriage were a legal option. In any case, same-sex marriage does not appear to be politically feasible at the current time. A 1998 poll revealed that only 29% of the general public approved of legally sanctioned same-sex marriage.[13] Consistent with these views, Congress recently passed the Defense of Marriage Act, which denies federal recognition of same-sex marriages and allows states to refuse to recognize same-sex marriages authorized in other states.[14]

The rising number of heterosexual cohabitors represents persons who choose not to marry or choose to significantly delay marriage. Cohabita-

---

8. Arland Thorton, *Changing Attitudes Toward Family Issues in the United States*, J. MARRIAGE & FAM. 873, 887 (1989).

9. *See* LARRY L. BUMPASS & JAMES A. SWEET, NSFH WORKING PAPER NO. 65, COHABITATION, MARRIAGE AND UNION STABILITY: PRELIMINARY FINDINGS FROM NSFH2 6 (1995).

10. *Id.*

11. *See, e.g.*, Nitya Duclos, *Some Complicating Thoughts on Same-Sex Marriage*, 1 LAW & SEXUALITY 31 (1991); Mary C. Dunlap, *The Lesbian and Gay Marriage Debate: A Microcosm of Our Hopes and Troubles in the Nineties*, 1 LAW & SEXUALITY 63 (1991); Paula L. Ettelbrick, *Since When is Marriage a Path to Liberation?*, *in* FAMILY AND PERSONAL RELATIONSHIPS 76 (Gloria W. Bird & Michael J. Sporakowski eds., 1997); Nan D. Hunter, *Marriage, Law, and Gender: A Feminist Inquiry*, 1 LAW & SEXUALITY 9 (1991); Rob Claus, Letter to the Editor, *Can a Law Help Ease Pain of Divorce? Gay Marriage Debate*, N.Y. TIMES, July 2, 1997, at A22; Gustav Niebuhr, *Laws Aside, Some in Clergy Quietly Bless Gay 'Marriage'*, N.Y. TIMES, Apr. 17, 1998, at A1.

12. *See, e.g.*, Ettelbrick, *supra* note 11.

13. John Cloud, *For Better or Worse: In Hawaii, a Showdown over Marriage Tests the Limits of Gay Activism*, TIME, Oct. 26, 1998 at 43.

14. 1 U.S.C. § 7 (Supp. 1997); 28 U.S.C.A. § 1738C (West Supp. 1997).

tion is more common among those who have been previously married,[15] many of whom presumably hesitate to remarry. Among separated or divorced persons under age thirty-five, approximately two-thirds have cohabited.[16] Cohabitation for the majority of opposite-sex couples tends to be short term, ending in marriage or the termination of the relationship.[17] However, for a significant minority, cohabitation is a long-term arrangement. Bumpass, Sweet, and Cherlin found that 20% of cohabiting couples have lived together for five or more years.[18]

II. Legal Treatment of Unmarried Committed Partners

Because unmarried committed partners are not legally married, they are not entitled to many of the benefits that arise automatically for married partners. For example, the default property rights of married persons in the event of the dissolution of the marriage[19] or in the event that one of the partners dies[20] are statutorily defined. This is not the case for nonmarital partners. While married persons have the option of relying on statutory provisions or of entering into private agreements, nonmarital partners generally must enter into private agreements to define their property rights. Similarly, nonmarital partners must proactively consider their long-term health care if they want to ensure the participation of their partners in their health care decision making. The following sections describe a number of areas in which the rights of unmarried committed partners differ from those of married persons and that raise planning issues unique to nonmarital relationships.

A. Property Division

In every state, marriage entitles each partner in the marriage to statutorily defined property rights. If the marriage results in divorce and the parties do not come to their own agreement regarding the division of their assets, the distribution of property is determined by a court in accordance with state

---

15. Bumpass & Sweet, *supra* note 7, at 619.

16. *Id.*

17. Larry L. Bumpass et al., *The Role of Cohabitation in Declining Rates of Marriage*, 53 J. Marriage & Fam. 913, 919 (1991).

18. *Id.*

19. *See infra* notes 21-41 and accompanying text.

20. *See infra* notes 50-63 and accompanying text.

statute.[21] Each state provides for the division of property acquired during the marriage by reference to either the rules of community property or the notion of equitable distribution.[22] These systems of distribution assume that persons who are married act as "economic partners" during the marriage.[23]

In contrast, there are no state statutes that define the property rights of persons living in unmarried committed relationships.[24] The earnings of each party in the relationship and anything purchased with those earnings belong to that party; the partner has no defined statutory rights to that property.[25] Instead, the property rights of unmarried committed partners have been loosely defined through diffuse and inconsistent court opinions.[26] "Change occurs state by state; thus, change occurs slowly and in piecemeal fashion. Consequently, couples who cohabit rather than marry are likely to find themselves in a position of uncertainty with respect to their legal rights."[27]

Traditionally, courts found cohabitation to be immoral and refused to grant rights to partners in such relationships, even when the parties had an express agreement.[28] Courts often refused to enforce contracts between cohabiting partners "to the extent that they were based on meretricious sexual services (i.e., prostitution)."[29] More recently, however, most courts will enforce express property agreements between unmarried committed partners and some courts will enforce contracts that are implied from the conduct of the partners.[30] While most of the cases have involved oppo-

---

21. Monica A. Seff, *Cohabitation and the Law*, *in* FAMILIES AND LAW 141, 149 (L.J. McIntyre & M.B. Sussman eds., 1995).

22. Hara Jacobs, *A New Approach for Gay and Lesbian Domestic Partners: Legal Acceptance Through Relational Property Theory*, 1 DUKE J. GENDER L. & POL'Y 159, 161 (1994).

23. David L. Chambers, *What If? The Legal Consequences of Marriage and the Legal Needs of Lesbian and Gay Male Couples*, 95 MICH. L. REV. 447, 478 (1996).

24. Seff, *supra* note 21, at 149.

25. Chambers, *supra* note 23, at 480.

26. Jacobs, *supra* note 22, at 159.

27. Seff, *supra* note 21, at 149.

28. Chambers, *supra* note 23, at 480.

29. Seff, *supra* note 21, at 149. *See, e.g.*, Hewitt v. Hewitt, 394 N.E.2d 1204 (Ill. 1979); McCall v. Frampton, 415 N.Y.S.2d 752 (1979).

30. Chambers, *supra* note 23, at 480. *See, e.g.*, Wilcox v. Trautz, 693 N.E.2d 141, 146 (Mass. 1998) ("unmarried cohabitants may lawfully contract concerning property, financial, and other matters relevant to their relationship"); Beal v. Beal, 577 P.2d 507, 510 (Or. 1978) ("[C]ourts, when dealing with the property disputes of a man and a woman who have been living together in a nonmarital domestic relationship, should distribute the property based upon the express or implied intent of those parties."); *In re* Marriage of Lindsey, 678 P.2d 328, 331 (Wash. 1984) ("courts must examine the relationship and

site-sex couples, a few cases have addressed the property rights of same-sex couples.[31]

One of the earliest and most famous cases that acknowledged the property rights of unmarried committed partners was *Marvin v. Marvin*[32] In Marvin, the parties had lived together for seven years; all the property acquired during this relationship was acquired in the defendant's name. The plaintiff alleged that she and the defendant had orally agreed that they would "share equally" in the property accumulated, that the defendant would support the plaintiff for the rest of her life, that they would hold themselves out as husband and wife, that the plaintiff would give up her entertainment career, and that she would serve as "companion, home-maker, housekeeper and cook" to the defendant.[33]

The court concluded that "courts should enforce express contracts between nonmarital partners except to the extent that the contract is explicitly founded on the consideration of meretricious sexual services."[34] Moreover, the court found that

> [i]n the absence of an express contract, the courts should inquire into the conduct of the parties to determine whether that conduct demonstrates an implied contract, agreement of partnership or joint venture, or some other tacit understanding between the parties. The courts may also employ the doctrine of quantum meruit, or equitable remedies such as constructive or resulting trusts, when warranted by the facts of the case.[35]

The court, thus, recognized the validity of implied contracts and other equitable remedies for protecting the lawful expectations of unmarried committed partners. The court noted that

---

make a just and equitable disposition of the property"); Goode v. Goode, 396 S.E.2d 430, 438 (W. Va. 1990) ("[A] court may order a division of property acquired by a man and a woman who are unmarried cohabitants, but who have considered themselves and held themselves out to be husband and wife. Such order may be based upon principles of contract, either express or implied, or upon a constructive trust.").

31. Chambers, *supra* note 23, at 480. *See also* Ireland v. Flanagan, 627 P.2d 496 (Or. App. 1981). *Compare* Jones v. Daly, 122 Cal. App. 3d 500 (1981) (refusing to enforce oral "cohabitatants agreement" between two males because the sexual relationship was inseparable) *with* Whorton v. Dillingham, 202 Cal. App. 3d 447 (1988) (finding oral cohabitants agreement between two males enforceable although the sexual relationship was express part of consideration).

32. 557 P.2d 106 (Cal. 1976).

33. *Id.* at 110.

34. *Id.*

35. *Id.*

although parties to a nonmarital relationship obviously cannot have based any expectations upon the belief that they were married, other expectations and equitable considerations remain. The parties may well expect that property will be divided in accord with the parties' own tacit understanding and that in the absence of such understanding the courts will fairly apportion property accumulated through mutual effort. We need not treat nonmarital partners as putatively married persons in order to apply principles of implied contract, or extend equitable remedies; we need to treat them only as we do any other unmarried persons.[36]

Cases such as Marvin have given unmarried committed partners some property rights in the event of the breakup of the relationship. However, unmarried partners generally do not have clearly defined property rights in the absence of an express agreement.[37] As the court noted in *Goode v. Goode*, the

evidence [presented at trial] must prove that the parties' nonmarital cohabiting relationship was based upon a valid contract, either expressly or one which may be inferred from the evidence. Similarly, in the absence of a valid contract, a party claiming relief must demonstrate that equitable principles would provide the relief being sought.[38]

Express agreements, often called cohabitation contracts, are agreements between unmarried committed partners that specify the property rights of the partners during and after the relationship and are intended to be legally binding.[39]

Cohabitation contracts are quite flexible and can be tailored to each individual relationship, defining the rights and obligations of each partner.[40] In particular, cohabitation contracts might be useful for couples who are planning for long-term relationships, who wish to make major purchases together, who make decisions that involve one partner moving and/or giving up a job, or who have a relationship that is supported financially by one partner.[41]

Several commentators have suggested points that ought to be included in a cohabitation contract: (1) the rights of each partner to the property

---

36. *Id.* at 121.

37. Chambers, *supra* note 23, at 481.

38. Goode v. Goode, 396 S.E.2d 430, 438-39 (W. Va. 1990).

39. Seff, *supra* note 21, at 154.

40. Adam Chase, *Tax Planning for Same-Sex Couples*, 72 DENV. U. L. REV. 359, 373-74 (1995).

41. Seff, *supra* note 21, at 156.

and income of the other;[42] (2) the ownership of assets;[43] (3) responsibility for debts;[44] (4) how assets acquired together shall be titled;[45] (5) consideration for the agreement;[46] (6) how property will be divided in the event of a breakup;[47] (7) provisions for the care of children from this and previous relationships;[48] and (8) provisions for the termination of the agreement (for example, death or marriage).[49]

B. Intestate Succession

Unmarried committed partners must also address the issue of their respective property rights upon the death of one partner. The system of property succession in the United States is based on the premise that individuals ought to be able to freely dispose of their property.[50] Accordingly, individuals are largely free, with a few exceptions,[51] to determine who will succeed to their accumulated wealth. The testator determines who shall receive his or her accumulated wealth upon his or her death and makes these wishes known through the execution of a will. However, if a decedent failed to execute a will, the state law of intestate succession governs who shall receive the decedent's property.[52] These laws provide a substitute estate plan for those who have not specifically provided their own plan by executing a valid and enforceable will.

Despite the increasing number of people involved in unmarried committed relationships, intestacy laws currently only recognize marital, blood, or adoptive relationships in defining the heirs of a person who dies intes-

---

42. LENORE J. WEITZMAN, THE MARRIAGE CONTRACT: SPOUSES, LOVERS, AND THE LAW 264-65 (1981).

43. *Id.* at 266-67.

44. Raymond C. O'Brien, *Domestic Partnership: Recognition and Responsibility*, 32 SAN DIEGO L. REV. 163, 214 (1995).

45. WEITZMAN, *supra* note 42, at 268-69; Seff, *supra* note 21, at 155.

46. WEITZMAN, *supra* note 42, at 257.

47. *Id.* at 286-90; Seff, *supra* note 21, at 155.

48. WEITZMAN, *supra* note 42, at 279-80; Seff, *supra* note 21, at 155.

49. WEITZMAN, *supra* note 42, at 285; Seff, *supra* note 21, at 155.

50. THOMAS E. ATKINSON, HANDBOOK OF THE LAW OF WILLS 35 (2d ed. 1953).

51. For example, freedom of testation is limited by the spouse's elective share on grounds of public policy. Based on the need to protect spouses against disinheritance, elective share statutes give the surviving spouse the right to take under the decedent's will or to take a statutorily defined share of the decedent's estate. JOHN RITCHIE ET AL., DECEDENTS' ESTATES AND TRUSTS 162-63 (8th ed. 1993).

52. ATKINSON, *supra* note 50, at 60; WILLIAM M. McGOVERN ET AL., WILLS, TRUSTS, AND ESTATES 2 (1988).

tate.[53] Accordingly, if a decedent is not married to his or her committed partner,[54] that partner is not considered an heir of the decedent.[55] Therefore, a decedent's unmarried committed partner does not receive a share of the decedent's estate under the laws of intestacy.[56] Instead, the decedent's property is distributed to his or her lineal descendants (children, grandchildren, etc.). If the decedent with no surviving spouse is not survived

---

53. *See, e.g.*, UNIF. PROBATE CODE §§ 2-102, 2-103 (amended 1993). *See also, e.g.*, Peffley-Warner v. Bowen, 778 P.2d 1022 (Wash. 1989).

54. An alternative would be for one of the partners to adopt the other. If such an adoption were allowed, the partners would be entitled to the rights of intestate succession as would a parent and child. *Compare In re* Adoption of Swanson, 623 A.2d 1095 (Del. 1993) (allowing the adoption), *with In re* Adoption of Robert Paul P., 471 N.E.2d 424 (N.Y. 1984) (denying the adoption).

55. Two exceptions are Oregon and New Hampshire. Oregon's intestacy statute, enacted in 1993 and amended in 1995, defines the surviving spouse of a decedent to include some committed partners:

For purposes of [intestate succession], a person shall be considered the surviving spouse of a decedent under either of the following circumstances:

(1) The person was legally married to the decedent at the time of the decedent's death.

(2) The person and the decedent, although not married but capable of entering into a valid contract of marriage under ORS chapter 106, cohabited for a period of at least 10 years, the period ended not earlier than two years before the death of the decedent, and

(a) During the 10-year period, the person and the decedent mutually assumed marital rights, duties, and obligations;

(b) During the 10-year period, the person and the decedent held themselves out as husband and wife, and acquired a uniform and general reputation as a husband and wife;

(c) During at least the last two years of the 10-year period, the person and the decedent were domiciled in this state; and

(d) Neither the person nor the decedent was legally married to another person at the time of the decedent's death.

OR. REV. STAT. § 112.017 (1995). The statute requires that the parties must have been capable of entering into a valid contract of marriage, excluding same-sex couples, and must have cohabited for at least ten years, excluding those who have not been together this long.

The New Hampshire statute provides: "Persons cohabiting and acknowledging each other as husband and wife, and generally reputed to be such, for the period of 3 years, and until the decease of one of them, shall thereafter be deemed to have been legally married." N.H. REV. STAT. ANN. § 457:39 (1992).

56. Challenges to the exclusion of committed partners as heirs have been unsuccessful. *See, e.g., In re* Petri, N.Y.L.J., Apr. 4, 1994 at 29; *In re* Estate of Cooper, 592 N.Y.S.2d 797 (N.Y. App. Term. 1993).

by any lineal descendants, the property passes to the decedent's parents, if either has survived, or to the descendants of the parents.[57]

Married people are protected against disinheritance by their spouses by "elective share" statutes, which permit a surviving spouse to either take what was provided in the decedent's will or elect to take a forced share of the estate (typically one-third).[58] As in the case of intestacy, unmarried committed partners do not receive the same protection in this area as do spouses; they do not have the right to an elective share of their partner's estate.

Although unmarried committed partners are not generally provided for under state intestacy schemes, a substantial segment of the general public (60-70%) and of committed partners themselves (70-85% of persons with opposite-sex partners; 93-100% of persons with same-sex partners) would give some portion of the estate of a decedent with a committed partner to the partner.[59] A 1992 *Newsweek* poll found that 70% of registered voters approved of inheritance rights for gay "spouses," even though support for gay marriage fell far short of this.[60]

Professor Lawrence Waggoner, a preeminent wills and trusts scholar, has recently suggested that committed partners be allowed to share in their partner's intestate estate.[61] Under the Working Draft of Waggoner's proposal, a committed partner is defined as a person who is an unmarried adult, who would not have been prohibited from marrying the decedent by reason of a blood relationship with the decedent, and who shared a common household with the decedent in a marriage-like relationship.[62] A non-exclusive list of factors for determining whether a relationship was "marriage-like" is provided. These factors include the duration of the relationship, whether the parties intermingled their finances, whether the parties participated in a commitment ceremony, and whether one or both parties

---

57. *See, e.g.*, UNIF. PROBATE CODE § 2-103 (amended 1993).

58. RITCHIE ET AL., *supra* note 51, at 162-63. *See, e.g.*, UNIF. PROBATE CODE, Part 2 (amended 1993).

59. Mary Louise Fellows et al., *Committed Partners and Inheritance: An Empirical Study*, 16 LAW & INEQ. J. 1 (1998). Respondents were presented with a series of hypothetical scenarios in which they were asked how they would divide the property of a decedent among survivors identified in terms of their familial-type relationship with the decedent.

60. *Gays Under Fire*, NEWSWEEK, Sept. 14, 1992, at 35.

61. Lawrence Waggoner, *Waggoner Working Draft: Intestate Share of Committed Partner* (1995) (reproduced in Fellows et al., *supra* note 59, at 92-94) [hereinafter Waggoner, *Working Draft*]. *See also* LAWRENCE W. WAGGONER ET AL., FAMILY PROPERTY LAW: CASES AND MATERIALS ON WILLS, TRUSTS, AND FUTURE INTERESTS (2d ed. 1997); Lawrence W. Waggoner, *Marital Property Rights in Transition*, 59 MO. L. REV. 21 (1994).

62. Waggoner, *Working Draft*, *supra* note 61, at 92.

named the other as a primary beneficiary of a life insurance policy. The Waggoner Working Draft would apply to both opposite-sex and same-sex committed partners.[63]

In the absence of state law provisions to include unmarried committed partners in intestacy statutes, committed partners must execute wills to protect their testamentary preferences if those preferences include their partners. While it is advisable for married persons to execute wills that give effect to their precise testamentary preferences, for unmarried committed partners, executing a will or engaging in other estate planning techniques (such as obtaining life insurance or jointly owning property) is essential to ensure that property will pass to the partner.

C. Health Care Planning

An additional planning issue that nonmarital partners must face involves the eventuality that one of the partners may become unable to direct his or her own health care. Each state provides statutes that grant health care decision making power to relatives if a person becomes incompetent to make such decisions.[64] If the person is married, these statutes usually designate the person's spouse as the substitute decision maker.[65] However, if the person is not married, a parent, child, or other relative is typically designated as the surrogate decision maker.[66] For example, the Uniform Probate Code specifies the order of preference for those who could be a guardian of an incapacitated person as: the person's spouse or person nominated by will, the person's adult child, and then the person's parent.[67] Statutes designating the incompetent person's spouse as surrogate decision maker are premised on the assumption that the spouse is most likely to know what the person would have wanted and to have the person's best interests in mind.[68] However, the same could likely be said about a person's committed partner as well.

A few states do include unmarried committed partners among the persons to be considered as a surrogate decision maker in the absence of a specific designation by the patient. For example, New Mexico's health care decision making statute gives priority over everyone other than a spouse to "an individual in a long-term relationship of indefinite duration with the patient in which the individual has demonstrated an actual com-

---

63. *Id.*

64. *See, e.g.*, KY. REV. STAT. ANN. § 311.631 (Michie 1995).

65. *See* Chambers, *supra* note 23, at 454-55.

66. *See id.*

67. UNIF. PROBATE CODE § 5-305(c) (amended 1993).

68. *See* Chambers, *supra* note 23, at 456.

mitment to the patient similar to the commitment of a spouse and in which the individual and the patient consider themselves to be responsible for each other's well-being."[69] However, most states do not provide for unmarried committed partners to act as surrogate decision makers.

Failure to designate the incompetent person's partner as a surrogate decision maker may be "doubly unfortunate" for persons in homosexual relationships. First, failure to designate the person's partner as the surrogate decision maker may mean that the person to whom he or she is closest will not be making decisions about his or her care. Moreover, because homosexuals are somewhat more likely to be estranged from their immediate families,[70] it is possible that the person who is designated as the surrogate decision maker is not close to the incompetent person. In addition, the surrogate decision maker may refuse to allow the partner to participate in the decision making or to visit the ill partner.[71]

The extensive litigation involved in the case of Sharon Kowalski[72] provides a vivid example of these dangers. In 1983, Kowalski suffered severe brain injuries as a result of an automobile accident.[73] At the time of the accident she was living with her lesbian partner, but she had not disclosed her sexual orientation or the relationship to her parents. Following the accident, the animosity between Kowalski's parents and her partner resulted in a series of legal battles regarding who would be Kowalski's guardian.[74] Kowalski's partner was prohibited from visiting her for three years and she did not succeed in becoming Kowalski's guardian until more than eight

---

69. N.M. STAT. ANN. § 24-7A-5(B)(2) (Michie 1997). An Arizona Statute provides that, if the patient has not designated an agent and the court has not appointed a guardian for the purpose of making health care decisions, a patient's domestic partner can act as the surrogate decision maker; however, such a person is given a lower priority than a spouse, an adult child, or a parent. ARIZ. REV. STAT. ANN. § 36-3231 (West 1995). Other statutes allow a person who has exhibited special care for the patient and who is familiar with the patient's values to serve as a surrogate decision maker, but only if the listed family members are unavailable. See, e.g., DEL. CODE ANN. tit. 16, § 2507 (1998); ME. REV. STAT. ANN. tit. 18-A, § 5- 805 (West 1997).

70. See KATH WESTON, FAMILIES WE CHOOSE: LESBIANS, GAYS, KINSHIP (1997).

71. See Chambers, supra note 23, at 457-58.

72. In re Guardianship of Kowalski, 478 N.W.2d 790 (Minn. App. 1991); In re Guardianship of Kowalski, 392 N.W.2d 310 (Minn. App. 1986); In re Guardianship of Kowalski, 382 N.W.2d 861 (Minn. App. 1986).

73. Kowalski was both physically and mentally impaired. She was confined to wheelchair, had difficulty communicating, and had the mental capacity of a child between 4 and 6 years of age. Kowalski, 382 N.W.2d 861.

74. Kowalski, 478 N.W.2d 790; Kowalski, 392 N.W.2d 310; Kowalski, 382 N.W.2d 861.

years after Kowalski's accident, even though she was the only person who was willing and able to care for Kowalski outside of an institution.[75]

As in the context of property rights, married persons can choose whether to rely on the statutory designation or to execute a private document designating a substitute decision-maker. However, persons in unmarried committed relationships who want their partners to act as their surrogate health care decision-makers must make use of private agreements. A durable power of attorney for health care is a mechanism that can be used by unmarried committed partners to maximize the likelihood that their wishes regarding long-term health care will be followed.[76] Using a durable power of attorney for health care, a competent person can appoint another person to make health care decisions in the event that the person becomes unable to direct his or her own care.[77] The power granted to the surrogate decision maker may be detailed to the extent desired by the individual, but no specific direction is required. When the durable power is in effect, the appointed decision-maker has the legal authority to make health care decisions on behalf of the principal and health care providers are required to honor those decisions. Financial durable powers of attorney can also be executed so that one partner has the authority to direct the person's or the couple's finances during the period of the other's incapacity.[78]

All states have provisions for durable powers of attorney. However, not all states have expressly determined whether a durable power of attorney may be used for health care decision making.[79] Approximately one-half of states specifically permit the designation of an individual to make health care decisions, eight states have interpreted their durable power statutes to

---

75. *Kowalski*, 478 N.W.2d at 791.

76. Another mechanism by which a competent person can express his or her wishes regarding long-term health care is a living will or advance directive. An advance directive for mental health care might also be considered. *See* Bruce J. Winick, *Advance Directive Instruments for those with Mental Illness*, 51 U. MIAMI L. REV. 57 (1996). *See* Dennis P. Stolle, *Advance Directives, AIDS, and Mental Health: TJ Preventive Law for the HIV-Positive Client*, PSYCHOL. PUB. POL'Y & L. (forthcoming 1999) (discussing advance directives for mental health care in the context of HIV-infection and possible estrangement from family).

77. HAYDEN CURRY ET AL., A LEGAL GUIDE FOR LESBIAN AND GAY COUPLES 4-19 (1993); BARRY R. FURROW ET AL., BIOETHICS: HEALTH CARE LAW AND ETHICS 275 (1991).

78. CURRY ET AL., *supra* note 77, at 4-21.

79. Ann Lorentson Friedman & Rosemary B. Hughes, *AIDS: Legal Tools Helpful for Mental Health Counseling Interventions*, 16 J. MENTAL HEALTH COUNS. 291, 295 (1994).

permit the designation of a health care decision maker, and an additional eight states allow the designation of an individual to make health care decisions other than the withdrawal or withholding of life support.[80]

Thus, through the execution of a durable power of attorney for health care, a person living in an unmarried committed relationship can designate his or her partner as his or her legal health care decision-maker. In this way, a person can, if he or she wishes, ensure that the partner, rather than another family member, will be allowed to make health care decisions when and if necessary. In addition, durable power of attorney can help prevent the exclusion of the partner from the health care decision making process and from access to the ill partner.[81]

D. Employment Benefits and Legal Registration

Finally, another issue related to both property and health care planning involves the availability to partners of benefits provided by employers. Generally, the employment benefits provided in both the private and public sectors are extended only to the spouses and dependents of employees. However, a few municipalities and corporations have granted some benefits to the nonmarital committed partners of their employees.[82] These

---

80. *Id.*

81. *See, e.g.,* CURRY ET AL., *supra* note 77, at 4-2.

82. A number of cities (e.g., Berkeley, CA; Laguna Beach, CA; Los Angeles, CA; San Francisco, CA; Santa Cruz, CA; West Hollywood, CA; Cambridge, MA; Tacoma Park, MD; Ann Arbor, MI; Minneapolis, MN; Ithaca, NY; New York City, NY; Seattle, WA; Madison, WI), one state (Vermont), and a number of businesses and universities (e.g., APA Insurance Trust, Apple Computer, Ben and Jerry's, Columbia University, HBO, IBM, Microsoft Corp., Levi Strauss & Co., Lotus, Princeton University, Stanford University, University of Colorado, University of Iowa, University of Minnesota, the Village Voice, and Walt Disney) offer some benefits to domestic partners. *See* CURRY ET AL., *supra* note 77, at 1-9 to 1-13; Rebecca L. Melton, *Legal Rights of Unmarried Heterosexual and Homosexual Couples and Evolving Definitions of "Family"*, 29 J. FAM. L. 497, 503 (1990-1991); Seff, *supra* note 21, at 157; Sue Spielman & Liz Winfeld, *Domestic Partner Benefits: A Bottom Line Discussion*, 4 J. GAY & LESBIAN SOC. SERV. 53, 54-55 (1996) ("[B]etween 1990 and 1994, the number of businesses, universities, and municipalities that have chosen to offer domestic partner benefits inclusive of medical benefits has increased from under 5 to over 130. And the number that offer employee benefits exclusive of medical coverage is close to three times that number." (citation omitted)); Mary Patricia Treuthart, *Adopting a More Realistic Definition of "Family"*, 26 GONZ. L. REV. 91, 100-05 (1990-1991); Jeff Barge, *More Firms Offer Benefits for Gay Couples: Managers Say Fairness Concerns Prompted Change: Low Cost was a Surprise*, A.B.A. J., June 1995, at 34; Kirk Johnson, *Gay Divorce: Few Markers in This Realm*, N.Y. TIMES, Aug. 12, 1994, at A20.

ordinances or corporate rules allow couples in committed relationships to receive the benefits that are extended to married couples.[83] These benefits typically include access to company events and facilities, bereavement and sick leave, employee assistance and counseling, relocation assistance, and health and dental insurance coverage.[84]

Ordinances or corporate rules granting benefits to domestic partners typically define what it means to be a domestic partner. These requirements often include a minimum time that the partners must have been in the relationship, evidence of financial interdependence, the sharing of a joint residence, relationship boundaries (for example, exclusivity, no close blood relationship, and no current legal marriage), and the naming of the partner as a beneficiary of life insurance or pension plans.[85]

One state has now implemented provisions under which some unmarried committed partners can register as domestic partners in order to receive employment benefits and other legal protections. In 1997, in response to a series of state court decisions,[86] the Hawaii legislature, in a political compromise, passed two bills.[87] These bills proposed an amendment to the Hawaii constitution giving the legislature the power to limit marriage to

---

83. Chase, *supra* note 40, at 378.

84. O'Brien, *supra* note 44, at 207. While only 35% of registered voters approved of "legally sanctioned gay marriages" and only 32% approved of adoption rights for gay spouses, 67% approved of health insurance for gay spouses and 58% approved of social security for gay spouses. *Gays Under Fire*, *supra* note 60, at 37. A more recent poll of Californians found that while 60% disapproved of same-sex marriage, nearly two-thirds approved of recognizing the rights of partners to hospital visitation rights, medical power of attorney, and conservatorship; 60% approved of allowing partners to received pension benefits, health benefits, and family leave benefits, and 55% approved of legal domestic partner registration. Philip J. Trounstine, *Californians oppose gay marriage but favor limited legal rights, poll finds*, KNIGHT-RIDDER/TRIB. NEWS SERVICE, Mar. 2, 1997, at 302K2618.

85. O'Brien, *supra* note 44, at 181.

86. In *Baehr v. Lewin*, 852 P.2d 44 (Haw. 1993), the Hawaii Supreme Court held that the state was regulating access to the status of married persons on the basis of sex and that, therefore, the state was required to demonstrate a compelling state interest in accordance with the Equal Protection Clause of the Hawaii Constitution, HAW. CONST. Art I, § 5. On remand in *Baehr v. Mike*, Civ-No. 91-1394, 1996 WL 694235, at *20 (Haw. Cir. Ct. Dec. 3, 1996), the trial court ruled that the state had failed to sustain its burden by demonstrating a compelling state interest. Therefore, the court ruled that the sex-based classification was unconstitutional as violative of equal protection. *Id.* at *22.

87. H.B. No. 117, A Bill for an Act Proposing a Constitutional Amendment Relating to Marriage, 19th Leg., Reg. Sess. (Haw. 1997); H.B. No. 118, Act Relating to Unmarried Couples (Reciprocal Beneficiaries) (Haw. 1997), codified at HAW. REV. STAT. ANN. § 572C-1 to § 572C-7 (Michie Supp. 1997).

opposite-sex couples[88] but provided that certain couples could register as "reciprocal beneficiaries."[89] The law "extend[s] certain rights and benefits which are presently available only to married couples to couples composed of two individuals who are legally prohibited from marrying under state law."[90] Included is the right of each "reciprocal beneficiary" to receive a share of the other's intestate estate as would a surviving spouse, to participate in family health coverage, to hospital visitation, to make health care decisions as would a spouse, and to employee benefits such as funeral leave for the death of the reciprocal beneficiary.[91]

Under the Hawaii legislation, reciprocal beneficiaries must be at least eighteen years old; must not be married nor parties to other reciprocal beneficiary relationships; must be legally prohibited from marrying each other under state law; must not consent to the relationship as a result of force, duress, or fraud; and must sign a declaration of a reciprocal beneficiary relationship.[92]

Unlike Waggoner's Working Draft for intestacy, the Hawaii provisions do not apply to opposite-sex unmarried couples because reciprocal beneficiaries must be prohibited from marrying under Hawaii law. However, other unmarried adults, such as siblings, may register as reciprocal beneficiaries under the legislation. The Hawaii legislation and the Waggoner Working Draft also differ in their approach to the determination of whether two people are committed partners. The Waggoner Working Draft provides criteria by which to determine whether or not a couple is sufficiently committed to be included within its provisions. Conversely, the Hawaii legislation allows couples to define themselves as committed partners as long as they meet the stated minimum criteria. Self-definition allows couples to choose whether or not to be registered as committed partners. However, because partners who fail to file have no rights as reciprocal beneficiaries, such a system may miss those committed partners who are not informed about the provisions or who do not have other contacts with the legal system through which they can learn about the option to register.

Without a doubt, persons in nonmarital committed relationships face difficulties in relation to their long-term planning needs that are not encountered by married couples. In planning for their combined futures, the partners must address a host of interrelated legal and psychological questions. By using an approach to lawyering that combines the perspectives of TJ-preventive law, attorneys who work with clients who are in nonmarital

---

88. H.B. No. 117.
89. H.B. No. 118.
90. *Id.* § 1.
91. *Id.*
92. *Id.* § 4.

relationships may be better able to provide more effective legal services that are also therapeutic to the clients' psychological well-being.

III. Therapeutic Jurisprudence/Preventive Law

A. Therapeutic Jurisprudence

Therapeutic jurisprudence is the study of the law as a therapeutic agent.[93] A perspective centered around therapeutic jurisprudence considers how the law might be used to achieve therapeutic objectives.[94] Acknowledging that the law inevitably functions as a therapeutic agent, impacting on the psychological and physical health and well-being of those with whom it comes into contact, therapeutic jurisprudence seeks to engage in systematic study of these effects.[95] To do so, therapeutic jurisprudence seeks to utilize the interdisciplinary perspectives and techniques of legal and policy studies, psychiatry, philosophy, and the behavioral sciences, particularly clinical, social, and experimental psychology, to evaluate the therapeutic and the anti-therapeutic effects of substantive laws, legal procedures, and legal roles.[96] While the therapeutic jurisprudential perspective first emerged in analyses of mental health law,[97] the approach has broadened to include a wide range of legal domains and a focus on the general psychological and physical well-being of ordinary individuals.[98]

A perspective based on therapeutic jurisprudence recognizes that the law can serve any number of potential ends, some of which will inevitably come into conflict.[99] Thus, therapeutic jurisprudence acknowledges the potential for conflict between the use of the law to achieve therapeutic

---

93. David B. Wexler & Robert F. Schopp, *Therapeutic Jurisprudence: A New Approach to Mental Health Law*, in HANDBOOK OF PSYCHOLOGY AND LAW 361, 362 (D.K. Kagehiro & W.S. Laufer eds., 1992).

94. *Id.*

95. Stolle et al., *supra* note 2, at 17; David B. Wexler, *Applying the Law Therapeutically*, in LAW IN A THERAPEUTIC KEY: DEVELOPMENTS IN THERAPEUTIC JURISPRUDENCE 831 (David B. Wexler & Bruce J. Winick eds., 1996); Bruce J. Winick, *The Jurisprudence of Therapeutic Jurisprudence*, 3 PSYCHOL. PUB. POL'Y & L. 184, 187 (1997).

96. DAVID B. WEXLER, THERAPEUTIC JURISPRUDENCE: THE LAW AS A THERAPEUTIC AGENT (1990); DAVID B. WEXLER & BRUCE J. WINICK, ESSAYS IN THERAPEUTIC JURISPRUDENCE (1991).

97. WEXLER, *supra* note 96, at 4.

98. See the breadth of the topics addressed in LAW IN A THERAPEUTIC KEY: DEVELOPMENTS IN THERAPEUTIC JURISPRUDENCE, *supra* note 95.

99. *See* Robert F. Schopp, *Therapeutic Jurisprudence and Conflicts Among Values in Mental Health Law*, 11 BEHAV. SCI. & L. 31, 31-32 (1993).

objectives and other values important in the law, such as individual liberty. However, therapeutic jurisprudence "suggests that, other things being equal, positive therapeutic effects are desirable and should generally be a proper aim of law, and that anti-therapeutic effects are undesirable and should be avoided or minimized."[100]

In recent years, there has been increasing interest in a dimension of therapeutic jurisprudence that takes the law as given and explores ways in which existing law might be applied most therapeutically.[101] For any particular state of the law, there may be a wide degree of latitude for applying the law more therapeutically and less anti-therapeutically.[102] Thus, "[t]he actual legal practice of therapeutic jurisprudence will principally involve lawyers working with clients to apply existing law in a manner likely to promote psychological well-being."[103] In accordance with this approach, we assume that the state of the law as just described will continue. That is, we examine the ways in which lawyers can work with nonmarital partners given that same-sex marriage is not recognized, that the property rights of unmarried couples remain uncertain, that state intestacy laws have not been altered to include unmarried committed partners, that there continue to be few opportunities for legal registration, and that nonmarital partners are generally not statutorily defined surrogate decision makers.[104] Practitioners will be best able to work with unmarried com-

---

100. Winick, *supra* note 95, at 188.

101. Stolle et al., *supra* note 2, at 18. *See also* Rose A. Daly-Rooney, *Designing Reasonable Accomodations Through Co-Worker Participation: Therapeutic Jurisprudence and the Confidentiality Provision of the Americans with Disabilities Act*, 8 J. L. & HEALTH 89 (1993-1994); David Finkelman & Thomas Grisso, *Therapeutic Jurisprudence: From Idea to Application*, *in* LAW IN A THERAPEUTIC KEY: DEVELOPMENTS IN THERAPEUTIC JURISPRUDENCE 587, *supra* note 95; Dennis P. Stolle, *Professional Responsibility in Elder Law: A Synthesis of Preventive Law and Therapeutic Jurisprudence*, 14 BEHAV. SCI. & L. 459 (1996); Wexler, *supra* note 95.

102. Winick, *supra* note 95, at 201.

103. David B. Wexler, Practicing Therapeutic Jurisprudence: Psycholegal Soft Spots and Strategies (1998) (unpublished manuscript, on file with author).

104. Any changes that might occur are likely to occur slowly and could be either favorable or unfavorable to nonmarital partnerships. We have noted several reform efforts beneficial to unmarried committed partners. *See supra* notes 61-63 and accompanying text (describing the Waggoner intestacy working draft), notes 86-92 and accompanying text (describing the Hawaii reciprocal beneficiary legislation). There have also been efforts directed toward reforms such as prohibiting same-sex marriages. *See* Dunlap, *Fearing a Toehold*, *supra* note 1. Indeed, the recently enacted Defense of Marriage Act denies federal recognition of same-sex marriages and permits states to decline to recognize same-sex marriages as well. 1 U.S.C. § 7 (Supp. 1997); 28 U.S.C. § 1738C (Supp. 1997).

mitted partners as clients in this context by engaging in the practice of preventive law.

B. Preventive Law

Preventive law is "a branch of law that endeavors to minimize the risk of litigation or to secure more certainty as to legal rights and duties."[105] Accordingly, the "objective of the lawyer practicing preventive law on behalf of a client is to work with that client in arranging his or her affairs, through the use of legal techniques and documents, in such a way as to maximize the probability of achieving the client's objectives and, in doing so, to minimize legal risks and costs associated with those objectives."[106] A preventive law approach is proactive; it emphasizes planning and prevention and focuses on the "careful private ordering of affairs."[107] In order to appropriately consider the client's long-term interests and how to most effectively protect those interests and avoid future legal problems, a preventive lawyer must make effective use of client intake forms, client counseling, and legal check-ups.[108] As described below, a preventive law approach can also provide an opportunity in which to practice therapeutic jurisprudence.

C. Synthesis

Stolle has suggested that good preventive lawyers should be sensitive to the therapeutic and anti-therapeutic effects of the law and legal planning on their clients.[109] Thus, he proposes an integration of therapeutic jurisprudence and preventive law such that attorneys will engage in a systematic application of both preventive law and therapeutic jurisprudence principles.[110] In such an integration of perspectives, preventive law pro-

---

105. Stolle et al., *supra* note 2, at 16 (citing Honorable Edward D. Re, *The Lawyer as Counselor and the Prevention of Litigation*, 31 Cath. U. L. Rev. 685, 692 (1995)).

106. *Id.* at 33-34.

107. *Id.* at 16. *See also* Louis M. Brown & Edward A. Dauer, Perspectives on the Lawyer as Planner (1978).

108. Scott E. Isaacson, *Preventive Law: A Personal Essay*, 9-Oct. Utah B. J. 14 (1996).

109. Stolle, *supra* note 101, at 469.

110. Stolle et al., *supra* note 2, at 20. Discussion of the integration of therapeutic jurisprudence and preventative law can be found in Stolle, *supra* note 101; Stolle, *supra* note 76; Dennis P. Stolle & David B. Wexler, *Thearpeutic Jurisprudence and Preventative Law: A Combined Concentration to Invigorate the Everyday Practice of Law*, 39 Ariz. L. Rev. 25 (1997).

vides the framework — the law office practice — and therapeutic jurisprudence draws on an interdisciplinary approach and provides the objectives — therapeutic outcomes.[111]

Thus, while a client may enter a law office with a particular question or issue, a lawyer working from a TJ-preventive law perspective can use the preventive law tools of client intake and counseling to help the client identify "psycholegal soft spots," for instance, relationships, goals, or psychological and value issues that should be considered when contemplating any legal action or non-action.[112] Then, the practitioner can use preventive legal documents (in the present context these include cohabitation contracts, wills, durable powers of attorney, legal registration, life insurance, etc.) to maximize the likelihood that therapeutic outcomes will result from the transaction.[113]

Stolle frames the TJ-preventive law approach as comprising four stages. First, psycholegal soft spots must be identified. Second, the legal documents or procedures that are most likely to result in therapeutic outcomes must be selected. Third, these preventive legal documents and procedures must be employed to maximize therapeutic outcomes and to minimize anti-therapeutic outcomes. Finally, the attorney and client should engage in on-going legal check-ups so that "unanticipated life changes" are taken into account in reformulating the preventive documents to ensure that they remain legally effective and therapeutic.[114]

The integration of therapeutic jurisprudence and preventive law is growing and has now been applied in a number of legal domains including elder law, HIV/AIDS law, family law, and corporate and business planning law.[115] We propose that long-term property and health care planning, particularly for those persons in unmarried committed relationships, is an area that can benefit from a TJ-preventive law approach.

One approach to the complex issues faced by unmarried committed partners is to advocate reform of the law. Such legal reform could range from allowing committed partners to register as reciprocal beneficiaries for limited benefits to allowing same-sex marriage. In this vein, Waggoner and Fellows and her colleagues suggest reform of state intestacy laws to provide for unmarried committed partners.[116] In the absence of legislative or policy reform, however, another approach is for individuals to engage in the private ordering of their own affairs, attempting to address their needs

---

111. Stolle, *supra* note 76.

112. Stolle et al., *supra* note 2, at 42-43.

113. *Id.* at 25.

114. Stolle, *supra* note 101, at 469.

115. See review in Stolle et al., *supra* note 2, at 20-32.

116. Fellows et al., *supra* note 59, at 89-91; Waggoner, *Working Draft, supra* note 61, at 78-80.

proactively by using a preventive law approach. The preventive law emphasis on planning and prevention through the use of legal instruments can be used to accurately reflect the goals and circumstances of an unmarried committed couple.

Many of the challenges that nonmarital couples will face both during and after their committed relationships are of both legal and psychological importance. During the relationship, the ways in which couples structure their finances, handle joint participation in the rearing of children, and approach possible estrangement from their families can have both legal and psychological repercussions. Similarly, at the end of the relationship, whether it ends by the choice of one or both partners or upon the death of one of the partners, the legal disposition or division of assets can be an emotional process that can become even more difficult if family conflict arises. Health care decision making, likewise, involves the psychological issues surrounding illness and human decision making in the context of legal rights. Some of the therapeutic outcomes that can result from careful legal planning in these areas include acknowledging the relationship, avoiding leaving a partner unprovided for, ensuring that health care decision making power is held by the person that the individual wishes, and avoiding future conflict. Melton notes:

> Property ownership and beneficiary designations are the most valuable estate planning tools that unmarried heterosexual and same-sex couples have at their disposal. A surviving joint owner, or the beneficiary of a life insurance policy or trust, will receive the designated property in the event of death, regardless of the existence or non-existence of a traditional family relationship with the decedent. Same-sex couples can effectuate a legal relationship through such devices as reciprocal wills, naming each other beneficiaries of insurance policies, and executing powers of attorney for one another.[117]

In order to begin providing information to practitioners who may have occasion to encounter unmarried committed partners in their legal practices, we report the results of the following empirical study, which examines the current estate, financial, and health care planning practices of a sample of unmarried committed partners.

IV. Empirical Study

The present study provides an opportunity to examine the long-term property and health care planning practices of unmarried committed part-

---

117. Melton, *supra* note 82, at 507.

ners in both opposite-sex and same-sex relationships and some of the reasons for those practices.

A. Design and Method

The survey data were collected by the Minnesota Center for Survey Research in the fall of 1996. Telephone surveys were completed by 256 Minnesota residents over the age of 25, including a random sample of the general public (N=87), and samples of persons in opposite-sex committed relationships (N=33), of women in same-sex committed relationships (N=85), and of men in same-sex committed relationships (N=51).[118] The data from the sample of the general public are not discussed in the present paper.

The sample of persons with opposite-sex committed partners was generated by asking general public respondents (generated via random digit dialing) and subsequent respondents in the committed partner samples to provide the name of someone they knew in an unmarried opposite-sex committed relationship. Due to the difficulties in generating a random sample of same-sex committed couples, volunteers were solicited for these samples.[119] Flyers were placed in the Twin Cities in bookstores, cafes, bars, and other businesses that the lesbian, gay, bisexual, and transgender communities support. Advocacy groups throughout the state were also contacted and asked for help in generating names. A few radio stations and newspapers ran community service advertisements about the study. Finally, names were generated by word of mouth as people became aware of the project.

A self-definition of committed relationship was used for eligibility. Not all of the sample respondents in committed relationships were cohabiting with their partner at the time of the survey. Eleven (33.3%) respondents with opposite-sex partners, five (5.9%) female respondents with same-sex

---

118. More detailed descriptions of the sample can be found in Fellows et al., *supra* note 59, and in Monica K. Johnson & Jennifer K. Robbennolt, *Using Social Science to Inform the Law of Intestacy: The Case of Unmarried Committed Partners*, 22 LAW & HUM. BEHAV. 479 (1998).

119. Relative to the population of the United States, few persons are in same-sex relationships. In addition, very few persons are willing to identify themselves as lesbian, gay, bisexual, or transgender to a poller over the phone due to fear of discrimination. Therefore, random digit dialing is not a feasible means of identifying potential respondents. In one national phone survey, for example, it took 1650 calls to Kansas, a total of 55 hours of dialing, before pollers found the first person willing to identify himself or herself to a poller as being gay or lesbian. *See* Chambers, *supra* note 23, at 449 (citing Larry Hatfield, *Methods of Polling*, S.F. EXAMINER, June 5, 1989, at A20).

partners, and three (6.0%) male respondents with same-sex partners were not living with their partner at the time of the study. Respondents with opposite-sex partners had been in their current relationships for an average of 5.5 years. Respondents with same-sex partners had been in their current relationships for an average of 8.5 years.

Interviewers indicated that they were calling from the University of Minnesota and told respondents that they were conducting a study regarding attitudes about inheritance rights of couples who are living together without being married. They used a standardized questionnaire to conduct the interviews and recorded responses directly. Information was gathered regarding respondents' personal relationships, wealth accumulation, estate planning instruments, and children. Demographic information was also gathered on all respondents.[120]

B. Findings

1. Written Agreements

In the present study, interviewers asked respondents whether they had entered into written property agreements with their partners. Approximately 29% of the sample (48 respondents) had executed formal written property agreements with their partners. One of the primary reasons given for entering into a written agreement was to make the partners' understandings and wishes explicit in order to avoid later problems. As one participant responded, a written agreement was necessary "to establish some sense of order." In addition, participants cited the need to legally protect their partner given current law. Another commonly cited reason for entering into a written agreement was that one or both partners did not trust their respective families or felt a need to protect the other partner. This particularly concerned many people in unmarried committed relationships who did not have the support of their families.[121] Finally, a few participants indicated that their written agreements were prompted by a major transition affecting the committed relationship.[122]

Twenty percent of the sample (33 respondents) indicated that they had considered entering into a written agreement with their partners but had

---

120. In addition, respondents were presented with a series of hypothetical scenarios in which they were asked to divide the property of the decedent among survivors identified in terms of their familial-type relationship with the decedent. These results are reported in Fellows et al., *supra* note 59, and in Johnson & Robbennolt, *supra* note 118.

121. *See supra* notes 70-75 and accompanying text.

122. One example of such a transition is the purchase of a house or the decision to have a child.

decided against it. When asked why they decided not to enter into a written agreement, approximately one-half of these respondents indicated that they had not had time to make these arrangements or had otherwise "not gotten around to it." One person indicated that the couple was still thinking about entering into a contract but had not yet made a decision. These responses cannot be considered actual rejections of having written property agreements. Perhaps many of these respondents would enter into written agreements with their partners if the process was facilitated in some way.

Among those who had considered but decided against entering into a written agreement, the reasons varied. Several people indicated that such an agreement was not needed because they had faith in their relationship, trusted their partner, or were very clear with each other about property ownership. Along these lines, several respondents indicated that they had decided not to enter a written agreement because they did not foresee the relationship ending. Comparing a written agreement to a prenuptial agreement, one of these respondents explained that one only entered into these types of agreements if one planned to break up. One gay man who had been in his current relationship for twenty-one years explained, "Our lawyer advised it, but after so many years, it didn't seem relevant." Two respondents explained that they intended to execute written agreements after they had been in their relationships longer. One respondent indicated that his or her partner did not want a written agreement. Finally, one respondent indicated that a lawyer had advised against it since each party had a will.

The remaining 52% of the sample (88 respondents) had never considered executing a written agreement with their partners. It is possible that many of these people had not yet encountered any of the events that typically trigger consideration of an agreement, such as the joint purchase of a home or a relocation. It is also possible that the need for an agreement had not been suggested to them by an attorney or other trusted source. It may be less common for a partner in a committed unmarried relationship to initiate consideration of an agreement than for an event or outside suggestion to raise the issue.

In a series of analyses, we sought to outline some of the characteristics of respondents who had written agreements, wills, and other legal arrangements with their partners. We considered a number of socio-demographic factors, including gender, age, estate size, education, and personal income. We also considered a number of characteristics of the respondents' current relationship. These factors include whether the couple had held a commitment ceremony or exchanged a symbol of the relationship (for example, rings); the duration of the relationship; whether the couple made joint charitable gifts; whether the couple was financially interdependent as measured by having a joint bank account, joint investment, or joint credit card; whether the couple had joint ownership of a pet, a motor vehicle, or a home; and whether a child (either the respondent's or the partner's) lived in the household (for at least two months during the year). In the tables, we present only the data for those characteristics that significantly predicted having a written agreement, will, or other legal arrangement.[123]

Several of the demographic and relationship characteristics were associated with whether respondents had entered written agreements with their partners.[124] Due to the small number of respondents who had entered into written agreements, the sample groups are considered together for this analysis. Age and education were both positively associated with having a written agreement; older and more highly educated people were more likely to have written agreements. Estate size also had a significant positive effect; those persons with an estate of less than $50,000 were particularly unlikely to have written agreements. Although income was positively associated with having a written agreement, this relationship did not achieve statistical significance.

Similarly, several of the relationship characteristics were related to having a written agreement. Having held a commitment ceremony or exchanged a symbol of the relationship was strongly related to having a written agreement; those engaging in such activities were more likely to have agreements. Similarly, the duration of the relationship was also positively related to having a written agreement; those who had been in their relationships for a longer period were more likely to have written agreements. Financial interdependence and joint ownership of a home were both related to having a written agreement; financially interdependent couples were more likely to have formal agreements, as were those who jointly owned a home. This is consistent with the respondents' stated reasons for having written agreements, including the need to financially protect a partner and the purchase of a home as prompting the execution of a written agreement. Finally, having a child who lived in the household was negatively related to having a written agreement; those who had a child living in the household were less likely to have entered into written agreements with their partners.[125]

---

123. Many of these socio-demographic and relationship characteristics are correlated with one another (e.g., age and estate size). Due to limitations in sample size for the groups of interest, the statistical tests (2) reported in the following sections do not correct for this collinearity. Thus, we do not identify the unique contribution of each variable.

124. *See* Table 1.

125. Gender was not related to whether respondents had written agreements. In addition, there were no significant effects of having made joint charitable gifts, jointly owning a motor vehicle, or jointly owning a pet.

Extensive information was gathered on the nature of the written agreements.[126] Just over one-half (52.1%) of the agreements had a provision for dividing property if the relationship were to end. Of these, most contained a provision regarding the home. It was also quite common for these agreements to contain a provision for the division of other mutually owned property. Less frequently, these agreements contained provisions regarding pension and retirement benefits and separately owned property. Most of the agreements (91.7%) addressed the division of property in the event of the death of one of the partners. Again, nearly all of these agreements included a provision for the disposition of the home. Just under one-half (41.7%) contained provisions regarding pensions or retirement benefits, the partners' separate property, and mutually owned property.

Slightly over one-half (54.2%) of the agreements designated that property brought to the relationship would become mutually owned by both partners. One-third of the agreements designated that property brought to the relationship would remain separately owned by each partner. The few remaining respondents did not know the terms of their agreement on this matter. With respect to property acquired during the relationship, three-quarters (75.0%) of the agreements designated that this be mutually owned. Only 6.4% of agreements designated that property acquired during the relationship remain the separate property of each partner, and the remaining few respondents did not know the terms of their agreement on this matter. Less than one-third of the written agreements addressed the issue of property that was received as a gift or inheritance during the relationship. Those agreements addressing this situation were approximately equally likely to designated such property as the separate property of the partner who received it (N=6) as to designated it as mutually owned by both partners (N=8).

Written agreements also addressed a number of other issues. One-fourth of the agreements outlined general duties of support and maintenance between the partners during the relationship and 35.4% outlined these responsibilities for the period following the termination of the relationship. Only seven agreements (14.6%) provided for the support and maintenance of children (N=5) or other family members (N=2) during the relationship, after the termination of the relationship, or after the death of one partner.

Respondents were asked to explain any other provisions in the written agreement that had not been covered. Fifteen respondents indicated that their agreement included other provisions. Six agreements designated a health care decision-maker (in all but one case this was the partner) and

---

126. *See* Table 2.

four agreements established the partner as having a general power of attorney. Three agreements established who would get the pet(s), two named other guardians for children in the event of death, and one established joint custody and minor guardianship for a child due in several weeks.[127]

2. Wills

Interviewers asked respondents whether they had a will and whether they had updated their will since their committed relationship began. Among respondents with opposite-sex partners, one-third had wills and only 40% of those had updated their will since their committed relationship began. Respondents with same-sex partners were more likely to have wills; 60% (81 respondents) had wills, and most (87.7%) had updated their will since their committed relationship began. Of those respondents who had wills, respondents with same-sex partners were also more likely to designate their partner as a beneficiary in their will. Over 90% of respondents with same-sex partners (77 respondents) included their partner as an heir; 40% of respondents with opposite-sex partners (4 respondents) did so.

The rate of testacy among opposite-sex partners appears to be similar to that found for the general population in previous studies. The proportion of intestate decedents has varied across studies, with estimates ranging from 21% to 46%.[128] In previous telephone surveys, 46% to 49% of respondents had wills at the time of the interview.[129] However, the rate of testacy among same-sex couples in this sample appears to exceed even the highest estimates from the general population.

Interviewers also asked respondents a series of questions designed to test respondents' knowledge of common-law marriage and intestacy laws. The interviewers asked respondents with opposite-sex partners whether common-law marriages were recognized in their jurisdiction (Minnesota)

---

127. Four additional provisions were mentioned by one respondent each: living will provisions, making the partner responsible for funeral arrangements, forgiving business partnership debts, and requiring notice to terminate the agreement.

128. Olin L. Browder, Jr., *Recent Patterns of Testate Succession in the United States and England*, 67 MICH. L. REV. 1303, 1306 (1969); Contemporary Studies Project, *A Comparison of Iowans' Dispositive Preferences with Selected Provisions of the Iowa and Uniform Probate Codes*, 63 IOWA L. REV. 1041, 1070-76 (1978); Allison Dunham, *The Method, Process and Frequency of Wealth Transmission at Death*, 30 U. CHI. L. REV. 241, 246-47 (1963); John R. Price, *The Transmission of Wealth at Death in a Community Property Jurisdiction*, 50 WASH. L. REV. 277, 297 (1975).

129. Contemporary Studies Project, *supra* note 129, at 1070; Rita J. Simon et al., *Public Versus Statutory Choice of Heirs: A Study of Public Attitudes About Property Distribution at Death*, 58 SOC. FORCES 1263, 1264 (1980).

and whether they believed they were in a common-law marriage. Although common-law marriages are not legally recognized in the jurisdiction, over two-thirds of the respondents did not know this—30% (9 respondents) indicated that they believed that common-law marriages were recognized and 36.7% (11 respondents) indicated that they did not know. However, only one person who believed common-law marriages were possible, mistakenly believed she was currently in one. Thus, it is unlikely that these respondents were relying on common-law marriage to define their respective property rights.

Respondents were also asked whether they knew who would inherit their property if they died without a will. The majority of respondents in each sample indicated that they knew who would inherit their property.[130] Many of these respondents, however, mistakenly believed that their partner would be among their heirs.[131] In a similar study based on interviews of married persons, only 44.6% of respondents who thought they knew who would inherit their property if they died without a will were correct or nearly so.[132]

Respondents with wills were less likely to mistakenly believe that their partner would inherit their property if they died intestate. For the total sample, 34 of 73 persons without wills (47%) and 17 of 89 persons with wills (19%) mistakenly thought their partner would inherit their estate under the laws of intestate succession.[133] Limiting the comparison to only those respondents who claimed to "know" who would inherit their estate, 34 of 52 persons without wills (65%) and 17 of 65 persons with wills (26%) thought their partner would inherit their estate.[134] Thus, knowledge of intestacy laws and testacy appear to coincide. Accordingly, many people in unmarried committed partnerships without wills may not recognize the need under existing laws to specifically designate their partner as the beneficiary of their property if they so desire.

---

130. 60% of respondents with opposite-sex partners (18 respondents) responded that they knew who would inherit their property; 72.8% of respondents with same-sex partners (99 respondents) similarly responded.

131. 33.3% of respondents with opposite-sex partners (6 respondents) and 45.5% of respondents with same-sex partners (45 respondents) mistakenly believed that their partner would be among their heirs. This provides a minimum indication of error in respondents' knowledge of intestacy laws. Aside from naming their partner, respondents gave other incorrect answers of various kinds.

132. Mary Louise Fellows et al., *Public Attitudes About Property Distribution at Death and Intestate Succession Laws in the United States*, 1978 AM. B. FOUND. RES. J. 319, 340.

133. $\chi^2(1)=18.08$, p<.001.

134. $\chi^2(1)=14.03$, p<.001.

As shown in Table 3, several demographic and relationship characteristics are related to whether or not the respondent included the partner as
an heir in his or her will. Again, only the significant effects are presented.
Women in the sample were significantly more likely than men to include
their partners as heirs in their wills. In fact, all but two women who had
wills named their partners as beneficiaries. Respondents with higher levels of education were also more likely to include their partners in their
wills. With respect to relationship characteristics, having held a commitment ceremony or exchanged a symbol of the relationship (for example,
rings) was strongly related to including the partner as a beneficiary. Current financial ties between the partners also predicted the content of their
wills. Respondents in relationships in which they made joint charitable
gifts, were financially interdependent, jointly owned a motor vehicle, or
jointly owned a home were more likely to name their partners as beneficiaries. Finally, respondents who had been in their relationships for five
or more years were more likely to have included their partners in their
wills.[135]

3. Life Insurance

One widely used estate planning device is life insurance. An insured
who names his or her committed partner as the beneficiary of his or her
life insurance policy can accomplish a transfer of wealth to the partner at
the death of the insured.[136] Respondents were asked whether they had life
insurance and whether their partners were named as beneficiaries of those
policies. Over three-quarters of the respondents had life insurance policies.[137] In addition, respondents with same-sex partners were considerably
more likely to include their partner as a beneficiary.[138]

Only one demographic characteristic of respondents was significantly
related to whether those with life insurance named their partner as a ben-

---

135. A number of demographic and relationship characteristics were not significantly
related to whether or not the partner was named as a beneficiary and are thus not presented in Table 3. Estate size, income, age, joint ownership of a pet, and having a child in the
household were not associated with naming the partner as a beneficiary in a will.

136. Chase, *supra* note 40, at 388. In most instances, one partner cannot buy life
insurance on the life of his or her partner. An alternative is for each partner to buy a life
insurance policy on his or her own life and to name the other partner as the beneficiary.
Seff, *supra* note 21, at 157.

137. 76.7% of respondents with opposite-sex partners (23 respondents) and 78.5% of
respondents with same-sex partners (106 respondents) had life insurance policies.

138. Of those with life insurance policies, 43.5% of respondents with opposite-sex
partners (10 respondents) and 88.7% of respondents with same-sex partners (94 respondents) designated their partner as a beneficiary.

eficiary.[139] Among respondents with opposite-sex partners, those with at least a college degree were much more likely to have included their partner as a beneficiary. In addition, several characteristics of the relationship were significantly related to whether the partner was named as a beneficiary. Financial interdependence, making joint charitable gifts, and joint ownership of a home were significant predictors of whether the partner was named as a beneficiary among respondents with opposite-sex partners. For respondents with same-sex partners, having held a commitment ceremony or exchanged a symbol of the relationship and joint ownership of a motor vehicle each had a significant positive relationship with whether the partner was named as a beneficiary.[140]

4. Health Care Decision-Making

Respondents were asked to indicate whether they had named their partner as a surrogate health care decision maker.[141] Designating a partner as one's health care decision maker was much more common among respondents with same-sex partners than among respondents with opposite-sex partners.[142] Because respondents were only asked whether they had named their partner as their health care decision maker, this does not reflect the total number of people who had made arrangements for a health care decision maker.

Among respondents with opposite-sex partners, women were much more likely to have named their partners as their surrogate health care decision makers.[143] The only other demographic characteristic that significantly predicted whether the partner was named as a health care decision maker was income, and again, this was only for respondents with opposite-sex partners and the data did not show a clear linear trend. However, a number of relationship characteristics predicted whether the partner was named as a health care decision maker. For respondents with opposite-sex partners, those who made joint charitable gifts were substantially more likely to have made this arrangement. Financial interdependence, joint ownership of a motor vehicle, and joint ownership of a home were also moderately associated with naming the partner as health care deci-

---

139. *See* Table 4.

140. The duration of the relationship, having a child in the household, and joint ownership of a pet did not have significant effects for either group.

141. It should be noted that respondents were not asked whether they had named someone other than their partner as their surrogate health care decision maker.

142. 26.7% of respondents with opposite-sex partners (8 respondents) and 71.1% of respondents with same-sex partners (96 respondents) designated their partner as their surrogate health care decision maker.

143. *See* Table 5.

sion maker but did not achieve statistical significance. For respondents with same-sex partners, owning a pet together, making joint charitable gifts, financial interdependence, and joint ownership of a motor vehicle or a home significantly predicted naming a partner as a surrogate health care decision maker. Long term relationships (five or more years) were also significantly predictive of whether the partner was named as a health care decision maker.[144]

5. Legal Registration

A number of the respondents in same-sex relationships lived in a municipality that allows domestic partner registration (Minneapolis). Approximately one-third (36.3%; 29 respondents) of those who were eligible to register their partnership had done so.

None of the demographic characteristics significantly predicted domestic partner registration. However, several characteristics of respondents' relationships were important predictors.[145] Respondents who had held a commitment ceremony or had exchanged a symbol of their relationship were twice as likely to have registered their partnership with the city. It is likely that many of these couples held their ceremony in conjunction with domestic partnership registration. Joint ownership of a home, a motor vehicle, and a pet were each significant predictors of domestic partner registration. Both the duration of the relationship and financial interdependence were moderately associated with registering the partnership, but neither achieved statistical significance.[146]

6. Association Among Legal Options

It is possible that once an unmarried committed couple has made contact with the legal system in relation to executing any one of these legal instruments (for example, a will), they are more likely to also use other legal instruments to order their affairs. This could be because they have made contact with a legal professional who can counsel them about additional measures that can be taken to prevent future legal difficulties or because they have independently decided to take advantage of multiple opportunities for planning. Combining the information gathered on each of the legal options described above, it is possible to determine the extent to which respondents with any one of these options have also taken advantage of the other options. This may provide a rough indication of the extent

---

144. The effects of having held a commitment ceremony, exchanging a symbol of the relationship, and having a child live in the household were not significant for either group.

145. See Table 6.

146. The effects of having a child in the household and of making joint charitable gifts were not significantly associated with registration.

to which preventive law is already actively being practiced and of the degree to which there is room for improvement.

The use of each legal instrument was significantly related to the use of the other instruments.[147] For example, respondents who had executed wills were more likely to also have made use of other planning documents, such as written agreements, than were respondents who had not executed wills. Of the instruments examined in this study, three are more likely to involve some contact with an attorney: wills, cohabitation agreements, and health care decision maker designations. Over one-half (51.5%; 17 respondents) of respondents with opposite-sex partners and 79.4% of respondents with same-sex partners (108 respondents) had executed at least one of these.

V. Discussion

Unmarried committed partners invariably encounter a myriad of inter-related legal and psychological issues as they weave their way through the intricacies of their intimate relationships and intertwined emotional and financial lives. Particularly because they must navigate a system that generally does not offer legal recognition of their relationships, long-term planning for such couples is at once increasingly necessary and fraught with pitfalls. The situations nonmarital partners face both during and after the relationship are clearly of both psychological and legal importance. Each of these situations can be addressed in a therapeutic manner as an attorney engaged in the practice of preventive law helps the partners to recognize and plan for those issues that are relevant to their circumstances.

Chase notes that a well-planned nonmarital relationship ought to include plans for how to handle the cohabitation, the couple's finances and property ownership (including insurance and pensions), the parties' parenting roles, medical emergencies and periods of incapacity, and the eventual termination of the relationship either through dissolution or death.[148] Working through each of these issues allows the partners to clarify their expectations about the relationship and to communicate those expectations to each other.[149] Identifying and solving problems before they arise can provide a guide for future interactions, reduce the anxiety and anger that may

---

147. p<.05. There was one general exception: domestic registration was not significantly related to any of the other options, most likely because fewer respondents were eligible to exercise this legal option.

148. Chase, *supra* note 40, at 373.

149. WEITZMAN, *supra* note 42, at 232-33.

arise if the issues are not addressed, and increase the predictability and stability of the relationship itself.[150]

In particular, planning for the termination of the relationship, either as a result of the death of one partner or the dissolution of the relationship, is important. The termination of a committed relationship is inevitably emotionally difficult whether the couple is married or cohabiting. A study of gay and lesbian couples who separated found that, similar to opposite-sex couples, the parties experienced strong emotional responses to the break-up.[151] These emotions including loneliness, relief from conflict, and personal growth.[152] Partners also experienced happiness, confusion, independence, anger, guilt, helplessness, and nervousness.[153] Respondents who had been in long-term relationships and who had been in relationships in which the parties pooled their finances had more difficult periods of psychological adjustment.[154] This is likely due to the greater emotional investment in longer-term relationships and to the difficulties inherent in sorting out finances following a separation. Pooling finances may be one indication of the commitment to the relationship. One study of gay and lesbian couples found that couples who did not pool their finances were more likely to separate than were couples who did pool their finances.[155] Thus, ending a relationship in which the parties' finances have been intertwined may be more difficult, not only because of the financial decisions that must be made, but also because the relationship was more deeply committed at one time. In addition, one of the most common problems encountered by partners who separated was financial stress.[156]

Not only is the end of a committed relationship fraught with psychological, financial, and potential legal issues, but in the absence of a legal marriage, there is no clear procedure that provides a formal end to the relationship. Formal legal procedures are provided to structure the dissolution of a marriage, and while still difficult for the parties, the rules are at least

---

150. *Id.* at 232-37.

151. Lawrence A. Kurdek, *The Dissolution of Gay and Lesbian Couples*, 8 J. Soc. & Pers. Rel. 265, 273, 275 (1991). *See also* Lesbians and Gays in Couples and Families: A Handbook for Therapists (Joan Laird & Robert-Jay Green eds., 1996).

152. Kurdek, *supra* note 154, at 273.

153. *Id.* at 271.

154. Letitia Anne Peplau et al., *Gay and Lesbian Relationships, in* The Lives of Lesbians, Gays, and Bisexuals: Children to Adults 250, 264 (Ritch C. Savin-Williams & Kenneth M. Cohen eds., 1996) (citing Kurdek, *supra* note 154).

155. *Id.* at 263 (citing P. Blumstein & P. Schwartz, American Couples: Money, Work, Sex (1983)).

156. Kurdek, *supra* note 154, at 273.

somewhat defined. In contrast, nonmarital partners do not have clear boundaries to guide them legally or emotionally. As described above, the property rights of unmarried partners upon the termination of the relationship are unclear and piecemeal.[157] Moreover, because there is no formal or legal end to the relationship, such as a divorce decree, the parties may not experience a clear psychological end to the relationship. One commentator noted:

> Because gay people cannot be legally married anywhere in the United States, there is, for starters, no access to divorce court.
>
> As a result, every gay settlement is different, a cobbled agreement that can involve some combination of negotiation or mediation in court.
>
> "I used to say, 'Why do we want to get married? It doesn't work for straight people,'" said [an attorney] who specializes in gay and lesbian issues. "But now I say we should care: They have the privilege of divorce and we don't. We're left out there to twirl around in pain."[158]

Similarly, termination of the relationship due to the death of one partner is an emotional time for the surviving partner and for the rest of the decedent's family. Conflict over issues of health care decision making prior to the death and inheritance rights and funeral arrangements following the death only compound the partner's and the family's suffering.

A practitioner operating from a TJ-preventive law perspective can provide services to unmarried couples that, although not eliminating the psychological distress inherent in these situations, can reduce the anti-therapeutic effects of many of these possible outcomes. Indeed, some of the actions that can be encouraged and facilitated by the lawyer, such as clarifying and embodying expectations in a formal agreement, can be therapeutic for the couple and help to prevent future conflict. Helping the partners to recognize and make decisions regarding their relative rights to and obligations for their individual and separate property, income, assets, and debts during and after the relationship may assist the couple in communicating about, planning for, and ultimately avoiding future problems.

Clearly, there are opportunities for TJ-preventive law to operate in this context. Only 29% of unmarried committed partners in the present study had written agreements regarding their property. The majority of respondents (52%) had not even considered the utility of having an agreement with their partner. This is consistent with what attorneys see in practice. One family law specialist noted: "I see very bright educated people who entered into their relationship with only very vague ideas about the rights accrued when and if the relationship ends. . . . They're stunned when they find they

---

157. *See supra* notes 21-41 and accompanying text.
158. Johnson, *supra* note 82, at A20.

can't walk into divorce court like any other citizen."[159] An attorney acting in a TJ-preventive lawyering role can educate clients about their rights and responsibilities in the relationship and about what legal protections they do and do not have. Further, the attorney can suggest the possibility of formalizing an agreement.

Twenty percent of the respondents in the present study had considered whether to have a written agreement and decided against it. Although some of these partners may have fully considered this option and made a decision not to execute an agreement, others gave reasons such as procrastination or that they were not planning to end the relationship. Practitioners can encourage the client not to delay drafting an agreement and can explain the benefits of a written agreement, even for couples who are committed to a long-term relationship. Moreover, even among those who did have written property agreements, almost one-half (48%) did not have provisions for property division at the end of the relationship and more than one half (64.6%) did not have provisions for maintenance and support. Again, most couples do not expect the relationship to end, but a sensitive practitioner concerned about the overall well-being of the clients can articulate both the benefits of including such provisions in an agreement and the lack of protection that can occur in the absence of such provisions.[160]

Assisting the couple to draft wills and take advantage of other estate planning techniques, though forcing the couple to confront their own mortality, helps to ensure that their testamentary preferences are known and effectuated. Clearly stated preferences can help to reduce conflict upon the death of one of the partners, particularly potential conflict between the surviving partner and the decedent's family. A practitioner operating from a TJ-preventive law perspective can help clients avoid potential disputes over estate distribution, funeral arrangements, and other decisions surrounding the death. Minimizing conflict at the time of death will ultimately be therapeutic for the surviving partner and both partners may secure peace of mind knowing that they have taken steps to prevent such discord. Many respondents did not have wills and many of those who were testate had not updated their wills to reflect their committed relationships. As with other written agreements, previous studies have found that "laziness" is the reason most people do not execute wills.[161] Effective practi-

---

159. *Id.*

160. *See* WEITZMAN, *supra* note 42, at 241 ("[T]he positive advantages of open and honest communication facilitated by precontract negotiations would seem to more than offset the temporary jolt that comes from anticipating a grim possibility.").

161. Rita J. Simon et al., *Public Opinion About Property Distribution at Death*, 5 MARRIAGE & FAM. REV. 25, 27 (1982).

tioners might be able to encourage their clients, particularly those in unmarried committed relationships, to execute wills and to do so in a timely fashion.

Similarly, discussing the naming of a surrogate health care decisionmaker by executing a durable power of attorney for health care is an important service that practitioners can provide to clients in committed relationships. As described above, partners, not automatically considered as surrogate decision makers under most state statutes, have been excluded from health care decisions regarding their partners and have been denied the right to visit their partners.[162] The practitioner can suggest the benefits of naming a health care decision maker and can use the durable power of attorney for health care to designate a substitute decision maker. One study of gay men with AIDS found that making arrangements for advance directives gave the men a sense of accomplishment and control and that thinking about advance directives did not cause them to lose all hope.[163] Thus, raising the issue of planning for death was not anti-therapeutic for this sample and the act of taking control had therapeutic effects.

In serving clients who are in unmarried committed relationships, the attorney must be aware of the potential for conflicts of interest between the partners and should discuss these potential conflicts with the clients.[164] For example, if a wide disparity exists in the financial assets brought by the partners to the relationship, the legal interest in protecting the financial assets of the wealthier partner may conflict with the legal interest of securing support for the less financially secure partner. Further, if one partner

---

162. *See supra* notes 64-81 and accompanying text.

163. Jill Littrell et al., *Negotiating Advance Directives for Persons with AIDS*, 23 Soc. Work Health Care 43, 47-48, 55 (1996).

164. Rule 1.7 of the Model Rules of Professional Conduct provides:

(a) A lawyer shall not represent a client if the representation of that client will be directly adverse to another client, unless:

(1) the lawyer reasonably believes the representation will not adversely affect the relationship with the other client; and

(2) each client consents after consultation.

(b) A lawyer shall not represent a client if the representation of that client may be materially limited by the lawyer's responsibilities to another client or to a third person, or by the lawyer's own interests, unless:

(1) the lawyer reasonably believes the representation will not be adversely affected; and

(2) the client consents after consultation. When representation of multiple clients in a single matter is undertaken, the consultation shall include explanation of the implications of the common representation and the advantages and risks involved.

Model Rules of Professional Conduct Rule 1.7 (1995).

has greater resources (education, financial assets, etc.) than the other, that partner may have greater bargaining power.[165] Similarly, when considering the therapeutic and anti-therapeutic consequences of a particular course of legal action, the attorney and the couple must consider *for whom* the result is therapeutic or anti-therapeutic.[166] The legal and therapeutic interests of the two individuals and of the couple may not always coincide. Thus, attention should be paid to both the legal and therapeutic interests of each partner and of the partnership, particularly when there is inequity in the power held by the partners in the relationship.[167] Coinciding and divergent interests should be considered when selecting and using any of the preventive law instruments discussed here.

The preventive law technique of engaging in annual legal check-ups can be effective in relation to each of the potential estate planning tools.[168] A legal check-up provides the attorney an opportunity to update the clients about developments in the law and provides the clients with an opportunity to update the attorney about changes that have taken place in their lives. For example, the attorney could alert the couple if the possibility for legal registration as domestic partners became available. Two respondents in the instant study indicated that they had considered entering into a written property agreement but that they had not been in the relationship long enough. A lawyer could discuss the possibility of executing an agreement with the clients and, if they decide to wait until the relationship is sufficiently developed, could consult with the clients at a later date to formalize an agreement.

Similarly, a large number of respondents had not updated their wills since their relationships began. Unfortunately, the data do not indicate

---

165. Peplau, *supra* note 157, at 255-56. Indeed, some suggest that each partner should be represented by independent counsel. *See, e.g.*, Mike McCurley, *Same-Sex Cohabitation Agreements*, in PREMARITAL AND MARITAL CONTRACTS: A LAWYER'S GUIDE TO DRAFTING AND NEGOTIATING ENFORCEABLE MARITAL AND COHABITATION AGREEMENTS 195, 207 (Edward A. Winer & Lewis Becker eds., 1993).

166. David B. Wexler, *Reflection on the Scope of Therapeutic Jurisprudence*, in LAW IN A THERAPEUTIC KEY: DEVELOPMENTS IN THERAPEUTIC JURISPRUDENCE, *supra* note 95, at 815-16 (noting that there may be "a clash whereby a legal rule is therapeutic for one person or participant and anti-therapeutic for another").

167. *See generally* Elizabeth Kingdom, *Cohabitation Contracts and Equality*, 18 INT'L J. SOC. L. 287 (1990) [hereinafter Kingdom, *Cohabitation Contracts and Equality*]; Elizabeth Kingdom, *Cohabitation Contracts: A Socialist-Feminist Issue*, 15 J. L. & SOC'Y 77 (1988).

168. Stolle notes that this type of ongoing consultation with existing clients does not constitute an improper solicitation of business. Stolle, *supra* note 76. *See also* Louis M. Brown, *The Scheme: Maximize Opportunities, Minimize Future Legal Trouble*, 6 PREVENTIVE L. REP. 17, 19 (1987).

whether these respondents had considered updating their wills and chosen not to or had not entertained the possibility of an update. Nonetheless, the fact that substantial numbers of opposite-sex partners and some same-sex partners had not updated their wills since they began their relationships suggests that a lawyer operating from a TJ-preventive law perspective could help the clients respond effectively to life changes. The lawyer can ensure that the client is aware of the effects of including the partner in his or her will and can help the client effectuate his or her testamentary preferences, whether or not those preferences include the partner as a beneficiary. The data do not indicate how many of the respondents had updated their designation of a health care decision-maker but presumably some had not. Thus, as with wills, the lawyer can help clients ensure that their wishes regarding the participation of their partners in their health care are expressed and followed.

In order for a TJ-preventive law approach to be successful in the estate planning context, as well as in other areas, the practitioner must have some kind of contact with the client. That is, before a lawyer can make use of the preventive law tools of client intake, client counseling, and the legal checkup, the client and the lawyer must have some initial professional interaction. Many of the respondents in the present study likely had made some contact with an attorney. Of respondents with opposite-sex partners, one-third had wills and 26.7% had named their partner as their health care decision-maker. Of respondents with same-sex partners, 60% had wills and 71.1% had named their partner as their health care decision-maker. Overall, 29% of respondents had written property agreements. Over one-half of each group[169] had executed at least one of these three instruments. However, while having any one of the instruments made it more likely that the respondent also had another, only 18.3% of the sample reported having all three. Thus, even those committed partners who have made contact with the legal system and have begun to engage in long-term planning may not have comprehensive protection. The practice of TJ-preventive law can help to fill these gaps using client counseling to appraise the full range of the partners' planning needs. Accordingly, the practitioner can introduce a couple who came into the office for wills to the possible range of other planning tools, such as written agreements and durable powers of attorney for health care.

It appears that persons in same-sex committed relationships are more likely to have made contact with the system than are those in opposite-sex committed relationships. Same-sex respondents were more likely to have wills, to have updated those wills, and to have designated their part-

---

169. 51.4% of respondents with opposite-sex partners and 79.4% of respondents with same-sex partners had executed at least one of the above instruments.

ners as their substitute decision-makers than were opposite-sex respondents. Several possible reasons for these differences exist. First, opposite-sex nonmarital partners have the option of marrying. Some may have rejected the institution of marriage, while others may not feel that their relationship has risen to the level of commitment required for marriage. In contrast, same-sex partners cannot be joined by a legally recognized marriage. Thus, it is possible that greater numbers of same-sex couples are in "marriage-like" committed relationships than are opposite-sex couples. Second, a great deal of political activism and education have surrounded the issues of gay marriage and gay rights in general.[170] Thus, same-sex partners may be more aware of the lack of legal protections for nonmarital partners and the resulting necessity for private arrangements.

However, it is likely that some percentage of both groups have not made contact with an attorney or with the legal system in relation to their committed relationships. Some of these may consult an attorney for assistance in matters not ostensibly related to their relationship, such as the purchase of a home or other property. The lawyer can then use client intake and interviewing techniques to ascertain whether to suggest the exploration of estate planning issues. Other individuals may not have occasion to have any direct contact with the legal system. Lawyers should, therefore, engage in general community education activities related to these issues.

In particular, the results of the present study indicate that people who are younger, less educated, and with smaller estates are less likely to have cohabitation contracts with their partners. Therefore, education activities specifically targeted at these groups might be particularly effective. Because younger people and those with smaller estates are also less likely to have wills,[171] efforts to educate these groups about the importance of long-term financial and health care planning are likely to provide benefits to a wide range of people, in addition to those who are in committed partnerships. Moreover, the results of the current study indicate that a substantial number of persons in nonmarital committed relationships hold mistaken beliefs about common-law marriage and about who would inherit their property if they died intestate. Importantly, those without wills were most likely to hold these mistaken beliefs. Helping to educate nonmarital couples about their rights and the need for careful planning could become an important extension of the practice of TJ-preventive law.

---

170. *See, e.g.*, CURRY ET AL., *supra* note 77; LAMBDA LEGAL DEFENSE AND EDUCATION FUND, INC., AIDS LEGAL GUIDE (Abby R. Rubenfeld ed., 2d ed. 1987); MARK S. SENAK, HIV, AIDS, AND THE LAW: A GUIDE TO OUR RIGHTS AND CHALLENGES (1996); Paula L. Ettelbrick, *Legal Issues in Health Care for Lesbians and Gay Men*, 5 J. GAY & LESBIAN SOC. SERV. 93 (1996).

171. Johnson & Robbennolt, *supra* note 118, at 484.

We have applied the perspective of TJ-preventive law to the issues involved in the long-term planning and protection of unmarried committed partners. Consistent with this perspective, we have attempted to demonstrate the differences in the way the law treats married and unmarried partners as well as the ways in which the conscientious practice of TJ-preventive law can maximize the therapeutic potential of estate planning and minimize the possibility for future conflict between the partners and with third-parties. However, this approach should be used in conjunction with efforts aimed at legal reform. Fellows and her colleagues noted that "[a]lthough persons in committed relationships can protect their respective interests under current law through private agreements, the protections fall short of the predictability and enforceability provided to persons who are married."[172] Previous research has demonstrated that even people who are aware of the ramifications of failing to engage in long-term planning are reluctant to consider the issues involved (for instance, death or the break-up of the relationship) or are lazy about taking action.[173] This is one justification for statutory protection for spouses in these areas: to fill the gaps that occur when the parties do not plan sufficiently. Moreover, statutory protections can address issues of power and inequality between the partners that may be stumbling blocks to the sufficient private ordering of affairs.[174]

VI. Conclusion

In recent years, increasing numbers of people are living in unmarried committed partnerships. Whether they live in these relationships because they choose to or because the option of legal marriage is not available to them, differences in the legal treatment of married and unmarried partners make long-term financial and health care planning of the utmost importance. Both during and after the relationship, the financial and health care issues faced by nonmarital partners have important legal and psychological facets. Legal practitioners can assist clients who are in unmarried committed relationships in using the appropriate preventive law tools, such as contracts, wills, and durable powers of attorney, to meet their legal needs and to promote their psychological well-being.

The data presented here suggest that a notable number of people in unmarried committed partnerships have not engaged in beneficial legal planning. Moreover, many of those who have taken some steps toward

---

172. Fellows et al., *supra* note 59, at 18.

173. Chambers, *supra* note 23, at 457; Fellows et al., *supra* note 133, at 339.

174. *See* Kingdom, *Cohabitation Contracts and Equality*, *supra* note 170.

planning for their long-term future, still may not be thoroughly prepared. The perspective of TJ-preventive law suggests that practitioners should educate those who could profit from legal planning about the need for and benefits of estate and health care planning. Moreover, practitioners should use client counseling and legal check-ups to maximize the likelihood that their clients are advised about the most appropriate preventive strategies. Ultimately, the practitioner can use the instruments of preventive law to help persons in unmarried committed relationships navigate the uncertainties in their legal environment and to execute legally effective documents that will maximize the therapeutic potential of long-term planning and minimize the possibility for future conflict and litigation.

Table 1
Significant Predictors of Having a Written Agreement Regarding Property[1]

	All Respondents	Total N
Age		
25-34	13.6	44
35-44	31.0	71
45+	40.0	50
	$\chi^2(2)=8.73^{**}$ / $\gamma=.39$	
Estate Size		
<$50,000	12.1	33
$50,000–100,000	26.5	34
$100,000–200,000	37.2	43
$200,000–400,000	40.0	30
$400,000+	33.3	18
	$\chi^2(4)=8.62^{*}$ / $\gamma=.30$	
Education		
< college degree	12.5	24
college degree	26.1	46
> college degree	34.7	95
	$\chi^2(2)=5.39^{*}$ / $\gamma=.33$	
Ceremony/exchange Symbol		
No	14.9	67
Yes	38.8	98
	$\chi^2(1)=11.63^{****}$ / $\gamma=.57$	
Financial Interdependence		
No	13.6	44
Yes	34.7	121
	$\chi^2(1)=7.68^{***}$ / $\gamma=.54$	
Joint Ownership of Home		
No	17.8	73
Yes	38.5	91
	$\chi^2(1)=8.63^{***}$ / $\gamma=.49$	
Length of Relationship		
0-4 years	19.6	51
5+ years	33.3	114
	$\chi^2(1)=3.37^{*}$ / $\gamma=.34$	
Child in Household		
No	33.1	130
Yes	14.3	35
	$\chi^2(1)=5.24^{**}$ / $\gamma=.50$	

---

* p<.10   ** p<.05   *** p<.01   **** p<.001

---

1. Table 1 is based on 165 written agreements. Information about the respondent's estate size is missing for seven of these agreements, and information about whether the respondent jointly owned a home with his or her partner is missing for one agreement.

Table 2
Summary of Written Agreement Provisions

	% of Agreements	(N)
Total Number of Written Agreements		48
Contains Provisions Regarding the Division of Property if the Relationship Ends	52.1	25
Home	43.9	21
Mutually Owned Property	33.3	16
Separate Property	25.0	12
Pension	8.3	4
Contains Provisions Regarding the Division of Property at One Partner's Death	91.7	44
Home	81.3	39
Mutually Owned Property	39.6	19
Separate Property	41.7	20
Pension	41.7	20
Property Brought to the Relationship is:		
Separate	34.0	16
Mutually Owned	55.3	26
Don't Know	10.6	5
Property Acquired During the Relationship is:		
Separate	6.3	3
Mutually Owned	76.6	36
Don't Know	17.0	8
Property Acquired as Gift or Inheritance is:		
Separate	42.9	6
Mutually Owned	57.1	8
Don't Know	0.0	0
Support and Maintenance During Relationship	25.0	12
Support and Maintenance After Relationship Ends	35.4	17
Support and Maintenance of Children	10.4	5
Support and Maintenance of Other Relative	4.2	2
Other Provisions	31.3	15

Table 3

Significant Predictors of Naming Partner as Beneficiary in Will

RESPONDENTS WHO HAD WILLS (N=91)

	% Naming Partner	Total N
Gender		
Male	77.8	36
Female	96.4	55
	$\chi^2(1)=7.70^{***}$ / $\gamma=.77$	
Education		
< College Degree	66.7	9
College Degree	81.8	22
> College Degree	95.0	60
	$\chi^2(2)=6.88^{**}$ / $\gamma=.65$	
Ceremony/Exchange Symbol		
No	74.2	31
Yes	96.7	60
	$\chi^2(1)=10.08^{***}$ / $\gamma=.82$	
Make Joint Charitable Gifts		
No	76.2	21
Yes	92.9	70
	$\chi^2(1)=3.95^{**}$ / $\gamma=.60$	
Financial Interdependence		
No	70.6	17
Yes	93.2	74
	$\chi^2(1)=5.83^{**}$ / $\gamma=.70$	
Joint Ownership of a Motor Vehicle		
No	79.2	48
Yes	100.0	43
	$\chi^2(1)=13.90^{****}$ / $\gamma=1.00$	
Joint Ownership of Home		
No	73.5	34
Yes	98.2	57
	$\chi^2(1)=13.66^{****}$ / $\gamma=.91$	
Length of Relationship		
0-4 Years	79.2	24
5+ Years	92.5	67
	$\chi^2(1)=2.89$ / $\gamma=.53$	

*p<.10   **p<.05   ***p<.01   ****p<.001

Table 4
Significant Predictors of Having Named Partner as a Beneficiary of Life Insurance[2]

	RESPONDENTS WITH OPPOSITE-SEX PARTNERS		RESPONDENTS WITH SAME-SEX PARTNERS	
	% with life insurance to partner	Total N	% with life insurance to partner	Total N
Education				
< college degree	12.5	8	—	—
college degree	60.0	5	82.1	39
> college degree	60.0	10	92.5	67
	$\chi^2(2)=5.27*$		$\chi^2(1)=2.59$	
	$\gamma=.61$		$\gamma=.46$	
Ceremony/ Exchange Symbol				
No	33.3	15	77.1	35
Yes	62.5	8	94.4	71
	$\chi^2(1)=1.81$		$\chi^2(1)=6.46**$	
	$\gamma=.54$		$\gamma=.6\,6$	
Make Joint Charitable Gifts				
No	18.2	11	85.2	27
Yes	66.7	12	89.9	79
	$\chi^2(1)=5.78**$		$\chi^2(1)=0.42$	
	$\gamma=.80$		$\gamma=.21$	
Financial Interdependence				
No	26.7	15	85.0	20
Yes	75.0	8	89.5	86
	$\chi^2(1)=5.10**$		$\chi^2(1)=0.31$	
	$\gamma=.78$		$\gamma=.20$	
Joint Ownership of Motor Vehicle				
No	42.1	19	82.5	57
Yes	50.0	4	95.9	49
	$\chi^2(1)=0.08$		$\chi^2(1)=5.22**$	
	$\gamma=.16$		$\gamma=.67$	
Joint Ownership of Home				
No	27.8	18	83.3	36
Yes	100.0	4	91.4	70
	$\chi^2(1)=8.50***$		$\chi^2(1)=1.48$	
	$\gamma=1.00$		$\gamma=.36$	

*p<.10   **p<.05   ***p.01   ****p<.001

2. Table 4 is based on the 23 respondents with opposite-sex partners and the 106 respondents with same-sex partners who had life insurance. For one respondent with an opposite-sex partner, information about joint home ownership is missing.

Table 5
Significant Predictors of Having Named Partner as Health Care Decision-Maker[3]

	RESPONDENTS WITH OPPOSITE-SEX PARTNERS		RESPONDENTS WITH SAME-SEX PARTNERS	
	% named partner	Total N	% named partner	Total N
Gender				
Male	7.7	13	65.3	49
Female	41.2	17	78.0	82
	$\chi^2(1)=4.71$**		$\chi^2(1)=2.50$	
	$\gamma=.79$		$\gamma=.31$	
Income				
<$20,000	42.9	7	58.8	17
$20,000-30,000	22.2	9	78.9	19
$30,000-40,000	60.0	5	68.4	38
$40,000-50,000	—		77.3	22
$50,000+	0.0	6	79.4	34
	$\chi^2(3)=6.99$*		$\chi^2(4)=3.30$	
	$\gamma=-.32$		$\gamma=.18$	
Own Pet Together				
No	29.4	17	57.1	35
Yes	23.1	13	79.2	96
	$\chi^2(1)=0.15$		$\chi^2(1)=6.01$**	
	$\gamma=-.16$		$\gamma=.48$	
Make Joint Charitable Gifts				
No	5.9	17	60.0	30
Yes	53.8	13	77.2	101
	$\chi^2(1)=9.24$***		$\chi^2(1)=3.22$*	
	$\gamma=.90$		$\gamma=.39$	
Financial Interdependence				
No	17.6	17	57.7	26
Yes	38.5	13	77.1	105
	$\chi^2(1)=1.63$		$\chi^2(1)=3.76$*	
	$\gamma=.49$		$\gamma=.42$	

	RESPONDENTS WITH OPPOSITE-SEX PARTNERS		RESPONDENTS WITH SAME-SEX PARTNERS	
	% named partner	Total N	% named partner	Total N
Joint Ownership of Motor Vehicle				
No	20.8	24	63.2	76
Yes	50.0	6	87.3	55
	$\chi^2(1)=1.91$		$\chi^2(1)=10.11$***	
	$\gamma=.58$		$\gamma=.60$	
Joint Ownership of Home				
No	21.7	23	64.6	48
Yes	50.0	6	78.3	83
	$\chi^2(1)=1.76$		$\chi^2(1)=2.87$*	
	$\gamma=.57$		$\gamma=.33$	
Length of Relationship				
0-4 years	29.4	17	51.5	33
5+ years	23.1	13	80.6	98
	$\chi^2(1)=0.15$		$\chi^2(1)=9.96$***	
	$\gamma=-.16$		$\gamma=.59$	

*p<.10   **p<.05   ***p<.01   ****p<.001

---

3. Table 5 is based on the 30 respondents with opposite-sex partners and the 131 respondents with same-sex partners who had named their partner as their surrogate health care decision-maker. Information about income is missing for three respondents with opposite-sex partners and for one respondent with a same-sex partner. Information about joint home ownership is missing for one respondent with an opposite-sex partner.

Table 6
Significant Predictors of Domestic Partner Registration

ELIGIBLE RESPONDENTS WITH SAME-SEX PARTNERS (N=83)

	% registered	Total N
Ceremony/Exchange Symbol		
No	20.0	25
Yes	4.14	58
	$\chi^2(1)=3.72^*$	
	$\gamma=.48$	
Own Pet Together		
No	14.3	21
Yes	41.9	62
	$\chi^2(1)=5.86^{**}$	
	$\gamma=.63$	
Joint Ownership of Motor Vehicle		
No	22.2	45
Yes	50.0	38
	$\chi^2(1)=7.06^{***}$	
	$\gamma=.56$	
Joint Ownershiip of Home		
No	20.7	29
Yes	42.6	54
	$\chi^2(1)=4.17^{**}$	
	$\gamma=.48$	

$^*p<.10$ $^{**}p<.05$ $^{***}p<.01$ $^{****}p<.001$

Chapter 6

Preventive Lawyering Strategies to Mitigate the Detrimental Effects of Clients' Divorces on their Children

Kathryn E. Maxwell

I. Introduction

Psychological and sociological research is rife with evidence of the disastrous effects that divorce can have upon the children of divorcing parents. When a client seeks legal assistance in obtaining a divorce, the relationship between the spouses is already none too amicable. Our judicial system then pits the divorcing spouses against each other as adversaries in a battle over property, child custody, visitation, and child support. Given this climate of antagonism and hostility during the divorce process, cooperation for the sake of the children may be all but impossible after the divorce.

Perhaps there is another way: By taking a therapeutically oriented, preventive approach, the divorce lawyer may be able to mitigate the detrimental effects of divorce on children. This article examines what divorce lawyers could and should do to minimize the negative effects of clients' divorces on their children.

The first section of this paper examines the detrimental effects of parents' divorces on their children, and the second section identifies the three principal causes of these detrimental effects. The third section discusses fairly recent changes in the law made to mitigate those effects on children. In the fourth section, the lawyer's role in the divorce process is examined, and, in the fifth section, concrete strategies are proposed that lawyers should or could use in order to minimize the negative effects of divorce on children.

The strategies proposed in this paper are intended to address only the "average" divorce scenario, not situations involving domestic violence and/or child sexual abuse. Though mediation is one of the suggested strategies, where a serious power imbalance exists between divorcing spouses, mediation may merely afford a domineering spouse yet another opportunity to bully and intimidate the oppressed spouse.[1]

---

1. *See, e.g.,* Trina Grillo, *The Mediation Alternative: Process Dangers for Women,* 100

II. The Effects of Divorce On Children

An impressive body of empirical studies shows the detrimental effects that parents' divorces may have on their children, among them, depression, aggression, antisocial and/or self-destructive behavior, and diminished academic performance.

Children of divorced parents suffer more emotional problems than do children of married parents. In her ten-year study of children of divorce, Judith Wallerstein noted "moderate to severe depression in over one-third of the entire original sample of the five-year mark," including the preschool children.[2] Another study found that children from divorced homes are less self-confident than children of married parents. The researchers found that "recent divorce appears to be related to adolescent self-perceived competence."[3]

Children from single-parent households do not perform as well academically as do children from two-parent households. Children who reside with both biological parents are only half as likely to have repeated a grade in school as are children who live in one-parent families.[4] As a rule, the longer a child has lived in a single-parent family, "the greater the reduction in educational attainment."[5] A recent review of the available research on the academic performance of children of divorce concluded that children of divorce "receive lower scores on standardized tests and lower school grades" than children from non-divorced families.[6] Stevenson and Black noted that children whose parents are divorced "complete fewer years of schooling than offspring from non-divorced families."[7]

YALE L.J. 1545 (1991); Penelope E. Bryan, *Killing Us Softly: Divorce Mediation and the Politics of Power*, 40 BUFF. L.REV. 441 (1992).

2. Wallerstein found this result especially troubling "since all of the children in the study had been drawn from a nonclinical population and were youngsters who, prior to the marital rupture, had not been identified as needing psychological help by either their mothers or their teachers." Judith Wallerstein, *Children of Divorce: Preliminary Report of a Ten-Year Follow-Up of Young Children, in* READINGS IN FAMILY LAW 77, 78(Frederica K. Lombard ed., 1990).

3. Rex Forehand et al., *Divorce and Marital Conflict: Relationship to Adolescent Competence and Adjustment in Early Adolescence, in* IMPACT OF DIVORCE, SINGLE PARENTING, AND STEPPARENTING ON CHILDREN 155, 164 (E. Mavis Hetherington and Josephine D. Arasteh eds., 1988).

4. Nicholas Davidson, *Life Without Father: America's Greatest Social Catastrophe*, 51 POL'Y REV. 40, 41-42 (1990).

5. Sheila Fitzgerald Krein & Andrea H. Beller, *Educational Attainment of Children From Single-Parent Families: Differences by Exposure, Gender, and Race*, 25 DEMOGRAPHY 221, 228 (1988).

6. MICHAEL R. STEVENSON & KATHRYN N. BLACK, HOW DIVORCE AFFECTS OFFSPRING 72 (Michael Lange ed., 1995).

Furthermore, children of divorce are at increased risk of antisocial and self-destructive behavior, such as drug abuse and promiscuity.[8] Children, especially boys, of divorced parents are more prone to exhibit aggressive behavior.[9] Studies have linked the absence of fathers following divorce to an increased risk of adolescent drug use and to adolescent crime, particularly in boys.[10] An analysis of current research found children of divorce "more likely than offspring of non-divorced families to use controlled substances...."[11] Stevenson and Black's review of existing studies concluded that children in one-parent families "are more likely to misbehave or be delinquent than offspring in two-parent families."[12] The same review of available research found that children of divorce "become involved in sexual relationships earlier than offspring in non-divorced families."[13]

✗ Researchers have looked beyond the broad generalization that divorce is detrimental to children and have attempted to isolate specific elements present during divorce that cause the negative effects on children.[14]

III. The Primary Causes of the Adverse Effects on Children

Researchers have identified three factors as the most important predictors of negative effects on children of divorce: instability in the child's life,

---

7. *Id.* at 72.

8. Stevenson and Black concluded that following divorce, "there is a greater likelihood that offspring will exhibit some acting out behaviors that will be disturbing to those around them and in some instances potentially harmful to the child. This includes an increase in physical aggression toward others, running away from home, and substance abuse." *Id.* at 111.

9. "Children who had positive relationships with both parents, in comparison with children who had a negative relationship with one or both parents, had lower ratings on stress and aggression and higher ratings on work effectiveness and social relations with peers." W. Glenn Clingempeel & N. Dickon Reppucci, *Joint Custody After Divorce: Major Issues and Goals for Research, in* READINGS IN FAMILY LAW, *supra* note 2, at 163.

10. STEVENSON & BLACK, *supra* note 6, at 101-02.

11. *Id.* at 112.

12. The researchers went on to note that "the difference is small and is not likely to be the result of the divorce per se....Delinquent behavior is more likely the result of economic hardship, parental pathology, or conflict than of parental divorce." *Id.*

13. *Id.* at 99.

14. Stevenson and Black concluded that "for externalizing and internalizing problems, divorce per se does not necessarily produce long-term problems. However, it is clear that the population of divorcing adults and divorcing families may well be at risk because of other variables that often accompany divorce." *Id.* at 118.

interparental conflict, and an absence, at least temporarily, of effective parenting.[15]

A. Instability

The financial decline resulting from divorce often precipitates a chain of events that undermine stability in many aspects of the child's life.[16] The financial decline associated with most divorces often forces the custodial parent to move the child out of the family home, away from friends and

---

15. Wallerstein summarizes the causes of adverse effects on children of divorce as follows: "The lasting danger lies in the disrupted parenting that so often follows in the wake of marital breakdown, in the parental conflicts that can remain and become chronic within the postdivorce family, in the flawed or tragic role models provided by parents who fail over many years to reconstitute or stabilize their lives, in the overall diminished quality of life, the economic deprivation, and the curtailed educational and social opportunities for the children that represent the legacy of divorce in so many postdivorce families." Judith S. Wallerstein et al., *Children of Divorce: A 10-Year Study, in* IMPACT OF DIVORCE, SINGLE PARENTING, AND STEPPARENTING ON CHILDREN, *supra* note 3, at 212. Robert Emery states: "The quality of ongoing family relationships is a key predictor of more or less adequate adjustment to divorce among children. Parental conflict throughout the divorce transition is a consistent predictor of maladjustment among children, as is the less adequate parenting that characterizes most divorces, at least temporarily. Economic problems strain all members of the divorced family system..." ROBERT E. EMERY, RENEGOTIATING FAMILY RELATIONSHIPS 217 (1994). Stevenson and Black conclude that "[differences between offspring of divorced and those of non-divorced parents may be attributed to parental discord and poor relationships with the parents rather than to divorce." STEVENSON & BLACK, *supra* note 6, at 99.

16. Lenore Weitzman states: "The statistics suggest that we are sentencing a significant proportion of the current generation of American children to lives of financial impoverishment." Lenore Weitzman, *The Divorce Revolution: The Unexpected Social and Economic Consequences for Women and Children, in* READINGS IN FAMILY LAW, *supra* note 2, at 90."Decreased income can cause mother-only families to live in economically and socially isolated neighborhoods, which lowers opportunities for economic mobility and raises the likelihood of children dropping out of school and of offspring becoming teen parents. These neighborhoods also provide fewer safe places for children to play." STEVENSON & BLACK, *supra* note 6, at 130. Emery writes that "declining living standards can set into motion a series of changes that tax children's coping resources. Important life changes include moving from the family home, changing schools, losing contact with old friends, spending more time in child care settings while their mother is working, and dealing with their parents' preoccupation with and conflict over financial matters." EMERY, *supra* note 15, at 214.

neighbors, and into a different school district. Frequently, the divorced mother must increase her working hours, and, consequently, the child spends more time in a daycare setting. Thus, economic decline not only takes a serious financial toll on the child, but also robs the child of the support network necessary to cope with the emotional fallout of the divorce. Weitzman was not surprised to find "a strong relationship between the economic and psychological effects of divorce on children."[17]

B. Interparental Conflict

Interparental conflict, especially in front of the child, is detrimental to the child, whether the parents remain married or are divorced.[18] Researchers characterize parental conflict as strongly associated with the post-divorce adjustment of children.[19] Further research shows that the occurrence of parental conflict in the presence of the child "is associated with the most detrimental effects on children."[20] Mnookin found that teenagers who felt they were caught in the middle of parental conflict "showed more symptoms of maladjustment (for example, depression, deviant behavior) than those who did not."[21] Another study concluded that the extent to which parents can cooperate after the divorce and the manner in which they resolve their conflicts with each other affect the child's post-divorce adjustment.[22] Specifically, "the father's use of verbal attack predicted children's behavioral problems and aggressiveness."[23]

---

17. WEITZMAN, *supra* note 16, at 92.

18. "Ongoing high conflict in intact or divorced homes produces lowered self-esteem, greater anxiety, and less feelings of control." Elisa J. Slater & Joel D. Haber, *Adolescent Adjustment Following Divorce as a Function of Familial Conflict,* 52 J. CONSULTING AND CLINICAL PSYCHOL. 920 (1984). Emery stated that "conflict in the co-parental relationship consistently has been found to be associated with an increase in child behavior problems." Robert E. Emery, *Interparental Conflict and the Children of Discord and Divorce,* 92 PSYCHOL. BULL. 310 (1982). Family conflict contributes to many problems in social development and cognitive skills, and these effects continue long after the divorce is finalized. Lawrence A. Kurdek, *An Integrative Perspective on Children's Divorce Adjustment,* 36 AM. PSYCHOL. 856 (1981).

19. DESMOND ELLIS & NOREEN STUCKLESS, MEDIATING AND NEGOTIATING MARITAL CONFLICTS 137 (1996).

20. Forehand, *supra* note 3, at 156.

21. ELEANOR E. MACCOBY & ROBERT H. MNOOKIN, DIVIDING THE CHILD 248 (1992).

22. "The degree of interparental cooperation in the postdivorce period, as well as the conflict resolution styles used by each spouse to regulate disagreements, appear to be

Studies also reveal a correlation between interparental conflict and a decline, over time, in visitation with the non-custodial parent.[24] This drop off in visitation not only can leave the child feeling abandoned,[25] but is also associated with reduced compliance with child support awards.[26] Thus, inter-parental conflict can directly affect the child's emotional well-being and indirectly detract from the child's financial stability.

C. Absence of Effective Parenting

During and after divorce, many children must endure, at least temporarily, an absence of effective parenting due to one or both parents' preoccupation with their own stress. Parents are often less consistent in maintaining the child's routine, monitoring the child's whereabouts and activities, enforcing discipline, and maintaining a positive outlook toward the child.[27] Less effective parenting may partially be due to the custodial parent's abrupt assumption of both parents' roles. Other research, showing that the manifestations of diminished parenting vary as between male and female parents, would appear to support that hypothesis: While newly divorced fathers reported difficulties in monitoring their children's whereabouts and activities, newly divorced mothers reported problems in remain-

---

important factors that determine the children's psychosocial adjustment two years following the divorce." Kathleen A. Camara & Gary Resnick, *Interparental Conflict and Cooperation: Factors Moderating Children's Post-Divorce Adjustment, in* IMPACT OF DIVORCE, SINGLE PARENTING, AND STEPPARENTING ON CHILDREN, *supra* note 3, at 191-192.

23. *Id.* at 192.

24. "Moreover, it has been shown that high rates of continued aggression and conflict between the divorced parents is associated with the gradual loss of contact of the noncustodial parent..." Eileen Mavis Hetherington et al., *Divorced Fathers, in* READINGS IN FAMILY LAW, *supra* note 2, at 55.

25. Susan Steinman, *The Experience of Children in a Joint-Custody Arrangement, in* READINGS IN FAMILY LAW, *supra* note 2, at 155.

26. Judith S. Wallerstein & Shauna Corbin, *Father-Child Relationships After Divorce: Child Support and Educational Opportunity, in* READINGS IN FAMILY LAW, *supra* note 2, at 99.

27. "Sometimes temporarily and sometimes permanently, divorced parents are likely to have problems meeting all of the responsibilities of healthy parenting. Houses may not be kept clean; bedtime and mealtime routines may disappear; homework may not be checked. Children may in general not be supervised, and parents may be more critical and less positive." STEVENSON & BLACK, *supra* note 6, at 42.

ing firm and patient. The researchers concluded that each parent was manifesting difficulties in assuming the other's pre-divorce parenting role.[28]

Ineffective parenting may also be a function of the custodial parent's mental state. Wallerstein found that parents' failure to adjust to the divorce caused maladjustment in the children.[29] The same study revealed a strong correlation between a parent's continued conflict with his or her ex-spouse and that parent's emotional instability.[30] Two independent studies found that irritability, depression, and anxiety in the custodial parent are predictors of inept discipline.[31] One of these studies established a direct path from the mother's affective state to the child's antisocial behavior.[32]

Hetherington noted a tendency in adolescents of divorced parents to detach themselves prematurely from their parents. The researcher concluded that this premature detachment could be detrimental if the poorly supervised teen substitutes for his family ties an attachment to a negative peer group or is involved in antisocial behavior.[33] Premature adolescent

---

28. "Fathers were somewhat more likely than mothers to report difficulty with monitoring their children's whereabouts, activities, and school progress. Mothers, for their part, reported more difficulty than fathers in remaining firm and patient. These differences, though small, are significant, and we believe they reflect the different parental roles typically carried out by each parent before the separation." MACCOBY & MNOOKIN, *supra* note 21, at 245.

29. Wallerstein noted that "[a] central cause of poor outcome for the children and the adolescents was the failure of the divorce to result in a reasonable adjustment to it by the parents." Judith S. Wallerstein & Joan B. Kelly, SURVIVING THE BREAKUP—HOW CHILDREN AND PARENTS COPE WITH DIVORCE 224 (1980).

30. "Continued friction between parents who had long been divorced was significantly linked to psychological instability, psychiatric illness, and, most particularly, to the loneliness of one or both adults." *Id.* at 224.

31. These studies found that "heightened levels of maternal negative affectivity [i.e. irritability, depression, and anxiety] indirectly influenced child behavior as a result of inept discipline…". M. S. Forgatch et al., *A Mediational Model for the Effect of Divorce on Antisocial Behavior in Boys, in* IMPACT OF DIVORCE, SINGLE PARENTING, AND STEPPARENTING ON CHILDREN, *supra* note 3, at 144. Gene H. Brody & Rex Forehand, *Multiple Determinants of Parenting: Research Findings, in* IMPACT OF DIVORCE, SINGLE PARENTING, AND STEPPARENTING ON CHILDREN, *supra* note 3, at 129.

32. Forgatch et al., *supra* note 31, at 144.

33. "If this disengagement leads to greater involvement in a prosocial peer group, school attainment, or nurturant, constructive relationships outside of the family, this can be an adaptive, positive coping mechanism. If, however, it is associated with involvement in antisocial groups and activities with little adult concern or monitoring, the outcomes can be disastrous." Eileen Mavis Hetherington et al., *Marital Transitions, A Child's Perspective, in* READINGS IN FAMILY LAW, *supra* note 2, at 49.

detachment could explain why children of divorce may succumb more easily to pressure from peers to engage in antisocial behavior.[34]

IV. Innovations Made in the Law to Help Children

Three major changes in the law have emerged, intended to mitigate the negative effects of divorce on children: the "best interests of the child" standard, a preference in some jurisdictions for joint custody, and divorce mediation.

A. The "Best Interest of the Child" Standard

The "best interest of the child" standard, a product of social and psychological research,[35] is law in all jurisdictions. In spite of legislative attempts to enumerate factors that define what is in the child's best interest, the "standard" remains vague, subjective, and open to broad judicial discretion. The Uniform Marriage and Divorce Act set forth factors to be considered in determining the best interests of children in custody disputes.[36] Courts are to consider:

1. the parents' wishes;
2. the child's wishes;
3. the child's interaction and interrelationship with his parents, siblings, and anyone else who might significantly affect the child's best interests;
4. the child's adjustment to his home, school, and community; and
5. the mental and physical health of all individuals involved.

Most state legislatures have codified identical or similar factors.[37] In spite of statutes and case law, the decision as to what is in the best interest of the child is complex and depends largely upon the individual facts in any given case.[38]

---

34. STEVENSON & BLACK, *supra* note 6, at 110.

35. *See* JOSEPH GOLDSTEIN ET AL., BEYOND THE BEST INTERESTS OF THE CHILD (1979).

36. UNIF. MARRIAGE AND DIVORCE ACT § 402, 9A U.L.A. 561 (1982).

37. *See, e.g.* CAL. FAM. CODE APP. § 4600.5 (West 1994).

38. Elizabeth Scott & Andre Derdeyn, *Rethinking Joint Custody*, 45 Ohio St. L. J. 455, 466 (1984). David L. Chambers, *Rethinking the Substantive Rules for Custody Disputes in Divorce*, 83 MICH. L. REV. 477, 481 (1984).

The "best interests of the child" standard is well-intentioned, but is so vague that it invites litigation, allows into evidence any allegations of a parent's character defects, and leaves judges with little guidance as to what exactly is in the child's "best interests". Judges have discretion to determine which, if any, of the statutory factors should carry the most weight and how the factors apply in a given case. Thus, the "best interests of the child" standard leaves custody determinations in the hands of very human, often subjective, and sometimes biased judges and provides no standard for appellate review.[39] Furthermore, vague standards create the potential for frustrated expectations and lingering resentment in both spouses.[40] As noted by Lenore Weitzman, "custody laws that designate clear priorities and minimize litigation are clearly preferable."[41]

In conclusion, the "best interest of the child" standard, though a good idea in theory, is a concept too amorphous and illusive to be of much practical use in guiding judges' difficult decisions and shaping parents' realistic expectations as to custody.

B. Joint Custody

Today, joint custody is recognized as a viable custody arrangement in all states,[42] and some state legislatures have enacted a statutory presumption that joint custody is in the best interest of the child.[43] One researcher found that "about 80 percent of our sample families now have joint legal custody..."[44]

The wide-spread preference for joint custody grew out of sociological researchers' belief that joint custody would promote cooperative co-parenting after divorce and, thus, benefit the children of divorce.[45]

The same researchers who originally promoted joint custody now realize that it is not a panacea and that joint custody may indeed be the worst possible custody arrangement if the parents maintain a high level of open hostility and conflict after divorcing.[46] One researcher concluded that "only certain families can make joint legal custody a positive and relatively stress-

---

39. EMERY, *supra* note 15, at 67.

40. *Id.* at 67.

41. Weitzman, *supra* note 16, at 93.

42. *See, e.g.* ARIZ. REV. STAT. ANN. § 25-403 (West Supp. 1996).

43. IDAHO CODE § 32-717B.

44. MACCOBY & MNOOKIN, *supra* note 21, at 112.

45. "Wallerstein's work quickly attracted the attention of lawmakers. She advocated more father involvement after divorce, and the Legislature approved joint custody." Barbara Mahan, *But What About the Kids?*, 14 MAY CAL. LAW. 52, 54 (1994).

46. EMERY, *supra* note 15, at 77.

free experience."[47] Judith Wallerstein, originally an ardent proponent of joint custody as a means of tempering the effects of divorce on children, has since acknowledged that joint custody, in and of itself, does not mitigate the detrimental effects of divorce on children.[48]

In fact, joint custody is more of a legal label than a reality. In most cases, the joint custody arrangement very closely resembles a traditional sole custody arrangement where the child lives with one parent and where the other parent has visitation.[49] Mnookin explains that of all "joint custody" children, over seventy percent live primarily with their mothers, about ten percent reside primarily with their fathers, and only the remaining one-eighth actually have dual residences and spend four or more nights within each two-week period with each parent.[50] Another study found that only ten percent of joint legal custody arrangements actually involved joint physical custody.[51] The authors noted that much of the research literature and most of the popular press do not draw a distinction between joint

---

47. Amy Koel et al., *A Comparison of Joint and Sole Legal Custody Agreements, in* IMPACT OF DIVORCE, SINGLE PARENTING, AND STEPPARENTING ON CHILDREN, *supra* note 3, at 86.

48. "Two years after divorce, children raised in joint custody households are no better adjusted than children raised in sole custody homes. Despite more or less access to both parents, joint custody children show neither less disturbance nor better social adjustment than sole custody children. Unfortunately, joint custody does not minimize the negative impact of divorce on children during the early postdivorce years. The custody arrangement itself exerts but a minor influence on the psychological adjustment of children. Other, more familiar factors weigh more heavily: the mother's anxiety or depression, the parents' emotional functioning at separation, the amount of conflict between the parents a year later, the age and sex of the children, and the children's temperaments." Judith S. Wallerstein & Sandra Blakeslee, *Second Chances: Men, Women and Children A Decade After Divorce, in* READINGS IN FAMILY LAW, *supra* note 2, at 161.

49. EMERY, *supra* note 15, at 76.
"Most parents with joint custody actually share only joint legal custody, and many such arrangements resemble traditional custody and visitation in terms of children's actual residence (e.g., one parent sees the children every other weekend.)" Maccoby et al., *Custody of Children Following Divorce, in* IMPACT OF DIVORCE, SINGLE PARENTING, AND STEPPARENTING ON CHILDREN, *supra* note 3, at 112.

50. Mnookin stated: "Although there's been an enormous increase in what's now known as joint legal custody, that's only a legal label for the most part and has nothing to so with a child's day-to day life." Robert Mnookin, *in* DIVORCE: AN ORAL PORTRAIT 196 (George Feifer ed., 1995).

51. "Of the 199 joint legal custody cases, only 10% received joint physical custody. In the families granted joint legal custody, most mothers received physical custody (71.4%) whereas few fathers did (13.6%)." Koel et al., *supra* note 47, at 79.

legal custody and joint physical custody.[52] Even in jurisdictions where the statutes codify a presumption in favor of joint custody, equal allotment of the child's time between the two parents is not mandated.[53] (Nor would an equal allotment of the child's time be practical.)

Though joint custody, in and of itself, has not proven to be the panacea and though it is more of a label than a reality, joint custody appears to produce at least two indirect beneficial effects for the children of divorce: better long-term emotional adjustment to the divorce and better child support compliance. Both of these benefits stem from the fact that, over time, non-custodial fathers with joint custody drop out of their children's lives less frequently than their sole custody counterparts.[54]

Research shows that the right to participate in a decision making process fosters higher compliance and satisfaction with the decision itself.[55] A non-custodial father's dropout could be a function of frustration at having no legal say in his child's upbringing. Legally lacking the right to participate in decisions affecting his child, the non-custodial father may feel less inclined to *actually* participate in the child's life.[56] Labeled a non-parent in the eyes of the law, he gradually comes to behave as a non-parent in fact. The legal label becomes reality.

In general, preventing non-custodial parent dropout emotionally benefits the children of divorce. Those children, whose non-custodial parents remain involved, do not feel as rejected and abandoned as do those whose non-custodial parents drop out.[57] Research shows that, in most cases, children's post-divorce adjustment is better when frequent interaction with the non-custodial parent is maintained.[58]

Reducing parental dropout can also result in financial benefits to children. Research shows a strong correlation between non-custodial parents' visitation and their compliance in making child support payments. Waller-

---

52. *Id.* at 80.

53. Ariz. Rev. Stat. Ann § 25-403 (West Supp. 1996).

54. The researchers found that "the fathers in joint custody families are more committed to their children. None has 'dropped out' or stopped the visiting [of their children]…" Wallerstein & Blakeslee, *supra* note 48, at 161.

55. Tom R. Tyler, *The Psychosocial Consequences of Judicial Procedures: Implications for Civil Commitment Hearings,* 46 SMU L. Rev. 433, 440 (1992).

56. Judith Brown Greif writes that "these fathers see themselves less and less as parents and eventually act in accordance with the role that has been assigned to them: the absent parent." Judith Brown Greif, *Fathers, Children and Joint Custody, in* Readings in Family Law, *supra* note 2, at 22.

57. Steinman, *supra* note 25, at 155.

58. Clingempeel & Reppucci, *supra* note 9, at 163.

stein's ten-year study found that, over time, non-custodial parents who visited less paid less child support.[59]

In summary, joint custody parents drop out of their children's lives less frequently than do parents without joint custody, and this reduction in dropout benefits children in two ways: emotionally, through more interaction with the parent without physical custody, and financially, through more child support from that parent. Thus, perhaps joint custody *is* more than "just a legal label."

C. Divorce Mediation

Divorce mediation intuitively seems more likely than adversarial negotiations or litigation to foster interparental cooperation[60] and yet research has not conclusively established a correlation between mediation and better co-parenting after divorce.[61]

However, as mentioned above, studies show that participation in a decision making process produces a higher level of satisfaction and compliance with the decision itself.[62] Thus, better compliance with child support awards is likely when the payor has participated in mediation leading to an agreement as to the amount. Available research confirms that fathers who mediated felt more in control of their divorce and more satisfied with both the process and the outcome than fathers who participated in negotiation through their lawyers.[63] Another study found that fathers who mediated were more satisfied, solely because of the feeling of control and participation in the process. The increased satisfaction was not attributable to better outcomes, since these fathers' initial requests differed substantially from what they actually received.[64] According to a 1996 review of avail-

---

59. "The relationship between child support and visiting, while of little moment at the time of the separation, grew increasingly important over the years that followed within the postdivorce family." Wallerstein & Corbin, *supra* note 26, at 99.

60. Emery writes that "it seems reasonable to hypothesize that adversary procedures increase conflict and stress to the detriment of family members." Robert E. Emery, *Mediation and the Settlement of Divorce Disputes, in* IMPACT OF DIVORCE, SINGLE PARENTING, AND STEPPARENTING ON CHILDREN, *supra* note 3, at 57.

61. "The whole global psychological impact of mediational and adversarial dispute settlement procedures is one that is in need of much further investigation." *Id.* at 67.

62. Tyler, *supra* note 55, at 440.

63. "Client satisfaction varies with the dispute resolution process they participated in, with mediation clients being more satisfied than lawyer clients." ELLIS & STUCKLESS, *supra* note 19, at 90.

64. The study found that "differences in men's satisfaction between groups can be attributed to procedural, not distributive, factors. The fathers in our study were more satisfied when they experienced the increased control and participation allowed in mediation,

able research on mediation versus negotiation, "[c]lient satisfaction does not vary with participation in voluntary or mandatory mediation."[65] This finding negates the notion that any differences in client satisfaction were due to self-selection of the mediation samples.

One study found that non-custodial parents who felt in control of the divorce process and its outcomes were "more likely to make their child support payments regularly and on time."[66] Mediation clients in Toronto reported "higher levels of compliance with the terms of the agreements by their ex-partners" than did clients who had participated in the adversarial process.[67] A recent review of available research studies concluded that mediation is "more effective than lawyer negotiations in preventing non-compliance with agreed-on custody and support arrangements..."[68] Ellis and Stuckless intuited that mediation increases compliance because it reduces interparental conflict.[69] Greater child support compliance could also be attributed to the fact that mediation fathers remain more involved with their children, and greater involvement is associated with better compliance.[70]

Moreover, fathers who go through mediation are more likely to be awarded joint custody than fathers who do not. An analysis of the existing research concluded that joint legal custody "is far more likely to be reached through mediation than through lawyer negotiations."[71]

Mothers who mediate are likely to get more adequate child support awards than mothers who do not mediate. Ellis and Stuckless' survey of studies found that mothers who participate in mediation "are more likely than females involved in lawyer negotiations to get the level of child support they want."[72]

Since joint custody fathers are more likely to pay their child support than non-custodial fathers and since mediation promotes joint custody,

---

even though in nearly all cases they received outcomes that departed substantially from their initial request." Katherine M. Kitzmann & Robert E. Emery, *Procedural Justice and Parents' Satisfaction in a Field Study of Child Custody Dispute Resolution*, 17 LAW AND HUM. BEHAV. 553, 554 (1993).

65. ELLIS & STUCKLESS, *supra* note 19, at 103.

66. *Id.* at 136.

67. *Id.* at 116.

68. *Id.*

69. The authors write that "mediation makes a greater contribution to reducing parental conflict, including economic conflict, and should therefore facilitate greater compliance with child support and access arrangements." *Id.* at 136.

70. "Some evidence indicated that fathers who mediated remained more involved with their children than did fathers who litigated." EMERY, *supra* note 15, at 191.

71. ELLIS & STUCKLESS, *supra* note 19, at 88.

72. *Id.*

mediation would seem to foster not just higher child support awards but also better compliance.

Divorce mediation is not a zero-sum proposition: One spouse's gain does not necessarily result in the other spouse's loss in an equal amount.[73] Researchers conclude that "gains in fathers' satisfaction following mediation are produced by a 'win-win' outcome, not by a loss for mothers."[74]

To summarize, in the average divorce case, the father who mediates feels more in control, gets "joint custody", maintains contact with his children, and pays more child support. The mother who mediates still gets actual physical custody (essentially identical to traditional sole custody with father visitation) and gains higher compliance with an often higher child support award. In addition, both parents can reap the benefits of lower legal fees.

V. How Do Lawyers Fit In?

Research substantiating divorce lawyers' legendary combative attitudes and underhanded tactics and establishing any resulting negative impact on clients' future co-parenting relationships is nonexistent.

However, the American Academy of Matrimonial Lawyers (AAML), though not directly accusing lawyers of unduly acrimonious behavior, did publish a voluntary code of conduct for divorce lawyers. The code encourages matrimonial lawyers to adhere to a higher standard of behavior than the minimum dictated by the mandatory ethical rules. Pursuant to the AAML voluntary code, a lawyer:

1. should "encourage the settlement of marital disputes through negotiation, mediation, or arbitration" to prevent the detrimental effects on the children of "protracted, adversarial proceedings between the spouses;"[75]
2. should "consider the welfare of the children;"[76]

---

73. "First, fathers were significantly and substantially more satisfied with mediation than with litigation in virtually every domain of the assessment.... Second, few differences were found between mothers in terms of the satisfaction with mediation or litigation that they reported.... Third, whether they mediated or litigated their custody dispute, mothers were more satisfied than fathers with the process, outcome, and input of the dispute settlement." These findings were consistent across the initial study, a replication study, and a 1 year longitudinal follow-up. EMERY, *supra* note 15, at 185.

74. *Id.* at 191.

75. AMERICAN ACADEMY OF MATRIMONIAL LAWYERS, THE BOUNDS OF ADVOCACY 22, Rule 2.15.

76. *Id.* at 27, Rule 2.23.

3. should "not contest child custody or visitation for either finan-
    cial leverage or vindictiveness;"[77] and
4. should "refuse to assist in vindictive conduct toward a spouse
    or third person and should not do anything to increase the emo-
    tional level of the dispute."[78]

The mere fact that the AAML perceived the necessity to publish these
rules is a strong indication that matrimonial lawyers recognized a serious
problem among their ranks.

Lawyers and judges provide ample anecdotal evidence of the existence
of lawyers whose overly zealous advocacy unnecessarily heightened the
acrimony between divorcing spouses. Melvin Belli, an experienced divorce
lawyer, warns consumers to "[b]eware of 'barracuda' lawyers who fan
adversarial flames."[79] In response to researchers' queries, lawyers in New
Jersey cited undue competitiveness in opposing counsel as the most common problem in divorce practice.[80] Thirty-eight percent of lawyers attributed the undue combativeness to opposing counsel's greed.[81]

Mnookin and Kornhauser warned that lawyers may be inclined to use
threats and exaggerated demands in order to maximize the outcome for their
clients.[82] The sparse research has identified that lawyer behavior falls on a
spectrum ranging from the role of counselor on one extreme to the role of
zealous advocate on the other.[83] According to Kressel, counselors encourage agreement, avoid using threats, and realistically appraise the value of
a case. "Their strategy is to approach negotiation in an objective, fair,
trustworthy way and to seek agreement by the open exchange of information."[84] Advocates, on the other hand, have "a principal objective of
outdoing or outmaneuvering their opponent, ... to score a clear victory."[85]
In one article, the list of unfair lawyer tactics includes: condoning "freeze

---

77. *Id.* at 28, Rule 2.25.

78. *Id.* at 29, Rule 2.27.

79. The quoted comment is all the more interesting coming from Mr. Belli, perhaps the
most famous "barracuda lawyer" of our time. MELVIN M. BELLI, SR. & MEL KRANTZLER,
DIVORCING 75 (St. Martin's Press, 1988).

80. KENNETH KRESSEL, THE PROCESS OF DIVORCE: HOW PROFESSIONALS & COUPLES
NEGOTIATE SETTLEMENTS 163 (Basic Books, 1985).

81. *Id.* at 164.

82. Robert Mnookin and Lewis Kornhauser, *Bargaining in the Shadow of the Law:
The Case of Divorce*, 88 YALE LAW JOURNAL 950, 985-987 (1979).

83. The author writes that "our research has succeeded in identifying in a crude, but
basically accurate fashion, two relatively stable and sharply contrasting approaches to
legal work in divorce." KRESSEL, *supra* note 80, at 150.

84. *Id.* at 152.

85. *Id.* at 153.

and starve techniques" that deprive the opponent of the basic means of support and arguing frivolous positions, and engaging in unnecessary vindictiveness to prolong the proceedings and to generate higher legal fees.[86]

The Canons of Ethics create an obligation of zealous advocacy,[87] but neither the rules nor the adversarial system, which the rules were promulgated to facilitate, address the special circumstances surrounding divorce. Divorces, especially those involving children, differ from other types of litigation in significant respects: First, the litigants share an intimate past relationship, which may heighten one or both spouses' sense of abandonment, loss, bitterness and/or betrayal. These intense emotions increase the likelihood of hostility between the divorcing spouses.[88] Second, because the parties share a child, they will necessarily be forced to interact with each other for years to come, whether they like it or not. Third, while the parties are at polar opposites during the case, they are expected to put aside their animosity and work together as parents as soon as the proceedings end.

Research has documented both lawyers' and divorcing individuals' belief that the adversarial system "promotes conflict and emotional difficulty or, at least, fails to minimize those deleterious outcomes...."[89] In its purest form, zealous advocacy is also at odds with the informal pressures to produce settlements and unclutter judicial dockets.[90]

A lawyer may voluntarily adopt a higher standard of conduct and play a "kinder, gentler" role, while still operating within the bounds of her ethical obligations. The American Academy of Matrimonial Lawyers code exemplifies standards of lawyer conduct that meet the requirements of the ethical rules yet promote more therapeutic outcomes for post-divorce families. Rather than waiting for a change in the law, the code advocates apply-

---

86. Richard E. Crouch, *The Matter of Bombers: Unfair Tactics and the Problem of Defining Unethical Behavior in Divorce Litigation*, 413 Family Law Quarterly, Vol. XX, Number 3, Fall 1986, at 420-431.

87. American Bar Association, Code of Professional Responsibility, Canon 7 (1969), stating that "a lawyer should represent a client zealously within the bounds of the law."

Rule 1.3 of the Model Rules of Professional Conduct substitutes reasonable diligence and promptness for zeal.

88. Lois A. Weithorn, Psychology and Child Custody Determinations 26-27 (University of Nebraska Press, 1987).

89. Emily Hancock, *Sources of Discord Between Attorneys and Therapists in Divorce Cases, in* Therapists, Lawyers, and Divorcing Spouses 99, 110 (Judy L. Perlman ed., 1982).

90. Kressel writes that "while the official code of conduct prescribes a zealous pursuit of the client's interests, the informal norms and the realities of professional life prompt compromise and cooperation. Unfortunately, clear guidelines for helping attorneys decide which path to take are nonexistent." Kressel, *supra* note 80, at 159.

ing existing law therapeutically.[91] To meet the needs of clients and protect the best interests of their children, lawyers, as a whole, must embrace a more preventive/therapeutic role in divorce cases.

Modern legal instruction typically takes one of two distinct directions: a very pragmatic approach or a more theoretical, interdisciplinary approach. Therapeutic jurisprudence, the study of the law as a therapeutic agent, involves "the use of social science to study the extent to which a legal rule or practice promotes the psychological or physical well-being of the people it affects."[92] A symbiosis between therapeutic jurisprudence and preventive law could bridge the gap between the two directions of legal instruction and infuse the study and the practice of law with a very practical, human dimension, benefiting students, lawyers and clients alike.[93]

Recent scholarship in family law has proposed that judges take "[a]n approach to family law jurisprudence that structures decision making by applying the ecology of human development paradigm, buttressed by notions of therapeutic jurisprudence" in order to improve outcomes for individuals and families.[94]

---

91. David B. Wexler, *Applying the Law Therapeutically*, 5 APPLIED & PREVENTIVE PSYCHOL. 179 (1996), *reprinted in* LAW IN A THERAPEUTIC KEY: DEVELOPMENTS IN THERAPEUTIC JURISPRUDENCE (David B. Wexler & Bruce J. Winick eds., 1996).

92. Christopher Slobogin, *Therapeutic Jurisprudence: Five Dilemmas to Ponder*, 1 PSYCHOL. PUB. POL'Y, AND L. 196 (1995).

93. The authors found that throughout divorce lawyer-client conferences, "the lawyer encourages the client to be clear headed and to grant priority to monetary issues. By defining the ultimate goal as the resolution of the case and resolution in terms of the division of property, and by seeking to exclude the emotional focus that the client continues to provide, he expresses the indifference of the law to those parts of the self that might be most salient at the time of the divorce. The legal process of divorce becomes at best a distraction, at worst an additional trauma." A therapeutically-oriented, preventive approach focused on the client's children might provide a mutually satisfactory middle ground between the lawyer's and the client's respective positions. The approach acknowledges the client's emotions as a human being and as a parent. Rather than excluding entirely the client's emotional focus, the preventive/therapeutic approach attempts to subordinate the client's self-centered emotions to his parental need to protect his children. The approach, in effect, focuses the client on his more "rational" emotions while coloring the lawyer's rational, outcome-oriented position with more overt compassion for the children and validating the client's feelings as a parent. Dennis P. Stolle & David B. Wexler, *Therapeutic Jurisprudence and Preventive Law: A Combined Concentration to Invigorate the Everyday Practice of Law*, 39 ARIZ. L. REV. 25 (1997). *See also* Austin Sarat & William L.F. Felstiner, *Law and Strategy in the Divorce Lawyer's Office*, 20 L. & SOC. REV. 93 at 132 (1986).

94. Barbara A. Babb, *An Interdisciplinary Approach to Family Law Jurisprudence: Application of an Ecological and Therapeutic Perspective*, 72 IND. L. J. 775, 802 (1997).

This paper proposes that divorce lawyers adopt a therapeutically oriented, preventive role in order to mitigate the detrimental effects of clients' divorces on the clients' children.

VI. Lawyer Strategies to Mitigate Negative Effects on Children

This last section of the paper proposes concrete strategies that the lawyer can use to help prevent the client's divorce from negatively affecting the client's children.

A caveat: The proposed strategies may be difficult to implement if opposing counsel is overly adversarial or bows to his client's vindictive desire to abuse, demean, and embarrass your client. One article provides the following suggestions when faced with the unfair tactics of a "Rambo litigator" adversary. First, confirm all verbal agreements in writing. Second, conduct yourself in a professional manner. Third, "bring deceit and unfair tactics to the attention of the judge" whenever possible.[95] The author, a judge for the United States Court of Appeals, concludes that unfair "Rambo" tactics often backfire by inviting unsympathetic attention from judges and juries. "Tricks, pretense, and the slightest sign of unfairness invite rejection.... Rambo may succeed in the theater, but he self-destructs in the courtroom."[96] The judge cites cases where one lawyer's civility prevailed over the other's obnoxious behavior.[97]

"Rambo litigator" opponents aside, here are strategies that the lawyer can use to mitigate the negative effects of her client's divorce on the client's children:

1. Select Like-Minded Clients:
    a) The lawyer could advertise her preference for child-friendly divorce, in order to attract like-minded clients and avoid future conflicts with contrary clients.[98]
    b) The lawyer should screen potential clients by clearly explaining her philosophy from the outset and by conditioning her retain-

---

95. Thomas M. Reavley, *Rambo Litigators: Pitting Aggressive Tactics Against Legal Ethics*, 17 Pepp. L. Rev. 637, 651 (1990).

96. *Id.* at 655.

97. *Id.*

98. For example, a lawyer's ad might say:
Getting a divorce? Taking your ex to the cleaners might put your kids through the wringer. For your child's sake, try divorce on the delicate cycle: Call 1 800 THE DOVE.

er on the client's agreement with that philosophy.[99] The letter of retainer should fully disclose to the client the lawyer's child-centered focus and document the client's consent to that approach.[100]

2. Educate the Client:[101]

    a) The lawyer should paint for the client a realistic picture of the likely outcome of a divorce dispute and dispel any illusions of absolute victory that the client may entertain.

    b) The lawyer should provide materials and advice to educate the client about the detrimental effects of divorce on children.

    c) The lawyer should emphasize to the client that the principal causes of those harmful effects are instability, interparental conflict, and the temporary absence of effective parenting.

    d) The lawyer should inform his custodial client that frequent visitation, especially overnight, prevents drop off in visitation by the non-custodial parent and the correlated decline in child support compliance.

    e) The lawyer should inform her custodial client that mediation and joint custody foster higher child support awards and better compliance.

    f) The lawyer should read and have the client read "Getting to Yes"[102] in preparation for mediation.

    g) The lawyer should tell the client that encouraging the child's contact with the non-custodial parent promotes stability for the child and alleviates the child's problems of divided loyalties.

    h) The lawyer should provide the client with information about community-based and/or school support groups for parents and/or children going through divorce.

3. Plan a Strategy for the Benefit of the Child:

    a) The lawyer should plan a strategy that will maximize the child's post-divorce standard of living and prevent the instability that

---

99. For example, a philosophy statement may read as follows:
In representing a parent in a divorce, I always consider the welfare of the children. Because protracted hostility between divorcing parents is detrimental to their children, I encourage the settlement of marital disputes through negotiation or mediation I will not contest child custody for vindictiveness or for financial leverage. I will not purposefully increase the emotional level of the dispute between divorcing parents.

100. Full disclosure and informed consent are of the essence from the outset in undertaking this departure from the more traditional client-centered approach described in Robert D. Dinerstein, *Client-Centered Counseling: Reappraisal and Refinement,* 32 ARIZ. L. REV. 501 (1990).

101. *See* Appendix.

102. ROGER FISHER & WILLIAM URY, GETTING TO YES (Bruce Patton, ed., 1981).

accompanies a sudden financial decline. In doing so, the lawyer should use a checklist and anticipate in the agreement the child's every foreseeable financial need.

b) The lawyer should plan a strategy to promote stability in the child's social and emotional life. Keeping the child in the same home, neighborhood, school, church and/or activities helps the child feel a sense of stability in a time of overwhelming change and crisis. Researchers recognize the importance of the child's continuing contact with friends and relatives as a factor facilitating the child's post-divorce adjustment.

c) The lawyer should adopt a strategy that discourages conflict between the client and the client's ex-spouse, especially in front of or involving the children.

   i) The lawyer should discuss setting up a weekly time for the two parents to speak with each other on the telephone about the child, when the child is not present.

   ii) The lawyer should negotiate a very specific and comprehensive agreement to eliminate future misunderstandings and/or conflicts over ambiguous or omitted details.

   iii) The lawyer should plan for eventual changes due to moves, job changes, shift changes, the child's wishes and/or family reconfigurations such as remarriage.

d) The lawyer should remind the client to remain an effective and involved parent throughout the divorce process and beyond.

   i) Early in the representation, the lawyer should have the client document the client's involvement in the child's weekly routine and use it as a frequent reminder to the client to maintain at least the same level of involvement after the marital separation. This documentation would also prove valuable in the event of a custody battle.

   ii) The lawyer could provide the client with a self-test that would help the client evaluate, monitor, and adjust her co-parenting style.[103]

   iii) The lawyer could provide the client with a "child's progress chart" to help the client identify tell-tale signs of distress in the child.

   iv) The lawyer should inform the client that by continuing to support and attend the child's routine activities, both parents can promote the child's positive social activities and practice involved parenting.

---

103. *See, e.g.*, Separate Houses: A Practical Guide for Divorced Parents (New York: Prentice Hall Press, 1989).

Appendix

Important Information for Divorcing Parents

A. How Parents' Divorces Can Affect Their Children

When parents divorce, their children's world is abruptly torn apart. No matter how old they are, children may feel afraid, depressed, angry, lonely, and/or insecure. Depending on the child's age, he might act out in various ways, such as regressing in his potty training, underachieving in his school work, hanging around with an undesirable peer group, or experimenting with alcohol and/or drugs.

B. The Real Culprits

According to a huge body of social science research, the negative effects of divorce on children are caused mainly by three things: instability, ineffective parenting, and interparental conflict.

I. *Instability in the child's life*: Often, after divorce, the custodial parent and the child can't afford to stay in the same house or neighborhood as before the divorce. The child not only loses a parent from the home but also loses her home, her familiar surroundings, and her neighborhood friends. Often, she has to go to a different school and/or church, as well. Almost everything the child has known is gone. Of course the child is devastated.

II. *Ineffective Parenting*: During and after divorce, most parents are emotionally upset. Some are so miserable themselves that they don't focus on their child's needs as much as they normally would. Some have to work longer hours to make ends meet and have less time and energy for the children. Others have trouble adjusting to suddenly being single parents. For any, or all, of these reasons, people going through divorce are often not the most effective parents. Ineffective parenting can leave children lonely, hurt, and unsupervised.

III. *Interparental Conflict*: Conflict between two parents, especially in front of the child, is harmful to the child. Children whose parents are openly hostile to each other are more likely to have problems. They may act aggressively, defy authority, and/or engage in any number of undesirable behaviors.

C. How To Prevent Instability, Ineffective Parenting, and Interparental Conflict From Hurting The Children

I. *Prevent Instability*: Stability is very important to children. The more stable you can keep your child's life, the better adjusted he will be after the divorce.

Stability means maintaining regular contact with the absent parent, other relatives, and friends. List the important people and activities in your child's life. During the divorce process, this list will serve as a reminder of what you are trying to preserve for the child. In addition, after the divorce, you can periodically compare the pre-and post-divorce lists to see how stable your child's life is.

Stability means following a familiar routine. Document your child's day-to-day routine and your involvement in her routine. In the event that we have to go to court over custody, this information will help the judge decide which parent should have primary physical custody of the child. If we don't end up in court, this chart will remind you of your child's normal routine. You should strive to preserve that routine as best you can in negotiations or mediation with your spouse.

Stability means staying in familiar surroundings, such as the same home, the same school, and the same daycare facility as before the divorce. Whether or not you can give your child the stability of familiar surroundings depends largely on financial factors. To prevent financial instability, the child's post-divorce standard of living should be maximized.

Fathers who mediate, fathers who have joint legal custody, and fathers who get lots of visitation (especially overnight) are more likely to behave as responsible fathers. They are more likely to maintain regular contact with their children, which helps the children feel less abandoned and hurt. They are also more likely to pay their child support, which helps the children financially. In other words, if a man is told by the law that he has a legal right to participate in his child's life, he feels more responsibility toward the child and acts accordingly.

Mediation is a good idea for both parents. Dads who mediate are more likely to get joint legal custody than dads who fight in court over custody. While moms who are willing to mediate are less likely to get sole custody, moms who mediate are more likely to get the amount of child support they want, and joint custody dads are more likely to actually pay their child support over the years. For each spouse, mediation can be a first step toward cooperating with the other. Additionally, both spouses can benefit from lower legal fees, since mediation costs less than a long custody battle.

Before going to mediation, you should read "Getting to Yes". This book will help you understand and prepare for the mediation process. In mediation, use the enclosed checklist and make sure your divorce agreement resolves all of the issues listed, plus any additional issues you can think of.

II. *Prevent Ineffective Parenting*: Use the chart of your child's routine as a reminder to remain as involved in his every-day life as you were before the divorce. Participate in and support your child's positive activities as you did before the divorce. Encouraging his participation in good activities prevents his involvement in bad activities. Be reasonable, but consistent, in enforcing rules. Seek help from friends, family, and/or support groups if you feel overwhelmed as a single parent. Call your child's school about support groups for children of divorce. Find self-help books in your local library or book store. Tell your child that the divorce is not her fault. Show your child each day that you love her and will be there to take care of her.

III. *Prevent Interparental Conflict*: Use the enclosed checklist and get a detailed custody agreement. Hammering out all of the details now will prevent future arguments over unforeseen or ambiguous issues. Thus, getting a detailed agreement will make cooperation between you and your ex, easier in the long run. Your child will adjust to life after divorce best if you and your ex cooperate.

Arrange for a regular time *when your child is not present* for you and your ex-spouse to discuss the child. Discuss your child at least once every week. Remember, if you and your ex don't communicate with each other, your only means of knowing what goes on when the child is at your former spouse's house is the child. Failing to communicate with your ex will, in effect, make your child the messenger between you and your ex-spouse. Your child may feel he is betraying you by talking to your ex about you, and vice versa. Also, the information you get through your child may not always be reliable. A teenager, for example, may use his parents' ignorance of his whereabouts and activities to his advantage. Share important information about the child's progress and problems. Work together to help the child adjust to the divorce.

If you and your ex-spouse absolutely cannot cooperate for the sake of your child, learn to be disengaged from your ex rather than openly hostile. In other words, if you can't say anything nice, don't say anything at all. If you can't meet each other without arguing, arrange for the child to be picked up for visitation and returned at a neutral location (the daycare center, the school, or grandma's house, for example). Fighting with your ex during transitions can cause your child to feel terrible anxiety and stress before each transition. Though co-parenting with an ex from whom you are disengaged is not as beneficial for the children as cooperation, it is still better than open conflict.

No matter how you feel about your ex-spouse, you must separate those feelings from your role as a parent. Don't let your hostility interfere with your child's relationship with her other parent. Never threaten to withhold visitation. Never fight in front of the child. Never speak badly of your ex in front of the child, and never allow others to do so. Never pump your child for information about your ex. Never use your child as a messenger between you and your ex. And never treat your child as an adult confidant to whom you tell all of your adult troubles.

Some divorcing parents engage in long, drawn-out divorce litigation. Often, these court battles are a waste of time and money, based on one or both spouses' belief that they will eventually "win." Sometimes a spouse's expectations are unrealistic. Before you put your time, energy, emotions, and money into litigation, get a realistic idea of the likely outcomes.

D. What Can I Realistically Expect?

Even though custody statutes are now sex-neutral, mothers still typically get physical custody of the children. About two thirds of divorced moms have physical custody of their children. In one study, eighty-one percent of judges surveyed still felt that maternal custody was in the child's best interest. Another study explains that kids may live with their moms because mothers have more experience as primary caretakers and because mothers have often already made child-centered career choices and day-to-day arrangements. Generally, the parent who has been the child's primary caretaker is most likely to get physical custody of the child in court.

When divorcing parents litigate over custody, moms are more likely to get sole custody. When divorcing parents mediate, dads are more likely to get joint legal custody.

Checklist of Items to get in your Divorce Agreement

1. Who has legal custody of the child? In other words, who has the legal right to make decisions about how your child will be raised, educated, etc.? If you and your ex have joint legal custody, you both have the right to participate in those decisions.
   a. Will one parent have the ultimate decision-making power as to some aspects of the child's life and the other parent have the last word as to other aspects? If so, spell out who decides what in your agreement.
2. Who has physical custody of the child? In other words, where does the child primarily reside?
3. When does the noncustodial parent have visitation? (Be as specific as you can to prevent conflict later.)
   a. Where will the child spend holidays and birthdays?
4. How much notice must each parent give the other before taking the child on a vacation?
   a. What will be the time limit, if any, on the length of the vacation?
   b. Will trips out of the country be allowed?
   c. Will the vacationing parent provide an itinerary with phone numbers and addresses so that the other parent can contact the child during the trip?
5. Where will the parents exchange the child before and after visitation?

6. When will the child spend time with grandparents and other relatives?
7. Who will provide daycare for the child when the custodial parent is not available?
   a. Will the other parent have the right of first refusal as to child-care when one parent is not available?
8. What are acceptable hours for one parent to call the child or the other parent?
9. Who will provide medical and dental insurance for the child?
10. Who will pay for uninsured health-care expenses such as co-payments, eye care, orthodontics, and counseling?
11. Does either parent have life insurance benefiting the child in the event one parent dies?
12. Who will pay educational expenses such as private school tuition and registration fees?
13. Who will provide the child's sex education?
14. In which religion will the child be raised?
15. Does the parent who will be transporting the child to and from school and activities have reliable transportation?
16. How much child support will the parent without physical custody pay?
17. Who will pay for the child's post-secondary education (college, trade school, etc.)?
18. Who will pay for the teenager's car registration, car insurance, car repairs, and gas?
19. When is a good time each week for the two parents to discuss the child outside of the child's presence?
20. How will the parenting arrangement change if the parent with physical custody has a change in working hours?
21. How will the custody arrangement change if the parent with physical custody has to move to another location?
22. How will the custody arrangement change if the child decides to live with the noncustodial parent?
23. Will the parents get together to review the parenting agreement once every year and make sure it still meets the child's needs?
    a. Will all agreed-upon changes be in writing?
24. How will the two parents resolve future conflicts? (mediation? arbitration?)
25. What behavioral rules will the parents expect the child to follow?
    a. How will the parents reward the child for good behavior?
    b. What consequences will the parents impose on the child for bad behavior?
26. What will be the child's last name?
27. What is the parents' position on underage marriage?

Chapter 7

Collaborative Law: What It Is and Why Lawyers Need to Know About It

Pauline H. Tesler

Introduction

Any lawyer who has practiced family law for long knows some uncomfortable facts about this area of specialty. Of course, the entire picture is not bleak. To begin with the disclaimers: most family law attorneys work hard to do a good job for their clients, and as a result, they settle a high percentage of cases. When cases must be tried, family lawyers often achieve good results for clients and sometimes make new law. Each of us gets our share of reasonable, civilized clients and opposing attorneys, the people who make the practice of family law satisfying.

Despite those comforting facts, the evidence suggests disturbing trends that family law attorneys wanting to anticipate the need for change in their mode of practice ought to be aware of. Put baldly, current research tells us that our clients are unhappy with us—and we are unhappy with them and with ourselves.

Collaborative Law, the subject of this article, is a thoughtful, forward-looking response to the current state of affairs in the area of family law. Before looking at exactly what it is, it would be helpful to understand the context that makes awareness of Collaborative Law potentially so important to family lawyers.

Unhappy Clients, Unhappy Lawyers

Unhappy Clients

Our clients and potential clients, generally speaking, do not trust us very much, and for good reasons. This is evident from considering the growing percentage of divorcing couples who are well able to afford lawyers, but who just say "no." Although the number of divorces annu-

ally has risen by 67% between 1970 and 1990,[1] more and more potential clients are deciding to eschew professional legal representation altogether.[2] In California,[3] family law judges deplore the clogging of their court
dockets with unrepresented *in propria persona* litigants who file papers
that are substantively and procedurally flawed, and who flounder help-
lessly attempting to secure custody, support, and restraining orders on their
own.[4]

This refusal to secure needed legal advice cannot be dismissed as a reflection of poverty or lack of complexity. Many of these unrepresented litigants need legal advice, and can afford it.[5] They are staying away from
lawyers because they believe they and their loved ones are better off without our help. One need only read the daily newspapers, listen to the jokes
being told at the water-cooler, or scan the internet humor websites, to
appreciate the depth of fear and scorn felt toward lawyers. [6]

---

1. U.S. COMMISSION ON CHILD AND FAMILY WELFARE, PARENTING OUR CHILDREN:
IN THE BEST INTEREST OF THE NATION (1996), at 12.

2. Some of them may be seeking out mediators; some may be using freelance parale-
gals who skirt the area of unlicensed practice of law. Some may be securing "unbundled"
legal advice without retaining counsel of record. Many are buying "do it yourself"
divorce manuals and going it alone. For people with short marriages, and those without
children and without significant income or assets, the issues may be simple enough that a
lawyer is an unnecessary luxury. But for many, negotiating without legal advice spawns
unfair agreements, inadequate support, and future post-judgment conflicts that may give
rise to otherwise avoidable litigation.

3. California is so populous, has such a high divorce rate, and has been the source of
sufficient trends in family law, that lawyers from other regions might be wise to look at
reports from this state as "the canary in the coalmine."

4. Contested family law cases involving pro per litigants create substantial problems
for judges and court personnel as well as the litigants themselves. *See* Roderic Duncan,
Pro Per Do-It-Yourself Divorce, CALIFORNIA LAWYER 44 (January 1998).

5. Some commentators have estimated that as many as 70% of California divorces
proceed to judgment without attorneys of record. Of these, it is further estimated that
half—35% or so of all divorcing couples—can readily afford lawyers but refuse to retain
them.

6. Popular humor websites generally have a special category for jokes about lawyers;
see, e.g., scroom.com/humor/lawyer/html; netfit.com; and humor.com. No other profession is singled out for this attention. Even legal research websites put forth the same scorn-
ful lawyer jokes; *see, e.g.,* nolo.com/humor, and counselquest.com/jokes.htm. The jokes
have numbingly repetitive themes: lawyers are greedy, unethical, crooked; they will do
anything to keep litigation going and build up higher fees. They cheat their clients and
anyone else they deal with. They are routinely compared to rodents, snakes, and other
vermin and found to be less admirable. Many of the jokes involve killing lawyers, with the
punch lines suggesting that nobody could possibly grieve for them and that a service to
society has been done thereby. This is chilling material when read alongside the disturbing-

Instead of simply wringing our hands about how misunderstood and disliked we are, it is a useful exercise to play what Professor Deborah Tannen calls "the believing game"[7] about this situation. What if our clients feel this way about lawyers for good reasons? What might those reasons be, and what might we want do about the problem?

The Gladiator Model

The first thing that might cause clients to fear, distrust, and avoid family lawyers is that we, as a profession, are a great deal more adversarial in our thinking and behavior than our clients need or want.[8] We over-litigate, exacerbating intrafamilial stress when we could be calming it. And as a result, we charge our clients a high emotional and financial price that few can afford. We do this not because we wish to harm our clients or their families, but because we believe that is what lawyers are supposed to do.

We have absorbed from movies, television, novels, the newspapers, and our law school education a gladiatorial model for our professional role that is so deeply imbedded in our definition of what it means to be a lawyer that most of us do not even see it. It is invisible, the water we swim in and the air we breathe; and consequently, we reconsider our automatic adversarial behaviors just about as often as we remind ourselves to breathe.

The research also shows remarkably clearly that as a profession, we lawyers generally are poorly suited, by both temperament and training, to

---

ly frequent news reports of lawyers being shot and killed by clients and adverse parties. In California, the two courtrooms that routinely have metal detectors at the entrance are the criminal and the domestic relations departments.

7. DEBORAH TANNEN, THE ARGUMENT CULTURE (1998) at 273.

8. *See, e.g,* Susan Daicoff, *Lawyer, Know Thyself: A Review of Empirical Research on Attorney Attributes Bearing on Professionalism,* 46 AM. U. L. REV. 1337 (1997); Stephen Reich, *California Psychological Inventory: Profile of a Sample of First-year Law Students,* 36 PSYCHOL. REP. 871-874 (1976); Carl Hosticka, *We Don't Care About What Happened, We Only Care About What is Going to Happen: Lawyer-Client Negotiations of Reality,*26 SOC. PROBS. 599 (1979); Paul J. Spiegleman, *Integrating Doctrine, Theory and Practice in the Law School Curriculum: The Logic of Jake's Ladder in the Context of Amy's Web,* 38 J. OF L.EDUC. 243-270 (1988); Deborah Rhode, *Ethical Perspectives on Legal Practice,* 37 Stan. L.Rev. 589 (1985); Susan P. Sturm, *Gender and the Higher Education Classroom, in Maximizing the Learning Environment: From Gladiators to Problem-Solvers: Connecting Conversations About Women, the Academy, and the Legal Profession,*4 DUKE J. GEN. L. & POL'Y 119 (1997); Jack Himmelstein, *Reassessing Law Schooling: An Inquiry into the Application of Humanistic Educational Psychology to the Teaching of Law,*53 N.Y.U. L. REV. 514, 533-39 (1978); Lani Guinier, Michelle Fine, and Jane Balin, *"Hey! There's Ladies Here!"* 73 N.Y.U.L.Rev. 1022, 1035 (1998); Janet Weinstein, *And Never the Twain Shall Meet: The Best Interests of the Children and the Adversary System,* 52 UNIV. MIAMI L. REV. 79 (1997).

deal effectively with strong emotions.[9] Strong emotion, of course, is the currency that our family law clients are richest in: they are in the midst of one of the most stressful life passages that people can go through, second only to the death of a spouse, and consequently our clients often are awash in fear, anger, guilt, grief, shame, and remorse, sometimes even to the point of diminished capacity to cope with the ordinary demands of life.[10] In that state, they enter the unfamiliar world of law, and in that state they must make decisions that will affect themselves and their children for the rest of their lives. Although divorce is a major life passage, as big a piece of a person's life history as marriage, our clients commonly have only us, the family law attorneys, to help them through it.[11]

---

9. Daicoff, *supra* note 8; *Reich, supra* note 8. *See also* Susan Daicoff, *Asking Leopards to Change Their Spots: Should Lawyers Change? A Critique of Solutions to Problems With Professionalism By Reference to Empirically Derived Attorney Personality Attributes*11 GEORGETOWN J. LEG. ETHICS 547 (1998).

10. In the words of one custody expert, "I have seen normal people become neurotic, and neurotic people become psychotic, as a direct result of embroilment in adversarial proceedings associated with their divorces." Richard A. Gardner, M.D., *My Involvement in Child Custody Litigation*, 27 FAM. & CONCILIATION CTS. REV. 1, 3-9 (1989). Another noted specialist in high-conflict divorces notes, "…[E]ntrenched disputes often represent a response to overpowering feelings of shame and vulnerability which are evoked by the marital separation as well as by the perception that professionals are increasingly in charge of what was once the family's private life. Vulnerable parents frequently manage these feelings of shame and helplessness by projecting all incompetence and badness onto the former spouse and holding all competence and goodness for themselves. From this dynamic evolves a wish that the judge, Solomon-like, will erase the shame by publicly answering, once and for all, the question of which parent is good and competent and which parent is bad and incompetent." Vivienne Roseby, Ph.D., *Uses of Psychological Testing in a Child-Focused Approach to Child Custody Evaluations*, 29 FAM. L. Q. 97, 98 (1999).

11. It is beyond the scope of this article to pursue the implications of this fact, but they are significant. Our culture has prescribed ceremonies and rituals to assist people in handling the sometimes-overwhelming emotions that accompany major life transitions. For births, weddings, and deaths, there are religious and social ceremonies and customs that provide support and aid participants in understanding the larger meaning of the event and one's own place in it. In Joseph Campbell terms, these ceremonies help people fit themselves and these events into their own personal myths. No such traditions have evolved to support people through divorce, though most people will experience divorce either directly or in their immediate families during their lifetimes. Most people go through divorce without the help of mental health professionals; *see* Austin Sarat and William Felstiner, *Law and Society in the Divorce Lawyer's Office*, 20 LAW AND SOC'Y REV. 93 (1986). The divorce lawyer is the de-facto priest assigned the full cultural weight of bringing clients through this intensely destabilizing experience, and the trial is the only ceremony offered. Divorce for us is a set of legal issues; for our clients, it is a multi-dimensional experience

Poor Preparation for the Complexities of Divorce

How well prepared are we for this momentous task? Not well at all. We studied contracts and civil procedure in law school, and perhaps even domestic relations law. If our law school was forward-looking and we are not too old, we may have been exposed to courses in negotiations and mediation—or even a clinical semester.

Most of us have studied little or nothing about the psychodynamics of the divorce process and of family breakdown and restructuring. We are largely ignorant of the predictable stages of grief and recovery, and consequently cannot incorporate proper attention to that reality into our pacing of the legal divorce process. What we know about child development we most often learned by preparing adversarial experts for contested custody trials, a perspective that oversimplifies reality, weeds out inconvenient facts and theories, and leaves us unaware of, perhaps even indifferent to, the catastrophic impact of the divorce process itself—especially high-conflict divorce—upon children. We delude ourselves that such concerns are outside the lawyer's purview, ignoring the unpleasant fact that what we do during the course of our representation may cause far more injury to the children than what led up to their parents' decision to divorce.[12]

---

that begins long before and ends long after the legal divorce, including emotional, spiritual, physical, financial, familial, relational, and ethical dimensions. Generally, there is no other professional assisting clients through this complex experience, and generally, we lawyers deal with this complex transition by defining most of it as irrelevant.

12. One commentator observes, "litigation itself is often demeaning, as litigants attempt to exaggerate each other's flaws and reopen old wounds in order to win points for themselves. Further, the process is disempowering as it forces the parties to place their fates in the hands of their attorneys and the court. In the process, the family's resources are expended and depleted with no beneficial outcome for the child or the parents." Weinstein, *supra* note 8, at 133. Despite the fact that children need extra attention from their parents during the upheavals of divorce, they get less because litigation drains the personal and emotional as well as financial resources of their parents. JUDITH S. WALLER-STEIN AND JOAN BERLIN KELLY, SURVIVING THE BREAKUP: HOW CHILDREN AND PARENTS COPE WITH DIVORCE (1980), at 30. Andrew Schepard puts it this way: "Despite a child's overriding need for conflict management, the prevalent adversarial model of courtroom confrontation rewards parental conflict....Precisely when children need parents to lessen the degree of hostility and behave cooperatively, the specter of courtroom combat—and especially the conflict over the vague legal standard of the "best interests of the child"—encourages conflict....The adversarial process encourages parents to denigrate one another, rather than to cooperate on the essential task of post-divorce child rearing....the custody dispute also drains resources from limited marital assets at a time when those assets could better be used to preserve the family's standard of living." *War and P.E.A.C.E.: A Preliminary Report and a Model Statute on an Interdisciplinary Education-*

Our ignorance of the psychological dimensions of divorce leads us to inflict other avoidable harms. Because most of us don't know nearly enough about the psychological phenomena of splitting, transference, and counter-transference, we may jump unthinkingly onto white horses in full battle array when that might be the very worst thing we can do for our clients.[13] Later, we wonder why, since we won such a powerful legal victory in court, our client is nonetheless furious.[14]

The Duty of Zealous Representation

Another reason why our clients may be right to distrust lawyers is that, over the course of this century, we lawyers have learned to misread our duty of zealous representation in the narrowest possible fashion. Wanting to do the best possible job, and being most comfortable with outcomes that are measurable, and least comfortable with the fuzzy, the emotional, the illogical, the relational,[15] lawyers can easily find themselves focusing considerable legal efforts on achieving very small increments of financial gain. In doing so, it is rare for a lawyer to think much about the corollary damage caused by that narrow focus.

The very process of what lawyers refer to as "spotting the issues," which is what we do in the preliminary stages of a representation, involves excluding as legally irrelevant those parts of the client's actual concerns that do not fit in the "lawyer's comfort zone":[16] the realm of the logical, the measurable, and the quantifiable. In so doing, we ignore, and often do irreparable harm to, the nonquantifiable human concerns that may well have far greater impact on the quality of our clients' lives long after the legal divorce is over than any marginal financial gain we might achieve at trial. These concerns — which we would learn are of immense importance to our clients, if we would ask and then listen — often include questions like these:

> Will my spouse and I be able to parent our children adequately after the divorce? Can we shield them from the harms that seem to afflict children of divorce? Will fighting about every last cent of sup-

---

al Program for Divorcing and Separating Parents, 27 U. Mich. J. L. Reform 131, 145-47 (1993).

13. See Roseby, supra note 10.

14. Cf. Marygold S. Melli, et al., The Process of Negotiations: an Exploratory Investigation in the Context of No-Fault Divorce, 40 Rutgers L. Rev. 1133, 1143-44, 1160 (1988).

15. See supra, notes 8 and 9. Also illustrative are the conclusions of clinical law professor Alan Lerner, Law and Lawyering in the Workplace: Building Better Lawyers by Teaching Students to Exercise Critical Judgment as Creative Problem-Solvers, 32 Akron L. Rev. 107, 114- 117 (1999).

16. See Hosticka, supra note 8.

port and every last dollar of assets permit any of the remaining good faith between us to survive? Can I protect my interests without becoming my spouse's enemy?

Will it be possible for my spouse and me to meet at graduations, weddings, births, deaths, with any civility or sense of mutual pride? Is there anything I can do to enhance that possibility?

Will the grandparents, aunts, uncles, and cousins who have close connections to my children be able to sustain these relationships after a divorce? Can I remain close to the in-laws and extended family that I love, even though I am losing my spouse?

Will our friends be able to avoid choosing between my spouse and me? Will I have any friends left after a contested divorce?

Can the legal process allow room for my personal values of ethical dispute resolution, privacy and self-determination?

Will I be able to look back upon how I conducted myself during this divorce process with pride and a sense of integrity?

Insufficient Counseling About Dispute Resolution Options

Any experienced family law attorney knows that for most clients who take their divorce issues to court for resolution, the answers to the foregoing questions are overwhelmingly negative. Yet, in most parts of the country, it is rare indeed for family lawyers to begin their representation by inviting clients to consider what kind of a divorce experience they want, and how they might best go about achieving it, or to give clients a realistic picture of how adversarial dispute resolution typically affects families.[17] While many individual attorneys may be exceptions to this rule, we as a profession overwhelmingly fail to take any ethical or moral leadership in counseling our clients that there is a way to divorce with dignity and integrity if they want that outcome sufficiently, and that we are available to show them how. We are the only ones who can tell them the truth about what really happens when divorcing couples take their issues to court.[18]

---

17. A fair analogy in the medical field would be the failure to advise critically ill patients about the range of treatment options and the risks commonly associated with each—a failure most lawyers would consider to be at least arguably malpractice. Surely our own standard of care requires no less. *See, e.g.,* Robert F. Cochran, Jr., *Must Lawyers Tell Clients About ADR?* ARBITRATION JOURNAL 8 (June 1993).

18. For a vivid judicial snapshot of what is wrong with court-based family dispute resolution, *see* the comments of family law judge Ann Kass, in *Clinical Advice from the Bench,* 7 J. OF CHILD AND ADOLESCENT PSYCHIATRIC CLINICS OF N. AM. 247 (1998), at 251-53 ["[T]oo few judges and lawyers have examined their personal beliefs, attitudes, and expectations about family matters in any depth, and that leaves them vulnerable to

Yet, unless we have something better to offer clients, it would make little sense to speak so candidly about the adversarial paradigm. And since there has been little else to offer,[19] family lawyers have for the most part trudged forward to court with their clients, feeling little confidence that anything fundamentally satisfying will come of it, but unwilling to say so. In this, we resemble physicians who must treat patients with dreadful, incurable diseases. With no cure to offer, the choice is to officiate at the patient's death with false hope, or with honest, detached gloom.[20]

---

becoming emotionally entangled in divorce and custody cases, sometimes quite unconsciously.... What does reach their conscious awareness is that they are extremely uncomfortable, but they haven't the skills to reflect on their discomfort through introspection. In short, family law has the propensity to diminish objectivity and blur boundaries for judges and lawyers and thus cause emotional overload." Worse yet, the art of "building and maintaining appropriate boundaries is missing from legal education, so we find lawyers and judges who assume the inappropriate roles of rescuer and avenger." Communication about hard facts is often "tied to fault and blame," and lawyers and judges communicate in "linear and triangular patterns with little understanding that doing so causes misinterpretations, suspicion, and confusion."] Janet Johnston and Vivienne Roseby deplore the faulty reasoning involved in asking courts and judges to "take on and resolve family dilemmas that other professionals and the community at large have failed to resolve—cases that attorneys have failed to negotiate and mediators have failed to settle, for families that counselors and therapists have failed to help. Inexplicably, there is an assumption that judges have some special capacity to resolve the most difficult, the most complex of all family problems. Is it any wonder that family court assignments for judges are so unpopular, so often avoided, and usually staffed by rotating assignments to prevent burnout?" IN THE NAME OF THE CHILD (1998) at 223. Retired California Court of Appeals Justice Donald M. King made the point more succinctly: "Family court is where they shoot the survivors." King, address at *New Ways of Helping Children and Families Through Divorce*, a conference sponsored by Judith Wallerstein Center for the Family in Transition and University of California, Santa Cruz; Quail Lodge, Carmel Valley, California (November 21, 1998).

19. We do, of course, settle many cases, but we do so in a litigation-driven matrix in which much of the harm of adversarial wrangling has already occurred before settlement discussions begin. In recent years, mediation has been an option, but for many (though certainly not all) couples, it may provide insufficient protections and controls to be a wise dispute resolution choice. For an example of feminist critique of mediation which includes some cautions about who should not mediate, see, *e.g.*, Penelope E. Bryan, *Reclaiming Professionalism: The Lawyer's Role in Divorce Mediation*, 28 FAM. L. Q. 177 (1994), at 193-207.

20. There is, however, an important difference. If the physician's treatments should cause additional harm to the patient, the patient with the fatal illness does not survive to chastise him. Family law clients who are injured by the dispute resolution process selected or imposed by the lawyer will live to mull about who is to blame for the pain they experienced.

Whether we win or whether we lose, the sad reality is that at the end of many litigated divorces, our clients will be unhappy.[21] As an experienced civil and family litigator, with a successful track record in trial and appellate courts, I have come to understand that however big a "win" I may have obtained from the lawyer's perspective, it is invariably less than or other than my client secretly expected, and it comes at a tremendous financial and emotional cost. As one respected family law judge in my county used to tell litigants at the start of trials, "If anyone leaves this courtroom happy, I've made a dreadful error."

Unhappy Lawyers

The commentators generally agree that the well of client dissatisfaction, and the stresses and incivilities of litigation, are getting worse, not better. The consequences hurt not only clients; they can be nearly catastrophic for the mental and physical health of lawyers.

Many of us went to law school for idealistic reasons, thinking we were joining a helping profession. We saw ourselves as gladiatorial heroes, who would fight on the side of the angels (our clients), using our intellects and our passion to win their just causes. In law school we were taught to win via the dominant paradigm for dispute resolution, the zeitgeist that Deborah Tannen refers to "the argument culture." In that model, the lawyer is the dispassionate warrior, advancing the client's self-identified goals with total zeal, passion, and guile.[22] In that model, we learned to follow agreed rules of combat (the code of civil procedure) in our march toward the courthouse, where the judge would ascertain the truth, find out who was at fault, and dispense impartial justice (trial and judgment). In this dominant paradigm, the role of the lawyer is to remain morally disengaged, to become the extension of the client's legal and moral personality.[23] The lawyer, in this gladiatorial role definition, is expected to take no moral

---

21. *See generally*, Stephen Erickson, *ADR and Family Law*, 12 Hamline J. Pub. L. & Pol'y 5 (1991); Bruce Winick, *Integrating Preventive Law and Therapeutic Jurisprudence: A Law and Psychology Based Approach to Lawyering*, 34 Cal. W. L. Rev. 15 (1997).

22. *See supra* notes 8, 9, 15.

23. *See* Deborah Rhode, *Ethical Perspectives on Legal Practice*, 37 Stan. L. Rev. 589 (1985); Richard Wasserstrom, *Lawyers as Professionals: Some Moral Issues*, 5 Hum. Rts. 1(1975); Gerald J. Postema, *Moral Responsibility in Professional Ethics*, 55 N. Y. U. L. Rev. 63 (1980); Rand Jack and Dana Crowley Jack, Moral Vision and Professional Decisions: The Changing Values of Women and Men Lawyers (1989); Richard Zitrin and Carol M. Langford, The Moral Compass of the American Lawyer: Truth, Justice, Power, and Greed (1999).

responsibility for the purposes to which the lawyer's services are put. We park our moral consciousness in the courthouse parking lot, and pick up the lawyer's substitute for a conscience, the "duty of zealous representation."

This role-defined morality is superficially seductive; it allows us as family lawyers to float above the inherent messiness of human relationships as they unravel. In its seductiveness, it can link up with our buried idealism and with the zero-sum game that is adversarial engagement, causing us to cast our clients' stories in black and white, and to ignore the relativity and situational complexity of human relationships. If our job is to march forward zealously to achieve our client's goals, whatever they may be, we are a good deal more comfortable as gladiators if we can convince ourselves that we are acting on behalf of angels.[24] An all-out custody battle is easier to mount if the lawyer believes what he will have to prove, that his client is a superb parent and the other is a danger. Our role definition, in other words, encourages us to oversimplify reality.

For these same reasons, we are far more comfortable with goals that have clear bottom lines that are readily quantifiable because they lend themselves readily to adversarial simplification. It's easy to tell who won, and by how much, when the issues are confined to money and hours. We define the legally cognizable issues this way, and we know which gladiator won (and did a better job for the client) by the size of the bottom line. Since we played by the rules, we are comfortable with the outcome, because justice was done: it emerged from the judge's application of fair general rules to the messy facts of our clients' lives, which we so capably simplified at trial.

Another factor operating in this dominant paradigm is that our clients' goals, which are the holy grail of the gladiator's duty of zealous representation, tend to be identified in a process marred by diminished capacity on the part of the clients, and shaped by transference and countertransference that neither the lawyer nor the client is generally much aware of.[25]

Family law clients do not call their lawyers to report that everything is fine, that they are getting along well with their spouses, and that their ability to work out issues on their own is improving. Those moments do occur during the course of many divorces, but clients typically call their divorce

---

24. What the better family lawyers understand, after some years in the practice of law, is that in reality there are very few angels hiring us to represent them, and very few devils on the opposing side. As the saying in the San Francisco legal community goes, "Snow White rarely marries Hitler." The vast majority of our clients are simply good people going through a very bad time in their lives, and sooner or later most of us realize that casting their stories in black and white, win-lose terms does their families no service.

25. The family law client, from this perspective, looks to the lawyer and the court system to assuage unbearable narcissistic wounds. Roseby, *supra* note 10.

lawyers only when things are worst, when they or their spouses are locked in the grip of primitive emotion and they are paralyzed by grief, fear, anxiety, remorse, shame, guilt, or anger. In that state, it is the rare client who has sufficiently clear insight into her own needs or the needs of the others who are most important to her; it is the rare client who can take the long view and consider with the lawyer what outcomes will serve her interests best fifteen or twenty years from now. Instead, most clients sit down with the lawyer in this flood of overwhelming negative emotion to identify goals and priorities, and to plan strategies. Inevitably, things get better, but the client does not typically call the lawyer back to report the improvement and reconsider the litigation plan.[26] The other client and lawyer are planning goals and strategies in a similar state.

It should be apparent with a moment's reflection that there is no room in this model for consideration of a client's long-term enlightened self-interest, whether financial or emotional. Very few family law attorneys expect their clients to ponder the larger questions in setting goals and strategy, questions such as, "Should I be seeking this? How will it further my overall health and welfare, and the best interests of those I care about, if I achieve this goal?"

In short, our clients frequently come to us gripped by a "shadow state" of powerful negative emotions, and we insist that they set major life goals in that state. Once those goals have been defined, we set out to win them for the client. To do so, we take control so that we can maximize the possibility of a win. We see other professionals (therapists, mediators) as meddlers who are compromising our ability to win big for our client by blurring the neat black and white lines we are drawing. We discourage direct negotiations between the clients, for this too will undercut our trial strategies. We take our instructions from our clients in their least functional state, and are surprised that later, they don't appreciate our efforts. Sooner or later, all but those at the far ends of the bell-shaped curve will recover from the immediate divorce trauma and resume a more normal, balanced state of functioning most of the time. Many of them at that point will look back on the divorce process with pain for the rest of their lives.[27]

---

26. First, it is costly to spend any time with a lawyer, and therefore, paying money to report good news probably does not occur to clients. Second, meetings with the lawyer tend to be painful and fraught with anxiety and therefore are to be avoided if possible. Third, clients too absorb the dominant gladiatorial model. Lawyers are hired warriors who go to battle for you against a demonized spouse. Why call on them for assistance when a hired gun isn't needed?

27. If they are reflective and mature, they may look back with a mixture of shame, remorse, regret, and guilt at their own contribution to a "bad divorce." If they are by nature more primitive in emotional development, they may carry forward from the wreckage of their divorce a permanent, unchangeable picture of themselves as victim and

For all these reasons, not only do many of our clients fear and dislike us, but also we fear our clients. We know that they may well end the legal divorce process angry and frustrated, and looking for someone to blame. Experienced family lawyers can attest that many clients retain us but don't pay us. Fee disputes are common in family law, not only because money tends to be scarce when two households form out of one, but also because family law clients tend to be unhappy with the results, however a good job their lawyers may have done. When our clients have run up large bills — an error lawyers try to but cannot always avoid — fee disputes and the reverse side of that coin, malpractice suits, are common.[28] Lawyers who have made the mistake of acting as their clients' alter egos, stoking their anger or fear and raising unreasonable expectations from the adversarial process, are particular targets of this pool of anger.

And in California, where I practice, a fee dispute or malpractice action is far from the worst the family lawyer needs to guard against. Clients have brought their guns and shot the lawyers who epitomize for them all that is wrong with how our legal system handles the breakdown and restructuring of families.[29]

It is small wonder that many family lawyers regret their choice of profession, are leaving the field of law in unprecedented numbers, and report that they would not advise their children to choose law as a career.[30] Even more troubling are the high drug and alcohol abuse rates for attorneys and their disturbingly high rates of clinical depression.[31] These reports confirm what many of us know from first-hand experience: family lawyers as a group have difficulty taking pride and satisfaction in their work, however well they are doing it. When we look in the mirror, we are not happy with what we see.

---

the ex-spouse as demon, a stance that thwarts their own personal growth and the emotional development of any children of the marriage.

28. According to one large malpractice carrier, Lawyers' Mutual Insurance Company, "experience has shown us that a cross-complaint for malpractice is not an unusual concomitant to a fee dispute between attorney and client." 10 Law. Mutual Ins. Company Bul. (1995).

29. Gardner, supra note 10, observes that the stresses of litigation can produce rage so extreme it induces serious urges to murder, a risk recognized by the California court system in installing metal detectors at the entrance to many family law departments. *See* Weinstein, *supra* note 8, at 133, n.178.

30. Joseph Bellacosa, *A Nation Under Lost Lawyers*, 100 Dick. L. Rev. 505 (1996); Mary Jordon, *More Attorneys Making a Motion for the Pursuit of Happiness*, Washington Post, September 4, 1993.

31. *See* Association of American Law Schools, *Report of AALS Special Committee on Substance Abuse in the Law Schools*, 44 J. Legal Educ. 35, 41-46 (1994); Connie J.A. Beck et al., *Lawyer Distress: Alcohol-Related Problems and Other Psychological Concerns Among a Sample of Practicing Lawyers*, 10 J. L. & Health 1, 45-58 (1995-96).

A New Paradigm with New Possibilities

Out of this ferment (client and attorney malaise, dissatisfaction with the obvious shortcomings of adversarial litigation as a way of helping families resolve the inevitable disputes attendant upon family restructuring in divorce, and recognition of the limitations of existing alternate dispute resolution models), the new paradigm of Collaborative Law emerged in the early 1990's. It was the inspiration of a single disgusted family lawyer practicing in Minneapolis.[32]

Very rapidly, lawyers learned about this new way of practicing family law and began spreading the model to other parts of the country.[33] Presentations about Collaborative Law have been offered in recent years at a number of conferences sponsored by organizations including the American Bar Association, the Association of Family and Conciliation Courts, The American Academy of Matrimonial Lawyers, The American Psychological Association, The University of California, the Judith Wallerstein Center for the Family in Transition, and the American Institute of Collaborative Professionals.

What Collaborative Law Is: The Bare Bones

Collaborative Law consists of two clients and two attorneys, working together toward the sole goal of reaching an efficient, fair, comprehensive

---

32. Stuart Webb describes his inspiration simply. He was so fed up with family law and its inconsistency with his personal ethics that he decided he would simply have to stop practicing law. Then it struck him that if he was willing to give up law altogether, there was no reason why he couldn't first try to reshape what was wrong about it and see if he could devise a mode of family law practice that made more sense to him. Pauline H. Tesler, *Collaborative Law: Where Did It Come From, Where Is It Now, Where Is It Going?* 1 The Collaborative quarterly 1 (1999).

33. Groups of collaborative lawyers formed in California and Ohio in the early nineties. By the mid-nineties, several experienced collaborative lawyers were offering trainings around the country. In Northern California, a parallel development among financial and mental health professionals called "Collaborative Divorce" emerged, opening for the first time the possibility of a well-trained interdisciplinary team of lawyers and other divorce professionals working in collaboration to help couples achieve a settlement entirely outside the court system, with all the benefits of sophisticated professional advocacy and support. Stuart Webb and the author are now offering trainings in conjunction with the originators of the Collaborative Divorce model, for interdisciplinary groups of lawyers, financial professionals, and mental health professionals. (*See* the Collaborative Divorce website at collaborativedivorce.com for information.)

settlement of all issues.[34] Each party selects independent collaborative counsel. Each lawyer's retainer agreement specifies that the lawyer is retained solely to assist the client in reaching a fair agreement, and that under no circumstances will the lawyer represent the client if the matter goes to court. If the process fails to reach agreement and either party then wishes to have matters resolved in court, both collaborative attorneys are disqualified from further representation. They assist in the orderly transfer of the case to adversarial counsel. Experts are brought into the collaborative process as needed, but only as neutrals, jointly retained by both parties. They, too, are disqualified from continuing work and cannot assist either party if the matter goes to court. The process involves binding commitments to disclose voluntarily all relevant information, to proceed respectfully and in good faith, and to refrain from any threat of litigation during the collaborative process.

The process moves forward via carefully managed four-way settlement meetings, preceded by considerable groundwork between lawyer and client, and between lawyer and lawyer. The lawyer's job is challenging: in addition to the usual identification, investigation, and development of issues and proposals for settlement, the lawyer must also work with the client and the other lawyer to anticipate and manage conflict, and to guide the negotiation process. The lawyer also must encourage the client to take a considered and broad view in setting goals and priorities, and must teach the client how to use interest-based rather than positional bargaining.[35]

---

34. The model first emerged in connection with divorce, but can be applied in any situation where preservation of an ongoing relationship between the parties is an important objective. This article focuses on the model as it is applied in divorce and other family law matters, but it certainly should be considered an option in probate and commercial matters as well.

35. Positional bargaining is most easily described as horse trading, or "Mediterranean marketplace" bargaining, which proceeds via choreographed presentation of a sequence of unreasonable positions, always moving closer toward an intermediate reasonable compromise that often can be predicted by looking at the parties' opening positions. Some theorists also describe and avoid "Scandinavian bargaining" (in which a party decides what is the right and fair outcome, proposes it, and refuses to deviate from it, because it is fair and right), and "Soviet cold-war" bargaining (in which ultimatums and threats replace reasoned negotiations). Interest-based bargaining is more complex. The lawyer works with her own client to examine how a given goal or objective will help the client, and why, and whether there are other ways that could also achieve the same or better ends. The lawyer does not bring the issue to the bargaining table until it can be explained persuasively why the client needs whatever is being sought, and why the other party ought to consider it a reasonable goal. The collaborative process includes commitments to respect the legitimate settlement objectives of the other party, and to attempt to find win-win solutions that achieve the legitimate goals of both whenever possible. Thus, the primary

Before any negotiating session, the collaborative lawyers generally meet and confer, sharing information that will assist them both in managing conflict and in setting the agendas for four-way meetings. The skill here is to manage agendas in such a way that the clients experience success during the early meetings, thereby building in the clients a sense of confidence, safety, and competency that will serve them as more difficult issues are tackled.

An important element of collaborative representation is the lawyers' commitment to manage conflict creatively. To do so effectively, the lawyer needs a whole new array of understandings and skills. Without this new toolbox, the lawyer runs the risk of promising more than can be delivered and disappointing clients. Given the unconscious, knee-jerk adversarial proclivities of most lawyers, this is easier said than done. The "retooling" needed to become excellent at collaborative law can be described in four stages:[36]

1. Retooling how one thinks, speaks, and behaves.
2. Retooling how one relates to the client.
3. Retooling how one relates to the other attorney, the other party, and other professionals.
4. Retooling how one conducts settlement meetings.

The questions most often asked about collaborative law are: (1) I already settle cases, and I'm a reasonable lawyer; so isn't it true that I'm already doing what you do, only by a different name? And (2) isn't this really just like mediation? The answer to both questions is "no."

The best family lawyers have always offered settlement-oriented representation where appropriate, wherein discovery is voluntary, and agreements are more common than trials. Collaborative Law differs in several important respects from that pragmatic orientation toward settling cases. The differences arise from the profound effects that the formal written commitments made at the start of the process have upon the state of mind of the parties and their attorneys. *First*, both parties entering a Collaborative Law dissolution process commit to selecting counsel on both sides who willingly bind themselves to pre-arranged ground rules. Ideally, the clients

---

importance of working first with one's own client to be sure that true interests, not artificial negotiating positions, are being presented

36. I am indebted to my colleague, Laurence Wilson, for giving me permission to use and adapt this theoretical framework. The actual work of retooling in the four stages is subtle and fascinating, and cannot be mastered from reading an article or book. Trainings that include role-playing and critique are the most efficient way to learn these skills. It can be done independently through a combination of working with trusted colleagues and studying with mental health and communications professionals, but the learning curve will be considerably slower and more of the learning will be via trial and error.

choose attorneys who have a history of working cooperatively and effectively as opposing or collaborative counsel.[37] *Second*, everyone signs a stipulation about how the process will be conducted, which remains in effect so long as all participants conduct themselves in good faith. *Third*, a core element of the stipulation is that the process continues only so long as no one threatens litigation as a means of conducting negotiations, nor takes any steps to bring the matter into the court's litigation process. *Fourth*, if the process breaks down, either because of bad faith or because one party or the other feels obliged to turn to the courts for relief, the attorneys must withdraw, and thereafter cannot represent either party against the other. While departing Collaborative Law counsel will assist in an orderly transition to litigation counsel, the financial and emotional costs of starting over with new representation will usually be significant.

These stipulated commitments become powerful "carrots" and "sticks" encouraging immediate engagement in good faith problem-solving on all sides, and discouraging the parties from lightly electing to litigate. Suspicion and paranoia decline dramatically; this is both because most of the process takes place in the presence of both parties, and because the explicit commitment on both sides is that Collaborative Law counsel will withdraw if they have any reason to doubt the good faith of their own clients.

The transformation that often occurs in the attorneys' capacity to find creative solutions to thorny issues in collaborative practice simply must be experienced to be believed, and the essential key to entering this "creative hyperspace" is the disqualification stipulation. Without it, you may have something cordial and reasonably effective in settling cases, but you do not have Collaborative Law. When the attorneys' range of options no longer includes going to court, the thought process changes from: "Well, we can always see what Judge Smith will do with this problem," to: 'If I don't come up with a way to solve this problem that the other three participants find acceptable, I've failed and I will have to withdraw." In Collaborative Law, if I cannot find a good solution for the other party's legitimate needs that is also acceptable to my client, the process ends just as surely as if my own client's problems are not being attended to sufficiently.

For those reasons, in a collaborative representation involving difficult issues, there is often a distinct moment when everyone around the table recognizes that either the four of them must figure out a solution, or the process ends and someone else will do the deciding.[38] At that point, instead

---

37. *See* Ronald J. Gilson and Robert H. Mnookin, *Disputing Through Agents: Cooperation and Conflict Between Lawyers in Litigation*, 94 COLUM. L. REV. 509 (1994).

38. It is important to emphasize that the clients are not giving up their right to have their dispute adjudicated in court. Either party can terminate the collaborative process and go to court at any time. The lawyers, however, cannot go with them. In this respect,

of the oppositional negotiations that characterize litigation-dominated settlement conferences, it often happens that both parties and both lawyers enter a creative problem-solving mode in which all build on the ideas emerging around the table. In that situation, surprising solutions can emerge that would have been unimaginable in a conventional negotiation. The process encourages imaginative lateral thinking at a high level among all four participants from the start. None of these effects is impossible to achieve in a traditional settlement negotiation, but nothing about the traditional lawyer-client relationship fosters these effects as Collaborative Law does.

Mediation, too, can be an effective dispute-resolution mode,[39] but it, too, lacks the powerful problem-solving potential that is at the structural core of Collaborative Law. First, in mediation, a single neutral mediator manages the negotiations and conflicts. Whether or not the clients have independent counsel assisting them, it is not the job of either the mediator or the attorneys to work privately with a very unreasonable or upset client so that productive negotiations can resume. Such problems can sink a mediation permanently. Second, the mediator is not able, as collaborative lawyers can, to deal well with one-sided delay, resistance, withholding of information, and similar problems that can impair the integrity and efficiency of the process. In Collaborative Law, the lawyers place their own integrity on the line, committing not to continue to represent a client who refuses to abide by the good faith commitments contained in the stipulation. Third, the single talent that lawyers most often bring to a dispute is creative problem-solving skill. With two lawyers working together to find mutually acceptable solutions, both clients benefit from the double professional talent engaged toward the same goal.

In short, Collaborative Law melds vigorous attorney advocacy and advice with a very sophisticated dispute resolution process that, at its best,

---

collaborative law is a "limited purpose retention." That being so, it is particularly important that the retention agreement is drafted clearly and that the clients fully understand and agree that should they go to court, they will need to retain new counsel.

39. Though not for all clients. In the family mediation model most prevalent in Northern California, attorneys do not participate directly in the process and are not present during mediation. Where there are significant imbalances in financial sophistication, negotiating skill, or emotional comfort about the divorce, or if serious emotional disturbance is present, it can be difficult for a neutral mediator to maintain the level playing field that is essential if a fair agreement is to result. Either an unfair agreement may result, or one or the other of the parties may perceive the mediator as biased and the process may end. Consequently, mediation may be best suited for the higher functioning divorcing spouses, those who are capable of handling conflict and strong feelings without losing their ability to negotiate.

engages the highest intentions and creativity of the participants. Many lawyers who are practicing Collaborative Law report a degree of enthusiasm and gratification from their work that had long been missing. Their clients genuinely appreciate the lawyers' work, and are quick to recognize that the risk of failure is being distributed to the attorneys as well as the parties.[40] Surprisingly often, the experience of solving problems without the emotional toll exacted in prior efforts to negotiate with the spouse leads clients to acts of spontaneous generosity at the bargaining table. More reconciliations have occurred during my six years of collaborative practice than in my preceding thirteen years in family law.[41]

Collaborative Law is not a panacea; nothing is. It isn't for every client, and it isn't for every lawyer.[42] There will always be clients who need to take their cases to trial, and there will always be lawyers ready and willing to assist them. For those lawyers who worry about the damage done to clients, their families, their lawyers, and our communities from unthink-

---

40. One client of mine, a successful forensic physician with a well-honed suspicion of lawyers, was especially delighted with this aspect of Collaborative Law. "If you guys can't solve the problem, you're out of a job!" he chortled. The lawyers, of course, tend to emphasize how effectively Collaborative Law provides incentives for difficult clients to behave reasonably. Both are true.

41. I attribute this to the fact that effective collaborative lawyers model and demonstrate good problem-solving skills and succeed in eliciting both spouses' positive participation in that process. Where there is a residual core of positive affection between the parties—and that is often present, but extinguished early in the conventional legal process—successful, cordial problem solving together sometimes moves couples to try again.

42. Collaborative Law requires basic honesty, self-respect, and at least a modicum of respect for the other spouse. It is inconsistent with active domestic violence and with certain kinds of mental illness and character disorders. For the process to work well, both parties need to trust the other's fundamental honesty as to assets, debts, and income; both need to take considerable personal responsibility for their own behavior; both need the ability to control emotions under stress sufficiently so that unacceptable outbursts do not fatally undermine the process. Further qualities correlated with successful collaborative representations include: that each party value integrity, civility, and a mutually fair outcome more than getting the biggest share of the pie above all else, and that each party be able to prioritize, and to take ultimate responsibility for devising and accepting their own terms for settlement. Not all clients can do these things. Nor can all lawyers engage in the self-examination, self-criticism, and retraining required to undo the instinctive, unreflective behavior of the career gladiator. Further, there will always be clients who prefer not to take so much responsibility for their own destinies, who would rather turn their cases over to lawyers and judges. And from time to time (but probably far less often than we might imagine) there will be, with all the good faith that could be desired, still an issue that cannot be resolved except via third-party decision-making. There are ways consistent with the collaborative process to contain resolution of those disputes and avoid runaway litigation, but discussion of them is beyond the scope of this article.

ing, avoidable adversarial conflict in divorce, Collaborative Law is a model worth learning about. It looks very much as if it could be the wave of the future.

Chapter 8

A Therapeutic Jurisprudence and Preventive Law Approach to Family Law

Stephen J. Anderer

David J. Glass

Introduction

As an introduction to the application of therapeutic jurisprudence and preventive law to the practice of family law, we will begin with a brief story involving the first author's wife and his older daughter, Arielle, who at the time was 2-1/2 years old.

When the first author was at work, Arielle would often ask the question, "Where is Daddy?" On more than one occasion his wife said, "He had to go to talk to the judge." Being at an inquisitive stage, Arielle asked, "What does that mean?" The author's wife, who is a licensed psychologist, said, "When people are having an argument, the judge helps them find solutions." That interesting description of the judge's role developed into a game whereby, seemingly out of the blue, Arielle would approach her father and say, "Let's fight over Blankie, Daddy. Mommy, you be the judge."

Arguments might start with the following exchange: "It's mine. No, it's mine." Then they might get more sophisticated: "Well, I had it first" and "But you're not using it." As the judge, mommy would then say, "Arielle, tell me what happened." After Arielle told her what happened, the judge would say, "How did that make you feel?" This was intriguing to the first author because he didn't think that judges or lawyers trying to teach about the legal system would ask the question, "How did that make you feel?"[1]

The judge, mommy, then asked daddy as the litigant to tell her what happened and how that made him feel. As the next step in the process, she asked both litigants: "What can we do so that both of you feel happy?"

_____

1. He subsequently realized that lawyers and judges interested in therapeutic jurisprudence might ask that question.

Daddy and Arielle tried to come up with as many choices as possible. In some cases, proposed solutions involved sharing the blankie or taking turns with the blankie. Sometimes, there were more creative solutions. For example, in one case where Arielle was fighting with daddy over milk, she kept the milk but went to get daddy a cracker as a way of solving the problem.

Once different alternatives were generated, one was selected as the best and again mommy asked, "How does that make you feel?" A lawyer or judge explaining the legal process would probably say that the question should be, "Do you think that's fair?" A therapeutic jurisprudence approach would entail asking both of these questions in determining whether the legal system is constructed in the best fashion.

The more we have thought about this vignette, the richer it has become. It is useful to examine our approach to dispute resolution through a developmental lens or through the eyes of a child. We're using the story here to illustrate two primary points. The first point is the importance of attending to emotion. The second point is the utility of a problem solving approach. In part, what the first author's wife was doing comes from a problem solving model and a specific program developed for children called Interpersonal Cognitive Problem Solving (ICPS; also known as "I Can Problem Solve.")[2] There is a rich literature on teaching problem solving skills as a therapeutic tool. That literature is fairly robust in suggesting that teaching problem solving has positive therapeutic effects.[3]

When the first author told his wife that he was going to use this example, she said, "Have I been practicing therapeutic jurisprudence?" Many of us involved in conflict resolution, whether from psychology or law, have been practicing therapeutic jurisprudence and preventive law to varying degrees, although most of us have been doing so without conscious awareness of doing so. We believe it is helpful to make the integration of therapeutic jurisprudence and preventive law with family law *explicit* and not simply *implicit*. We also believe that a more systematic approach to the integration is warranted. Finally, we believe that research and science should inform the integration.

---

2. Myrna B. Shure and George Spivack, *Interpersonal Cognitive Problem Solving and Primary Prevention: Programming for Preschool and Kindergarten Children*, Journal of Clinical Child Psychology 89 (Summer 1979).

3. *See, e.g.*, Arthur M. Nezu and Christine M. Nezu (Eds.), Clinical Decision Making in Behavior Therapy: A Problem-Solving Perspective (1989); Arthur M. Nezu et al., Problem-Solving Therapy for Depression: Theory, Research and Clinical Guidelines (1989).

The Developmental Model
Applied to Family Law

In thinking developmentally, we began our analysis by asking: "Where do family law disputes start and where do these disputes fit into peoples lives?" A developmental approach is important because it provides us with information about where we might intervene to address problems in a therapeutic manner, consistent with therapeutic jurisprudence, and also to prevent problems, consistent with preventive law. Figure one below shows our beginning efforts to construct a developmental model that will aid in thinking about a preventive law and therapeutic jurisprudence approach to family law.

Figure 1
Family Law Case Development

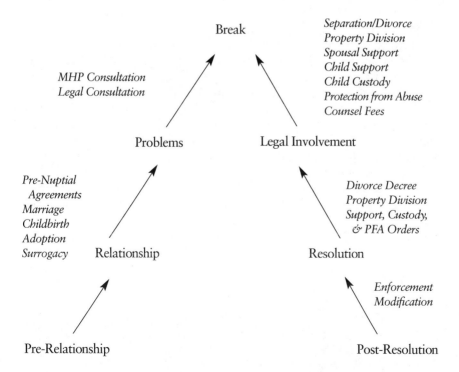

Each of the stages in figure one—from "Pre-Relationship" to "Post-Resolution"—are distinct periods at which attorneys, mental health professionals, and judges have the potential to intervene. Consistent with therapeutic jurisprudence and preventive law approaches, each step represents an opportunity to head-off disputes or steer matters toward a more satisfactory process or result. It is important to note that our model begins *not* with the initiation of the marital relationship or some other legally relevant relationship, even though the formation of such relationships typically begin a couple's interaction with the legal system. Rather, the model begins with the pre-relationship period. Also, it is important to note that most lawyering occurs on the down slope of this model, shortly after the point where the relationship has broken—the "Break" stage in figure one. Not enough attention is paid to the stages on the upward slope or to the stage at the very end of the down slope-the "Post-Resolution" stage.

As noted above, the first stage in the model is the "Pre-Relationship" stage. The pre-relationship factors affecting the development of family law problems include familial, cultural, educational and societal factors (*e.g.*, the media) as well as individual personality and temperament. Preventive interventions might address any of these factors. For example, programs have been developed to teach children relationship skills in school, with the purpose of preventing later marital disputes.

The next stage in the model is the "Relationship" stage. Legally relevant relationships can be formed through marriage, childbirth, adoption, pre-nuptial agreements, or surrogate parenting contracts, among other ways. Some examples of preventive interventions at this stage are pre-marital counseling, marriage contracts, adoption agreements, childbirth classes, parenting classes and childrearing agreements. Pre-nuptial agreements themselves might even be used as a preventive intervention.[4] In fact, an explicit purpose for most pre-nuptial agreements is to reduce the potential for future litigation.

The "Problems" stage is a stage at which there is a strong likelihood that there will be consultations with mental health professionals or lawyers. The consultations may occur when the problems have begun, but before someone has made a decision to break the relationship, or they may occur after the break. Lawyers and mental health professionals already are inter-

---

4. Florence Kaslow, *Enter the Pre-Nuptial: A Prelude to Marriage or Remarriage*, 9 BEHAVIORAL SCIENCES & THE LAW 375 (1991) (suggesting that the benefits of pre-nuptial agreements include: increased knowledge of each other, dispelling of the illusions of the other party so that a foundation of trust, integrity, love and respect can be substituted).

vening during this stage, and the question is how these interventions can be made more preventive and therapeutic. Specifically, what can be done by lawyers and mental health professionals to keep the relationship problems from turning into a formal legal dispute (*e.g.*, a divorce or child custody action)? Also, if the formal legal dispute is going to occur regardless of the efforts made by lawyers or mental health professionals, what can be done to make the process less emotionally traumatic for everyone involved?

In this model, the "Break" stage is the stage at which it is established that the parties' current relationship is at an end and the parties' are headed toward a new status (*e.g.*, separation, divorce, a custody arrangement, etc.). The break may or may not be a discrete point in time. The manner in which the break occurs can have profound implications for the development of and nature of later legal disputes between the parties and the therapeutic outcomes for the parties. Therefore, the principles of preventive law and therapeutic jurisprudence suggest that lawyers and mental health professionals may want to attempt to influence the manner in which the break occurs, if it is possible to do so.

More Formal Legal Involvement

After the "Break" stage comes a period of more formal involvement with the legal system, a stage we therefore call "Legal Involvement." In cases of divorce, the legal involvement can involve all of the issues listed in figure one, including actual separation and divorce, division of property, monetary support for the spouse and a child or children, child custody, protection from abuse and payment of counsel fees. It is during this stage that traditional methods of legal dispute resolution are engaged. There is room for therapeutic jurisprudence and preventive law thinking within the traditional legal framework, and such thinking is discussed herein. However, consideration should also be given to changing the traditional legal framework, and potential changes also are discussed herein.

The "Resolution" stage is the stage at which the dispute comes to an end, recognizing that the end may be uncertain, tentative or unstable. The resolution typically involves an agreement or an order from a court. Some resolutions may be more therapeutic than others, and some may be more in keeping with preventive law in preventing future legal disputes.

The "Post-Resolution" stage may involve issues of implementation, enforcement or modification of orders or agreements. Our focus is on what can be done both before and during this stage to ensure more therapeutic outcomes (*e.g.*, outcomes that maximize the psychological well-being of the parties) and to ensure fewer future disputes.

Focusing within the Legal Involvement Stage

Looking within the developmental model at the Legal Involvement stage, figure two shows the sub-stages of legal involvement.

We believe it is useful to break down the Legal Involvement stage into these sub-stages because each of these sub-stages presents discrete types of opportunities for intervention. Typically, legal involvement starts with an initial consultation, and the first sub-stage is therefore entitled "Initial Consultation." Even if a party is unrepresented by a lawyer, there is generally some consultation with someone within the legal system, be it a court intake worker or a judicial or quasi-judicial official. This first consultation sets the tone for all future interactions relating to the parties' dispute. We don't believe the importance of this initial consultation can be underestimated.

After the initial consultation, a decision generally needs to be made about contact with the other party. As discussed in more detail below, the manner in which this contact is initiated has profound implications for the

Figure 2
Sub-Stages of Legal Involvement

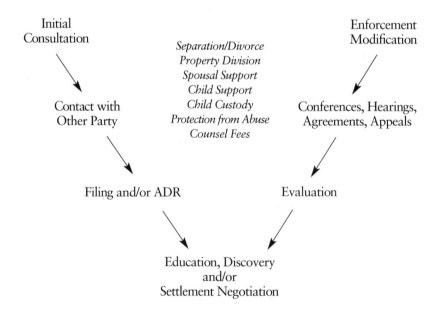

future course of the parties disputes and the therapeutic or anti-therapeutic nature of the process and outcomes of those disputes. Thus, although it is generally a fairly discrete step, we consider "Contact with Other Party" a separate sub-stage.

The next sub-stage is entitled "Filing and/or Alternative Dispute Resolution." In order to move a legal dispute toward resolution, one option is to file with the court in the traditional fashion starting with a pleading sometimes referred to as a "complaint." However, another option may be to initiate a form of alternative dispute resolution ("ADR"), such as mediation or arbitration.[5] Generally, parties must enter into an agreement to submit their dispute to mediation or arbitration, although some jurisdictions have developed programs that make mediation mandatory in specified circumstances. Here again, the decisions that are made about filing a complaint (*e.g.*, whether to file, when to file, the content of the filing, etc.) or the initiation of alternative dispute resolution will resonate throughout the future dispute resolution process, and therapeutic jurisprudence and preventive law dictate that the decisions be made with full consideration of their consequences.

Following the contact with the other party, and, in most cases, following filing and/or initiation of ADR, there is a period of "Education, Discovery and/or Settlement Negotiations." There are a variety of avenues for preventive law and therapeutic jurisprudence interventions during this period, not all of which are unique to family law. However, in family law disputes, there are often evaluations — of the parties, the children or the assets. The ubiquitous nature of these evaluations in family law disputes merits their inclusion as a separate "Evaluation" substage. It is widely assumed that evaluations can serve a preventive law function of reducing litigation. The evaluations also can serve therapeutic ends. All too often, however, a poorly executed evaluation process can have anti-therapeutic effects.

The next sub-stage of Legal Involvement in our model is entitled "Conferences, Hearings, Agreements and Appeals." Unless and until an agreement is reached between the parties to a family law dispute, they will participate in a legal process involving conferences and hearings with third party decision-makers (*e.g.*, masters or judges). Those may result in a court order, which may then be appealed. It is during this sub-stage that the lawyer who is attempting to approach dispute resolution from therapeutic jurisprudence and preventive law perspectives is most constrained by the existing legal framework and may find him or herself frustrated by the status quo of legal rules, procedures and institutions. A therapeutic jurispru-

---

5. Leonard B. Loeb, *New Forms of Resolving Disputes—ADR*, 33 FAMILY LAW QUARTERLY 581 (1999).

dence and preventive law approach to family law disputes requires consideration of changes to existing legal rules, procedures and institutions.

Even after an agreement is reached or there is a final order (in Figure one, this is at the "Resolution" stage after the "Legal Involvement" stage), enforcement or modification issues may arise (in Figure one, these issues fall within the "Post-Resolution" stage). Our focus is on what can be done both before and during this period to ensure more therapeutic outcomes and to ensure fewer future disputes.

Following a Child Custody Case through the Developmental Model

What follows is a more detailed analysis of a preventive law and therapeutic approach to one area of family law — child custody. At each stage, we need to think about what can be done to prevent future problems and improve the therapeutic outcomes, and, specifically, what we can do as legislators, court administrators, lawyers, mental health professionals, judges and members of society. The discussion is primarily based upon our clinical experience as attorneys, but the need for attorneys to inform their clinical practices through research is a theme throughout.

Figure 3
Child Custody from Start to Finish

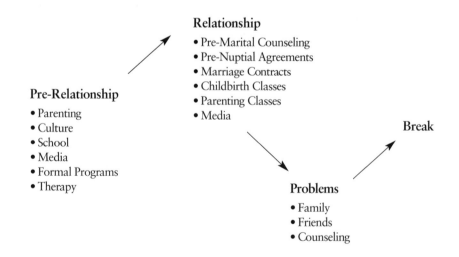

Relationship
- Pre-Marital Counseling
- Pre-Nuptial Agreements
- Marriage Contracts
- Childbirth Classes
- Parenting Classes
- Media

Pre-Relationship
- Parenting
- Culture
- School
- Media
- Formal Programs
- Therapy

Break

Problems
- Family
- Friends
- Counseling

Pre-Relationship

Looking at the "Pre-Relationship" stage in figure three, the listed factors are just some of the factors that may affect a couple's development of later disputes, and specifically child custody disputes. These factors also may influence the manner in which couples approach the resolution of those disputes. For example, what we teach as parents—for example, what we teach our children about parental roles, about conflict resolution, et cetera—will have an impact on whether our children have disputes over child custody when they become parents and how they handle those disputes that do arise. More broadly, cultural factors, not only differences among countries, but also differences among sub-cultures within a country result in differing approaches to parenting and dispute resolution.[6]

If we view preventive law approaches as including efforts at primary prevention, then interventions designed to address any of the listed pre-relationship factors fall within the preventive law framework. The failure of lawyers to consider the potential for early interventions to reduce family law disputes is analogous to the failure of physicians to consider the potential for vaccinations and education about healthy diets, hygiene and exercise to reduce disease. We are remiss if we don't consider that school programs teaching children about parenting and conflict resolution may serve to prevent later child custody litigation. We also are remiss if we don't consider the messages that we send through the popular media about disputes over child custody (*e.g.*, that fleeing with your children is an acceptable alternative to a flawed legal process) or that are more broadly transmitted by our culture (*e.g.*, that there is something wrong with a woman who does not have primary custody of her children or that there is something wrong with a man who chooses childrearing over a career).

---

6. *See, e.g.*, Benjamin Silliman & Walter R. Schumm, *Client Interests in Premarital Counseling*, 21 JOURNAL OF SEX & MARITAL THERAPY 43 (1995) (survey results show that subjects with more supportive family backgrounds were more likely to participate in premarital counseling programs and religious subjects tended to want longer and mandatory programs for persons seeking to marry); Lee M. Williams, *Premarital Counseling: A Needs Assessment Among Engaged Individuals*, 14 CONTEMPORARY FAMILY THERAPY 505 (1992) (subjects specific requests from premarital counseling included keeping romance alive, handling anger or silence, learning how to resolve differences, and the effect of children on marriage); Jeffrey H. Larson, *"You're My One and Only": Premarital Counseling for Unrealistic Beliefs About Mate Selection*, 20 AMERICAN JOURNAL OF FAMILY THERAPY 242 (1992) (detailing cognitive therapy techniques for use in premarital counseling for unrealistic beliefs such as the perfect self, the perfect mate, the perfect relationship, the try harder, the love is enough, the cohabitation, the opposites complement each other, and the choosing should be easy).

Relationship

There are a variety of interventions by lawyers, mental health professionals and others that take place at or around the time a legally relevant relationship is formed through marriage or childbirth. Some of these interventions are listed under the "Relationship" heading in figure three. Although future child custody disputes may not be the focus of these interventions, these established interventions provide a potential avenue for a preventive law and therapeutic jurisprudence approach designed to reduce future child custody disputes and minimize psychological trauma in disputes that do arise.

A host of research papers have examined the effectiveness of premarital counseling or educational programs.[7] The general finding has been that although the concept of preparation for marriage is good, the current value of these programs is limited. Several studies have examined issues of couple compatibility and the prediction of satisfaction with the marital relationship.[8] Likewise, another list of papers has examined the predictive

---

7. *See, e.g.,* Christine Senediak, *The Value of Premarital Education*, 11 AUSTRAILIAN & NEW ZEALAND JOURNAL OF FAMILY THERAPY 26 (1990) (current premarital education program typically suffer from lack of specific goals in the program format and poor evaluation procedures to examine effectiveness); Walter R. Schumm, Gary Resnick, Benjamin Silliman, & D. Bruce Bell, *Premarital Counseling and Marital Satisfaction Among Civilian Wives of Military Service Members*, 24 JOURNAL OF SEX & MARITAL THERAPY 21 (1998) (where both parties attended and enjoyed premarital counseling, parties reported higher level of marital satisfaction); Eddie W. Parish, *A Quasi-Experimental Evaluation of the Premarital Assessment Program for Premarital Counseling*, 13 AUSTRALIAN & NEW ZEALAND JOURNAL OF FAMILY THERAPY 33 (1992) (evaluation of a premarital psychoeducational program aimed at reducing the prevalence of marital dysfunction showed that program that stressed communication associated with greatest rate of relationship success); Russell D. Bishop, *An Evaluation of Premarital Counseling from an Adlerian Perspective*, 49 INDIVIDUAL PSYCHOLOGY 294 (1993).

8. Blaine J. Fowers, Kelly H. Montel & David H. Olson, *Predicting Marital Success for Premarital Couple Types Based on PREPARE*, 22 JOURNAL OF MARITAL AND FAMILY THERAPY 103 (1996) (subjects grouped into four premarital types—vitalized, harmonious, traditional, and conflicted—and relationship outcome over 3 year period tested, revealing that conflicted subjects most likely to separate or divorce, and vitalized subjects had the highest levels of satisfaction); Thomas B. Holman & Bing Dao Li, *Premarital Factors Influencing Perceived Readiness for Marriage*, 18 JOURNAL OF FAMILY ISSUES 124 (1997) (readiness of subjects for marriage depend largely on contextual issues, such as family of origin and sociodemographic characteristics and on the quality of couple interaction); Renate M. Houts, Elliot Robins, & Ted L. Huston, *Compatibility and the Development of Premarital Relationships*, 58 JOURNAL OF MARRIAGE AND THE FAMILY 7 (1996) (the more similar subjects role performance preferences and leisure interests were to those of the partner, the more compatible the couple reported themselves).

nature of a diverse assortment of premarital factors from premarital cohabitation to something else.[9] An intriguing question is how these programs and factors affect the later development and resolution of custody disputes. Similarly, it would be worthwhile to examine the manner in which prenuptial agreements, marriage contracts, childbirth classes and parenting classes affect the later development and resolution of custody disputes. Ultimately, it is worthwhile considering how these established interventions can serve preventive law and therapeutic jurisprudence ends in relation to child custody disputes.

Problems

As noted above, it is at the "Problems" stage that couples are most likely to consult with lawyers or mental health professionals. The consultations with lawyers may be informal information gathering meetings. Consultations at this stage-when problems have developed but the relationship has not yet reached the breaking point-may be crucial in determining the future course of the relationship. For that reason, these consultations are deserving of systematic study. It would be useful to know what does happen in these consultations, whether with lawyers or mental health professionals, and what the impact is of the various things that these professionals say and do. Does consulting with a lawyer when problems develop make it more or less likely that parties will proceed toward a formal break in the relationship and litigation? What is the impact of consulting with a mental health professional? Do prior consultations with either lawyers or mental health professionals affect the course of the litigation or its emotional impact?

Although there is consensus that the formal legal system for family law problems needs improvement, there is room for improvement in the places where much of the work is done-in the offices of attorneys and mental health professionals and in their interactions with clients and one another outside of court. These interactions can be every bit as therapeutic or counter-therapeutic as what transpires in court.

If data were gathered about the types of clients who come into custody disputes, and it were possible to track these types of clients longitudinal-

---

9. Vijaya Krishnan, *Premarital Cohabitation and Marital Disruption*, 28 JOURNAL OF DIVORCE & REMARRIAGE 157 (1998) (women whose marriages were preceded by cohabitation more likely to break their marriages and frequent attenders of church services less likely to report marital disruption); David A. Smith, Dina Vivian & K. Daniel O'Leary, *Longitudinal Prediction of Marital Discord from Premarital Expressions of Affect*, 58 JOURNAL OF CONSULTING & CLINICAL PSYCHOLOGY 790 (1990) (affective features of dyadic communication bear importantly on relationship satisfaction).

ly over the course of the dispute resolution and beyond, the data would be of great utility to lawyers. In effect, attorneys might be able to anticipate that when a particular type of client comes in, there are particular things to look out for, there are particular questions that might best be asked, and there is a particular approach that will be most helpful.[10] Ideally, attorneys would have a literature base to consult so they are not taken by surprise when problems develop.

The interventions of lay persons also are deserving of study. For example, once problems are encountered in a relationship, how do family and friends contribute to the problems or mediate the effects of the problems? Of even more basic importance — what is the impact of marriage or relationship counseling? What do that data say about the success rate for avoiding divorce through counseling? What kinds of people enter marriage or relationship counseling?[11] How much does marriage counseling really help?[12] Turning the focus back to child custody specifically, to what

---

10. Robert M. Counts & Anita Sacks, *Profiles of the Divorce Prone: The Self Involved Narcissist*, 15 JOURNAL OF DIVORCE & REMARRIAGE 51 (1991) (describing the typical family, past history, and marital history of a subgroup of identified divorce-prone persons); Toni L. Thiriot & Eugene T. Buckner, *Multiple Predictors of Satisfactory Post-Divorce Adjustment of Single Custodial Parents*, 17 JOURNAL OF DIVORCE & REMARRIAGE 27 (1991) (strongest single predictor of divorce adjustment was the custodial parent's own subjective sense of well-being; other significant factors included sense of social status and economic position, who initiated the divorce, and employment satisfaction).

11. Judith M. Larson, *Examining Reconciliation*, 11 MEDIATION QUARTERLY 95 (1993) (examines the misconception of divorce as the only outcome after marital problems); Suzanne Freedman, *Forgiveness and Reconciliation*, 42 COUNSELING & VALUES 200 (1998) (offering guidelines for counselors for teaching how the concepts of forgiveness and reconciliation differ); Howard Wineberg, *An Examination of Divorced Women Who Attempted a Marital Reconciliation Before Becoming Divorced*, 22 JOURNAL OF DIVORCE & REMARRIAGE 129 (1995) (The age of female subjects negatively correlated with attempts to achieve reconciliation before becoming divorced; likewise educational level and age homogamy were significantly related to the increased reconciliation behavior); Howard Wineberg, *The Prevalence and Characteristics of Blacks Having a Successful Marital Reconciliation*, 25 JOURNAL OF DIVORCE & REMARRIAGE 75 (1996) (age at separation and premarital fertility the only significantly related variables for successful reconciliation out of a battery of variables tested); Howard Wineberg, *Association Between Having a Failed Marital Reconciliation in the First Marriage and Dissolution of the Second Marriage*, 27 JOURNAL OF DIVORCE & REMARRIAGE 39 (1997) (women who attempted reconciliation in first marriage and failed were more likely to show marital instability in their second marriage as compared to similarly previously divorced and later re-married women).

12. Robert L. Smith, Jon Carlson, Patricia Stevens-Smith & Michelle Dennison, *Marriage and Family Counseling*, 74 JOURNAL OF COUNSELING & DEVELOPMENT 154 (1995)

extent are parenting issues a focus and how are they affected by counseling?

For example, does the experience of going through marriage counseling and learning how to argue fairly and how to resolve disputes affect co-parenting in the future?[13]

Figure 4
Child Custody from Start to Finish

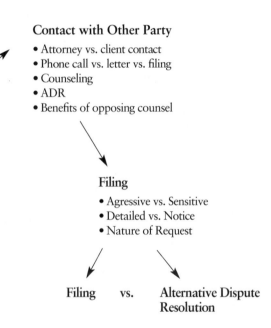

Contact with Other Party
- Attorney vs. client contact
- Phone call vs. letter vs. filing
- Counseling
- ADR
- Benefits of opposing counsel

Initial Consultation
- Pre-set attitude vs. client driven
- Approach to reconcilaiton
- Referral for counseling
- Use of educational materials
- Proposal of ADR
- Fact-gathering
- Focus on emotional issues
- Focus on relationship issues
- Legal and practical advice

Filing
- Agressive vs. Sensitive
- Detailed vs. Notice
- Nature of Request

Filing   vs.   Alternative Dispute Resolution

(provides a good overview of marriage and family counseling, including standards for training and credentialing and special ethical considerations for clinicians).

13. Julianne M. Serovich, Sharon J. Price, Steven F. Chapman & David W. Wright, *Attachment Between Former Spouses: Impact on Co-Parenting Communication and Parental Involvement*, 17 JOURNAL OF DIVORCE & REMARRIAGE 109 (1992) (attachment may not be an adequate predictor in how involved divorced males are with their children—rather, family boundary ambiguity in divorced families may contribute to low parental involvement and poor co-parental communication); Donna Hendrickson Christenson & Kathryn D. Rettig, *The Relationship of Remarriage to Post-Divorce Co-Parenting*, 24 JOURNAL OF DIVORCE & REMARRIAGE 73 (1995) (remarriage associated with less frequent co-parental interaction, less reported parenting support from the former spouse, and more negative attitudes about the other parent for both women and men).

Initial Consultation

After the break in the relationship, at the stage where there is more established involvement of lawyers and the legal system, there often is a more formal "Initial Consultation" with a lawyer. This consultation sets the tone for all future interactions relating to the parties' dispute. Figure four lists some of the factors that we think about clinically, but also that we think need to be researched. A few of these factors are worth highlighting. For example, what kind of educational materials should be provided to people at that initial consultation? How should the potential for reconciliation be approached? Under what circumstances is it appropriate to recommend counseling, whether individual or marital counseling? When should alternative dispute resolution be proposed? To what extent should emotional issues and how the client feels be a focus of the consultation? To what extent should advice be given, and what effect does that advice have? These are clinical questions, but they could be informed by research. The question of the psychological impact on clients of the manner in which an attorney approaches the initial consultation can be answered empirically.

Our training in therapy gives us a clinical predisposition as attorneys toward focusing on emotions and empathizing with clients. Moreover, we adopt a problem-solving approach in our consultations with clients.[14] (Recall the vignette with which this article began). During the initial consultation a lawyer has the opportunity to help the client better define the problem he or she is facing. The attorney also can offer, or better, help the client develop options for dealing with those problems. In the terms of problem-solving therapy, the lawyer can help the client "generate alternative solutions" to the problem. Following a preventive law approach, the alternative solutions that are generated should include solutions outside the strict legal framework (*e.g.*, direct discussion with the other party, intercession of a trusted family advisor or family member, consultation with a mental health professional, etc.). The lawyer can also help the client understand the potential consequences-risks and benefits-of the various alternative solutions. Following a therapeutic jurisprudence approach, the potential consequences that are identified should include the emotional and relational consequences.[15]

---

14. *See, e.g.,* Thomas J. D'Zurilla & Arthur M. Nezu, *Development and Preliminary Evaluation of the Social Problem-Solving Inventory*, 2 PSYCHOLOGICAL ASSESSMENT: A JOURNAL OF CONSULTING AND CLINICAL PSYCHOLOGY 156 (1990) (discussing a well-developed model of social problem-solving).

15. Dennis P. Stolle et al., *Integrating Preventive Law and Therapeutic Jurisprudence: A Law and Psychology Based Approach to Lawyering*, 34 CALIFORNIA WESTERN LAW REVIEW 15 (1997). This article by Stolle et al. also discusses the joint decision-making

Although the attitude with which we approach the initial consultation is in part pre-determined by our problem solving approach, there must be a balance between that pre-determined attitude and the needs and desires of the client. For example, we frequently get referral requests from colleagues that say a friend or family member needs "an aggressive lawyer" or a "shark." Along those lines, we get clients who come in and say "I'm going to get her" or "I'm not going let him get away with this." On the one hand, a lawyer who simply says, "That's right, we're going to get him (her)" may be doing his or her client a disservice. There are costs associated with "getting" the other party. Apart from the financial costs of protracted litigation, there are emotional costs associated with that litigation. Maintaining anger toward the other party, and even increasing it through aggressive litigation tactics, may not be best for the client's psychological well-being. The available research suggests that protracted litigation may have negative effects on the psychological well-being of children.[16]

On the other hand, the client has a need for understanding of, and empathy with, his or her point of view. If we as lawyers do not acknowledge our client's perspectives, then the attorney-client relationship, if it is ever established, will inevitably be troubled. Moreover, as lawyers, we have a duty to pursue the objectives of our clients, within limits, rather than our own.

In attempting to strike the proper balance, we have found that although clients in the heat of marital disputes often have difficulty recognizing the negative effect their conduct has on their children, they may understand that acting aggressively will make them look bad in the eyes of a judge who hears their custody case. Furthermore, they may accept that an aggressive strategy will make it more difficult to develop a working co-parenting relationship with the other parent and to get cooperation on a variety of issues (e.g., where the child goes to school, child support, etc.). The initial consultation may be a time to explore these potential unintended consequences. If the client then says that he or she thought about those consequences but this is the strategy he or she wants to pursue, then it may be appropriate to take an aggressive advocacy approach. The lawyer may not make the ultimate choice, but he or she should offer the alternatives and make sure the client's choice is informed.

The issue of timing is pervasive in family law. At the initial consultation the client might not be in the emotional state (e.g., because of anger, depression, anxiety) to be receptive to thinking about some of these other

---

process used by lawyers and clients in preventive law, a process that is consistent with the problem-solving approach discussed above. *Id.* at 16- 17.

16. *See, e.g.,* Janet R. Johnston et al., *Ongoing Post-Divorce Conflict: Effects on Children of Joint Custody and Frequent Access,* 59 AMERICAN JOURNAL OF ORTHOPSYCHIATRY 576 (1989).

issues. However, research suggests that people's attitudes and emotions change over the course of a break-up and eventual divorce.[17]

Contact with the Other Party

As noted above, the stage at which an attorney makes contact with the other parent (*see* Figure 4) is a sensitive point in the development of the case and is worthy of significant attention.[18] How should the attorney handle it? Should the attorney make the initial contact without warning or should the client him or herself speak to the other party to say, "We're heading toward divorce.[19] I've spoken to an attorney, and he will be getting in touch with you." For example, in a case where a client is still living with her husband and has only spoken to him vaguely about the idea of separating, it may not be the best approach to have a process server show up with legal papers and hand them to her husband. We have heard people after the fact say things such as, "I'll never forgive you for the way you notified me about this," or "You never said anything to me, I saw you the night before, I saw you that day, and you didn't say anything before this guy showed up."

Also, other details are deserving of attention-whether the attorney begins with a telephone call, a letter, or the filing of a formal complaint. Treating the other person with dignity can have long-term benefits as to what direction a dispute takes. Having the client say to her spouse, "Look, there's will be some papers coming; here's what they're all about," may set the right initial tone.[20]

Non-lawyers might believe that lawyers like it when there is no attorney on the other side and a person is representing himself or herself, because it could appear to give the lawyer a chance to really take advantage of the other party. In fact, most lawyers find that there are benefits to having

17. Shelley Day Sclater, *Narratives of Divorce*, 19 JOURNAL OF SOCIAL WELFARE AND FAMILY LAW 423 (1997) (divorce process described in developmental terms and compared to people's recovery after traumatic events and grieving); Michael S. Kolevzon & Susan J. Gottlieb, *The Impact of Divorce: A Multivariate Study*, 7 JOURNAL OF DIVORCE 89 (1983) (surveyed members of a divorced parents' group to test the validity of existing theories regarding the phases of emotional readjustment after divorce).

18. In the terms of Stolle et al., this point is a "psycholegal soft spot." Stolle et al., *supra* note 16, at 42-44.

19. Or "We need to get a child custody order."

20. Our department chair, who has been in practice for more than 35 years, has said that there are certain days not to serve people with divorce papers, or custody papers: birthdays (whether the other parent's or a child's), wedding anniversaries, Valentine's Day and April Fool's day, among others.

attorneys on both sides, because attorneys should help to modulate the emotions of the parties and bring some rationality and predictability to the process. Lawyers can help by imposing some structure imposed during a chaotic period when the parties don't know what's going to happen or who is in charge.

However, having opposing counsel is not always a benefit. One of the best predictors of what route a case is going to take is who the attorney is that the opposing party hires. With certain attorneys, it may inevitably be a knock-down-drag-out fight, and every issue, no matter how insignificant may be contested. There are limits to a lawyer's ability to prevent litigation when opposing counsel is uncooperative, and the counter-therapeutic actions of opposing counsel can more than neutralize a lawyer's therapeutic efforts.

It is not uncommon to hear clients say, "We're too nice, they're aggressive and they get whatever they want." It may appear that way to certain clients even when it is not accurate, and it is necessary to display an appropriate amount of forcefulness in pursuing the client's objectives. However, in some cases, it may be possible to redirect the client who insists on "fighting fire with fire" by reminding that client that sometimes the best way to fight a fire is with water. Ideally, it will be possible to reassure the clients that the judge hearing the matter is a good judge who will not tolerate inappropriately aggressive or unprofessional advocacy and who will respect, and possibly reward, a more reasonable approach.

Filing

As discussed above, the decisions that are made about filing a complaint (*e.g.*, whether to file, when to file, the content of the filing, etc.) will resonate throughout the future dispute resolution process, and therapeutic jurisprudence and preventive law dictate that the decisions be made with full consideration of their consequences. Figure four lists some of the issues that should be considered by the attorney as he or she thinks about the content of any filing in a child custody action. Should the lawyer take an aggressive approach, or should the lawyer take a more sensitive approach and try to keep matters amicable? For example, in the initial filing, it may or may not necessary to lay out the opposing party's mental health problems and substance abuse history and strenuously attack that party's parenting capacity.

Also, what should the attorney request in his or her pleading with the court? For example, if a father really wants to have substantial partial physical custody of the child but recognize that the mother should have primary physical custody, should the father's attorney nevertheless take an aggressive approach and ask that the father have the child most of the time because that will give the father more negotiating leverage? That is an approach that may in fact be counterproductive in leading to greater litigation and higher emotional as well as financial costs for both parties, but it is one that many lawyers take.

Alternative Dispute Resolution

Alternative dispute resolution methods such as arbitration and mediation have been promoted as less expensive than traditional litigation.[21] Many advocates of alternative dispute resolution also assert that a major advantage of alternative dispute resolution is that it is less psychologically traumatic than traditional litigation.[22] It is assumed that the children as well as the parties will benefit psychologically by avoiding traditional litigation.

One question that is still on the research agenda is whether there are certain types of cases that are not appropriate for mediation.[23] There is some literature, and many commentators have said, that domestic violence cases may not be appropriate for mediation. Also, in some cases, the two parties may be so far apart that they need a judge to intervene and make an authoritative determination. Courts can prolong the resolution of some matters by forcing mediation on the assumption that the parties "should be able to work this out." The delay in resolution is often associated with the anti-therapeutic consequences of continued uncertainty and turmoil for the parties and the children.

For example, we had a case in which one parent lived in Hawaii, and one parent lived in Pennsylvania, thousands of miles apart. The issue of with whom the child was going to reside primarily during the school year was never going to be solved by mediation, and the interim resolution of six

---

21. Joan B. Kelly, *Is Mediation Less Expensive? Comparison of Mediated and Adversarial Divorce Costs*, 8 MEDIATION QUARTERLY 15 (1990) (compared subjects going through these two routes for divorce; found that the 2-attorney adversarial process involved 134% more in total fees than couples using a comprehensive divorce mediation to resolve all issues).

22. Loeb, *supra* note 6, at 582-83.

23. Sam Margulies & Anya Luchow, *Litigation, Mediation, and the Psychology of Divorce*, 20 JOURNAL OF PSYCHIATRY & LAW 483 (1992) (providing detailed criticism of how the adversarial legal system is poorly designed to meet the psychological needs of families); Craig A. McEwen, Lynn Mather & Richard J. Maiman, *Lawyers, Mediators, and the Management of Divorce Practice*, 149 LAW & SOCIETY REVIEW 149 (1994) (concluding that lawyers, as a group, suffer from the widespread misassumption that divorce mediation and divorce lawyers are incompatible; also reporting results from a mandatory mediation program in Maine)

Figure 5
Child Custody from Start to Finish

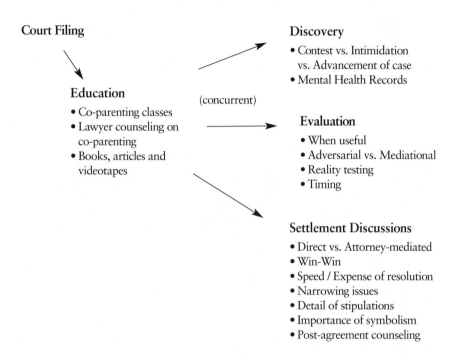

Court Filing

Education
- Co-parenting classes
- Lawyer counseling on co-parenting
- Books, articles and videotapes

(concurrent)

Discovery
- Contest vs. Intimidation vs. Advancement of case
- Mental Health Records

Evaluation
- When useful
- Adversarial vs. Mediational
- Reality testing
- Timing

Settlement Discussions
- Direct vs. Attorney-mediated
- Win-Win
- Speed / Expense of resolution
- Narrowing issues
- Detail of stipulations
- Importance of symbolism
- Post-agreement counseling

months in Hawaii and six months in Pennsylvania was traumatic for everyone involved. Once a judge made the basic decision about where the child was going to be primarily, then the rest of the details could be mediated. This was a matter that needed to be resolved by a third party decision maker.

In some cases, the parties may need a full-blown trial to get the feeling that they did everything they could, that they got to fully speak their minds, that their concenrs were considered or that they simply "had their day in court." In sum, more information is needed on whether mediation is more appropriate for some cases than for others.

Education

Figure five shows some of the activities that might occur following a court filing. Lawyers, courts and mental health professionals may make efforts to educate the parties, and in some cases, their children. Some courts have instituted mandatory videotapes, educational sessions or co-parenting classes or counseling. Notwithstanding the good intentions of such mandates, it is an open question whether coerced education or counseling is effective.[24] At the point of filing a divorce when so much else is going on, are there benefits to getting the people into a co-parenting class that teaches them what to expect, how to talk to their children about divorce, et cetera? Are there benefits to ordering parents into "co-parenting counseling?" How does the coercive element of the court mandating attendance affect people's attitudes going in and coming out? Do these efforts at education and counseling reduce future litigation?

Discovery

In Pennsylvania, the courts have chosen to limit discovery in child custody cases on the assumption that the harm caused by allowing open discovery in those cases will outweigh the benefits. However, the impact of allowing discovery in custody cases is an empirical question. The process of discovery can become a contest or the tools of discovery can be used by attorneys to intimidate a party. On the other hand, discovery also can be used to advance the case toward the search for the best interests of the child.

A common and instructive example arises when one parent has been in mental health treatment. The records of that treatment may be relevant to the best interests of the child. In some cases, their release may even lead to a negotiated resolution by providing reassurance to the other parent that the treated parent is psychologically fit to care for the children. However, those records can also be sought with an improper motive-to harass and intimidate. Moreover, the release of such records may defeat the purpose of privilege laws designed to facilitate therapy.

Once again, we are confronted with unanswered empirical questions. Does allowing discovery lead to greater litigation or more frequent settlements? What therapeutic and counter-therapeutic effects does discovery have?

Child Custody Evaluations

The provision of psychological and psychiatric child custody evaluations has becoming a booming business in the United States. Very often

---

24. Second author David Glass conducted his dissertation research on coercion to drug treatment. Judges frequently ordered that part of a person's probation was going to drug treatment, and questions arose as to how that coercion affected the actual therapy that occurred. Dr. Glass conducted empirical research on the impact of various forms of coercion on the drug treatment. Similar research could be conducted to evaluate co-parenting classes or counseling.

mental health professionals are asked to do evaluations of the parties and the children in a custody dispute to come up with recommendations for the courts. There is a lot more that needs to be done to help us determine when such evaluations are useful and exactly how those evaluation should be done-for example, what kind of approach they should take. Some empirical research has at least begun to examine the practices followed by child custody evaluators.[25]

The evaluation process may provide another opportunity for preventive law and therapeutic jurisprudence interventions. When the report comes back from the mental health professional, there may be an opportunity for some reality checking. Typically, the report will point out the strengths and weaknesses of both parties and some clients may be receptive to that feedback. For example, "Did you see what your psychologist said about your wife, that she had a very good bond with the child, and she is especially good at working with homework." Some clients may even be able to acknowledge the good points of the spouse. It also may provide a reality test for the client's objectives. For example, maybe he or she is pushing for primary custody, and that might not be a realistic goal in light of the factors set forth in the evaluators report and to be considered by the court. The client may be able to see another point of view and other options. Furthermore, the receipt of the custody evaluation also provides an opportunity to discuss with the client the effect that the custody litigation could be having on the children.[26]

Settlement Discussions

Figure five highlights a number of different aspects of settlement discussions. In some cases, it may be more "therapeutic" for the parties to conduct settlement discussions directly between themselves whereas in

---

25. Marc J. Ackerman & Melissa C. Ackerman, *Child Custody Evaluation Practices: A 1996 Survey of Psychologists*, 30 FAM. L.Q. 565, 572 (1996). *But see* Chery Hysjulien, Barbara Wood & G. Andrew Benjamin, *Child Custody Evaluations: A Review of Methods Used in Litigation and Alternative Dispute Resolution*, 32 FAMILY & CONCILIATION COURTS REVIEW 466 (1994) (concluding that although psychological tests, semi-structured interviews and behavioral observations of parents and children are often used in child custody disputes, there is little empirical evidence to support the efficacy of methods typically used by professionals making recommendations to the courts).

26. *See* Kathryn E. Maxwell, *Preventive Lawyering Strategies to Mitigate the Detrimental Effects of Clients' Divorces on Their Children*, 67 REVISTA JURIDICA UNIVERSIDAD DE PUERTO RICO 137 (examining preventive and therapeutic strategies for lawyers to attempt to minimize the anti-therapeutic effects of divorce on their clients' children) (1998).

other cases it may be best to have the settlement discussions mediated by the attorneys. Even if the attorneys are going to conduct the settlement discussions, a variety of options are available. For example, the discussions may be in-person, with or without the parties being present; they may be by telephone; or they may be conducted through letters or e-mail. Although some attorneys may have an intuitive sense of which method is best for a particular case, more often the method may be selected by happenstance. The decision on how to conduct settlement discussions is deserving of thought, and should be informed by the available research. There is an extensive literature on how to conduct settlement negotiations, and a therapeutic approach to family law involves drawing particularly on that literature advocating "win-win" solutions.[27]

We have encountered certain practices in communications from attorneys that are destructive. It is all too common for lawyers to use sarcasm and make gratuitous insults (*i.e,* "Your client never gave a damn about the children when the parties were married," "Your client isn't working, so you would think she'd be able to take care of the children better," or "Your client is an irresponsible drunk."). Clients who are accustomed to social conventions of being polite and exercising good manners are shocked by this behavior by attorneys, and it can create anger and resentment as the clients feel their integrity is being challenged. We often hear clients say, "How does he (or she) get away with it?" or "Can't I complain to the bar association?" While the rules of battle may apply once the parties are in court, there is virtually[28] no purpose that is served by these types of comments in letters from attorneys. In fact, because these communications engender hostility, they are counterproductive.

Two additional aspects of settlement discussions should be highlighted. One is the importance of symbolism. In the United Kingdom and in some jurisdictions within the United States, there have been changes from using terms such as "custody" toward using terms such as "parenting arrangement" or "parenting plan." In some states, there has been a big movement toward the idea of shared parenting, or shared custody. We've found that the language attorneys use in the agreement, or even in the negotiations, can have tremendous impact on the other party. An attorney can present the same physical arrangement, but if the agreement states that the parties have "shared" physical custody rather than that one party

---

27. *Id.* at 157 (advocating that lawyers and clients read ROGER FISHER & WILLIAM URY, GETTING TO YES (Bruce Patton, ed., 1981)).

28. I say virtually no purpose because abusive comments may temporarily appease the client, who may be angry or even abusive. However, the comments inevitably provoke a response that only angers the client further.

has "primary" physical custody and the other party "partial" physical custody, a party can feel much better about it. Conversely, one party may object to the "shared" language, and it may be best to leave out any reference to that. The use of terms such as "primary," "shared," or "partial" custody can have significance to parents, and lawyers need to be attuned to that.

Other opportunities for a therapeutic jurisprudence and preventive law approach present themselves when attorneys are negotiating the specific terms of a stipulation for custody. In some cases, the parties may be working together reasonably well, and it may be best for attorneys to prepare a "bare bones" stipulation with a provision that other aspects of the custody arrangement shall be "as the parties can agree." The parties are encouraged to work out the remaining details over time in recognition that forcing them to haggle over the details at the present time may lead to a deterioration of their cooperative relationship.

In other cases, or at other points in time, it may be worthwhile to prepare a detailed stipulation that goes beyond a simple statement of the schedule, such as, "Father will have the children on alternate weekends and Wednesday night for dinner." The parties may need more guidance, with exact times and directions for pick-up and delivery of the children. They may need to be directed to share information about schooling, religious classes and extra-curricular activities. There may need to be language stating that the parties will consult with each other before any major decision-making affecting the child. The parties may need provisions with times for telephone calls and what is to be done if the children are not at home at the scheduled time for a call. The stipulation may have provisions reminding parents that when they have the child the other parent should have access by mail or e-mail, and that the other parent should be notified if one parent takes the children out of town.

It is a matter of being attuned to the parties with whom the attorney is dealing, and also, again, it is a timing issue. With some people once the basic agreement is down, if you give them some time they can work out the rest. Other parties will never be able to work out any details on their own, and the attorney will need to specify everything.

Hearings/Conferences

The discussion above demonstrates that many of the opportunities for taking a therapeutic jurisprudence approach present themselves well before the parties enter a court or hearing room. Even more obviously, preventive law approaches strive to avoid formal legal proceedings. Nevertheless, family law cases can and do proceed to court. As noted above, that is

Figure 6
Child Custody from Start to Finish

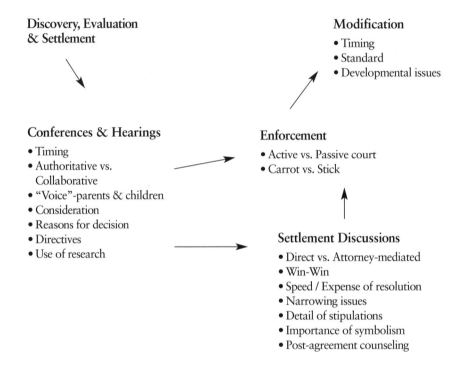

Discovery, Evaluation
& Settlement

Modification
• Timing
• Standard
• Developmental issues

Conferences & Hearings
• Timing
• Authoritative vs.
  Collaborative
• "Voice"-parents & children
• Consideration
• Reasons for decision
• Directives
• Use of research

Enforcement
• Active vs. Passive court
• Carrot vs. Stick

Settlement Discussions
• Direct vs. Attorney-mediated
• Win-Win
• Speed / Expense of resolution
• Narrowing issues
• Detail of stipulations
• Importance of symbolism
• Post-agreement counseling

where therapeutic jurisprudence and preventive law practitioners frequently encounter frustration with existing court procedures.

In part because of frustration with the counter-therapeutic impact of existing legal procedures, there has been a great deal of discussion in recent years about reforming the procedures followed in family law cases. In addition to calling for greater use of alternative dispute resolution, commentators and advocates have promoted various procedural models as part of the movement for a "Unified Family Court."[29] Other advocates and commentators have proposed models such as "collaborative divorce" and "legal therapy counseling." It is beyond the scope of this chapter to discuss the full scope of the problems with current legal procedures in fami-

---

29. Catherine J. Ross (Ed.), *Symposium on Unified Family Courts*, 32 FAMILY LAW QUARTERLY (1998).

ly courts and the numerous proposals for, and experiments with, reform.[30] However, we do want to highlight some aspects of family law proceedings that raise particular procedural justice concerns.

The classic research on procedural justice measured litigants' satisfaction with the process and outcome of litigation. Researchers found that litigants' satisfaction with outcomes is influenced by their perceptions of the fairness of procedures used to decide those outcomes, and the perception of fairness depends on factors such as accuracy, consistency, ethicality, bias suppression, correctability and representativeness/voice.[31] In family law, the same important factors of perceived procedural fairness contribute to litigants' perceptions of outcomes.[32] How do the procedures followed at conferences and hearings in family law cases measure up on these factors, such as voice? How do people feel after family law conferences and hearings?

A typical family law procedural justice problem is presented when a judge decides, often with the best of intentions, decides, "I don't need to see the clients, let's just have counsel in the back room and we're going to hash this out." Counsel may then go into the judge's robing room or chambers with the judge but without their clients, and may emerge with a decision. What effect does it have on a client who is waiting in the outside room when his or her attorney comes out and says, "This is the deal." It may be a good resolution, but the client may wonder whether the attorney advocated for him or her or "sold out." The client may ask, "Did you tell the judge about this?" or "What about that?" "How could you decide this without us being in there?" A client may feel that, "I never got my say." In sum, the client may not perceive the procedure as fair and may have a negative emotional reaction to it.

---

30. For a survey and analysis of family law adjudicatory systems across the United States, see Barbara A. Babb, *Where We Stand: An Analysis of America's Family Law Adjudicatory Systems and the Mandate to Establish Unified Courts*, 32 FAMILY LAW QUARTERLY 31 (1998).

31. Tom R. Tyler, *The Psychosocial Consequences of Judicial Procedures: Implications for Civil Commitment Proceedings*, 46 SMU L. REV. 433 (1992); E. LIND & TOM R. TYLER, THE SOCIAL PSYCHOLOGY OF PROCEDURAL JUSTICE (1988); J. THIBAUT & L. WALKER, PROCEDURAL JUSTICE: A PSYCHOLOGICAL ANALYSIS (1975).

32. Katherine M. Kitzmann & Robert E. Emery, *Procedural Justice and Parents' Satisfaction in a Field Study of Child Custody Dispute Resolution*, 17 LAW & HUMAN BEHAVIOR 553 (1993); Kathryn Rettig & Carla M. Dahl, *Impact of Procedural Factors on Perceived Justice in Divorce Settlements*, 6 AMERICAN PSYCHOLOGIST 301 (1993) (developing a theoretical organization and code to include procedural fairness principles as applied to legal decision making in divorce; also describing the perceptions of divorcing people about the violations of procedural fairness principles in their own divorce proceedings).

In contrast, we have seen cases in which, even though there is a general sense among the litigants and counsel of what the end result will be, the judge allows each party to get up and make a statement. That can be very powerful in terms of the client getting a sense of relief, feeling, "At least I had a chance to speak my peace." The issue of giving child custody litigants' voice is a very sensitive and important one. Moreover, the voice that we give to children in custody disputes and the impact of giving children a voice or denying them that voice could be the topic of a chapter in and of itself. Notwithstanding its importance, bear in mind that voice is only one procedural justice factor to be considered.

There are deontological reasons for saying that feelings do matter as well as consequential reasons. From a deontological standpoint, the legal system should care about whether people are harmed psychologically by the legal procedures followed for the same reasons it should care about whether people's bones are broken-concern for the well-being of others is fundamental to our jurisprudence. From a consequential standpoint, if the legal system concerns itself with the feelings of litigants, there may be residual benefits, such as: fewer appeals; greater compliance with orders; fewer enforcement actions; and fewer modification actions. It is an empirical question whether there will be such residual benefits, but the existing literature on procedural justice gives us reason to believe that there may be.

Existing family law procedures should be examined systematically to determine how they rate on procedural justice criteria, and changes to those procedures should be examined to see how well they fare on the same criteria.

Enforcement/Modification/Appeals

All too often agreements and orders are viewed as the final goal of litigation. However, family lawyers, and lawyers in child custody disputes in particular, need to look beyond the agreement or order because of the frequency with which enforcement and modification issues arise. Apart from seeking to prevent appeals of orders, the family lawyer who takes a preventive law approach will want to consider methods for reducing enforcement problems and future modification actions. Given the many ways that families change over the years that a child custody agreement or order may be in place, it may not be possible to prevent all future problems, but even for those cases where problems will arise, it may be possible to put mechanisms in place for resolving those problems (*e.g.*, an order could provide for a period of co-parenting counseling that is designed to help the parties learn to resolve parenting issues that arise or the order could include a provision that future disputes will first go to a mediator for an attempt at resolution).

In many cases, it may be appropriate to establish a "legal check-up system" for periodic review of the custody agreement or order.[33] In child custody cases, the legal check-ups might be tied to developmental events in the life of the child (*e.g.*, when the child reaches school age and the custody schedule must be coordinated with the school schedule; when the child reaches an age that he may go away to overnight camp necessitating a change to the summer schedule; when the child is able to travel on his or her own from one parent's home to the other; etc.). The legal check-ups might also take into account developmental events in the life of the parent, such as the planned completion of a residency or school program, after which the parent anticipates relocating. Of course, some changes may not be anticipated, but may require legal consultation (*e.g.*, a child who has always lived primarily with one parent asserts upon reaching adolescence that he or she wants to live with the other parent). However, clients should be counseled that such unforseen changes may occur.

In sum, more attention needs to be paid to factors and methods that lead to prevention of future litigation and long-term therapeutic outcomes.[34]

Research Agenda

There are a number of different areas in which research needs to be done, some of which are highlighted above. Moreover, the research that is available needs to be brought to bear on these issues and disseminated in a manner that is accessible to practicing attorneys and mental health professionals and not simply scholars.[35] Lawyers need to be informed about how to incorporate the available knowledge and therapeutic jurisprudence and preventive law principles into their practices. Research about what is effective also could help motivate courts and legislatures to provide funding for effective procedures and programs.

We don't think the research can answer the normative questions for us, for example whether therapy should be a goal or what weight therapeutic outcomes should have but they can tell us to what degree those goals are served. As noted above, beyond the deontological reasons for caring about therapeutic outcome—*i.e*, because it is the right thing to do if we care about people—research may show that concerning ourselves with

---

33. *See* Stolle et al., *supra* note 16, at 16-17, 26-27.

34. *See* Stolle et al., *supra* note 16, at 16 (discussing the importance in preventive law of focusing on the client's long term goals and interests) .

35. *See* Stolle et al., *supra* note 16, at 42 (discussing the need for an empirical research base that can be used by lawyers taking a therapeutic jurisprudence and preventive law approach).

therapeutic outcomes leads to fewer people returning to court and less use of court resources to resolve these matters. Even from a business perspective, a concern with therapeutic outcomes may be warranted because attorneys who have that concern will provide a better service to the client through looking at the whole person, including their emotional and relationship issues and not just the strict traditional legal issues.

Conclusion

As discussed above, it is worthwhile to look at the whole process of family law disputes developmentally, starting with all of those pre-relationship factors that affect whether a dispute will arise and how it will be resolved. More attention needs to be paid to intervention opportunities both before and after the traditional scope of legal involvement. More attention needs to be paid to the activities of mental health professionals and lawyers at each stage of disputes, and research needs to be conducted on the therapeutic effects of those activities.

At the risk of sounding paternalistic, pun intended, we'd like to return to the vignette with which we began this chapter. One way to evaluate our family law system is to ask, "What would I want to happen to my child should my child have to go through this?" Also, "How do I prevent my children from going through this?" We'd like the system, and the actors within that system, to be more proactive (not just reactive) and more sensible and sensitive by the time our children, including Arielle, reach adulthood.

III.

Criminal Practice

Chapter 9

Relapse Prevention Planning Principles for Criminal Law Practice

David B. Wexler

The intersection of therapeutic jurisprudence and preventive law has often been discussed in the context of legal counseling, and that context typically involves a general civil office practice. But a therapeutic/preventive paradigm is equally applicable to criminal law practice.

This essay samples a bite-size piece of the criminal law pie. It looks at how the behavioral science literature on rehabilitation and relapse prevention can be used by criminal defense attorneys and their clients to propose plausible probationary dispositions.[3]

---

1. *E.g.*, PRACTICING THERAPEUTIC JURISPRUDENCE (Dennis P. Stolle et al., eds., forthcoming); Dennis P. Stolle et al., *Integrating Preventive Law and Therapeutic Jurisprudence: A Law and Psychology Based Approach to Lawyering*, 34 CAL. W. L. REV. 15 (1997).

2. Indeed, one can envision a criminal lawyer with a therapeutic jurisprudence/preventive law concentration. *See, e.g.*, Peggy Fulton Hora et al., *Therapeutic Jurisprudence and the Drug Court Movement: Revolutionizing the Criminal Justice System's Response to Drug Abuse and Crime in America*, 74 NOTRE DAME L. REV. 439 (1999); Thomas J. Scheff, *Community Conferences: Shame and Anger in Therapeutic Jurisprudence*, 67 REVISTA JURIDICA UPR 95 (1998); Thomas J. Mescall II, *Legally-Induced Participation and Waiver of Juvenile Courts: A Therapeutic Jurisprudence Analysis*, 68 REVISTA JURIDICA UPR 707 (1999). *See also*, LAW IN A THERAPEUTIC KEY: DEVELOPMENTS IN THERAPEUTIC JURISPRUDENCE (David B. Wexler & Bruce J. Winick eds., 1996) [hereinafter Key] (containing many criminal law chapters).

3. Much of the thesis would apply as well to so-called "intermediate" sanctions (such as intensive probation supervision), to juvenile transfer issues, and (assuming attorney availability) to parole. *See*, David B. Wexler, *Therapeutic Jurisprudence and the Criminal Courts*, in KEY, *supra* note 2 at 157, 168-69 (intermediate sanction); Mescall II, *supra* note 2 (juvenile transfer); David B. Wexler, *How the Law Can Use What Works: A Therapeutic Jurisprudence Look at Recent Research on Rehabilitation*, 15 BEHAV. SCI. & L. 365, 368-69 (1997) (parole).

I. A Sketch of the Rehabilitative Principles

After approximately two decades of discouraging reports from the community of correctional researchers regarding the potential of rehabilitative programs, there is finally some empirical evidence that suggests real promise for at least some rehabilitative approaches. The most successful approaches, recently synthesized in British psychologist James McGuire's edited collection entitled *What Works: Reducing Reoffending,*[6] are of the "cognitive-behavioural"[7] variety. These are "treatments that have a more concrete behavioural or skills-oriented character,"[8] such as the "Reasoning and Rehabilitation" cognitive skills training package now widely in use.[9]

Reasoning and Rehabilitation-type programs proceed from the premise that "for many persistent offenders, a central problem that is linked to their offending behaviour is their lack of, or failure to apply, a number of problem-solving skills."[10] These skills "include the ability to identify when they have a problem, to think of alternative courses of action, to plan the steps toward solution of a problem, to anticipate consequences and to consider the effects of their actions upon others."[11]

In order to increase offender self-control and to reduce impulsivity, successful relapse prevention programs seek to develop an internal self-management system "designed to interrupt the seemingly inexorable chain of events that lead to an offense."[12] Once the chain of events culminating in criminal behavior is identified, "two interventions are employed: (a) strategies that help the offender avoid high-risk situations, and (b) strategies that minimize the likelihood that high-risk situations, once encountered, will lead to relapse."[13]

Relapse prevention principles are central to many current correctional programs. For example, the Cognitive Self Change program in Vermont institutions teaches offenders "to observe their own thinking, to recognize

---

4. Robert Martinson, *What Works? Questions and Answers About Prison Reform*, 10 PUB. INTEREST 22 (1974).

5. WHAT WORKS: REDUCING REOFFENDING (James McGuire ed., 1995). For a recent skeptical view, *see*, Leonore J. Simon, *Does Criminal Offender Treatment Work?*, 7 APP. & PREV. PSYCHOLOGY 137 (1998).

6. WHAT WORKS: REDUCING REOFFENDING (James McGuire ed., 1995).

7. *Id.* at 16.

8. *Id.* at 74.

9. *Id.* at 18-19. *See*, Robert R. Ross et al., *Reasoning and Rehabilitation*, 32 INT'L. J. OFFENDER THERAPY & COMP. CRIMINOLOGY 29 (1998).

10. WHAT WORKS: REDUCING REOFFENDING, *supra* note 6 at 117.

11. *Id.*

12. *Id.* at 166.

13. *Id.*

the consequences of that thinking, and to learn specific skills for controlling that thinking." After learning to observe and report on the content of their thinking, each offender must:

(1) Identify the patterns of thinking that have led him or her to perform acts of crime and violence in the past and that pose a risk of such behaviours in the future;

(2) Learn specific skills for intervening in and controlling these patterns of thinking; and

(3) Summarize these patterns and interventions in the form of a plan for controlling their high-risk thinking in the community. This becomes his or her 'relapse prevention plan.'[15]

In Vermont, offenders ultimately released back into the community apply their relapse prevention plans and meet to evaluate their efforts at controlling their thinking. And in south Wales, the courts often order probationers to hone problem-solving skills by participating in the successful probation-officer taught Reasoning and Rehabilitation-type STOP (Straight Thinking On Probation) program.[16]

II. The Law and the Rehabilitative Principles

The Vermont and south Wales experiences illustrate how, at the most obvious level, these promising rehabilitative principles may be brought into the legal system. In Vermont, a promising program has been created and made available to the prison population. In south Wales, courts in appropriate circumstances take the further step of ordering probationers to avail themselves of such services. A more interesting therapeutic jurisprudence inquiry, however, is how the legal system might be restructured so that the system *itself* might facilitate rehabilitation through the process of offender reasoning.

For example, courts could themselves become acquainted with the rudimentary principles of relapse prevention and cognitive self change. In a situation of probation eligibility and a reasonable likelihood of probation being awarded, a court could encourage the development of appropriate problem-solving skills by requiring the defendant, with the help of counsel (and others),[17] to prepare and submit a relapse prevention plan as the

14. *Id.* at 141.

15. *Id.*

16. *Id.* at 118.

17. Probation personnel may be of major assistance, as may other community resources available to the court. And some defendants may be able to obtain private con-

basis of a possible probationary sentence. The plan should address methods—and relevant release conditions[18]—for avoiding (e.g., remaining home on weekend nights) or coping with (e.g., making an excuse to avoid partying at Joe's place) high-risk situations.

As part of the plan preparation process, family, friends, neighbors, and community members can be spoken with by the defendant and defense counsel. Their recommendations—and cooperation—can be solicited. These persons may be spoken with individually or, on appropriate occasions, in the setting of a community conference. When possible, the victim's input can be obtained by the defendant and counsel (or, of course, by the court, before finally deciding on probationary release), and the plan can seek to include conditions for assuring the victim's safety.[19]

In advance of the hearing, defense counsel should discuss the process with the defendant, including the anticipated concerns of the court and the victim. The defendant should be prepared to specify how the proposed plan addresses those concerns or how it might be modified to do so. At the sentencing hearing itself, the court could question the offender about the plan, could solicit the views and concerns of the victim,[20] could discuss its own concerns about high-risk situations and behaviors, and could hear from the offender about how such situations would expectedly be avoided or confronted.

With that input, the court could decide whether to grant probation and, if so, whether to accept the submitted relapse prevention plan or a revised one based upon concerns expressed at the hearing. Note that conditional release conditions derived from the dialogue at the hearing would basically be conditions suggested by the offender personally to cope with anticipated high-risk situations. By tailoring those conditions specifically to the

---

sultation from psychologists, social workers, and other rehabilitative/correctional professionals.

18. Of course, participation in a full-blown Reasoning and Rehabilitation program, assuming one is available in the location (as is the case in south Wales), could constitute one of the proposed conditions. Indeed, sentencing might even be deferred until the defendant completes the program and prepares a relapse prevention plan. Moreover, the post-offense rehabilitative effort might itself constitute grounds for imposing a lighter sentence than might have initially been imposed. *See*, Bruce J. Winick, *Redefining the Role of the Criminal Defense Lawyer at Plea Bargaining and Sentencing: A Therapeutic Jurisprudence/Preventive Law Model*, 6 Psychology, Public Policy and Law (forthcoming March 2000).

19. This path would draw some restorative justice methods into the therapeutic jurisprudence/preventive law mix. *See*, Scheff, *supra* note 2.

20. *See*, Richard R. Wiebe, *The Mental Health Implications of Crime Victim Rights*, in Key, *supra* note 2, at 213.

offender's situation, and by giving the offender "voice"[21] in crafting the conditions, we should expect the offender not to regard the conditions as particularly unjust,[22] and, relatedly, we should expect the process to facilitate an offender's compliance with the conditions.

In addition, by responding to concerns and defending the plan, the defendant will be anchoring himself or herself in the position that the proposed plan is workable—and in this respect different from the situation that landed him or her in court in the first place. This process—of defending one's proposed course of action when presented with "mild counterarguments"—has also been linked to increased treatment compliance.[23] Indeed, the recommended procedure as a whole taps nicely into principles for promoting offender compliance.[24]

III. Lawyering

Courts seem increasingly interested in the therapeutic jurisprudence perspective.[25] They—or at least some of them—may accordingly take the lead in explicitly incorporating relapse prevention planning in the probationary process. If courts require the preparation and submission of such plans as a prelude to considering conditional release, lawyers will expectedly quickly acquire a familiarity with the area.

Even if courts do not take the lead, however, criminal defense attorneys could themselves profitably introduce the procedure. If a defendant,

---

21. Tom R. Tyler, *The Psychological Consequences of Judicial Procedures: Implications for Civil Commitment Hearings*, 46 SMU. L. Rev. 433 (1992) (relationship of procedural justice and therapeutic jurisprudence).

22. What Works: Reducing Reoffending, *supra* note 6 at 142.

23. Donald Meichenbaum & Dennis C. Turk, Facilitating Treatment Adherence: A Practitioner's Guidebook 176 (1987). *See also*, David B. Wexler, *Therapeutic Jurisprudence and the Criminal Courts*, in Key, *supra* note 2, at 166.

24. Psychological principles, borrowed from the health care context, regarded as likely to increase treatment compliance include: engaging the patient in a respectful dialogue, involving family members and friends, signing a behavioral contract, making a public commitment to comply, and confronting the patient with mild counterarguments regarding the patient's probably compliance. *See*, Donald Meichenbaum & Dennis C. Turk, Facilitating Treatment Adherence: A Practitioner's Guidebook (1987); David B. Wexler, *Therapeutic Jurisprudence and the Criminal Courts*, in Key, *supra* note 2, at 157, 165-70. These health care compliance principles have been utilized here in devising the proposed procedure for preparing, defending, revising, and approving relapse prevention/probation plans.

25. Hora Et Al, *supra* note 2, at 439; Michael D. Zimmerman, *A New Approach to Court Reform*, 82 Judicature 108 (1998).

with the assistance of defense counsel and other professionals, were to prepare and submit a relapse prevention plan as the basis of a proposed probationary disposition, the judicial stage would be set for the court to consider the matter seriously, to question the defendant regarding concerns and likely compliance, and to decide whether to accept, reject, or modify the proposed plan.

A court is likely to take the matter seriously because the relapse prevention principles seem to comport with judicial common sense. The ordinary plan will not propose a probationary disposition on condition that the defendant submit to some little-understood therapy. Instead, the typical plan will expectedly cover, albeit in a rather careful and systematic manner, the sorts of concerns a court is ordinarily likely to harbor: Can the offender be released without posing an undue risk to public safety? On what conditions? Can the defendant be expected to comply with the conditions?

Counsel may at times be tempted by considerations of efficiency personally to prepare a proposal and to involve the client only to obtain the client's acquiescence with regard to the proposed plan. Such a course of action would be a serious mistake. The psychological principles of compliance and of relapse prevention rather clearly call for the plan to be basically designed by the *client*, although the actual drafting can of course be performed by counsel. It is the client, not counsel, who needs to undergo cognitive self change. It will often be the client who will be called upon to respond to questions from the court. It is the client who needs to regard the plan as fair. It is the client who, as a party to a behavioral contract, is to comply with its conditions—or suffer the consequences of noncompliance. And it is the *lawyer* who will lose credibility with the courts if his or her clients continually find themselves subject to probation revocation for failure to complete the terms of conditional release.

IV. Conclusion

By engaging the client to think through his or her behavioral patterns that lead to criminality, by engaging the client then to devise ways both to avoid high-risk situations and also to cope with such situations should they arise, a criminal lawyer will in essence be engaging the client in the cognitive/behavioral change process of relapse prevention planning. If such action leads to more[26]—and more successful—probationary sentences, this

---

26. Of course, in many cases, probation will not be granted. While this will obviously be a major immediate setback for the defendant, the preparation of the relapse prevention plan may nonetheless eventually prove useful. If the defendant has gained insight into how cognitive and behavioral processes have contributed to criminality, perhaps he or she will

sort of lawyering may come to constitute a highly challenging and rewarding form of criminal law practice.[27]

---

begin to follow the revised reasoning process in prison. The plan, moreover, may serve as
the basis of a later parole proposal, and, in any event, can guide the offender's behavior
when he or she is ultimately released into the community. This, in fact, is how the Vermont plans are now used. They are prepared during incarceration, and serve to guide the
offender's behavior after the ultimate return to the community. WHAT WORKS: REDUCING
REOFFENDING, *supra* note 6 at 141-47.

[27] Lawyers desiring to specialize in this sort of work might receive training on the
principles and content of a Reasoning and Rehabilitation (or comparable) model, as probation officers do in south Wales. WHAT WORKS: REDUCING REOFFENDING, *supra* note 6
at 118. In terms of time and effort, such training would probably be similar to mediation
training taken by lawyers who wish to practice as mediators.

Chapter 10

Redefining the Role of the Criminal Defense Lawyer at Plea Bargaining and Sentencing: A Therapeutic Jurisprudence/Preventive Law Model

Bruce J. Winick

I. Introduction

Several recent developments suggest the need for rethinking the role of the criminal defense lawyer at plea bargaining and sentencing. The defense attorney's traditional function at sentencing is to present arguments to mitigate sentence designed to either obtain a term of probation or (where imprisonment is likely) to minimize the term of imprisonment imposed. The traditional role of counsel at plea bargaining is to work out the best possible deal for the client in the circumstances, and it frequently involves making to the prosecutor similar arguments in mitigation of sentence. Rehabilitation has always been one of the important aims of criminal sentencing.[1] Since the mid-1970s, however, the rehabilitative ideal has not been taken seriously. Scholarly work in the early 1970s on the efficacy of correctional rehabilitation seemed to conclude that nothing worked.[2] This

---

1. *See generally* ARTHUR W. CAMPBELL, LAW OF SENTENCING §2.4, at 29 (2d ed. 1991) (the country's dominant sentencing rationale until the late 1970s); ROBERT O. DAWSON, SENTENCING: THE DECISIONS AS TO TYPE, LENGTH, AND CONDITIONS OF SENTENCE 3 (1969) (one of the "major goals of the correctional process"); HERBERT L. A. HART, PUNISHMENT AND RESPONSIBILITY: ESSAYS IN THE PHILOSOPHY OF LAW (1968); WAYNE R. LaFAVE & AUSTIN W. SCOTT, JR., SUBSTANTIVE CRIMINAL LAW 1, 5, 38-40 (1986); HERBERT L. PACKER, THE LIMITS OF THE CRIMINAL SANCTION 35-61 (1968); BRUCE J. WINICK, THE RIGHT TO REFUSE MENTAL HEALTH TREATMENT 303 (1997); Kent Greenawalt, *Punishment*, 74 J. CRIM. L. & CRIMINOLOGY 343 (1983); Marc Miller, *Purposes of Sentencing*, 66 S. CAL. L. REV. 413, 414 (1992) (one of the traditional purposes of sentencing).

2. *See, e.g.*, DOUGLAS S. LIPTON ET AL., THE EFFECTIVENESS OF CORRECTIONAL TREATMENT (1975); Robert Martinson, *What Works?—Questions and Answers About Prison Reform*, 35 PUB. INTEREST 22 (1974); S. REP. NO. 225, 98th CONG., 2d SESS. 51

conclusion now seems to have been premature.[3] Perhaps the most that could accurately have been said at that point is that we could not answer the question of what works in correctional rehabilitation and that we simply did not know. This was the analysis of a National Academy of Sciences panel that studied the issue of correctional rehabilitation and its alternatives.[4]

Recently, however, some studies have provided more optimistic evidence concerning the prospects for rehabilitation of criminal offenders. A chapter in this volume by David Wexler brings to our attention a recent synthesis of the most successful rehabilitative approaches that have been reported in the current literature.[5] This synthesis appeared in British psychologist James McGuire's edited book, *What Works?: Reducing Reof-*

---

at (1984), *reprinted in* 1984 U.S. CODE CONG. & ADMIN. NEWS 3220, 3221; SUBCOMM. ON PENITENTIARIES AND CORRECTIONS OF THE SEN. COMM. ON THE JUDICIARY, ANNUAL REPORT, S. REP. NO. 95-909, 95TH CONG., 1ST SESS. (1978); *but see* TTED PALMER, CORRECTIONAL INTERVENTION AND RESEARCH 15-36 (1978) (presenting a more optimistic view). Although noting that more recent programs may show more promise, a study of offender rehabilitation performed under the auspices of the National Academy of Sciences found that the negative conclusions concerning the effectiveness of correctional rehabilitation contained in the studies published at the time to be "reasonably accurate and fair." PANEL ON RESEARCH ON REHABILITATIVE TECHNIQUES OF THE NATIONAL RESEARCH COUNCIL, THE REHABILITATION OF CRIMINAL OFFENDERS: PROBLEMS AND PROSPECTS 5 (Lee B. Sechrest et al. eds., 1979) [hereinafter Rehabilitation of Criminal Offenders]. However, the study found that Palmer's "optimistic view cannot be supported." *Id.* at 31.

3. John Q. La Fond & Bruce J. Winick, *Foreword: Sex Offenders and the Law,* 4 PSYCHOL. PUB. POL'Y & L. 3, 19 (1998) ("We concluded, too hastily, that nothing works in the way of correctional transformation.").

4. The National Research Panel study concluded:

The entire body of research appears to justify only the conclusion that we do not now know of any program or method of rehabilitation that could be guaranteed to reduce the criminal activity of released offenders. Although a generous reviewer of the literature might discern some glimmers of hope, those glimmers are so few, so scattered, and so inconsistent that they do not serve as a basis for any recommendation other than continued research.

REHABILITATION OF CRIMINAL OFFENDERS, *supra* note 3, at 3. For a critical analysis of the then existing evaluation literature finding most studies inadequate for failure to measure the "strength" or intensity of the treatment or its "integrity" or consistency in administration, *see* Lee B. Sechrest & Robin Redner, *Strength and Integrity in Evaluation Studies, in* HOW WELL DOES IT WORK: A REVIEW OF CRIMINAL JUSTICE EVALUATION 1978 (1978).

5. David B. Wexler, *Relapse Prevention Planning Principles for Criminal Law Practice,* Chapter 9.

fending.[6] McGuire trumpeted the promise of <u>cognitive behavioral meth-</u><u>ods, including the reasoning and rehabilitative cognitive skills training</u> <u>package now widely in use.</u> These programs involve a variety of techniques designed to make the individual aware of existing behavior patterns and of alternative problem-solving approaches. In particular, <u>they involve</u> <u>relapse prevention models designed to develop in the offender an internal</u> <u>self-management system</u> that allows the individual to <u>identify those situ-</u><u>ations</u> and events <u>that</u> often <u>lead to criminal behavior</u> and to <u>develop and</u> <u>use strategies for avoiding high-risk</u> situations or minimizing the likeli-hood that they trigger the individual's customary behavior patterns.[7]

These promising new models pose significant new opportunities for rehabilitating offenders that, particularly in this age of prison overcrowding, many judges will greet with interest and even enthusiasm. These cognitive self-change and relapse prevention methods join a variety of promising models used by judges in fashioning creative community alternatives to incarceration that include <u>alcohol and other drug treatment,</u> <u>counseling</u> <u>programs,</u> home <u>confinement and electronic monitoring,</u> <u>restitution, and</u> <u>community service.</u>[8] <u>Criminal defense attorneys need to understand these</u> <u>new approaches and to use them to help fashion rehabilitative plans for their</u> <u>clients that can be urged as the basis for a more advantageous plea bargain</u> <u>or probation or more lenient sentencing.</u>

Several additional new developments magnify the importance of crim-inal defense attorneys becoming acquainted with these new rehabilitative methodologies. Post-offense rehabilitation has traditionally served as a

---

6. WHAT WORKS?: REDUCING REOFFENDING (James McGuire ed., 1995); *see also* TED PALMER, THE RE-EMERGENCE OF CORRECTIONAL INTERVENTION (1992); EDGARDO ROTMAN, BEYOND PUNISHMENT: A NEW VIEW ON THE REHABILITATION OF CRIMINAL OFFENDERS (1990); TREATING ADULT AND JUVENILE OFFENDERS WITH SPECIAL NEEDS (Jose B. Ashford et al., eds., forthcoming); Paul Gendreau & Robert Ross, *The Revivifica-tion of Rehabilitation: Evidence from the 1980s,* 4 JUSTICE Q. 349 (1988); Ted Palmer, *The Effectiveness of Intervention: Recent Trends and Current Issues,* 37 CRIME & DELIN-QUENCY 330, 342 (1991); David B. Wexler, *How The Law Can Use What Works: A Therapeutic Jurisprudence Look at Recent Research on Rehabilitation,* 15 BEHAV. SCI. & L. 365 (1997) (book review); *but see* Lenore J. Simon, *Does Criminal Offender Treat-ment Work?,* 7 APP. & PREV. PSYCHOL. 137 (1998) (presenting a skeptical view).

7. Wexler, *supra* note 5.

8. *See* United States v. Flowers, 983 F. Supp. 159, 162 (E.D.N.Y. 1997) (discussing these approaches, including probation, house arrest, and electronic monitoring used in lieu of incarceration, community service orders, "shock" sentencing to a short term of mili-tary-style boot camp, and pretrial diversion or deferred prosecution). *See generally* COM-MUNITY CORRECTIONS: PROBATION, PAROLE, AND INTERMEDIATE SANCTIONS (Joan Petersilia ed. 1998) (reviewing recent trends in community corrections).

ground for mitigating sentence in both federal and state courts. For the past 15 years, however, at the federal level and increasingly in the states, criminal sentencing has been dominated by approaches using sentencing guidelines that significantly limit the discretion of trial judges in the setting of criminal sentences.[9] These approaches were designed to emphasize a just desserts approach to criminal punishment, to remedy what had been the growing problem of sentencing disparity (in which trial judges were generally perceived as sentencing similar defendants committing similar crimes to widely differing terms of imprisonment), and to increase sentences in part as a result of the perception that some judges were "soft on crime."

Yet tensions have remained between the goal of avoiding sentencing disparity and that of accomplishing individualized justice, leading many sentencing judges to seek to manipulate such sentencing guidelines by granting downward departures from the range of sentences contemplated when special circumstances justified such departures. The extent to which federal sentencing judges enjoyed this power was controversial, but in the 1996 case *Koon v. United States*[10] the U.S. Supreme Court broadly sanctioned the ability of sentencing judges to grant such departures and adopted a narrow abuse of discretion standard to govern appellate review of departure decisions. Moreover, although the Supreme Court has not spoken to the issue, federal circuit and district courts have increasingly recognized that post-offense rehabilitation itself may qualify as a ground for a downward departure.[11] In addition, this development has taken on added significance with the issuance of a 1997 opinion by District Judge Jack B. Weinstein in *United States v. Flowers*,[12] which recognizes that sentenc-

---

9. The Federal Sentencing Guidelines, applicable to cases adjudicated in federal court, are the best known of sentencing guidelines approaches. *See* United States Sentencing Comm'n, Federal Sentencing Guidelines Manual, ch. 1, pt. A, at 1 (Nov. 1998) [hereinafter U.S.S.G.]; *see also* Marvin E. Frankel, *Sentencing Commissions and Guidelines*, 73 Geo. L. J. 225, 243-46 (1984) (summarizing guideline system); Daniel A. Rezneck, *The New Federal Criminal Sentencing Provisions*, 22 Am. Crim. L. Rev. 785, 785-90 (1985) (same). Sentencing guideline approaches are also increasingly being used in the states. Yale Kamisar et al., Modern Criminal Procedure: Cases — Comments — Questions 1539 (9th ed. 1999) (almost half of the states have sentencing guidelines). Perhaps the best known of these state sentencing guideline approaches is that of Minnesota, the first state to have adopted such guidelines. *See id.*; Andrew Ashworth, *Three Techniques for Reducing Sentence Disparity, in* Principled Sentencing 282, 286-88 (Andrew von Hirsch & Andrew Ashworth, eds. 1992) (discussing Minnesota's presumptive sentencing guideline system).

10. 518 U.S. 81 (1996).

11. *See infra* Part III.

12. 983 F. Supp. 159 (E.D.N.Y. 1997); *see infra* Part IV.

ing judges enjoy broad discretion to postpone or defer sentencing in appropriate cases in order to allow the defendant to commence a rehabilitative program that, if successful, might provide the basis for a downward departure. These developments under the Federal Sentencing Guidelines and parallel possibilities under their state counterparts place a new premium on criminal defense attorneys understanding the new rehabilitative approaches, being able to persuade their clients of their value, helping those who are interested to fashion rehabilitative and relapse prevention plans, and being able to present the facts of their clients' rehabilitation more effectively to prosecutors in plea bargaining negotiations, to probation officers who design presentence reports and make recommendations to sentencing judges concerning appropriate Guideline ranges, and to sentencing judges concerning the justifications for granting downward departures.

These new skills apply as well in the context of defense attorneys representing corporations and other organizations that have been or may be the subject of criminal prosecution. The 1991 amendments to the *United States Sentencing Guidelines* contain special provisions governing the sentencing of corporations and other organizations that present significant opportunities for organizational clients to minimize the potential of heavy fines if they can demonstrate the existence of legal compliance mechanisms and relapse prevention plans to deter and prevent reoccurrence of illegality.[13] These new developments emphasize the need for defense attorneys in these contexts to develop similar understandings concerning the new rehabilitative approaches and how to advocate to their clients, to prosecutors, to probation officers, and to sentencing courts concerning them.

The confluence of these recent developments call for a rethinking and broadening of the role of criminal defense attorneys in the plea bargaining and sentencing process. Not only do these attorneys need to develop new skills, but they need to think of themselves in new ways. They need to understand the vocabulary and techniques of these new rehabilitative approaches. They need to develop techniques for dealing with their clients about the issue of rehabilitation with a higher degree of psychological sensitivity. They need to understand that, whether they know it or not, they are functioning as therapeutic agents in their interactions with their clients, particularly in the plea and sentencing process. They need to recognize the opportunities that these new developments provide to offer new modes of assistance to their clients that can promote both their interests in maintaining their liberty and in achieving a higher degree of psychological well-

---

13. U.S. Sentencing Comm'n, federal sentencing Guidelines Manual § 2E1.1 (Nov. 1991); Molly E. Joseph, *Organization Sentencing*, 35 Am. Crim. L. Rev. 1017 (1998); *infra* Part V.

being. Moreover, they need to understand that playing these new roles can have important positive effects for their own mental health and personal and professional satisfaction. In short, they need to understand the insights of therapeutic jurisprudence[14] and preventive law[15] and to see themselves as therapeutically oriented preventive lawyers.[16]

In this chapter, I explain the new integrated therapeutic jurisprudence/preventive law model and describe how it can apply in the context of criminal sentencing to help reshape the role of the criminal defense practitioner. In Part II, I discuss the new approach and its application to the plea bargaining and sentencing process. The discussion uses developments under the *United States Sentencing Guidelines* and their judicial construction as illustrative of the new opportunities defense lawyers enjoy, but parallel opportunities exist under state sentencing guidelines and in states that do not constrain sentencing discretion through sentencing guidelines; instead, they leave wide discretion in the hands of sentencing judges. In these jurisdictions judges possess even more discretion to reduce sentence on the basis of successful rehabilitation, presenting even greater opportunities for creative lawyering. Furthermore, these opportunities exist for criminal defense attorneys in other countries, in which rehabilitation similarly figures prominently in the exercise of sentencing discretion.[17]

---

14. *See generally* DAVID B. WEXLER & BRUCE J. WINICK, ESSAYS IN THERAPEUTIC JURISPRUDENCE (1991); LAW IN A THERAPEUTIC KEY: DEVELOPMENTS IN THERAPUTIC JURISPRUDENCE (David B. Wexler & Bruce J. Winick, eds., 1996) [hereinafter LAW IN A THERAPEUTIC KEY]; Bruce J. Winick, *The Jurisprudence of Therapeutic Jurisprudence*, 3 PSYCHOL. PUB. POL'Y & L. 184 (1997).

15. *See generally* LOUIS M. BROWN & EDWARD A. DAUER, PLANNING BY LAWYERS: MATERIALS ON A NON-ADVERSARIAL LEGAL PROCESS (1977); ROBERT M. HARDAWAY, PREVENTIVE LAW: MATERIALS ON A NON-ADVERSARIAL LEGAL PROCESS (1997).

16. Dennis P. Stolle, David B. Wexler, Bruce J. Winick & Edward A. Dauer, *Integrating Preventive Law and Therapeutic Jurisprudence: A Law and Psychology Based Approach to Lawyering*, 34 CAL. W. L. REV. 15 (1997); Dennis P. Stolle & David B. Wexler, *Therapeutic Jurisprudence and Preventive Law: A Combined Concentration to Invigorate the Everyday Practice of Law*, 39 ARIZ. L. REV. 25 (1997); Dennis P. Stolle, *Professional Responsibility in Elder Law: A Synthesis of Preventive Law and Therapeutic Jurisprudence*, 14 BEHAV. SCI. & L. 14 (1996); Dennis P. Stolle & David B. Wexler, *Preventive Law and Therapeutic Jurisprudence: A Symbiotic Relationship*, 16 PREVENTIVE L. REP. 4 (1997); David B. Wexler, *Practicing Therapeutic Jurisprudence: Psycholegal Soft Spots and Strategies*, 67 REVISTA JURIDICA U.P.R. 317 (1998); Bruce J. Winick, *Client Denial and Resistance in the Advance Directive Context: Reflections on How Attorneys Can Identify and Deal with a Psycholegal Soft Spot*, 4 PSYCHOL. PUB. POL'Y & L. 901 (1998).

17. *See* PRINCIPLED SENTENCING (Andrew von Hirsch & Andrew Andrew Ashworth, eds. 1992) (discussing sentencing practices of various countries); SENTENCING REFORM: A

In Part III, I describe the new developments enabling sentencing judges to consider post-offense rehabilitation as a ground for a downward departure under sentencing guidelines. In Part IV, I describe the *Flowers* case and the new discretion it affords sentencing judges in granting deferred sentencing to enable the commencement of rehabilitative efforts and to facilitate their successful completion. Part V provides analysis of the special role for defense counsel representing corporations and other organizations involved in the criminal sentencing process. In Part VI, I provide a discussion of various psychological principles that can be adapted to facilitate what are certain to be highly sensitive attorney/client conversations about the advisability of the client's coming to terms with his or her criminal and related psychological problems and obtaining rehabilitation. In the final section, Part VII, I offer some concluding thoughts concerning the applicability of the proposed model to attorneys practicing in related areas and about the limits of the model.

II. The Therapeutic Jurisprudence/ Preventive Law Model

An emerging literature seeks to integrate the separate fields of therapeutic jurisprudence and preventive law to provide a law and psychology-based approach to the everyday practice of law.[18] Therapeutic jurisprudence is a field of interdisciplinary scholarship with a law reform agenda that focuses attention on the consequences of law for the psychological functioning and emotional well-being of the people effected.[19] Therapeutic jurisprudence sees the law and the way in which it is applied by various legal actors, including lawyers, as having inevitable consequences for psychological well-being that should be studied with the tools of the behavioral sciences. It suggests that these consequences should be taken into account in reforming law, when consistent with other important normative

---

CANADIAN APPROACH, REPORT OF THE CANADIAN SENTENCING COMMISSION 139 (1987) ("the individualized sentence is a tool for the rehabilitation of offenders and this goal ought to be achieved through non-custodial programs."); Andrew von Hirsch, *Federal Sentencing Guidelines: The United States and Canadian Schemes Compared* (occasional papers from the Center for Research in Crime and Justice, New York University School of Law, 1988) (comparing U.S. Federal and Canadian sentencing practices); Gilles Renaud, R. v. Fuller: *Time to Brush Aside the Rules Prohibiting Therapeutic Remands?*, 35 CRIM. L. Q. 91 (1992) (discussing Canadian and British Commonwealth law regarding the appropriateness of pre-sentence remand to craft individualized sentences).

18. *See, e.g.,* sources cited in *supra* note 16.

19. *See, e.g.,* BRUCE J. WINICK, THERAPEUTIC JURISPRUDENCE APPLIED: ESSAYS ON MENTAL HEALTH LAW (1997); LAW IN A THERAPEUTIC KEY, *supra* note 14.

values, in the direction of making it less antitherapeutic and more therapeutic. It is a mental health approach to law and the way it is applied, suggesting the need for law makers and law appliers to be sensitive to law's
impact on psychological health and to perform their roles with an awareness of basic principles of psychology.

Preventive law is an approach to legal practice that attempts to avoid
legal problems and litigation through the creative application of legal
planning, legal drafting, and alternative dispute resolution techniques.[20] It
seeks to minimize the risk of litigation and other legal difficulties and to
provide increased certainty concerning legal rights and duties and enhanced
personal and business opportunities. It is a preventive approach to lawyering that emphasizes the lawyer's role as a planner. Preventive law is the
legal analog of preventive medicine, and it makes use of periodic legal
checkups to monitor client activities in order to avoid legal difficulties.

The integrated approach envisions therapeutically oriented preventive
lawyers who practice preventive law with an awareness of the client's psychological and emotional needs and to the significance of the attorney-
client interaction on the emotional well-being of both client and attorney.
These lawyers are psychologically minded and sensitive to the emotional
climate of the attorney/client relationship. They are "relational lawyers"[21]
or "affective lawyers."[22] They practice law with an ethic of care,[23] attempting to use their interpersonal skills to enhance the emotional well-being of
their clients. They are alert to what the emerging literature concerning this
integrated model calls *psycholegal soft spots,* the way in which certain
legal issues, procedures, or interventions may produce or reduce anxiety,
distress, anger, depression, hard or hurt feelings, and other dimensions of
law-related psychological well-being.[24]

---

20. *See, e.g.,* BROWN & DAUER, *supra* note 15; HARDAWAY, *supra* note 15.

21. Stephanie Stier, *Essay Review: Reframing Legal Skills: Relational Lawyering,* 42 J.
LEGAL EDUC. 303 (1992).

22. Peter Margulies, *Representation of Domestic Violence Survivors as a New Paradigm of Poverty Law in Search of Access, Connection and Voice,*63 GEO L. REV. 1071
(1995); Carrie J. Menkel-Meadow, *Narrowing the Gap by Narrowing the Field: What's
Missing from the MacGrate Report—Of Skill, Human Science and Being a Human
Being,* 69 WASH. L. REV. 593 (1994); Linda G. Mills, *On the Other Side of Silence: Affec-
tive Lawyering for Intimate Abuse,* 81 CORNELL L. REV. 1225 (1996); Linda G. Mills,
Affective Lawyering: The Emotional Dimensions of the Lawyer-Client Relation, in PRAC-
TICING THERAPEUTIC JURISPRUDENCE (Dennis P. Stolle, David B. Wexler and Bruce J.
Winick, eds. forthcoming).

23. Winick, *supra* note 16, at 903.

24. Mark W. Patry et al., *Better Legal Counseling Through Empirical Research: Identifying Psycholegal Soft Spots and Strategies,* 34 CAL. W. L. REV. 439 (1998); Stolle et al.,
supra note 16, at 42-43; Wexler, *supra* note 16; Winick, *supra* note 16, at 903.

The therapeutically oriented preventive lawyer has a heightened sensitivity to the psychological dimensions of the attorney/client relationship and uses insights from psychology in interviewing and counseling clients. Formal training in psychology and social work is not a prerequisite, but the preventive law function is enhanced when the attorney understands some basic principles of psychology. Attorneys do not need to be therapists, but they do need to have emotional intelligence[25] or interpersonal intelligence[26] and to be psychologically minded. Just as a basic understanding of the principles of economics can improve the functioning of an antitrust lawyer or business lawyer generally, an understanding of psychology can increase the effectiveness of the preventive lawyer.[27]

Dealing with their criminal charges can be a highly emotional experience for most defendants. Moreover, when the behavior that resulted in criminal charges is related to substance abuse, mental illness, or psychologically maladaptive behavior patterns, confronting the existence of such a problem and coming to terms with the need to deal with it can produce considerable psychological distress. Dealing with the issue of rehabilitation and relapse prevention in the context of plea bargaining or sentencing thus may be regarded, within the terminology of therapeutic jurisprudence/preventive law, as a psycholegal soft spot.[28] Attorneys involved in these processes need to be sensitive to the emotional difficulties that dealing with such issues can produce, to be able to identify a client's psychological distress, and to be able to deal with it effectively within the attorney/client relationship. Attorneys who ignore the emotional dimensions of dealing with clients in these contexts risk a serious loss of effectiveness in representing them at plea bargaining and sentencing. They also risk alienating clients, who might interpret their lack of interest in the emotional aspects of the situation as coldness, insensitivity, callousness, or even antagonism. Clients tend to be more distrustful of such attorneys and are less likely to cooperate fully with them, to have full and frank communications with them, and to value their advice. They may regard them as part of the problem, not part of the solution, with the result that they may miss substantial opportunities to deal effectively with their problems and to reduce their risk of imprisonment or of more lengthy imprisonment.

---

25. *See* Daniel Goleman, Emotional Intelligence (1997); Daniel Goleman, Working With Emotional Intelligence (1998); Marjorie A. Silver, *Emotional Intelligence and Legal Education*, 5 Psychol. Pub. Pol'y & L. ___ (forthcoming).

26. Howard Gardner, Multiple Intelligences: The Theory in Practice 9 (1993) ("Interpersonal intelligence is the ability to understand other people: what motivates them, how they work, how to work cooperatively with them.").

27. Winick, *supra* note 16, at 904.

28. *See supra* note 22 and accompanying text.

By contrast, attorneys who are sensitive to the emotional aspects of dealing with clients facing these issues can function more effectively in playing their roles in the plea bargaining and sentencing process and can offer their clients an opportunity to turn their lives around, to face and deal effectively with their problems, and to achieve a genuine degree of rehabilitation that will reduce any future loss of liberty and increase their potential for happiness and effective functioning. The criminal defense attorney can thus function as a therapeutic agent in helping clients face and deal with problems that, if not confronted, can lead to greater difficulties, future criminal charges, and greater punishment. In short, criminal defense lawyers understanding the insights of therapeutic jurisprudence and preventive law can function more effectively in the plea bargaining and sentencing process without any sacrifice to the client's interests. By applying a therapeutic and preventive approach in the plea and sentencing process, such lawyers can take a holistic approach to the representation of the client, seeking to understand and be interested in all aspects of the client, not only his or her legal problems. In this manner, attorneys can help their clients to face and deal with a variety of other problems in ways that also help them to avoid serious future legal difficulties.

III. Post-offense Rehabilitation as a Basis for a Downward Departure under the Federal Sentencing Guidelines

A. The Federal Sentencing Guidelines

Although the rehabilitative ideal has been in sharp decline since the mid-1970s,[29] rehabilitation unquestionably remains one of the principal aims of criminal sentencing.[30] Prior to the 1980s, sentencing judges enjoyed wide discretion in determining whether and for how long a convicted offender should be incarcerated.[31] Sentencing statutes at the time typically authorized indeterminate sentencing, setting a wide range of sentencing options and leaving the sentencing judge with the discretion to sentence

---

29. *See generally* FRANCIS A. ALLAN, THE DECLINE OF THE REHABILITATIVE IDEAL: PENAL POLICY AND SOCIAL PURPOSE (1981); Robert A. Burt, *Cruelty, Hypocrisy, and the Rehabilitative Ideal in Corrections*, 16 INT'L J.L. & PSYCHIATRY 359 (1993).

30. *See generally* sources cited in *supra* note 1.

31. Koon v. United States, 518 U.S. 81, 92 (1996); Mistreta v. United States, 488 U.S. 361, 363 (1989); FAIR AND CERTAIN PUNISHMENT: REPORT OF THE TWENTIETH CENTURY FUND TASK FORCE ON CRIMINAL SENTENCING 3 (1976) [hereinafter FAIR AND CERTAIN PUNISHMENT]; PIERCE O'DONNELL ET AL., TOWARD A JUST AND EFFECTIVE SENTENCING SYSTEM 1 (1977).

the offender, within this range, according to his or her determination of what would be appropriate in the circumstances.[32] This wide discretion led to the problem of sentencing disparity, in which judges meted out widely differing sentences to similar offenders convicted of identical offenses.[33]

Congress responded to this problem by passing legislation creating the United States Sentencing Commission and delegating to it the responsibility for adopting a comprehensive set of sentencing guidelines.[34] After several years of work, the Commission promulgated the *United States Sentencing Guidelines*.[35] The Guidelines specify an appropriate range of possible sentences for each class of convicted offenders on the basis of various factors relating to the offense and the offender. The Guidelines significantly curtail the discretion of the sentencing judge, requiring the judge to impose a sentence within the applicable range that is specified. The judge is instructed to identify the base offense level for the crime in question, adjust the level as the Guidelines specify, and determine the offender's criminal history category.[36] The adjusted offense level is then coordinated with the criminal history category to yield the appropriate sentencing range.[37] In the ordinary case, the sentencing judge must sentence the offender to a term of imprisonment falling within the applicable range produced by this calculation.

B. Downward Departures

The Sentencing Reform Act of 1984, however, did not eliminate all discretion on the part of the sentencing judge. Rather, the Act acknowledged the desirability and even necessity of sentencing procedures that take into account individual circumstances.[38] Congress therefore permitted the sentencing judge to depart from the applicable guideline range if the court finds the existence of an aggravating or mitigating circumstance of a kind,

---

32. *See* Fair and Certain Punishment, *supra* note 31, at 11.

33. Koon v. United States, 518 U.S. 81 (1996), *citing* S. Rep. 98-225, at 38 (1983); Marvin E. Frankel, Criminal Sentences: Law Without Order 21 (1973); O'Donnell et al., *supra* note 31, at 10.

34. 28 U.S.C. § 994 (1988).

35. The current version of the Guidelines is set forth in U.S.S.G., *supra* note 9. *See also* Frankel, *supra* note 9, at 243-46 (summarizing guideline system); Rezneck, *supra* note 9, at 785-90 (same); *Project, Seventeenth Annual Review of Criminal Procedure: United States Supreme Court and Courts of Appeal, 1986-1987, Sentencing, Probation, and Parole*, 76 Geo. L. J. 1073 (1988).

36. U.S.S.G., *supra* note 9, § 1 1.1.

37. *Id.*

38. *Koon*, 518 U.S. at 93, *citing* 28 U.S.C. 991 (b)(1)(B) (1992).

or to a degree, that it determines should result in a sentence higher or lower than that called for by the Guidelines.[39] The Commission did not adequately take unusual cases into account, and factors that make a case unusual therefore may be considered as appropriate grounds for a Guideline departure by the sentencing court. The introduction to the Guidelines explains:[40]

> The Commission intends the sentencing courts to treat each guideline as carving out a heartland, a set of typical cases embodying the conduct that each guideline describes. When a court finds an atypical case, one to which a particular guideline linguistically applies but where conduct significantly differs from the norm, the court may consider whether a departure is warranted.

The Commission listed several factors that would never serve as a basis for departure—race, sex, national origin, creed, religion, socioeconomic status, lack of guidance as a youth, drug or alcohol dependence, and economic hardship.[41] With these exceptions, however, the Commission did not limit the factors that could be considered as grounds for a departure in unusual cases.[42] The Commission provided guidance to sentencing judges concerning which cases should count as atypical for this purpose by listing certain factors as either encouraged or discouraged bases for a sentencing departure. Encouraged factors are those the Commission has not been able fully to take into account in formulating the Guidelines, such as victim provocation of the offense, which should count as a ground for a downward departure, and offender disruption of a governmental function, which should count as a ground for an upward departure.[43] Even if such a factor is "encouraged," it is not necessarily an appropriate one on which to base a departure. When the applicable Guideline has already implicitly taken the encouraged factor into account, a court may depart on the basis of such a factor only if it is present to a degree substantially in excess of that which is ordinarily involved in the offense.[44] Discouraged

---

39. 18 U.S.C. § 3553 (b) (1992).

40. U.S.S.G., *supra* note 9, at ch. 1, pt. A, intro, cmt. 4(b).

41. *Id.* § 5H1.4 (drug or alcohol dependence); *id.* § 5h1.10 (race, sex, national origin, creed, religion, socioeconomic status); *id.* at § 5H1.12 (lack of guidance as a youth); *id.* § 5K2.12 (economic hardship); *see Koon*, 518 U.S. at 93.

42. U.S.S.G., *supra* note 9, at ch. 1, pt. A, intro. cmt. 4(b).

43. *Id.* § 5K2.10; *id.* § 10.

44. *Id.* § 5K2.7.

factors, such as the defendant's family ties and responsibilities; educational or vocational skills; and military, civic, charitable, or public service record, ordinarily should not be considered as grounds for a departure, but may be so considered in exceptional cases.[45]

If a factor is not mentioned in the Guidelines (*i.e.,* it is neither an encouraged nor a discouraged factor) the sentencing court must consider whether it is sufficiently atypical to justify a departure as "outside the Guideline's heartland," after considering "the structure and theory of both relevant individual Guidelines and the Guidelines taken as a whole...."[46] Departures based on grounds not mentioned in the Guidelines are intended to be "highly infrequent."[47]

In a significant 1996 case, *Koon v. United States,* the U.S. Supreme Court broadly endorsed the discretion of sentencing judges to depart from the Guideline ranges in accordance with these principles and adopted a narrow abuse of discretion standard by which appellate courts could review their exercises of discretion.[48] A sentencing court's departure decision, the Court noted, "involves the consideration of unique factors that are little susceptible of useful generalization."[49] Whether a factor that purportedly justifies departure is within or without the "heartland," given all the cir-

---

45. *Id.* at ch. 5, pt. H, intro. cmt.; *id.* §§ 5H1.6, 5H1.2, 5H1.11. The U.S. Supreme Court recently summarized its understanding concerning factors that could be taken into account by sentencing judges in determining whether to depart from the Guideline range:

> If the special factor is a forbidden factor, then the sentencing court cannot use it as a basis for departure. If the special factor is an encouraged factor the court is authorized to depart if the applicable guideline does not already take it into account. If the special factor is a discouraged factor, or an encouraged factor already taken into account by the applicable guideline, the court should only depart if the factor is present to an exceptional degree or in some other way makes the case different from the ordinary case where the factor is present.

Koon, 518 U.S. at 96.

46. *Id.* at 93.

47. *Id.* at 96, *citing* U.S. Sentencing Comm'n, Federal Sentencing Guidelines Manual ch. 1, pt. A, at 6 (Nov. 1995).

48. *Id.* at 95-96. The *Koon* Court specified standards governing when a judge can support a departure from the Guidelines:

> What features of this case, potentially, take it outside the Guidelines' "heartland" and make of it a special, or unusual, case? Has the Commission forbidden departures based on those features? If not, has the commission encouraged departures based on those features?

Id. at 95.

49. *Id.* at 99, *citing* Cooter Gell v. Hartmarx Corp., 496 U.S. 384 (1990).

cumstances of the case, varies considerably from case to case and therefore is a factual matter left largely to the trial court's discretion.[50]

C. Can Post-offense Rehabilitation Serve as the Basis for a Downward Departure?

Under this framework, applicable to federal courts and in varying degrees to state courts using similar sentencing guideline schemes, the offender's post-offense rehabilitation can be argued, in appropriate cases, to constitute grounds for a downward departure from the sentencing range set forth in the Guidelines. Post-offense rehabilitation was not mentioned in the original Guidelines or the commentary thereto.[51]

Can post-offense rehabilitation be considered a sufficiently atypical factor to justify a downward departure? Although the U.S. Supreme Court has not addressed the issue, every circuit court of appeal to have considered the question has determined that in appropriate cases post-offense rehabilitation can justify a downward departure under the Guidelines.[52] One of the

---

50. *Id.* at 98.

51. The U.S. Sentencing Commission is an on-going body that may, over time, amend the Guidelines or issue new clarifying commentary. *Koon*, 518 U.S. at 93. A 1992 amendment to the commentary for the first time mentioned post-offense rehabilitation in connection with the availability of an adjustment in the level of the offense on the basis of the offender's acceptance of responsibility. *See infra* notes 62-73 and accompanying text.

52. *E.g.,* United States v. Pickering, 178 F.3d 1168, 1174 (11th Cir. 1999) ("a truly extraordinary post-arrest, pre-sentence [rehabilitation]" may be considered as a ground for a downward departure) (dicta); United States v. Simms, 174 F.3d 911 (8th Cir. 1999) (defendant's post arrest rehabilitation conduct can be a basis for a downward departure if sufficiently atypical) (dicta); United States v. Green, 152 F.3d 1202 (9th Cir. 1998) (defendant's post sentencing rehabilitation was "highly successful" and "exceptional" and thus warranted a downward departure from sentencing guidelines); United States v. Whitaker, 152 F.3d 1238 (10th Cir. 1998) (downward departure authorized for post-offense rehabilitation); United States v. Rhodes, 145 F.3d 1375 (D.C. Cir. 1998) (sentencing courts may consider post-conviction rehabilitation at resentencing; rejecting contentions that downward departure for post-offense rehabilitation would revive the parole system abolished by Congress and would usurp the power of the Bureau of Prisons to grant good time credit). United States v. Kapitzke, 130 F.3d 820 (8th Cir. 1997) (upholding downward departure based on defendant's "extraordinary post-offense rehabilitation" and his showing of "guilt and regret for his conduct beyond that normally seen by the court"); United States v. Sally, 116 F.3d 76 (3d Cir. 1997) (upholding departure on the basis of defendant's post-offense rehabilitation); United States v. Brock, 108 F.3d 31 (4th Cir. 1997) (upholding downward departure on the basis of defendant's acceptance of responsibility and rehabilitation); United States v. Barton, 76 F.3d 499 (2d Cir. 1996) (upholding downward departure on the basis of defendant's voluntarily seeking therapy, publicly acknowledging

first circuit court opinions to do so was *United States v. Maier*,[53] in which the court concluded that Congress must have intended that sentencing judges would use their authority, in appropriate cases, to place defendants on probation in order to allow them to obtain medical care or other correctional treatment in the most effective manner. The defendant in *Maier* had been given a downward departure because of her extraordinary efforts to overcome her heroin addiction. "Though drug dependence is not a reason for a departure," the court noted, "the related awareness of one's circumstances and the demonstrated willingness to achieve rehabilitation, thereby benefiting the individual and society, is such a reason."[54] A downward departure would not be upheld, the court noted, merely because a defendant had entered a drug treatment program. More would be required. On the facts, the court upheld the lower court's downward departure because that court had conscientiously examined all of the pertinent circumstances, including the nature of the defendant's addiction, the characteristics of the program she had entered, the progress she had made, the objective indications of her determination to rehabilitate herself, and her therapist's assessment of her progress toward rehabilitation and the hazards of interrupting that progress.[55]

The mere willingness of defendants to acknowledge their disorders and seek treatment may not suffice, however. In *United States v. Barton*,[56] the district court had granted a downward departure on the basis of the public acknowledgement by the defendant, convicted of knowingly receiving child pornography, of his disorder, his voluntary willingness to enter therapy, and a letter from his psychiatrist attesting to the defendant's commitment to rehabilitation. The circuit court reversed because of the factual insufficiency of the evidence relied on by the district court to support its conclusion. Although rejecting a downward departure on the facts, the

---

his disorder, and demonstrating his commitment to rehabilitation); United States v. Maier, 975 F.2d 944 (2d Cir. 1992) (upholding downward departure on the basis of defendant's efforts to overcome her heroin addiction); United States v. Sklar, 920 F.2d 107 (1st Cir. 1990) (evidence sufficient to justify downward departure); United States v. Maddalena, 893 F.2d 815 (6th Cir. 1989) (rehabilitation is grounds for departure).

53. 975 F.2d 944 (2d Cir. 1992). Several circuit courts had earlier reached this conclusion. *E.g.*, United States v. Harrington, 947 F.2d 956 (D.C. Cir. 1991); United States v. Sklar, 920 F.2d 107 (1st Cir. 1990); United States v. Maddalena, 893 F.2d 815 (6th Cir. 1989); *see* Patricia H. Brown, *Considering Post-Arrest Rehabilitation of Addicted Offenders Under the Federal Sentencing Guidelines*, 10 YALE L. & POL'Y REV. 520, 528-30 (1992).

54. *Id.* at 948.

55. *Id.*

56. 76 F.3d 499 (2d Cir. 1996).

circuit court concluded that as a matter of law a defendant convicted of receiving child pornography may be entitled to a downward departure in light of his or her rehabilitative efforts, provided those efforts are "extra-ordinary."[57]

✳ What factors would make a case sufficiently extraordinary to justify such a downward departure? One court has stated that the district court must find that a defendant must have achieved "concrete gains" in reha-bilitating himself.[58] The court must determine whether the defendant's post-conviction rehabilitation efforts are "remarkable and indicate real, positive behavioral change."[59] This downward departure possibility has been described as "a chance for truly repentant defendants to earn reduc-tions in their sentences based on a demonstrated commitment to repair and rebuild their lives."[60]

A 1992 amendment to the commentary in the Guidelines for the first time mentioned post-offense rehabilitation, listing it not as a separate ground for a downward departure, but as a factor to be considered in determining the availability of a reduction in the level of offense on the basis of the separate category of acceptance by the defendant of responsibility for the offense.[61] Although two of the circuit courts of appeal had originally con-strued this amendment to foreclose consideration of post-offense rehabil-itation as a basis for a departure beyond that authorized for acceptance of responsibility, these cases have more recently been overruled. [62] Every circuit court of appeals to have addressed the issue has now rejected this analysis, holding instead that this amendment was not intended to foreclose sentencing judges from considering rehabilitation as the basis for a sepa-rate downward departure.[63]

---

57. *Id.* at 503.

58. United States v. Sally, 116 F.3d 76, 80 (3d Cir. 1997).

59. *Id.* at 81.

60. *Id.*

61. U.S. SENTENCING COMM'N. FEDERAL SENTENCING GUIDELINES MANUAL § 3E1.1 cmt., n(1)(b) (Nov. 1992) ("Post-offense rehabilitative efforts (*e.g.*, counseling or drug treatment") are an appropriate consideration in determining whether the defendant accepted responsibility for the offense) (*quoted in* United States v. Ziegler, 1 F.3d 1044, 1048 (10th Cir. 1993); U.S.S.G., *supra* note 9, § 3E1.1(a) provides for a two-level reduc-tion in the offense level "if the defendant clearly demonstrates a recognition and affirma-tive acceptance of personal responsibility for his criminal conduct."

62. United States v. Ziegler, 39 F.3d 1058 (10th Cir. 1994), *overruled,* United States v. Whitaker, 152 F.3d 1238 (10th Cir. 1998); United States v. Van Dyke, 895 F.2d 984 (4th Cir. 1990), *overruled,* United States v. Brock, 108 F.3d 31 (4th Cir. 1997).

63. *E.g.*, United States v. Pickering, 178 F.3d 1168 (11th Cir. 1999); United States v. Roberts, 166 F.3d 1222 (10th Cir. 1999); United States v. Green, 152 F.3d 1202 (9th Cir. 1998); United States v. Whittaker, 152 F.3d 1238 (10th Cir. 1998); United States v. Core,

The approach set forth in the U.S. Supreme Court's 1996 decision in *Koon v. United States*, although it does not address this issue, supports the virtually consistent recognition by the circuit courts that a downward departure is authorized on the basis of post-offense rehabilitation notwithstanding the fact that such rehabilitation is now an encouraged factor that the commentary to the Guidelines explicitly permits to be taken into account in determining whether to allow an acceptance of responsibility adjustment in the level of offense. *Koon* focuses the inquiry on whether a potential basis for a departure was adequately considered by the Commission in formulating the Guidelines in a way that was intended to preclude additional consideration. The question under *Koon* is whether the Guidelines, policy statements, or official commentary address the factor, and whether it is encompassed within the "heartland" of situations to which the Guidelines are intended to apply.[64] When a factor is not categorically forbidden to be considered by the Commission, it becomes a potential basis for departure, depending on the category in which it falls—encouraged, discouraged, or unmentioned. Rehabilitation is not a forbidden category and (since 1992) has been an encouraged category in connection with considering the availability of an acceptance of responsibility adjustment in the level of offense. As a result, the availability of a downward departure on rehabilitative grounds depends on whether post-offense rehabilitation is present in the particular case to such an exceptional degree that the situation could not be considered typical of those circumstances in which an acceptance of responsibility adjustment is appropriate. Because post-offense rehabilitation is now "an encouraged factor already taken into account by the Guidelines, the court should only depart if the factor is present to an exceptional degree...."[65]

This analysis of *Koon* was the basis of the Fourth Circuit Court of Appeals' 1997 decision in *United States v. Brock*.[66] Brock was convicted on the basis of his guilty plea to two counts of credit card fraud. His presentence report recommended a Guideline range of 12-18 months imprisonment and concluded that no basis for a downward departure existed. Brock asserted that the district court should grant a downward departure because of his rehabilitative efforts. The district court rejected this assertion, feeling itself constrained by the prior Fourth Circuit decision in *United States v. Van Dyke*, holding that post-offense rehabilitative efforts may be considered for an acceptance of responsibility adjustment

---

125 F.3d 74 (2d Cir. 1997); United States v. Brock, 108 F.3d 31 (4th Cir. 1997); United States v. Evans, 49 F.3d 114 (3d Cir. 1996).

64. *Koon*, 518 U.S. at 93-94.

65. *Koon*, 518 U.S. at 96.

66. 108 F.3d 31 (4th Cir. 1997).

but may not also constitute a basis for a downward departure.[67] The Fourth Circuit reversed, finding that the U.S. Supreme Court's decision in *Koon* had effectively overruled the circuit's prior decision in *Van Dyke*.[68] Applying the analysis of *Koon*, the court in *Brock* found that because the Commission has not expressly forbidden consideration of post-offense rehabilitation efforts, they may potentially serve as a viable basis for a departure provided that, when present, they are of such an exceptional degree that the situation cannot be considered typical of those circumstances in which an acceptance of responsibility adjustment is authorized.[69]

This analysis seems correct and has been followed by every circuit court of appeals to have considered the issue.[70] Allowing a downward departure on the basis of rehabilitation is not inconsistent with the adjustment in level of offense authorized by §3E1.1. The two-level adjustment authorized by this section is earned simply by a defendant's guilty plea and expression of remorse. To qualify a defendant must simply say "I violated the law and I am sorry."[71] The successful completion of a course of rehabilitation is a significant accomplishment above and beyond the acceptance of responsibility for the offense and accordingly should be recognized as the basis for an additional sentence reduction.[72] Allowing a downward departure to reward such successful rehabilitative efforts encourages offenders to seek rehabilitation and to achieve the rehabilitative goal and therefore is supported by considerations of therapeutic jurisprudence.

As a result of these developments district judges are increasingly granting downward departures for post-offense rehabilitation.[73] The Commis-

---

67. 895 F.2d 984 (4th Cir. 1990); *accord*, United States v. Ziegler, 39 F.3d 1058 (10th Cir. 1994).

68. United States v. Brock, 108 F.3d 31 (4th Cir. 1997).

69. *Id.* at 31; *accord*, United States v. Whitaker, 152 F.3d 1238 (10th Cir. 1998).

70. Cases cited in *supra* note 52.

71. *Brown, supra* note 53, at 530.

72. *Id.*

73. *See, e.g.*, United States v. McBroom, 991 F. Supp. 445, 451 (D.N.J. 1998) (a chance for truly repentant defendants to earn reductions in their sentences based on a demonstrated commitment to repair and rebuild their lives); United States v. Janus, 986 F. Supp. 328 (CD. Md. 1997) (defendant's acceptance of responsibility and post-offense efforts were exceptional and removed her case from the heartland); United States v. Flowers, 983 F. Supp. 159 (E.D.N.Y. 1997) (post-offense, pre-sentence rehabilitation is factor that may be considered in granting downward departure from Guidelines range); United States v. Griffiths, 954 F. Supp. 254 (D. Vt. 1997) (granting downward departure for post-offense rehabilitation). The latest statistices available from the U.S. Sentencing Commission show that defendants received downward departures in 32.9% of cases, Figure G, Percent of Offenders Receiving Each Type of Departure, *in* U.S. Sentencing Commission,

sion has thus far left these recent developments undisturbed. Its silence in the face of consistent judicial recognition of rehabilitation as a ground for a downward departure constitutes an implicit acceptance of this approach.

D. A Rehabilitative Role for Defense Attorneys

These recent developments thus provide a new opportunity for criminal defense lawyers to assist their clients to obtain post-offense rehabilitation and to urge in plea bargaining discussions and at sentencing hearings that their clients' rehabilitative efforts should constitute grounds for a downward departure from the sentencing range they otherwise would have received under the Guidelines. To effectively play this role, defense attorneys need to familiarize themselves with the full range of rehabilitative opportunities that might be available in their community, the conditions for eligibility for admission into these programs, and the mechanics of assisting their clients to gain entry into them. They need to consider at an early point in the professional relationship, preferably at the initial client interview, whether the client is a suitable candidate for rehabilitation and desires or can be persuaded to undertake rehabilitative efforts. They should advise their clients of the value of such rehabilitative efforts in the plea bargaining and sentencing process. They should assist willing clients to enter such programs or otherwise obtain needed rehabilitative or therapeutic services at an early point. In appropriate cases, they should assist the client to design a rehabilitative program tailored to the client's needs and interests. They should monitor their clients' progress in these programs, periodically reminding them of the value they may provide both in obtaining more favorable sentencing and in adjusting to post-sentence life. When clients have successfully completed such rehabilitative efforts or are making encouraging progress in them, defense attorneys should bring this to the attention of prosecutors in the plea bargaining process, urging such rehabilitative efforts as a ground for a plea bargained sentence lower than that otherwise authorized under the Guidelines, or a lowered sentence recommendation on the part of the prosecutor.[74] They should inform

---

Annual Report, 1998 in <http://www.ussc.gov/ANNRPT/1998/fig-g.pdf>, consulted Jan. 28, 2000, and that offender rehabilitation constituted a ground for a downward departure in 1.5% of cases. Table 25, Reasons Given by Sentencing Courts for Upward and Downward Departures, Fiscal Year 1998, *in* U.S. Sentencing Commission, Annual Report, 1998, in <http://www.ussc.gov/ANNRPT/1998/tab2425.pdf>, consulted Jan. 28, 2000.

74. Defense counsel should bring this information to the attention of the prosecutor in a way that is calculated to affect the mind and heart of a busy prosecutor. An experienced criminal defense attorney makes the following suggestions:

the court's probation department about such rehabilitative efforts, because the department often prepares a pre-sentence report for the court, and its recommendation concerning the range of sentences authorized under the Guidelines and the appropriate sentence in the particular case is frequently given great weight. In cases in which a plea bargain does not specify a particular sentence, defense attorneys should focus on such rehabilitative efforts at their presentation at the sentencing hearing, urging them as a basis for a downward departure. Even in the case of clients who had been convicted following trial, any post-offense rehabilitative efforts that have occurred may similarly be urged at the sentencing hearing as a basis for a reduced sentence. In addition, there may be opportunities to raise rehabilitation as a basis for a post-sentencing motion to reduce sentence. For example, many states' codes of criminal procedure allow the court to use "shock probation" or "shock sentencing." In these situations, the sentencing judge retains plenary jurisdiction over the case for a certain period of time after the defendant has been incarcerated. At any time during this jurisdictional period, the court can conduct a hearing to determine whether the defendant should be subjected to further incarceration. Furthermore, for defendants who have been sentenced to a term of imprisonment, their participation in rehabilitative efforts within the correctional setting can be urged as a basis for resentencing should appellate review of their conviction or sentence result in a resentencing proceeding.[75] Even

---

One of my pet peeves is that many defendants work hard to rehabilitate themselves post-offense, and their lawyer simply mentions it to the prosecutor in the course of hurried negotiations during a chaotic docket call when the prosecutor has dozens of other things on his or her mind. It has long been my practice to prepare a bound packet of information documenting the defendant's rehabilitative success, and present this packet with great pride and enthusiasm to the prosecutor at a time when I have his or her attention. Where appropriate, I include pictures of the defendant's family and find other ways to humanize him or her. I brag about my client's courageous efforts with the same love and delight I display when recounting the achievements of my marvelous children and grandchildren. I tell the prosecutor that a dramatic healing miracle is unfolding and invite him or her to become part of the miracle by recommending a disposition which will be therapeutic for the defendant and everyone else involved. This approach has led to many excellent outcomes for clients and other people impacted by the cases.

Personal communication from John V. McShane, Esq., Dec. 7, 1999, at 5-6.

75. United States v. Cornielle, 171 F.3d 748 (2d Cir. 1999) (rehabilitative efforts made that may entitle defendant to a downward departure from Sentencing Guidelines range must be shown to be extraordinary); United States v. Green, 152 F.3d 1202 (9th Cir. 1998) (defendant's post- sentence rehabilitation was "highly successful" and "exceptional," and thus warranted downward departure from Sentencing Guidelines for resentencing); United States v. Rhodes, 145 F.3d 1375 (D.C. Cir. 1998) (post-sentencing rehabilita-

when resentencing does not occur, these prison rehabilitative efforts can favorably impress the parole board when the defendant becomes eligible for parole consideration.

In all of these circumstances, attorneys can assert, when appropriate, the rehabilitative efforts of their clients as grounds for a sentence of probation rather than of imprisonment. In these times of overcrowded prisons, sentencing judges are especially interested in rehabilitative alternatives to incarceration. Prisons, particularly those that are overcrowded and underfunded and can offer little in the way of rehabilitation, may be criminogenic, schooling inmates in the ways of crime and breeding anger and resentment that are not conducive to rehabilitation. Allowing offenders to continue to remain in the community, particularly if residing with their family or other support group, permits them to engage or continue to engage in productive employment, helping to earn funds to make restitution to the victim or pay fines or court-imposed costs. Probation can also allow offenders to remain in a rehabilitative, treatment, or educational program in which they already are engaged, and continuation in such a program can be made a condition of probation.

In all of these contexts, defense arguments based on client rehabilitation may be met by a degree of cynicism. Prosecutors in plea bargaining, judges engaged in sentencing, and probation officers making recommendations to the courts may be skeptical concerning the genuineness of the defendant's asserted rehabilitation. What can defense counsel do to meet this skepticism? Clients themselves can be placed on the stand and their personal testimony can reveal the genuineness of their rehabilitation. A heart-felt apology can be made to the victim and to the court.[76] Moreover, letters from program staff, family members, and even victims can be introduced, where appropriate, to help to demonstrate the genuineness of rehabilitative efforts and of apology. In addition, where the question is raised as to whether participation in rehabilitation or the making of an apology has not been genuine, defense counsel may consider the use of an expert

---

tion may be the basis for a departure only if it is present to "an exceptional degree"); United States v. Core, 125 F.3d 74 (2d Cir. 1997) (concluding that "acceptance of responsibility" and a successful rehabilitation goes beyond what is required to qualify for the reduction in level of offense under Guidelines § 3E1.1); United States v. Barry, 961 F.2d 260 (D.C. Cir. 1992) (approving resentencing when the district court permitted defendant to provide "updated information" concerning his rehabilitation efforts and the community service he had performed between the first and second sentencings).

76. For recent work on the value of apology in various legal context, see Jonathan R. Cohen, *Advising Clients to Apologize*, 72 S. CAL. L. REV. 1009 (1999); Steven Keeva, *Does Law Mean Never Having to Say You're Sorry?*, 85 ABAJ 64 (Dec. 1999); Daniel W. Shuman, *The Role of Apology in Tort Law*, 83 JUDICATURE 180 (2000).

witness on malingering. In recent years, psychiatrists and psychologists have developed increased ability to detect deception and malingering and a variety of psychometric instruments for this purpose.[77] In adducing expert testimony that the defendant's rehabilitative efforts or apology are genuine, defense counsel should use an expert who is independent of the treatment process. A clinician involved in the defendant's treatment may not be placed in the role of validating the genuineness of efforts consistent with the requirements of professional ethics.[78]

The redefined role for counsel proposed in this chapter may not be an altogether new role for some criminal defense attorneys, but it is for many. Moreover, the new opportunities made possible by recent case law developments authorizing a downward departure for rehabilitative efforts make it imperative that all criminal defense attorneys master this role. Playing this role and playing it well can not only significantly reduce the sentence a client might otherwise receive, but it can provide the attorney an opportunity to assist clients to turn their lives around in ways that safeguard both their future liberty and their future health and happiness. Moreover, making such a contribution can bring a measure of personal and professional satisfaction that many criminal defense lawyers rarely experience. These are the dividends of being a therapeutically oriented preventive lawyer.

IV. Deferred Sentencing to Enable Rehabilitation to Commence and to Facilitate Its Successful Completion

When an offender desires to (or can be persuaded to) engage in rehabilitative efforts but there is insufficient time between the offense and the commencement of plea discussions or the occurrence of sentencing, defense counsel may have little more than the client's good intentions to use in support of arguments to mitigate sentence on rehabilitative grounds. Good intentions alone will not suffice, however, Unless a period of meaningful

---

77. *See, e.g.,* CLINICAL ASSESSMENT OF MALINGERING AND DECEPTION (Richard Rogers ed. 1997); Sherrie Bourg et al., *The Impact of Expertise and Sufficient Information on Psychologists' Ability to Detect Malingering,* 13 BEHAV. SCI. & L. 505 (1995); Douglas Mossman & Kathleen J. Hart, *Presenting Evidence of Malingering to Courts: Insights from Decision Theory,* 14 BEHAV. SCI. & L. 271 (1996); Richard Rogers & Randall T. Salekin, *Research Report Beguiled by Bayes: A Re-analysis of Mossman and Hart's Estimates of Malingering,* 16 BEHAV. SCI. & L.147 (1998).

78. Daniel W. Shuman, *The Use of Empathy in Forensic Examinations,* 3 ETHICS & BEHAV. 289 (1993).

engagement in rehabilitation has occurred in which the defendant has had
the opportunity to demonstrate a significant degree of rehabilitative progress,
prosecutors and judges rarely are willing to take such efforts into account
in a material way in their plea bargaining and sentencing decisions.[79] In
addition, absent such progress, sentencing judges certainly will not find
that post-offense rehabilitation is present to the exceptional degree necessary to take it outside the heartland of the *Guidelines* and hence to justify a downward departure on this basis. [80]

What can the defense attorney do in these circumstances? Brief post-
ponements of the sentencing hearing can usually be obtained, but time
usually runs out before serious rehabilitative efforts can occur or bear
fruit. The solution to this dilemma may be to seek a deferred sentencing to
enable the defendant to achieve what at that point may seem only a potential for successful rehabilitation.

The deferred sentencing option was the subject of a recent significant and
highly creative opinion by one of the nation's most well-regarded federal
judges, Federal District Judge Jack B. Weinstein. In *United States v. Flowers*,[81] the court faced the question of first impression of whether, under the
Guidelines, a court may defer sentence to assure itself that the defendant has
been rehabilitated.[82] The defendant, a 21-year-old single mother of a 4-year-
old child, lived in a two-room apartment in Brooklyn. Her father, an alcoholic,
had abandoned the family when she was 2. She worked at many short-term,
low-paying positions without chance for advancement. The sole support of
her minor child, she succumbed to a suggestion made by a friend of a friend
that she act as a drug courier for money. The defendant was arrested at the
airport when she returned from Barbados with 3.77 kilograms of cocaine
secreted in her luggage. She pled guilty to one count of conspiracy to import,
distribute, and possess cocaine. In the courtroom, the defendant appeared to
be contrite, nervous, soft-spoken, and "somewhat naïve, a person open to
suggestion."[83] Because of the amount of drugs involved, even after a downward departure for acceptance of responsibility and minimal participation, she
faced a prison sentence of between 37 and 46 months, which would separate
her from her child during some of the most important years of the child's life.

The court found that rehabilitation "seems to be well under way" but
that further time would be necessary to determine its extent before decid-

---

79. *See* Simon, *supra* note 6, at 152 ("Given the small treatment effects and the lack of
definitive knowledge about what treatments work, it would be a mistake to base sentencing policy on the offender's willingness to enter into treatment.").

80. *See supra* notes 40, 44, and 46 and accompanying text.

81. 983 F. Supp. 159 (E.D.N.Y. 1997).

82. *Id.* at 160.

83. *Id.*

ing on whether a downward departure to a lesser term of imprisonment or to probation with conditions was appropriate.[84] The court granted a deferral of sentencing, noting that deferring final adjudication to allow a defendant time needed to improve her circumstances was not new to the law.[85] Reasonable delay, the court found, "may help insure that the sentence fit both the crime and the circumstances of the defendant and her family."[86]

In a lengthy, scholarly opinion, Judge Weinstein reviewed the history of innovative alternative sentencing designed to achieve rehabilitation and to protect the public by effectively preventing crime.[87] These have included probation,[88] house arrest and electronic monitoring used in lieu of incarceration,[89] community service orders,[90] "shock" sentencing to a short term of military-style boot camp,[91] and pretrial diversion or deferred prosecution.[92] These differing models of providing alternatives to incarceration

---

84. *Id.* at 161.

85. *Id.*

86. *Id.*

87. *Id.*; *see, e.g.*, ABA STANDARDS FOR CRIMINAL JUSTICE SENTENCING xix (3d ed. 1994) (encouraging the use of "alternative sanctions" instead of "total confinement in prisons and jails or probation" to "create criminal justice systems that are more flexible, responsive, and effective"); ANDREW R. KLEIN, ALTERNATIVE SENTENCING: A PRACTITIONER'S GUIDE 87-136 (1988) (providing examples of alternative sentencing in a wide range of cases).

88. Probation, in which the offender is released to the community with a variety of conditions, sometimes under the supervision of a court probation officer, was the "original" and probably is the most often used form of "alternative" sentencing. KLEIN, *supra* note 87, at 91.

89. House arrest and electronic monitoring are now often imposed in lieu of incarceration. PAUL J. HOFER & BARBARA S. MEIERHOEFER, HOME CONFINEMENT: AN EVOLVING SANCTION IN THE FEDERAL CRIMINAL JUSTICE SYSTEM (Federal Judicial Center ed., 1987) (home confinement as an alternative to traditional imprisonment). *See* U.S.S.G., *supra* note 9, at § 5 F1; *see also* Steven J. Rackmill, An Analysis of Home Confinement as a Sanction, *in* CRIMINAL JUSTICE: CONCEPTS AND ISSUES 229-39 (Chris W. Eskridge, ed., 2d ed. 1997) (discussion of use of home confinement and electronic monitoring) (hereinafter CRIMINAL JUSTICE).

90. Terms of community service are also increasingly being imposed by sentencing judges. *See* U.S.S.G., *supra* note 9, § 5 F1.3; *see also* Malcolm M. Feeley et al., *Between Two Extremes: An Examination of the Effectiveness of Community Service Orders and Their Implications for the United States Sentencing Guidelines*, 66 S. CAL. L. REV. 155 (1992).

91. *See Flowers*, 983 F. Supp. at 162; U.S.S.G., *supra* note 9, § 5F1.7; Doris Layton MacKenzie, *Results of a Multistate Study of Boot Camp Prisons, in* CRIMINAL JUSTICE, *supra* note 82, at 240, 240-47.

92. *See* WAYNE R. LAFAVE & JEROLD H. ISRAEL, CRIMINAL PROCEDURE § 13.6, at 217 (1984) (diversion permitted by individual prosecutors informally when defendant makes

have allowed judges to fashion creative conditions that must be complied with by the offender, including the payment of restitution, the maintenance of employment, attendance at alcohol and other drug treatment or other counseling programs, and the performance of community service.[93] These creative approaches have allowed countless offenders, particularly first offenders, to avoid the harsh consequences of imprisonment and to achieve rehabilitation in the community.

In his opinion in *Flowers,* Judge Weinstein rejected the contention that the Federal Sentencing Guidelines were designed to give rehabilitation a subsidiary role in sentencing.[94] Noting the increasing recognition of post-offense rehabilitation as a ground for a downward departure under the Guidelines,[95] the court then considered whether a deferral of sentencing to enable an offender to demonstrate sufficient rehabilitative efforts to qualify for a downward departure on this basis would be permissible under the Federal Rules of Criminal Procedure.

The Federal Rules of Criminal Procedure do not explicitly authorize a delay in sentencing at the request of the defendant. However, the text in history of Rule 32 contemplate an exercise of discretion by the trial judge in determining when sentencing shall occur.[96] The original version of Rule 32 (a) called for imposition of sentence "without unreasonable delay," necessitating a degree of discretion by the trial judge in determining what was reasonable in the circumstances. [97] The 1987 amendments to the Federal Rules changed the language to provide that sentencing shall occur "without unnecessary delay, but the court may, upon motion that is jointly filed by the defendant and the attorney for the government and that asserts a factor important to the sentencing determination is not capable of being resolved at that time, postpone the imposition of sentence for a reasonable time until the factor is capable of being resolved."[98] In 1989, the Rule was again modified, this time eliminating the requirement that both

---

restitution to the victim or does some other act, such as attending a rehabilitative program); Bruce J. Winick, *Legal Limitations on Correctional Therapy and Research*, 65 MINN. L. REV. 331, 333 (1981); Note, *Pretrial Diversion from the Criminal Process*, 83 YALE L.J. 827 (1974). Two of the most well-known versions of diversion and their history are extensively discussed in *Flowers*, 983 F. Supp. at 162-164 (New York State's Adjournment in Contemplation of Dismissal and the Federal system's "Brooklyn Plan").

93. *Flowers,* 983 F. Supp. at 161.

94.*Id.* at 165. Rehabilitation traditionally has been an important standard of the American criminal justice system. *See supra* note 1 and accompanying text.

95. *Flowers,* 983 F. Supp. at 166. *See supra* Part III.

96. *Flowers,* 983 F. Supp. at 167.

97. FED. R. CRIM. P. 32 (a) (1944 version).

98. FED. R. CRIM. P. 32 (a) (1) (1987 version).

parties request and agree on a delay in sentencing.[99] The legislative history of this amendment demonstrated that it was intended to dispel any implication that a motion for a delay made by one party only might be considered unreasonable and explicitly noted the intention to provide the sentencing judge with "desirable discretion to assure that relevant factors are considered and accurately resolved."[100] This amendment restored the district judge's previous discretion and stressed the importance of leaving such discretion in the hands of the judge in order to allow full consideration of all factors that might be relevant to the sentencing task made more complicated by the Guidelines.[101]

The Rule was revised once again in 1994. The current version retained the sentencing judge's power to postpone sentencing, but it substituted a "good cause" standard governing such discretion.[102] None of the reasons motivating the 1994 amendment purport to limit the trial judge's discretion in setting a sentencing date.[103] Moreover, what constitutes "just cause" to authorize a delay must be considered in light of the greater complexity of the sentencing hearing necessitated by the Guidelines regime, and this has been recognized by a variety of courts.[104] In addition, the post-Guideline amendments to Rule 35 of the Federal Rules of Criminal Procedure substantially restricted the previous ability of the trial judge to correct a sentence already imposed,[105] therefore making it "imperative that judges have the full picture at the time of sentencing."[106]

Judge Weinstein therefore concluded that federal judges possess a wide discretion to postpone sentencing to enable full consideration of all issues that might be relevant concerning sentencing under the Guidelines. When the defendant seeks such a postponement, whatever limitations imposed on this discretion by the defendant's constitutional right to speedy trial are absent.[107] Noting that pre-sentence rehabilitation is an important consideration for the sentencing judge to take into account, Judge Weinstein granted a 1-year postponement of sentencing to allow the defendant to

---

99. FED. R. CRIM. P. 32 (a) (1) (1989 version).

100. FED. R. CRIM. P. 32 (a) (1) (1989 Advisory Comm. Note), *in 109* S. Ct. 72, 99-100 (1988).

101. *Flowers*, 983 F. Supp. at 169.

102. FED. R. CRIM. P. 32 (a) (1) (1994 version)..

103. *Flowers*, 983 F. Supp. at 170.

104. *Id.*, *citing* United States v. Lopez, 26, F.3d 512, 523 (5th Cir. 1994).

105. FED. R. CRIM. P. 35.

106. *Flowers*, 983 F. Supp. at 172.

107. *Id.*

demonstrate her entitlement to a downward departure on this basis. It is the duty of sentencing judges to consider every possible ground for a departure from the sentencing range set forth in the Guidelines, he noted,[108] and the facts of this case made it appropriate to provide the defendant an opportunity to engage in rehabilitative efforts that seemed likely to succeed and therefore to constitute a basis for a possible downward departure. Judge Weinstein's pioneering decision in _Flowers_ thus provides sentencing judges with wide discretion to postpone sentencing in appropriate cases to allow defendants to engage in rehabilitative efforts that seem likely to provide an ultimate basis for a downward departure on the basis of their post-offense rehabilitation. This possibility provides defense attorneys a broad opportunity to develop rehabilitative plans in conjunction with their clients that can provide significant therapeutic and legal value to them. The combination of the downward departure possibility for post-offense rehabilitation and the possibility that _Flowers_ suggests to obtain a postponement of sentencing to enable such rehabilitative efforts to demonstrate success before sentencing occurs constitutes an important new tool for the criminal defense lawyer. This tool enables a significant expansion of the role of the criminal defense lawyer at sentencing, permitting such attorneys to realize the advantages, for both their clients and themselves, of becoming therapeutically oriented preventive lawyers.

V. Representing Corporate and Other Organizational Defendants

A. Increased Prosecution of Organizations

In this era of increasing concern with white collar crime, attorneys will more frequently find themselves representing corporations and other organizations that are or could be involved with criminal prosecution. Keeping such organizations from violating criminal prohibitions through counseling concerning the requirements of law, periodic legal checkups, and compliance monitoring has been a traditional role of the preventive lawyer.[109] Recent developments involving the adoption of special sentencing guidelines for organizations give this role added importance and provide

---

108. _Id._

109. _See, e.g.,_ BROWN & DAUER, _supra_ note 15; HARDAWAY, _supra_ note 15; Richard S. Gruner & Louis M. Brown, _Organizational Justice: Recognizing and Rewarding the Good Citizen Corporation,_ 21 J. CORP L. 731 (1996)

new opportunities for attorneys to keep their clients out of trouble and to minimize their difficulties when criminal charges have been filed.

With increasing frequency, state-end federal prosecutors are targeting corporations and other organizations, as well as their executives, for the suspected criminal acts of their employees.[110] These include securities and antitrust violations, regulatory and environmental transgressions, fraud, money laundering, and even murder and manslaughter.[111] A corporation or other organizational entity may be held criminally responsible for acts of misfeasance, malfeasance, or nonfeasance even though the act complained of requires a specific intent or was accomplished through unauthorized conduct.[112] In addition, a corporation or other entity may be held criminally liable for the acts of an agent who has been vested with the authority to act on behalf of the entity within the sphere of the entity's business in which the criminal act was committed.[113]

Although at common law, criminal responsibility for corporations and other entities was unthinkable,[114] this common law rule was gradually eclipsed, and in 1909, the U.S. Supreme Court case of *New York Central and Hudson River Railroad Company v. United States* finally rejected it.[115] This landmark case ushered in a new era of corporate criminal liability

---

110. A recent example was the criminal indictment charging manslaughter and murder against SabreTech, an aircraft maintenance company involved in the 1996 ValuJet crash in the Florida Everglades that killed 110 people. Ina Paiva-Cordle, *Murder Charged in Plane Crash: SabreTech Targeted in Glades Disaster*, MIAMI HERALD, July 14, 1999, at 1. Although SaberTech was acquitted on several counts, it was found guilty on several counts of recklessly violating hazardous materials regulations and failing to properly train workers. Ina Paiva-Cordle, *Jury Convicts Firm in Vauljet Crash Two Workers are Exonerated*, MIAMI HERALD, December 7, 1999 at 1. [hereinafter *Jury Convicts*].

111. *See, e.g., Jury Convicts, supra* note 110, at 1 (corporation charged in state court with 110 counts of third-degree murder, 110 counts of manslaughter, and 1 count of unlawful transportation of hazardous materials in ValuJet crash).

112. State v. Shaouse, 177 So. 2d 724 (Fla. 2d DCA 1965).

113. West Valley Estates, Inc. v. State, 286 So. 2d 208 (Fla. 2d DCA 1973).

114. *See, e.g.,* 1 WILLIAM BLACKSTONE, COMMENTARIES 476 (1765) ("A corporation cannot commit treason, or felony, or other crime, in its corporate capacity....How could anyone think differently?").

115. 212 U.S. 481 (1909). The railroad was charged with violation of the Elkins Act on the basis of actions of its agent. The railroad argued that Congress lacked the constitutional authority to impute criminal guilt to the corporation, particularly to its innocent stockholders. The Court rejected this argument based on considerations of public policy and affirmed the corporation's conviction. Because corporations already were liable in tort under the principle of *respondeat superior*, the Court found it obvious that they also could be convicted criminally. *Id.* at 494.

based on principles of vicarious responsibility for the acts of the organization's agents.[116]

B. The Organizational Sentencing Guidelines

Although vicarious criminal liability tends to be broad in scope, until
recently the penalties imposed on corporations were not particularly large.
Corporations typically were subject to the same penalties as individuals,
and because maximum fines were usually set with individuals in mind,
they were relatively low. However, in 1984 Congress enacted statutory
provisions designed to increase corporate criminal sanctions.[117] In 1991,
the United States Sentencing Commission promulgated Guidelines to govern the sentencing of organizations in federal court.[118] The Guidelines
apply to the sentencing of organizations for federal felonies and Class A misdemeanors, including antitrust offenses, bribery, kickbacks, fraud, money
laundering, theft, and tax violations.[119] The Guidelines define an organization broadly as "a person other than an individual."[120] This definition
thus applies to associations, corporations, joint stock companies, partnerships, pension funds, trusts, governments, and unions.[121]
In general, the Guidelines were developed to promote consistency in
sentencing.[122] In line with this general aim, the Guideline provisions governing corporations require courts to sentence organizational defendants
in a systematic and uniform manner.[123] Under the Guidelines, corporate fines
are calculated on the basis of the greatest of (a) the pecuniary gain to the
organization from the offense; (b) the pecuniary loss to others from the
offense (to the extent the loss was caused intentionally, knowingly, or
recklessly); or (c) an amount determined by a table contained in the Guidelines corresponding to the offense level of the crime. This calculation results
in the base fine. To determine the actual fine, the Guidelines provide that

---

116. *See, e.g.*, Kathleen Brickey, *Corporate Criminal Liability: A Primer for Corporate
Counsel*, 40 Bus. L. 129 (1984).
117. Criminal Fine Enforcement Act of 1984, Pub. L. No. 98-596, 98 Stat.
3134, *codified in* 18 U.S.C. § 3565 (1998).
118. U.S. Sentencing Comm'n, Federal Sentencing Guidelines Manual
§ 2E1.1 (Nov. 1991).
119. U.S.S.G. *supra* note 9, § 8A1.1 cmt. 2.
120. *Id.* § 8A1.1 cmt. 1 (1998).
121. Joseph, *supra* note 13, at 1018.
122. U.S.S.G., *supra* note 9, § 8. C2.59 (b)-(g) (setting forth provisions by which an
organization's culpability score may be increased or decreased).
123. *Id.* § 8C2.5(a).

the court must adjust this base fine by a multiplier that reflects the corporation's level of culpability, unless the corporation demonstrates entitlement to relief under the Guidelines' mitigation provisions.[124] The multiplier generally exceeds one and may be as high as four. In addition to increasing and standardizing organizational sanctions, the Guidelines introduced an important innovation—explicit provisions regarding fine mitigation for corporations that have "effective monitoring programs" and that report violations promptly to the government.[125]

The Commission has indicated that the Guidelines were designed to provide "just punishment, adequate deterrence, and incentives for organizations to maintain internal mechanisms for preventing, detecting, and reporting criminal conduct."[126] According to the Commission, the Guidelines reflect several principles: The Guidelines are designed to encourage the organization to remedy any harm caused by the offense.[127] The resources expended to remedy the harm are not viewed as punishment, but rather as a means of compensating victims for the harm caused. If the organization operated primarily for a criminal purpose or primarily by criminal means, the Guidelines recommend that the fine be set sufficiently high to divest the organization of all its assets.[128] The fine range for any other organization is based on the seriousness of the offense and the culpability of the organization.[129] The seriousness of the offense generally is taken into account by considerations reflected in the calculation of the base fine. Culpability generally is determined by the steps taken by the organization prior to consideration of the offense to prevent and detect criminal conduct, the level and extent of involvement in or tolerance of the offense by certain personnel, and the organization's actions after an offense has been committed.[130] Probation is a contemplated sentence for an organizational defendant when needed to ensure that another sanction is fully implemented or that steps will be taken within the organization to reduce the likelihood of future criminal conduct.[131]

---

124. *Id.* §§ 8C2.5, 8C2.6.

125. *Id.* § 8C2.6. However, the mitigation provisions are inapplicable to situations in which the crime was committed by a senior employee with managerial authority. *Id.* § 8C2.5.

126. *Id.* § 8 C2.5(g)(1).

127. *Id.*

128. *Id.*

129. *Id.*

130. *Id.*

131. *Id.*

C. A Rehabilitative and Preventive Law Role for Attorneys

The Guidelines provisions applicable to corporations and other organizations provide a number of opportunities for the therapeutically oriented preventive lawyer to offer significant services to the organizational client. For clients charged with offenses, the attorney can play an important advocacy role with the court's probation department and with the sentencing judge in helping the court to calculate the appropriate sentencing range. Because offense severity largely is a factor of the offense and the pecuniary gain to the client and loss to the victim, the attorney's most important role is advocacy concerning how to evaluate the client's culpability, which entails a consideration of the organization's compliance program, past history, extent of involvement in the offense, and cooperation once the offense has been discovered. After the court determines the base fine level, it must determine the organization's culpability.[132] Under § 8C2.5 of the Guidelines, the court begins with five culpability points and can then consider whether to add or subtract points for specific factors.[133] Factors such as whether the organization was part of the criminal activity or tolerated that activity may increase the organization's culpability score.[134] The court then reviews the organization's prior history and increases the culpability score by one or two points if there is evidence of prior similar misconduct within the previous 5 or 10 years.[135]

Counsel can also point to a number of factors that under the Guidelines can reduce the client's culpability score.[136] For instance, an organization can qualify for a reduction in its culpability score if it reports the unlawful conduct, cooperates in the investigation, and accepts responsibility for the criminal activity.

[137] An organization has "accepted responsibility" for an offense when it has admitted involvement in the offense and related conduct and has pled guilty to the offense prior to trial.[138]

---

132. *Id.* § 8C2.5(a).

133. *Id.; see id.* § 8C2.5(b)-(g) (setting forth provisions by which an organization's culpability score may be increased or decreased).

134. Joseph, *supra* note 13, at 1025 (An organization can be found to have been "involved" in the criminal activity if its managers were willfully ignorant of, condoned or participated in the criminal conduct.).

135. U.S.S.G., *supra* note 9, § 8C2.5(c)(1)(2).

136. *Id.* § 8C2.5(f)(g) (providing for reductions in culpability scores for effective compliance programs that prevent and detect violations and encourage self-reporting and acceptance of responsibility).

137. *Id.* § 8C2.5(g)(1).

138. *Id.* § 8C2.5 cmt. 13.

Another way an organization may reduce its culpability score is by having had in place an effective compliance program at the time of the unlawful conduct.[139] The existence of an effective compliance program reduces the culpability score by three points, which may achieve up to a 60% reduction of the minimum fine and up to 120% of the maximum possible fine.[140]

By assisting the organizational client to develop an effective compliance program, the attorney can play a significant preventive law role. The Organizational Sentencing Guidelines provide a "carrot and stick" approach to motivating organizations to police themselves and become aware of any of its agents involved in criminal activity at the workplace. Preventive lawyers can assist their organizational clients to understand this "carrot and stick" approach and can provide them with the tools to anticipate illegal activity, assist them to implement procedures to identify and prevent it, and affect sentencing when conviction of the organization has occurred. The most common and effective method of accomplishing this task is the development and implementation of compliance programs.

Even though the Guidelines provide strong incentives for the adoption of compliance plans,[141] the existence of a compliance program does not insulate an organization from prosecution. Although "the existence of a *bona fide* compliance program may exert a favorable influence on prosecutorial discretion" and should serve to mitigate whatever sentence the client might receive, it also may produce a risk of disclosing offenses that would not have been detected and of waiving confidential communications.[142] Counsel should point out to the client both these advantages and risks but suggest that the minimization or avoidance of the risk of criminal liability argues strongly for the adoption of such a plan.

To succeed in achieving a mitigation of sentence under the Guidelines, a compliance program must be "reasonably designed, implemented, and

---

139. *Id.* § 8C2.5(f).

140. U.S.S.G., *supra* note 9, § 8c 2.5(f) (1998); Joseph, *supra* note 13, at 1034 n.77; *see* U.S.S.G. *supra* note 9, § 8C2.6 (providing table for determining maximum and minimum multipliers based on culpability score). The advantages of having an effective compliance program are graphically illustrated by a hypothetical set forth in Charles H. Rositacher & Aileen M. Reilly, *Federal Sentencing Guidelines and Organizational Defendants,* ABA. Ctr. for Continuing Legal Education Nat'l Inst., WL N98GENB ABALGLED D-11 (April 16- 17, 1998) (comparing two fact patterns involving organizations convicted of money laundering in which the organization with a compliance plan is eligible for a fine of between $1,365,000 and $2,600,000 less than its counterpart, which had no compliance plan).

141. Joseph, *supra* note 13, at 1030.

142. *Id.*

enforced so that it generally will be effective in preventing and detecting criminal conduct."[143] Due diligence, not success, is the hallmark of an effective compliance program.[144] Such a program "is a mitigating factor despite its failure to prevent a criminal offense from occurring because of the recognition that even the most diligent corporate monitor may fail to catch every violation."[145]

To succeed in achieving mitigation under the Guidelines, a compliance program should ensure that the organization exercises "due diligence in seeking to prevent and detect criminal conduct" and demonstrate that the organization is not indifferent to the law but has taken reasonable steps to comply with it.[146] The Guidelines identify seven factors that a qualifying compliance program should meet.[147] The organization must (a) enact standards and procedures "that are reasonably capable of reducing the prospect of criminal conduct;"[148] (b) assign a high-level employee to supervise the compliance program;[149] (c) use "due care not to delegate substantial discretionary authority to individuals whom the organization knew, or should have known through the exercise of due diligence, had a propensity to engage in illegal activities;"[150] (d) effectively communicate the standards and procedures of the compliance program to all of its employees;[151] (e) enforce the program through "monitoring and auditing systems;"[152] (f) consistently enforce the program through "appropriate disciplinary mechanisms;"[153] and (g) (if an offense has been detected) take "all reasonable steps to respond appropriately to the offense and to prevent further similar offenses—including any necessary modifications to its program."[154]

The Guidelines require that compliance programs be tailored to the circumstances and potential problems of the particular organization.[155] For example, when many employees have the authority to discuss and/or decide

---

143. U.S.S.G., *supra* note 9, § 8A1.2 cmt..3(k).
144. *Id.*
145. Joseph, *supra* note 13, at 1028.
146. *Id.*
147. U.S.S.G., *supra* note 9, § 8A1.2 cmt. 3(k)(1)-(7).
148. *Id.* § 8A1.2 cmt. 3(k)(1).
149. *Id.* § 8A1.2 cmt. 3(k)(2).
150. *Id.* § 8A1.2 cmt. 3(k)(3).
151. *Id.* § 8A1.2 cmt. 3(k)(4).
152. *Id.* § 8A1.2 cmt. 3(k)(5).
153. *Id.* § 8A1.2 cmt. 3(k)(6).
154. *Id.* § 8A1.2 cmt. 3(k)(7).
155. Steven M. Kowal, *Corporate Compliance Programs: A Shield Against Criminal Liability*, 53 Food & Drug L.J. 517, 523 (1998).

the price of a product, the compliance program should be developed with antitrust considerations in mind.[156]

Although the attorney should counsel the organizational client about the need for the development of a compliance program and the requirements that it must meet to qualify for mitigation of sentence under the guidelines, counsel should not simply prepare the plan for the client. Rather, counsel should involve the client and its employees in the process of the plan's development. As David Wexler suggested, preventive lawyers should resist the temptation to take over the drafting of such compliance or relapse prevention plans; they should encourage the client to play the major role in preparing them.[157] Design of the plan by the client itself is called for, as Wexler suggested, by the psychological principles of compliance and relapse prevention.[158] Client design of the plan better produces the needed cognitive self-change and is more likely to produce feelings of fairness and participation that in turn are likely to bring about greater compliance.[159] Counsel can play a role, but the setting of standards and procedures should be done with the active participation of the client's officers and employees.

In the case of large organizations, counsel can suggest the use of survey teams in the development, implementation, and maintenance of compliance programs. These teams, composed of outside and in-house counsel and the members of the organization's human resources department, can identify potential problem areas, review past civil and administrative difficulties experienced by the organization, and consider problems confronted by other industry members, governmental interests and regulations, and future development plans, *such as* corporate acquisitions.[160] The determi-

---

156. *Id.*

157. Wexler, *supra* note 5.

158. *Id.*

159. *Id.*; Bruce J. Winick, *Therapeutic Jurisprudence and the Civil Commitment Hearing*, 10 J. CONTEMP. L. ISSUES 37 (1999) (arguing that when patients subjected to civil commitment proceedings experience feelings of fairness and participation, they are likely to experience greater satisfaction with the outcome of the proceeding and to comply more readily with it, thereby increasing the efficacy of the hospitalization to which they may be subjected); Bruce J. Winick, *Coercion and Mental Health Treatment*, 74 DENVER L. REV. 1145 (1997) [hereinafter *Coercion*] (same); Bruce J Winick, *Sex Offender Law in the 1990s: A Therapeutic Jurisprudence Analysis*, 4 PSYCHOL. PUB. POL'Y & L. 505, 565-66 (1998) (sex offenders who experience hearings on whether they are or continue to be sexually violent predators and concerning their risk level for purposes of community notification who perceive such hearings as fulfilling their interests in fairness and participation are likely to respond better to sex offender rehabilitative efforts).

160. Kowal, *supra* note 155, at 524.

nations and recommendations of this survey team can then be used to develop the design of an effective compliance program.[161]

✗ However the plan is developed, counsel should impress on the client that merely designing a compliance plan is not sufficient; it must be implemented with policies and procedures that provide constant monitoring and review.[162] Counsel should be aware of a number of potential problems in the implementation and maintenance of compliance programs. Major problems can occur when top management is not committed to the compliance program.[163] In this situation lower level employees sense the lack of commitment, thus ensuring the program's failure. When this occurs and prosecution results, federal investigators are quick to assert that the compliance program was a "sham" or just "window dressing" from the start.[164] Problems also can occur when the appointed compliance officer has no background in compliance issues or does not regularly communicate with the board of directors, thereby undermining the effectiveness of the compliance program;[165] when the company undergoes a merger or acquisition and does not revise its policies and procedures to reflect the new entity or its compliance needs;[166] when the organization fails to document its compliance program efforts; when the policies and procedures are not circulated to all employees; and when the organization does not regularly reevaluate the program.[167]

The danger always exists that employees do not take the compliance program seriously. Not only must the plan be distributed to all relevant employees and made the subject of training programs where appropriate, but the corporate culture must embrace the plan and communicate the seriousness of the compliance goal throughout the organization. How can mechanisms be put into place to assure that this occurs?

✗ Therapeutic jurisprudence/preventive law has much to contribute to the solution of this problem. Preventive law is often compared with preventive medicine.[168] This is an area where lawyers may be able to learn much from physicians and other healers. Patient noncompliance with the recommendations of their health care providers is a significant problem that has provoked much discussion in the medical literature. The field of behavioral

---

161. *Id.* at 525.

162. *Id.*

163. Robert W. Tarun, *Unlucky Side Effect—13 Common Problems With Compliance Programs*, 13 CORP. COUNS. 1 (1998).

164. *Id.*

165. *Id.*

166. *Id.*

167. *Id.*

168. *See* Stolle et al., *supra* note 16, at 16.

medicine has much to contribute to the resolution of this problem.[169] In a useful book, psychologists Donald Michenbaum and Donald Tork review a variety of health care compliance principles and how they can be employed by health care providers to increase the likelihood that their patients follow their recommendations.[170] Preventive lawyers can adapt these principles in counseling their clients concerning compliance with plans developed to insure that the organization fulfills legal requirements and to avoid a repetition of any past wrongdoing. Indeed, existing therapeutic jurisprudence work has adapted these principles for use in a variety of legal areas—in insanity defense acquitee conditional release decision making and the setting of conditions of probation[171] and in facilitating drug treatment, teaching job training skills to those on welfare, and reducing truancy on the part of public school students.[172] These principles can be adapted to advantage in the design of organizational compliance programs and of relapse prevention plans for organizations pleading guilty to criminal wrongdoing

A technique of behavioral psychology known as *behavioral contracting* or *contingency management* captures many of these compliance principles and may be helpful in ensuring that employees of the organization adhere to the compliance program.[173] This approach is based on an explicit, formal agreement where the contracting parties obligate themselves to achieve specified goals.[174] Motivation to achieve the goal is facilitated through contract terms providing for a combination of agreed-on rewards for success and penalties or aversive consequences for failure.[175] Indeed, the Organizational Sentencing Guidelines themselves can be viewed as a form of contingency management in which the government offers to enter into

---

169. *See, e.g.*, DONALD MICHENBAUM & DONALD TURK, FACILITATING TREATMENT ADHERENCE: A PRACTITIONER'S GUIDEBOOK (1987).

170. *Id.*

171. David B. Wexler, *Health Care Compliance Principles and the Insanity Acquitee Conditional Release Process, in* DAVID B. WEXLER & BRUCE J. WINICK, ESSAYS IN THERAPEUTIC JURISPRUDENCE, 199 (1991); Wexler, *supra* note 6.

172. Bruce J. Winick, *Harnessing the Power of the Bet: Wagering With the Government as a Mechanism for Social and Individual Change*, 45 U. MIAMI L. REV. 737, 772-88, 793-97 (1991).

173. *See id.* (describing this approach, analyzing the psychological principles on which it is based, and illustrating its application). This approach can be used as well in the representation of an individual criminal client. For example, the attorney can insert a provision in the retainer agreement in which the client agrees to abide by the terms of the rehabilitation program and the attorney is permitted to withdraw from the case if the provision is breached.

174. *Id.* at 739.

175. *Id.*

an agreement with its citizen corporations by providing special incentives, including a reduction in sentence, in exchange for the organization's commitment to implement and monitor a compliance program. To assure compliance with the plan by its employees, the organization can enter into a behavioral contract with them by providing motivational incentives. For example, monetary bonuses may be offered periodically to divisions, sectors, or other identifiable subgroups that remain in compliance for a specific period of time. Non-monetary incentives may be even more effective. These can include time off from work; points accumulated toward a larger office, new desk, or file cabinet, or a faster computer; installation of a coffee or soda machine at the workplace; tickets to sporting events, movies, or concerts; added discounts on the company's products; and other creative possibilities. The employees might agree that if violations of the compliance plan occur by them or under their watch, they suffer a penalty, such as a fine, extra duty, or loss of certain benefits. The combination of positive reinforcement to encourage compliant behavior and aversive conditioning to decrease or extinguish non-compliant behavior can be quite effective and serves as the basis for behavioral contracting, a technique frequently used in clinical practice. Moreover, the office behavioral contract can provide not only rewards or penalties for achievement or non-achievement of a long-term goal (like compliance for a 5-year period), but also on the occurrence or nonoccurrence of intermediate goals. Behavioral contracts between the organization and its employees that contain these features can be an effective means to increase employee commitment and motivation to adhere to the plan.

By understanding the organizational sentencing provisions of the Guidelines, the preventive lawyer can thus offer a variety of significant services to the client. The lawyer can audit the client's operations to insure that the organization is in compliance with various legal requirements and assist the organization to develop, monitor, and maintain effective compliance plans. Increasingly, the violation of a wide variety of federal and state legal requirements can expose the client to potential criminal liability. Preventive lawyers can play their roles best by suggesting ways of preventing any failures to comply with legal requirements, thereby avoiding the occurrence of potentially serious legal problems, including criminal ones. This is a classic role not only of the preventive lawyer, but of all good lawyers—the identification and prevention or minimization of risk.

Some clients may object that they do not think they need such a compliance audit and do not want to pay for it. Preventive lawyers need to educate their clients concerning the high value of such preventive services. Compliance audits and the adoption of such plans can be justified not only by the interest in avoiding criminal liability, but also by the interests of the directors of the organization in avoiding their own potential civil liability.[176] Repairing a stitch in the hem of one's clothing also may cost money, but far less money than nine stitches. The client, and business and other kinds of organizations generally, need to understand the costs and burdens of being involved in legal proceedings with the government, and criminal proceedings in particular. The legal fees involved in fighting such proceedings can often be astronomical, far more than the cost of compliance audits. There are other, serious costs as well. Being involved in litigation can be a nasty and vexatious business. It can drain away the resources of the organization in defensive efforts, in compliance with discovery requests, in attending meetings with lawyers and making appearances in court, and in responding to press inquiries. Moreover, there are often serious emotional costs. Legal proceedings are intensely stressful and can create feelings of fear, anger, anxiety, and depression. In short, they are highly antitherapeutic. In addition, being publicly charged by the government with unlawful activity can be highly damaging to the reputation of the organization. Indeed, accusation of serious wrongdoing and criminal violation can produce a lasting stigma that may seriously diminish the organization's business and other activities. Mending a bridge or a highway in need of repairs can also be expensive, but society justifies the expense as necessary to prevent disaster. Being a defendant, even an organizational defendant, in a criminal prosecution is nothing less than a disaster.

There still will be clients who do not see the light and decline their attorney's suggestion of the need for a compliance audit and the development of a compliance plan. Perhaps they fully are in compliance, and their compliant behavior is already adequately assured by procedures that are well in place or by some other viable review mechanism. If this is so, there may be no need to have the attorney double-check their compliance. Other clients simply do not want to spend the money, or may wish to remain in denial concerning their non-compliant behavior or about procedures within the organization that might (even inadvertently) encourage such behavior. Sometimes it is the duty of lawyers to make their clients face their denial. Doing so may often require a degree of psychological skill, understanding, and sensitivity, particularly if their denial has a psychological basis, as it often does.[177] Dealing with clients about such issues is chal-

---

176. The business judgment rule, which for many years had shielded directors from liability for acts done in good faith, has more recently been eclipsed by case law developments imposing an affirmative duty of care on directors, including the use of compliance and reporting systems designed to prevent wrongdoing. See In re Caremark Int'l, Inc. Derivative Litigation, 698 A. 2d 959 (Del. Ch. 1996); Joseph F. Savage, Jr., The Caremark Decision: Director's Fiduciary Duty in a Sentencing Guidelines World, 11 CORP. COUNS. 8, 9 (1997).

177. See generally Winick, supra note 16 (making suggestions concerning how attor-

lenging work; it demands a high degree of psychological skill and judgment and the ability to listen to the client, to make the client feel comfortable, to communicate empathy, and to understand the social psychology of persuasion. These psychological skills, all of which can and should be taught in continuing legal education programs and clinical legal education, are considered in more detail in Part VI of this chapter.[178] These are skills that therapeutic jurisprudence brings to the attention of lawyers and nicely illustrate the advantages of their integration into a model of lawyering that champions the principles of preventive law and the psychology mindedness of therapeutic jurisprudence.

Not only do preventive lawyers counseling corporations and other types of organizations need to understand the workings of the Guidelines governing organizations, but all business lawyers, government lawyers, lawyers representing not-for-profit organizations, and criminal lawyers need to understand them. Criminal lawyers in particular, because of their already existing familiarity with how sentencing guidelines work, possess the natural ability to develop an expertise in how the organizational guidelines function as well. Moreover, by learning the lessons of therapeutic jurisprudence and preventive law, such criminal lawyers could offer their services to what for many might be a new clientele—the organizational defendant. They could be of particular service when organizations face criminal prosecution. Such organizations need to retain the services of criminal defense lawyers to determine whether the charges can be fought or whether the organization should plead guilty or *nolo contendere*, to engage in plea bargaining discussions, and to provide representation at the sentencing hearing. Criminal lawyers performing these functions can only benefit from the insights of therapeutic jurisprudence and preventive law. These insights can inform and improve their functioning with significant benefits for their clients and themselves.

VI. Attorney/Client Conversations About Rehabilitation: Applying Insights from Psychology

Criminal defense lawyers who apply a therapeutic jurisprudence/preventive law model in the plea bargaining and sentencing process therefore

---

neys can identify and deal with denial on the part of their clients); *infra* Part VI.

178. *See id.* (discussing psychological principles that can be adapted by attorneys to facilitate such attorney/client conversations).

have much to offer their clients. There are many advantages to counseling appropriate clients about the benefits of rehabilitative programs and of presenting such rehabilitative options to prosecutors, probation officers, and sentencing judges as bases for plea bargains and reduced sentencing. A significant period of post-offense rehabilitation can be asserted as a ground for a downward departure under sentencing guidelines; when insufficient time between the offense and the scheduled sentencing hearing has passed to enable significant rehabilitative efforts to have occurred, a deferred sentencing can be sought to facilitate the rehabilitative process. This device presents an exciting opportunity for the attorney working with the client to fashion a creative rehabilitative program that has a high potential for success. Sentencing judges convinced of this potential can grant a deferral of sentencing, permitting a rehabilitative plan to commence and bear fruit. Successful efforts can ultimately qualify for a downward departure under sentencing guidelines, earning probation or a substantially reduced sentence. Furthermore, in the case of corporations or other organizational clients, preventive approaches such as compliance audits, effective compliance programs, and relapse prevention plans for those who have been convicted can produce a substantial reduction in any fine imposed and succeed in avoiding future problems.

A. Psycholegal Soft Spots in the Attorney/Client Dialogue

However, holding conversations with clients about the value of rehabilitative efforts can trigger negative emotional reactions on the part of the client if not done with sensitivity. Many clients resist having such conversations or are uncomfortable and experience psychological distress during them. Therapeutically oriented preventive lawyers recognize these conversations as psycholegal soft spots.[179] How should attorneys deal with them? What insights does psychology have for the conduct of these sensitive conversations? How far should the attorney go in counseling the client in the direction of seeking rehabilitation, and how should such counseling occur?

In a variety of criminal cases, it may be fairly clear to the attorney that the client has a psychological problem that relates to his or her criminality. Perhaps the client is a substance abuser who commits theft offenses in order to support a drug habit. Perhaps the client is an alcoholic whose drinking contributes to repetitive acts of domestic violence,[180] impaired

---

179. *See supra* note 23 and accompanying text.

180. The co-occurrence of alcohol and other drug abuse and domestic violence appears common, with 94% of perpetrators and 43% of victims using such substances at the time of the offense. DANIEL BROOKOFF, NATIONAL INSTITUTE OF JUSTICE RESEARCH

driving, or assault. Perhaps the client's pedophilia coupled with cognitive distortions and denial about his culpability or the pain that his conduct causes his child victims contributes to his repetitive acts of sexual violence directed at children. Perhaps the client suffers from pyromania which contributes to crimes of arson, or kleptomania which contributes to repetitive shoplifting, or compulsive gambling which contributes to illegal gambling and crimes of theft or embezzlement designed to obtain funds needed for gambling activity. Perhaps the client suffers from schizophrenia or other mental illness, and the client's refusal to take needed medication contributes to the repetitive commission of various nuisance offenses such as trespassing, loitering, or urinating in public. Although the attorney may correctly analyze the client's repetitive criminality as a product of psychological or behavioral problems that could successfully respond to a variety of rehabilitative efforts, attorney/client conversations about these issues are bound to be highly sensitive and to touch a number of emotional issues that are the subject of client denial, suppression, or repression.[181] These are conversations that must be engaged in with a high degree of psychological sensitivity.

B. Avoiding Paternalism and Coercion

At the outset, attorneys must be careful to avoid being paternalistic with their clients in such counseling sessions. These are contexts in which it is easy for the attorney to respond paternalistically. The attorney may be strongly convinced, often correctly, that the client suffers from an emotional problem that produces repetitive criminality and that could respond effectively to available rehabilitative programs. The attorney, therefore, may think that if only the client could see the light (*i.e.*, could understand matters in the way that the attorney does), the client would agree to obtain needed help. However, paternalism, particularly on the part of those who are not close family members or friends (and sometimes even then), is often experienced as offensive by its recipients. Moreover, because people often resent being the subject of paternalism, a paternalistic approach on the part of the attorney may backfire, producing a psychological reac-

---

IN PROGRESS SEMINAR SERIES, DRUG USE AND DOMESTIC VIOLENCE (1996). However, substance abuse may not "cause" domestic violence, because stopping substance abuse may not stop domestic violence. National Institute on Alcohol Abuse and Alcoholism, *Alcohol Alert* 3 (October 1997). Other treatment approaches also may be needed.

181. See Winick, *supra* note 16, at 904-06 (discussing denial, repression, and suppression occurring in attorney/client conversations about the advisability of advance directive instruments for health and mental health care).

tance to the advice offered that might in fact be counterproductive.[182] In addition, many offenders in these circumstances are in denial about their alcoholism and other drug abuse or other psychological or behavioral problems that contribute to their repetitive offending. Paternalism on the part of the attorney is unlikely to succeed in allowing clients to deal with such denial and may instead provoke anxiety and other psychological distress that simply drives them out of the attorney's office.

How can attorneys avoid the spectre of paternalism in their conversations with clients about the desirability of engaging in rehabilitative efforts? Rather than being committed to a traditional legal counseling model that assumes that clients are passive and implicitly delegate decision-making authority to their lawyers, therapeutically oriented preventive lawyers are committed to the model of client-centered counseling.[183] Under this model, the attorney is the agent of the client, and the client, rather than the lawyer, makes the critical decisions. This model is based on deference to client autonomy and is designed to foster client decision making.[184] It seeks to provide opportunities for client self- determination, allowing clients to make decisions for themselves rather than to have them made by others, such as the attorney.[185] Under this approach to the attorney/client relationship, the lawyer's role is to engage the client in an exploration of possible alternatives and the advantages and disadvantages of each.[186] Together, the attorney and client identify and evaluate the legal, social, economic, and

---

182. *See* SHARON S. BREHM & JACK W. BREHM, PSYCHOLOGICAL REACTANCE: A THEORY OF FREEDOM AND CONTROL 300-01 (1981).

183. Michael L. Perlin et al., *Therapeutic Jurisprudence and Civil Rights of Institutionalized Mentally Disabled Persons: Hopeless Oxymoron or Path to Redemption?* 1 PSYCHOL. PUB. POL'Y & L. 80, 85 (1995) ("In therapeutic jurisprudence, the client's perspective should determine the therapeutic worth or impact of a particular course of events."); Winick, *supra* note 16, at 916-17 (therapeutically oriented preventive lawyers should apply a client-centered approach). For discussions of the concept of client-centered counseling, *see* DAVID A. BINDER ET AL., LAWYERS AS COUNSELORS: A CLIENT-CENTERED APPROACH 16-24 (1991); ROBERT M. BASTRESS & JOSEPH D. HARBAUGH, INTERVIEWING, COUNSELING, & NEGOTIATING SKILLS FOR EFFECTIVE REPRESENTATION 334-38 (1990); Robert D. Dinerstein, *Client-Centered Counseling: Reappraisal and Refinement,* 32 ARIZ. L. REV. 501 (1990); Winick, *supra* note 16, at 916-17 .

184. Richard Marsico, *Working for Social Change and Preserving Client Autonomy: Is There a Role for "Facilitating" Lawyering?,* 1 CLINICAL L. REV. (1995); Stier, *supra* note 21, at 304-11 (attorneys should respect client autonomy); Note, *Lawyers and Clients,* 34 UCLA L. REV. 717 (1987) (discussing client autonomy in lawyer/client interviewing); *cf.* Francis Peabody, *The Care of the Patient,* 88 JAMA 887 (1927) (discussing doctor/patient relationship).

185. *Id.*

186. *Id.*

psychological consequences of available alternative courses of action.[187] The lawyer is the agent of the client, helping the client to reach the best decision in the circumstances. The attorney guides the client through the decision-making process but allows the client to make the ultimate decision. This conception of the role of the attorney parallels that of the clinician applying what Carl Rogers called "client-centered therapy."[188] The Rogerian approach to therapy and the client-centered approach to lawyering are both based on the premise that individuals can achieve their full potential for self-actualization when facilitated by a relationship with a helping person who is genuine, empathic, and nonjudgmental.[189]

Even when the attorney has what he or she is convinced is a superior understanding of the situation, the attorney must be careful to cede choice to clients. Rather than dictating a course of action in a way that seems to clients to be an exercise in power subordination, the attorney should state that the ultimate decision is up to them. This approach can be empowering to clients who often feel powerless and helpless, fostering the value of individual autonomy and helping to achieve the goal of preventive law.

The function of the criminal defense attorney attempting to suggest to the client the value of obtaining rehabilitation is properly regarded as one of persuasion, not coercion.[190] In this context, lawyers should be aware of

---

187. *Id.*

188. CARL R. ROGERS, CLIENT-CENTERED THERAPY (1951).

189. Winick, *supra* note 16, at 916-17. *See also* BINDER et al., *supra* note 183, at chs. 3-4, 7. An experienced criminal defense attorney makes the following suggestions concerning how to avoid paternalism in the attorney/client relationship:

I spend some quiet time before each client interview saying "goodbye" to my predispositions and preconceptions about the client, my judgments, my ego and need to be right, and my fear. When I have a clean slate upon which the client can write his or her story, I am much less likely to be paternalistic. I also use all of my interpersonal skills to help the client relax. If the client is not in jail, I interview him or her in a living room type, conversation area setting which I have set up in my office for this purpose. I find that the client bonds with me and trusts me much more quickly if I am sitting in a chair next to him or her rather than behind my big executive desk.

Most criminal defense attorneys do not appreciate the devastating impact of shame on the psyche and spirit of the defendant. The difference between guilt and shame is often illustrated as follows: Guilt means, "I made a mistake." Shame means, " I am a mistake." The criminal defense attorneys need to realize that most of the defendants they meet are shame-based persons with very low self-esteem. Therefore, it is important to be an affirming presence in the lives of these clients. I try to "catch my clients doing something right" as often as possible.

Personal communication from John V. McShane, Dec. 7, 1999, at 6.

190. *See* WINICK, *supra* note 1, at 327-44; Winick, *Coercion, supra* note 159 (dis-

the psychological value of choice.[191] Attorneys counseling clients in the criminal justice context need to understand that client self-determination is an essential aspect of psychological health and that people who make their own choices (if perceived by them as non-coerced) function more effectively and with greater satisfaction. They need to realize that people who feel coerced, by contrast, may respond with a negative psychological reactance[192] and may experience a variety of other psychological difficulties.[193] Attorneys therefore need to communicate to their clients their views concerning the client's best interests, but to do so in a way that makes clear that this is solely the attorney's view and that the decision is up to the client.[194] Moreover, the psychological value of choice should be considered in the design of a rehabilitative plan. There typically may be many options available in fashioning the plan, including variations in rehabilitative techniques and service providers. The attorney can lay the options out for the client, who then can exercise choice. The individual's choice concerning the various issues that arise in the design of the plan can itself influence the likelihood of success.[195]

The line between coercion and choice can be a narrow one. The therapeutically oriented preventive lawyer counseling clients in the criminal sentencing context concerning the advantages of rehabilitative efforts must therefore understand what makes people feel coerced and what makes them feel that they have acted voluntarily. They should understand the implications of recent research on coercion conducted under the auspices of the MacArthur Network on Mental Health and the Law.[196] This research studied the causes and correlates of what makes people feel coerced and

---

cussing differences between coercion and persuasion).

191. *See generally* WINICK, *supra* note 1, at 327-44; Winick, *Coercion, supra* note 159; Bruce J. Winick, *On Autonomy: Legal and Psychological Perspectives*, 37 VILL. L. REV. 1705 (1992).

192. BREHM & BREHM, *supra* note 182.

193. *See generally* Bruce J. Winick, *The Side Effects of Incompetency Labeling and the Implications for Mental Health Law*, 1 PSYCHOL. PUB. POL'Y & L. 6 (1995).

194. Winick, *supra* note 16, at 916-17.

195. *See* Kathy Cerminara, *Protecting Participants in and Beneficiaries of ERISA-Governed Managed Health-Care Plans*, 29 U. MEMPHIS L. REV. 317, 339-40 (1999) (discussing therapeutic value of giving patients treatment choices).

196. *See* Nancy S. Bennet et al., *Inclusion, Motivation, and Good Faith: The Morality of Coercion in Mental Hospital Admission*, 11 BEHAV. SCI. & L. 295 (1993); William Gardener et al., *Two Scales for Measuring Patient Perceptions of Coercion During Mental Hospital Admission*, 11 BEHAV. SCI. & L. 307 (1993); Steven K. Hoge et al., *Perceptions of Coercion in the Admission of Voluntary and Involuntary Psychiatric Patients*, 20 INT'L J. L. & PSYCHIATRY 167 (1997); Charles W. Lidz et al., *Perceived Coercion in Mental Hospital Admission: Pressures and Process*, 52 ARCH. GEN. PSYCHIATRY 1034 (1995);

determined that, even when people are subjected to legal coercion, such as involuntary civil commitment, they feel non-coerced when they are treated with dignity and respect by people who they perceive as acting with genuine benevolence and who accord them a sense of *voice*, the ability to have their say, and *validation*, the impression that what they say is taken seriously. In the attorney/client dialogue concerning rehabilitation, attorneys should always respect the dignity and autonomy of their clients. They should remind their clients that, as attorneys, they are agents whose professional responsibility is to safeguard their clients' best interests, and that the attorney's advice is given in furtherance of their fiduciary duty to their clients and not based on other considerations, such as the interests of the state, the community, or the victim. The attorney's task is to communicate to the client that counsel's professional advice is based on the attorney's perceptions of what would be best for the client legally (and when relevant, economically, socially and psychologically), but that the ultimate decision is that of the client.[197] The attorney should give the client ample opportunity to express his or her views (voice) and should take those views seriously (validation).

If handled properly by counsel, conversations about rehabilitation can be an opportunity for empowering the client in ways that can have positive psychological value. During the attorney's initial interview with a client, the attorney typically seeks to ascertain whether the client is guilty of the crime. When the client admits guilt to counsel, counsel can point out that the one part of the criminal justice system in which the client can be powerful and proactive and create favorable evidence is the sentencing process. With regard to the guilt or innocence issue, the client lacks the ability to change the evidence as it existed at the time of the offense. The fingerprint, bloodstain, DNA sample, eyewitness, and smoking gun are what they are. Defense counsel and the client cannot ethically manufacture new evidence to change much of anything about this phase of the case. By entering rehabilitation programs and successfully completing them, the

---

John Monihan, *Coercion and Commitment: Understanding Involuntary Mental Hospital Admission*, 18 INT'L J. L. & PSYCHIATRY 249 (1995).

197. Attorneys need to resist the urge to be directive to clients in connection with the client's rehabilitation. Criminal defense attorneys would do well to take some basic coaching courses in the art of "leading from behind." The assumption in this training is that clients have intuitive wisdom and ability to act in their own best interest if these competencies can be emancipated and facilitated by a skilled professional. *See* GERARD EGAN, THE SKILLED HELPER: A PROBLEM-MANAGEMENT APPROACH TO HELPING (1998) (providing a number of practical methods for facilitating clients in setting their goals, marshalling the resources for the accomplishment of the goals, and developing an action plan to see them through).

client thereby can create facts, documents, testifying expert witnesses, testifying fact witnesses, and a positive theme for his case through his own efforts. Clients often are excited and energized by the sense of power and control that is produced when counsel points out this aspect of what they can do for themselves.

Criminal defense attorneys engaged in these attorney/client conversations should also have an awareness of the social psychology of persuasion.[198] This body of psychological research identifies three elements of the persuasion process as critical—source, message, and receiver.[199] The likelihood of persuasion is significantly influenced by both the content of the message and the way it is delivered. Persuasion theory has postulated an elaboration likelihood model.[200] Under this model, certain persuasive elements are seen as being influenced by the extent to which the receiver of information is actively involved in the processing of the information presented. The literature on the psychology of persuasion distinguishes between two differing routes to persuasion—central and peripheral. Central route persuasion focuses on the content of the message and postulates that the potential for persuasion is maximized when the receivers of the information have a high likelihood of elaboration, that is, when they engage in issue-relevant thinking about the content of the message itself. The potential for persuasion is heightened if the message has personal relevance to the recipients and the recipients have prior knowledge about the issue.[201] It can be assumed that clients facing criminal sentencing wish to minimize their risk of imprisonment and value strategies that achieve this result. Thus, attorneys can explain to their clients how the Guidelines work, how they would apply to the client's situation, the range of possible sentences authorized by the Guidelines in the client's case, and the possibility of obtaining a downward departure from this authorized range based on post-offense rehabilitation.[202] Attorneys can also explain the

---

198. Daniel J. O'Keefe, Persuasion: Theory and Research 130-39 (1990); R.E. Petty & John T. Cacioppo, Communication and Persuasion: Central and Peripheral Routes to Attitude Change (1986); Winick, *supra* note 16, at 914-15.

199. O'Keefe, *supra* note 198.

200. Petty & Cacioppo, *supra* note 198, at 125-28.

201. Wendy Wood, *Retrieval of Attitude-Relevant Information From Memory: Effects on Susceptibility to Persuasion and on Intrinsic Motivation*, 42 J. Personality & Soc. Psychol. 798 (1982); Wendy Wood & Carl A. Kallgren, *Communicator Attributes and Persuasion: Recipients' Access to Attitude-Relevant Information in Memory*, 14 Personality & Soc. Psychol. Bull. 172 (1988).

202. *See supra* Part III.

option of seeking deferred sentencing to allow rehabilitative efforts to commence so as to develop a basis for such a downward departure.[203] In addition, when representing corporations or other organizations, attorneys can explain the special provisions contained in the Guidelines that allow a reduction in sentence because of the existence of organizational compliance programs designed to avoid unlawful conduct and to prevent its repetition.[204] Clients understanding these considerations can then be left free to engage in instrumental thinking concerning the value to themselves of making rehabilitative efforts. After explaining these possible avenues to a reduction of sentence, attorneys can ask their clients whether they think that any of these options might be available in their cases, allowing the clients to engage in their own processing of the information conveyed to them and apply their own preferences to the decision of whether to pursue these options.

Allowing clients to think through for themselves the value to them of undertaking rehabilitative efforts after supplying them with several of the factual and legal premises necessary to a consideration of the issue is fully consistent with principles of client-centered counseling and can be an effective means of persuading clients to accept rehabilitation. Indeed, it can be more effective than pressuring the client to seek rehabilitation or presenting arguments that spell out in detail why the attorney thinks this course would be preferable. Moreover, allowing clients to come to such decisions for themselves can permit them more effectively to internalize the rehabilitative goal and can increase their intrinsic motivation to achieve it. Thus, effective use of the likelihood elaboration model in this manner not only can persuade the client to seek rehabilitation, but can do so in a way that is more likely to be successful. Particularly for cognitive behavioral approaches, those that are seen as most likely to be effective in offender rehabilitation,[205] the motivation and commitment to succeed of the individual are crucial to success.[206] Thus, allowing clients to come to the decision to engage in rehabilitation for themselves would be more effective than pressuring them to do so. Moreover, as Wexler pointed out, allowing clients to develop their own rehabilitative and relapse prevention plans rather

---

203. *See supra* Part IV.

204. *See supra* Part V.

205. *See* WHAT WORKS?: REDUCING REOFFENDING (James McGuire ed., 1995); *supra* notes 6-7 and accompanying text.

206. WINICK, *supra* note 1, at 327-44 (analyzing why verbal psychotherapy and behavioral treatment approaches are more effective when engaged in voluntarily rather than through coercion); WINICK, *supra* note 14, at ch. 3 (same).

than having the attorney do it for them can also increase the likelihood of positive results.[207] Furthermore, it would increase the willingness of sentencing judges to view the offender's rehabilitative efforts as genuine and to take them into account favorably in their sentencing decisions.

A variation on the likelihood elaboration model of persuasion can be used by lawyers counseling corporate and other organizational clients who have been found guilty or have pled guilty or *nolo contendere* in response to criminal charges. These lawyers can use a standard preventive law technique with their clients, the rewind technique.[208] The client can be asked to engage in a thought experiment in which the scene prior to the occurrence of the violation is imagined and the client is asked what could have been done differently to have prevented the result that occurred. This technique can help the client to understand the need for a relapse prevention plan and to design one more effectively. Indeed, this technique can also be helpful in counseling individual criminal defendants and in similarly helping them to identify the need for relapse prevention plans and to design such plans in ways that are likely to increase their effectiveness and the potential that sentencing courts would be willing to rely on them in granting probation or a downward departure from the range of imprisonment authorized under sentencing guidelines[209] or in granting a deferral of sentencing in order to allow such a plan to be implemented.

Attorneys also should be aware that there are peripheral routes to persuasion that can supplement the likelihood elaboration technique discussed above. When clients seem uninterested in the content of the message the attorneys seek to communicate relating to the advantages of rehabilitation, the likelihood of central route persuasion occurring is significantly diminished. In such cases, the client may simply wish to defer to the attorney in the same way that patients frequently defer to the judgment of their physicians. In these instances, the client's decision-making process may be influenced largely by some heuristic principle unrelated to the content of the message. Two common heuristic principles are applied by most people—the credibility heuristic and the liking heuristic.[210] The former is grounded in the assumption that a message delivered by a credible source can be trusted; the latter, by the assumption that a message delivered by a liked source is agreeable.[211] Attorneys intuitively understand these insights of psychology. In accordance with these insights, attorneys should attempt

---

207. Wexler, *supra* note 5.

208. Patry et al., *supra* note 24, at 441.

209. *See supra* Part III.

210. O'KEEFE, *supra* note 198, at 106.

211. Shelly Chaikin, *The Heuristic Model of Persuasion*, 5 SOC. INFLUENCE: THE ONTARIO SYMP. 3 (1987).

to be both credible and likeable in their conversations with clients concerning the advisability of engaging in rehabilitative efforts. They should dress appropriately and professionally and should act in ways calculated to increase client confidence and trust. They should communicate clearly, cogently, and authoritatively.[212] They should be warm, gracious, and friendly. They should create for their clients an image of competence and expertise, thereby enhancing their perceived credibility.[213] They should appear knowledgeable and trustworthy and give the impression that they are presenting information accurately and without distortion.[214] In their conversations with clients, attorneys should avoid lack of fluency in speech, including repetition, inarticulateness, and misstatement, all of which may tend to decrease perceived competence.[215] Attorneys should be prepared to back up their factual and legal assertions with credible sources of information, thereby increasing their credibility and ultimate persuasiveness. To the extent that the attorney shares a common background, outlook, or set of values with the client, at least on some matters, these commonalties should be demonstrated to the client, thereby increasing the attorney's likeability and consequent persuasiveness. For example, if the attorney has recovered from alcoholism or other drug abuse, he or she can share these experiences with the client, and such sharing can help to forge an emotional connection that can increase attorney persuasiveness. These suggestions for increasing persuasiveness are common sense to most attorneys,[216] but they are useful reminders of how to act in the professional relationship when discussing sensitive subjects.

C. Improving Interviewing, Counseling, and Interpersonal Skills

A special sensitivity to the client's pain, shame, sadness, and anxiety in coming to terms with the existence of psychological or behavioral prob-

---

212. Winick, *supra* note 16, at 915.

213. *Id.*

214. Alice H. Eagly & Shelly Chaikin, An Attribution Analysis of the Effect of Communicator Attractiveness (1975); O'Keefe, *supra* note 198, at 132.

215. J. Michael McCroskey & Robert Samuel Mehrley, The Effects of Disorganization and Nonfluency on Attitude Change and Source Credibility (1969); Gerald R. Miller & Murray A. Hewgill, The Effect of Variations in Nonfluency on Audience Ratings of Source Credibility (1964).

216. *See, e.g.,* Joseph Bellacosa, *A Nation Under Lost Lawyers,* 100 Dick. L. Rev. 505, 547-49, 553 (1996); Robert Burt, *Conflict and Trust Between Attorney and Client,* 69 Geo. L. J. 1015, 1016-18, 1040-46 (1981); Timothy P. Terrell & James Wildman, *Rethinking Professionalism,* 41 Emory L. Rev. 403, 470-72, 482-83, 486-88 (1992).

lems that have produced criminality and the victimization of others is called for in determining what to say to the client and how to say it.[217] Criminal defense attorneys performing this function need to improve their interviewing, counseling, and interpersonal skills. Even though attorneys at times may strongly disapprove of the conduct of the client, they must strive in the attorney-client dialogue to be supportive, empathic, warm, and good listeners. These are highly sensitive conversations, and clients are disinclined to engage in them with attorneys they perceive to be cold, insensitive, or judgmental.

A willingness to deal with the strong feelings that coming to terms with their criminality may produce requires an environment in which the client feels safe and comfortable. Perhaps the most important way in which the attorney can create such an environment is through the conveyance of empathy. Empathy involves the ability to enter another person's feelings and to see the world through that other person's eyes.[218] Empathy has both cognitive and affective components.[219] The attorney must convey both an intellectual response to the client, communicating the sense that he or she understands the client and the client's predicament, as well as an emotional response, communicating the sense that the attorney shares the client's feelings. In discussing rehabilitation with their clients, attorney should communicate a sense of caring, sympathy, genuineness, and understanding.[220] Only then can they hope to create a comfortable space in which clients can feel free to express their emotions and deal effectively with them.

Attorneys also need to be sensitive to the psychological mechanisms of transference and counter-transference and how they can affect communication in the attorney/client relationship. Transference is the tendency of people to project on to a current relationship feelings that originated in prior relationships with others, notably parents and siblings.[221] Counter-

---

217. *See* BASTRESS & HARBOUGH, *supra* note 183 (discussing lawyer interviewing and counseling techniques); THOMAS L. SHAFFER & JAMES R. ELKINS, LEGAL INTERVIEWING AND COUNSELING IN A NUTSHELL (1987) (same); Clark D. Cunningham, *Evaluating Effective Lawyer-Client Communication: An International Project — Moving From Research to Reform,* 67 FORDHAM L. REV. 1959 (1999) (same).

218. Winick, *supra* note 16, at 916-17.

219. GERALD A. GLADSTEIN, UNDERSTANDING EMPATHY: DEVELOPMENT, TRAINING AND CONSEQUENCES (1983); Shuman, *supra* note 78.

220. As Marjorie A. Silver noted, attorneys must convey empathy to their clients but also keep a sense of distance, not becoming overinvolved in their problems or overidentifying with them. Silver, *supra* note 25.

221. *See* Marjorie A. Silver, *Love, Hate, and Other Emotional Interference in the Lawyer/Client Relationship,* 6 CLINICAL L. REV. 259 (1999) (discussing transference in

transference can occur when the attorney transfers feelings onto the client that stem from the attorney's own prior relationships.[222]

The attorney should be sensitive to the possibility of transference on the part of the client and seek to avoid negative transference and to induce positive transference when possible. For example, clients who have experienced repeated exposure to the criminal justice system on the basis of their repeated acts of criminality are likely to have been unsuccessfully lectured in the past by a variety of parents or other family members, teachers, police officers, or judges concerning their need to shape up and obtain rehabilitation. To the extent that these "lectures" have been infected with a paternalistic tone, they might have stimulated feelings of resentment or humiliation or produced a degree of resistance or psychological reactance. The criminal defense attorney needs to figure out how to avoid having attorney/client conversations about the possibility of rehabilitation tainted by the negative feelings and relational images that these prior conversations might have produced. Unlike these others, criminal defense attorneys have a professional duty to the client and a duty of confidentiality that prevents communications from being divulged, even under subpoena. The attorney is the professional ally or champion of the defendant, an agent with a fiduciary duty of undivided loyalty to protect and secure the client's interests in accordance with the client's wishes. By making this professional role clear, the attorney can help to avoid such potential negative transference based on the defendant's prior relations with others. Many criminal defense clients have had few such fiduciary relationships in the past, and to the degree that the attorney can engender the client's trust and confidence in the initial stages of the relationship, the attorney may be able to avoid these negative relational images and perhaps even remind the client emotionally of trusted and respected others in the client's past.

In addition, attorneys should be sensitive to the possibility of countertransference on their own part, which can inhibit their ability to express empathy and develop rapport with the client. Criminal defense attorneys probably have had numerous experiences with prior clients that may have engendered in the attorney an assortment of negative emotional reactions directed at them. Attorneys may feel a degree of anger and resentment toward clients whom they think are guilty and have harmed others yet whom they are professionally required to defend. Although it is the role of the criminal defense attorney to provide a zealous defense even to those who may be guilty, fulfilling this role in cases in which the attorney strongly

---

the attorney/client relationship); Stier, *supra* note 21, at 310; Winick, *supra* note 16, at 911.

222. *See* sources cited in *supra* note 221.

dislikes the client and feels that he or she is a bad person can produce emotional conflicts in the attorney that at times are troubling.[223] Many attorneys may be in denial about these feelings or suppress or repress them. The reemergence of these negative feelings engendered in prior professional relationships may produce a negative counter-transference on the part of the attorney directed at the present client that may interfere with the attorney's ability to effectively play the therapeutic and preventive role in the plea bargaining and sentencing process. Attorneys must be on their guard to avoid such counter-transference, to avoid associating the client they are counseling with prior clients who may have invoked such negative emotional reactions.

In attempting to create a safe environment in which clients can express their emotions and thereby increase the likelihood of coming to grips with their criminality and underlying psychological or behavioral problems, attorneys need to be good listeners.[224] Attorney/client communications concerning such sensitive issues are occasions for dialogue, not for speeches. Such conversations need to occur in a quiet room when the attorney can be assured of being free of distractions and interruptions. The client must be encouraged to speak, and this often requires the attorney to stop speaking, thereby signaling to the client that what he or she has to say is important. Attorneys need to convey to their clients that they genuinely wish to hear them and are interested in their problems and in helping to solve them. Attorneys need to listen to their clients in a manner that is attentive, nonjudgmental, and sympathetic. Techniques of active listening and passive listening may be helpful in this connection.[225]

Creating such a safe and comfortable environment also involves the ability on the part of the attorney to read the client's non-verbal communications and to interpret his or her underlying feelings.[226] Non-verbal forms of communication, such as facial expression, body language, and tone of voice, can be important vehicles for understanding the client's emo-

---

223. These conflicting feelings have been the frequent theme of a popular ABC television show about criminal defense attorneys, *The Practice*, which appears on Sunday evenings. Even though empirical evidence concerning the prevalence of such conflicting feelings on the part of members of the criminal defense bar might be lacking, the portrayal of this problem in the media suggests that it is not uncommon.

224. *See* Steven Keeva, *Beyond the Words: Understanding What Your Client Is Really Saying Makes for Successful Lawyering,* ABAJ 60 (Jan. 1999) (providing pointers on good listening techniques for attorneys to use in lawyer/client conversations); Silver, *supra* note 25, at 912-13 (suggesting that lawyers practice active listening) .

225. BINDER ET AL., *supra* note 183, at 52-57; Winick, *supra* note 16, at 912-13.

226. Stier, *supra* note 21, at 313-14.

tions and determining how to respond to them. In holding these sensitive conversations with their clients, attorneys need to listen beyond their clients' words.[227]

In short, attorneys engaged in conversations with clients about the advisability of their accepting responsibility for their conduct and attempting rehabilitation need to develop their human relations skills, their communication skills, and their counseling skills. To do so requires a degree of psychological sensitivity to the client that is the hallmark of the therapeutically oriented preventive lawyer. Which of these psychological techniques work or work best in attorney/client conversations about rehabilitation is, of course, an empirical question. Criminal defense lawyers need to share their experiences with one another concerning techniques used in such conversations and how they worked. This is a much understudied aspect of the attorney/client process, and I hope that the suggestions in this chapter receive the attention of lawyers seeking to improve their effectiveness. I also hope that they will inspire social scientists to engage in a new and important form of legal profession empiricism.

Analogous areas in the attorney/client relationship in the criminal process should be explored. For example, how do criminal defense attorneys conduct conversations with their clients concerning the advisability of their accepting diversion from the criminal process to drug treatment court, alcohol or other drug treatment, or other treatment or rehabilitative programs? How do criminal defense attorneys conduct conversations with their clients concerning the advisability of accepting a guilty plea, including one that requires some form of community treatment as a condition of probation? How do criminal defense attorneys conduct conversations with their clients about the issue of restitution to the victim of the crime or of making an apology to him or her? These are sensitive conversations that require a high degree of psychological mindedness. Too little is known about these aspects of the attorney/client relationship and the criminal process, yet there is much to be gained by the sharing of information among attorneys concerning successful strategies in these and similar contexts and what they might suggest for the context of conversations with clients concerning rehabilitation in the sentencing process. All of these can be considered to be psycholegal soft spots within the vocabulary of the integrated therapeutic jurisprudence/preventive law model,[228] and there is a need

---

227. *See* Keeva, *supra* note 224. *See also* Gay Gellhorn, *Law and Language: An Empirically Based Model for the Opening Moments of Client Interviews*, 4 CLINICAL L. REV. 321 (1998); Gay Gellhorn et al., *Law and Language: An Interdisciplinary Study of Client Interviews*, 1 CLINICAL L. REV. 245 (1994).

228. *See supra* note 24 and accompanying text.

for a new focus on such questions, their consideration in continuing legal education programs and in clinical legal education, and their attention by scholars of the legal profession.

D. Psychological Benefits for the Attorney

An additional point is worth making concerning the psychological effects of restructuring attorney/client interactions in the way I am proposing in this chapter. Not only can the therapeutic jurisprudence/preventive law model produce many benefits for the client, but playing this new role can also benefit the attorney's own health and happiness. Many criminal defense lawyers become jaded and cynical. Many of their clients, they know, are guilty and have perpetrated significant harm on a variety of innocent victims. Although functioning as their champion in court is essential to our adversary system and to the protection of the rights of their clients, some attorneys experience emotional conflicts as a result of the role they play.[229] Some attorneys may experience feelings of guilt or shame or become anxious or depressed. Some may experience a feeling of incongruity between their personal and professional lives that may contribute to unhappiness, distress, and professional burnout.

Practicing therapeutic jurisprudence/preventive law can help to reduce these problems. Counseling clients who may need it to accept rehabilitation and helping them to secure it and to succeed in it can be both professionally and personally rewarding. It can allow criminal defense lawyers to see themselves as members of a helping profession. They can make a real difference in the lives of their clients and help them avoid future problems for themselves and others. Helping people in these ways can produce a measure of professional and personal satisfaction that can bring a new sense of joy to their professional lives and significant benefits for their own emotional well-being.

VII. Conclusion: The Breadth and Limits of the Model

I have proposed a redefinition of the role of the criminal defense attorney at plea bargaining and sentencing. A broadening of that role has been suggested, with attorneys being sensitive to their ability to carry out their responsibilities in ways that value the psychological health and emotional well-being of their clients and stress the prevention of future legal prob-

---

229. *See supra* note 223 and accompanying text.

lems. These are the promises of the therapeutic jurisprudence/preventive law model.

What is the breadth of this model, and what are its limitations in the criminal context? I have focused on applying this model in the plea bargaining and sentencing process, but it also has applications in other aspects of criminal representation. The proposed model certainly can inform the process of client interviewing, especially the first client interview, when foundations are put into place that either do or do not support client trust and confidence in the attorney.[230] The model certainly should inform attorney/client discussions about the possibility of entering into a plea bargain and the terms of such an arrangement. Sentencing guidelines constrain prosecutorial discretion, but attorneys using the approaches suggested here can attempt to persuade prosecutors to help to fashion and to accept plea arrangements that include significantly reduced sentences in exchange for the client's willing and genuine participation in rehabilitative efforts. The therapeutic jurisprudence/preventive law approach also can be highly advantageous in the context of attorney/client conversations about the client's participation in diversion programs and negotiations with probation departments and prosecutors concerning the terms of such participation and their willingness to allow the client to enter a program as an alternative to prosecution. When clients who have pled not guilty are convicted following trial, the proposed approach also can inform attorney/client discussions about the meaning of the conviction and the client's future options.

Moreover, the new model proposed here for the role of counsel has many potential applications outside the area of traditional criminal practice. It can apply in the representation of clients whose cases are processed in the variety of specialized courts that have been established in recent years. These include courts for those charged with driving while intoxicated, drug treatment court (a specialized diversion program in which the judge plays a key role in the drug treatment process), domestic violence court, and mental health court (dealing with people with mental illness charged with nonviolent misdemeanors and petty offenses).[231] It also can be used in a variety of family court and juvenile court contexts, including

---

230. *See* Gellhorn, *supra* note 227.

231. *See, e.g.,* Pamela Casey & David B. Rottman, *Therapeutic Jurisprudence and the Emergence of Problem-Solving Courts,* NAT'L INST. JUST. J. 13 (July 1999); Randall B. Fritzler & Leonore M.J. Simon, *Bringing About Change in Judicial Practice in Domestic Violence Cases: Combat in the Trenches,* 37 COURT REV. 28 (Spring 2000); Peggy Fulton Hora et al., *Therapeutic Jurisprudence and the Drug Treatment Court Movement: Revolutionizing the Criminal Justice System's Response to Drug Abuse and Crime in America,* 74 NOTRE DAME L. REV. 439 (1999). *See generally* Special Issue on Therapeutic Jurisprudence, 37 COURT REV. 1-68 (Spring 2000).

the representation of clients charged with child abuse or neglect and juvenile delinquency. The model also has applications in various civil contexts, including the representation of clients involved in disciplinary proceedings at state licensing boards and those charged in administrative or judicial proceedings with failure to comply with a variety of regulatory requirements.

The juvenile justice system would be a particularly fertile area for lawyers applying a therapeutic jurisprudence/preventive law approach. The proposed model's utility can be seen by considering the role of counsel in the representation of juveniles whose cases are sought to be transferred to adult criminal court. Juvenile transfer has increasingly been the legislative remedy for the explosion in juvenile violence that has occurred in recent years.[232] Statutory responses to the rising tide of juvenile violence have delegated enlarged discretion to judges and prosecutors to transfer the cases of juveniles at increasingly younger ages. Sometimes there is a hearing concerning the transfer decision, but sometimes this decision is made without a hearing.

Attorneys representing juveniles in the transfer process will find the techniques of therapeutic jurisprudence and preventive law particularly useful. An important ingredient of the transfer decision is whether the juvenile is fit for rehabilitation. Encouraging and assisting the juvenile to develop a rehabilitative plan or a relapse prevention program can thus be extremely helpful in avoiding transfer, which carries the likelihood of more punitive sentencing. Once developed, such plans can be the basis for advocacy designed to avoid transfer. That the juvenile himself has developed such a plan is strong evidence of motivation for rehabilitation and of potential success. Even in situations in which no provision is made for a hearing on transfer at which evidence can be presented, defense counsel can present these arguments in informal discussions with prosecutors concerning their exercise of transfer discretion. A hearing at which the juvenile bears the burden of demonstrating his or her potential for rehabilitation may itself be therapeutic, engaging the juvenile's motivation and commitment and providing a formal occasion for the juvenile to agree to comply with program goals, thereby increasing the likelihood that they are achieved.[233]

---

232. *See, e.g.,* Jeffrey Fagan & Elizabeth P. Deschenes, *Determinants of Judicial Waiver Decisions for Violent Juvenile Offenders*, 81 J. CRIM. L. & CRIMINOLOGY 314 (1990); Cynthia R. Noon, *"Waiving" Goodby to Juvenile Delinquents, Getting Smart vs. Getting Tough*, 49 U. MIAMI L. REV. 431 (1994); Richard E. Redding, *Juveniles Transferred to Criminal Court: Legal Reform Proposals Based on Social Science Research*, 1997 UTAH L. REV. 709 (1997).

233. *See* Thomas J. Mescall II, *Legally Induced Participation and Waiver of Juvenile Courts: A Therapeutic Jurisprudence Analysis*, 68 REVISTA JURIDICA U.P.R. 707 (1999).

Moreover, even in situations in which such a hearing is not required, defense counsel can advocate to prosecutors that they afford the juvenile an informal hearing concerning transfer because of the rehabilitative potential that such a hearing may provide. In addition, when juveniles have been transferred to adult criminal court for the adjudication of their charges, in many jurisdictions judges retain the flexibility to apply the more rehabilitative-oriented sanctions of the juvenile court in lieu of sentencing the convicted offender to the penitentiary.[234] Thus, even if the juvenile has been convicted in adult criminal court, defense counsel may advocate the availability of a community-based rehabilitative program or relapse prevention plan as a basis for a less severe sentence.

The reconceptualization of the role of the criminal defense lawyer that I suggest in this chapter thus has broad implications both within and without the criminal justice system. What are the limits that should be placed on lawyers seeking to play this new role? Although lawyers applying the therapeutic jurisprudence/preventive law model can be therapeutic agents for their clients, they should remember that they are lawyers, not therapists. Lawyers in the plea bargaining and sentencing process should be knowledgeable about principles of therapy and rehabilitation and the various rehabilitative programs that exist in their communities, but they should keep clear the professional boundary between lawyer and therapist. Although principles of psychology should inform their interactions with clients, they should not pretend to be psychologists. Lawyers playing this new role can benefit from professional associations with clinicians in the community, and when appropriate they should consult with such clinicians concerning issues that arise in their relationship with clients that might benefit from such clinical input. Some public defender programs employ social workers to assist defense lawyers in performing a variety of functions in the criminal process, and in general, criminal defense attorneys of all kinds have much to gain through increasing their relations with social workers, psychologists, psychiatrists, and specialists in alcohol and other drug treatment and in consulting with them when needed.

What are the limits imposed by principles of professional responsibility on lawyers applying the therapeutic jurisprudence/preventive law model? Is this new therapeutic and preventive role consistent with the criminal defense attorney's traditional function as the client's champion? It is entirely the client's decision, of course, whether to plead guilty or not guilty.[235] When the client has decided to plead not guilty, the attorney owes the

---

234. *E.g.*, FLA. STAT. § 985.233 (1) (1998); Noon, *supra* note 232, at 458-59.

235. Jones v. Barnes, 465 U.S. 745, 751 (1983) (dictum); ABA STANDARDS FOR CRIMINAL JUSTICE § 45:2, at 21-22 (2d ed. 1980).

client a duty of zealous representation, even when the attorney thinks or knows that the client is in fact guilty.[236] When the attorney has counseled the client concerning the advisability of pleading guilty and entering into rehabilitation but the client has resisted, the attorney must respect the client's decision and challenge the prosecution's evidence.[237] When the client has been found guilty notwithstanding the attorney's best efforts, it is the attorney's role to represent the client zealously at sentencing in an effort to minimize the client's loss of liberty. To the extent that the attorney can persuade the client to enter into a rehabilitative program, advocacy to the sentencing judge that such efforts should be considered in mitigation of sentence is fully consistent with the attorney's professional responsibility to the client at sentencing. Indeed, failure to explore this option with the client would seem highly inappropriate given the potential sentencing advantages that might result, even apart from the therapeutic and psychological benefits that could occur.

I do not suggest a role for defense counsel that in any way subordinates the client's constitutional rights and liberty interests to the attorney's conception of what is truly in the client's best interests. The therapeutic jurisprudence/preventive law model is committed to the notion of client-centered counseling,[238] which respects the client as the ultimate decision maker. As long as the attorney adheres to the model of client-centered counseling, no ethical dilemmas are raised by the attorney's attempt to convince the client to obtain rehabilitation, particularly if needed, and particularly when this could provide a basis for a lesser sentence or a sentence of probation. Therapeutic jurisprudence favors lawyering practices that help to achieve therapeutic effects for clients, but only when to do so does not conflict with other important normative values, such as clients' due process rights.[239] Therapeutic jurisprudence seeks convergence between therapeutic and other important values.[240] The approach of client-centered counseling facilitates the achievement of such a convergence of values. Sometimes clients'

---

236. *See* MODEL RULES OF PROFESSIONAL CONDUCT, preamble (1983); *id.* at Rule 1.3, cmt.

237. *Id.* at Rule 1.2(a) ("A lawyer shall abide by a client's decisions concerning the objectives of representation,...and shall consult with the client as to the means by which they are to be pursued").

238. *See supra* notes 183-89 and accompanying text (discussing client-centered counseling); Winick, *supra* note 16, at 916-17 (noting that the therapeutic jurisprudence/preventive law model is committed to client-centered counseling).

239. WEXLER & WINICK, LAW IN A THERAPEUTIC KEY, *supra* note 14, at xvii; Winick, *supra* note 16, at 190-91.

240. *Id.* at 197-200; *see, e.g.,* WINICK, *supra* note 19 (illustrating convergence approach in the context of proposals for reforming mental health law).

therapeutic interests may clash with their legal rights and interests. In such cases, the client-centered approach allows the client to resolve the conflict. For example, clients who have been charged with drug offenses may have the opportunity of pleading guilty and accepting diversion to drug treatment court.[241] Such diversion can provide an offender who is motivated to get off drugs the opportunity to achieve a recovery from addiction.[242] Moreover, if the defendant successfully completes the drug treatment court program, criminal charges are dismissed. As a result, the defendant may feel that accepting diversion to drug treatment court can be both therapeutically and legally advantageous. If the defendant does not feel this way, however, and instead would prefer to fight the criminal charges in the hope of obtaining a verdict of not guilty or a dismissal of the charges on legal grounds, such as the suppression of crucial evidence that was obtained illegally, the defendant will wish to decline the drug treatment court possibility and plead not guilty. This is the defendant's legal right, and an attorney following the approach of client-centered counseling must respect it, even if he or she is convinced that this course is not in the client's best interests. The attorney can explain the alternative possibilities to the client and help the client to understand the advantages and disadvantages of each, but must defer to the client's decision.

Even when the defendant opts for diversion to drug treatment court in order to achieve its presumed therapeutic advantages, the concern may be raised that this course is more onerous than a plea of guilty or a decision to face the risks of going to trial inasmuch as drug treatment court necessitates that a defendant whose guilt has not been determined spend between 1 1/2 to 2 years in drug treatment under close judicial supervision.[243] Viewed in this way, drug treatment court may present a conflict between the defendant's therapeutic and legal interests, achieving a result that is beneficial to the client, but at the expense of a waiver of trial rights and the acceptance of a more intrusive disposition than might have occurred had the attorney zealously asserted those rights. Under the approach of client-centered counseling, it is the client, not the attorney, who must resolve this conflict. The attorney may have views concerning how this conflict should be resolved, and if asked by the client, should express those views.[244] How-

---

241. *See* Hora et al., *Supra* note 231, at 448-49 (describing drug treatment court).

242. *Id.* at 448.

243. *See* Richard C. Boldt, *Rehabilitative Punishment and the Drug Treatment Court Movement*, 76 WASH. U.L.Q. 1205, 1256-57 (1998).

244. Some attorneys will have strong opinions concerning such issues. Indeed, their views may be so strong that they make it their practice to decline to accept the cases of clients who do not share their views. Thus, some attorneys may decline to represent clients accused of drug offenses or driving while intoxicated unless they agree to plea

ever, the weighing of advantages and disadvantages must be performed by the client.[245] When the client decides to forgo his or her legal rights in order to obtain the advantages of drug treatment court or some other therapeutic intervention, and can do so competently and without coercion, no conflict is presented between the client's therapeutic and legal interests. Legal rights, including a defendant's due process rights in the criminal process, may be waived by the client consistent with principles of justice as long as done freely and competently.[246]

Reconceptualizing the role of the criminal defense attorney at plea bargaining and sentencing in the way I proposed in this chapter can thus allow the attorney to function as a therapeutic agent for the client consistent with principles of justice and professional responsibility. In general, it is outside the role of counsel to make recommendations to clients concerning their health. When such recommendations can also serve the client's legal

---

guilty and accept treatment. If these are private attorneys who make their practices known in advance to prospective clients, there would seem to be no violation of professional ethics. Prospective clients who do not wish to accept these conditions are free to seek other counsel, and attorneys who conduct their practice in these ways should make this clear in the initial client interview. In general, attorneys are free to refuse to accept certain types of cases altogether, and some attorneys never accept criminal cases, or particular types of criminal cases, such as those involving defendants accused of rape or child molestation. A public defender's office could not take this position because of its duty to represent indigent criminal defendants who are not otherwise represented. However, private attorneys do not have an ethical responsibility to accept clients they do not wish to represent, with the possible exception of situations in which they are court appointed.

245. Defendants who are significantly impaired by mental illness may not be able to engage in rational decision making. In such cases, the question of whether they are competent to stand trial or plead guilty typically is raised. *See Drope v. Missouri*, 420 U.S. 162, 181 (1975) ("A trial court must always be alert to circumstances suggesting a change that would render the accused unable to meet the standards of competence to stand trial."); WINICK, *supra* note 19, at 239; *see* Bruce J. Winick, *Incompetency in the Criminal Process: Past, Present, and Future*, in LAW, MENTAL HEALTH, AND MENTAL DISORDER 310 (Bruce D. Sales & Daniel W. Shuman eds., 1996). Few defendants, however, are so impaired as to be found incompetent. Even those suffering from a variety of psychological or behavioral problems that contribute to their criminal conduct are rarely so impaired as to be found incompetent. As long as they are not incompetent, attorneys should defer to their autonomy in making crucial decisions concerning the resolution of their criminal charges, such as those involved in deciding how to plead and whether to accept diversion. Impairment not rising to the level of incompetence may impose a special responsibility on the defense attorney to assist the client in the decision-making process, but as long as the client is not so grossly impaired as to be incompetent, the attorney should follow a client-centered approach in the attorney/client relationship.

246. *See* Winick, *Coercion*, *supra* note 159 (discussing principles of constitutional waiver, including the waiver of constitutional rights that occurs in plea bargaining).

interests, however, attorneys do not exceed the scope of their professional role when they advocate such measures to their clients. In light of the significant benefits in plea bargaining and sentencing that recent legal developments provide for clients who successfully undergo rehabilitation, raising the subject with clients would seem a wholly appropriate aspect of effective representation. So long as this task is not pursued in ways that are inconsistent with the defense lawyer's function and professional responsibility, the attorney can provide a service to the client that perhaps few others are able to offer. Clients may be able to hear advice from their own attorneys in ways that they simply cannot hear when offered by friends, family members, clergy, teachers, or court officials. Attorneys may therefore have a special opportunity to offer advice and counseling that may provide significant help in turning their clients' lives around. Helping the client in this way has not usually been seen as the role of the criminal defense lawyer,[247] but playing this role can be highly beneficial to the client. The defense function is usually conceptualized too narrowly as fighting the criminal charges and attempting to obtain as lenient a sentence as possible.[248] However, the client's interests extend beyond the case at hand. Many defendants, if their problems remain unchanged, reoffend and face even more serious charges and more harsh penalties. The attorney may not succeed where others have failed in attempting to change the defendant's life, but there may be no harm in trying. Clients who are unwilling to hear this message probably make this clear to the attorney.

As long as the attorney has approached the issue with sensitivity and in a manner that is not paternalistic and judgmental, the attorney's counseling about the advisability of the client obtaining rehabilitation should not interfere with the performance of the attorney's traditional role. When the client protests his or her innocence, it may be inappropriate to interject advice about the benefits of rehabilitation, at least until after conviction, if it should occur. However, when the client has been convicted or admits guilt to the attorney, legal counseling about the advantages of entering into rehabilitation, as long as done with sensitivity, would seem consistent with both clients' legal interests and their future health and happiness.

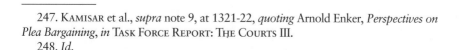

---

247. KAMISAR et al., *supra* note 9, at 1321-22, *quoting* Arnold Enker, *Perspectives on Plea Bargaining, in* TASK FORCE REPORT: THE COURTS III.
248. *Id.*

IV.

Litigation

Chapter 11

Therapeutic Jurisprudence and the Role of Counsel in Litigation

Bruce J. Winick

I. Introduction: Advocacy at the Airport

We were wait-listed on the flight to Suroui and came to the airport in Biak at 5:30 A.M., as the Air Merpati agent had suggested the day before. "Not possible today," said the man at the Merpati ticket counter who finally looked up after I had stood there waiting for what seemed like half an hour. He showed me the passenger list, which revealed that all 17 seats had been sold. "Is it possible some of them won't come?" I asked. "Possible," he replied, "come back at 10:00."

Mike, the Pentecostal missionary we had met three weeks before when we arrived at the Biak airport, passed by. He remembered me and I thought I would ask for his help. Mike looked more like a high school gym coach than a missionary. Stocky in build, about 60 years old, and almost completely bald, he was talkative and friendly. Mike seemed to be a fixture at the airport, where he functioned as a facilitator for travelers, most of whom, presumably, were church connected.

Mike was happy to help. He proceeded to engage the ticket agents in a long conversation in Bahasa Indonesian, which he spoke flawlessly, having spent about 35 years in Irian Jaya. His argument, as best I could follow it, was that the airline should give a preference to international travelers, and somehow make room for us on the flight. The ticket agent smiled gently, but persisted in his response that the flight was sold out and that he could do nothing. Mike was animated and forceful, but his argument ultimately seemed unconvincing, not only to the ticket agents, but to me as well. "Come back at 9:00 and we'll see if there are cancellations," was the conclusion.

Mike's argument, I thought, was like that often made by lawyers. Full of sound and fury, but signifying nothing. A show for the client more than serious persuasion. But there is an element of persuasion in a show itself, sometimes even if the content of the argument lacks substance. The Merpati ticket agents knew Mike, after all (as the judges often know the lawyers appearing before them). Mike's presence and the argument he made, even

309

if unconvincing, functioned as a reminder that the airline personnel should exercise whatever discretion they may have had in our favor, and that a knowledgeable observer would be aware and might complain if they failed to do so. As such, perhaps Mike's intervention would be helpful. Much of what lawyers do may be helpful to their clients in precisely this way.

Moreover, Mike's efforts on our behalf reflected another important function played by lawyers. Even if his argument did not materially contribute to the result, Mike's efforts gave us a sense of having participated in the decision-making process. People like the opportunity to participate in a process that affects them; they dislike being excluded from participating. This participatory or dignitary value of process produces litigant satisfaction and a greater degree of acceptance of and compliance with the ultimate decision reached. This value is usually served by counsel selected by the parties to represent their interest in the proceedings.[2] The parties participate through a counsel they have themselves selected, generally one they regard as a trusted professional who they can count on to seek their interest zealously, free of conflicting loyalties. Moreover, just as Mike spoke the language (Bahasa Indonesian) of the Merpati agents, a language we could speak and understand only in part, the lawyer speaks the specialized language of the court (or administrative body), a language that often is largely beyond the full comprehension of the litigants.

Hence, whatever the result, we were happy to have Mike's assistance and advocacy. We felt that the ultimate decision would be made fairly and with proper consideration of our interests. Even though his argument was a make-weight which to us lacked substance and persuasive force, the mere fact of his advocacy was felt by us to be helpful and to satisfy our psychological interest in participating. We felt we had taken our best shot, and we could accept whatever the outcome might be.

We ultimately got on the flight; two of the ticketed passengers did not show up. We had been lucky. Although we attributed our success to luck rather than to Mike's efforts, during the advocacy phase of the process, when psychological unease and anxiety are at their highest, and during the interval that followed, we felt better as a result of his advocacy. More-

---

1. *See* DAVID B. WEXLER & BRUCE J. WINICK, ESSAYS IN THERAPEUTIC JURISPRUDENCE 307 (1991). An important developing body of social psychology research examines these issues. *See infra* note 26 and accompanying text.

2. *See* Bruce J. Winick, *Forfeiture of Attorneys' Fees Under RICO and CCE and the Right to Counsel of Choice: The Constitutional Dilemma and How to Avoid It*, 43 U. MIAMI L. REV. 765, 801-06 (1989) (analyzing the participatory value of the right to counsel of choice).

over, we felt better for reasons that I think apply more generally to advocacy by counsel in a variety of legal contexts.

This psychological function of counsel, apart from the content of the
arguments they make, is an important and under-examined part of the
lawyering process. Whether intended or even recognized by attorneys, the
way they act in the presence of their clients has an inevitable psychological or therapeutic impact. This occurs in non-advocacy contexts, of course,
and a developing literature discusses the psychological role of counsel in
interviewing and counseling the client.[3] But it also occurs when lawyers
play a litigation role, and the psychological or therapeutic impact of the
lawyer on the client in litigation contexts has rarely been discussed. This
chapter examines these psychological or therapeutic effects, exploring the
underexamined subject of the psychological role of counsel in litigation.
My hope is to create a new awareness of this role, and in the process, to
reframe lawyers' conceptions of the role of the trial attorney in ways that
can have significant benefits for both their clients and themselves.

The approach of therapeutic jurisprudence[4] is used to examine counsel's role in the litigation process. Therapeutic jurisprudence is the study of
law's healing potential. It is an interdisciplinary approach to legal scholarship
that has a law reform agenda. It seeks to examine the therapeutic and
counter-therapeutic impact of law and how it is applied, and to effect legal
change that will minimize antitherapeutic consequences, and when possible, maximize law's healing potential.

The way lawyers' play their role in the litigation process has inevitable
therapeutic consequences for the client. This chapter provides a preliminary
analysis of these consequences and offers suggestions as to how lawyers
playing this role can help to promote their clients' emotional wellbeing.
The litigation process is riddled with what in therapeutic jurisprudence
terms has been referred to as "psycholegal soft spots," potential trouble
points that can produce anger, anxiety, stress, hurt and hard feelings, and

---

3. *See, e.g.,* Marjorie A. Silver, *Love, Hate and Other Emotional Interference in the
Lawyer/Client Relationship,* 6 Clin. L. Rev. 259 (1999); Dennis P. Stolle et al., *Integrat-
ing Preventive Law and Therapeutic Jurisprudence: A Law and Psychology Based
Approach to Lawyering,* 34 Cal. W. L. Rev. 15 (1997); Bruce J. Winick, *Client Denial
and Resistance in the Advance Directive Context: Reflections on How Attorneys Can
Identify and Deal with a Psycholegal Soft Spot,* 4 Psychol. Pub. Pol'y & L. 901 (1998).

4. *See generally* David B. Wexler & Bruce J. Winick, Law in a Therapeutic Key:
Developments in Therapeutic Jurisprudence (1996); Bruce J. Winick, *The Jurisprudence of Therapeutic Jurisprudence,* 3 Psychol. Pub. Pol'y & L. 184 (1997). For a comprehensive bibliography of therapeutic jurisprudence work, see <http://www.law.
arizona.edu/upr-intj>.

other strongly negative emotional reactions that can diminish the client's psychological wellbeing. [The trial process also may present the attorney with what might be called "psycholegal opportunity spots," points in the professional relationship in which the psychologically sensitive trial lawyer can act in ways that will achieve psychological benefits for the client.] Trial lawyers need to identify these trouble spots and opportunity points occurring in the litigation process. They also need to devise and apply strategies for avoiding or minimizing the adverse impact that such trouble spots can impose on their clients. Although it does not purport to conduct a systematic analysis of the emotional aspects of the litigation process, this chapter seeks to alert counsel to the existence of a number of important trial-related psycholegal soft spots and opportunity points and to discuss strategies that may be used in dealing with them.

II. The Stress of Litigation and How Counsel Can Help Reduce It

Being a party in litigation is an extremely stressful event. It ranks near the death of a loved one, the loss of a job, and the experience of a grave illness.[6] Indeed, Judge Learned Hand complained that " as a litigant I should dread a lawsuit beyond almost anything else short of sickness and death."[7] There is little worse than being sued. Litigation requires the expenditure of huge sums of money and takes the litigant away from employment and personal endeavors. It is particularly difficult for the defendant, who is involuntarily made to play this role. But it may be almost as stressful to be the plaintiff in a lawsuit. Plaintiffs have been harmed in some fashion, and rather than putting the pain and loss behind them and beginning the healing process, a lawsuit makes them relive the painful episode in ways that may prevent healing.

The costs and burdens of being involved in legal proceedings with the government, and criminal proceedings in particular, are especially high.

---

5. Mark W. Patry et al., *Better Legal Counseling Through Empirical Research: Identifying Psycholegal Soft Spots and Strategies*, 34 CAL. W. L. REV. 439 (1998); Stolle et al., *supra* note 3; David B. Wexler, *Practicing Therapeutic Jurisprudence: Psycholegal Soft Spots and Strategies*, 67 REVISTA JURIDICA U.P.R. 317 (1998); Winick, *supra* note 3.

6. Barbara S. Dohrenwend et al., *Exemplification of a Method for Scaling Life Events: The PERI Life Events Scale*, 19 J. HEALTH & SOC. BEHAV. 205 (1978).

7. Learned Hand, *The Deficiencies of Trials to Reach the Heart of the Matter,* address delivered before the Association of the Bar of the City of New York, Nov. 17, 1921, *quoted in* PLEADING AND PROCEDURE: STATE AND FEDERAL 36, 37 (David W. Louisell et al., eds. 6th ed. 1989).

The legal fees involved in fighting such proceedings can often be astronomical. There are other, serious costs as well. Being involved in governmental accusation and litigation can be a nasty and vexatious business. It can drain away the resources of the individual or organizational client involved in defensive efforts, in complying with discovery requests, in attending meetings with lawyers and making appearances in court, and in responding to press inquiries. Moreover, there are often serious emotional costs. Criminal and similar kinds of government legal proceedings are intensely stressful and can create feelings of fear, anxiety, and depression. In short, the are highly antitherapeutic. In addition, being publicly charged by the government with unlawful activity can be highly damaging to the reputation of the individual or organization. Indeed, accusation of serious wrongdoing and criminal violation can produce a lasting stigma that may seriously diminish the individual's or organization's business and other activities.

A lawyer representing a person or organization in a lawsuit can significantly diffuse the stress and pain of the litigation process. The lawyer is an ally, perhaps the only one that the litigant has. Even if the entire world seems allied against him, the client has his lawyer at his side, his defender, champion, gladiator, and guardian. The lawyer is an experienced guide across treacherous terrain. At least where the client feels trust and confidence in the lawyer, the lawyer's helpful presence and assistance can enable the weathering of the storm. The trial lawyer thus should avoid any conduct likely to shatter the client's trust and confidence or the sense that counsel is the client's devoted ally.

In addition, the lawyer, by providing information to the client about the meaning of the various stages of the litigation process, can provide an important measure of information control. The social cognition literature shows that the provision of needed information plays a significant role in stress reduction.[8] The unknown often inspires great fear and anxiety. Information enables us to adjust our expectations in a realistic way and to prepare emotionally to meet the challenges ahead.

Surely one of the most stressful emotional aspects of a lawsuit is when the client testifies at trial or has his or her deposition taken by the adverse party. The courtroom is a public place, and testimony is taken from the witness stand in the presence of a variety of strangers and enemies. Public speaking even in a friendly and supportive environment can produce great stress for those who are inexperienced in doing it. Playing such a key

---

8. *See* SUSAN T. FISKE & SHELLEY E. TAYLOR, SOCIAL COGNITION 122 (1984); Bruce J. Winick, *Thereapeutic Jurisprudence and the Civil Commitment Hearing*, 10 J. CONTEMP. L. ISSUES 37, 46-47 (1999).

speaking role on center stage in the courtroom can thus be a nightmare for many clients. Moreover, although a deposition typically is taken in a lawyer's office, the deponent's testimony will frequently be taken in front of strangers such as the court reporter and adversaries such as the other parties in the lawsuit and their attorneys.

How can trial lawyers deal with the intense stress and strong emotions that such testimony is likely to produce on the part of their clients? How can they deal with the intense stress that is likely to occur when the client is subjected to cross-examination by the adverse attorney, a process that explicitly attempts to impugn their honesty and credibility, sometimes in the most provocative and confrontational manner? Clients need to be able to think clearly and speak cogently during the taking of their testimony. They need to be calm and collected, to focus their attention, and to retrieve items from memory. These functions are associated with the prefrontal lobe portion of the brain, the brain area responsible for executive functioning.[9]

When an individual feels attacked, the portion of the brain known as the hypocampus takes over, producing a heightened sense of alertness that has been described as the "fight or flight" reaction, one that shuts off the executive functioning needed in testifying.[10] This "fight or flight" reaction, likely to be provoked by intense cross-examination, will produce extreme stress and anxiety and diminish the individual's ability to function effectively as a witness. When the amygdala is stimulated in this way, it causes the release of various stress hormones, including cortisol, which heightens the senses, dulls the mind, and steals energy resources from working memory and the intellect so that such energy may be used to prepare the individual either to fight or to run.[11] High cortisol levels produce mental errors, distraction, and impairment in the ability to remember and to process information.[12]

Thus, when a witness is subjected to the attack of cross-examination, the resulting emotional reaction will diminish his or her ability to think and remember. How can counsel help the client to avoid this reaction, leaving his or her executive functioning relatively free of the kinds of impairment that testifying or undergoing cross-examination may produce? Counsel needs to prepare the client for a deposition or court testimony by explaining what will probably occur, including the likely challenges that will come with cross-examination. Coaching the client on the process of examination and cross-examination will help to alleviate some degree of stress. Furthermore, counsel can engage in a role-play exercise with the client in which the client has the opportunity to rehearse his or her testimony, per-

---

9. DANIEL GOLEMAN, WORKING WITH EMOTIONAL INTELLIGENCE, ch. 5 (1998).
10. *Id.*
11. *Id.*
12. *Id.*

haps in front of a small audience. In addition, counsel can play the role of the adverse attorney and cross-examine the client vigorously, attempting to raise various questions likely to come up during the examination conducted by any opposing counsel. Such role playing can provide clients an opportunity to prepare to meet the worse that can be thrown at them by an adversary, formulate responses to predictable questions, avoid the anxiety of facing unanticipated challenges, and control their emotional reactions to the often offensive conduct of their interrogators. Such attorney-client discussions and role play exercises can provide clients with a significant degree of information control[13] over the often highly stressful event of providing testimony, allowing them to adjust their expectations and emotional responsiveness in ways that can help to avoid the anger and fear that can seriously diminish their effectiveness as witnesses.

When the opposing counsel asks an improper question at trial or deposition, the attorney will raise an objection. Such questions are not unusual, and may stray beyond the scope of relevance or may be repetitive, badgering, or otherwise inappropriate. Questions such as these can provoke extreme stress in the client, and to minimize such stress, the attorney should discuss with the client beforehand the possibility that such questions may arise and how the attorney will attempt to shield the client from them. The client should be instructed to slow things down in the event of such a question so as to give the lawyer an opportunity to raise an objection, and look to the attorney to see whether such an objection will be raised. In a deposition, where the largest percentage of live testimony by the client will typically occur, and which can be intensely stressful even to the experienced client, counsel can arrange to sit right next to the client at a closeness that ordinarily would be a bit uncomfortable. Counsel can explain to the client that he or she is doing this so that the opposing counsel, sitting across the table, never gets the sense he or she is talking only to the witness, but rather, always has the attorney clearly in his or her peripheral vision. The lawyer can also explain that this is done so that the client can see the attorney's hand movements or facial expressions. This can prevent the client from blurting something out before the attorney has the opportunity to make an objection and instruct the client not to answer the question. This technique can be reassuring to clients, making them feel that they are never alone, unrepresented, or unprotected during the stressful questioning that occurs at the deposition.

When the case goes to trial, there often is a gap between the completion of the presentation of the evidence and the final decision of the tribunal. The stress on the client can be particularly high during the period when

---

13. *See supra* note 8 and accompanying text.

the jury (or judge) is out. The lawyer and client have lived through the stress of the trial together, and this shared experience can produce an emotional bond that can be extremely comforting to the client during this period of uncertainty. It may therefore be comforting to the client for the lawyer to spend this period or much of it with the client, helping to deflect and dissipate the strong emotions that may arise while awaiting the decision.

It also is particularly important for the lawyer to be with the client when the decision is reached. What the decision may mean and what will happen next are themselves questions that can produce much stress and emotion. The lawyer can be of significant help in providing information control at this point and in helping the client to frame the decision in as positive a way as is possible. When the decision is unfavorable, sharing the loss with a trusted ally who has fought the battle with the client can help the client to survive the bitter experience and the difficult emotions it may produce far better than would facing it alone.

III. Helping the Client to Deal with Settlement Possibilities

An extremely high percentage of both civil and criminal cases are resolved through settlement rather than full dress trial. Even after a lawsuit has been filed, negotiation and settlement are likely to occur during the pretrial phase or even during the trial itself. In the criminal context, this occurs through plea-bargaining in which the prosecutor and defense attorney discuss the possibility of a reduction or dismissal of charges or a specified sentence or sentence recommendation as a condition for the defendant's agreement to plead guilty or *nolo contendere*.

In addition to avoiding the stress, delay, and expense of trial, settlement may pose a number of psychological advantages for the client. Negotiation can itself be a healing process, bringing together disputants to discuss and iron out their differences, and helping them to resolve their conflicts and to achieve reconciliation.[14] In general, people feel better about making their own decisions rather than having them imposed upon them by another. Exercising a degree of control and self-determination in significant aspects of one's life may be an important ingredient of psychological wellbeing.[15]

---

14. *See* Gerald R. Williams, *Negotiation as a Healing Process*, 1996 J. DIS. RESOL. 1.

15. BRUCE J. WINICK, THERAPEUTIC JURISPRUDENCE APPLIED: ESSAYS ON MENTAL HEALTH LAW 68-83 (1997); Bruce J. Winick, *On Autonomy: Legal and Psychological Perspectives*, 37 VILL. L. REV. 1705, 1755-68 (1992).

If the parties can come to their own solution to the controversy, they will likely feel better about it than when the judge does it for them. Moreover, settlement puts an end to the controversy and allows the parties to get on with their lives rather than being mired in it for what may well be the several year period that trial and potential appeal might take. It is unhealthy for the client to hold on to hatred, anger, and resentment during this several year period; giving it up can allow the client to experience a degree of peace, relaxation, and joy in life that might otherwise be impossible.[16] Helping clients to understand the emotional value of settlement and to achieve it can thus be an enormous contribution by lawyers to their clients' psychological well being.

For a variety of reasons, settlement therefore can have significant advantages over trial. Yet settlement often is difficult when emotions run high between the parties. Indeed, strong emotions provoked by the controversy or its antecedents or by the lawsuit itself may make it impossible for the parties even to meet in the same room to discuss their differences. In such cases, counsel can represent the client in settlement discussions conducted with opposing counsel. In addition, the services of a third-party mediator may be used. Counsel should be aware of the various modes of alternative dispute resolution[17]—negotiation, mediation, arbitration, and collaborative law[18]—and their benefits and disadvantages, and should counsel the client on these potential methods of avoiding trial.[19]

The possibility of engaging in settlement discussions or of using the differing techniques of alternative dispute resolution should be fully explored

---

16. *See* PHILLIP C. McGRAW, LIFE STRATEGIES: DOING WHAT WORKS, DOING WHAT MATTERS 201 (1999).

17. *See, e.g.*, STEVEN GOLDBERG, ET AL, DISPUTE RESOLUTION (3d ed. 2000); KIMBERLEE K. KOVACH, MEDIATION: PRINCIPLES AND PRACTICE (1994); Carrie Menkel-Meadow, *Pursuing Settlement in an Adversary Culture: A Tale of Innovation Co-Opted or "The Law of ADR"*, 19 FLA. ST. U. L. REV. 1 (1991); Judith Resnik, *Many Doors? Closing Doors? Alternative Dispute Resolution and Adjudication*, 10 OHIO ST. J. DISP. RESOL. 211 (1995).

18. Pauline H. Tesler, *Collaborative Law: A New Paradigm for Divorce Lawyers*, 5 PSYCHOL. PUB. POL'Y & L. ___ (1999); Pauline H. Tesler, *Collaborative Law: What It Is and Why Family Law Attorneys Need to Know About It*, 13 AM. J. FAM. L. 215 (1999).

19. *See* Andrea Kupfer Schneider, *The Intersection of Therapeutic Jurisprudence, Preventive Law and Alternate Dispute Resolution*, 5 PSYCHOL. PUB. POL'Y & L. ___ (1999) (discussing how the framework of therapeutic jurisprudence and preventive law can help lawyers counsel their clients in choosing between ADR methods and in designing dispute resolution systems).

with the client in conversations in which the attorney seeks to ascertain the client's interests and needs and what he or she will find minimally acceptable. In this connection, attorneys should be alert to the fact that clients often want more than merely financial compensation when they feel they have been wronged. For some, an acknowledgement of wrongdoing and an apology might be more important.[20]

If successful, settlement discussions will produce some form of compromise, less than the client may have been seeking or more than he or she contemplated paying. Even so, such compromises are often far better than would be the results of a full trial discounted by the emotional and financial wear and tear on the client that such trials produce. Helping the client to understand this and to evaluate the settlement proposal is an important role for counsel and one that requires a high degree of psychological sensitivity.

Notwithstanding the many advantages of settlement over trial, many clients will be too angry to deal effectively with the settlement process or will otherwise be unable even to consider the possibility as a result of various psychological problems. For example, many defendants in both civil and criminal cases are in denial concerning the existence or extent of their wrongdoing.[21] Many will display other psychological defense mechanisms such as minimization and rationalization that, like denial, might make it hard for them effectively to evaluate and decide about settlement issues as well as trial strategies generally. Some clients in divorce proceedings will be in denial concerning the fact that the relationship is over, and as a result may not be able to engage in settlement discussions or pretrial proceedings. Attorneys therefore need to be able to identify and deal with denial and other defense mechanisms that might prevent the reaching of a sensi-

---

20. There has been increasing recent interest in apology in various legal contexts. *See* Jonathan R. Cohen, *Advising Clients to Apologize*, 72 S. Cal. L. Rev. 1009 (1999); Steven Keeva, *Does Law Mean Never Having to Say You're Sorry?*, 85 ABAJ 64 (Dec. 1999); Daniel W. Shuman, *The Role of Apology in Tort Law*, 83 Judicature 180 (2000); Lee Taft, *Apology Subverted: The Comodification of Apology*, 109 Yale L.J. 1135 (2000); Carrie J. Petrucci, *Apology in the Criminal Justice Setting: Evidence for Including Apology as an Additional Component in the Legal System* (unpub. manuscript, Feb. 25, 2000, on file with the author). *See also* Nicholas Tavuchis, Mea Culpa (1991) (socialogical analysis); Jeffrie G. Murphy, *Forgiveness and Resentment, in* Jeffrie G. Murphy & Jean Hampton, Forgiveness and Mercy 14 (1988) (philosophical analysis); Steven J. Scher & John M. Darley, *How Effective Are the Things People Say To Apologize? Effects of the Realization of the Apology Speech Act*, 26 J. Psycholinguistic Res. 127 (1997) (psychological analysis).

21. *See* Winick, *supra* note 3 (discussing denial in the attorney/client relationship).

ble and advantageous settlement of a civil lawsuit or plea bargain in a criminal case.[22]

In order to deal effectively with these psychological mechanisms, the attorney needs to establish a relationship of trust and confidence with the client. In the initial client interview and in subsequent meetings, the attorney needs to be sensitive to the client's psychological state, to be supportive and non-judgmental, and to convey empathy.[23] The attorney needs to create a climate in which the client can feel comfortable in discussing highly personal and sensitive matters that produce intense emotional reactions. The attorney should explain the attorney-client privilege and the cloak of confidentiality that covers communications occurring within the professional relationship. The attorney should encourage the client to express his or her feelings about being sued or about the conduct of the other parties or their lawyers. Clients need to be made to feel that their attorneys are their allies and confidants, and that they should be free to share their thoughts and feelings with counsel, no matter what they are. To be successful in these conversations, attorneys need to develop their interpersonal skills. They need to be able to listen attentively to their clients and to pay attention not only to their verbal responses, but to their non-verbal forms of communication as well.[24] They need to develop their emotional intelligence[25] and be affective lawyers.[26] Lawyers need to convince their clients that they have the client's best interests at heart, and to suggest that they consider various issues that might provoke intense anxiety and denial and other forms of resistance in order that the client's interests may be achieved. They need to respect their clients' autonomy, persuading rather than coercing them to accept the advice the attorney thinks would be advantageous.

---

22. See Id. (discussing strategies for attorneys to use in dealing with denial and other forms of resistance on the part of the client).

23. Id. at 906-17.

24. Id. at 912-13.

25. See DANIEL GOLEMAN, EMOTIONAL INTELLIGENCE (1997); GOLEMAN, supra note 9; Marjorie A. Silver, Emotional Intelligence and Legal Education, 5 PSYCHOL. PUB. POL'Y & L. ___ (1999).

26. Peter Margulies, Representation of Domestic Violence Survivors as a New Paradigm of Poverty Law in Search of Access, Connection and Voice; 63 GEO. L. REV. 1071 (1995); Carrie J. Menkel-Meadow, Narrowing the Gap by Narrowing the Field: What's Missing from the MacGrate Report—Of Skill, Human Science and Being a Human Being, 69 WASH. L. REV. 593 (1994); Linda G. Mills, On the Other Side of Silence: Affective Lawyering for Intimate Abuse, 81 CORNELL L. REV. 1225 (1996); Linda G. Mills, Affective Lawyering: The Emotional Dimensions of the Lawyer-Client Relation, in PRACTICING THERAPEUTIC JURISPRUDENCE, Chapter 14 (Dennis P. Stolle, David B. Wexler & Bruce J. Winick, eds. 2000).

Attorneys who successfully develop and use these techniques can enable their clients to deal effectively and straightforwardly with the issues that arise in settlement discussions and the development of trial strategy, and to effect an advantageous settlement of the dispute or a course of action for the trial that can be enormously beneficial.

IV. The Psychology of Procedural Justice

Empirical studies of how litigants experience the litigation process has lead to the development of a literature on the psychology of procedural justice.[27] Litigants highly value the process or dignitary value of a hearing. People who feel they have been treated fairly at the hearing, with respect and dignity and in good faith, experience greater litigant satisfaction than those who feel treated unfairly, with disrespect, and in bad faith. People highly value "voice," the ability to tell their story, and "validation," the feeling that what they have had to say was taken seriously by the judge or other decision-maker. When people are treated these ways at a hearing, they often are satisfied with the result even if it is adverse to them, and comply more readily with the outcome of the hearing. Moreover, they experience the results of the proceeding as less coercive than when these conditions are violated, and even feel that they have voluntarily chosen the course that is judicially imposed.[28] Such feelings of voluntariness rather

---

27. *See, e.g.,* Edgar Allen Lind & Tom R. Tyler, The Social Psychology of Procedural Justice (1988); John Thibault & Laurens Walker, Procedural Justice: A Psychological Analysis 83-84, 94-95, 118 (1975); Tom R. Tyler, Why People Obey The Law (1990); Edgar Allen Lind et al., *Voice, Control, and Procedural Justice: Instrumental and Noninstrumental Concerns in Fairness Judgments,* 59 J. Personality& Soc. Psychology 952 (1990). For applications of these principles to the civil commitment hearing, *see* Tom R. Tyler, *The Psychological Consequences of Judicial Procedures: Implications for Civil Commitment Hearings,* 46 SMU L. Rev. 433 (1992); Winick, *supra* note 8 (discussing role of counsel in civil commitment).

28. Recent research by the MacArthur Network on Mental Health and the Law on patient perceptions of coercion found that people feel non-coerced even in coercive situations like civil commitment when they perceive the intentions of state actors to be benevolent and when they are treated with dignity and respect, given voice and validation, and not treated in bad faith. Nancy S. Bennett et al., *Inclusion, Motivation, and Good Faith: The Morality of Coercion in Mental Hospital Admission,* 11 Behav. Sci. & L. 295 (1993); William S. Gardner et al., *Two Scales for Measuring Patient Perceptions for Coercion During Mental Hospital Admission,* 11 Behav. Sci. & L. 307 (1993); Steven K. Hoge et al., *Perceptions of Coercion in the Admission of Voluntary and Involuntary Psychiatric Patients,* 20 Int'l J. L. & Psychiatry 167 (1997); Charles W. Lidz et al., *Perceived Coercion in Mental Hospital Admission: Pressures and Process,* 52 Arch. Gen. Psychiatry

than coercion tend to produce more effective behavior on their part.[29] For many litigants, these process values are more important than winning.

The trial lawyer can do much to help the client experience these process values. The lawyer typically functions as the instrument of the client's voice. It is the lawyer who articulates the client's position in the tribunal and who advances the client's story. Lawyers can enhance this role by making certain they understand their client's stories and what it is they wish to have conveyed. Clients will feel much better when they perceive that their lawyers understand them and their interests and values. It is important for the lawyer to spend time with the client at the early stages of the professional relationship, communicating with the client about these interests and listening to what the client has to say.

Many lawyers are not good listeners.[30] They are short on time and somewhat impatient, tending to jump quickly to conclusions at the early stages of the attorney/client dialogue, cutting the dialogue off because it is thought to be unnecessary to continue. But when the client is cut off in this way, the feeling may be created that the lawyer doesn't truly care about the client or about hearing the client's full story. Clients have a human need to tell their stories and to feel listened to by their lawyers in a way that is non-judgmental and empathic. The lawyer needs to convey sympathy and understanding. The lawyer needs to encourage the client to "open up," to communicate what has occurred and the feelings it produced.[31] Particularly when the client has been the victim of a crime or accident or other traumatic event, the need to talk about it with a trusted confidant who will be understanding and sympathetic, if fulfilled, can do much to allow the individual to get past it. By helping the client to put the events into perspective, the

---

1034 (1995); John Monahan et al., *Coercion and Commitment: Understanding Involuntary Mental Hospital Admission*, 18 INT'L J. L. & PSYCHIATRY 249 (1995) [hereinafter *Coercion and Commitment*]; John Monahan et al., *Coercion to Inpatient Treatment: Initial Results and Implications for Assertive Treatment in the Community, in* COERCION AND AGGRESSIVE COMMUNITY TREATMENT: A NEW FRONTIER IN MENTAL HEALTH LAW 13 (Deborah L. Dennis & John Monahan eds., 1996); *see, e.g.*, Bruce J. Winick, *Coercion and Mental Health Treatment*, 74 DENVER U. L. REV. 1145, 1158-59 (1997). Patients who are provided procedural justice in this sense, even if involuntarily committed or pressured by family members and clinicians to be hospitalized, reported experiencing considerably less coercion than patients who were not afforded procedural justice. Hoge et al., *supra*; Monahan et al., *Coercion and Commitment, supra*.

29. Winick, *supra* note 28, at 1155-59; *supra* note 15 and accompanying text.

30. *See* Steven Keeva, *Beyond the Words: Understanding What Your Client Is Really Saying Makes for Successful Lawyering*, ABAJ 60 (Jan. 1999).

31. JOHN PENNEBAKER, OPENING UP: THE HEALING POWER OF CONFIDING IN OTHERS (1990).

lawyer can do much to assist the client in undergoing a positive reframing of the incident and to deal effectively with what can and should be done thereafter.

Most disputes that go to litigation are resolved through settlement, thereby avoiding the stress and expense of a full dress trial. An important role of counsel therefore is to attempt to secure settlement as favorable to the client's position as possible. The preceding section of this chapter discusses some of the psychological roadblocks on the part of the client that may interfere with settlement, and how counsel can deal with them. The settlement process itself is an important opportunity for the lawyer to help the client satisfy the psychological need for procedural justice. The client should play an important participatory role in settlement discussions. Lawyers often conduct such discussions with opposing attorneys in ways that make the client feel frozen out of the process. There should be frequent consultation and information exchange between attorney and client in the settlement process. Clients deciding whether to settle need to feel that the offer under consideration is fair and either approximates what can be expected if the trial goes forward, discounted, of course, by the savings occurring from avoiding litigation, or reflects their interests or needs in the circumstances. Reassurance by an experienced and trusted lawyer that the proposed settlement is reasonable in the circumstances in view of the client's interests and needs can thus go a long way to making the client feel good about settling.

It is particularly important for the lawyer to permit the client to play a meaningful role in the selection of the legal strategy to be pursued in the litigation. Frequently the lawyer makes strategic determinations without consultation with the client, leading the client to feel a loss of control over the lawsuit. The lawyer's superior experience certainly indicates that the lawyer play the major role in designing the litigation strategy, but allowing the client's full participation can enhance the client's sense that the lawsuit is telling his or her story, rather than one that does not entirely capture it.

For similar reasons, a client should be consulted and given the opportunity to participate in the design of the opening and closing statements.[32]

---

32. Attorneys should anticipate that some clients might be perplexed at being consulted concerning the design of the litigation strategy or the preparation of the opening and closing statement. They may feel that this is the lawyer's job, and being consulted by the lawyer might undermine their confidence in the lawyer's ability. To avoid this concern, lawyers can tell their clients that it is their practice to involve the client in the design of these strategies to insure that the client is certain that they are consistent with the client's wishes. They should feel free to present their views on these strategies to the client, and to relate how similar strategies have been successful in prior cases. A parallel exists here between the lawyer-client relationship and the doctor-patient relationship. In providing the disclosure necessary for informed consent to treatment, the doctor frequently will (and

The opening statement frames the lawsuit, conveying to the judge or jury the broad outlines of the story that will follow. The closing argument summarizes what the evidence has shown from the party's perspective, seeking to have the trier of fact view the evidence through the lens provided by the party. The client's need for voice and validation - to tell his or her story and to feel that it is listened to in earnest - can be significantly frustrated if the story heard by the client in opening and closing argument is not his or her own, but rather, reflects a contrivance by the lawyer that tells a different story.

V. Conclusion

Many trial lawyers use psychology, implicitly if not explicitly, in their attempt to persuade judges and juries of the correctness of the positions they are advocating in court. The content of their arguments as well as the way in which they are presented and the credibility, appearance, communication skills, and the likeability of the lawyer all have an important impact on the ability to persuade.[33] However, many trial lawyers do not understand the psychology of dealing with their clients in the litigation process. How attorneys act and communicate with their clients prior to and during hearings or trials have important consequences for their clients' psychological functioning and emotional wellbeing during what is one of life's most stressful events. Lawyers therefore should be aware of this psychological impact of their role, and should attempt to play it in ways that reduce negative effects and produce positive results.

This chapter has conducted a preliminary analysis of the litigation process designed to sensitize trial lawyers to this rarely discussed aspect of how they play their roles. Litigators should be aware that how they relate to their clients and how they act in their presence during various

---

should) consult the patient on how the patient balances risks and benefits in the circumstances and what the patient thinks appropriate. The doctor, of course, will make recommendations concerning what he or she thinks is appropriate in the circumstances. Many patients may tell the doctor: "Whatever you think, Doc. You know best." In such circumstances, the patient in effect is waiving a greater participation in the decision making process. Similarly, clients may prefer to leave these matters entirely to the lawyer, but probably will feel better about being consulted than they would if not consulted at all.

33. Some trial lawyers will be familiar with the literature on the social psychology of persuasion. *See, e.g.,* DANIEL J. O'KEEFE, PERSUASION: THEORY AND RESEARCH (1990); R.E. PETTY & JOHN T. CACIOPPO, COMMUNICATION AND PERSUASION: CENTRAL AND PERIPHERAL ROUTES TO ATTITUDE CHANGE (1986); Winick, *supra* note 3, at 914-15. Others will understand these principles intuitively and apply them in courtroom settings.

aspects of the litigation process can have important psychological consequences for their clients. In this respect, whether they know it or not, trial lawyers function as therapeutic agents in regard to their clients. The trial process raises a variety of psycholegal trouble spots and opportunity points. This chapter has attempted to identify a number of these psychological soft spots and opportunity points and to offer suggestions as to how trial lawyers can act so as to help their clients to deal effectively with the stress of litigation and to increase their psychological functioning during and after the trial process.

I hope this chapter will provoke discussion in both the legal and psychological literature concerning these unexamined issues. Anecdotal accounts by lawyers of how they have dealt with these psychological issues can be instructive to the trial bar, heightening their awareness of these issues and of effective strategies for dealing with them. Moreover, psychologists and social workers can offer helpful commentary on how trial lawyers can face the challenges of playing their psychological role. There also is need for increased attention to these issues in trial advocacy instruction in law school and in continuing legal education programs designed for the trial bar.

Sensitizing lawyers to the psychological dimension of their role can itself improve attorney functioning and client satisfaction. In addition, it can spark a new and exciting form of interdisciplinary scholarship and legal and continuing legal education that can significantly improve the way lawyers function in the trial process and the ability of their clients to survive it.

Finally, it can help litigation attorneys to achieve a greater measure of professional and personal satisfaction in their work. Many trial attorneys experience professional burn-out, extreme stress, depression, and alcoholism and substance abuse. For trial lawyers who regard winning as everything, defeat may be emotionally unbearable. Helping their clients to adjust successfully to the litigation process and its results, whatever they may be, can bring immense satisfaction and emotional wellbeing for client and attorney alike.

V.

Attorney/Client Communications

Client Denial and Resistance in the Advance Directive Context: Reflections on How Attorneys Can Identify and Deal With a Psycholegal Soft Spot

Bruce J. Winick

Advance directive instruments represent an important future direction in legal planning. They can be used in a variety of contexts to enable clients to order their affairs and engage in present decision-making concerning crucial choices in the future. Because advancing age and potential infirmity may impair the ability to engage in rational decision-making at a time when crucial choices need to be made, it is wise for people to plan for the future and articulate how they presently envision what their preferences would be in various future situations. Advance directive instruments provide a legally enforceable mechanism for doing this. The instruments' most common use, of course, is in end-of-life decision-making, in which, through living wills, people can articulate their preferences concerning life-sustaining treatment and nourishment at a time when prolonging life is thought to be no longer desirable (American Medical Association Council on Ethical and Judicial Affairs, 1998; Cantor, 1998). These instruments, however, are increasingly being used in other contexts: future health care decisions (American Medical Association Council on Ethical and Judicial Affairs, 1998), mental health treatment and hospitalization decisions (Gallagher, 1998; R.D. Miller, 1998; Winick, 1996), nursing home admission decisions (Kapp, 1998), and decision-making by patients diagnosed as HIV positive (Stolle, 1998).

Because of the increasing utility and versatility of advance directive instruments, lawyers should become aware of their potential, and these instruments should become an important stock in trade of the preventive lawyer. The focus of preventive lawyering is the prevention of legal problems through careful drafting and planning (Brown & Dauer, 1978; Hardaway, 1997; Stolle, 1996; Stolle & Wexler, 1997; Stolle, Wexler, Winick,

& Dauer, 1997). The preventive lawyer seeks to avoid litigation and other legal problems and to maximize a client's opportunities through counseling, planning, and legal drafting. The analogy to preventive medicine is explicit. Indeed, preventive lawyers are urged to conduct periodic "legal check-ups" with their clients in order to identify and deal with future legal problems before they materialize and to engage in legal risk management. The advance directive instrument is an effective tool for realizing many of the preventive law goals, and preventive lawyers counseling clients who are growing older or who may have health or mental health problems should discuss the use of advance directive instruments at client counseling sessions.

It is estimated that in 1990, 13% of Americans were age 65 or older and that by the year 2050, 20% of the population will be in this category, 24% of whom will be age 85 or older (Mezzullo, 1991, p. 342). In 1988, approximately 5% of persons over age 65 resided in nursing homes, and it is now estimated that 49% of persons between the ages of 65 and 69 will spend at least some time in a nursing home and that 25% of those over age 85 currently reside in nursing homes (Mezzullo, 1991, p. 343). Additionally, it is estimated that each year more than 28% of adult Americans suffer from a diagnosable mental illness (Regier et al., 1993; Winick, 1996, p. 57). Conditions like Alzheimer's disease and other dementias seem to be increasing as our population ages. Moreover, dementia is a symptom of advanced AIDS (American Psychiatric Association, 1994), and medical conditions such as strokes that are more prevalent with the elderly produce various forms of cognitive impairment. Death is inevitable and occurs more frequently in the hospital. The increasingly technological nature of modern medicine and its high cost make planning for the end of life something that everyone should do.

Engaging in advance decision-making concerning death, medical and psychiatric care and hospitalization, and nursing home admission through the use of advance directive instruments can be extremely valuable. This type of decision-making can increase the likelihood that people will be dealt with in accordance with their wishes at times of vulnerability and distress, produce considerable cost savings, and avoid litigation and the need for guardianship proceedings and decision-making by guardians and other substitute decision makers that may not truly reflect the desires of the individual. In addition, the empowerment that advance directive instruments offer and the psychological benefits of engaging in advance planning for oneself can have considerable therapeutic value (Winick, 1996, pp. 81-96). As such, advance directive instruments can be seen as an important tool of preventive lawyering.

Although advance directive instruments present many advantages, they have been significantly underutilized (American Medical Association Council on Ethical and Judicial Affairs, 1998; Cantor, 1998). According to a 1990 Gallup Poll, 75% of Americans favored the use of advance directive instruments, yet only 20% had actually utilized one (Bowers, 1996, p. 691). Why is there such a disparity between attitudes and action in this area? There may, of course, be good reasons for not using advance directives. Service providers too often ignore them (American Medical Association Council on Ethical and Judicial Affairs, 1998). Some people may be satisfied with how the law will deal with their situation in the absence of an advance directive. Others may find the expense of the instruments' preparation (even if relatively modest) to be beyond their means or not worth it. However, some people may be unable to consider the merits of the use of these instruments as a result of the psychological stress that is produced by thinking about them. As one court has recognized, "the typically human characteristics of procrastination and reluctance to contemplate the need for such arrangements" makes the advance directive "a tool which will all too often go unused by those who might desire it" (*Barber v. Superior Court*, 1983, p. 1015).

This procrastination and reluctance to deal with anxiety-producing issues can be understood in psychological terms as an aspect of denial. Preventive lawyers attempting to advocate to their clients the desirability of advance directive instruments may be met with denial or resistance on the part of the client concerning the need for advance directives (or any other solution to what the client does not personally regard as a problem). Clients may be psychologically unable or unwilling to deal with their future death, illness, or incapacity. The anxiety that these issues produce in most people sets up psychological mechanisms for their avoidance. When an attorney raises the question of an advance directive instrument to deal with one of these troubling issues, he or she should not be surprised to encounter resistance or even denial.

Denial can take many forms and can produce a variety of cognitive distortions. The client can dismiss the suggestion of any need to discuss the area in question as being unnecessary, premature, or not applicable, at least not at the time. By touching such deep anxiety, the attorney's mere suggestion could provoke resistance, hostility, anger, and quick rejection. "I'm too busy," the client might say (or think). "I can't think about this now." "I'm too young [or healthy]. It can't happen to me, at least for many, many years."

Some people may wish to designate a family member or good friend whom they wish to take charge of their care to function as a health care surrogate. Surely in vulnerable times this is a rational approach. Yet the individual may not realize that unless they formally appoint a specific person as their health care proxy, a court may, in the event of their incompetency, choose someone else to play this role, perhaps someone unfamiliar with the person's values and preferences. The person also may not be aware that they can express their values and preferences in ways that will either bind or guide the proxy. For some, the psychological stress produced by thinking about the issue of incompetency brings about denial or some other form of resistance that prevents consideration of these possibilities.

In the face of resistance, denial, and cognitive distortion, how can an attorney persuade the client to consider the use of advance directive instruments or provide the information needed for intelligent decision-making? How can attorneys recognize denial, and how can they deal with it? Denial and other forms of resistance arising in the context of the attorney-client relationship can be regarded as an example of what the emerging literature on therapeutic jurisprudence and preventive law describes as a *psycholegal soft spot*—the way in which certain legal issues, procedures, or interventions may produce (or reduce) anxiety, distress, anger, depression, hard or hurt feelings, and other dimensions of law-related psychological well-being (Patry, Wexler, Stolle, & Tomkins, 1998; Stolle et al., 1997; Wexler, 1998). This chapter constitutes an exploration of the psycholegal soft spot of denial and related forms of resistance occurring in the attorney-client relationship. Therapeutically oriented preventive lawyers need to have a heightened sensitivity to the psychological dimensions of the attorney-client relationship. Although formal training in psychology or social work is not a prerequisite, the preventive law function will be enhanced if an attorney understands some basic principles of psychology. The suggestion is not that attorneys should be therapists, but rather, that they should be psychologically minded. Just as an understanding of the basic principles of economics can generally improve the functioning of an antitrust lawyer or a business lawyer, an understanding of psychology can increase the effectiveness of the preventive lawyer. This chapter, therefore, attempts to help attorneys functioning in this context to understand denial and related forms of resistance and makes a number of suggestions as to how attorneys might deal with denial and resistance in discussions relating to advance directives.

Understanding Denial and Related Forms of Client Resistance

Denial is a defense mechanism that operates unconsciously. It functions as a means to avoid inner conflicts and anxiety through the disavowal of thoughts, wishes, needs, or external reality factors that would be consciously intolerable (Edgerton, 1994, p. 37; Othmer, 1994, p. 81). Denial involves more than simply pretending that something is not as it truly is. In denial, unacceptable facts are vanished from awareness entirely, and the individual has no access to them (Gregory, 1968, p. 349). Although usually defined as an unconscious process, denial sometimes involves conscious mechanisms. It thus can be broadly understood as the conscious or unconscious repudiation of the meaning, or even occurrence, of an event to avoid anxiety or other unpleasant effects (Hackett, Cassem, & Wishnie, 1968, p. 1365).

The concept of denial is derived from the work of Sigmund Freud (1936, 1923/1961), who viewed denial as a protective personality mechanism that, by reducing anxiety, allows the individual to function. Under the classic psychoanalytic paradigm, denial is an unconscious process designed to protect and preserve the individual's functioning. Freud posited that the unpleasant feelings that create anxiety cause the ego to respond in a defensive manner (S. Freud, 1936, p. 97). Denial is thus an unconscious defense mechanism resulting from the ego's need to remove or rescue itself from actual or perceived danger (S. Freud, 1936, p. 86). The term is also sometimes used to describe the conscious process by which an individual protects himself or herself from a crisis and threat by consciously limiting the amount of information taken in (Taylor, 1983).

Denial can be a healthy coping mechanism by which an individual limits anxiety and maintains self-esteem and a sense of control (Forchuck & Westwell, 1987). For example, denial can frequently be a healthy defense mechanism early in the course of a terminal illness, allowing an individual to act on unrealistic plans and, thereby, function during a time when functioning is still possible. Denial can serve as a buffer to shield an individual from unexpected, shocking news, such as the diagnosis of a terminal illness (Kart, 1996, p. 501; Kubler-Ross, 1970, p. 35). It can allow a person "to collect himself" and, with time, mobilize other, less radical defenses (Kubler-Ross, 1970, p. 35). Denial can be an effective strategy for reducing or alleviating stress that can otherwise be debilitating (Kart, 1996, p. 192). Although it is generally best for an individual to face a problem and deal with it, there is increasing recognition that defensive maneuvers like denial may be extremely useful (Clausen, 1986). Denial of some deficits associated with old age, for example, may be less problematic for an individual than dwelling on the deficits, particularly if nothing can be done. Everyone experiences denial concerning some aspects of their life, and in some circumstances, it can be a healthy, functional means of coping with certain stressors, maintaining equilibrium, and going on with life.

On the other hand, denial can be unhealthy and harmful. It is inevitably distorting. It can prevent the individual from understanding reality and from dealing with it effectively. Denial may prevent seeking treatment that is needed, such as when a woman ignores the growing lump in her breast for many months, thereby reducing the effectiveness of any therapy undertaken (Wing & Hammer-Higgins, 1993). It can create a serious hazard for an individual and for others, as when an elderly person ignores serious visual or reflex deficits and continues to drive an automobile when it is no longer safe to do so.

Denial bears certain similarities to other defense mechanisms like repression and suppression (which is technically not a defense mechanism). Like denial, repression operates unconsciously. This defense mechanism vanishes unacceptable ideas, fantasies, affects, or impulses from consciousness (Edgerton, 1994, p. 117). Suppression, on the other hand, is the conscious effort to control and conceal unacceptable impulses, thoughts, feelings, or acts (Edgerton, 1994, p. 131). Repression, the fundamental defense mechanism that underlies all others, is like forgetting (Gregory, 1968, p. 52). Thoughts, memories, and feelings are forced by the conscious mind into the unconscious and actively kept out of awareness (S. Freud, 1915/1959, p. 91; Gregory, 1968, p. 52). According to Anna Freud, denial functions as a precursor to repression (Sandler & A. Freud, 1985, p. 340). An individual learns how to defend against distressing internal feelings that are triggered by external experiences by denying those external experiences. Denial of the external stimuli facilitates the repression of these internal feelings. Repression prevents the recognition of thoughts and feelings; denial prevents the recognition of external reality. So strong is the need to avoid inner pain or anxiety that an individual disbelieves a fact of external reality. To avoid these distressing feelings, an individual in effect lies to herself or himself (Sandler & A. Freud, 1985, p. 341). As a result, denial may produce grossly distorted thinking and behavior (Gregory, 1968, p. 53). For example, people are frequently in denial about the existence of a serious physical illness and may, as a result, delay consulting a physician about ominous symptoms until it is too late.

Denial concerning one's own death or related issues, such as disability, incapacity, and the need for hospitalization or nursing home admission, is normal and natural. In his theory of death, Freud (1915/1959, p. 313) contended that in the unconscious, human beings are convinced of their own immortality and cannot contemplate the cessation of their existence, except perhaps through accident or foul play (Neimeyer, 1994, p. 6). So fearful and anxiety producing is the thought of death, that a high degree of denial about the subject may be the natural state. Ernest Becker (1973, p. 27) observed that "everything that man does in his symbolic world is an attempt to deny and overcome his grotesque fate. He literally drives himself into a blind obliviousness with social games, psychological tricks, personal preoccupations so far removed from the reality of his situation that they are forms of madness...."

Self-denial about death produces a variety of psychological disturbances (Firestone, 1985, pp. 275-276). Striving to remove the concept of death from consciousness causes people to withhold their feelings from things and others in their lives who remind them of their own mortality; to limit their emotional, interpersonal, and professional growth; and to act in ways that deprive them of self-fulfillment and true happiness. The idea and the fear of death "haunts the human animal like nothing else" (Becker, 1973, p. ix).

Psychodynamic explanations of denial of death and its incidents and antecedents are reinforced by societal and cultural attitudes concerning death. In Western society, death is still largely in the closet. In some Eastern societies—India, for example—when someone dies, he or she is placed on a wooden pallet, wrapped in sheets, and carried through the streets to the burning grounds. In such cultures, death is public, not hidden away. Most people in these cultures die at home among their extended family members, with the result being that most people witness death and are not strangers to it. In such societies, death is a natural and familiar part of life. In Western society, by contrast, death remains hidden behind closed doors, under sheets, in closed coffins, and surrounded by a veil of silence. Many people in this culture have never been in the presence of someone who is dying and have never even seen a dead body. Death is so frightening and painful that it is rarely discussed. Even when people are dying, their caregivers and family members frequently practice a kind of deception, keeping the reality of the person's condition from him or her and from themselves (*see* Tolstoy, 1927). In this society, death is treated as a hated enemy and, for doctors and family members, constitutes a personal failure. In Western culture, societal attitudes about death thus coalesce with psychodynamic forces to produce a high degree of denial concerning this painful subject.

Dealing With Denial and Resistance in the Lawyer-Client Relationship

Given the combination of psychological and societal pressures, it should not be surprising that most people in Western culture are in considerable denial concerning their own death and the gradual loss of competency that often comes with old age and various physical and medical conditions. A preventive lawyer attempting to present to the client the advantages of having advance directive instruments for various purposes should therefore be prepared to confront denial and similar psychological mechanisms used to avoid thinking about these anxiety-provoking eventualities. How should an attorney deal with such client denial and resistance?

A word of caution is appropriate at the outset: What appears to be denial may actually be something else. Perhaps the client has good reason not to have an advance directive. Perhaps the client has thought about the matter and would prefer the way the law will deal with him or her in the absence of an advance directive. It would be offensive to such clients to suggest that although they think they have good reasons for preferring the status quo, in truth, they are in denial about the *real* reasons for their unwillingness to take the lawyer's advice. Here, the lawyer, if satisfied that the client has fully considered the question, should accept the client's decision. It may be appropriate to determine whether the client has considered certain issues that the attorney thinks may have been overlooked or misunderstood, but if this is not the case, the attorney should not assume that denial is the reason for the client's refusal to follow counsel's advice. The Freudian concept of denial assumes an objective reality that the individual fails to see or distorts for psychological reasons. Yet the client's reality may differ from the attorney's perception. Seeing something differently or evaluating it differently does not necessarily indicate denial on the part of the client. Attorneys need to be careful to eliminate other possible explanations for the client's disinclination to accept counsel's advice before jumping to the conclusion that denial is the culprit.

Denial should be suspected when the client is unwilling to engage in a discussion of the advance directive question without any apparent good reason. The attorney should observe the client carefully for signs of stress and anxiety. Only when a gentle probing of the client's unwillingness suggests that the client's stated reasons for not wishing to consider the matter are pretextual and, thus, grounded in the psychological distress presented by the issue should the attorney conclude that the client's resistance is psychologically based.

If this inquiry leads the attorney to conclude that the client's resistance is psychological, what should counsel do? It may be helpful for attorneys to consider how mental health clinicians deal with denial on the part of their patients. There are basically two schools of thought in dealing with denial. One method is to approach patients subtly, allowing them to deal with their feelings slowly. In the context of dealing with denial about impending death, this approach is associated with Elizabeth Kubler-Ross (1970), who recommended confronting such individuals but also giving them time to deal with feelings that were uncovered, like taking baby steps. This is a gradual approach in which the therapist is consistent, but it allows patients the time to pace themselves. The other leading approach is more direct and confrontational. This latter approach is identified with Robert Langs (1973-1974), who recommended an intervention in which everything is brought out at once and is dealt with accordingly. Clinicians have the professional ability to deal with the ramifications of this dramatic technique. However, lawyers (or at least those who have not had clinical training) do not possess the appropriate professional skills, and thus should avoid being so confrontational. Another reason for avoiding such a dramatic approach is that it will drive many clients from the lawyer's office rather than allowing them to see the benefits of entering into an advance directive instrument.

An attorney must be sensitive to the client's anxiety level. When acute anxiety is unleashed, a physician can prescribe medication, but a lawyer cannot. The attorney should observe the client carefully during the lawyer-client conversation for signs of agitation, anger, and distress. The attorney should proceed gently. This conversation is not a closing argument to a jury; it is a difficult discussion about an intimate and sensitive subject. The attorney should watch the client closely for such obvious signs of distress as teary eyes, fidgeting, and a shaky voice. If the attorney detects any of these warning signals or if the client seems to be behaving inappropriately, the attorney should consider a shift in tone or strategy. "Can we continue discussing this?," the attorney might say. "I can see that you're uncomfortable. Many people are uncomfortable discussing this subject. Can we continue?," the attorney might ask in a gentle voice. Or, perhaps, "I think it's worthwhile to continue even if you're uncomfortable, but what do you think? If it becomes too uncomfortable, let me know and we will stop. If so, you can think about what I said, and we'll talk about it another day."

Although lawyers are not clinicians, they can learn much from how clinicians deal with patients in similar circumstances. Clinicians dealing with patients who are dying are urged to be supportive, empathic, warm, and attentive (i.e., good listeners) (Tomb, 1995, p. 102-105). When denial and other defense mechanisms come up in the diagnostic interview, some therapists attempt to make their patients aware of their defenses, their underlying mechanism, and their unconscious origins (Othmer, 1994, ch. 3). The aim is to assist patients in gaining insight into their defenses and replace their defensive behavior with a more reality-oriented behavior.

Several management techniques are recommended to help the therapist handle denial and other defenses. These techniques include bypassing, reassurance, distraction, confrontation, and interpretation (Othmer, 1994, pp. 83-88). Sometimes clinicians are advised to "let sleeping dogs lie" and bypass or ignore the patient's distortions and defenses rather than confronting them. Reassurance is a technique designed to decrease the patient's anxieties and increase self-confidence by offering support. This technique works by viewing the defense mechanism from the patient's vantage point. It is especially useful when patients appear overwhelmed by their problems. This empathic approach conveys to patients the idea that they have an ally. Distraction is a technique used for patients who have an abnormal mood state due to a psychiatric disorder like mania or alcoholism. Strong stimuli such as calling the patient's name, shouting, or physical contact are used to distract the patient from an agitated state so that he or she may experience a degree of insight concerning his or her defenses. Confrontation involves drawing the patient's attention to a particular behavior with the expectation that he or she will recognize it and correct it. Provocative confrontations may cause the patient to inhibit emotion, and empathic confrontations may increase the patient's self- exploration. Interpretation involves the therapist offering an explanation concerning the patient's defenses. Interpretation usually follows confrontation because patients must first be made aware of their behavior. By offering a theory to explain the patient's behavior, the therapist invites the patient to examine and discuss it.

Some of these management techniques are beyond the ability of lawyers without clinical training, but many attorneys will be able to adapt one or more of these approaches in dealing with client denial in the law office. Interpretation and the appropriate time to offer it, for example, requires a significant amount of clinical skill and experience. In the context of denial concerning the need for advance directive instruments, however, the source of denial will ordinarily be fairly obvious. Raising and dealing with the issue when it arises in the attorney-client relationship should only rarely require clinical training and experience. When it does, of course, attorneys should consult with clinicians or refer their clients to them. Such referral discussions should be handled with great sensitivity, as many clients will be offended at the suggestion that they need therapy. It might be helpful for the attorney to recount prior experiences with other clients in which counseling proved helpful in dealing with issues arising in the attorney's representation, such as divorce counseling or counseling for depression accompanying loss of a job. The attorney can then gently suggest the possibility of a referral to a known and trusted psychologist or social worker to help the individual deal with the advance planning need identified by the attorney. Although such referrals may occasionally be desirable, other than in unusual circumstances, attorneys can and should attempt to deal with these issues themselves and should develop and improve the skills needed to do so.

There is a growing awareness of the need for lawyers to be sensitive to their clients' emotional needs and the psychological dimensions of the attorney-client interaction. In a book review of two recent law school coursebooks dealing with interviewing and counseling skills for lawyers— Bastress and Harbaugh (1990) and Binder, Bergman, and Price (1991)— Stier (1992) praised what she calls relational lawyering. The hallmark of this type of lawyering is that it values a professional relationship that is collaborative and mutually respectful (Stier, 1992, p. 303). Relational lawyering recognizes that the counseling process requires good interpersonal skills and a sensitivity to the emotional needs both of clients and lawyers. A related approach is what Mills (1996) has called *affective lawyering*. Mills conducted a critical review of work by legal practice theorists and public interest lawyers like Alfieri (1991), Lopez (1992), and Crenshaw (1991), suggesting that in their attempts to deal with the problem of public interest lawyers working with clients of a different race, gender, class, sexual preference, and/or disability than themselves, lawyers miss the critical need of clients for an emotional response from their attorneys. Mills seeks to reframe the role of lawyers, particularly those working with such clients of difference, into what she calls affective lawyers—those possessing the interpersonal skills necessary to deal with the anger, frustration, despair, or even indifference that legal encounters often produce. The term *affective lawyering* also appears in the work of Menkel-Meadow (1994) and Margulies (1995), who similarly call for lawyers with increased interpersonal skills and sensitivity.

An additional movement in the direction of reforming the lawyer's role in this way is what Stolle et al. (1997) have called the TJ (or therapeutically oriented) preventive lawyer. Their work is an attempt to integrate the field of therapeutic jurisprudence (Wexler & Winick, 1991, 1996; Winick, 1997b, 1997d) with that of preventive law (Brown & Dauer, 1978; Hardaway, 1997) to provide a law- and psychology- based approach to the everyday practice of law. Therapeutic jurisprudence sees the law and the way in which it is applied by various legal actors, including lawyers, as having inevitable consequences for the mental health and psychological functioning of those affected (Wexler & Winick, 1996; Winick, 1997d). The approach of preventive law sees the lawyer's role as preventing legal problems through such techniques as legal planning, legal drafting, and alternative dispute resolution (Brown & Dauer, 1978; Hardaway, 1997). A preventive lawyer armed with the insights of therapeutic jurisprudence is sensitive to the client's psychological and emotional needs and to the significance of the attorney-client interaction on the emotional well-being of both client and attorney (Stolle, 1996; Stolle & Wexler, 1997; Stolle et al., 1997).

Relational lawyers, affective lawyers, and therapeutically oriented preventive lawyers are all psychologically minded and sensitive to the emotional climate of the attorney-client relationship. They attempt to use their interpersonal skills to enhance the emotional well-being of their clients. All three types of lawyers attempt to impart a sense of empathic understanding to their clients. Just as empathy has been recognized to be an important ingredient in the professional relationship of physicians, psychologists, social workers, and nurses with their patients and clients, these psychologically minded lawyers understand the centrality of empathy in the attorney-client relationship. Because a central feature of the various techniques used by clinicians in dealing with denial on the part of their clients is empathy, this concept is especially significant to the preventive lawyer confronting client denial and resistance in the advanced directive context.

Empathy is the ability to enter another person's feelings and to see the world through that person's eyes. It is the ability to perceive the meanings of another person and to communicate that feeling back to the other person. The word *empathy* is derived from the Greek *empatheia*, which implies an act of appreciation of another person's feeling experience (Goldstein & Michaels, 1985). Empathy has both cognitive and affective components (Gladstein, 1983; Shuman, 1993). It involves both an intellectual response to the person, conveying the sense that the listener thinks the same way as the speaker, and an emotional response, conveying the sense that the listener feels the way the speaker does. The empathic listener should strive to convey a perception and understanding of the experiences of the other and communicate a "quality of felt awareness" of his or her experiences (Barrett-Leonard, 1981).

Psychotherapist Carl Rogers has had a major impact on our thinking about empathy in professional relationships (Gould, 1990). In his client-centered therapy, Rogers emphasized facilitating the growth and development of human personality toward its maximum potential (Rogers, 1975). Rogers (1958) posited that the ability of one individual to help another is dependent on the creation of a relationship fostering warmth, genuineness, sensitivity, and empathy. Buber (1955) challenged Rogers' view by distinguishing between self-transposal, an attempt to think oneself into the place of another in order to better understand the other person, and empathy, in which one individual crosses over into another individual's world of meaning.

Legal commentators have analyzed the importance of empathy in the attorney-client relationship (Binder et al., 1991; Henderson, 1987). According to Henderson (1987, p. 1574), empathy involves the capacity to perceive others as having goals, interests, and emotions similar to one's own; to imagine the situation of another; and to respond in ways calculated to ease the other person's pain. Empathy involves exuding a feeling of caring and sincerely trying to understand the other in a nonjudgmental and helping way (Goldstein & Michaels, 1985; Rogers, 1975). To be effective at expressing empathy, attorneys must learn to project themselves into the feelings and situations of their clients, expressing the warmth and understanding that create a comfortable space within which clients can express their own emotions. Empathy involves an openness to suffering that is most pronounced in people who themselves have experienced suffering in matters of separation and attachment (Mills, 1996). The role of empathy has been questioned by some legal commentators (Delgado & Stefanic, 1992; Massaro, 1989), but it has emerged as an important emphasis in progressive lawyering. Although lawyers who have experienced their own suffering may be better able to communicate empathy to their clients (Mills, 1996), the social science literature suggests that empathy can be taught (Carkhuff, 1969; Hoffman, 1981; Natale, 1972, p. 71).

Empathy involves the ability to become adept at reading another person's nonverbal communications and interpreting another's underlying feelings. Such feelings, of course, are not always expressed verbally; indeed, many clients will not be in touch with their own feelings and will have difficulty in talking about them. Human communication is a complex process that involves considerably more than verbal utterances. It involves many subconscious messages that are exchanged nonverbally (Stier, 1992, pp. 309-310). Nonverbal cues, such as the tone of voice and facial expression and body language of the speaker, are important ingredients in what is communicated. Also important is the context in which the communication is delivered, like the setting and expectation of the listener. Attorneys need to learn how to listen with their "third ear" to such meta-messages (Stier, 1992, p. 310). Though some attorneys may be instinctively sensitive to these subtle aspects of communication, many are not. These are skills that can and should be taught in law school and in continuing legal education. Indeed, several of the better coursebooks used in teaching counseling and interviewing skills in law school (Bastress & Harbaugh, 1990; Binder et al., 1991) emphasize these techniques and the importance of related psychological mechanisms such as transference and countertransference that occur in the professional relationship.

Transference, a psychoanalytic concept, occurs when the patient transfers or projects feelings onto the therapist that originated in prior relationships with others, notably parents and siblings (Adler, 1980; Greenson, 1965). Similarly, in the attorney-client relationship, clients may often transfer onto the attorney feelings relating to prior relationships (Mills, 1996; Silver, 1999; Stier, 1992, p. 310). These are relational images that we all carry and impose on new relationships. Negative transference occurs when a past experience produced negative emotions that are transferred onto the new relationship. When feelings that arose in the old relationship were positive and are transferred to the new relationship, it is considered positive transference. By being empathic, warm, and caring, the attorney can inspire positive transference, invoking feelings on the part of the client that may have been associated with a trusted grandparent, parent, friend, or teacher. These traits may also be the best defense against negative transference toward the attorney that some clients may have developed as a result of prior unpleasant experiences with other lawyers or negative associations with lawyers, generally stemming from negative portrayals of attorneys in the media and popular entertainment. "I'm not one of those aggressive Rambo litigators that you see on TV or in the movies, or one of those greedy lawyers that is the subject of the lawyer jokes you may have heard," the attorney can assure the client. "I see myself as a member of a helping profession, and I hope that is why you have sought my services."

In conducting the professional dialogue, an attorney must also be aware of the potential dangers of countertransference. Countertransference arises when the therapist (or lawyer) transfers feelings from a prior relationship of his or her own onto the patient (or client). An attorney should be sensitive to the possibility that his or her reaction to the client might be heavily colored by feelings engendered in a prior personal relationship, either positive or negative. Countertransference, occurring when the client reminds the lawyer of someone else and evokes in the lawyer feelings associated with that other person, may inhibit the attorney's ability to express empathy and to develop rapport with the client (Silver, 1999; Stier, 1992, p. 312).

Attorneys need to be able to develop techniques for putting the client at ease so that he or she can feel comfortable in expressing emotion. When the client holds on to strong feelings and does not express them, as will be the case when those feelings are repressed or denied, decision-making is inevitably distorted. Being able to express one's emotions has the salutary effect of freeing the individual to think more clearly (Stier, 1992, p. 312). Forging a connection with the client, an emotional bond that can be palpable, and experiencing an emotional and energetic exchange with the client can thus enable clients to touch their own fear and anxiety concerning death and its antecedent incapacities and disabilities. In this respect, the attorney can be an effective vehicle for the client's opening up (Pennebaker, 1990), enabling the expression of feelings that can then allow the client to deal more straightforwardly and rationally with the desirability of entering into advanced directive instruments for various purposes.

A number of approaches by the attorney may be helpful in facilitating the client's willingness to express emotions to the attorney. Lawyers need to learn how to be good listeners (Keeva, 1999a). To do so, attorneys need to understand that a lawyer-client counseling session is a dialogue, not a speech. To have a true dialogue, attorneys need to stop speaking at some point and allow the room to become silent, thereby encouraging the client to speak. Attorneys need to devote time exclusively to the client and eliminate distractions by conducting the counseling session in a quiet room, holding incoming telephone calls, and directing secretaries or other lawyers in the office not to disturb the conversation. Attorneys need to convey to their clients that they genuinely wish to listen to them and that they are eager to hear and understand their problems. In listening to their clients, attorneys need to be attentive, nonjudgmental, and sympathetic. The attorney should validate the feelings expressed by the client, making appropriate verbal and nonverbal responses that express interest, caring, warmth, and sympathy.

Several specific listening techniques for dealing with denial may be especially helpful. These techniques include the active listening response and the passive listening response (Binder et al., 1991, pp. 52-53). In what is known as passive listening, the lawyer allows periods of silence to punctuate the lawyer-client dialogue, thereby communicating to the client that the lawyer is listening and that the client is free to go ahead at his or her own speed. The lawyer also responds periodically with brief comments, indicating acknowledgment of the client's statements or feelings. These are noncommittal responses because they do not reveal how the lawyer feels about what the client has said but acknowledge that the attorney is listening. Open-ended questions, another technique of passive listening, encourage the client to tell his or her story in a narrative fashion without specific direction. These passive listening devices—silence, noncommittal acknowledgments, and open-ended questions—function to give the client space in the interview to truly express thoughts and feelings.

Active listening, developed by Carl Rogers, is the process of picking up what the client has stated and sending it back in a reflective statement that mirrors the content of what the client has said (Binder et al., 1991, pp. 52-59). By mirroring what has been said, the lawyer demonstrates that he or she has been listening intently and understands what the client has expressed. Moreover, this technique does not judge what has been said but merely accepts it and therefore constitutes an entirely empathic response. The lawyer's active listening response can be a particularly effective way of getting at the client's feelings, many of which may be withheld or only ambiguously stated. The lawyer's precise reflection of what he or she understands to be the feeling conveyed (*e.g.*, "Our discussion about death may make you feel angry...Did it?"; "That may have made you feel anxious.") helps the client to better understand his or her own emotional reactions. Identifying the client's feelings when they are unstated or only ambiguously stated may be difficult, but an experienced lawyer, skilled at interpersonal relations, will be able to form hypotheses based in part on what is said and in part on the client's visual and auditory (*i.e.*, nonverbal) cues. These techniques can be effective ways of expressing empathy and rapport and providing the client with a comfortable space in which to express his or her emotions. These techniques can sometimes be combined with motivational statements by which an attorney makes known to the client the benefits of expressing more fully the client's own thoughts and feelings (Binder et al., 1991, p. 34).

Other techniques for dealing with denial involve putting the client at ease. People are naturally reluctant to share their personal feelings with those who appear to be critical or unfriendly. The attorney, therefore, should greet the client warmly and offer coffee or a soft drink. A smile or a bit of humor can help to break the ice. Indeed, humor, even about as grim a subject as death, also can occasionally be used by the attorney to facilitate the client's ability to express feelings and focus on anxiety-provoking thoughts without causing distress (Gregory, 1968). The attorney can also put the client at ease by sharing something of herself or himself with the client. For clients who are religious or spiritual, the lawyer can share spiritual conceptions of death with the client that may produce some comfort. Death, after all, is a natural and inescapable part of life and the human condition. Attorneys dealing with advance directive instruments in these contexts should understand the literature on death and dying (*e.g.*, Kubler-Ross, 1970), including philosophical and religious conceptions of death. All human beings will die, and death need not be regarded as a frightful disaster or a personal failure.

Attorneys can share with their clients their own thoughts about death, how they have dealt with the issue of death and disability, and how they have planned for it through the use of advance directive instruments. To the extent that an attorney has had his or her own brush with death or disability, sharing those experiences with the client can facilitate the communication of empathy and the client's willingness to share his or her own fears and anxieties on the subject.

Lawyers need to resolve their own internal conflicts about death and disability in order to deal effectively with their clients concerning these issues. Lawyers should talk with colleagues who feel comfortable dealing with death and disability or with other professionals who work with the terminally ill, such as social workers, psychiatrists, or psychologists. Preventive lawyers dealing with advance directive instruments should also talk with trust and estate lawyers and business lawyers to see how they deal with parallel problems of denial and resistance arising in their practices. Denial is not uncommon in clients needing a will or estate plan and among people entering into a business relationship concerning the possibility of a future dissolution of the business and a falling out with trusted and esteemed partners (*see* Stolle et al., 1997, pp. 31-32). Lawyers can also tell their clients how they have drafted advance directive instruments for friends and other clients and for their own parents, grandparents, or other relatives, mentioning how such planning has had the effect of easing their own transition to old age and inevitable death. An attorney can use principles of modeling, pointing to other people respected by the client who have dealt with these issues effectively through the use of advance directive instruments (Bandura, 1971).

Attorneys can also use a variety of creative approaches to enable their clients to think more rationally about their anxiety relating to death and disability. For example, Stier discussed several creative interventions used by an attorney to help a client in a personal injury case confront her own anxiety about going to trial, a trial that the attorney believes will result in a considerably higher award of damages than could be obtained through negotiation. The lawyer might ask, Stier suggests, "If I could sell you a miracle pill that would take all your fear away, how much would you be willing to pay?" (1992, p. 312). If the client realizes that this amount is far less than the amount foregone by not going to trial, she may be willing to reconsider her initial judgment that trial is not a viable option, given the extent of the anxiety it provokes in her. Not only may this exercise allow her to decide to live with the anxiety of a trial, but it may also actually reduce her anxiety by empowering her to consider the financial costs of her anxiety and decide for herself whether to live with her fear. An attorney dealing with a client riddled with denial concerning death or incapacity can engage in a similar exercise with the client. Advance directives concerning the cessation of extraordinary treatment, future health care decisions to be made at a time of incapacity, or future nursing home admission, for example, may produce considerable financial advantages for the client and maximize the client's estate for ultimate distribution to heirs. A question by the attorney seeking to encourage the client to financially quantify the cost of his or her anxiety in dealing with these issues can similarly empower the client to engage in more rational decision-making about the issue, reducing anxiety in the process.

The task of convincing clients to deal with the denial that prevents them from thinking seriously about advance directive instruments and their value is essentially one of persuasion. Thus, an attorney engaged in this process should have a basic understanding of the social psychology of persuasion (O'Keefe, 1990, pp. 130-139; Petty & Cacioppo, 1986). The attorney should understand the powerful influence of conformity (Kiesler & Kiesler, 1969) and obedience to authority (Milgram, 1974). Attorneys can tell their clients that many of their other clients in similar situations are now using advance directive instruments and that the attorney's own family members and friends are doing so. This will set up a psychological pressure to conform to the social norm. Attorneys (who, for most clients, constitute authority figures) can strongly urge their clients to enter into advance directive instruments, thereby making use of the psychological pressure toward obedience to authority.

Persuasion theory identifies three elements of the persuasion process as critical: source, message, and receiver (O'Keefe, 1990). Both the content of the message and the process by which it is delivered are significant to the likelihood of persuasion. The elaboration likelihood model of persuasion is particularly useful in this context (Petty & Cacioppo, 1986, pp. 125-128). This model posits that the impact of certain persuasive elements will be influenced by the extent to which the audience is actively involved in the processing of the presented information. It is useful to distinguish two routes to persuasion: central and peripheral. Central route persuasion focuses on the content of the message itself and posits that persuasion is maximized when the audience has a high likelihood of elaboration (*i.e.*, engaging in issue- relevant thinking about the message itself). The likelihood of persuasion is maximized to the extent that the message has personal relevance to the audience and the audience has prior knowledge of the issue

(Wood, 1982; Wood & Kallgren, 1988). By asking questions of the client, the attorney can ascertain the extent to which the client is generally knowledgeable about the consequences of death, hospitalization, nursing home admission, incapacity, and disability. The attorney should be reasonably knowledgeable concerning the client's social and familial situation and values and can tailor the persuasive message so as to maximize the extent to which it has relevance to the client's situation.

Persuasion also occurs through peripheral routes. Even when the client appears uninterested in the content of the message the attorney is attempting to deliver, the attorney should be aware that the client may rely on some heuristic principle, based on peripheral cues, to engage in decision-making. Two common heuristic principles are applied by most people: the credibility heuristic and the liking heuristic (O'Keefe, 1990, p. 106). The former heuristic principle assumes that a message delivered by a credible source can be trusted; the latter assumes that the message of a liked source is agreeable (Chaiken, 1987). Attorneys, therefore, should strive to be both credible and likable in conversations with their clients. Attorneys should dress appropriately and conduct themselves in ways that maximize client confidence and trust. They should speak clearly, cogently, and with authority. Attorneys should be warm, gracious, and friendly. They should strive to present an image of competence and expertise, thereby enhancing the client's perception of their credibility (Chaiken, 1987). Attorneys should appear to be knowledgeable and trustworthy, giving the impression that they are presenting information without distortion (O'Keefe, 1990, p. 132; Eagly & Chaiken, 1975). Some clients may think that an attorney is advocating advance directive instruments for economic purposes. To anticipate and rebut such an inference of reporting bias, attorneys should remind their clients that although they charge money for their services, they are recommending the use of an advance directive instrument because of the client's needs and interests, not merely to collect a fee. Attorneys should acknowledge alternative viewpoints and act so as to avoid the inference that their recommendations are a product of ulterior motives or self-interest. The attorney should avoid dysfluencies in speech, including repetition, inarticulateness, hesitation, and misstatements, all of which will lessen perceived competence (see McCroskey & Mehrley, 1969; G. Miller & Hewgill, 1964). Attorneys should be prepared to cite credible sources of information in support of their assertions, thereby enhancing both persuasiveness and credibility. To the extent that the attorney knows the attitudes and values of the client, he or she should seek to show the client that they share certain attitudes and values, thus increasing likability and, consequently, persuasiveness.

Are attorneys who utilize these psychological techniques of persuasion manipulating their clients? The word *manipulation* is a pejorative term, suggesting an inappropriate form of persuasion. A lawyer convinced that a particular course of action is advantageous or disadvantageous for the client will naturally and properly attempt to convince the client of the wisdom of the offered advice. Indeed, in matters of consequence, attorneys who fail to do so or do so ineffectively may be open to the criticism that they have not performed their professional duty. To be an effective advocate for this advice, the attorney must understand and use these principles of persuasion. To some extent, this can be seen as a form of manipulation, but not necessarily an inappropriate one. As long as the lawyer genuinely believes that the advice offered is in the client's best interests and does not use deception or dishonesty in communicating with the client, the use of these techniques of persuasion would seem no different than what attorneys traditionally do in counseling their clients in estate planning and business contexts and, thus, would not violate principles of morality or professional ethics. When the attorney perceives that the client's ability to consider the wisdom of the advice offered is undermined by a psychological defense mechanism like denial, the use of psychological techniques designed to attempt to free the client of these impediments to the exercise of enlightened judgment would not seem improper.

Many of these principles of persuasion will be familiar to most lawyers, but understanding the psychological dimensions of persuasion and effective communication can greatly enhance the effectiveness of the client counseling process. This is especially important in the case of clients whose denial about death and infirmity pose a barrier to the consideration of legal advice that can prevent future legal, financial, health, and administrative problems. A special sensitivity to the client's pain, fear, and anxiety in dealing with these difficult issues is called for in determining what to say to the client and how to say it.

The value of using advance directives for various purposes, provided they are properly drafted, cannot be doubted. On the basis of any rational calculation of costs and benefits, these instruments would seem to be advantageous for many, if not most, clients. Yet, the strong emotions sometimes produced by facing the future can get in the way of rational decision-making by the client. Breaking through the denial and resistance that these strong emotions can bring about and persuading the client of the values of planning for the future and taking advantage of the opportunities that advance directive instruments offer for doing so is an important challenge for the preventive lawyer.

Even though the lawyer may be convinced of the benefits of the use of these instruments for the client, she or he should remember that a lawyer is an agent of the client and that, ultimately, the decision lies with the client. This is the essence of client-centered counseling (Bastress & Harbaugh, 1990, pp. 334-338; Binder et al., 1991, pp. 16-24). In this respect, the lawyer's role is parallel to that of the therapist, applying what Carl Rogers (1951) called client-centered therapy. The Rogerian approach is based on the premise that individuals can achieve their full potential or self-actualization when facilitated by a relationship with a helping person who is genuine, empathic, and nonjudgmental. Even though an attorney may think he or she knows best about what is good for the client and will often be entirely correct, the attorney must cede choice to the client. Indeed, reminding the client that the decision is up to him or her can not only foster the value of individual autonomy, but can also have the instrumental value of helping to achieve the preventive law goal. Lawyers should be aware of the psychology of choice (Winick, 1992; Winick, 1997c, ch. 17, pp. 327-344). Self-determination is an essential aspect of psychological health, and people who make choices for themselves function more effectively and with greater satisfaction. Moreover, people who feel coerced often display a negative psychological reactance (Brehm & Brehm, 1981) and may experience other psychological difficulties (Winick, 1995). People like to make decisions for themselves and resent coercion. "It's entirely your choice, but here's what I think...," the attorney should tell the client. The line between persuasion and coercion, of course, is sometimes a narrow one. Attorneys providing counseling in this context need to understand what makes people feel coerced and avoid acting in these ways. Recent research on coercion, conducted under the auspices of the MacArthur Network on Mental Health and the Law, is relevant in this respect (Bennett et al., 1993; Gardner et al., 1993; Hoge et al., 1997; Lidz et al., 1995; Monahan, 1996; see Winick, 1997a). People who are treated with dignity and respect by those whom they perceive as acting benevolently and who give them a sense of voice, the ability to have their say, and validation (i.e., the sense that what they say is taken seriously) generally do not feel coerced, even if legal coercion is being applied. In the counseling process, therefore, attorneys should always respect the dignity and autonomy of their clients. They should remind clients that they are agents and that their job is to help and protect their clients. They should remind clients that they are concerned with their welfare—their professional duty. "I am a professional with a fiduciary responsibility to act in your best interests," the attorney should tell them. "I charge for my time, but this is not why I am recommending this course of action. It is my professional duty that leads me to make this recommendation and not any narrow, pecuniary interest." Attorneys should remind their clients of any prior occasions in which they have helped them, even if for a fee. Attorneys should persuade their clients, not coerce them. "Now listen to what I have to say," the attorney should tell the client, "and you can decide whatever you want about it. The choice is yours." The attorney should make sure to give the client ample opportunity to express his or her views (i.e., voice) and should take those views seriously (i.e., validation). With these approaches, the attorney can make a client feel comfortable and increase client trust and confidence, thereby maximizing the chance that the client will be willing to face his or her denial.

Attorneys should be empathic listeners and persuasive speakers in dealing with client denial and resistance. They need a heightened sensitivity to the client's nonverbal communication and feelings. They need to be warm and understanding. In short, they need to develop their human relations and counseling skills.

Conclusion

There are many good reasons why advance directive instruments should be used as a way of preventing legal problems, increasing the likelihood that individuals experiencing a state of illness or incapacity in the future can be dealt with in accordance with their wishes, and saving the fiscal and emotional resources of individuals and their families at a time when they are experiencing highly distressing events. Advance directive instruments for use in dealing with end-of-life decision-making, health and mental health care, and nursing home admission, if properly drafted, can be legally effective mechanisms for achieving these objectives. There has been an increased public awareness of living wills involving end-of-life decision-making ever since the cases of Karen Ann Quinlan, Nancy Cruzan, and other similar human tragedies received considerable public attention. Yet, lawyers are just beginning to understand the potential use of this legal device for dealing with more far- reaching problems of health and human services. There is a significant disparity between the numbers of people answering surveys who indicate they are in favor of advance directives and those who actually use them (Bowers, 1996, p. 691). One reason for such underutilization is denial and other forms of resistance.

Denial and resistance, grounded in the client's anxiety in facing these difficult issues, are examples of what the literature on therapeutic jurisprudence and preventive law has termed a psycholegal soft spot. Attorneys need to be sensitized to the existence of the aspects of their practice that can cause or minimize stress and other emotional difficulties that arise in the professional relationship or in the events that have precipitated and will follow. To be effective preventive lawyers, indeed, to be effective lawyers, attorneys need to understand some basic principles of psychology and be sensitive to their clients' emotional needs. They need to be relational lawyers or affective lawyers or therapeutically oriented preventive lawyers.

Understanding the psychological mechanisms of denial and related forms of resistance and the various approaches for dealing with these mechanisms can benefit all lawyers. Denial and client resistance arise in numerous practice contexts. A client in need of estate planning who refuses to deal with it may be acting out of denial. Clients awash in the good feelings of a new partnership or business arrangement may be in denial about the need for taking protective measures and mechanisms for resolving controversies if things go awry. This chapter addresses only denial and resistance in the advance directive context, but the need to examine these psychological mechanisms in other legal contexts can be instructive for lawyers in all practice settings. In their chapter on integrating therapeutic jurisprudence and preventive law, Stolle et al. (1997) call for a new form of legal practice empiricism to examine how attorneys deal with psycholegal soft spots and encourage a dialogue in the professional literature (both legal and clinical) concerning how to deal with these soft spots. It would be useful, for example, to survey various samples of lawyers in differing legal practice contexts to identify instances of client denial (and other psycholegal soft spots) and ways in which attorneys deal with that denial. These issues can and should be the subject not only of scholarship, but also of law school training and continuing legal education. Legal education has focused almost entirely on teaching analytical and advocacy skills and substantive knowledge. Law school should broaden its educational mission to explicitly provide training and practice experience in interviewing and counseling skills and should sensitize students to the psychological aspects of the professional relationship.

Many attorneys will have good instincts about dealing with the psychological dimensions of the attorney-client relationship. Even for these attorneys, thinking more explicitly about the psychological aspects of the professional relationship can be helpful. Attorneys need to be good listeners, to be patient, to be kind, and to be empathic. Many lawyers do not possess these skills in abundance. They should work to acquire these traits, because it will both make them better lawyers and make them and their clients happier about the professional encounter and about themselves. Attorneys need to sharpen their interpersonal skills. They need to understand the whole client, not just his or her legal problem. Attorneys need to go beyond their clients' verbal statements and understand their nonverbal communications as well. They need to understand how to create a safe climate in which the client can feel comfortable about expressing emotions and talking about feelings.

There are times, of course, when an attorney should be alert to signs of emotional distress or psychological malfunctioning that are so serious that the services of a clinician are needed. Attorneys are not clinicians and should not try to function as such. Yet, attorneys need to understand the ways clinicians function and transplant some of these learnings into the attorney-client relationship. They need to understand the insights of psychology and apply those insights to their professional dealings, because lawyers, like clinicians, often function as counselors. Effective counseling skills are something that no good lawyer should be without.

This chapter illustrates a form of therapeutic jurisprudence scholarship that reviews principles of psychology developed in other contexts and suggests how these principles might apply in the legal arena. In short, the approach seeks to extrapolate from various psychological principles, suggesting how legal decision makers and lawyers can apply these principles in dealing with various problems. Will these principles apply in attorney-client interactions as suggested in this chapter? Informed speculation suggests that they will, but this, of course, is an empirical question. Whether the strategies suggested here will be effective means of dealing with denial and other forms of resistance in the attorney-client relationship is a matter that awaits empirical verification.

As with much therapeutic jurisprudence work, this chapter offers theoretical speculations that, I hope, will prompt empirical investigation. The integration of therapeutic jurisprudence and preventive law can help to frame many areas of fruitful empirical research into the practices of members of the legal profession, suggesting means to more effectively deal with clients' problems in ways that promote mental health and psychological functioning. I hope that explorations of psycholegal soft spots, such as those identified in this chapter, can become a new and highly valuable subject for professional dialogue and social science research, finding a way into the pages of both law reviews and psychology journals. Indeed, inspiring such interdisciplinary research is a major aim of therapeutic jurisprudence.

Theoretical, empirical, and interdisciplinary research into this largely ignored aspect of the lawyer—client relationship can improve legal practice in ways that abound to the benefit of the consumers of legal services. In addition, it can have an important impact on the mental health and psychological functioning of members of the profession as well. Lawyers are increasingly dissatisfied with law practice, encountering forms of distress that produce disproportionate levels of alcoholism, drug abuse, depression, and anxiety and professional burnout (Elwork & Benjamin, 1995). Lawyers are increasingly striving for better approaches that can more fully integrate their personal and professional lives (Keeva, 1999b). The integration of therapeutic jurisprudence and preventive law offers a new vision of the practicing lawyer that can be more personally and professionally fulfilling, one that is therapeutic for both lawyer and client alike.

References

Adler, A.A. (1980). Transference, real relationship and alliance. *International Journal of Psychoanalysis, 61*, 547-558.

Alfieri, A. (1991). Reconstructive poverty law practice: Learning lessons of client narrative. *Yale Law Journal, 100,* 2107-2147.

American Medical Association Council on Ethical and Judicial Affairs. (1998). Optimal use of orders not to intervene and advance directives. *Psychology, Public Policy, and Law, 4,* 668-675.

American Psychiatric Association. (1994). *Diagnostic and statistical manual of mental disorders* (4th ed.). Washington, DC: Author.

Bandura, A. (1971). *Psychological modeling: Conflicting theories.* Chicago: Aldine Atherton.

Barber v. Superior Court, 147 Cal. App. 3d. 1006 (1983).

Barrett-Leonard, J.T. (1981). The empathy cycle: Refinement of a nuclear concept. *Journal of Counseling Psychology, 28,* 91-100.

Bastress, R.M., & J.D. Harbaugh (1990). *Interviewing, counseling, & negotiating skills for effective representation.* Boston: Little, Brown.

Becker, E. (1973). *The denial of death.* New York: Free Press.

Bennett, N., Lidz, C., Monahan, J., Mulvey, E., Hoge, S., Roth, L., & Gardner, W. (1993). Inclusion, motivation, and good faith: The morality of coercion in mental hospital admission. *Behavioral Sciences and the Law, 11,* 295-306.

Binder, D.A., P. Bergman, & S.C. Price (1991). *Lawyers as counselors: A client-centered approach.* St. Paul, MN: West.

Bowers, V.J. (1996). Advance directives: Peace of mind or false security? *Stetson Law Review, 26,* 677-723.

Brehm, S., & J. Brehm (1981). *Psychological reactance: A theory of freedom and control.* New York: Academic Press.

Brown, L., & E. Dauer (1978). *Perspectives on the lawyer as planner.* St. Paul, MN: West.

Buber, M. (1955). *Between man and man.* Boston: Beacon Press.

Cantor, N.L. (1998). Making advance directives meaningful. *Psychology, Public Policy, and Law, 4,* 629-652.

Carkhuff, R.R. (1969). *Helping and human relationships: A primer for lay and professional helpers* (Vols. 1-2). New York: Holt, Reinhart & Winston.

Chaiken, S. (1987). The heuristic model of persuasion. *Social influence: The Ontario Symposium, 5,* 3-4.

Clausen, J.A. (1986). *The life course: A sociological perspective.* Englewood Cliffs, NJ: Prentice Hall.

Crenshaw, K. (1991). Mapping the margins: Intersectionality, identity politics, and violence against women of color. *Stanford Law Review, 43,* 1241-1299.

Delgado, R., & J. Stefanic (1992). Images of the outsider in American law and culture: Can free expression remedy systemic social ills? *Cornell Law Review, 77,* 1258-1296.

Eagly, A.H., & S. Chaiken (1975). An attribution analysis of the effect of communicator characteristics on opinion change: The case of communicator attractiveness. *Journal of Personality and Social Psychology, 32,* 136-144.

Edgerton, J.E. (Ed.). (1994). *American psychiatric glossary* (7th ed.). Washington, DC: American Psychiatric Press.

Elwork, A., & G.A. Benjamin (1995). Lawyers in distress. *Journal of Psychology and Law, 23,* 205-229.

Firestone, R. (1985). *The fantasy bond: Structure of psychological defenses.* New York: Human Sciences Press.

Forchuck, C., & J. Westwell (1987). Denial. *Journal of Psychological Nursing, 6,* 8-13.

Freud, S. (1936). *The problem of anxiety.* New York: W.W. Norton.

——— (1959). Repression. In *Collected papers,* Vol. 4. New York: Basic Books. (Original work published 1915)

——— (1961). The ego and the id. In J. Strachey (Ed. and Trans.), *The standard edition of the complete psychological works of Sigmund Freud* (Vol. 19, pp. 3-66). London: Hogarth Press. (Original work published 1923)

Gallagher, E.M. (1998). Advance directives for psychiatric care: A theoretical and practical overview for legal professionals. *Psychology, Public Policy, and Law, 4,* 746-787.

Gardner, W., S. Hoge, N. Bennett, L. Roth, C. Lidz, J. Monahan, & E. Mulvey, (1993). Two scales for measuring patients' perceptions for coercion during mental hospital admission. *Behavioral Sciences and the Law, 11,* 307-321.

Gladstein, G.A. (1983). Understanding empathy: Integrating counseling, developmental, and social psychology influences. *Journal of Counseling Psychology, 30,* 467-482.

Goldstein, A.P., & G.Y. Michaels (1985). *Empathy: Development, training and consequences.* Hillsdale, NJ: Erlbaum.

Gould, D. (1990). Empathy: A review of the literature with suggestions for an alternative research strategy. *Journal of Advanced Nursing, 15,* 1167-1174.

Greenson, R.R. (1965). The working alliance and transference analysis. *Psychoanalytic Quarterly, 34,* 155-181.

Gregory, I. (1968). *Fundamentals of psychiatry* (2nd ed.). Philadelphia: W. B. Saunders.

Hackett, T., N. Cassem, & H. Wishnie (1968). The coronary-care unit: An appraisal of its psychologic hazards. *New England Journal of Medicine, 25,* 1365-1370.

Hardaway, R.M. (1997). *Preventive law: Materials on nonadversarial legal process.* Cincinnati, OH: Anderson.

Henderson, L. (1987). Legality and empathy. *Michigan Law Review,* 85, 1574- 1653.

Hoffman, M.L. (1981). The development of empathy. In J.P. Rushton & R.M. Sorrentino (Eds.), Altruism and helping behavior: *Social, personality and developmental perspectives* (pp. 41-63). Hillsdale, NJ: Erlbaum.

Hoge, S., C. Lidz, M. Eisenberg, W. Gardner, J. Monahan, E. Mulvey, L. Roth, & N. Bennett (1997). Perceptions of coercion in the admission of voluntary and involuntary psychiatric patients. *International Journal of Law & Psychiatry, 20,* 167-181.

Kapp, M.B. (1998). "A place like that": Advance directives and nursing home admissions. *Psychology, Public Policy, and Law, 4,* 805-828.

Kart, C.S. (1996). *Realities of aging: An introduction to gerontology.* Needham Heights, MA: Allyn & Bacon.

Keeva, S. (1999a, January). Beyond the words: Understanding what your client is really saying makes for successful lawyering. *American Bar Association Journal,* pp. 60-63.

Keeva, S. (1999b). *Transforming practices: Finding joy and satisfaction.* Lincolnwood, IL: Contemporary.

Kiesler, C., & S. Kiesler (1969). *Conformity.* Reading, MA: Addison-Wesley.

Kubler-Ross, E. (1970). *On death and dying.* New York: Macmillan.

Langs, R.J. (1973-1974). *The technique of psychoanalytic psychotherapy.* New York: Jason Aronson.

Lidz, C., S. Hoge, W. Gardner, N. Bennett, J. Monahan, E. Mulvey, & L. Roth (1995). Perceived coercion in mental hospital admission: Pressures and process. *Archives of General Psychiatry, 52,* 1034-1039.

Lopez, G. (1992). *Rebellious lawyering: One Chicano's vision of progressive law practice.* Boulder, CO: Westview Press.

Margulies, P. (1995). Representation of domestic violence survivors as a new paradigm of poverty law in search of access, connection and voice. *George Washington Law Review, 63,* 1071-1104.

Massaro, T. (1989). Empathy, legal storytelling, and the rule of law: New words, old wounds? *Michigan Law Review, 87,* 2099-2151.

McCroskey, J., & R. Mehrley (1969). The effects of disorganization and nonfluency on attitude change and source credibility. *Speech Monographs, 36,* 13-21.

Menkel-Meadow, C.J. (1994). Narrowing the gap by narrowing the field: What's missing from the MacGrate Report—Of skill, human science and being a human being. *Washington Law Review, 69,* 593-624.

Mezzullo, L.A. (1991). Planning for senior citizens. *C658 ALI-ABA,* 337-533.

Milgram, S. (1974). *Obedience to authority: An experimental view.* New York: Harper & Row.

Miller, G., & M. Hewgill (1964). The effect of variations in nonfluency on audience ratings of source credibility. *Quarterly Journal of Speech, 50,* 36-44.

Miller, R.D. (1998). Advance directives for psychiatric treatment: A view from the trenches. *Psychology, Public Policy, and Law, 4,* 728-745.

Mills, L. (1996). On the other side of silence: Affective lawyering for intimate abuse. *Cornell Law Review, 81,* 1225.

Monahan, J. (1996). Coercion to inpatient treatment: Initial results and implications for assertive treatment in the community. In D.L. Dennis & J. Monahan (Eds.), *Coercion and aggressive community treatment: A new frontier in mental health law* (pp. 13-28). New York: Plenum Press.

Natale, S. (1972). *An experiment in empathy.* Slough, England: National Foundation for Educational Research in England and Wales.

Neimeyer, R.A. (Ed.). (1994). *Death anxiety handbook.* Washington, DC: Taylor & Francis.

O'Keefe, D. (1990). *Persuasion: Theory and research.* Newbury Park, CA: Sage.

Othmer, E. (1994). *The clinical interview using DSM-IV.* Washington, DC: American Psychiatric Press.

Patry, M.W., D.B. Wexler, D.P. Stolle, & A.J. Tomkins (1998). Better legal counseling through empirical research: Identifying psycholegal soft spots and strategies. *California Western Law Review, 44,* 439-455.

Pennebaker, J. (1990). *Opening up: The healing power of confiding in others.* New York: W. Morrow.

Petty, R., & J. Cacioppo (1986). *Communication and persuasion: Central and peripheral routes to attitude change.* New York: Springer-Verlag.

Regier, D.A., W.E. Narrow, D.S. Rae, R.W. Manderscheid, B.Z. Locke, & F.K. Goodwin (1993). The de facto US mental and addictive disorders service system. *Archives of General Psychiatry, 50,* 85-94.

Rogers, C.R. (1951). *Client-centered therapy.* Boston: Houghton Mifflin.

———— (1958). The characteristics of a helping relationship. *Personnel and Guidance Journal, 37,* 6-16.

———— (1975). Empathic: An unappreciated way of being. *Counseling Psychologist, 2,* 2-10.

Sandler, J., & A. Freud (1985). *The analysis of defense: The ego and the mechanisms of defense revisited*. New York: International Universities Press.

Shuman, D.R. (1993). The use of empathy in forensic examinations. *Ethics and Behavior, 3*, 289-302.

Silver, M. (1999). Love, hate, and other emotional interference in the lawyer/client relationship. *Clinical Law Review, 6*, 259-313.

Stier, S. (1992). Reframing legal skills: Relational lawyering. *Journal of Legal Education, 42*, 303-323.

Stolle, D.P. (1996). Professional responsibility in elder law: A synthesis of preventive law and therapeutic jurisprudence. *Behavioral Sciences and the Law, 14*, 459-478.

——— (1998). Advance directives, AIDS, and mental health: TJ preventive law for the HIV-positive client. *Psychology, Public Policy, and Law, 4*, 854-877.

———, & D.B. Wexler (1997). Therapeutic jurisprudence and preventive law: A combined concentration to invigorate the everyday practice of law. *Arizona Law Review, 39*, 25-33.

———, D.B. Wexler, B.J. Winick, & E.A. Dauer (1997). Integrating preventive law and therapeutic jurisprudence: A law and psychology based approach to lawyering. *California Western Law Review, 34*, 15-51.

Taylor, S. (1983). Adjustment to threatening events: A theory of cognitive adaptation. *American Psychologist, 38*, 1161-1173.

Tolstoy, L. (1927). *The death of Ivan Ilyitch*. New York: Dodd, Mead.

Tomb, D. (1995). *Psychiatry* (5th ed.). Baltimore: Williams & Wilkins.

Wexler, D.B. (1998). Practicing therapeutic jurisprudence: Psycholegal soft spots and strategies. *Revista Juridica UPR, 67*, 317-342.

———, & Winick, B.J. (1991). *Essays in therapeutic jurisprudence*. Durham, NC: Carolina Academic Press.

———, & Winick, B.J. (1996). *Law in a therapeutic key: Developments in therapeutic jurisprudence*. Durham, NC: Carolina Academic Press.

Wing, D.M., & P. Hammer-Higgins (1993). Determinants of denial: A study of recovering alcoholics. *Journal of Psychological Nursing and Mental Health Services, 31*, 13-17.

Winick, B.J. (1992). On autonomy: Legal and psychological perspectives. *Villanova Law Review, 37*, 1705-1777.

——— (1995). The side effects of incompetency labeling and the implications for mental health law. *Psychology, Public Policy, and Law, 1*, 6-42.

——— (1996). Advance directives for those with mental illness. *University of Miami Law Review, 51*, 57-95.

———— (1997a). Coercion and mental health treatment. *Denver Law Review, 74,* 1145-1168.

———— (1997b). The jurisprudence of therapeutic jurisprudence. *Psychology, Public Policy, and Law, 3,* 184-206.

———— (1997c). *The right to refuse mental health treatment.* Washington, DC: American Psychological Association.

———— (1997d). *Therapeutic jurisprudence applied: Essays on mental health law.* Durham, NC: Carolina Academic Press.

Wood, W. (1982). Retrieval of attitude-relevant information from memory: Effects on susceptibility to persuasion and on intrinsic motivation. *Journal of Personality and Social Psychology, 42,* 798-810.

————, & Kallgren, C. A. (1988). Communicator attributes and persuasion: Recipients' access to attitude-relevant information in memory. *Personality and Social Psychology Bulletin, 14,* 172-182.

Love, Hate, and Other Emotional Interference in the Lawyer/Client Relationship

Marjorie A. Silver

Introduction

In the summer before their first semester, most law schools encourage students to read a host of books to prepare for the enterprise ahead. While their friends are lying on the beach reading escape novels, prospective law students are reading such classics as *The Nature of the Judicial Process*[1] and lighter fare about lawyering like *The Buffalo Creek Disaster*[2] and *A Civil Action*.[3] Come late August, first-semester students are already tarrying to assimilate the lawyer's tools of logical analysis and seeking to absorb The Rule of Reason. Meanwhile, their friends are still at the beach, perhaps reading pop psychology. One of these books, *Emotional Intelligence*,[4] held a place on *The New York Times'* nonfiction best seller list for many months, and continues to be widely read.[5] As far as I know, no law schools have yet to add it to their recommended summer reading list.

---

1. Benjamin N. Cardozo, The Nature of the Judicial Process (1921).

2. Gerald M. Stern, The Buffalo Creek Disaster (1976).

3. Jonathan Harr, A Civil Action (1995).

4. Daniel Goleman, Emotional Intelligence (1997). The term "emotional intelligence" grew out of the work of Howard Gardner, a psychologist at the Harvard School of Education, who developed the theory of multiple intelligences. *Id.* at 37-39. It was further explicated by Yale psychologist Peter Salovey, who focused on how intelligence can be brought to bear on our emotions. *Id.* at 42.

5. *See* Warren Bennis, *It Ain't What You Know*, Book Review, N.Y. Times Oct. 25, 1998, at 50 (book review of Daniel Goleman, Working With Emotional Intelligence (1998) describing Goleman as the author of the "hugely popular" Emotional Intelligence); James Traub, *Multiple Intelligence Disorder*, The New Republic, Oct. 26, 1998, at 20, 21 (describing book as "wildly popular").

Perhaps they should. Lawyers need emotional intelligence as much as they need the other skills that make them Good Lawyers.[6] We are all simultaneously emotional and rational human beings, although some of us operate more comfortably at one extreme or the other.[7] In order to do our work well, we must be in touch with what we are feeling—and why.

This Article is about one aspect of the need for lawyers to confront their emotional side: their relationships with their clients. Specifically, it is about how that relationship may be enhanced by the lawyer's recognition and resolution of strong emotional reactions—positive or negative—towards a client. Conversely, a lawyer's inability to come to terms with such emotions may well adversely affect the representation.

---

6. Salovey described five main components of emotional intelligence, as recounted by Goleman:

1. *Knowing one's emotions.* Self-awareness—recognizing a feeling as it happens...
2. *Managing emotions.* Handling feelings so they are appropriate... 3. *Motivating oneself.* 4. *Recognizing emotions in others.* Empathy, another ability that builds one's emotional self-awareness, is the fundamental "people skill"... 5. *Handling Relationships.*

GOLEMAN, *supra* note 4, at 42-43. *See also* HARROP A. FREEMAN, LEGAL INTERVIEWING & COUNSELING 50 (1964) (describing HEP (Health Engendering Person), a term coined by F.E. Fielder to describe a person who has the qualities to be good at counseling, negotiating, mediating or doing therapy).

7. Carl Jung identified individuals as one type versus another: Extrovert vs. Introvert, Sensor vs. Intuitive, Thinker vs. Feeler. John E. Barbuto, Jr., *A Critique of the Myers-Briggs Type Indicator and Its Operationalization of Carl Jung's Psychological Types*, 80 PSYCHOL. REP. 611, 612 (1997); Robert R. McCrae & Paul T. Costa, Jr., *Reinterpreting the Myers-Briggs Type Indicator from the Perspective of the Five-Factor Model of Personality*, 57 J. PERSONALITY 17, 18-19 (Mar. 1989). According to Jung, one type predominates but individuals possess some degree of the other types. Jung noted that those "pure" types exist infrequently in actual life. Barbuto, *supra* at 613; David A. Cowan, *An Alternative to the Dichotomous Interpretation of Jung's Psychological Functions: Developing More Sensitive Measurement Technology*, 53 J. PERSONALITY ASSESSMENT 459, 462-63 (1989). The Myers-Briggs Type Indicator (MBTI) integrates Jungian theory on psychological types and aims to identify an individual's basic preferences as dichotomous in nature. *Id.* at 462; Barbuto, *supra* at 614. Criticism of the MBTI has focused on its forced choice-testing format, which is not continuous. *Id.* at 617-18. Continuous measurements would more accurately reflect individual personalities and account for an individual's preferences. *Id.* at 618. Some have stated that the dichotomous interpretation that the MBTI draws from Jungian theory is not in keeping with the theory itself. Cowan, *supra* at 461; McCrae & Costa, *supra* at 32. Various adjuncts have been proposed to improve the MBTI ability to evaluate individual differences along a continuum scale, so as to salvage important information lost in the current instrument's dichotomous approach. *Id.* at 36-37; Cowan, *supra* at 463-64; Barbuto, *supra* at 620-21.

The lawyer/client relationship, by its very nature, is usually character-ized by an imbalance of power.[8] Although for some sophisticated or wealthy clients, this imbalance may well be to the lawyer's disadvantage,[9] more often, the attorney holds the greater power.[10] In most cases, the client is a person with a problem that requires legal expertise, and is thus dependent on the attorney for redress.[11] The relationship between lawyer and client is often extremely intense; the degree, however, may vary with the nature of the representation.[12] A lawyer's representation of a client for a real estate closing may not be especially fraught with intensity.[13] Yet a client seeking to avoid deportation, incarceration or loss of custody of a child is likely to demand a great deal of attention from her attorney, not all of which will be of a legal nature. Unlike friendship, the obligations of caring are one-

---

8. *See* ABA Formal Op. 92-364 (1992):

The factors leading to the client's trust and reliance on the lawyer also have the potential for placing the lawyer in a position of dominance, and the client a position of vulnerability. All of the positive characteristics that the lawyer is encouraged to develop so that the client will be confident that he or she is being well served can reinforce a feeling of dependence.

9. *See* Stephen Ellmann, *The Ethic of Care as an Ethic for Lawyers*, 81 Geo. L.J. 2665, 2686 (1993) ("Rather than being dependent on their lawyers...some clients may wield such power or act with such insistence that they dominate and intimidate their legal agents.").

10. *Id.* at 2697. For a provocative challenge to the traditional role and privileged posi-tion of the lawyer in representation of subordinated people, see Gerald P. López, Rebel-lious Lawyering: One Chicano's Vision of Progressive Law Practice (1992):

Throwing around labels like "thoroughly oppressed" and "totally dominant" does seem to imply, after all, that power can sometimes reside on only one side of a rela-tionship.... [But p]ower necessarily runs in all directions within relationships. No person...is ever *absolutely* powerless in any relationship, not battered women and not low-income people of color....In fact, when we call a person or a group "subor-dinated" or victimized," we're always describing a state of relative powerlessness.
Id. at 41.

11. *See id.* at 54 ("For all their reluctance in seeking a lawyer's help, many clients virtu-ally turn over their situation to their lawyer and the legal culture.").

12. *See* Ellmann, *supra* note 9, at 2686 ("Lawyers and clients are thrown together by the client need that generates the relationship. From this more or less intimate encounter can come strong feelings, particularly from the client for his lawyer, on whom the client may be dependent for emotional sustenance and legal aid ranging from criminal defense to estate planning.").

13. *See id.* ("Some clients may need no personal sustenance from their lawyers, because they use the lawyers' services for entirely routine and unemotional transactions or projects.").

sided.[14] The lawyer's devotion to the client's needs is not reciprocated by the client. In these ways, the lawyer/client relationship mirrors other kinds of intense, non-reciprocal relationships involving inherent power imbalances: those of physician/patient, therapist/patient, pastor/counselee, and teacher/student. Such relationships inevitably invite misplaced emotional reactions. These misplacements are commonly known as transference and countertransference. It is the doctrine of countertransference—misplaced emotions by the attorney on her client—with which this Article is primarily concerned.

Part IA explores the phenomena of transference and countertransference. Part IB focuses primarily on how the imbalance of power that characterizes countertransference in most professional relationships creates a danger of sexual exploitation, and how the professions have responded to such problems. Part IC compares and contrasts the ways in which analysts and attorneys respond to countertransference and the disparity in their preparation for its occurrence.

Part IIA explores the importance of recognizing the emotional dimension in lawyering and the need for attorneys to accept and endeavor to understand their own emotional lives. As a vehicle for this discussion, this section uses a scenario involving a hypothetical lawyer experiencing different countertransference reactions to two clients. Part IIB explores why members of the legal profession resist accepting their emotional lives. Part IIC canvases the literature about lawyering and psychology in general, and lawyering and countertransference in particular. Part IID offers some reasons for optimism about the prospect that lawyers' resistance to acknowledging the power of their emotional lives and those of their clients may be softening. Such reasons include the evolving de-stigmatization of mental health issues among the population generally and the legal profession in particular, as well as the convergence of several schools of legal scholarship that embrace an awareness of the importance of psychological sensitivity and knowledge.

Part III suggests strategies for recognizing and resolving emotional interference in the lawyer/client relationship. Part IIIA identifies what individual attorneys can do to recognize countertransference reactions and diminish their power. As this section acknowledges, the diversity among lawyers and among different practice settings is likely to affect the incidence and intensity of problematic countertransference. Part IIIA then revisits the earlier hypothetical to suggest how an understanding of psychological

---

14. *See* Charles Fried, *The Lawyer as Friend: The Moral Foundations of the Lawyer-Client Relationship*, 85 YALE L.J. 1060, 1074 (1976). *See also* Ellmann, *supra* note 9, at 2697 ("[T]he client receives more care from the lawyer than the lawyer ordinarily receives from the client.").

processes might improve the outcome. Part IIIB offers some preliminary thoughts on what law schools and the practicing bar can do to help law students and lawyers cultivate their emotional intelligence.

I. Transference, Countertransference and the Attorney/Client Relationship

A. Psychoanalytical Transference and Countertransference

The concept of transference was first introduced by Sigmund Freud in 1910 in his lectures on psychoanalysis:

> In every psycho-analytical treatment of a neurotic patient the strange phenomena that is known as "transference" makes its appearance. The patient, that is to say, directs towards the physician a degree of affectionate feeling (mingled, often enough, with hostility) which is based on no real relation between them and which—as is shown by every detail of its emergence—can only be traced back to old wishful phantasies of the patient which have become unconscious.[15]

Although Freud focused on the manifestation of transference in psychoanalytic treatment, he observed that the phenomenon was not limited to psychoanalysis, and, indeed, was manifest in all human relationships.[16] Human beings carry emotional baggage from early relationships and unload that baggage in the relationships they form later in life. Transference may involve strong positive (love-transference)[17] or negative (hate-transference)[18] emotions. Freud cautioned analysts to resist urges to act on trans-

---

15. Sigmund Freud, *Five Lectures on Psycho-Analysis, Leonardo da Vinci, and Other Works, Fifth Lecture, in* XI The Standard Edition Of The Complete Psychological Works Of Sigmund Freud 51 (James Stachey ed., 1957) (1910).

16. *Id.* at 51-52. *See also* Lewis R. Wolberg, M.D., The Technique Of Psychotherapy 309 (1954).

17. Sigmund Freud, *Observations On Transference-Love, in* XII The Standard Edition Of The Complete Psychological Works Of Sigmund Freud 159-71 (James Stachey ed., 1957) (1911-13); Steven B. Bisbing, Linda Mabus Jorgenson & Pamela K. Sutherland, Sexual Abuse By Professionals: A Legal Guide 460 (1995); Leon J. Saul, *The Erotic Transference*, 31 Psychoanalytic Q. 54 (1962); H.F. Searles, *Oedipal Love in the Countertransference*, 40 Int. J. Psychoanal. 180 (1959).

18. Sigmund Freud, *Introductory Lectures on Psycho-Analysis* (Part III), *in* XVI The Standard Edition Of The Complete Psychological Works Of Sigmund Freud

ference, and encouraged them to learn to deal with it appropriately.[19] Although transference was first viewed as a hindrance to the work at hand, Freud and others later came to see it as an extremely useful tool to advance analysis.[20]

Freud soon named the related phenomenon of the analyst's response to the patient's transference: countertransference.[21] Yet not much beyond this naming occurred in the exploration of countertransference for the next forty years.[22] Since then, however, countertransference has received a great deal of attention, by Freudians and non-Freudians alike.[23]

The literature yields a wide range of definitions for both transference[24]

---

444 (James Stachey ed., 1957) (1916-17); D.W. Winnicott, *Hate in the Countertransference*, 3(4) J. PSYCHOTHERAPY PRAC. & RES. 350 (1994).

19. Freud, *Observations on Transference-Love, supra* note 17, at 170; Freud, *Introductory Lectures, Part III, supra* note 18, at 444.

20. Freud, *Introductory Lectures, Part III, supra* note 18, at 444; HEINRICH RACKER, TRANSFERENCE & COUNTERTRANSFERENCE 18 (1968); Joseph Sandler, *Countertransference and Role-responsiveness*, 3 INT. REV. PSYCHOANAL. 43 (1976).

21. Sigmund Freud, *Nuremberg Congress Paper: The Future Prospects of Psycho-analytic Theory, in* XI THE STANDARD EDITION OF THE COMPLETE PSYCHOLOGICAL WORKS OF SIGMUND FREUD 144-45 (James Stachey ed., 1957) (1910).

22. *See* RACKER, *supra* note 20, at 130; Therese Benedek, *Dynamics of the Countertransference*, 17 BULL. MENNINGER CLINIC 201 (1953). Benedek describes that the tradition of having the patient lie on a couch with the analyst sitting behind the patient grew out of Freud's concern about countertransference. "Freud frankly admitted that he used this arrangement inherited from the days of hypnosis, because he did not like 'to be stared at'; thus, it served him as a protection in the transference-countertransference duel." *Id.* at 202; Theodore J. Jacobs, *The Analyst and the Patient's Object World: Notes on an Aspect of Countertransference*, 31 JAMA 619, 620 (1983).

23. *See, e.g.*, Linda Mills, *On the Other Side of Silence: Affective Lawyering for Intimate Abuse*, 81 CORNELL L. REV. 1225, 1244-45 n.98 (1996) (quoting CARL G. JUNG, THE PRACTICE OF PSYCHOLOGY: ESSAYS ON THE PSYCHOLOGY OF THE TRANSFERENCE AND OTHER SUBJECTS, paras. 164-67 (Herbert Read et. al. eds. & R.F.C. Hull trans., 2d ed. 1966)). *See also* Thomas L. Shaffer, *Undue Influence, Confidential Relationship, and the Psychology of Transference*, 45 NOTRE DAME LAW. 197, 204-14 (1970) (discussing significance of transference throughout all schools of psychotherapy).

24. *See, e.g.*, ANDREW S. WATSON, THE LAWYER IN THE INTERVIEWING AND COUNSELING PROCESS 23-24 (1976) ("In the legal interview setting, [transference] includes all of the reactions stimulated by the reality of the lawyer's involvement as well as some unreal and distorted impressions derived from prior experiences and their resultant patterning of the client's psychic life."); WOLBERG, *supra* note 16; Jill M. Crumpacker, *Regulation of Lawyer-Client Sex: Codifying the "Cold Shower" or a "Fatal Attraction" Per Se?*, 32 WASHBURN L.J. 379, 391 (1993) ("'transference,' refers to the process by which a client projects onto a lawyer certain traits which may not be based in reality, but which stem from the client's pre-

and countertransference.[25] Some define countertransference narrowly as the professional's reaction to transference;[26] others describe it to include

vious associations with important persons in her life." (*citing* Lawrence Dubin, *Sex and the Divorce Lawyer: Is the Client Off Limits?*, 1 GEO. J. LEGAL ETHICS 605 (1988) (citing ANDREW WATSON, PSYCHIATRY FOR LAWYERS 4 (1978))). For additional interpretations, definitions & constructions of transference, see Shaffer, *supra* note 23, at 205-06.

25. *See* ROSEMARY MARSHALL BALSAM & ALAN BALSAM, BECOMING A PSYCHOTHERAPIST 92 (1974) ("The therapist, too, often experiences an uneven mixture of available and less available feelings while with the patient. The unconscious responses are most correctly called *countertransference*."); FREEMAN, *supra* note 6, at 50 (attorney's positive or negative responses to client); RACKER, *supra* note 20, at 127-29 (surveying various definitions of countertransference); HOWARD F. STEIN, THE PSYCHO-DYNAMICS OF MEDICAL PRACTICE: UNCONSCIOUS FACTORS IN PATIENT CARE 3 (1985) ("all nonrational elements of the physician's work;"); Eugene Baum, *Countertransference and the Vicissitudes in an Analyst's Development*, 64 PSYCHOANALYTIC REV. 539, 540 (1977) (countertransference as interference that needs to be worked through); Benedek, *supra* note 22, at 205-06 ("therapists reactions to transference of the patient" or "analyst's projection of an important person of his past into his patient."); Theodore Jacobs, *On Countertransference Enactments*, 34 J. AMER. PSYCHOANAL. ASS'N 289, 290 (1986) ("influences on [the therapist's] understanding and technique that stem both from his transferences and from his emotional responses to the patient's transferences"); Judy L. Kantrowitz, *Follow-up of Psychoanalysis Five-to-Ten Years After Termination: III. The Relationship of the Transference Neurosis to the Patient-Analyst Match*, 38 J. AMER. PSYCHOANAL. ASS'N 655, 656 (1990) (less inclusive than "all inadvertent expressions of personal characteristics"); Otto Kernberg, *Notes on Countertransference*, 13 J. AMER. PSYCHOANAL. ASS'N 38, 38-39 (1965) (summarizing others' definitions as unconscious reaction to patient's transference or total emotional reaction to patient); William D. Langford, Jr., *Criminalizing Attorney-Client Sexual Relations: Towards Substantive Enforcement*, 73 TEX. L. REV. 1223, 1239 (1995) (therapist's transfer of feelings about others onto patient); Margaret Little, *Counter-Transference and the Patient's Response To It*, 32 INT. J. PSYCHOANAL. 32, 32 (1951) (list of various definitions); Annie Reich, *Further Remarks on Counter-transference*, 41 INT. J. PSYCHOANAL. 389, 389-90 (1960) (term is wrongly defined by others as total response to patient; conscious responses only if they reach "an inordinate intensity or are strongly tainted by inappropriate sexual or aggressive feelings, thus revealing themselves to be determined by unconscious infantile strivings"); Owen Renik, *Analytic Interaction: Conceptualizing Technique in Light of the Analyst's Irreducible Subjectivity*, 62 PSYCHOANAL. Q. 553, 565 (1993) ("It has been said justifiably, that one person's countertransference is another person's empathy....What we have been used to calling countertransference in the widest use of the term, is the ever-present raw material of technique."); Searles, *supra* note 17, at 187 (transference responses "carried over from figure of analyst's own early years, without awareness that his response springs predominantly from an early life source, rather than being based mainly upon the reality of the present analyst-patient relationship"); Lucia E. Tower, *Countertransference*, J. AMER. PSYCHOANAL. ASS'N 224, 225-26 (1956) (surveying range of definitions).

26. *See, e.g.*, H.P. Blum, *Countertransference and the Theory of Technique: Discussion*, 34 J. AMER. PSYCHOANAL. ASS'N 309, 311 (1986) ("In Freud's formulation of the classical

the entire range of the professional's emotional responses to the client/patient.[27] Still others suggest that the term countertransference is a misnomer, and that countertransference occurs as an entirely distinct, independent phenomenon.[28]

As with transference, countertransference exists in all human relationships,[29] but is most notable and potentially problematic in those relationships involving an imbalance of power.[30]

B. Countertransference and Sexual Exploitation in Professional Relationships

Countertransference acquired notoriety in large measure due to its manifestation in scandalous and not infrequent sexual relationships between numerous therapists and their patients, often with dire consequences for

---

view, countertransference is an interfering counterreaction to the patient's transference which stems from the analyst's own unresolved intrapsychic conflicts."); Shirley Feldman-Summers, *Sexual Contact in Fiduciary Relationships, in* SEXUAL EXPLOITATION IN PROFESSIONAL RELATIONSHIPS 203 (Glen O. Gabbard ed., 1989) (reaction to patient's transference).

27. *See, e.g.*, Paul Heimann, *On Countertransference*, 31 INT. J. PSYCHOANAL. 81 (1950) (all feelings towards patient); Cynthia Mitchell & Karen Melikian, *The Treatment of Male Sexual Offenders: Countertransference Reactions*, 4(1) J. CHILD SEXUAL ABUSE 87, 87 (1995) (all of therapist's conscious and unconscious reactions to patient).

28. *See, e.g.*, STEIN, *supra* note 25:

Transference and countertransference can be identified dynamically as the same phenomenon: They both refer to how human beings use one another for unconscious purposes. They differ with respect to who is doing so, not what is being done. Transference in the clinical relationship denotes the patient's displacement and exteriorizing of internal issues onto the clinician; countertransference denotes the reverse.

J.T. McLaughlin, *Transference, Psychic Reality and Countertransference*, 50 PSYCHOANAL. Q. 637, 655-60 (1981). McLaughlin would not limit countertransference to the analyst's reactions to the patient or the analysis, but rather sees it as a ubiquitous phenomenon encompassing all of the analyst's psychic reality. *See also* Adolph Stern, *On the Counter-transference in Psychoanalysis*, 11 PSYCHOANAL. REV. 166, 167 (1924) (countertransference is "the transference that the analyst makes to the patient"). *Contra*, Hanna Segal, *Countertransference*, 6 INT. J. PSYCHOANALYTIC THEORY 31, 33 (1977) (countertransference and transference are *not* same phenomena).

29. *See* STEIN, *supra* note 25, at 47; Tower, *supra* note 25, at 232-34.

30. *See* Linda M. Jorgenson & Pamela K. Sutherland, *Lawyers' Sex with Clients: Proposal for a Uniform Standard*, 12 (11) FAIR$HARE 11 n.38 (Nov. 1992) (citing Schaffer, *supra* note 23, at 214-15 (quoting 16 COLLECTED WORKS OF CARL G. JUNG 218 (H. Read, M. Fordham & G. Adler, ed., 2d ed. 1966))).

the emotionally vulnerable patients.[31] Such relationships understandably were condemned by the profession. Both the American Psychiatric Association and the American Psychological Association adopted ethical rules forbidding such sexual relationships.[32] Psychotherapists have often faced

---

31. *See, e.g.,* MARILYN R. PETERSON, AT PERSONAL RISK 1-2 (1992); PETER RUTTER, SEX IN THE FORBIDDEN ZONE 5-6 (1989) (especially when male is in power position); Dean T. Collins, *Sexual Involvement Between Psychiatric Hospital Staff and Their Patients, in* SEXUAL EXPLOITATION IN PROFESSIONAL RELATIONSHIPS 159 (Glen O. Gabbard ed., 1989); Virginia Davidson, *Psychiatry's Problem with No Name: Therapist-Patient Sex,* 37 AM. J. PSYCHOANALYSIS 37, 46-47 (1977); Feldman-Summers, *supra* note 26, at 202-03; Paul N. Gerber, *Commentary on Counter-Transference in Working with Sex Offenders: The Issue of Sexual Attraction,* 4(1) J. CHILD SEXUAL ABUSE 117, 118-19 (1995) (in work with sex offenders); Kenneth S. Pope, *Teacher-Student Sexual Intimacy, in* SEXUAL EXPLOITATION IN PROFESSIONAL RELATIONSHIPS 172-73 (Glen O. Gabbard ed., 1989) (problem of not dealing with countertransference in training psychotherapists because of educator-student intimacy problems); Kenneth S. Pope, *Therapist-Patient Sex Syndrome: A Guide for Attorneys and Subsequent Therapists Assessing Damage, in* SEXUAL EXPLOITATION IN PROFESSIONAL RELATIONSHIPS 45, 46 (Glen O. Gabbard ed., 1989); Leonard L. Riskin, *Sexual Relations Between Therapists and Their Patients: Toward Research on Restraint,* 67 CAL. L. REV. 1000, 1003 (1979) (over 5% of male psychotherapists surveyed admitted to sexual intimacy with patients during treatment); Tower, *supra* note 25, at 230, 232. *See also* Robert D. Glaser & Joseph S. Thorpe, *Unethical Intimacy: A Survey of Sexual Contact and Advances Between Psychology Educators and Female Graduate Students,* 41 AM. PSYCHOLOGIST 43 (1986) (survey revealing prevalence of sexual contact between psychology educators and students). For additional articles, see MICHAEL L. PERLIN, 3 MENTAL DISABILITY LAW: CIVIL AND CRIMINAL § 12.09, at 29 n.180 (1989 & Supp. 1998).

32. American Psychiatric Association, *The Principles of Medical Ethics With Annotations Especially Applicable to Psychiatry,* 130 AM. J. PSYCHIATRY 1058, 1061 (1973); APA Ethical Standards for Psychologists, Principles 6 ("sexual intimacies with clients are unethical") (APA 1977); *id.* at 7 ("psychologists do not exploit their professional relationships with clients, supervisees, students, employees, or research participants sexually or otherwise") (APA 1981). *See* Glaser & Thorpe, *supra* note 31, at 43; Linda Fitts Mischler, *Reconciling Rapture, Representation and Responsibility: An Argument Against Per Se Bans on Attorney-Client Sex,* 10 GEO. J. LEGAL ETHICS 209, 215 n.26 (1996). Although the ancient Hippocratic Oath proscribed sexual relations between physicians and their patients, *see* Phyllis Coleman, *Sex in Power Dependent Relationships: Taking Unfair Advantage of the "Fair" Sex,* 53 ALB. L. REV. 95, 110 (1988); Riskin, *supra* note 31, at 1000, not until 1989 did the American Medical Association's Council on Ethical and Judicial Affairs issue Opinion 8.14 on Sexual Misconduct, which explicitly codifies such a prohibition. *See* Paul S. Applebaum, Linda M. Jorgenson and Pamela K. Sutherland, *Sexual Relationships Between Physicians and Patients,* 154 ARCHIVES OF INTERNAL MED. 2561 (1994); ABA Formal Op. 92-364, n.18 (1992) (adopted by the AMA House of Delegates on December 4, 1990, "finding all sexual relationships between doctor and patient to be potentially exploitative and detrimental to the physician's medical judgment

civil liability for sexual liaisons with their patients.[33] Recently, a number of jurisdictions have moved towards criminalization of such relationships.[34]

Sexual relationships are problems in other professions as well.[35] The greater the degree of power-dependency, the higher the incidence of exploita-

---

and to the patient's trust). *See also* BISBING, JORGENSON & SUTHERLAND, *supra* note 17, at 26. The American Medical Association stated with respect to idealization:

> The professional physician-patient relationship frequently evokes strong and complicated emotions in both the physician and patient. It is not unusual for sexual attraction to be one of these emotions. Many commentators agree that sexual or romantic attraction to patients is not uncommon or abnormal; &elip; . The emotions of admiration, affection, and caring that are part of a physician-patient relationship can become particularly powerful when either party is experiencing intense pressures or traumatic or major life events.

American Medical Association's Council of Ethical and Judicial Affairs, *Sexual Misconduct in the Practice of Medicine*, 266 JAMA 2742 (1991). Other professional codes contain similar proscriptions, *See* Riskin, *supra* note 31, at 1003, as do a number of state statutes. *See, e.g.,* Sexual Exploitation in Psychotherapy Act, ILL. REV. STAT. ch. 70, pr. 801 *et seq.* (1989). *But see* Andrew S. Watson, *Lawyers and Professionalism: A Further Psychiatric Perspective on Legal Education*, 8 U. MICH. J. L. REF. 248, 251 (1975) (ethical codes help professionals ignore underlying emotional issues).

33. *See, e.g.,* Simmons v. United States, 805 F.2d 1363 (9th Cir. 1986); Corgan v. Muehling 173 Ill.2d 296, 574 N.E.2d 602, 606-07 (1991); Cotton v. Kamby, 101 Mich. App. 537, 300 N.W. 2d 627 (1980); Zipkin v. Freeman, 436 S.W.2d 753 (Mo. 1968). *See also* Coleman, *supra* note 32, at 99 (recommending civil liability and professional discipline as well as criminal charges); Linda Mabus Jorgenson & Pamela K. Sutherland, *Fiduciary Theory Applied To Personal Dealings; Attorney Client Sexual Contact*, 45 ARK. L. REV. 459, 468 (1992).

34. *See* PERLIN, *supra* note 31, § 12.09, at 305.

35. *See* RUTTER, *supra* note 31, at 6; SEXUAL EXPLOITATION IN PROFESSIONAL RELATIONSHIPS, xi-xii, *passim* (Glen O. Gabbard ed., 1989); Ann H. Britton, *Sexual Abuse in the Professional Relationship*, 11 HAMLINE L. REV. 247 (1988) (surveying problems of professional sexual abuse and their outcomes); Coleman, *supra* note 32, at 95; Feldman-Summers, *supra* note 26, at 202; Leslie R. Schover, *Sexual Exploitation by Sex Therapists, in* SEXUAL EXPLOITATION IN PROFESSIONAL RELATIONSHIPS (Glen O. Gabbard ed., 1989). For discussion of problems in the pastoral relationship, see BISBING, JORGENSON & SUTHERLAND, *supra* note 17; Marie Fortune, *Boundaries or Barriers? An Exchange*, 111 THE CHRISTIAN CENTURY, No. 18, at 5 (1994); William E. Hulme, *Sexual Boundary Violations of Clergy, in* SEXUAL EXPLOITATION IN PROFESSIONAL RELATIONSHIPS (Glen O. Gabbard ed., 1989); Doe v. Samaritan Counseling Center, 791 P.2d 344 (Alaska 1990) (defendant Counseling Center may be liable for mishandling of transference phenomenon by pastoral counselor who engaged in sexual relations with plaintiff); Langford v. Roman Catholic Diocese of Brooklyn, 177 Misc.2d 897, 677 N.Y.S.2d 436 (Sup. Ct. Kings County 1998) (dismissing parishioner's claim against pastor for alleged sexual molestation due to First Amendment religion clause constraints). For problems of teacher/student sexual exploitation, *see* Pope, *supra* note 31. Pope notes special problems in Psychology Ph.D programs. *Id.* at 171.

tive sexual encounters between professionals and the recipients of their services.[36] We rarely if ever hear about sexual relationships gone wrong between mail carriers and letter receivers, butchers and their customers, or even hair dressers and their clients. There appears to be something inherent in the power relationship of caring professions that fosters opportunities for abuse.[37]

In recent years, the problem has been an especially grave one for lawyers,[38] who have faced disciplinary charges[39] and civil liability[40] for

---

36. *See* Coleman, *supra* note 32, at 95-97 (describing continuum of presumption of exploitation based on power dependency). *But see* Mischler, *supra* note 32, at 245-49 (arguing that power imbalance is not as pronounced in attorney/client relationships as it is in other professional relationships).

37. *See* PETERSON, *supra* note 31, at 34.

38. *See* Caroline Forell, *Lawyers, Clients and Sex: Breaking the Silence on The Ethical and Liability Issues*, 22 GOLDEN GATE U. L. REV. 611 (1992) (overview of California, Oregon, and Illinois attempts to address attorney-client relations as well as stimulus for those attempts); Jorgenson & Sutherland, *supra* note 30, at 12-13; Thomas Lyon, *Sexual Exploitation of Divorce Clients: The Lawyer's Prerogative?*, 10 HARV. WOMEN'S L.J. 159 (1987).

39. *See* Jorgenson & Sutherland, *supra* note 33, at 499 n.11 (informal survey of state bar associations' disciplinary proceedings dealing with sexual harassment and contact by attorneys). *See e.g.*, People v. Zeilinger, 814 P.2d 808 (Colo. 1991) (public reprimand for engaging in sexual relations with client in marital dissolution action); People v. Gibbons, 685 P.2d 168 (Colo. 1984) (disbarring suspended attorney for, *inter alia*, engaging in covert sexual relation with client); Committee on Professional Ethics and Conduct of the Iowa State Bar Association, 436 N.W.2d 57 (Iowa 1989) (suspending license for three months for violation of DR 1-102(A)(3) and (6) for having sex with client whom lawyer represented in custody proceedings); Drucker's Case, 577 A.2d 1198 (N.H. 1990) (two-year suspension for, *inter alia*, sexual relations with client); In the Matter of Feinman, 225 A.D.2d 200 (N.Y. 4th Dep't 1996) (six-month suspension for, *inter alia*, sexual relationship with client whom attorney represented in criminal matter,); In the Matter of McClure, 204 A.D.2d (N.Y. 3d Dep't 1994) (prosecutor suspended for five years for having sex with 20 year old defendant); In the Matter of Bowen, 542 A.D.2d 45 (N.Y. 3d Dep't 1989) (two-year suspension for, *inter alia*, sexual misconduct with client). *See also, e.g.*, following cases involving sexual harassment of clients: In the Matter of Darrell Adams, 428 N.E.2d 786 (Ind. 1981); In re Raymond Howard, 912 S.W.2d (Mo. 1995) (indefinite suspension for, *inter alia*, unwanted sexual advances); Matter of Bernstein, 237 A.D.2d 89 (N.Y. 2d Dep't 1997) (attorney disbarred for ten counts of making sexually suggestive remarks to female clients); In the Matter of Romano, 231 A.D.2d 299 (N.Y. 1st Dep't 1997); In the Matter of Gilbert, 194 A.D.2d 262 (N.Y. 4th Dep't 1993) (one-year suspension for making unwanted and unsolicited sexual advances to clients and secretaries); Matter of Rudnick, 177 A.D.2d 121 (N.Y. 2d Dep't 1992) (two-year suspension for, *inter alia*, having coercive sexual relations with client); State *ex rel.* Okla. Bar Ass'n v. Sopher, 852 P.2d 707 (Okla. 1993) (public reprimand for unwanted sexual advances towards client).

40. *See, e.g.*, Catherine Holand Petersen & Candace Mathers, *Developing Per-*

sexual liaisons with their clients. The most egregious cases tend to arise in family law practice.[41] In 1992 the ABA issued formal opinion 92-364, which, while not prohibiting sexual liaisons between lawyers and clients outright, strongly discouraged them and identified various problems that could result in a violation of rules of professional responsibility.[42] The opinion concluded that in disciplinary or other proceedings, an attorney who has engaged in sexual relations with a client would have the burden to prove such relations *did not* impair the representation.[43] Some state codes of professional responsibility now include sexual relationships between lawyer and client in the categories of sanctionable conduct.[44] Pro-

---

sonal Relationship, Impairing Attorney-Client Relationship, 14(2) FAIR$HARE 26 (Feb. 1994) (discussing specific malpractice case finding liability). *But see* Kling v. Landry, 226 Ill. App. 3d 329 (1997); Suppressed v. Suppressed, 206 Ill. App. 3d 918 (1990) (no cause of action stated by plaintiff's allegations of seduction by attorney in absence of actual harm to representation). While there may be overlap, consensual relations between attorneys and clients are distinguishable from sexual harassment and sexual assault of clients by attorneys. *See, e.g.,* Matter of Bernstein, 237 A.D.2d 89 (N.Y. 2d Dep't 1997) (attorney disbarred for ten counts of making sexually suggestive remarks to female clients); In the Matter of Romano, 231 A.D.2d 299 (N.Y. 1st Dep't 1997) (attorney suspended for personally conducting physical examination of clients).

41. *See, e.g.,* Lyon, *supra* note 38 (exploring causes and effects of sexual relations between divorce lawyers and their clients and comparing them to therapist-client relationship). Currently, New York's absolute ban against sexual relationships between lawyers and clients applies only in matters involving domestic relations. 22 NYCRR § 1200.3 [DR 1-102(A)(7)]. The genesis of this prohibition was a 1993 report issued by the Chief Judge's Committee to Examine Lawyer Conduct in Matrimonial Matters. *See* e-mail correspondence between Kathleen R. Mulligan Baxter, Counsel, New York State Bar Association and Sandra Maliszewski, 9/29/98 (on file with author).

42. ABA Formal Op. 92-364 (1992).

43. *Id. See* Jorgenson & Sutherland, *supra* note 30, at 13 (proposing rebuttable presumption as least restrictive way to deal with problem).

44. A survey of the States reveals a variety of approaches to regulation of attorney-client sexual relations: CALIFORNIA: CAL. CODE RPC 3-120 & CAL. BPC § 6106.9 (1997)): attorneys are prohibited from requiring or demanding sex from client incident to or as condition of representation, employing coercive influence over client to enter sexual relations, or maintaining preexisting relationship which would violate other rules of professional conduct); FLORIDA: F.S.A. BAR RULE SEC. 4-8.4(I): attorneys are prohibited from engaging in sexual relations with clients that exploit lawyer/client relationship, excluding preexisting sexual relationships); MINNESOTA: M.S.A. RPC 1.8(k): attorneys are prohibited from having sex with current clients unless there is preexisting sexual relationship); New York: 22 NYCRR § 1200.29-a (eff. June 30, 1999): attorneys are prohibited from requiring or demanding sexual relations as condition of representation, employing coercion, intimidation or undue influence in entering into sexual relations,

posals for adding such prohibitions are pending in other jurisdictions.[45] The literature—academic and other—is rife with recommendations pro and con the regulation of sexual liaisons between attorneys and clients.[46]

---

or, in domestic relations matters, having sexual relations with client that begin after representation commences; OREGON: ORCPR DR5-110: attorneys cannot engage in sexual relations with current clients or with representatives of current clients except for preexisting relationships; DR5-101(B): prohibits maintaining preexisting sexual relationship that could prejudice client's case and create conflict of interest); WEST VIRGINIA: WV RPC 8.4(g): prohibits lawyer from having sexual relations with client unless preexisting consensual relationship). *See* Appelbaum, Jorgenson & Sutherland, *supra* note 32, at 2563-65 nn.31-33 and accompanying text; Abed Awad, *Attorney-Client Sexual Relations*, 22 J. LEGAL PROF. 131 (1998); Michael Daigneault, *Client-Attorney Relationships: The Danger of "Going To Far,"* THE FEDERAL LAWYER, June 1995, at 13, 15.

45. The Kansas Bar Association recently approved Rule 1-17, which is pending before the Kansas Supreme Court. The proposed rule prohibits an attorney from engaging in a sexual relationship with a current client or a representative of the client if the contact would or is likely to damage or prejudice the client, excluding preexisting sexual relationships. *See Item of Interest-Board Seeks Comments on Sex with Clients Proposal*, 66 J. KAN. B. ASS'N 3 (1997). The Pennsylvania State Bar's Ethics Committee published a proposal to prohibit attorney/client sexual relations similar to that issued by Kansas, but it was later withdrawn. Instead, it was issued as an ethical opinion. *See* PA Ethical Op. 97-100, 1997 WL 671579. The ABA's Ethics 2000 Commission has floated a similar rule for comment. Proposed Rule 1.8(k), Attorney/Client Sexual Relationships (lawyers prohibited from having sexual relations with client unless consensual sexual relationship preexisted commencement of lawyer-client relationship). Other states have issued ethics opinions containing similar prohibitions, including Kansas (Kansas Ethics Op. 94-13: sexual relations which post-date representation are prohibited) or have disciplined attorneys for sexual relationships with clients even in the absence of a specific rule, *see, e.g.*, Disciplinary Counsel v. DePietro, Ohio S. Ct. No. 92-56 (Dec. 30, 1994); State *ex rel*. Okla. Bar Ass'n v. Sopher, 852 P.2d 707 (Okla. 1993).

46. *See, e.g.*, Jeffrey A. Barker, *Professional-Client Sex: Is Criminal Liability an Appropriate Means of Enforcing Professional Responsibility?*, 40 UCLA L. REV. 1277 (1993) (focusing on the legal and medical professions and questioning the adoption of criminal penalties for professional-client sexual relations); Crumpacker, *supra* note 24, at 379; Yael Levy, *Attorneys, Clients and Sex: Conflicting Interests in the California Rule*, 5 GEO. J. LEGAL ETHICS 649 (1992) (proposing to limit California rule to banning attorney-client sexual relationship only when client is "vulnerable" or when nature of care is emotional); Lyon, *supra* note 38, at 159 (regulation perpetuates stereotype of women as unable to resist sexual advances); Mischler, *supra* note 32, at 209 n.3 (and sources cited therein); Joanne Pitulla, *Unfair Advantage*, A.B.A. J. 76 (Nov. 1992) (reluctance of legal profession to acknowledge problem of attorney-client sexual relations).

At least one commentator has recommended criminal liability for such abuses of the fiduciary relationship.[47]

Indeed, the relationship among transference, countertransference and sexual relations has received a good deal of attention in legal scholarship, case law, and as the subject of regulation.[48] It is not my intention to reiterate that discussion here. Rather, I wish to shift the focus away from the sexual culmination of transference/countertransference and examine instead the ways in which a variety of powerful emotions may affect lawyers in their relationships with their clients, so that attorneys may learn to understand, harness and handle such emotional reactions in more positive and constructive ways.

C. Countertransference in Practice

Not all emotional engagement between lawyer and client is inappropriate or harmful. It is important to distinguish, for example, empathy from countertransference. Despite some intimations in the psychoanalytic literature to the contrary,[49] empathy—an aspect of good counseling[50] and good lawyering[51]—is not the same as countertransference.[52] Empathy is the quality of metaphorically walking in someone else's shoes so as to understand that person's needs and desires.[53] Although similarities exist

---

47. Langford, *supra* note 25, at 1223.

48. *See, e.g.*, Mischler, *supra* note 32.

49. *See* RACKER, *supra* note 20, at 135-36 ("[I]t should be borne in mind that the disposition to empathy...springs largely from the sublimated positive countertransference, which likewise relates empathy with countertransference in the wider sense.").

50. *See* A.M. Cooper, *Some Limitations on Therapeutic Effectiveness: The "Burnout Syndrome" in Psychoanalysis*, 55 PSYCHOANALYTIC Q. 576, 579 (1986) ("psychoanalysis will fail if the analyst cannot find points of empathic contact with his patient").

51. *See* Peter Margulies, *Re-Framing Empathy in Clinical Legal Education*, 5 CLIN. L. REV. 605, 605 (1999) ("There are two important things to remember about empathy—it is necessary, and it is impossible."); Bruce J. Winick, *Dealing With Client Denial in the Advance Directive Context: A Challenge for the Therapeutically-Oriented Preventive Lawyer*, 4 PSYCHOL. PUB. POL'Y & L. (forthcoming, 1999) (citing commentators who have emphasized importance of empathy in lawyer/client relationships). *But see* Mills, *supra* note 23, at 1243-44 n.91 (citing critiques of value of empathy in lawyering).

52. *See* FREEMAN, *supra* note 6, at 15, 50 ("Good interviewing is empathy....Empathy is shared identification. It is to 'feel with' rather than 'sorry for' a person....Either emotional over or under involvement is detrimental."); LEWIS R. WOLBERG, 2 THE TECHNIQUE OF PSYCHOTHERAPY 143 (4th ed. 1988); Blum, *supra* note 26, at 322-23 ("In both adult and child analysis, countertransference confuses empathy and should not be confused with empathy").

53. *See* DAVID A. BINDER, PAUL BERGMAN & SUSAN C. PRICE, LAWYERS AS COUNSELORS: A CLIENT-CENTERED APPROACH 40 (1991) (citing CARL ROGERS, *in* G. EGAN,

between countertransference and empathy, it is for our purposes useful to view countertransference as unharnessed emotions—emotional responses gone awry.[54] Empathy is an important tool for The Good Lawyer and should be cultivated; countertransference, unchecked, is likely to cause problems.[55]

In the practice of psychoanalysis and psychotherapy, countertransference may manifest itself in a variety of ways, as positive (love)[56] or negative (hate).[57] For the therapist, understanding its operation is essential,[58]

THE SKILLED HELPER 87 (3d ed. 1986)):

> Empathy in its most fundamental sense…involves understanding the experiences, behaviors, and feelings of others as they experience them. It means that [lawyers] must, to the best of their abilities, put aside their own biases, prejudices, and points of view in order to understand as clearly as possible the points of view of their clients. It means entering into the experience of clients in order to develop a feeling for their inner world and how they view both this inner world and the world of people and [events] around them.

See also Ellmann, *supra* note 9, at 2681, 2699-700.

54. See Baum, *supra* note 25, at 540.

55. See Joan S. Meier, Notes *from the Underground: Integrating Psychological and Legal Perspectives on Domestic Violence in Theory and Practice*, 21 HOFSTRA L. REV. 1295, 1366, n.183 (1993) ("Once the professional has 'worked through' his or her counter-transference reactions, he or she is best situated to form a professionally 'empathic relationship' with the patient. In contrast, professionals who deny that they have any personal responses to clients, and therefore do not work them through, are likely to be somewhat handicapped in their professional interactions with the client."); Winick, *supra* note 51 (countertransference as inhibiting empathy). *But see* Meier, *supra* at 1352 ("In the legal profession, counter-transference is operating beneficially wherever people are personally committed to their work due to strong empathy for the population they serve. For instance, womens' identification with womens' rights issues such as domestic violence can fuel a strong empathy for battered women clients, conviction about their cause and strong advocacy on their behalf.").

56. See Crumpacker, *supra* note 24, at 391("[E]ighty seven percent of therapists report having sexual feeling[s] toward clients…[t]he other thirteen percent are liars." (quoting Dr. Glen Gabbard of the Menninger Clinic of Topeka, Kansas, in Gordon Slovut, *Therapists Who Have Sex With Patients Betray A Trust*, MINNEAPOLIS-ST. PAUL STAR TRIB., Oct. 15, 1992, at 1E)).

57. See Winnicott, *supra* note 18, at 350 ("However much [the therapist] loves his patients he cannot avoid hating them, and fearing them, and the better he knows this the less hate and fear will be the motive determining what he does to his patients"). *See supra* notes 17-18 and accompanying text.

58. See FRIEDA FROMM-REICHMAN, PRINCIPLES OF INTENSIVE PSYCHOTHERAPY 3-4 (1950); STEIN, *supra* note 25, at 4; WOLBERG, *supra* note 52, at 142; Richard Almond, *The Analytic Role: A Mediating Influence in the Interplay of Transference and Countertransference*, 43(2) J. AM. PSYCHOANALYTIC ASS'N 469, 471, 484 (1995); Gerber, *supra*

both to avoid impairment of the therapy,[59] as well as to use countertransference affirmatively in furthering the therapy's progress.[60] The literature abounds with case studies of therapists recognizing and wrestling with countertransference responses with varying degrees of success.[61] While there is debate about its utility, there is near universal acceptance that countertransference exists and that it is a force with which to contend. For effective psychotherapy, an understanding of countertransference must be both doctrinal and personal. Analysts-in-training, for example, both study the theory and then explore their own countertransference responses in their personal analysis and re-analysis.[62] Neither law students nor attorneys

note 31, at 117-18; Mitchell & Melikian, *supra* note 27, at 90-92 (in treating male sex offenders); Renik, *supra* note 25, at 554 (describing prevailing view); Saul, *supra* note 17; Segal, *supra* note 28, at 36; Jenny Smith, Coll Osman & Margaret Goding, *Reclaiming the Emotional Aspects of the Therapist-Family System*, 11(3) AUSTL. & N.Z. J. FAM. THERAPY 140, 146 (1990).

59. *See* FROMM-REICHMAN, *supra* note 58, at 198-99; LEON J. SAUL, PSYCHODYNAMICALLY BASED PSYCHOTHERAPY 329-30 (1972); Freud, *Nuremberg Congress Paper, supra* note 21, at 144-45; Kantrowitz, *supra* note 25, at 657; Hans W. Loewald, *Transference-countertransference*, 34 J. AM. PSYCHOANALYTIC ASS'N 275, 275 (1986); Pope, *supra* note 31, at 50; Kenneth S. Pope & Glen O. Gabbard, *Individual Psychotherapy for Victims of Therapist-Patient Sexual Intimacy, in* SEXUAL EXPLOITATION IN PROFESSIONAL RELATIONSHIPS 99 (Glen O. Gabbard ed., 1989); Annie Reich, *On Countertransference*, 32 INT. J. PSYCHOANAL. 25, 28 (1951); Reich, *supra* note 25, at 389, 392; Martin A. Silverman, *Countertransference and the Myth of the Perfectly Analyzed Analyst*, 54 PSYCHOANALYTIC Q. 175, 175-77 (1985); Stuart W. Twemlow & Glen O. Gabbard, *The Lovesick Therapist, in* SEXUAL EXPLOITATION IN PROFESSIONAL RELATIONSHIPS 86 (Glen O. Gabbard ed., 1989).

60. *See* GREGORY P. BAUER, THE ANALYSIS OF THE TRANSFERENCE IN THE HERE AND NOW 79 (1993); PETER L. GIOVACCHINI, 2 TACTICS AND TECHNIQUES IN PSYCHO-ANALYTIC THERAPY x (1975); Heimann, *supra* note 27, at 81, 83; Judy L. Kantrowitz, *The Beneficial Aspects of the Patient-Analyst Match*, 76 INT'L J. PSYCHO-ANALYSIS 299, 302 (1995); Kernberg, *supra* note 25, at 43; Loewald, *supra* note 59, at 282; Searles, *supra* note 17, at 180; Winnicott, *supra* note 18, at 351.

61. Case studies of avoiding its interference with the therapy: *see, e.g.,* Almond, *supra* note 58, at 484-86; Maxine Anderson, *The Need for the Patient to be Emotionally Known: The Search to Understand a Counter-Transference Dilemma*, 8(3) BRIT. J. PSYCHOTHERAPY 247 (1992); Silverman, *supra* note 59, at 181-97; Gertrude R. Ticho, *Cultural Aspects of Transference and Countertransference*, 35 BULL. MENNINGER CLINIC 313, 318-22 (September 1971); Tower, *supra* note 25, at 231. Case studies on its utility to advance the therapy: *see, e.g.,* Theodore Jacobs, *Posture, Gesture, and Movement in the Analyst: Cues to Interpretation and Transference*, 21 J. AMER. PSYCHOANAL. ASS'N 77, 90 (1973); Kantrowitz, *supra* note 60, at 303-07; Sandler, *supra* note 20, at 45-47.

62. *See* FROMM-REICHMAN, *supra* note 58, at 42; Pope & Gabbard, *supra* note 59, at 100; Reich, *supra* note 59, at 28. *But see* Twemlow & Gabbard, *supra* note 59, at 85

generally receive any such training, however, and thus they generally have no access to a structured protocol for addressing countertransference.

Countertransference, insufficiently understood, creates the danger of boundary violations, which both therapists and lawyers alike must avoid. Boundary violations are the crossing of the line between professional and client that defines the helping relationship within which they interact.[63] Sexual intercourse with a distraught and emotionally vulnerable patient or client is a relatively obvious example of such a boundary violation. Yet boundary violations certainly may occur even without sexual transgressions.[64] It is not sufficient merely to resist sexual impulses towards one's patient or client.[65] Harm to the relationship and consequent harm to the victim may happen without any physical or sexual component.[66] And liability may accompany that harm, even in the absence of sexual contact.[67]

("offenders were more likely than non-offenders to have undergone therapy or analysis").

63. *See* PETERSON, *supra* note 31, at 74-75:

Boundaries are the limits that allow for a safe connection based on the client's needs. When these limits are altered, what is allowed in the relationship becomes ambiguous. Such ambiguity is often experienced as an intrusion into the sphere of safety. The pain from a violation is frequently delayed, and the violation itself may not be recognized or felt until harmful consequences emerge.

64. *See* BISBING, JORGENSON & SUTHERLAND, *supra* note 17, at 461, 463-64; PETERSON, *supra* note 31, at 3; Carter Heyward, Book Review, *When Boundaries Betray Us: Beyond Illusions of What is Ethical in Therapy and Life, by Marie Fortune,* THE CHRISTIAN CENTURY, May 18, 1994, at 524; Hulme, *supra* note 35, at 185-86 (clergy-counselor); Twemlow & Gabbard, *supra* note 59, at 86.

65. *See* RUTTER, *supra* note 31, at 195; WATSON, INTERVIEWING AND COUNSELING, *supra* note 24, at 85.

66. See Zipkin v. Freeman, 436 S.W.2d 753 (Mo. 1968):

Once Dr. Freeman started to mishandle the transference phenomenon . . . it was inevitable that trouble was ahead. It is pretty clear from the medical evidence that the damage would have been done to Mrs. Zipkin even if the trips outside the state were carefully chaperoned, the swimming done with suits on, and if there had been ballroom dancing instead of sexual relations.

Id. at 761.

67. *See id.;* BISBING, JORGENSON & SUTHERLAND, *supra* note 17, at 1423 (citing *Zipkin*). Most malpractice is likely the product of shoddy or dishonest lawyering; boundary violations represent a different kind of malpractice, potentially less obvious as a transgression of one's fiduciary duty. That is, there is an inherent distinction between that which we must presume to be a *conscious* abuse of the lawyer's fiduciary duty, and that which may result from an unconscious succumbing to countertransference feelings. For therapists at least, there is no insurance coverage for boundary violations. BISBING, JORGENSON & SUTHERLAND, *supra* note 17, at 468 n.72 (quoting from Am. Psych. Assoc.-Sponsored Professional Liability Insurance Program, description of coverage). *See* New Mexico Physicians Mutual Liability Co. v. LaMure, 860 P.2d 734, 742 (N.M. 1993). *But see* St.

It may well be that such boundary violations are more likely to result in liability when the actor is a psychotherapist.[68] However, attorneys, too, are not without risk of incurring liability for boundary violations short of sexual relations.[69] Recent attempts to regulate sexual relations between lawyers and clients, however, fail to account for such other kinds of boundary violations.[70] Nonetheless, lawyers need to be sensitive to the possible crossing of boundaries *before* the fiduciary relationship is abridged.[71]

Avoidance of liability is certainly one reason why it is critical that we understand how our unconscious processes may impair our lawyering abilities. But malpractice liability and disciplinary sanctions need not be—indeed, they should not be—the major impetus. To strive to be the best lawyers we can be, we must learn to be self-aware and to develop the ability to critically analyze our participation in the lawyer/client relationship.

Paul Fire and Marine Insurance Co. v. Mitchell, 296 S.E.2d 126 (Ga. App. 1982) (psychiatrist's mishandling of transference by having sexual relations with client was within malpractice insurer's duty to defend, but genuine issues of material fact existed as to whether act constituted medical malpractice or intentional sexual assault).

68. *See* Zipkin v. Freeman, 436 S.W.2d 753 (Mo. 1968).

69. *See* Daigneault, *supra* note 44, at 15:

And what about the instance of non-sexual relationships between attorneys and their clients? If states are concerned that an attorney will become too emotionally involved, therefore prejudicing the client or the representation, then prohibiting only "sexual relations" does not completely address the problem in its entirety. Two adults are capable of engaging in a passionate relationship without engaging in physical intimacy. One might speculate as to how the states intend to prove that introducing sex into a relationship between the attorney and client is what places the professional representation at risk.

70. Arguably, therefore, they may be under-inclusive. *See* Daigneault, *supra* note 44, at 15. *See* also Langford, *supra* note 25, at 1240 (citing Jorgenson & Sutherland, *supra* note 33, at 478-79). They may be over-inclusive as well. *See* Mischler, *supra* note 32 (arguing against regulatory prohibitions on all attorney/client sexual liaisons).

71. Professor Lawrence Dubin's excellent video, WHAT WENT WRONG? CONVERSATIONS WITH DISCIPLINED LAWYERS (1985), exposes an example of another kind of boundary violation. One lawyer speaks of his emotional over-involvement with an emotionally unbalanced client who was a victim of rape. He allowed the client to use him as a round-the-clock confidant, social worker, as well as lawyer. He describes how he feared that this client—who had called him several times to take her to the hospital after suicide attempts—was too emotionally vulnerable to withstand either a criminal rape trial or civil litigation arising out of the rape. Thus he let the statute of limitations in both the criminal and civil cases pass without telling her so until it was too late. *See also* Gerald R. Williams, *Negotiation as a Healing Process*, 1996 J. DISP. RESOL. 1, 64 ("In addition to sexual violations, the most frequent boundary infractions are financial or emotional exploitation of clients.").

II. Confronting the Emotional Dimension in Lawyering

A. The Importance of Confronting Emotions in Lawyering

"Know thyself."[72] "The unexamined life is not worth living."[73] Much of the advice offered in the literature develops from these ancient and fundamental tenets.[74] In both our personal and professional lives, looking inward is necessary for self-actualization.[75] One cannot know whether a decision is rational or otherwise appropriate unless one looks within to examine the irrational forces bearing on that decision.[76] Lawyers must develop awareness of the unconscious behavioral traits and impulses that affect their interactions with clients[77] and others.[78]

---

72. Inscription at the Delphic Oracle, from PLUTARCH, MORALS *in* JOHN BARTLETT, FAMILIAR QUOTATIONS, 62 (15th ed. 1980).

73. Socrates *in* PLATO, APOLOGY, 38a, *in* THE OXFORD DICTIONARY OF QUOTATIONS 512 (3d ed. 1986).

74. *See, e.g.*, GOLEMAN, *supra* note 5, at 46; RACKER, *supra* note 20, at 20; WATSON, INTERVIEWING AND COUNSELING, *supra* note 24, at 24, 80; Andrew S. Watson, *The Lawyer as Counselor*, 5 J. FAM. L. 7, 18 (1965) ("In the last analysis, skillful interviewing is intimately related to self-awareness....It is jokingly said, that the principal barrier to self-analysis rests in the blindness of the analyst.").

75. Self-actualization, as defined by the founder of Humanistic Psychology Abraham Maslow, is the coming together of a person

in a particularly efficient and intensely enjoyable way...in which he is more integrated and less split, more open for experience, more...fully functioning, more creative,...more ego-transcending, more independent of his lower needs, etc. He becomes in these episodes more truly himself, more perfectly actualizing his potentialities, closer to the core of his Being, more fully human.

ABRAHAM H. MASLOW, TOWARDS A PSYCHOLOGY OF BEING 97 (2d ed. 1968).

76. *See* James R. Elkins, *The Legal Persona: An Essay on the Professional Mask*, 64 VA. L. REV. 735, 756-57 (1978) (quoting C.G. Schoenfeld, *Law and Unconscious Motivation*, 8 HOW. L. REV. 15, 25-26 (1962)).

77. *See* FREEMAN, *supra* note 6, at 7; MARK K. SCHOENFIELD & BARBARA PEARLMAN SCHOENFIELD, INTERVIEWING AND COUNSELING CLIENTS IN A LEGAL SETTING, 313, 325 (1977); Elkins, *supra* note 76, at 760-61; Robert S. Redmount, *Attorney Personalities and Some Psychological Aspects of Legal Consultation*, 109 U. PA. L. REV. 972, 985 (1961); Watson, *Lawyer as Counselor, supra* note 74, at 16.

78. *See, e.g.*, John Mixon & Robert P. Schuwerk, *The Personal Dimension of Professional Responsibility* 58 LAW & CONTEMP. PROBS. 87, 103 (1995):

[A]n otherwise mature lawyer who responds to authority figures with the patterns

Thus it would behoove lawyers to understand basic psychological concepts,[79] not so that we may become therapists[80] but so that we might be better legal counselors. We serve our clients best if we have emotional intelligence, if we are able to understand their fears, hopes and dreams. In fact, whether we undertake the task consciously or otherwise, when we counsel our clients we are dealing with their psyches.[81] The Good Lawyer must be accountable for this responsibility.[82]

Furthermore, to avoid boundary violations, lawyers must acknowledge that emotional responses are triggered in virtually every human encounter.

---

of response used in relating to a father, mother, or sibling (with, for example, belligerence, anger, excessive submissiveness, or passive aggressiveness) cannot deal effectively with judges, police, senior partners or opposing lawyers.
See also WATSON, INTERVIEWING AND COUNSELING, *supra* note 24, at 147 (among members of law firm).

79. *See* ROBERT M. BASTRESS & JOSEPH D. HARBAUGH, INTERVIEWING, COUNSELING, AND NEGOTIATING 19 (1990); WATSON, INTERVIEWING AND COUNSELING, *supra* note 24, at 11, 26. The body of scholarship known as "Therapeutic Jurisprudence" argues for bringing social science in general, and psychology in particular, to bear on both our system of laws and the individual practice of law, so as to maximize therapeutic and minimize anti-therapeutic consequences. *See, e.g.*, David B. Wexler, *New Directions in Therapeutic Jurisprudence: Breaking the Bounds of Conventional Mental Health Law Scholarship*, 10 N.Y. L. SCH. J. HUM. RTS. 759, 759-62 (1993); David B. Wexler, *Reflections on the Scope of Therapeutic Jurisprudence*, 1 PSYCHOL. PUBL. POL'Y & L. 220, 231 (1995).

80. *See* BASTRESS & HARBAUGH, *supra* note 79, at 20-21; FREEMAN, *supra* note 6, at 7, 51; WATSON, INTERVIEWING AND COUNSELING, *supra* note 24, at 11; James R. Elkins, *A Counseling Model for Lawyering in Divorce Cases*, 53 NOTRE DAME LAW. 229, 264 (1977-78); Shaffer, *supra* note 23, at 237. In fact, the lawyer as counselor is engaged in a distinctly different task than the therapist as counselor; nonetheless there is much that the lawyer may learn from the therapist regarding technique, skills and attitudes. *See* Hugh Brayne, *Counselling Skills for the Lawyer: Can Lawyers Learn Anything from Counsellors?*, 32 THE LAW TEACHER 137 (1998).

81. *See* BASTRESS & HARBAUGH, *supra* note 79, at 25; FREEMAN, *supra* note 6, at 49-52; WATSON, INTERVIEWING AND COUNSELING, *supra* note 24, at 149; WATSON, PSYCHIATRY FOR LAWYERS, *supra* note 24, at 9; Harriet F. Pilpel, *The Job Lawyers Shirk*, 220 HARPERS 67, 70 (1960) ("[W]e are virtually the only profession dealing with people that makes no attempt to learn anything about them.").

82. In addition to helping a lawyer understand and deal with transference and countertransference in the lawyer/client relationship, an understanding of psychological principles will help a lawyer in interviewing and fact-gathering. *See* BASTRESS & HARBAUGH, *supra* note 79, at 26; WATSON, PSYCHIATRY FOR LAWYERS, *supra* note 24, at 11. It also will enable a lawyer to determine when to refer a client to a professional in another field, such as a psychotherapist. FREEMAN, *supra* note 6, at 232-33; WATSON, INTERVIEWING AND COUNSELING, *supra* note 24, at 149.

The goal need not be—indeed could not be—to eradicate these responses. Rather the goal should be to recognize them, analyze how, if at all, they may affect the lawyer/client relationship, and resolve them appropriately.[83] Therefore the lawyer must understand the dynamics of transference and countertransference in lawyer/client relationships. Whether or not we so acknowledge, our unconscious exerts powerful force on our thoughts and actions.[84] Of course not all acting up of the unconscious and not all emotional reactions are problematic. But acceptance that they *might* be problematic is an essential first step in recognizing the situations in which they may impair the representation, and identifying means to avoid such impairment.[85]

It seems likely, for example, that for every lawyer who succumbs to a sexual liaison with a client, a hundred are tempted but resist. Imagine such a lawyer, and observe where countertransference might cause problems:

Love Countertransference

Adam is a 50 year-old lawyer with a mainly criminal law practice and a solid reputation as an ethical, competent and thorough attorney. Belle seeks representation for a felony drug charge. She is young, lovely, and treats Adam with awe. Adam finds himself strongly attracted to her. He looks forward to their meetings. It comes to pass that the prosecutor offers Belle

---

83. *See* Watson, *supra* note 32, at 268 ("While the conflicts will arise regardless of how they are handled, the way they are normally resolved when not understood is to banish them from awareness through one of the psychological defense mechanisms."). Peterson notes the relevance of this insight to all of the helping professions:

We also relate to professionals out of our childhood experiences with authority figures. If we were abused in our family, we may be careful not to question the professional. If we were neglected, we may hunger after a warm and sympathetic ear. If we fought our parents for control, we may respond combatively and battle the professional for the power. If the professional does not understand the origin of our presumptive response, has no limits, or is frightened of our anger, he or she may inadvertently feed our paranoia or encourage the negative ways we express our entitlement.

PETERSON, *supra* note 31, at 39.

84. *See* FREEMAN, *supra* note 6, at 50; WATSON, INTERVIEWING AND COUNSELING, *supra* note 24, at 93; David B. Saxe & Seymour F. Kuvin, Note*s on the Attorney-Client Relationship*, 2 J. PSYCHIATRY & L. 209, 209-10 (1974); Watson, *supra* note 74, at 11.

85. *See* PETERSON, *supra* note 31, at 40-41; SCHOENFIELD & SCHOENFIELD, *supra* note 77, at 315; Shaffer, *supra* note 23, at 214, 236. For the importance of understanding unconscious processes in order to avoid such impairment in negotiations, see Melissa L. Nelken, *Negotiation and Psychoanalysis: If I'd Wanted to Learn About Feelings, I Wouldn't Have Gone to Law School*, 46 J. LEGAL EDUC. 420, 423 (1996).

a plea deal. Adam discusses the deal with Belle, but for some reason does not push it very hard (as he might with other clients). Belle denies her guilt to him. Adam believes her. He tells her that if she is innocent, then they should go to trial. Placing her trust in his advice, she agrees. They go to trial. Belle is convicted and sentenced to twice the time she would have served had she accepted the deal the prosecutor offered.

Hate Countertransference

Now imagine Adam with a different client, Carl. Carl shares two characteristics with Belle. He is the same age, and has also been arrested on a felony drug charge (no relationship to Belle's alleged offense). Carl has a strong effeminate affect. Adam finds Carl annoying and obsequious, and dreads their encounters. Despite Carl's claim of innocence—Carl says he was framed by a neighborhood miscreant who threatened "I'm gonna get you, faggot"—Adam pushes the deal offered by the prosecution. Carl begins to cry. This annoys the hell out of Adam, who yells at the young man for crying and tells him to "grow up and act like a man." Carl, cowed, agrees to the plea. Now both of these scenarios might profitably be analyzed in terms of lawyer ethics and professional responsibility. Did Adam provide competent representation?[86] Did Adam adequately investigate the charges against Belle and Carl before rejecting or pushing the plea deals offered by the prosecution in their respective cases?[87] Should he be accountable for these actions? What if Carl was in fact innocent? However, the question with which we are here concerned is *why* Adam acted so differently in the two situations. If Adam did breach his professional responsibilities in these cases, what is the explanation?

It might be useful to know more about Adam. He has been married to the same woman for twenty years. His marriage has reached the comfort and complacency of its middle years. Also, Adam has a twelve-year-old son who cries easily when his feelings are hurt. If we knew something about countertransference, we might be able to proffer a good guess as to why Adam behaved in these situations as he did.[88] And if Adam acquired

---

86. *See* AMERICAN BAR ASSOCIATION, MODEL RULES OF PROFESSIONAL CONDUCT, Rule 1.1 (1983).

87. *See id. See also* AMERICAN BAR ASSOCIATION, STANDARDS RELATING TO THE ADMINISTRATION OF CRIMINAL JUSTICE, Ch. 4, *The Defense Function*, 4-4.1 (Duty to Investigate) (1992).

88. *Cf.* T.P. Hackett, *Which Patients Turn You Off? It's Worth Analyzing*, 46(15) MED. ECON. 94, 96 (1969):

A doctor who remains oblivious of his bias may not only be less able to help a patient, but may literally hurt him. For instance, I recall the surgery instructor who taught us how to use a sigmoidoscope. He was a burly guy who still looked like the

a degree of self-awareness, he might know as well, and perhaps avoid such aberrant behaviors.[89]

B. Resistance to Emotional Awareness

Most of us have difficulty acknowledging the influence of the unconscious in our daily lives.[90] Inappropriate emotional responses may befall any professional in a caring relationship with someone over whom he has power.[91] Among the helping professions, lawyers tend to be especially resistant to acknowledging the power of the unconscious.[92]

The genesis of this Article grew out of that resistance. I teach Professional Responsibility, a required upper-level course at Touro College Law Center. Several years ago, in one particular class, we were examining regulation of sexual relations between attorneys and clients. We were discussing ABA formal opinion 92-364 and its reasoning as to how sexual relations between lawyers and clients may cause attorneys to violate their fiduciary responsibilities.[93] A question popped into my head that I tossed out to the students: "What if an attorney has strong amorous feelings

---

football player he'd been in college. I observed — as did other interns — that when he performed sigmoidoscopies on effeminate men, he would never use enough lubricant, thus causing them considerable and unnecessary pain. I give him the benefit of the doubt and say he was unaware of what he was doing. He made no derisive comments about such men, but what he did to them spoke the true feelings he couldn't acknowledge: He needlessly hurt them. It wasn't malpractice, but it was not good medicine.

89. *See infra* text at notes 217-35.

90. *See* Freud, *Fifth Lecture, supra* note 15, at 52:

We must, I think, take into account two special obstacles to recognizing psychoanalytic trains of thought. In the first place, people are unaccustomed to reckoning with a strict and universal application of determinism to mental life; and in the second place, they are ignorant of the peculiarities which distinguish unconscious mental processes from the conscious ones that are familiar to us.

91. Problems that befall lawyers also befall medical practitioners. *See* STEIN, *supra* note 25, at 38, 47, 68, 184, *passim*; G.L. Bibring, *Psychiatry and Medical Practice in a General Hospital*, 254 N. ENGL. J. MED. 366 (1956); James E. Groves, *Taking Care of the Hateful Patient*, 298 NEW ENG. J. MED. 883 (1978); Hackett, *supra* note 88; Solomon Papper, *The Undesirable Patient*, 22 J. CHRONIC DISEASES 777, 779 (1970); KATHY ZOPPI, *Sexuality in the Patient-Physician Relationship*, 268 JAMA 3142, 3142, 3146 (1992).

92. *See* Charles Lawrence, *The Id, the Ego, and Equal Protection: Reckoning with Unconscious Racism*, 39 STAN. L. REV. 317, 329 (1987) (denial of unconscious and irrational as underpinning of legal system).

93. *See supra* note 8.

towards a client but refrains from acting on them? Might that not muck up the competency of the representation, even without physical consummation?" The reaction of the class was swift and strong. "1984!," exclaimed one student. "Thought police!," cried another.[94]

This led me to contemplate lawyers' intolerance for believing in the power of emotions, as well as our inherent antipathy towards crediting psychic influences on how we perform our craft. There are a number of possible explanations for the scope and intensity of this resistance. First, the psychological profile of the typical law student or lawyer is of one who is drawn to logical thinking and rationality.[95] Studies using the Myers-Briggs personality indicators[96] have found that the great majority of high-functioning law students and lawyers are "thinkers" rather than "feelers."[97]

---

94. *See* Daigneault, *supra* note 44, at 15:

And what about the instance of non-sexual relationships between attorneys and their clients? If states are concerned that an attorney will become too emotionally involved, therefore prejudicing the client or the representation, then prohibiting only "sexual relations" does not completely address the problem in its entirety. Two adults are capable of engaging in a passionate relationship without engaging in physical intimacy. One might speculate as to how the states intend to prove that introducing sex into a relationship between the attorney and client is what places the professional representation at risk.

95. *See* Watson, *supra* note 74, at 9; Andrew S. Watson, *The Quest for Professional Competence: Psychological Aspects of Legal Education*, 37 U. Cin. L. Rev. 91, 101-02 (1968).

96. For a discussion of the Myers-Briggs assessment tool, see *supra* note 7.

97. *See* Susan Daicoff, *Lawyer, Know Thyself: A Review of Empirical Research on Attorney Attributes Bearing on Professionalism*, 46 Am. U. L. Rev. 1337, 1361-62 (1997) (describing studies indicating that "lawyers who are more objective, rational, and logical in decision-making style were the most satisfied"); *id.* at 1365-66, 1392-93 (describing studies showing that law students and lawyers differ from general population by "marked preference for Thinking over Feeling," and that this "has remained a constant over time, independent of gender influences"); Deborah Cassens Moss, *Lawyer Personality*, A.B.A. J. 34 (Feb. 1991) ("The truly happy lawyers tend to be logical, dispassionate problem solvers."); Paul Van R. Miller, *Personality Differences and Student Survival in Law School*, 19 J. Legal Educ. 460, 463-65 (1967):

A &elip; basic difference&elip;arises from the existence of two distinct and sharply contrasting ways of coming to conclusions. One way is by the use of *thinking*, which is a logical process, aimed at an impersonal finding. The other way is by the use of *feeling*, which is the process of appreciation, equally reasonable in its fashion, bestowing on things a personal, subjective value.

Id. at 463 (quoting Isabel B. Myers, The Myers-Briggs Type Indicator 52 (Princeton, N.J.: Educational Testing Service, 1962). For a discussion of the Myers-Briggs dichotomy, see *supra* note 7.

Such thinkers tend to devalue emotional responses.[98] This is then reinforced throughout traditional legal education by means such as the Socratic Method,[99] and its emphasis on the Rule of Reason.[100] In most traditional law school classes, students who proffer their "feelings" about a legal principle or outcome—without supporting such feelings with "rational" arguments—risk facing condescension, if not outright ridicule, from professors and peers alike.[101] Upon graduation and admission to the bar, most lawyers

---

98. *See* Daicoff, *supra* note 97, at 1372-73; Amiram Elwork & G. Andrew H. Benjamin, *Lawyers in Distress, in* DAVID B. WEXLER & BRUCE J. WINICK, LAW IN A THERAPEUTIC KEY: DEVELOPMENTS IN THERAPEUTIC JURISPRUDENCE 569, 574-76 (1996).

99. *See* Bernard L. Diamond, *Psychological Problems of Law Students, in* LOOKING AT LAW SCHOOL 69-70 (Stephen Gillers ed., 4th ed. 1997):

> Certainly, if Anna Freud's principle of identification with the aggressor holds as true for the educational process as it does for the developmental process of the child, the Socratic method must provide the major source of the lawyer's notorious insensitivity to the fine points of human emotional relationships. The Socratic method is a marvelous device for the emphasis of the purely logical, abstract essence of the appellate case. The deductive precision of such Socratic dialogue can further the illusion, claimed by Langdell, that law is a true science.

The process described in the text has a disproportionate impact on women. *See* LANI GUINIER, MICHELLE FINE & JANE BALIN, BECOMING GENTLEMEN: WOMEN, LAW SCHOOL, AND INSTITUTIONAL CHANGE 66-67 (1997) ("The way things are done in law school (the Socratic method, time issue-spotting exams, large classrooms, unpatrolled and informal networks) devalues and distorts those characteristics associated with women, such as empathy, relational logic, and nonaggressive behavior."). The Socratic method is also used to teach psychiatrists. WATSON, PSYCHIATRY FOR LAWYERS, *supra* note 24, at xix (preface to 1968 edition).

100. *See* Mixon & Schuwerk, *supra* note 78, at 95; Watson, *supra* note 74, at 11; Andrew S. Watson, *Some Psychological Aspects of Teaching Professional Responsibility*, 16 J. LEGAL EDUC. 1, 12-13 (1963):

> The anxiety-muting defensive maneuvers, instead of settling on the specific stress situations of the classroom, will be generalized progressively to block emotional awareness. Many law students will progressively surround themselves with a suit of psychological armor that makes them more and more impervious to the emotional aspects of most, if not all, situations.

See also Eleanor M. Fox, *The Good Law School, The Good Curriculum, and the Mind and the Heart*, 39 J. LEGAL EDUC. 473 (1989):

> From the nineteenth century, law school faculties have tended to favor mind over heart, except for the 1960's, when we sacrificed mind to heart. We have tended to ignore the student as whole human being. A change may be on the horizon. For the 1990's, there is a call for interrelatedness, for experience-based talking and listening, and for a new sensitivity.

Id. at 482.

101. *See* Paul N. Savoy, *Toward a New Politics of Legal Education*, 79 YALE L.J. 444, 461-62 (1970):

may find little if anything in daily practice that validates or rewards emotion rather than reason.[102]

Thus the disposition with which the average student enters the study of law, the training received in law school, and the reinforcement that comes with practice, all contribute to lawyers' inclinations to deny the power or influence of their emotions. Lawyers, therefore, are likely more resistant than professionals in other fields (doctors,[103] teachers, pastors) to acknowledge the force of the unconscious on the decisions they make or to recognize countertransference reactions they visit on their clients.

Such repression of emotions takes its toll.[104] It is no secret that the practice of law can be extremely stressful.[105] The quantity of work, the pressure from clients, the high stakes involved, the worry over making

---

The trouble with our existing forms of education is that they are anchored to a dualistic vision of man that forces the splitting and polarization of "intellect" and "feeling," of "mind" and "body." To be rational, to control yourself, to be objective and uninvolved, is good. To be irrational, to lose your head, to be subjective and emotionally involved, is bad.

* * *

Neither the legal tradition nor the liberal temperament, which feeds a large part of contemporary legal theory, has ever been very hospitable to the life of feeling. Daicoff, *supra* note 97, at 1381 (law school exacerbates Thinking over Feeling tendencies, resulting in emotional distress); *id.* at 1405 (citing study concluding that Feelers are often criticized for being overly sentimental); Robert S. Redmount, *Humanistic Law Through Education*, 1 Conn. L. Rev. 201, 203 (1968) ("The student's more natural and untutored sensitivities to facts and to the psychology of experience are blunted rather than developed. His regard for such matters as the human consequences of law may be deemed irrelevant unless it fits the narrower institutional framework of rights and wrongs as determined by law and equity.").

102. *See* Daicoff, *supra* note 97, at 1405 (citing study concluding that adversarial mentality wears on lawyers who are Feelers); Schoenfield & Schoenfield, *supra* note 77, at 325; Watson, Psychiatry for Lawyers, *supra* note 24, at 3. Shaffer & Elkins suggest that emotions are generally given no thought in professional relationships outside of therapy. Thomas L. Shaffer & James R. Elkins, Legal Interviewing & Counseling 56 (3d ed. 1997). "In the world of feeling, a lawyer has no more expertise or knowledge than the client." *Id.* at 60. *But see* Carrie Menkel-Meadow, *Portia Redux: Another Look at Gender, Feminism, and Legal Ethics*, 2 Va J. Soc. Pol'y & L. 75 (1989) (describing studies and literature supporting theory that women bring ethic of care to legal practice which is responsive to clients' needs, including emotional needs).

103. *But see* Stein, *supra* note 25, at 36-37 (suggesting reasons why physicians resist acknowledging countertransference responses to patients).

104. Professor Daicoff describes studies demonstrating that "more of the Feeling law students dropped out of law school than did the Thinking types, suggesting that Feeling may be more incompatible with the study of law, and suggesting that attorneys who preferred Feeling were less likely to be content in law practice." Daicoff, *supra* note 97, at 1366 n.149.

105. A 1990 study found that attorneys experienced depression at a higher rate than

payroll, all contribute to this stress. Added to these real-life, tangible pressures is the moral conflict that arises over the value of the lawyer's work.[106] The need to make decisions based on reason and role and to deny emotional conflict eats away at the attorney.[107] Commentators have noted that the inattention to interpersonal skills in law school contributes to the impairment of psychological well-being among law students and lawyers.[108] This undoubtedly contributes to the high rate of substance abuse and clinical depression among lawyers.[109] It likely also

---

any of 104 other occupations studied. Arleen Jacobius, *Coming Back From Depression*, A.B.A. J. 74 (April 1996). *See also* G. Andrew H. Benjamin & Bruce D. Sales, *Lawyer Psychopathology: Development, Prevalence, and Intervention*, in JAMES R.P. OGLOFF, LAW AND PSYCHOLOGY: THE BROADENING OF THE DISCIPLINE 281 (1992); Ellen I. Carni, *Stress and Productivity: For Better or Worse*, N.Y.L.J., Nov. 26, 1996, at 5, col. 1 (citing studies finding that U.S. lawyers suffer from clinical depression twice as often as general population).

106. *See* Watson, *supra* note 74, at 14:

The legal counselor in his professional operations, has from the offset a potentially difficult problem in that he must serve the best interests of his client, and at the same time maintain his responsibility to the bar. Thus he serves two masters who may have different goals and thus places him in the psychologically difficult position of balancing and judging the merits and relationships between these competing claims. I do not suggest that this is inappropriate or undesirable, but merely wish to point out that if one were to contrive a psychological situation which would produce great stress and anxiety, this set of circumstances could hardly be improved upon.

See also Amiram Elwork, *From Stress and Depression to Contentment: Psychology Can Change Your Life*, 13 COMPLEAT LAW. 54, 54-55 (1996) ("[M]any lawyers are…conflicted about their roles in society. Their duty to zealously promote their clients' special interests creates hostility directed toward them by the general public and reduces their own sense of self-esteem.").

107. *See* Daicoff, *supra* note 97, at 1401-02 (describing study suggesting that "submerging or denying one's care orientation and adopting a rights orientation in order to 'fit in' may result in psychological discomfort").

108. *See* Benjamin & Sales, *supra* note 105, at 289-90. "Conventional legal education that concentrates on the development of analytic skills while ignoring interpersonal development may increase distress levels and prevent the alleviation of symptoms." *Id.*

109. *See id.* at 296 (noting that one-third of practicing lawyers at any given time are likely suffering from depression, alcohol or drug addiction); Deborah Brooke, *Impairment in the Medical and Legal Professions*, 43 J. PSYCHOSOMATIC RES. 27, 27-29 (1997); Susan Daicoff, *Asking Leopards to Change Their Spots: Should Lawyers Change? A Critique of Solutions to Problems with Professionalism by Reference to Empirically-Derived Attorney Personality Attributes*, 11 GEO. J. LEGAL ETHICS 547, 555-57 (1998) (summarizing studies demonstrating high incidence of depression, alcoholism and other psychological problems among lawyers); Susan Daicoff, *Making the Practice of Law Therapeutic*

helps explain why so many lawyers are discontented with the practice of law.[110]

Lawyers' resistance to acknowledging the power of their emotional lives may help explain something else as well. There appears to be little awareness within our profession of the writings of those who have urged previous generations of lawyers, legal educators and law students to learn about basic psychology and the operation of unconscious processes in the practice of law.[111] The next section will examine that literature.

C. Writings on Lawyering and Emotional Intelligence, 1930 to the Present

Jerome Frank's *Law and the Modern Mind*, published in 1930, was perhaps the first important American work to incorporate Freud's teach-

---

for Lawyers: Lawyer Distress & Lawyering 2000 (presentation at the AALS Annual Meeting, New Orleans, LA, January 9, 1999) (graphs demonstrating disproportionate incidence of alcoholism, depression and other psychological distress among lawyers as compared to the general population). *See also* Carl Anderson, Thomas G. McCracken & Betty Reddy, *Addictive Illness in the Legal Profession: Bar Examiners' Dilemma*, 7 PROF. LAW. 16, 18 (1996):

> According to the "Report of the AALS Special Committee on Problems of Substance Abuse in the Law School" (1994), the Law Student Survey showed significantly higher usage rates by law students of alcohol and drugs, such as tranquilizers, barbiturates and marijuana, for each of three periods (lifetime, past years and past months) than by the high school or college graduates who also were surveyed.

110. *See* ABA SEC. LEGAL EDUC. & ADMISSIONS TO THE BAR, LEGAL EDUCATION AND PROFESSIONAL DEVELOPMENT—AN EDUCATIONAL CONTINUUM: REPORT OF THE TASK FORCE ON LAW SCHOOLS AND THE PROFESSION: NARROWING THE GAP 220-21 (1992) (*hereinafter* "MACCRATE") (citing numerous bar association studies documenting significant job dissatisfaction among attorneys); Moss, *supra* note 97, at 34 (noting high incidence of dissatisfaction with practice of law, especially by women); Daicoff, *Asking Leopards, supra* note 109, at 3-4 (summarizing studies demonstrating rise in lawyer dissatisfaction); Daicoff, *Lawyering 2000, supra* note 109 (charts demonstrating lawyer dissatisfaction). *See also* Debra Baker, *Cash-and-Carry Asociates*, A.B.A. J. 40-44 (May 1999) (describing large number of associates cashing out after a few years due in significant part to dissatisfaction with grueling schedules and lack of training and mentors).

111. I count myself as one among the ignorant majority. Before I began my research, I was unaware that anyone had thought or written about countertransference in the lawyer/client relationship, and I was certainly surprised at the extent of such literature. However, my former colleague, Michael Perlin, who has a much better memory than I, insists we once discussed the subject around the faculty lunchtable at New York Law School in 1986 or 1987.

ings into legal jurisprudence.[112] Judge Frank recommended that judges receive training in psychology so as to better understand not only the motivations of others, but their own less conscious tendencies:

> [T]he judge should be not a mere thinking-machine but well trained, not only in rules of law, but also in the best available methods of psychology. And among the most important objects which would be subject to his scrutiny as a psychologist would be his own personality so that he might become keenly aware of his own prejudices, biases, antipathies, and the like, not only in connection with attitudes political, economic and moral, but with respect to more minute and less easily discoverable preferences and disinclinations.[113]

Frank fostered a school of legal realists who explored psychological aspects of jurisprudence.[114] In 1953, Judge Frank participated in a symposium in the Ohio State Law Journal on Psychology and Law.[115] In his foreword to that symposium, Professor Warren Hill wrote:

> It is small wonder...that [Freud's] formulations and insights which have so drastically altered thinking in other significant social disciplines have begun to seep through the conservative barriers of the legal profession, which, preeminently, has always concerned itself with attempting to understand and control human behavior through the use of various sanctions and rewards.[116]

The relevance of such theory to skills training was noted by Dean Erwin Griswold, formerly dean of the Harvard Law School. In a 1955 speech delivered in St. Louis, Missouri, Dean Griswold called upon the bar and the legal academy to recognize the need for human relations training in law school.[117] Dean Griswold urged lawyers to study social science liter-

---

112. Jerome Frank, The "Conceptual" Nature of Psychological Explanations, in LAW AND THE MODERN MIND 356-61 (2d printing 1930). In 1943, Harold Lasswell and Myres McDougal had a vision of introducing the social sciences into legal education, at least at Yale. The revolution never came, and the experiment was pronounced a failure. See Fox, supra note 100, at 476.

113. Frank, supra note 112, at 147 n.*.

114. See James A. Elkins, A Humanistic Perspective in Legal Education, 62 NEB. L. REV. 494, 505 n.45 (1983).

115. Jerome N. Frank, Judicial Fact-Finding and Psychology, 14 OHIO ST. L.J. 183 (1953).

116. Warren P. Hill, Foreword, 14 OHIO ST. L.J. 2, 117-18 (1953).

117. Erwin N. Griswold, Law Schools and Human Relations, 37 CHI. B. RECORD 199, 201 (1956).

ature on human relations.[118] Noting that the average lawyer spent far more time interacting with people than reading and arguing appellate cases, Dean Griswold argued that such training might help lawyers understand their clients' emotional needs, and keep their own in check.[119]

Dean Griswold's speech inspired Professor Howard Sacks, now Professor Emeritus at the University of Connecticut School of Law, to offer an experimental human relations course at Northwestern Law School during the 1957-58 school year.[120] The course, entitled Professional Relations, was apparently the first course at any law school to endeavor to apply human relations training to lawyers.[121] The experience persuaded Professor Sacks that further experimentation should continue.[122]

Professor Andrew Watson, a psychiatrist who later held a joint appointment at the University of Michigan law and medical schools, participated in a similar experiment first at the University of Pennsylvania, and later at Michigan.[123] In his endeavors to bridge the gap between psychiatry and the practice of law, Watson published numerous articles[124] and two books[125] for a legal audience over a twenty-year period commencing in 1958. His work explored the clinical application of psychotherapeutic insights to legal education and the practice of law.[126] Watson repeatedly urged legal edu-

---

118. *Id.* at 202-04.

119. *Id.* at 203-04.

120. Howard R. Sacks, *Human Relations Training for Students and Lawyers*, 11 J. LEGAL EDUC. 316, 317 (1959).

121. *Id.* at 321 n.13.

122. *Id.* at 321. The course, offered without credit, was given for a total of eight hours in two-hour sessions over the span of two weeks. *Id.* at 322. Professor Sacks expressed the hope that other law teachers would join in the experiment, both in offering stand-alone courses such as Professional Relations and in integrating human relations training into the regular curriculum. *Id.* at 343.

123. Andrew S. Watson, *The Law and Behavioral Science Project at the University of Pennsylvania: A Psychiatrist on the Law Faculty*, 11 J. LEGAL EDUC. 73 (1958); Andrew S. Watson, *Teaching Mental Health Concepts in the Law School*, 33 AM. J. ORTHOPSYCH. 115, 120 (1963).

124. Watson, *Law and Behavioral Science Project, supra* note 123; Watson, *Teaching Mental Health Concepts, supra* note 123; Watson, *supra* note 100, at 1; Watson, *supra* note 74, at 7; Watson, *supra* note 95, at 91; Watson, *supra* note 32, at 248, 265-78.

125. WATSON, INTERVIEWING AND COUNSELING, *supra* note 24; WATSON, PSYCHIATRY FOR LAWYERS, *supra* note 24.

126. Professor Watson wrote extensively about transference and countertransference in the lawyering process. *See, e.g.,* WATSON, INTERVIEWING AND COUNSELING, *supra* note 24, at 23-26, 146-53; WATSON, PSYCHIATRY FOR LAWYERS, *supra* note 24, at 8-11.

cators to incorporate exposure to basic psychiatric tenets, including countertransference, into mainstream legal education.[127]

In 1964, Harrop Freeman, a Cornell law professor, published the first coursebook devoted to the techniques and psychology of interviewing and counseling clients.[128] In a preface to the book, Dean Griswold praised the work for recognizing the importance of cultivating interpersonal skills for the effective practice of law.[129] Dean Griswold opined that by seeking to fill a void in legal education—a field devoted until then almost entirely to the Langdellian case method—Freeman's contribution was "almost as much a pioneering book as was Dean Langdell's Cases on Contracts."[130] In addition to introducing students to the psychological aspects of the lawyering skills of interviewing and counseling, the book contained numerous case studies exploring transference and countertransference in actual lawyer/client interactions.[131]

Another important contributor to the field was Alan Stone, Professor of Law and Psychiatry at Harvard University.[132] In a 1971 law review article, Professor Stone lamented that sixteen years had passed since Dean Griswold had made his oft-cited declaration that legal education neglected human relations training. "In spite of Dean Griswold's enthusiasm," Professor Stone wrote, "law schools &elip; have largely ignored the responsibility of teaching interviewing, counseling, negotiating, and other human relations skills, and Harrop Freeman's work has not generated a new Langdellian dynasty."[133] Professor Stone noted some attempts (such as

---

127. WATSON, INTERVIEWING AND COUNSELING, *supra* note 24, at 81-82; WATSON, PSYCHIATRY FOR LAWYERS, *supra* note 24, at 14; Watson, *Law and Behavioral Science Project, supra* note 123, at 74-75; Watson, *supra* note 32, at 265-78; Watson, *supra* note 100, at 16-20.

128. FREEMAN, *supra* note 6. Although not technically a *case*book—at least not in the traditional sense of the word—the book was published as part of West Publishing Co.'s American Casebook Series.

129. *Id.* at ix.

130. *Id.* at x.

131. *Id.* at 59-229.

132. ALAN STONE, LAW, PSYCHIATRY, AND MORALITY 199 (1984); Alan Stone, *Legal Education on the Couch*, 85 HARV. L. REV. 392 (1971).

133. Stone, *Legal Education, supra* note 132, at 428. Professor Stone notes the limitation of the Freeman book's case studies:

Cases like those collected by Professor Freeman do have some utility, but often they neither have the psychological depth nor the complexity that allows for rigorous analysis; nor do they involve the student personally in a way which permits the psychological elements to come to life and be comprehended at the level of emotionally significant learning.

those by Professor Watson) to introduce law students to psychoanalytic theory and the emotional dimensions of lawyering.[134]

A 1970 law review article by Professor Thomas Shaffer of Notre Dame Law School appears to have been the first to use transference/counter-transference theory to inform legal doctrine rather than legal technique.[135] The article made several important contributions. It provided a detailed overview of psychoanalytic literature on transference and displacement as manifest in the lawyer/client relationship.[136] It suggested how transference could cause a grateful patient or client to leave a generous bequest to the helping professional, and offered a framework for how a court might decide whether such transference constitutes undue influence.[137] Additionally, noting Dr. Watson's then recently published work, *Psychiatry for Lawyers*, it cautioned attorneys to recognize that transference (or countertransference) may occur in their relationships to their clients.[138]

Id. at 429. Professor Stone discusses the relevance of the work of Carl Rogers—"one of the leading figures in the area of psychological counseling"—on "congruence" to lawyering skills. *Id.* at 433-34. As explained by Stone:

> Rogers' concept of "congruence" involves an attempt by the interviewer to experience the feelings of the moment, to attain an awareness of the flux of emotional responses that ordinarily are dampened or go on outside the scope of attention, and to be willing and able to express these feelings to the client. . . . Rogers does not assume that this always, or even ever, is completely achieved, but it is a goal toward which the interviewer strives. It is the emotional compass which guides him in his counseling behavior. If congruence were adopted as a goal by the new generation of lawyers, it would obviously imply a totally new professional demeanor which would have as its most salient feature the encouragement of human intimacy.

Id. at 434.

134. "A number of techniques have been introduced at law schools to meet the need. These range all the way from course work entirely devoted to psychoanalytic theory and legal counseling to innovations which are directed at making law students more sensitive to emotional issues. The latter, more recent innovations, seem to be aimed at providing the future lawyer with some insight into his own emotional reactions. . . . Over the past few years a number of enterprising professors of law have adapted these group experiences [used by Watson in large criminal law classes] for small second and third-year elective courses." *Id.* at 436-37. For a review of Law & Psychiatry courses at American law schools as of 1965, see John M. Suarez, *Reciprocal Education—A Key to the Psychiatrico-Legal Dilemma*, 17 J. LEGAL EDUC. 316 (1965).

135. Shaffer, *supra* note 23, at 197.

136. *Id.* at 204-18.

137. *Id.* at 218-35.

138. "Annoyance or impatience or anxiety in the lawyer…affects his clients far more than he realizes." *Id.* at 235-36. *See supra* note 125.

In 1976, Professor Shaffer published *Legal Interviewing and Counseling in a NutShell*, part of the West Publishing nutshell series.[139] Unlike most nutshells, however, the material in this work *supplemented*, rather than summarized, available texts. In a subchapter entitled "Dependence," Professor Shaffer wrote extensively about transference, referencing the work of Freud, Jung, Rogers and others.[140] Interestingly, the word "countertransference" does not appear in these original materials.[141] Professor Shaffer, together with Professor James Elkins of the West Virginia University College of Law, revised these materials twice: once in 1987[142] and again in 1997.[143] These later editions each contained a separate section on countertransference.[144]

In addition to co-authoring the nutshell, Professor Elkins made several other contributions to the literature in which he advocated training in human relations and specifically noted problems of transference and countertransference.[145] Professor Elkins discussed the importance of self-awareness and insight for the practicing attorney, arguing that "[t]hrough self-study, the lawyer achieves a greater awareness of unconscious behavioral traits that affect interactions with clients."[146] In an article on counseling in divorce cases, Professor Elkins cautioned attorneys to be aware of inappropriate emotional responses on the part of both attorney and client, and made suggestions for resolving such problems.[147]

In a 1983 law review article, Professor Elkins argued for the revitalization of a humanistic perspective in legal education.[148] He observed that a psychoanalytic approach, popular in the jurisprudence of the 1960's and early 1970's, had fallen into disfavor by the 1980's.[149] Professor Elkins

---

139. THOMAS L. SHAFFER, LEGAL INTERVIEWING AND COUNSELING IN A NUTSHELL (1976).

140. *Id.* at 160-80.

141. Shaffer does, however, write about the need for the lawyer to have self-awareness. *Id.* at 181-93.

142. SHAFFER & ELKINS, LEGAL INTERVIEWING AND COUNSELING (2d ed. 1987).

143. SHAFFER & ELKINS, *supra* note 102.

144. SHAFFER & ELKINS (2d ed.), *supra* note 142, at 66-71; SHAFFER & ELKINS (3d ed.), *supra* note 102, at 56-61. This material draws heavily on the work of Saxe & Kuvin, *supra* note 84.

145. Elkins, *supra* note 80; Elkins, *supra* note 76; Elkins, *supra* note 114.

146. Elkins, *supra* note 76, at 760.

147. Elkins, *supra* note 80, at 243-44. In this article, Professor Elkins discusses at length Andrew Watson's work on recognizing and resolving transference and countertransference in the lawyer/client relationship. *Id.*

148. Elkins, *supra* note 114.

149. *Id.* at 508. *See, e.g.*, JAY KATZ, JOSEPH GOLDSTEIN & ALAN M. DERSHOWITZ, PSYCHOANALYSIS, PSYCHIATRY AND LAW (1967); Redmount, *supra* note 101.

speculated that the loss of interest might have been due to a growing real-ization among academics that psychoanalytic and humanistic perspectives were unlikely to engender substantial change in legal education.[150] "[L]egal educators," he said, moved to take up other concerns as they realized, "conscious[ly] or unconscious[ly], that counseling was not going be the catalytic agent for change."[151]

Continuing what Professors Freeman, Shaffer and Elkins had begun, Professor Robert Bastress, also of West Virginia University College of Law, and Professor Joseph Harbaugh, now Dean at Nova Southeastern University Law Center, published a text on interviewing, counseling and negotiation that is now widely used in clinical courses to teach these skills and to introduce students to the various schools of psychotherapy.[152] As the authors explained, the text was designed to attune students to the less conscious variables of lawyering:

> Awareness of psychological forces, personality makeup, and human motivation makes it more likely that you can accurately perceive the nature and extent of a client's problem and can formulate a responsive strategy. *That knowledge also allows you to more easily recognize what is going on inside your own mind and how your feelings or needs could affect your handling of a case and your relations with others. That self-insight is essential to effective lawyering.*"[153]

Other writers, too, have noted the relationship of the unconscious, transference and countertransference to the practice of law.[154] For example, a 1977 law review article co-authored by Mark K. Schoenfeld, a law professor, and Barbara Pearlman Schoenfield, a social worker, offered practical advice for recognizing and resolving "emotional interference" in the lawyer/client counseling relationship.[155] A 1993 article by Professor Joan Meier dis-

---

150. Elkins, *supra* note 114, at 508 n.56.

151. *Id.* For a thoughtful analysis of why the profession and the academy have subordinated mental disability law scholarship and belittled its significance, see Michael Perlin, *Mental Disability, Sanism, Pretextuality, Therapeutic Jurisprudence, and Teaching Law*, Presentation at the Society of American Law Teachers Conference (SALT), Minneapolis, MN (Sept. 1994) (on file with the author).

152. BASTRESS & HARBAUGH, *supra* note 79. Their book is one of two clinical texts regularly used in courses on interviewing, counseling and negotiating. The psychological dimension of the book may well contribute to its popularity among clinicians.

153. *Id.* at 19 (emphasis added).

154. *See, e.g.*, Joseph Allegretti, *Shooting Elephants, Serving Clients: An Essay on George Orwell and the Lawyer-Client Relationship*, 27 CREIGHTON L. REV. 1, 6-7 (1993); Saxe & Kuvin, *supra* note 84, at 209-10; Schoenfeld, *supra* note 76, at 25.

155. Mark K. Schoenfeld & Barbara Pearlman Schoenfield, *Interviewing and Counseling Clients in a Legal Setting*, 11 AKRON L. REV. 313 (1977).

cussed the importance of educating clinic students about the operation of countertransference in representation of domestic violence victims.[156] Professor Melissa Nelken authored a 1996 article on psychoanalysis and negotiation, that focused on the importance of lawyers' self-understanding to avoid counterproductive behavior.[157] Even more recently, Professor Linda Mills has written of the need for state actors to recognize and resolve their own traumatic countertransference reactions in interactions with victims of intimate abuse.[158]

D. Overcoming Resistance to the Emotional Dimension of Lawyering

As the preceding discussion suggests, many writers have attempted to educate the bar and the academy about the importance of understanding the operation of the unconscious on the practice of law. Yet most of this literature appears to be largely unknown outside of a small community with a particular interest in or inclination towards psychology. It is likely that the earlier-discussed phenomenon of resistance within the profession[159] is at least partly responsible for the relative obscurity of these writings.

There are several reasons for guarded optimism that the profession and the academy may be increasingly inclined to give credence to the power of psychic forces. One pragmatic impetus for lawyers is the greater awareness, if not greater incidence, of sexual abuse of clients.[160] Increased regulation of and sanctions for such relationships inevitably heighten interest in the root causes of the problems. But there are other, more hopeful signs that, as we enter the twenty-first century, emotional intelligence may come into its own as a recognized and essential attribute for lawyers. One such sign is the movement towards mainstreaming public discourse about mental and emotional illness. The second is a convergence of several threads of scholarship that focus on bringing humanism to bear on the lawyer/client relationship.

1. The Mainstreaming of Mental Health

Both society in general and the Bar in particular are increasingly receptive to examining and addressing issues of mental health and well-being.

---

156. Meier, *supra* note 55, at 1349-56.

157. Nelken, *supra* note 85.

158. LINDA G. MILLS, THE HEART OF INTIMATE ABUSE: NEW INTERVENTIONS IN CHILD WELFARE, CRIMINAL JUSTICE, AND HEALTH SETTINGS 111-13, 116-18, 128, 150-51 (1998); Linda G. Mills, *Killing Her Softly: Intimate Abuse and the Violence of State Intervention*, 113 HARV. L. REV. (forthcoming Dec. 1999).

159. *See supra* notes 90-104 and accompanying text.

160. *See supra* notes 38-40 and accompanying text.

In recent years, for example, there has been a burgeoning of programs offered by bar associations to address emotional problems such as depression, alcoholism and substance abuse experienced by their members.[161] As more of us encounter such problems among ourselves, our families, friends and colleagues, we are less likely to view such problems as moral failings, and more likely to see them as illnesses requiring appropriate attention and treatment.

Our culture in general is progressing towards de-stigmatization and increasingly open dialogue about emotional and mental problems. That

---

161. See discussion of the problem at notes 105, 109 and accompanying text. Benjamin and Sales discuss the importance of effective Lawyer Assistance Programs (LAPs). Benjamin & Sales, *supra* note 105, at 297-301. Such programs now exist in all 50 states. Anderson, McCracken & Reddy, *supra* note 109, at 19; Robert A. Stein, *Aiding the Practice Impaired*, A.B.A. J. 82 (May 1999). The ABA publishes a directory of approximately 100 LAPs run by state and local bar associations. ABA Commission on Lawyer Assistance Programs, Directory of State and Local Lawyer Assistance Programs (1998). The New York State Bar Association's LAP, for example, was established in 1990 to aid attorneys and their family members to deal with alcoholism and drug abuse. Tracey Tully, *Guiderland Judge Cited for Outreach,* Times Union, May 15, 1997, at B2. Since its inception the Lawyer Assistance Program has assisted approximately 350 attorneys a year with alcohol and drug abuse. More recently, the LAP has been focusing on broader issues for attorneys, such as depression. Telephone interview with Ray Lopez, Director of the New York State Bar Association Lawyer Assistance Program (August 7, 1998). Recent efforts to limit inquiry by bar examiners into an applicant's mental health history are yet another example of increasing de-stigmatization of emotional problems. *See* H. Rutherford Turnbull III, *Limiting Mental Health Inquiries: ABA urges bar examiners to narrow focus to current, recent disabilities*, A.B.A. J. 131 (April 1995); Allison Wielobob, *Bar Application Mental Health Inquiries: Unwise and Unlawful*, 24 Hum. Rts. 12 (Winter 1997); *See also* Anderson, McCracken & Reddy, *supra* note 109 (advocating rehabilitative approach to character and fitness inquiries into applicants' mental health and substance abuse problems). A 1994 resolution of the ABA House of Delegates provides as follows:

BE IT RESOLVED that the American Bar association recommends that when making character and fitness determinations for the purpose of bar admission, state and territorial bar examiners, in carrying out their responsibilities to the public to admit only qualified applicants worthy of the public trust, should consider the privacy concerns of bar admission applicants, tailor questions concerning mental health and treatment narrowly in order to elicit information about current fitness to practice law, and take steps to ensure that their processes do not discourage those who would benefit from seeking professional assistance with personal problems and issues of mental health from doing so.

Id. at 17.

trend is evident, for example, in recent legislation requiring greater parity in health insurance benefits for the treatment of emotional and mental illness.[162] We can find evidence as well in electoral politics. Once, the revelation that a candidate for public office had sought counseling or medication for treatment of clinical depression would likely have ended his or her campaign.[163] In recent years, a candidate's history of emotional illness might give voters pause, but perhaps no more so than would a history of physical illness. In any event, it would not constitute a *per se* disqualification from holding office.[164]

---

162. *See* Mental Health Parity Act of 1996, 29 U.S.C. § 1185(a). The Act does not, however, require a health plan to include mental health benefits. *Id.*, § 1185(a)(b)(1). Furthermore, it does not apply to businesses employing fewer than 50 people. *Id.*, § (c)(1). According to *The Wall Street Journal*, the Act does not prohibit higher deductibles or co-payments for mental health treatment, and allows employers to limit hospital stays or the number of therapy sessions for psychiatric illness. Nancy Ann Jeffrey, *Court Allows Mental-Illness Benefit Caps*, WALL ST. J., Oct. 5, 1997, at B1. According to the *L.A. Times*, this "victory was largely symbolic" as it exempts any employers whose health care costs rise by 1% or more in a year. Don Morian & Julie Marquis, *State Senate OK's Insurance Bill on Mental Health*, L.A. TIMES, June 12, 1998, at A1 (*available in* 1998 WL 2436461). The Clinton administration is drafting standards to require complete parity in private health insurance plans for federal employees. Robert Pear, *Equal Coverage of Physical and Mental Ills is White House Goal for Federal Employees*, N.Y. TIMES, May 25, 1999, at A22, col. 1. Many states already provide for greater parity. Maryland, Minnesota, Vermont and Arkansas apply their parity statutes to all mental illnesses. *Perspectives: States Forge Ahead of Feds on Parity*, 51 MED. & HEALTH 48 (December 15, 1997). And, with the exception of Arkansas, these states require parity for substance abuse disorders as well, which the Federal Legislation does not. *Id.* Bills are pending in other states. *See* Richard Locker, *Equality in Mental Coverage Nearly Law*, COM. APPEAL (Mem. TN), Apr. 24, 1998 at B1 (*available in* 1998 WL 11202157). In May 1998, Tennessee Governor Sundquist signed into law Tennessee HB 3177/SB 2798, applying to employers of 25 or more employees. *See Consumer Protections Mandated Under Massachusetts Governor's Executive Order*, 6 WASH. HEALTH WK. 20 (June 8, 1998). In California, the State Senate approved mental health parity legislation, 1997 California Assembly Bill No. 1100, on June 11, 1998, which Governor Pete Wilson vetoed. *See* Julie Marquis & Lisa Richardson, *Wilson Vetoes Mental-Illness Coverage Bill Health*, L.A. TIMES, Sept. 30, 1998, at A3.

163. Thomas Eagleton was forced off the Democratic ticket as a vice-presidential candidate upon the revelation that he had once been hospitalized for depression. *See* CARL BERNSTEIN & BOB WOODWARD, ALL THE PRESIDENTS' MEN 45 (1974); Frank Rich, *The Last Taboo*, N.Y. TIMES, Dec. 23 1997, at A19, col. 1.

164. Michael Dukakis' ratings went down upon the revelation that he had seen a psychiatrist after his brother died, Rich, *supra* note 163, but he remained a strong presence in the presidential race. Lynn Rivers, congresswoman from Ann Arbor, Michigan, revealed

Lately, it is not uncommon for reputable journalists to air their family's and their own histories of depression and addiction in the popular media.[165] And in 1997, a major league baseball player went public with his own diagnosis and treatment of clinical depression—a rare and noteworthy event.[166]

If we are able to accept that any one of us is at risk of serious emotional dysfunction,[167] it should not be difficult to accept that some lesser impairments caused by unconscious forces may affect many of us in our ordi-

---

that she suffered from a bipolar mood disorder, and was nonetheless re-elected. *Id.* Governor Lawton Chiles of Florida was twice elected despite his revelation in 1987, during his term as a United States senator, that he had sought medical treatment for depression and had taken antidepressants. "Although questions were raised about Mr. Chiles's mental health during the 1990 campaign for governor, he was elected handily and re-elected in 1994." Richard Grayson, Letter to the Editor, N.Y. TIMES, Dec. 27, 1997, at A10, col. 6. *But see* Francis X. Clines, *Does Clinton Need to Turn to Ministers, or a Psychotherapist, Too?* N.Y. TIMES, Sept. 17, 1998, at A27, col. 1 ("For many veterans of the political wars, the merest hint of any psychological flaw is the ultimate taboo."). For a thoughtful, albeit somewhat whimsical, exploration of whether a psychiatrist should occupy a full-time position in the White House, *see* David Wallis, *Every First Family is Unhappy in Its Own Way,* N.Y. TIMES, March 14, 1999, sec. 4, at 4, col. 1. Mr. Wallis' essay gives credence to the increasing destigmatization of emotional and mental health issues, while at the same time underscoring how far we as a nation have yet to go. It is interesting to compare the American experience with that of Norway. *See Norwegian Premier's Illness Prompts Sympathy and Worries,* N.Y. TIMES, Sept. 20, 1998, at A12, col. 1 (describing Norwegians' sympathy with Prime Minister's several weeks of sick leave for depression). "It must be allowed for a politician also to show that people can get sick and react to stress." *Id.* (quoting Norwegian schoolteacher).

165. *See, e.g.,* Elisabeth Bumiller, *Funny Columnist With a Melancholy Bent,* N.Y. TIMES, Sept. 15 1998, at B2, col. 4 (about columnist Art Buchwald's struggle with depression); Frazier Moore, *Wallace Talks About the Pain of Depression in HBO's* Dead Blue, AP, 1998 WL 3132501 (describing Mike Wallace's HBO special, *Dead Blue: Surviving Depression,* Jan. 6, 1998, and Wallace's own struggle with depression); David Samuels, *Saying Yes to Drugs,* THE NEW YORKER, Mar. 23, 1998, at 48 (about Bill Moyers PBS series on addiction, and Moyers' son's own struggle with addiction). *See also* WILLIAM STYRON, DARKNESS VISIBLE: A MEMOIR OF MADNESS 1990 (recounting author's struggle with incapacitating depression).

166. *See* Frank Rich, *Harnisch's Perfect Pitch,* N.Y. TIMES, May 1, 1997, at A27, col. 5 (about New York Mets pitcher Pete Harnisch). *See also* Clines, *supra* note 164 (quoting home run king Mark McGuire, who ascribed his success to psychotherapy: "Guys tell me, 'I'll never go to therapy,'...Hey, everybody needs therapy.").

167. *See* Michael Perlin, *Competency, Deinstitutionalization, and Homelessness: A Story of Marginalization,* 28 HOUS. L. REV. 63, 93 n.174 (1991) ("It is probably worth pointing out that, while race and sex are immutable, we all *can* become mentally ill....").

nary relationships.[168] We must be open to the possibility that emotions we don't understand, and of which we are often oblivious, may affect how we act towards our clients.

2. Law and Humanism Revitalized

Recent scholarship suggests still another reason for optimism. We can identify both a burgeoning and a convergence of scholarship from several different schools of thought, all revealing an awareness of the importance of psychological sensitivity and knowledge—of emotional intelligence—in the practice of law.[169] Among these are Therapeutic Jurisprudence,[170] especially in its intersection with preventive lawyering,[171] affective lawyering,[172] lawyering with an "ethic of care"[173]

---

168. *See* Shaffer, *supra* note 23, at 237:
Lawyers are not analysts and clients are not in the law office for analysis. But people who come to law offices are troubled, and the lawyers who talk to them—whether they admit it or not—are also troubled.

169. *See* Carrie Menkel-Meadow, *Narrowing the Gap by Narrowing the Field: What's Missing from the MacCrate Report—Of Skill, Legal Science and Being a Human Being*, 69 WASH. L. REV. 593, 602 (1994). Professor Menkel-Meadow cites "[r]ecent scholarship which seeks to explore the emotional, empathic, and human side of law and lawyering" as evidence of increasing interest in what she characterizes as the "art" of lawyering. *Id. See also* Winick, *supra* note 51 (describing several approaches to lawyering that share concern with psychological sensitivity to "emotional climate of the attorney-client relationship").

170. *See supra* note 79.

171. *See, e.g.*, Marc W. Patry, David B. Wexler, Dennis P. Stolle & Alan J. Tomkins, *Better Legal Counseling Through Empirical Research: Identifying Psycholegal Soft Spots and Strategies*, 34 CAL. W. L. REV. 439 (1998); Dennis P. Stolle, David B. Wexler, Bruce J. Winick & Edward A. Dauer, *Integrating Preventive Law and Therapeutic Jurisprudence: A Law and Psychology Based Approach to Lawyering*, 34 CAL. W. L. REV. 15 (1997); David B. Wexler, *Practicing Therapeutic Jurisprudence: Psycholegal Soft Spots and Strategies*, 67 REVISTA JURIDICA U.P.R. 317 (1998); Winick, *supra* note 51.

172. *See, e.g.*, Menkel-Meadow, *supra* note 169, at 606-07, 619 (comparing Professor Tony Kronman's prescription for teaching affective skills of lawyering in law school with its absence in MacCrate report); *id.* at 610 (criticizing MacCrate report as advocating instrumental approach to counseling, as opposed to affective approach that "attends to emotional and interpersonal factors that might be affecting the communication," expresses "caring" for client's concerns, puts the client at ease, and actively listens "so as to create a relationship, not just to process information"); Mills, *supra* note 23, at 1225 (arguing that clients who are victims of domestic violence are better served by "affective lawyers" who are able to transcend differences and find emotional commonality with clients).

173. *See* Daicoff, *supra* note 97, at 1398-1400 (describing studies suggesting gender differ-

and Creative Problem Solving.[174]

Therapeutic Jurisprudence calls for an examination of the therapeutic and anti-therapeutic consequences of laws, legal systems and practices, with the goal of increasing psychological well-being, consistent with protecting legal rights.[175] What preventive lawyering adds to that is counseling and planning to *anticipate* "psycholegal soft spots" in order to eliminate or ameliorate potential problems.[176] An oft-used example is a case that involved an "undue influence" challenge to a will.[177] The decedent had left her modest estate, including her home, to her daughter. The daughter, who lived with her mother during the latter years of the mother's life, had limited resources and no home of her own. The son, a person of independent means and owner of his own home, challenged the will, claiming undue influence by the daughter. The judge rejected the challenge and, ruling from the bench, said something akin to the following:

> From what I can see, your mother wasn't an easy person. In fact she could be a very difficult person, who seldom showed her emotions. I imagine she wasn't someone who told her children she loved them very often. But just because she left her estate to your sister, and not to you, doesn't mean she didn't love you very much.

At that point, according to the judge, the son put his head in his hands and sobbed.[178]

---

ence in incidence of "ethic of care" among lawyers, that women law students rated contextual factors such as relationships, care and communication more highly than male law students); Ellmann, *supra* note 9 (examining how lawyer who seeks to practice with ethic of care and connect emotionally with clients and other persons might exercise professional responsibilities under existing norms); Theresa Glannon, *Lawyers and Caring: Building an Ethic of Care into Professional Responsibility*, 43 HASTINGS L.J. 1175 (1992) (discussing strategies utilized by author to integrate ethic of care pedagogy into first-year law school curriculum); Menkel-Meadow, *supra* note 169, at 620. The term "ethic of care" was originally coined by Carol Gilligan in her work on gendered differences in moral reasoning. CAROL GILLIGAN, IN A DIFFERENT VOICE: PSYCHOLOGICAL THEORY AND WOMEN'S DEVELOPMENT 3 (1982).

174. *See, e.g.*, James M. Cooper, *Towards a New Architecture: Creative Problem Solving and the Evolution of Law*, 34 CAL. W. L. REV. 297 (1998); Janeen Kerper, *Creative Problem Solving vs. The Case Method: A Marvelous Adventure in Which Winnie-the-Pooh Meets Mrs. Palsgraf*, 34 CAL. W. L. REV. 351 (1998).

175. *See* Wexler, *Reflections, supra* note 79, at 228.

176. *See* Wexler, *supra* note 171, at 320; Winick, *supra* note 51, at 4.

177. *See, e.g.*, Patry *et al.*, *supra* note 171, at 443-45; Marjorie Silver, *TJ: Where the Law Meets the Behavioral Sciences*, L.I. BUSINESS NEWS, Aug 17-23, 1998, at 48 (describing presentation by Judge Peggy Fulton Hora at First International Conference on Therapeutic Jurisprudence in Winchester, England in July, 1998).

178. *Id.*

A lawyer helping a client draw up a will should not only explain the legal consequences of implementing the client's wishes but also explore with the client the likely effect of those actions on the client's next of kin. In the above example, a lawyer sensitive to Therapeutic Jurisprudence might have explored with the mother the likely reaction of her son to being excluded from the will. A lawyer sensitive to Therapeutic Jurisprudence hopefully would have helped the son examine his motives for challenging his mother's will. Thus, Therapeutic Jurisprudence could have been brought to bear not only by the judge but also by at least two lawyers significantly earlier in the process. Had that happened, perhaps such a lawsuit—one that inevitably would create (or deepen) rifts between brother and sister—might have been avoided altogether.

Affective lawyering and lawyering with an ethic of care both focus on the importance of the emotional nexus between lawyer and client. As described by Professor Mills in her work on representing victims of domestic violence, affective lawyers are those who are able to transcend differences and find emotional commonality with their clients.[179] Professor Menkel-Meadow, who writes of both affective lawyering and lawyering with an ethic of care,[180] describes the affective approach to counseling as one that "attends to emotional and interpersonal factors that might be affecting the communication" with the client.[181] She notes the importance of caring for the client's concerns, of caring that the client is put at ease, and learning how to listen actively so as to create a relationship and not merely to process information.[182]

Creative Problem-solving, as described by Professor James Cooper, represents a convergence of numerous disciplines including the social sciences and the humanities to address the plethora of problems facing our technological and media-saturated society as we approach the next century.[183] It includes within it other schools of thought, like Therapeutic Jurisprudence and Preventive Lawyering, that "recognize that psychological and sociological perspectives must be addressed" throughout the legal system.[184] According to Professor Cooper, it is broader, however, in that it looks beyond the client's interests to recognize the impact a client's decision may have on the profession, community and society in general.[185] As described

---

179. Mills, *supra* note 23, at 1257-59.

180. Menkel-Meadow, *supra* note 169, at 619-20.

181. *Id.* at 610.

182. *Id.*

183. *See* Cooper, *supra* note 174, at 301.

184. "Creative Problem Solving is the umbrella under which Preventive Law, Therapeutic Jurisprudence, Holistic Lawyering, and Restorative Justice schools of thought rest." *Id.* at 322.

185. *Id.* at 320-21. "Creative Problem Solving is…about healing society, reconstructing the social contract, and strengthening community bonds, big and small." *Id.* at 322.

by Professor Kerper, "[c]reative problem solving assumes that not all problems require legal solutions; and not all legal problems require a lawsuit."[186]

These schools of thought and method, together with the growing body of other clinical and lawyering scholarship, evidence increasing attention to strategies which may enable lawyers to interact more effectively with clients, other lawyers, and judges.[187] Such strategies call for understanding the psychological processes—such as countertransference and denial[188]—that affect human relationships generally and lawyers' relationships in particular.

III. Lawyering and Emotional Intelligence: A Prescription for the 21st Century

A. The Self-Aware Lawyer

1. Lawyering with Self-Awareness

Whatever the reasons for emotional interference in the lawyer/client relationship, it is important that the lawyer strive to insure that the com-

---

186. Kerper, *supra* note 174, at 354. This article is a plea to balance the litigious thrust of legal education with non-litigation problem-solving skills.

187. Another sign of the times was the excellent program co-sponsored by the sections on Law and Mental Health and ADR at the January 1999 AALS Annual Meeting, entitled *Lawyering 2000: Should it Look More "Alternative"?* The program description was as follows:

> The legal profession is under attack in the late 20th century. Lawyer dissatisfaction appears to be rampant, and it may be related to a high incidence of psychological distress in the legal profession. Is it possible that "new" or "alternative" approaches to practicing law—that of Therapeutic Jurisprudence/preventive law and the use of mediation to resolve disputes—hold promise as templates for lawyering in the next millennium?

See also GUINIER ET AL., *supra* note 99, at 69-70 ("Another argument for changing legal education is that it currently overemphasizes the adversarial nature of lawyering. Legal education may be inadequate where it focuses on legal issues exclusively or primarily in the context of resolving disputes through litigation. The law school's definition of lawyering potential—as measured by a single evaluative methodology and one dominant pedagogy—may simply be outmoded in light of contemporary professional developments, which include alternative dispute resolution, emphasis on negotiation rather than litigation, and client counseling.").

188. *See* Winick, *supra* note 51.

petency of the representation is not compromised. There is no magic bullet for eviscerating emotional responses that interfere with our abilities to function as we would like. In an ideal world, perhaps we would all have the time and money to undergo personal analysis, to explore our hopes, dreams and fantasies with a well-trained guide. Perhaps every lawyer's training for the practice of law should include analysis or extensive psychotherapy.[189] However, as this is neither feasible nor essential for most of us, it is fortunate that less costly and time-consuming alternatives are available.[190]

When countertransference troubles a therapist or an attorney, a range of responses is possible. The efficacy of any response may well depend on the severity of the problem.[191] The first step, of course, is recognition that a problem or potential problem exists. The goal is to make the Unconscious conscious.[192] The mere acknowledgment of uncomfortable feelings may suffice to render such feelings more manageable.[193] In their clinical

---

189. See WATSON, INTERVIEWING AND COUNSELING, *supra* note 24, at 82:

I have often been queried about whether or not lawyers, judges, and other professionals should be "psychoanalyzed." My response has been that under ideal circumstances, because lawyers are constantly serving as counselors, and since the subjects of their work are always people, they and their profession would profit much by that form of learning and experience.

Elkins, *supra* note 76, at 758-59 ("The essential unresolved questions is whether insight for effective self-scrutiny is possible without the encouragement and guidance of an experienced psychoanalyst or psychotherapist."); Saxe & Kuvin, *supra* note 84, at 216 ("[I]t is respectfully submitted that optimally the prototypical attorney should himself have undergone some formal psychoanalysis or psychotherapy.").

190. See WATSON, INTERVIEWING AND COUNSELING, *supra* note 24, at 82 ("Needless to say, to require such a learning experience would be totally infeasible.").

191. See WATSON, PSYCHIATRY FOR LAWYERS, *supra* note 24, at 21; Silverman, *supra* note 59, at 177.

192. See RACKER, *supra* note 20, at 16; Renik, *supra* note 25, at 558-59; SCHOENFIELD & SCHOENFIELD, *supra* note 77, at 329; Allegretti, *supra* note 154, at 13 (quoting WATSON, PSYCHIATRY FOR LAWYERS, *supra* note 24, at 7); Freud, *Introductory Lectures, Part III, supra* note 18, at 435.

193. See WATSON, PSYCHIATRY FOR LAWYERS, *supra* note 24, at 8:

Since transference is unconscious, the question arises whether one can do anything about it. The answer is something of a paradox. The mere acknowledgment of the possibility of such unconscious reactions permits the participants to look more objectively at relationships and to question causes. The capacity to accept the possibility that one's feelings about another may be due to unconscious and unrealistic coloring rather than to the other's reality traits, is a major step toward understanding. Without awareness of transference phenomena, people are over- or under-con-

education materials, Bastress & Harbaugh suggest the lawyer start by asking the following series of questions, designed by psychotherapist Lewis
Wolberg, to elicit evidence of countertransference:[194]

1. How do I feel about the client?
2. Do I anticipate the client?
3. Do I over-identify with, or feel sorry for, the client?
4. Do I feel any resentment or jealousy toward the client?
5. Do I get extreme pleasure out of seeing the client?
6. Do I feel bored with the client?
7. Am I fearful of the client?
8. Do I want to protect, reject, or punish the client?
9. Am I impressed by the client?

If any of questions two through nine elicit an affirmative response, one
must then ask "Why"?[195] We might recognize that the client reminds us of

---

vinced by their own emotional response and have no opportunity to work out any
understanding of them.

194. BASTRESS & HARBAUGH, *supra* note 79, at 297, *citing* WOLBERG, *supra* note 16;
Allegretti, *supra* note 154, at 13 (footnote citing BASTRESS & HARBAUGH and WOLBERG).
See also Saxe & Kuvin, *supra* note 84, at 212-15 (canvasing variety of reactions that
should alert attorney to possible existance of neurotic conflicts affecting representation):
1. Feelings of depression or discomfort (anxiety) during or after time spent with
certain clients.... 2. Carelessness with regard to keeping appointments with the
client or allowing trivial maters that could easily be postponed to interfere with
time apportioned to the client. 3. Repeatedly experiencing affectionate feelings
toward the client.... [T]his affectivity may cause the attorney to prolong the case as
a rationalization to maintain the interpersonal relationship and further may eventually lead to seduction. 5. Repeated neglect by the attorney of certain files.... 7. A
conscious awareness, that the attorney is deriving satisfaction from the client's
praise, appreciation and other evidences of affection. 8. Becoming disturbed, consciously, by the client's persistent reproaches and evident dissatisfaction with the
merits of the case. 9. Perhaps the most important of all responses to which the
attorney should be alert, is a feeling of boredom or drowsiness when either he talks
or listens to the client.
SCHOENFIELD & SCHOENFIELD, *supra* note 77, at 329 (list of danger signals to alert attorney to own emotional interference in interviewing); SHAFFER & ELKINS, *supra* note 142,
at 58-59 (citing Saxe & Kuvin). In my opinion, the precise list of questions is of far less
import than the attorney's acknowledgment that good practice requires attention to one's
emotional reactions provoked by the representation.
195. Wolberg follows his list of questions with the following advice to the therapist,
advice that is beneficial to the attorney as well:
Should answers to any of the above point to problems, then ask why such feelings
and attitudes exist. Is the patient doing anything to stir up such feelings? Does the
patient resemble anybody the therapist knows or has known, and, if so, are any

a close family member and that we are revisiting an emotional pattern played out with a parent or sibling.[196] However, it is altogether possible that we will not have a clue as to why we are experiencing such an intense, troubling reaction to the client. Nonetheless, recognizing that a problem exists in our emotional response to the client may suffice to obtain control over the problem.[197] It may be unnecessary to identify the source; the very act of raising the reaction to a conscious level may make it possible to control the feeling or diffuse its force sufficiently to avoid problems in the representation.

But what if that is not enough? A psychotherapist would likely seek advice from a trusted friend or colleague to help gain perspective.[198] We lawyers, however, are far more likely to seek legal advice than personal advice on such matters. But given that interpersonal skills are as important to effective legal representation as is knowledge of legal strategies and doctrine, lawyers need to overcome that resistance. The process of telling a friend or colleague about one's emotional reactions to a client may enable a lawyer to gain the requisite perspective on and control over countertransference reactions.[199]

A therapist who finds that strong emotional reactions are interfering with the therapy may seek guidance through consultation[200] or reanalysis.[201] If still unable to surmount such difficulties, the therapist may find it necessary to refer the patient to someone else for treatment.[202] Likewise,

---

attitudes being transferred to the patient that are related to another person? What other impulses are being mobilized in the therapist that account for the feelings? What role does the therapist want to play with the patient? Mere verbalization to himself of answers to these queries, permits of better control of unreasonable feelings. Cognizance of the fact that he feels angry, displeased, disgusted, irritated, provoked, uninterested, unduly attentive, upset or overly attracted, may suffice to bring these emotions under control. In the event untoward attitudes continue, more self-searching is indicated. Of course it may be difficult to act accepting, non-critical and non-judgmental toward a patient who is provocatively hostile and destructive in his attitudes towards people, and who possesses disagreeable traits which the therapist in his everyday life would criticize.

WOLBERG, *supra* note 16, at 491.

196. *Id.*

197. *See id. See also* Kernberg, *supra* note 25, at 42.

198. *See* Kernberg, *supra* note 25, at 52; Meier, *supra* note 55, at 1354; Schover, *supra* note 35, at 147; Silverman, *supra* note 59, at 198.

199. *See* WATSON, INTERVIEWING AND COUNSELING, *supra* note 24, at 25, 81; WATSON, PSYCHIATRY FOR LAWYERS, *supra* note 24, at 10-11; Elkins, *supra* note 80, at 244.

200. *See* Loewald, *supra* note 59, at 275.

201. *See* Schover, *supra* note 35, at 147; Silverman, *supra* note 59, at 177.

202. *See* WOLBERG (4th ed.), *supra* note 52, at 488; Cooper, *supra* note 50, at 581; Kantrowitz, *supra* note 60 (on analyst/analysand match); Schover, *supra* note 35, at 147.

if a lawyer is unable to gain control over emotional responses to the client, it may be necessary to refer the client elsewhere for representation.[203]

And although therapy or analysis may not be necessary for all lawyers, lawyers who find they repeatedly experience problematic emotional reactions to clients that interfere with their practice may require professional treatment.[204]

2. Different Lawyers, Different Clients

Our individual psyches affect the intensity of countertransference in our professional lives. Each of us brings to the representation some unresolved—perhaps unconscious—biases in favor of or against persons based on their individual or group characteristics.[205] We may have emotional reactions to a client based on any number of variables: race, gender, sexual orientation, age, physical or mental disability, substance abuse problem or economic status. These reactions—again, often unknowingly—may affect the quality of our representation.

Another variable affecting countertransference is the kind of representation involved. The greater the degree of power imbalance and emotional intensity of the situation, the greater the likelihood that transference and countertransference may interfere with competent representation.[206] Thus countertransference is likely to pose the greatest problems in the con-

---

203. *See* Watson, Psychiatry for Lawyers, *supra* note 24, at 21; Binder, Bergman & Price, *supra* note 53, at 64 (recommending, where possible, referral to another attorney if lawyer lacks all empathy for client). *Cf.* Dr. Ruth Westheimer's presentation at January 1998 NYSBA Annual Meeting, Panel on Regulation of Sexual Relationships Between Lawyers and Clients. Dr. Ruth, a self-described romantic, thought it was absolutely wonderful for lawyer and client to establish an intimate relationship—as long as the lawyer then terminates the legal representation and refers the client to another lawyer. In fact, Dr. Ruth opined that if the attorney develops strong feelings for a client, the lawyer should own up to them and explain to the client the need for changing counsel. In certain kinds of representation, however, referral may be less viable. Clients represented by Legal Aid lawyers or Public Defenders may have nowhere else to go, unless they can be transferred to a different staff attorney in the same office. Furthermore, the socioeconomic disparities between lawyers and clients in such cases may exacerbate countertransference problems. For these attorneys, training in handling countertransference may be critical.

204. *See* Schoenfield & Schoenfield, *supra* note 77, at 331; Watson, Psychiatry for Lawyers, *supra* note 24, at 11.

205. *See* Lawrence, *supra* note 92, at 330.

206. *See supra* notes 8-13 and accompanying text. *See also* Gerber, *supra* note 31, at 120 (describing intensity of countertransference in work with sex offenders).

texts of child abuse, domestic violence,[207] criminal defense,[208] immigration, matrimonial practice,[209] and representation of mentally ill persons.[210]

In certain areas of practice, maintaining empathy may be difficult.[211] In connection with this project, I conducted several interviews with clinical colleagues of mine to discuss their own and their students' emotional reactions to clients. Several of them acknowledged the challenges of representing the difficult client.[212] Marianne Artusio, Director of Clinical Programs, spoke of an elder law client for whom the clinic had done an enormous amount of work, including nonlegal work, such as cleaning out and selling the client's home, a home she had not occupied for several years due to hospitalizations. The students were appalled at the client's lack of gratitude. When a client is difficult or demanding, it is hard for the students to maintain their zeal and to know when they have achieved completeness. Although Professor Artusio tries to work with the students on

---

207. *See* Meier, *supra* note 55.

208. *See supra* notes 8-13 and accompanying text. Death penalty representation would be a subset of criminal defense work likely to provoke even more powerful emotional reactions.

209. *See* Steven A. Ager, *Do Divorce Lawyers Really Have More Fun?*, 15(6) FAIR$HARE 7 (1995); Elkins, *supra* note 80; Jorgenson & Sutherland, *supra* note 30, at 11; Allwyn J. Levine, *Transference and Countertransference: How it Affects You and Your Client*, 15 FAM. ADVOC. 14 (Fall 1992):

> In no other field of jurisprudence is one dealing with the most private aspects of people's lives and their most precious possessions—their children. Divorce, in and of itself, is a psychologically draining experience. For all clients, it stirs up feelings of abandonment, separation, dependency, and anxiety—unmatched intensity by any other situation. A matrimonial lawyer is thus thrust into a veritable minefield of psychological traps and pitfalls.

210. *See* Michael Perlin, *Ethical Issues in the Representation of Individuals in the Commitment Process*, 45 L. & CONTEMP. PROBS. 161, 163 (1982) ("[I]ssues raised by investigating ethical standards in civil commitment representation may dredge up unconscious feelings which lead to avoidance—by clients, by lawyers, and by judges—of the underlying problems."). *See also* Winnicott, *supra* note 18 (discussing negative (hate) countertransference in treatment of psychotic patients):

> However much he loves his patients he cannot avoid hating them, and fearing them, and the better he knows this the less hate and fear will be the motive determining what he does to his patients.

Id. at 350.

211. *See also* FROMM-REICHMAN, *supra* note 58, at 198-99 (on psychiatrist's discomfort working with patients who have attempted suicide).

212. Author's interviews with Professors Marianne Artusio (July 9, 1997), Bill Brooks (July 3, 1997), Rhonda Shepardson (Sept. 2, 1998) and Lewis Silverman (June 26, 1997).

these issues, she is aware that she, too, is affected by a client's difficult personality. Time spent on an ungrateful client or a client whom the lawyer or student regards as "unworthy" takes time away from helping someone else, someone about whom a lawyer can feel good. Sometimes it is obvious how one's emotional reaction to a client affects the representation. Other times, it is less so.[213]

Some clients may act in obnoxious or hostile ways that would cause virtually any attorney to dread their interpersonal encounters. Negative feelings towards such a client might be an entirely reasonable reaction, rather than a manifestation of countertransference. Many clients hold views or have committed acts that most lawyers find abhorrent. The majority of civil liberties lawyers likely detest the racists and neo-nazis whose first amendment rights they attempt to vindicate. Criminal defense attorneys who represent persons charged with committing especially heinous crimes often face the challenge of providing zealous representation to clients they would otherwise despise. This problem is most acute when the lawyers or their loved ones have been the victims of similar crimes.[214] Nonethe-

---

213. Artusio interview, *supra* note 212.

214. Randy Bellows writes of how, as a young public defender in Washington D.C., he came to terms with representing accused rapists even after a close family relative was robbed and raped at knife point. Describing the rage he felt towards someone who had hurt a person he loved ("I loathe that person; I want him punished; I want no escape routes to grace his path."), Bellows wrote that if he neither knew nor thought too much about the victim, "then it is possible to do my job," and even develop the empathy necessary to effectively represent his client:

> While it is often impossible not to feel sympathy for the victim, this is not an emotion you can afford to nurture or encourage. To put it simply, it is not easy to develop warm feelings [towards your client] when your focus is on the devastation which your client has left in his wake. It makes a difficult job nearly impossible.

Randy Bellows, *Notes of a Public Defender, in* THE SOCIAL RESPONSIBILITIES OF LAWYERS 69, 78-79 (Philip B. Heymann & Lance Liebman eds., 1988). Bellows admits that even when the victim is a stranger, developing such empathy is not always possible. "In one case, for example, my client was charged with robbery. I was told in discovery that my client had robbed a pregnant woman, threatening to kick the woman in the stomach if she did not turn over her purse. At the time, my wife was six months pregnant. At the first opportunity, I pulled out of the case." *Id.* Professor Charles Ogletree describes a painfully similar reaction to learning that while he, too, was a public defender in Washington, D.C., his younger sister, a police officer, was stabbed to death in her apartment:

> When it came to my sister's murder, I did not want any procedural safeguards for the criminal. I wanted the state to use all evidence, obtained by any means whatsoever, to convict her attacker. I wanted the satisfaction of knowing that the person responsible for her death would be brought to justice. I wanted retribution.

Charles J. Ogletree, Jr., *Beyond Justifications: Seeking Motivations to Sustain Public Defenders*, 106 HARV. L. REV. 1239, 1262 (1993). After her murder, Ogletree struggled

less, lawyers must resolve these feelings in order to continue representing the client competently.[215]

3. Two Stories, Redux

What if Adam, the fifty-year old criminal defense attorney,[216] had been schooled in the ways of the psyche and understood countertransference? Imagine he had read the following account by psychoanalyst Theodore Jacobs:

> During the course of the analysis of a highly attractive young woman, I became aware of the unusual correctness of my posture as I greeted her. I made few spontaneous movements, and both my gait and posture conveyed a certain stiffness. I noticed, too, that the muscles of my arms and trunk were not relaxed as I sat in my chair, and that my tone conveyed a more formal quality than was true with other patients. Some self-analysis of these observations made clear to me what I had sensed in myself but had not sufficiently focused on; that I was responding to the patient's considerable charms by a defense of physical and emotional distance. My anxiety over my own positive feeling for her had led, not only to an exaggerated and rather sterile analytic stance, but to inadequate analysis of the patient's seductiveness both as a character trait and a resistance.[217]

Dr. Jacobs found himself responding to the charms of his patient by distancing himself from her, rather than by being drawn in to her seduction. He observed that he treated her differently from his other patients, to the

---

with the decision of whether to return to the public defenders' office. *Id.* at 1263. Ogletree ultimately transcended his emotional pain and did return, but not without intense conflict. Could he continue to zealously represent a client accused of rape and murder: "Might I subconsciously harbor unacknowledged resentments that would lead me to be underzealous in [my client's] defense?" *Id.* at 1264.

215. *See* Winnicott, *supra* note 18, at 351:

> If the analyst is going to have crude feelings imputed to him he is best forewarned and so forearmed, for he must tolerate being placed in that position. Above all he must not deny hate that really exists in himself. Hate that is justified in the present setting has to be sorted out and kept in storage and available for eventual interpretation.

Rhonda Shepardson, who runs Touro's housing rights clinic, shared how she steels herself for representing clients who she feels are "using her as a tool to rip off the system" or who are suspected spouse or child abusers. "I just focus on the legal issue, and make it all about winning. I focus on the *fight*." She finds it easier to do when her opponents are also not likable. Shepardson interview, *supra* note 212.

216. *See* text accompanying notes 85-89 *supra*.

217. Jacobs, *supra* note 61, at 90.

detriment of the analysis. Recognizing what was going on enabled him to dissipate his anxiety, and work with her effectively. In this instance, it was Dr. Jacobs' observation of his *physical* response to his patient that opened the door to his awareness:

> While the analyst seeks, in every case, to become cognizant of feelings in himself that may interfere with his analytic work, these may, as we know, become blocked off from consciousness and remain undetected for lengthy periods of time. Observation of his bodily reactions as they manifest themselves in posture, gesture, and movement enables him to enlarge the scope of his self-awareness and, at times, to gain access to attitudes and conflicts of which he is unaware.[218]

The psychoanalyst Lucia Tower reported that "in [her] experience virtually all physicians, when they gain enough confidence in their analysts, report erotic feelings and impulses toward their patients, but usually do so with a good deal of fear and conflict."[219]

Dr. Gertrude Ticho, an analyst who practiced in three different countries and wrote about cultural assumptions and countertransference,[220] shared two personal stories of how her own cultural biases threatened to derail the analytical relationship.[221] In one instance, a young South American man sought treatment from her for severe anxiety reactions, which worsened as his commitment to his fiancee grew stronger.[222] In one session he came to Dr. Ticho's office excitedly describing an accident he had had on his way to his weekly visit to a house of prostitution. This was the first mention of such visits in the eight or nine months of analysis, and Dr. Ticho first assumed that the patient's failure to disclose this information before that time was rife with psychological significance. Only later did she come to understand that these visits to the brothel were culturally bound, that they had been taking place for some ten years since the patient had first been taken to the house of prostitution by an uncle when the patient was seventeen years old, and that they held no relevance to the patient's relationship with his fiancee or his feelings about her.[223]

Dr. Ticho's second story concerned the treatment of a seventeen-year-old patient who was referred due to her promiscuity and suddenly failing

---

218. *Id.* at 88.

219. Tower, *supra* note 25, at 230. Tower concludes that this phenomenon, although widely condemned, is likely ubiquitous. *Id.*

220. Ticho, *supra* note 61.

221. *Id.* at 318-21.

222. *Id.* at 318. He did, however, report strongly erotic (albeit unconsummated) feelings towards his fiancee.

223. *Id.* at 318-19.

grades.[224] The patient (who was black) spoke passionately and politically about white racism and frequently accused Dr. Ticho (who was white) of such racism.[225] Dr. Ticho reported failure in her attempts to encourage the patient to examine her feelings about herself and the therapy.[226] Dr. Ticho believed herself to be free of racial prejudice, until a certain occurrence caught her quite by surprise:

> At the end of the tenth session with this patient, the patient was hesitant about leaving the office and suddenly said: "Last year there was a German girl in my class. She was quite all right. I kind of liked her." Whereupon, to my dismay, I made a typical beginner's mistake and said, "I am not a German, but an Austrian."

> How can one account for such a slip?

* * *

When the patient finally, for the first time, in the last second of that session, dared to indicate her positive feelings for the therapist, the therapist was caught unawares and heard only, "You are a German who has no regard for human beings, who even made human experiments with people of a 'lower race.'" To this the therapist reacted by saying, "No, I am not such a monster"; and, unfortunately, the technical blunder was committed. For a split second, the analyst's sensitivity toward the timid expression of the patient's positive feelings was lost, and so was her ability to identify with the patient.[227]

Love Countertransference Understood

Adam, had he read and understood the implications of Dr. Towers' work on erotic countertransference[228] and Dr. Jacobs' self-critique,[229] might have been conscious that he was drawn to Belle's "considerable charms," although his response was rather different than Dr. Jacobs'. Adam might have noticed that he contemplated their meetings with heightened anticipation. He then might have seen these deviations from his usual responses to clients as warning signs. If so, he likely would have responded differently than he did. He would probably have caught himself abandoning his usual—and usually appropriate—skepticism about his clients' protestations of innocence. Hopefully, he would have investigated the charges

---

224. *Id.* at 320.
225. *Id.* at 320-21.
226. *Id.* at 321.
227. *Id.*
228. Tower, *supra* note 25.
229. Jacobs, *supra* note 61.

against Belle more thoroughly. Were he then to conclude that strong evidence existed of Belle's culpability, he would probably have utilized his excellent powers of persuasion to convince Belle to accept the favorable plea offer.[230]

Hate Countertransference Understood

Acquiring awareness of his attraction to Belle probably would have been less of a stretch for Adam than confronting and understanding his more complicated feelings towards Carl—and their genesis. An understanding of Dr. Ticho's work[231] and an appreciation of the effects of unresolved conflicts or presumptions about differences in gender, race, culture or sexual orientation might have alerted Adam to examine his own conflicted feelings about homosexuality.[232] Individual analysis or therapy might have enabled Adam to understand his impatience with his twelve-year-old son who so easily dissolved in tears. Possibly, Adam might have come to realize that his anger at his son derived from insecurity about his own masculinity. Understanding countertransference, Adam might have realized that his disgust with Carl was triggered by his perception (conscious or not[233] and accurate or not) that Carl was gay, and derived from similar anxiety. If Adam came to understand these fears, they might have lost their powerful grip on him. Were he able to dispel his annoyance with Carl, he might have been able to hear and process Carl's claim of innocence, and, if warranted upon further investigation, he might have agreed with Carl's decision to proceed to trial.[234]

How is Adam to acquire such skills of self-awareness? Skills such as these evolve over a lifetime of experience. Ideally, one would commence this journey early in one's psychological development. But it is never too late to begin—even in law school or thereafter. Our aim as law school teachers must be to insure that knowledge of psychological processes and the skills needed to recognize and resolve psychological sore spots become basic learning objectives for all law students and lawyers.

---

230. *See* Bellows, *supra* note 214, at 89-90 (on critical importance of persuading client to accept favorable plea deal); Rodney J. Uphoff, *The Criminal Defense Lawyer as Effective Negotiator*, 2 CLIN. L. REV. 73, 97 & n.89, 130-32 (1995) (on obligation of defense counsel to attempt to persuade client to accept favorable plea bargain).

231. Ticho, *supra* note 61.

232. See discussion *supra* notes 86-89 and accompanying text.

233. *See* Lawrence, *supra* note 92.

234. Dr. Judy Kantrowitz suggests that a good "match" between analyst and patient may enable both parties to use countertransference positively so as to advance the analysis. *See* Kantrowitz, *supra* note 60, at 303-07. Arguably, a similar match might enhance the lawyer/client relationship. An attorney might find herself working harder on behalf of a client who reminds her of herself or someone close to her.

B. Cultivating Emotional Intelligence

1. Teaching Self-Awareness and Interpersonal Skills in Law School

Few would question the need for therapists or analysts to study interpersonal skills as a prerequisite for earning a license to practice their profession.[235] The requirement that analysts themselves submit to analysis before practicing, however, was a radical departure when first introduced.[236] "The idea of making a doctor into a patient before he can practice as a doctor is itself traumatic,"[237] and analysts are the only medical doctors who must submit to such treatment.

With the exception of psychotherapy—which is practiced by some medical doctors as well as other mental health professionals—the medical profession, like the legal profession, has virtually ignored emotional intelligence. Interpersonal skills are only rarely taught in medical school.[238] Most of us have likely experienced the frustration of encountering medical professionals who lack any measure of empathy.[239] Virtually all of us desire the assistance of medical professionals who can understand our pain and alleviate our anxiety. Our clients ask no less of us.

Apart from law school clinics—in which only a small proportion of law students participate[240]—law schools traditionally have paid little attention to skills training at all, let alone training in human relations skills.[241] As

---

235. *See supra* note 62 and accompanying text.

236. Tower, *supra* note 25, at 229.

237. *Id.*

238. *See* STEIN, *supra* note 25, at 172 ("Countertransference is a topic that should be introduced early in the education of medical students and continued throughout medical education."); Abigail Zuger, *When the Doctor and Patient Need Couple's Therapy*, N.Y. TIMES, Mar 31, 1998, at F4, col. 1 ("The current system of medical education leaves learning how to communicate well with patients entirely up to chance" (quoting Dr. Dennis Novack, professor of medicine at the Medical College of Pennsylvania-Hahnemann School of Medicine in Philadelphia)). *See also* Hulme, *supra* note 35, at 188, 191 (advocating education of seminarians about boundary violations).

239. *See* LOUISE HARMON, FRAGMENTS ON THE DEATHWATCH 128 (1998).

240. *See* MACCRATE, *supra* note 110, at 236-41.

241. At the time Harrop Freeman was writing about lawyer/client transference and countertransference, barely any attention was paid to the lawyering skills of interviewing and counseling, or to clinical education at all. FREEMAN, *supra* note 6, at 233; Diamond, *supra* note 99, at 67 ("The professional practice of law often requires nonlegal answers to human problems whose very existence seems not to be recognized by the legal curriculum."); Watson, *Teaching Professional Responsibility, supra* note 100. *See supra* notes 120-27, 132-34 and accompanying text for attempts at such training by Watson, Sacks

previously noted, Dean Griswold's 1955 call for human relations training in law school went largely unheeded.[242] Although some clinical materials (such as those of Bastress and Harbaugh[243]) do cover basic psychological principles, few law students are adequately exposed to human relations training.

Thanks in large measure to the impetus of the MacCrate Report,[244] law schools are increasingly integrating into their curriculum more courses on practice skills such as interviewing, counseling and negotiation to "bridge the gap" between school and practice.[245] But there has been little call for instruction on more subtle "practical" skills, such as training in human relations. In its compendium of core skills and values, MacCrate barely touches on the kinds of emotional intelligence needed for effective lawyering.[246] Yet emotional intelligence may be one of the most significant skills

---

and Stone. *See also* Elwork & Benjamin, *supra* note 98, at 583 (citing to others who have recommended law school training in human aspects of legal practice).

242. *See supra* note 133 and accompanying text.

243. *See supra* notes 152-53 and accompanying text.

244. MacCrate, *supra* note 110.

245. *See, e.g.*, Mischler, *supra* note 32, at Appendix (listing law schools offering courses in client counseling); Lawrence M. Grosberg, A Report on an Experiment Using "Standardized Clients" in Legal Education (unpublished manuscript, on file with the author).

246. The only intimations are found in the following two identified Fundamental Lawyering Skills:

Skill #5: Communication: 5.1 *Effectively Assessing the Perspectives of the Recipient of the Communication* (the client, decisionmaker(s), opposing counsel, witnesses, and so forth), and using this assessment to: (a) View situation, problems, and issues from the perspective of the recipient of the communication, while taking into account the possibility that one's ability to adopt the perspective of another person may be impeded by, *inter alia* (i) One's own partisan role and perspective; (ii) An insufficient understanding of the other person's culture, personal values, or attitudes. [ri]Skill #6: Counseling:6.2(c)(iii) The extent to which (and the ways in which) the client's perspective, perceptions, or judgment may differ from those of the lawyer because of: (A) Differences in personal values or attitudes; (B) Cultural differences; (C) Differences in emotional reactions to the situation; (D) Interpersonal factors in the relationship between attorney and client....

MacCrate, *supra* note 110, at 173, 179. One of the MacCrate Fundamental Values of the Profession may be read to include the need to recognize and resolve unconscious conflicts such as countertransference, but was likely intended to address the more obvious problems of substance abuse and mental depression:

Value #1: Provision of Competent Representation: 1.2(d) Maintaining the conditions of physical and mental alertness necessary for competence, including: &elip; (ii) To the extent that the lawyer's ability to provide competent representation is impaired, taking whatever steps are necessary to ensure competent representation of his or her clients, including.... [seeking treatment, soliciting assistance, referring

a lawyer can possess. In addition to helping the lawyer avoid boundary violations, it informs a myriad of other legal skills including, for example, counseling, mediation and negotiation.[247] Good Lawyers need to appreciate and respect their clients' emotional lives as well as their own.[248]

The law school of the 21st century should endeavor to insure that no graduate receive a law degree without exposure to the *psychology* of law practice. Ideally, all law students should leave law school and enter practice with an understanding of the techniques necessary to examine their own psychic tendencies, and an appreciation of the potential effects of the unconscious on the lawyer-client relationship.[249]

I do not wish to minimize the difficulty of such an accomplishment.[250] For one, there is the barrier of the overburdened curriculum. Although ideally a law student would arrive at law school already equipped with a grounding in psychology and psychological skills through prior education

---

client elsewhere].

Id. at 208-09. For a thoughtful critique of the MacCrate report in general, and its failure to address human relational skills in particular, see Menkel-Meadow, *supra* note 169. Professor Menkel-Meadow faults the MacCrate report—and legal education in general—for insufficient attention to "the human arts of lawyering." *Id.* at 619.

247. *See* Sacks, *supra* note 120, at 317-18; Interview with Stephen Reich, Ph.D., J.D. (July 7, 1997). Dr. Stephen Reich, a clinical psychologist who also holds a J.D. degree, graciously agreed to speak with me about my project. Dr. Reich shared his belief that the first interview with a client is essentially a psychotherapy session. A lawyer must listen carefully to the client to understand what it is that the client needs and wants. At each subsequent meeting with a client, a lawyer similarly should allow the client to have a psychotherapeutic experience in the course of the lawyer's acquiring necessary information from the client. For a discussion of the differences between the lawyer's role as counselor and that of a psychologist, see Meier, *supra* note 55, at 1360-61.

248. *See* Menkel-Meadow, *supra* note 169, at 620 ("the good lawyer needs to understand, from a human point of view, what the other wants to happen in the world"); Mischler, *supra* note 32, at 263 ("Both thinking and feeling must be engendered in the legal profession, as well as thinking *about* feelings.") (emphasis in original).

249. *See* WATSON, INTERVIEWING AND COUNSELING, *supra* note 24, at 82; Elkins, *supra* note 114, at 494; Watson, *Lawyers and Professionalism*, *supra* note 32, at 269, 275; Winick, *supra* note 51, at 13 ("These are skills that can and should be taught in law school and in continuing legal education."). Such skills would greatly assist lawyers in their dealings with judges, colleagues, bosses and adversaries as well. *See, e.g.*, Nelken, *supra* note 85 (importance of understanding unconscious processes in order to negotiate effectively with opponent).

250. *See, e.g.*, Sacks, *supra* note 120, at 320 n.10 ("In addition to data on the effectiveness of training, it will be necessary to consider such questions as the availability of faculty for this specialized type of course; the problem of already bulging law school curricula; the relative efficiency of training in law school as compared with post admission training, etc.").

and life experience, most law students have no such preparation.[251] Were basic undergraduate education to include human relations training, legal education could then focus on relating such knowledge and skills to the practice of law. However, as only a small percentage of entering law students have this kind of background, inevitably law schools would have to compensate. Moreover, successful education will require strategies for breaking down the *resistance* to crediting psychic life, which most law students bring with them to law school.[252] These are formidable obstacles.

As to the first concern, the curriculum is already overburdened. Many law professors are preoccupied with coverage and likely always will be. But as Dean Griswold recognized in 1955,[253] as Tony Amsterdam wrote in 1984,[254] and as Dean Feinman said in 1998,[255] no law school can or should hope to cover all the substantive knowledge that the law contains. Focusing on skill development, including the skills necessary to teach oneself, is far more essential.[256] And knowing how to bring emotional intelligence to bear on client problems is critically important. The prevailing skepticism regarding this assertion brings me to the second concern, and the greater challenge: overcoming resistance to crediting the importance of the psyche.

---

251. *See* Watson, *supra* note 95, at 98 (vast majority of law students have had no experience with behavioral sciences).

252. *See, e.g.*, Meier, *supra* note 55, at 1355 (discussing resistance of domestic violence clinic students to education about countertransference and other psychological processes in lawyer/client relationships); Stone, *Legal Education on the Couch, supra* note 132, at 438 ("[T]here is the considerable resistance of some faculty and students to what they consider to be either an amorphous learning experience or pseudotherapy.").

253. Griswold, *supra* note 117, at 207.

254. Anthony G. Amsterdam, *Clinical Education—A 21st Century Perspective*, 34 J. Legal Educ. 612, 618 (1984).

255. Jay M. Feinman, *The Future History of Legal Education*, 29 Rutgers L.J. 475, 479 (1998).

256. *See* MacCrate, *supra* note 110, at 211 (Commentary to Value #1): As Judge Judith S. Kaye [now Chief Judge] of the New York Court of Appeals has observed, "[t]he increasing codification and complexity of the law, the expansion of the law into wholly new societal areas, the heightened expectation of clients that their lawyers will know even arcane points of law of other jurisdictions in specialized areas, the new technology—all these serve to dramatize the eternal truth that ours is a profession that by its nature demands constant study in order to maintain even the barest level of competence." Kaye, *The Lawyer's Responsibility to Enhance Competence and Ethics, in* American Law Institute-American Bar Association Committee on Continuing Professional Education, CLE and the Lawyer's Responsibilities in an Evolving Profession: The Report on the Arden House III Conference 55, 56 (1988).

My colleague, Marianne Artusio, shared with me the difficulty of exploring psychological principles with the students in her clinics.[257] Professor Artusio uses the Bastress & Harbaugh materials,[258] but finds that students are enormously resistant to talking about, thinking about, or accepting the significance of transference and countertransference in the lawyer/client relationship. She introduces these issues at the beginning of the term and again at the end. By then, she finds the students a little more receptive, but not much more so.

I have suggested earlier that such resistance is breaking down in society generally, and in the legal profession in particular.[259] But this process is inevitably a slow one. It can be hastened by those of us who have the power to frame the discourse, especially those of us who teach in the first-year standard curriculum. As long as only a minority of law professors explores the relationship among emotions, the psyche, and the practice of law, students will reject such exploration as marginal and "soft," if not outright ridiculous. If students who self-select to take clinics are intolerant of psychological insights, it will surely be even harder to win over the many students who choose not to avail themselves of clinical opportunities.[260]

At least where I teach, however, even students who do not opt for clinics usually are eager nonetheless to learn lawyering skills. Most exhibit little if any resistance to learning "hard-core" skills like trial practice, negotiation and drafting, when offered as stand-alone electives or when introduced into traditional courses.[261] Students need to realize that interpersonal skills and the psychology that informs them are as "hard core" as these other skills. We, who teach them, must believe so, too.

We must teach these skills pervasively, throughout the curriculum. Students need to know from the first day of law school that understanding

---

257. Artusio interview, *supra* note 212.

258. *See supra* notes 152-53 and accompanying text.

259. *See supra* notes 159-168 and accompanying text.

260. This of course is a generalization. The reason at least some students do not avail themselves of clinical offerings is economics: many need to work at part-time jobs and lack the time for the all-consuming demands of clinical work.

261. For example, I teach Civil Procedure during the first year, and use the Lucy Lockett materials, created by Professor Phil Schrag of Georgetown University Law Center. PHILIP G. SCHRAG, CIVIL PROCEDURE: A SIMULATION SUPPLEMENT (1990). These materials consist of twelve discrete simulation exercises designed to teach procedure through the use of a simulated client. The exercises include interviewing the client, case planning, drafting a complaint, arguing a motion to dismiss, replying to a counterclaim, conducting discovery and negotiating a settlement. Students typically are very enthusiastic about the simulation.

basic psychological principles and processes is as important to the practice of law as understanding legal principles and processes.[262]

Ideally, a law school faculty should include a professional such as a psychiatrist, psychotherapist or social worker.[263] These professionals might be used in numerous ways. For example, they might teach stand-alone courses on human relations or interpersonal skills. They might co-teach clinics or skills courses.[264] They could consult with other faculty and help develop course materials and simulation components for the standard curriculum that will expose law students to psychological insights and processes necessary to the practice of law.

As with other skills training, the use of "hands on" instructional techniques will convey the desired lessons in the most effective and enduring manner. Simulations, the use of videotapes, videotaping and subsequent critiques of videotaped performances,[265] and other methods of problem-based learning[266] will be far more successful in integrating the necessary psychological skills than would more traditional pedagogical techniques. For

---

262. As with other skills and values—be they professional ethics, principles of justice, issues of diversity, or good writing—the failure to mainstream the lessons early and pervasively throughout the curriculum, creates a great risk of marginalizing their importance such that students consequently view them as "fluffy" and not "real law." *See, e.g.,* Margaret M. Russell, *Beginner's Resolve: An Essay on Collaboration, Clinical Innovation, and the First-Year Core Curriculum,* 1 CLIN. L. REV. 135 (1994) (discussing collaborative experiment integrating traditional doctrinal courses, clinical skills and issues of diversity in the first year curriculum); Russell G. Pearce, *Teaching Ethics Seriously: Legal Ethics as the Most Important Subject in Law School,* 29 LOY. U. CHI. L.J. 719, 737-38 (1998) (advocating pervasive teaching of legal ethics). *See also* DEBORAH L. RHODE, PROFESSIONAL RESPONSIBILITY: ETHICS BY THE PERVASIVE METHOD (2d ed. 1998).

263. *See* Diamond, *supra* note 99, at 75 ("Some of the top law schools now appoint psychiatrists and psychoanalysts to their faculties."); Watson, *The Law and Behavioral Science Project, supra* note 123, at 77-79 ("[A]n extremely important part of the plan was to place a psychiatrist on the faculty on a half-time basis. In the writer's estimation, this is a vital element in any undertaking where the integration of materials from two or more disciplines is to be attempted."); Watson, *supra* note 32, at 270 ("[I]t must be recognized that, at least for the present, most law schools will need outside, non-lawyer assistance to carry out this technique with skill and effectiveness."). Such professionals might also hold joint appointments at the law school and other schools within the same university, or, especially in the case of freestanding law schools, joint appointments at other institutions.

264. *See* Meier, *supra* note 55, at 1322-27 (discussing co-teaching domestic violence advocacy project with clinical psychologist).

265. *See* WATSON, INTERVIEWING AND COUNSELING, *supra* note 24, at 24 (suggesting videotape of interview interpreted by skilled professional; *id.* at 77-79 (relating specific examples of use of videotape in clinic).

266. For descriptions of problem-based learning in medical school education, see HOWARD S. BARROWS & ROBYN M. TAMBLYN, PROBLEM-BASED LEARNING: AN

example, simulated or "standardized" clients could be used to reveal manifestations of transference and countertransference, and strategies for their successful resolution.[267]

2. Continuing Education and Other Points on the Continuum

If students are pervasively exposed to psychological inputs before and during law school, inevitably that will affect how they think and act as practicing lawyers. However, the process of acquiring interpersonal skills should not end with law school. As with all other skills, acquisition and refinement must continue throughout the lawyer's career.[268] Bar associations and individual law firms can play an important role in facilitating this process.

Continuing legal education (CLE) is a place to begin. Today, more than three quarters of the states require lawyers to take CLE courses every year or two.[269] Most of the jurisdictions with mandatory CLE require a certain number of credits in a particular subject matter, most often ethics.[270] Some

---

Approach to Medical Education (1980); Steven Jonas, Medical Mystery: The Training of Doctors in the United States 352-56 (1978).

267. *See* Grosberg, *supra* note 245. Professor Lawrence Grosberg has been using standardized clients—based on standardized patients used in medical school clinical education—to offer quality skills practice and feedback to students. Currently, he is exploring cost-effective methods for using standardized clients for skills education of large numbers of students.

268. *See also* López, *supra* note 10, at 80-81:

You don't master lawyering... any more than you master living; it's not some knowable game about which you proclaim once and for all, "I got it." You plug along at it and try to improve the quality of your collaboration as you figure out new ways to change the world fundamentally. Even (or perhaps especially) when you've admirably re-inspired familiar and not-so-familiar practices with the aim to educate, you grow ever more aware of the need to stay alert and responsive to what you learn about yourself, about people and institutions, about how power operates in both large and small projects. In short, you understand just how integral education is to your conception of lawyering and living.

269. *See* Jonathan Lippman, *CLE: New York Bar has Reason to be Proud,* N.Y.L. J., Jan 27, 1998, at S1, col. 1.

270. American Law Institute, MCLE: A Coordinated Approach: Report and Recommendations, Table 5, Special Content Requirements 36-37 (1997). For example, New York State implemented mandatory CLE in 1997 for newly-admitted lawyers, who are required to take thirty-two hours in their first two years, including three hours of ethics and professionalism, six hours of skills (including writing, research and negotiation) and seven hours of practice management and other areas of professional practice. Part 1500, Mandatory Continuing Legal Education Program for Attorneys in the State of New York, § 1500.12 (minimum requirements for newly admitted attorneys). Effective Decem-

states also require courses on substance abuse and malpractice prevention.[271] Lawyers could be required or encouraged to take courses in human relations, or interpersonal skills, as well.[272]

In addition to their role as providers of CLE, bar associations might help in other ways. Bar associations could keep psychiatrists or psychologists on staff or on retainer and available for consultation by lawyers when psychological problems and questions arise in their practice.[273] Law firms, too, might retain professionals to consult with firm attorneys about emotional problems of their own or their clients that threaten to interfere with the professional relationship.[274]

---

ber 31, 1998, all attorneys in New York are required to complete a minimum of twenty-four hours of CLE biennially. *Id.,* § 1500.22

271. Arizona, New Hampshire, Ohio and Pennsylvania require substance abuse training as part of, in addition to, or as an alternative to ethics training. Arizona, Kansas, Missouri, and New Hampshire require malpractice prevention training as part of, in addition to, or as an alternative to ethics training. *Id.*

272. *See* Elwork & Benjamin, *supra* note 98, at 583 (["B]ar associations should consider approving continuing legal education credits for courses that focus on increasing interpersonal and psychological skills...."); Sanford M. Portnoy, *Responding To a Divorcing Client's Emotions,* MASS. LAW. WKLY., May 25, 1992, at 11, col. 4 (column and workshop offering advice regarding handling transference, recognizing and resolving countertransference by clinical psychologist). *See also* Watson, *supra* note 74, at 17 (discussing work with lawyers helping them analyze emotional interference in counseling relationships). Perhaps psychotherapy focused on professional relationship issues should also count for CLE credit.

273. *See* Pilpel, *supra* note 81, at 71 (describing New York City programs involving lawyers and psychotherapists). A psychologist serves on the Florida Bar's Professional Stress Committee. Jeff Schweers, *The Small Majority,* 68 JAN FLA. B.J. 14 (1994).

274. Some law firms currently have psychiatrists or psychologists on retainer for consultation and referrals for lawyers experiencing excessive stress. *See* Ellen I. Carni, *Stress and Productivity: For Better or Worse,* N.Y.L.J., Nov. 26, 1996, at 5, col. 1. *see also* WATSON, PSYCHIATRY FOR LAWYERS, *supra* note 24, at 17 n.5:

Information has come to the attention of the author about a law firm engaged in corporation practice, which worked out an arrangement with psychiatrists whereby they may call them into consultation in appropriate cases. When a situation arises where the lawyers believe that an emotional problem is the cause of the legal difficulty, it is suggested to the client that a psychiatric colleague be called into consultation. It is reported that results have been excellent in terms of salvaging clients' business relationships, and that all participants in the arrangement have regarded this procedure most favorably.

Divorce Lawyer Ronni Burrows employs "legal therapist counselors" to attend to the emotional needs of her clients while she concentrates on legal matters. *See* David E. Rovella, *"Therapizing" Divorce,* NAT'L L.J., Sept. 22, 1997, at 1.

Conclusion

Most lawyers have long resisted crediting the psychic forces in their lives, especially in their relationships with clients. Whether we acknowledge such forces or not, they exert a powerful influence on the quality of legal representation. Unconscious conflicts, inadequately resolved, threaten the competency of the lawyer/client relationship. These obstacles may be overcome by breaking down lawyers' resistance to acknowledging these problems and their root causes. Lawyers need to learn about the effects of the psyche on the practice of law. Among other things, lawyers need to understand how countertransference can interfere with their relationships with clients. Law schools have an obligation to provide this education. There is already a substantial body of literature available to inform this endeavor; hopefully more will be forthcoming. The challenge lies in developing successful methods for training in emotional skills. The organized bar should support the academy in this project and provide opportunities for lawyers to continue to cultivate their emotional intelligence beyond law school.

Chapter 14

Affective Lawyering:
The Emotional Dimensions
of the Lawyer-Client Relation

Linda G. Mills

In June, 1987, I met Elizabeth,[1] an African-American woman who was, as I was at the time, 30 years of age. When we met, I was a lawyer in the city of Richmond, California,[2] an African-American community where I represented people who were applying for Social Security disability benefits. As a lawyer with a master's in social work, a young, white woman raised in an upper middle class Jewish family, I knew my clients would suspect my intentions, and that I was not altogether qualified to understand theirs. However, I came to the work committed to alleviate the harshness of their oppression, with ten years of therapy, and some therapeutic training. None of this mattered though, according to my social work professors, who had prepared me for the harsh realities of cross-cultural work: the obvious differences between me and my clients meant that I could accomplish only the limited goal of obtaining Social Security disability benefits for the people I represented. I was, under no pretenses, emotionally, let alone culturally, prepared to intervene beyond my legal expertise. While in my heart I knew that I could offer more, I had neither the experience, nor the confidence to convince my professors otherwise.

So when Elizabeth, a new client,[3] arrived at my office and asked if she could hide under my computer table while we discussed the details of her case, I was not at all surprised by my conscious and deliberate effort to

---

1. The names of the clients have been changed, although their stories remain essentially true.

2. When I first started working in Richmond in the early 1980s, it was an exceptionally political environment. Confrontations with the police were not uncommon. To understand it's radical roots, it is helpful to note that a number of the Black Panthers and other radical civil rights groups were born and raised in Richmond, California.

3. I use the word client, not because of the subordinated role it has played historically in lawyer-client relationships, but rather, as a term which connotes respect; in other words, as the lawyer, you are there to serve them.

meet her "on her own ground." I asked her to pull up a pillow and make herself at home. I suspended all judgment, opened my heart, and heard her voice through my soul (all rather unconsciously). For quick reference, I scanned my experience for people I had known who had suffered traumas and tentatively assumed that her need for hard surfaces, for protection, was related to a previous assault, most likely in childhood. (A theory Elizabeth later confirmed.) Then I remembered Eileen, a client with whom I had worked previously, a woman with multiple personalities. Eighteen years of childhood trauma and 20 more years of abuse at the hands of her husband caused her to spend incalculable hours under her bed. Who wouldn't? But mostly, and most importantly, when Elizabeth asked if she could make her way under my computer table, I saw her terror in me.

Eight years later in Spring 1995, I taught an interdisciplinary course titled, "Social Advocacy and Domestic Violence" for UCLA social work and law students. When doing a mock interview with a battered woman in a restraining order clinic, I encouraged the law students who were practicing their skills to spend some time getting to know the client before discussing the legal issues with her. To "know" her, to befriend her,[4] to understand her experience, was to learn whether a restraining order was premature, unresponsive, or even dangerous. Imagine my surprise when my law students found this approach threatening; they argued that if they became "too involved emotionally"—they would not have the necessary distance to advise her from objectivity.[5] Perhaps more worrisome than

---

4. Charles Fried encourages lawyers to develop friendships with their clients in *The Lawyer as Friend: The Moral Foundations of the Lawyer-Client Relation*, 84 YALE L.J. 1060 (1976). My advice was given in a similar spirit, but with arguably greater emotional flavor. These issues are discussed in greater depth in the "Affective Lawyering" section. *See also*, Linda G. Mills, *On the Other Side of Silence: Affective Lawyering for Intimate Abuse*, 86 CORNELL L. REV. 102 (1996).

5. This sentiment is often echoed by law professors and clinic directors who work with law students. *See, e.g.*, GARY BELLOW & BEA MOULTON, LAWYERING PROCESS: CLINICAL INSTRUCTION IN ADVOCACY (1978); DAVID A. BINDER, PAUL BERGMAN, & SUSAN PRICE, LAWYERS AS COUNSELORS: A CLIENT-CENTERED APPROACH (1991). In one of my favorite stories in the latter book, Binder, Price, and Bergman advise other students to engage clients by asking them whether they found "good parking." The authors lay out the following interaction as an example of appropriate dialogue when meeting a client for the first time. "Lawyer: We can sit over here, Mr. Wilson [client]. You can put your coffee right here. Mr. Wilson: Thanks; say, that's a nice view you have. Lawyer: It is, and when things get crazy around here I like to stop and spend a few minutes just looking at the view; I find it's quite restful. Did you have any trouble parking? Mr. Wilson: None at all. Lawyer: Good. The parking situation in this building can be quite horrid at times and I feel badly when clients get delayed by the inefficiency of our parking service. I normally

their need to keep the interview free and clear of the complications feelings might engender, was their fear—they felt stymied by their differences with the women who sought their services. They worried how they could *really* understand just what the battered woman had gone through, if they themselves had never experienced abuse.

In general, the legal profession has resisted even the suggestion that emotion should play a role in the practice of law, especially in the interactions between lawyers and clients. While no one would probably deny that lawyers are actors in the legal dramas they produce, we are trained to believe that the advocate's job is to gather facts and to develop a reasoned strategy that will win a client's case. Distance and detachment remain the guiding principles of an effective practice.

Because of my sympathies to a more therapeutic approach, and my own experience as a therapist, I learned in my legal practice to rely on psychological skills to improve my effectiveness as a lawyer. What I found was that when I ignored the emotional dimensions of a case, I was not only less effective, but in some cases, incompetent. In this chapter, I will argue that the emotional alienation that is so often promoted by lawyers' formalist training, and the related problem of the obvious distance created by differences between lawyers and clients, has blinded many legal scholars and practitioners from seizing critical opportunities to meet the emotional, and hence, related financial, political, or cultural needs of their clients. In response, I propose an alternative method,[6] a postmodern[7] therapeutic jurisprudential approach,[8] a means and a passion for what I call "Affec-

---

warn new clients that parking may be a problem, and I realized I didn't say anything to you when you called. I'm glad things worked out well." *Id.* at 86. I am suggesting that feeling-oriented comments like "How are you doing with all your troubles?" or "It must be really hard to manage," might better serve the lawyer in negotiating a connection with the client; certainly this would be an improvement over questions about parking.

6. As Nietzsche put it, "The most valuable insights are methods." FRIEDRICH NIETZSCHE, THE ANTI-CHRIST. (Trans. Frederick Hollingdale 1972) 123.

7. By postmodern, I refer to the notion that lawyers would benefit from taking a "don't know" position. The operable assumption here is that legal advocates should abandon postures that claim to "know" how a client feels and instead adopt a position of not knowing. The client should supply the knowing the advocate seeks. My contention is that, at times, and especially in the domestic violence practice arena, the lawyer substitutes her position for that of the client. *See* Linda G. Mills, *Empowering Battered Women Transnationally: The Case for Postmodern Interventions*, 41 SOCIAL WORK 261 (1996); *see also*, LINDA G. MILLS, THE HEART OF INTIMATE ABUSE: NEW INTERVENTIONS IN CHILD WELFARE, CRIMINAL JUSTICE, AND HEALTH SETTINGS (1998).

8. Dennis P. Stolle, David B. Wexler, Bruce J. Winick, and Edward Dauer, *Integrating Preventive Law and Therapeutic Jurisprudence: A Law and Psychology Approach to Lawyering*, 34 CAL. WESTERN L. REV. 15 (1997).

tive Lawyering."[9] This method, like other psychology-based approaches to lawyering, suggests emotional ways for lawyers to meet their clients in the "space-in-between;"[10] an approach that helps lawyers acknowledge and work through the differences that all too often undermine their effectiveness as advocates. This method acknowledges that clients demand an emotional response, either explicitly or implicitly, and that lawyers must have the skills to address the anger, frustration, despair, or even indifference that legal interactions evoke.[11] Simultaneously, this method enables advocates to use the affective space created to ensure that a client's 'real' as opposed to superficial needs are met. This kind of practice[12] becomes possible, especially in emotionally charged legal interactions, when the client and the advocate spend time getting to know each other, that is, coming to understand one another in the context of the legal problem that brought them together.[13]

Recently, therapeutic jurisprudence and principles of preventive law have been developed and iterated to create a psychologically-oriented approach to lawyering.[14] These approaches provide promise for infusing affectivity into the lawyer-client dynamic and for improving outcomes and

---

9. The only reference, outside of my own work, I have seen to "affective lawyering" is in Peter Margulies, *Representation of Domestic Violence Survivors as a New Paradigm of Poverty Law: In Search of Access, Connection, and Voice*, 63 GEO. WASH. L. REV. 1071 (1995). Margulies uses the term "affective lawyering" interchangeably with such concepts as access, connection, and voice, contrasting it with other forms of lawyering, such as an instrumental approach. Margulies argues that an affective approach demands that an advocate spend "time" with her clients, that she be willing to self-disclose, and that she be attentive to the needs of these interpersonal relationships. Ultimately, Margulies argues for what he calls a "contextual approach." *See also*, Linda G. Mills, *On the Other Side of Silence*, note 4; Linda G. Mills, *Killing Her Softly: Intimate Abuse and the Violence of State Intervention*, 113 HARV. L. REV. 550 (1999).

10. Peter Goodrich, drawing on the French Derridean Luce Irigaray's work, uses this term to describe a third or distinct emotional space created by both parties to a relationship, *see*, LAW IN THE COURTS OF LOVE: LITERATURE AND OTHER MINOR JURISPRUDENCES (1996).

11. This is true whether the lawyer practices public interest or corporate law. The best attorneys respond not only to their clients legal needs, but also to their emotional demands. For an insightful political application of therapeutic techniques, *see generally* ANDREW SAMUELS, THE POLITICAL PSYCHE (1993).

12. Domestic violence, disability practice, and discrimination claims are a few of the kinds of cases that lend themselves to an affective practice.

13. Although this paper focuses on public interest practice examples, I believe that Affective Lawyering is appropriate in all practice circumstances. Given the limits of this chapter, I do not develop these ideas here.

14. Stolle, Wexler, Winick, and Dauer, *Integrating Preventive Law and Therapeutic Jurisprudence, supra* note 8.

satisfaction for clients in these interactions. Toward this end, Affective Lawyering is designed to be a form of preventive law practice insofar as it "secure[s] more certainty as to legal rights and duties" and teaches lawyers to learn more about the relevant events in clients lives in order to "improve decision-making and planning... reduce conflict, and increase life opportunities.[15] In addition, Affective Lawyering is therapeutic in its orientation to legal practice insofar as it is interdisciplinary, combining principles from law, social work, and psychology, and it is designed "to facilitate achievement of therapeutic" goals.[16] These aspects of Affective Lawyering distinguish it as both a method of preventive law practice and a form of therapeutic jurisprudence.

This chapter proceeds by presenting my own history, that is, how I came to appreciate the need for affective approaches in my legal work. In addition, I present a case example that suggests the importance of affective methods and what is lost when these approaches are not honored. Next, I analyze the issue of difference between lawyers and clients — differences that can be significant stumbling blocks to affectivity between lawyers and clients — and propose a method for acknowledging and working through those differences. Together, these pieces form the theoretical underpinnings of an Affective Lawyering approach that is modeled in a case example drawn from a domestic violence restraining order clinic.

Versie Hawkins

In 1983 I graduated from the University of California's Hastings College of the Law. I graduated confused, as most law students do, uncertain of everything except that I would practice public interest law.[17] I ultimately took a job representing Social Security disability claimants. Administrative law seemed familiar enough, and comfortable. Only a few judges were completely full of themselves, and only a handful wore robes. The judge at the close of my first Social Security hearing actually told me I had done a good job.

---

15. Stolle, Wexler, Winick, and Dauer, *Integrating Preventive Law and Therapeutic Jurisprudence, supra* note 8.

16. Stolle, Wexler, Winick, and Dauer, *Integrating Preventive Law and Therapeutic Jurisprudence, supra* note 8.

17. My experience of teaching in a law school setting is that much has changed in the sense that the course work is never explicitly racist or sexist as it was during my law school experience. However, as Patricia Williams has observed, while the most virulent examples of sexism and racism have been removed from legal discourse, an "unconsciously filtered vision remains with us in subtler form." *The Obliging Shell: An Informal Essay on Formal Equals Opportunity,* 87 MICH. L. REV. 2128, 2133 (1989).

On December 10, 1983, I was officially sworn in as a member of the California Bar. On December 11, 1983, my employer, Sandy Horwich, left for a six month tour around the world. My job was to represent the clients already on her caseload and to accept at least a few new cases each month. Only two warnings were issued: Accept only "winning" cases (the office supported itself on the contingency fees of successful claims) and don't spend too much time talking to clients (even then I had a propensity to chat).

In February 1984, I met Versie Hawkins.[18] At first blush, she seemed a typical Social Security client. She was 60 or so, African-American, a "retired" nurse's aide. She had applied for Social Security six years before and had been turned down, following four appeals, 16 months earlier. Sandy Horwich had previously represented her and had taken her appeal to federal district court. She had lost. Mrs. Hawkins had re-applied for benefits, as many claimants do, and had again been turned down. She had recently received notice that a hearing before an administrative law judge would be held in a few months, and wanted me to represent her. Mrs. Hawkins appeared in Sandy's office confident that I would take her case; Sandy had previously reassured Mrs. Hawkins that I was an excellent attorney, and that we would hopefully win this time around.

I perused Mrs. Hawkins' file from her previous case as she reiterated her troubles: Her back still hurt, her sugar was still bad, and she was tired all the time. According to Mrs. Hawkins, her medical condition had not changed since her previous appeal, except maybe that it had worsened. No, she was not seeing any new doctors, and she does not take anything stronger than Tylenol for her back pain. I told her that given that little had changed medically since her previous case, that I was inclined *not* to take it, that Sandy had not let me know that Mrs. Hawkins would be contacting me, and that I had been given strict instructions to accept only winning cases. Without new evidence, I said, or a much more severe condition, I was not confident that I would be successful. Mrs. Hawkins was devastated. She begged me, told me that I was her only chance, and that I would be forever remembered in her prayers. I attempted to put her back together, as best as a 25 year old inexperienced lawyer could, and sent her away. She would hear from me by mail.[19]

The next week was surprisingly hellish. I thought of Versie Hawkins at the oddest times. I kept coming back to it, haunted by these musings: Why practice law when even public interest did not spare you of these ethical or political dilemmas? To whom were my primary allegiances? Mrs. Hawkins, an African-American woman who endured a biography of rejections? To

---

18. Mrs. Hawkins name has not been changed. Mrs. Hawkins has given me permission to tell her story, as I do here.

19. Anthony Alfieri describes these ethical dilemmas at length in *The Ethics of Violence: Necessity, Excess, and Opposition*, 94 Colum. L. Rev. 1721-1750 (1994).

my office, a struggling public interest firm? Or, to the community as a whole, the other clients whose cases I would have to reject? Somewhat surprisingly (given my youth, the exigencies and demands of practicing public interest law, and given my formalistic and disengaged legal training), I made the right decision.

In March, 1984, I sent Mrs. Hawkins a letter telling her that I would accept her case and that we should get together soon to discuss any recent developments. Once I decided what to do, I treated it as just another case, until we met again. A week or two after my correspondence, Mrs. Hawkins arrived for her appointment. It was a typical appointment—I needed updated medical information, doctors, hospitals she had visited in the past few months, and anything else she thought was relevant. I elicited all the information I needed and then asked Mrs. Hawkins if there was anything else she had not told me. Well yes, she said, beginning to cry, "you know I've tried to finish things, get it all over." What did she mean? I asked with much trepidation. "You know," Mrs. Hawkins said, "I've tried to take my life."

She proceeded to share with me a suicide history that began with the first correspondence from Social Security some 8 years before. When the government had denied her application for benefits she felt a fraud, a liar, a fake. As her back condition worsened, she lost her ability to do much other than sleep. Mrs. Hawkins was fraught with guilt and overcome with desperation. She could not work and she could not support herself. She had never accepted welfare and was not going to start now. She was trapped. Suicide was her only option. What was so striking about Versie Hawkins' case was that we ultimately won her disability claim on the combined effect of her physical and emotional impairments. It was when Versie Hawkins felt comfortable enough divulging her emotional history, that we were poised to win her disability claim.

In 1986, The Hawkins Center of Law and Services for People with Disabilities was established in Mrs. Hawkins' honor and in her hometown, Richmond, California. It was to combine law and emotion, and it was to acknowledge and try to understand the differences that separate us. It was a center that would stake its success on winning claims on behalf of applicants by providing an environment that encouraged them to reveal what they needed to, and that together, lawyer and client, could forge through the legal process with an honesty that secured clients the benefits they desperately required. It was a place where people would tell the truth about the traumas that prevented them from working and where Elizabeth, if she needed one, would have a desk under which to hide.[20]

---

20. Fourteen years later, The Hawkins Center has represented over 2,500 people on Social Security disability claims, has a full-time social worker on staff to address clients'

Clients like Elizabeth, Versie Hawkins, and others showed me the legal value of recognizing, eliciting, and hearing the emotional subtext of our client's lives and using those painful and often humiliating realities as points of connection and as narratives for winning claims. In the moment Versie Hawkins shared her suicide history—race, class, and age did not separate us. Her honesty, that connection, became the basis both for a long term and deep relationship, and for creating an environment for building a successful claim *together*. The Affective Lawyering technique I map in this chapter presents the method I used for encouraging affective client interactions and for transforming meetings with clients into a more effective method of advocacy.

Conventional Theoretics of Practice

Affective Lawyering is both a reaction to an entrenched formalism of legal practice and an outgrowth of a new and evolving vein of psychologically-based approaches to lawyering.[21] Tracing a case example derived from a more traditional approach to lawyering provides the impetus for unveiling this new practice method that deliberately embraces the emotional dimensions of the dynamic between lawyer and client outlined in the next section.

Legal practice has been influenced most notably by the formalist tradition, the method applied both in the U.S. and England for some one hundred years. Its single-most defining feature is its emotional detachment— an unfaltering commitment to transcending the interests, especially the emotional interests of the parties involved. The alleged purpose of which is to legitimize the outcomes the law produces.[22] Justice Brennan, in his famous essay calling for a more passionate and engaged justice describes the formalist approach eloquently as "legal pharmaceutics," "dispensing the correct rule prescribed for the legal problem presented,"[23] like a chemist mixing the correct quotient of powder for a particular compound. Martha Minow and Elizabeth Spelman have similarly observed that

> [l]egal reasoning uses formal logic to proceed from premises, given at
> the start and to generate applications to new situations without reach-

---

emotional concerns, and has an attorney of the day hotline to answer the public's questions about disability programs.

21. For other examples of the application of therapeutic jurisprudence, *see* LAW IN A THERAPEUTIC KEY: THERAPEUTIC JURISPRUDENCE (David B. Wexler & Bruce J. Winick, eds., 1996).

22. Jane Flax, *Beyond Equality: Gender, Justice and Difference*, in BEYOND EQUALITY AND DIFFERENCE, 193, 195 (Gisela Bock & Susan James eds., 1992).

23. William Brennan, Jr., *Reason, Passion, and The Progress of Law*, 10 CARDOZO L. REV. 3, 4 (1988).

ing outside the given premises and without bypassing the demands of logical consistency. In law, for at least a century, the devotion to such a model of reason treats any attention to intuition, to experience ... [to] passions, as corruption. Emotion and passion signify evil, danger, and threat of disorder.[24]

Ironically, this approach adheres to the belief that success on a legal claim or action is most likely to be achieved through emotional distancing and the narrowing of the issues. I challenge this assumption and argue that in a number of instances exposing emotional issues may offer an exciting new tool to the advocate's toolbox, and to her overall effectiveness as a lawyer.

That the law ignores, deliberately disregards, and hence structurally represses the feelings of the people who come before it, that is, that it detaches rather than engages itself from those who seek its assistance, takes us one step closer to understanding just how lawyers, law students, and legal academics have consciously (and unconsciously) formulated how attorneys and clients should relate.[25] Beginning with the command that judges "reason" through and render emotionless decisions, attorneys are both directly admonished and indirectly counseled to present dispassionate, doctrinally relevant arguments upon which the detached decision-maker can judge. Lawyers are trained to seek only the details they need to formulate their narrow arguments and clients are, through this process, rendered emotionally silent and stifled by the weight of a fact-gathering[26] and precedent-oriented[27] system which, in its objectivity, produces an

---

24. Martha L. Minow & Elizabeth V. Spelman, *Passion for Justice*, 10 CARDOZO L. REV. 37, 38 (1988).

25. This is a generous interpretation of liberal or left-leaning academics who have not always been without culpability in struggles to do with hierarchy and repression. *See*, Peter Goodrich, *Sleeping with the Enemy*, 68 N.Y.U. L. REV. 389 (1992).

26. Lynne Henderson aptly describes the exclusion of feeling from case materials as a kind of exile: "Accordingly, the emotional, physical, and experiential aspects of being human have by and large been banished from the better legal neighborhoods and from explicit recognition in legal discourse (although they sometimes get smuggled in as "facts" in briefs and opinions.) Ironically, while emotion may generate laws via "politics," once those laws meet whatever criteria are necessary to constitute legitimacy in a system, they are cleansed of emotion under this vision of the Rule of Law. The law becomes not merely a human institution affecting real people, but rather the Law. *See*, *Legality and Empathy*, 85 MICH. L. REV. 1574, 1574 (1987).

27. Intrinsically detached from the parties involved, precedent is one of several means used to emotionally alienate people who seek the law's justice. Justice Brennan describes the history of the use of precedents as one cause of the judicial distancing process: "The number of reported cases had expanded seemingly exponentially over the years, and endless string cites of precedent began to dominate judicial opinions. The effect of this prac-

allegedly just result.[28] Deliberately promoted by the formalist tradition, emotional detachment whether rendering judgments, teaching case law,[29] or relating to clients, is touted as its panacea, the core of law's homosociality. John's case, described in detail below, provides an example of how lawyer and client are likely to relate when the emotional dimensions of a case are ignored.

John arrived at The Hawkins Center hoping to be represented on a Social Security disability claim. He was a shy 25-year old man who was alleging that he was unable to work due to a disabling depression. He came to my office to discuss his disability and to learn more about the hearing process. As in the Versie Hawkins story, it remains customary to "screen" Social Security disability cases to determine whether claimants' allegations and the medical evidence supporting their claims, will result in favorable decisions from judges. In general, lawyers practicing Social Security disability law accept cases they think they can win.

I was usually more liberal than most attorneys. I was liberal because I was running a not-for-profit legal and support services agency and hence more likely to take greater risks. In addition, I was more liberal because I had the unique ability and training to develop the emotional or psychological elements of a case; this supplemental evidence often bolstered the physical disability claims of my clients. My working hypothesis in my dis-

---

tice, of course, was to further distance the judge from the outcome of the case: it appeared that precedent alone determined each outcome. The rise of the legal treatise, with its strangely disembodied character, also contributed to this distancing process. The goal of the treatise—to classify reported cases into objective and determinative categories of legal principle—appealed to the positivist minds of the late-nineteenth century." *See supra* note 23.

28. Ironically this sanitized method provides only a mask, a cover for the judicial bias that is detectable in, but hidden by the formalist approach. *See, e.g.,* LINDA G. MILLS, A PENCHANT FOR PREJUDICE: UNRAVELING BIAS IN JUDICIAL DECISIONMAKING (1999), where I contend that impartiality, in the form in which doctrine has used it, is itself a type of bias, arguing that "a historically and contextually sensitive definition of bias, taking account of the communities and cultures that come to be judged in the legal system, must overcome the modern dualistic notion of impartiality as the exclusion of bias.... [t]o exclude bias is to engender prejudices in the form of what I will term repressed and therefore unconscious determinations of judgment" (at 13).

29. *See,* Peter Goodrich, *Maladies of The Legal Soul: Psychoanalysis and Interpretation in Law,* 54 WASH. & LEE L. REV. 1035, 1049 (1997) (discussing the significance of the grammatical deletion of the first person singular, the "I", in student law essays.). *See also,* Duncan Kennedy, *Legal Education as Training for Hierarchy,* in THE POLITICS OF LAW (ed. David Kairys 1992); and Gerald P. Lopez, *Training Future Lawyers to Work with the Politically and Socially Subordinated: Anti-Generic Legal Education,* 91 W. VA. L. REV. 305 (1989).

ability practice was that nearly all disability claimants were emotionally traumatized, in one way or another, by the process of becoming ill and also by applying for benefits. This trauma was caused either by the process itself (it could take up to 7 years to obtain benefits) or because the disability was so devastating that the claimant became depressed, suicidal, or even in some cases, psychotic simply from living with the illness or disease that disabled them. Having been trained as a social worker, I prided myself on my ability to elicit the emotional dimensions of a case. I felt particularly qualified to make psychological arguments on behalf of claimants and knew the judges respected my ability to do so.

When John arrived I was struck by his resemblance to a member in my family, however, I immediately repressed these feelings. What was also striking was that I was his peer—I was barely one year older than he was at the time that he was applying for benefits. John was obviously a very smart man. His problem: He had suffered from devastating sadness as far back as he could remember. This depression kept him from being functional—he had held only a few jobs since he graduated from high school. He obviously, as it was later revealed in our interaction, had feelings about uncovering his history to me.

I asked John about his psychological functioning. I was detailed and meticulous; I was persistent. I wanted to know why he thought the depression was disabling and how it affected every aspect of his life, including his relationships with other people. At the time, I noticed that my interrogation must seem scary. Despite this awareness, I justified my questions knowing that the judge would make a similar or equally offensive inquiry. I knew that John would have to sit through the judge's interrogatories, so why not test him now.

We met for a total of an hour. At the end of the interview, I could see that I did not need to gather his psychiatric records, or talk with his psychologist before making a decision on whether or not to take his case. I could see that he seemed a very scared young man, and that I had created a situation in which his terror was apparent. No doubt, I thought, that if I could replicate this experience in the hearing that I could convince the judge that John was totally disabled.

At the end of the interview, I told John that I would be happy to take his case and that we would proceed by collecting his medical records and other supporting documentation. He limply agreed, signed the papers, and smiled, all the while feeling terribly uncomfortable and seemingly devastated from the interaction. I knew, or thought I knew, what John was feeling, but I ignored the nagging sensation that I had violated him, that I had done violence.

As he was leaving my office, and we were saying goodbye, he turned back and said he had some reservations. I said, "Wow, okay, what's up?" He said, "I don't think I want to go through with this." I said, "With what?

Your disability claim?" He said, "No, with you representing me." "Oh," I said, "Why?" "I don't know. I just don't feel comfortable with you representing me." When I asked him if he could explain what he meant and inquired whether it would help to return to the privacy of my office, he said, "No." I asked him if he wanted a referral to another lawyer, and he said, "No." He walked out of my office.

This interaction shocked and devastated me. I was shocked because John had shown the strength to reject me, to react to my abuse in ways that were healthy. I was shocked because I knew that my interrogation of this very fragile man had caused him to feel so vulnerable. And I was shocked because I was so preoccupied with judging whether this claimant could present a winning claim to a judge, that I seemed unconcerned that my actions might exacerbate his suffering.

Eighteen or so years later, on reflection, this case presents several interesting concerns, and raises some important issues. To begin, I was aware that John reminded me of someone in my family, someone with whom I had had a conflicted relationship at best, and with whom I had felt victimized. Did the anger at my family member get "transferred" onto John? I think on reflection that there is no question that I felt less sympathetic to John's vulnerability because of my own family history that I had unconsciously associated with John.

Next, I was aware that John was likely to feel inadequate with me, given our closeness in age, and my obvious "success" when compared to his occupational "failure." He was obviously bright, but had floundered professionally because of his depression. I did nothing to assuage John's anxiety, to make him feel at ease; to feel unthreatened by me. Indeed, I may have even made things worse. By interrogating John in the way that I did, I may very well have made him feel more inadequate than he may have already felt.

Finally, my training as a lawyer gave me permission to abuse John, to treat him in the way that I did. Although I was unconscious of this at the time, I felt justified when making a decision whether or not to take a case, to take advantage of his vulnerabilities and to test his ability to withstand pressure. This approach helped me mimic work pressures and to determine John's ability to prove his disability. John was neither privy to my dirty little secret of testing him nor did he realize that the Social Security judge was likely to treat him in ways that were similarly abusive. Instead of easing the pain of the process, I exacerbated it and felt that good lawyering justified my reasons for doing so.

I have formulated three correlative critiques of current legal practice which I believe gave rise to my interaction with John. First, lawyers are trained to fear what they feel, to repress their feelings and, in general, to deny that their personal, let alone, emotional life plays a critical role in their work. This approach penetrates every dimension of the law school and practice experience. First year course content is static, and generally focuses almost exclusively on the "black letter law" as opposed to the facts of the cases which give rise to the lawsuit, or the idiosyncrasies or prejudices of the judges who decide them. Lawyering skills courses focus almost exclusively on the client's "problem" while students are discouraged from becoming too emotionally involved in the larger context of the client's life that motivates them to seek legal assistance in the first place. Even the more progressive professors teaching law school courses often structure them in a manner that is consistent with "training for hierarchy."[30] In addition, the practice of public interest law often prevents lawyers from extricating themselves from a legal services model that pressures them, institutionally speaking, both through high caseloads and a corresponding ethos that deters attorneys from exploring their own, or their client's feelings.

Second, students are nowhere encouraged to explore their own feelings, reactions, and traumatic experiences, and how these histories are evoked during interactions with clients. Transference and countertransference, terms used in psychoanalytic practice, are invisible to legal practitioners.[31] Transference refers to the feelings and history that clients may bring to the interactions with their therapists. Transference occurs when clients unconsciously transfer feelings evoked by a memory of people in their lives onto the psychoanalyst (or, in the case of a legal interaction, to the lawyer). Often, the therapist (or the lawyer) may in no real way resemble the person the client believes the analyst (or the lawyer) represents.[32] Countertransference refers to the reaction by the analyst (or the lawyer) to the client's account or problem, reactions that can take many forms including aroused emotion, or disturbed bodily and behavioral functioning.[33] Because

---

30. *See* Duncan Kennedy, *Legal Education as Training for Hierarchy, supra* note 29.

31. I have spoken at length about these issues in the domestic violence context in Linda G. Mills, *Killing Her Softly, supra,* note 9.

32. Transference, a mostly Freudian invention, occurs when the patient is in analysis and

"transfers" to the analyst the feelings that he experiences unconsciously for this or that character from her personal history. More precisely, he acts and repeats these motions in the current relation with the physician, rather than remembering the distant events that aroused them—the objective of the cure thus being to dissolve the transference by making it conscious.

Mikkel Borch-Jacobsen, Lacan: The Absolute Master (trans. by Douglas Brick, 1991).

33. Countertransference of Freudian origin, is well recognized in contemporary psychoanalytic theory and practice, and refers to an awareness that "[y]ou can exert no influence if you are not susceptible to influence.... The patient influences [the analyst] unconsciously.... One of the best-known symptoms of this kind is the countertransference

of their training to repress, and more profoundly to reproduce hierarchical relationships unconsciously through the law school experience, law students are discouraged from exploring how their own histories may emerge in interactions with clients, either evoked by themselves or by their clients, which may hinder, or even enhance their ability to meet in emotional spaces in which there is common language.

Third, given the repression of these feelings, it is not surprising that the differences (race, class, and education, to name a few) between lawyers and their clients cause tension, rather than facilitate connection. Outside of constitutional law and critical race theory courses, racial and other "differences" of clients are rendered invisible in the law school curriculum. Indeed, no cross-cultural or ethnic-sensitivity courses are taught, and hence, although some students will learn that race, and its intersection with other forms of oppression, must be acknowledged, they will not be taught how to make their way through an interaction that involves differences between the lawyer and the client. Combined with the fear I described, students graduate from law school not only terrified to express themselves emotionally, but incapable of doing so on the very issues to which their passion often speaks.

Affective Lawyering provides the psychological tools, as well as the emotional skills necessary to understand the client's layered experience, and the lawyer's conscious or unconscious reaction to it. Affective Lawyering teaches us the importance of valuing what we feel and what we have experienced, and using those feelings and experiences as the beginning points of a lawyer-client interaction or practice.

Affective Lawyering

Interactions with clients take many forms. Lawyers and clients meet in office settings, in community meetings, in jail and prison, and in court.

---

evoked by the transference." *See* ANDREW SAMUELS, THE PLURAL PSYCHE: PERSONALITY, MORALITY AND THE FATHER 147 (1989) (quoting CARL G. JUNG, HE PRACTICE OF PSYCHOTHERAPY: ESSAYS ON THE PSYCHOLOGY OF THE TRANSFERENCE AND OTHER SUBJECTS para. 163 (Herbert Read et al. eds. & R.F.C. Hull trans. 2d 3d. 1966)). *See also,* CARL B. JUNG, THE PRACTICE OF PSYCHOLOGY: ESSAYS ON THE PSYCHOLOGY OF THE TRANSFERENCE AND OTHER SUBJECTS paras. 164-167 (Herbert Read et al. eds. & R.F.C. Hull trans. 2d 3d. 1966).

Several practitioners have now addressed these issues in the jurisprudential literature. *See, for example,* Marjorie A. Silver, *Love, Hate and Other Emotional Interference in the Lawyer/Client Relationship,* 6 CLINICAL L. REV. 269 (1999).

They meet when the client expects something from the lawyer, that is, representation, or when the lawyer expects, or hopes to get something from the client, that is, their cooperation or assistance in a legal or organizing effort. Initial meetings can often be the most difficult, the most challenging, and the most revealing. In this section, I trace the nature of those interactions using an Affective Lawyering approach. I begin with an introduction to Affective Lawyering in general and explore how this method operates in theoretical terms. In addition, I begin to explore the challenges that race, gender, class and other differences present to lawyer-client relations, differences that so often underpin the unspoken dynamic of the largely liberal effort of privileged lawyers meeting their subordinated clients. I conclude by presenting an interaction between a lawyer and her client, and the struggles we face when meeting in the space in between.[34]

---

34. David Sibley in GEOGRAPHIES OF EXCLUSION (1995) describes a "space in between" most eloquently as "border crossings." "Crossing boundaries from a familiar space to an alien one which is under the control of somebody else, can provide anxious moments; in some circumstances it could be fatal, or it might be an exhilarating experience—the thrill of transgression."

Peter Goodrich first used the idea of "the space in between," or "the third space," when describing the 12th Century Courts of Love. Drawing on French Derridean Luce Irigaray's work, Goodrich argues for "laws that will help organize the relationships between women and men." In illuminating the usefulness or imagining a justice "in-between" parties, Goodrich suggests that the difference of such a justice resides in a fluidity or contingency that can only judge according to the sudden and future-oriented acts of a subjectivity created between two subjects: "a mixing of subjectivities or 'interpenetration,' a space between, a space—a touch, caress, body, or bond—that is not of itself but rather for the other." See, Goodrich, supra note 10 at 66.

The "space in-between" literature suggests that such a place is not only a phantasm of or between lovers, but rather that it is a function of everyday relationships. It suggests, as I do here, that however brief or insignificant an interaction, a distinct space is created which captures the energy of those moments. And when the two meet again, it is to that space that they return. In its most common sense, one might imagine one's relationship to a bank or grocery store teller. You meet, you exchange something special, a feeling stored with the previous expressions, content possibly irrelevant, but nonetheless distinct. It is yours together. Now imagine a client who has shared an experience, a trauma. You reserve a space for her, whether conscious or not, as she for you. Together you visit this space, with or without limits, with or without judgment, depending on what you bring along. Finally, imagine the space reserved for your friend, your lover, your spouse. It is distinct and separate, charged and safe, rainy and cloudless. But it is yours. This space in between marks the possibility of an affective or emotional relationship with clients; it recognizes the capacity and possibility of what we are intellectually constrained from realizing. Affective Lawyering gives us the permission to feel what we feel and to co-create the space in between.

Border Crossings to Affectivity

Affective Lawyering involves a deliberate attempt to reach our clients emotionally—to train ourselves to hear every syllable, every word, using every sense available to us, to understand first, and foremost, that every interaction contains an emotional subtext, second that in that subtext lies the key to a deeper relationship, a bridge, and finally, that the fruits of love and this project we are engaged in together can be found in the communication, in the shared language, in the space in between. I am arguing that two worlds—lawyer and client—can meet in a space in between no matter how diverse, and no matter how little time a lawyer may have to interact with a client.

The purpose of this approach is to find the affective common ground and to share in its possibility. It is on this emotional common ground that racial, class, neighborhood, education, and other differences can be bridged. Hence, Affective Lawyering involves understanding the emotional contours and the subjective and relational structure of the people with whom we are working. It is to train lawyers to be social workers, therapists, clinicians, or even friends[35]—whatever term one would use for people who listen for, understand, and respond to people's emotional lives. When these emotional divides are bridged through common experience, it is the beginning of a new way of relating. My argument is that to share these common histories is to reveal to subordinated people a very powerful secret: that privileged people also feel disempowered, even exposed, they just hide it better.

Commonality and Difference

We may not always meet in the same place, at the same time, as our clients. Internal and external forces such as race, class, and gender differ-

---

35. *See*, Charles Fried, *The Lawyer as Friend*, *supra*, note 4. Fried's basic thesis is that lawyers should be their client's "friend." He is specifically concerned with the question: How can lawyers justify taking a legal position, or working on behalf of clients, for ends that they themselves experience as morally undesirable? Defining the lawyer-client relationship as "special," Fried justifies the lawyer's morally reprehensible representation on the basis that the lawyer-client relationship is similar to that of a special friend or family member insofar as the duty, like with friends and family, involves an intense "identification with the client's interests." Fried rationalizes the lawyer's objectionable behavior by splitting the lawyer from himself, arguing that while "personal wrongs" committed by the lawyer-as-self are unacceptable, those performed within the adversarial system by the lawyer-in-lawyer role are justifiable given the overriding importance of advancing the interest and particularly the autonomy of the client.

ences may inhibit the opportunity to connect beyond the confines of a traditional lawyer-client relation. I am suggesting that despite these impediments, a shared mostly unspoken oppression often exist between lawyers and clients. That oppression might include experiences of domestic violence, death, or the passing of a relationship. Finding common ground in shared experiences of oppression is one therapeutic method for overcoming the race, class, and other boundaries between lawyer and client that impede effective practice.[36]

Affective Lawyering suggests that one method for working through the challenges race, class, and other differences impose is to meet at *common* threads of experience, experiences which may include the memory of sexual abuse, the loss of a child, or the threat of violence.[37] It is through the acknowledgment of similar experiences, either through deliberate sharing or unconscious validation, that the lawyer can connect with their constituents. When lawyers focus only on differences, I fear that alienation, not strength, ensues.[38] Only through connection, may the client realize her strength.[39] Affective Lawyering takes into consideration the intersection of race, gender, and class, by approaching differences with similarities, for the purpose of establishing the strength of connection, and hence to have the space in which to explore what separates us.

Three emotive or affective theoretical principles, including "shared suffering," "transference/countertransference," and "when and when not to share," underlie an affective practice, each of which converge with the race or difference issues raised by these reflections. I am suggesting that meeting on shared emotional ground, in spaces in between, enables us to get

---

36. For strength in this pursuit, I rely on Julia Kristera: "Every question, no matter how intellectual its content, reflects suffering." IN THE BEGINNING WAS LOVE: PSYCHOANALYSIS AND FAITH, xiii (Transl. by Arthur Goldhammer 1987).

37. For a discussion of the importance of recognizing race first, *see* Kimberle Williams Crenshaw, *Mapping the Margins: Intersectionality, Identity Politics, and Violence Against Women of Color*, 43 STAN. L. REV. 1241 (1991).

38. Kimberle Crenshaw's theory of intersectionality practice asks lawyers to focus on differences, rather than similarities. As a social work practitioner, I am sympathetic to this position. In Crenshaw's own words, she argues that "[t]hrough an awareness of intersectionality, we can better acknowledge and *ground the differences among us* and negotiate the means by which these differences will find expression...." *Ibid.* at 1299 (emphasis added). Crenshaw further suggests that "ignoring differences within groups contributes to tension among groups." *Id.* at 1242. I agree. I am arguing that the focus on difference should not preclude an effort to find points of connection.

39. This connection, or "relational cure" as Judith Herman has called it, can be the basis of an empowerment practice. JUDITH HERMAN, TRAUMA AND RECOVERY (1997). I have argued the importance of this connection in the domestic violence practice context. *See* Linda G. Mills, *Killing Her Softly, supra* note 9.

an edge on the usual barriers to communication such as race, class, gender, or educational differences. The issue is how does one create an environment, in a legal setting, for this possibility to occur.

Shared Suffering

Empathy is one avenue that legal advocates have relied on to meet clients in the space in between. Lynne Henderson, an advocate of a more personal and engaged theoretics of practice, explores how "empathy" might be employed to identify and improve the contours of the client-lawyer relationship.[40] I begin with Henderson's definition of empathy which provides a point of entry, and explore its relevance to an affective method.

Empathy, according to Henderson, involves the capacity to perceive others as having goals, interests, and affects similar to one's own. In addition, empathy involves the ability to imagine the situation of another. Finally, empathy translates into a "distress response" that accompanies this experiencing—which may (but not must) lead to action to ease the pain of another.[41]

Empathy, derived from an openness to suffering is, as Henderson describes it, most detectable in people whose early childhood experiences were characterized by some suffering, particularly as they relate to separation and attachment. This initial suffering, she argues, determines one's ability to "empathize" later in life. Empathic responses may often be hindered, Henderson argues, when it is inhibited by external conditions. Law school, for example, can cause one's empathy to be "foreclosed" or sent "underground."[42] It can also, I might add, in its alienation, rekindle a lost lifetime of suffering.[43]

Research reveals that individuals will have reduced empathic responses when they are instructed to see a victim in a detached way.[44] Given the

---

40. Empathy is a topic of much concern to the progressive lawyering community, generating debate on its practical merit. Few, if any, legal academics believe in it unconditionally. For the uses and limits of empathy, *see*, Richard Delgardo & Jean Stefancic, *Images of the Outsider in American Law and Culture: Can Free Expression Remedy Systemic Social Ills?*, 77 Cornell L. Rev. 1258 (1992).

41. Lynne Henderson, *Legality and Empathy*, *supra* note 27; *see also*, Lynne Henderson, *The Dialogue of Heart and Head*, 10 Cardozo L. Rev. 123 (1988).

42. Lynne Henderson, *Legality and Empathy*, *supra* note 26, at 1576 (citing A. Bandura, Social Foundations of Thought and Action: A Social Cognitive Theory 316 (1986)).

43. *See*, Peter Goodrich, *Twining's Tower: On Metaphors of Distance and the English Law School*, 49 Miami L. Rev. 901 (1995).

44. Drew Westen, Self and Society: Narcissism, Collectivism, and the Development of Morals 35 (1985).

difficulty the legal academy has had in recognizing that legal training priv-
ileges detachment over connection, disconnection over engagement, it is
helpful to decenter the empathy debate by situating it on new ground. Suffice it to say that empathy is relevant to an affective method insofar as it
begins with suffering. However, suffering, whether our clients or our own,
is a unitary process until one suffering being meets another in the space in
between. This geography suggests that the affective lawyer meet her client
not in the distance created or recognized by the conscious advocate aware
of the differences between them, or by the lawyer who finds friendship
through no fault or no effort of their own, but rather through the deliberate conscious or unconscious expression of shared suffering revealed in
the space in between.

Transference/Countertransference

So how do we share our suffering? This is best explored in the context
of two psychoanalytic principles: transference and countertransference.[45]
Transference refers to the experience of the patient in psychoanalysis, or
client in a legal setting. When the patient meets the therapist, or the client
the lawyer, she is encouraged to see the therapist as the person with whom
she has emotional conflict or attachment. I suggest that we might adapt
the principle of transference to legal interactions. Clients naturally engage
in transference with their therapists, and search for and even create emotional spaces in which to relate. Relying on this reality, it becomes possible for intimate meetings such as those between lawyers and clients to create the possibility of an affective base on which to connect.

Countertransference, on the other hand, exposes the fact that the therapist too is influenced by the patient, that the lawyer is affected by her
client.[46] Hence, countertransference encourages us to realize that every

---

45. For further use of these terms, and for applications of transference and countertransference in the legal context of domestic violence practice, *see* Linda G. Mills, *Killing
Her Softly, supra* note 9.

46. Marie Ashe, a legal postmodernist, and a lawyer who represents women who
abuse children argues that all our efforts ultimately lead to an affectivity which leads back
to ourselves. "When *I* seek to understand *my* own activity, when *I* attempt to construct
the meaning of *my* work, *I* am in need of interpretation that will take account of *my*
recognition of the power of horror and the pervasiveness of destruction. *I* am in need of
an ethic able to assert itself against the near nihilism that flashes and echoes through the
fragments, the flashings, and the sound waves of *my* children's lives and *my* student's
lives."

Ultimately, the reason Ashe's work is so compelling is that she is searching for a way to
understand why she loves her clients, even when they commit what appear to be inexplic-

interaction with a client could evoke a history which might and probably would directly affect how the lawyer reacts to her client's biography. Indeed, the principles of transference and countertransference provide the possibility that such an emotional connection can occur. The question is how.

Demeanor, body language, facial expressions, and conversational techniques all affect how we communicate with others. A softness, a comfort with oneself, a non-judgmental pose all contribute to creating a welcoming space, as does a recognition of the barriers when meeting someone different from oneself. However, none of these postures are possible without a desire and capacity to self-reflect. Knowing oneself well enough, what difference interactions "push your buttons," and the transference and countertransference issues likely to be evoked by one's own biography, are necessary components for creating a space for exploring the shared suffering. Self-reflection then is necessary to help understand and acknowledge the reality that transference and countertransference is operating, and hence can be more fully explored.

When and When Not to Say

While transference, countertransference, and self-reflection provides the spaciousness, the possibility for emotional meetings, it does not provide a blueprint for making those interactions a success. Indeed, most lawyers avoid the emotional realm altogether because they fear its negative emotional repercussions. (What if my efforts go wrong?)

Initially, it is helpful to remember that emotional interactions, like almost all meetings, begin with one's assessment of one's apparent differences (including race, class, education, etc.). On first contact, those differences are either reinforced or reified through judgment or rejection, or they are overcome through other means. Affirming a client's anger at the system, or sharing a history of child abuse, all the while feeling together helps make these efforts to connect a success. Next, this connection can only be achieved if lawyers reveal their own vulnerabilities, and expose their own weaknesses. They can do so with a glance, a story, a touch, or a word. But for the client to feel, the lawyer must also feel. And to feel usually means to know where, when, and how one hurts. This too is the job of the lawyer. Finally, once the feelings are exposed, it is to realize that dialogue can and should lead wherever. Never assume what your client is feeling. Navigate together and directly. It is the silence that oppresses, the unspoken subtext that denies. Go the conversational distance to know for sure that you

able and offensive acts against children. Marie Ashe, *Critical Theories and Legal Ethics: "Bad Mothers," "Good Lawyers," and "Legal Ethics,"* 81 GEORGETOWN L.J. 2533, 2536 (1993).

have met at a place at which the client chooses to go no further, do not stop before.

Meetings in Affectivity

To illustrate how an affective approach works, we will follow the interaction of a lawyer and client in a domestic violence restraining order clinic. I proceed first by presenting the lawyer's and the client's brief histories. I then present the text from their interaction and expose exactly how an affective dialogue unfolds. I model the Affective Lawyering approach and use "emotional subtext" to reveal the unspoken feelings of the lawyer.

Michelle and Lisa

I am Michelle, African-American, and 38 years old. I am married to Gary, a post-office employee and together we have four children. I have a GED and am currently enrolled in a paralegal program. For the past several years I haven't worked; I have remained at home to care for our kids. Last Saturday afternoon there was an incident. I arrived home late from school. My husband had said that he needed to use the car earlier that afternoon to run some errands, and that now I had made it impossible for him to take care of his business. He began to call me names like "fucking bitch," and made mean remarks to me like "can't you read a fucking clock." He kept saying that "if I would just keep my ass at home and pay more attention to the house and kids, none of this shit would happen." As I tried to explain why I was late, he punched me in the face above my left eye and said: "You better just shut the fuck up, or I will kick your ass." As I started bleeding, I screamed. Three of our children were home, playing in the back room. Eight-year old Lynn ran into the room. The neighbors must have heard because the police arrived shortly after the incident. In the meantime, my husband had left. The police took pictures and advised me to get a restraining order.

I am Lisa, a white middle-class woman, 32 years old and have had 6 years experience volunteering as a lawyer for battered women. I have been in group therapy regarding my own childhood and adult history of abuse and feel I have a good grasp of the issues that push my buttons. My first husband was physically and emotionally abusive. I decided not to get a restraining order against my ex-husband, but I do respect women who wish to do so. I do this work because I understand how victims of abuse feel and I want to help them make choices that they feel good about.

Here is a glimpse of the initial interview between Lisa and Michelle:

* * *

Lisa: Hi Michelle, please let's sit here. My name is Lisa.

Emotional Subtext (LISA): *I am aware that the restraining order clinic is busy this morning. There are at least 6 clients waiting and 4 volunteers working with women. There isn't much space to meet, except in a small corner in the office. I know I must work quickly to meet all the demands on my time.*

I notice that Michelle has a cut above her eye. I also notice that she is hesitant to be here. I know this because when she enters and I pull my chair forward to talk more privately, she pulls back. I sense she may be reluctant.

Michelle: Hi. What do I need to do?
Lisa: This is the Santa Monica Restraining Order Clinic. I'm a lawyer here and I want to help you. I'm willing to help however you'd like me to. I know this clinic is ridiculously small and not very private, but when it is this busy, usually no one is interested in what we are talking about. So hopefully you'll feel okay telling me your story. If not, stop me at any time. Should I continue?
Michelle: Sure, go ahead.
Lisa: I see your eye is cut. What happened?

Emotional Subtext (LISA): *At this point I hope that Michelle is feeling a little more comfortable. I deliberately reassure Michelle about the office space, although she still seems uncomfortable.*

Michelle: I had a fight with my husband on Saturday and he hit me. He can be such a jerk.
Lisa: Did you go to the doctor?

Emotional Subtext (LISA): *I have two choices at this point, affirm that men are jerks or encourage her to tell me more about the incident, and of course her history. I decide to ask if she went to the doctor, mostly to find out if there is any record of the abuse. There are two reasons I don't pursue the "jerk" comment. First, I don't know enough about Michelle's relationship with Gary, i.e., how long they've been together, how she feels about him, etc. I wonder if she is testing me. Do I hate men? Will I try to convince her to leave her husband? It's just too risky to respond to this comment with so little information at this point. Nonetheless, I give her a supportive glance to reassure her that her comment about her husband has registered.*

Michelle: No, I didn't. I went with my kids to my sister's house.
Lisa: Did the police come?
Michelle: Yes. They took pictures and prepared a police report. They told me to come here and get a restraining order.
Lisa: Did they arrest your husband?
Michelle: No, he wasn't home when they came.

Emotional Subtext (LISA): *This is a critical moment. I need to know more about how Michelle feels about her husband being arrested. What are the emotional, cultural, or financial issues that affect how Michelle relates to Gary. In the next micro-interaction I want Michelle to feel as comfortable as possible divulging this to me. Of course I can't assume that her husband is African-American. He might be white, Latino, or Asian... This may be relevant in terms of what she may feel she wants to do.*

Lisa: How are you feeling about all this?
Michelle: It's hard but I need to get some stuff resolved.

Emotional Subtext (LISA): *I sense now that Michelle doesn't want me to get into her feelings, that she is here to get some business done. I decide not to follow up with another feeling question.*

Lisa: Okay, so here are some options. We'll have to talk more about what happened on Saturday, and other previous incidents with your husband, if there are any, and decide whether you would like a restraining order. If not, you can leave here with the information you may need about how to get a restraining order at some later point.

Emotional Subtext (LISA): *Michelle seems relieved that she can get some advice on what to do, and where to go from here. I figure that once I give her the options, then she might feel more comfortable talking about what happened, and about her feelings. Also, giving her options will help her explore her feelings in concrete form, and she won't feel as though she has wasted the morning.*

Lisa and Michelle explore Michelle's options. She was afraid of her husband, it seemed, and she needed him for the income. She still loved Gary and she certainly did not want him to lose his job. She also didn't see herself relying on the "the system" to help her. She didn't trust cops or the courts. Bottom line, she didn't want Gary to get in trouble.

Lisa: So, you feel worried that if you get a restraining order and the neighbors call the police that they will take your husband away. Is that about right?

Michelle: Yes, I do not want to deprive my children of their father, and I do not see how I can support them without their father. I do not want him to get arrested because I do not want my husband's boss to find out about our problems. And I do not want to get welfare because I do not want to live off government money. I do not want to create any problems for my husband, I just want and need my own space for awhile.

Lisa: Here's one way of thinking about it: If you get a restraining order, it is more likely that your husband will be arrested if the police come to your home. You will be building a case against him. If you don't get a restraining order, the police may still arrest him if it looks like he has hurt you. In addition, if you don't get a restraining order, or take any other affirmative action, it could be that the Department of Child and Family Services ("DCFS") will conclude that you aren't doing enough to protect your children.[47] But even if you get a restraining order, it won't protect you. Oftentimes, leaving can be the most dangerous time.

Michelle: Yeah, I've threatened to leave before and he always gets more mad.

Michelle decides to get the restraining order, mostly because she is afraid that DCFS might threaten to take her children away if they find out about the abuse. She also decides to write Gary a letter telling him that she will stay away until the end of the month and then will expect him to find another place to live—at least temporarily. If he does not cooperate with her, she will send a copy of the restraining order to his boss. She feels that Gary is afraid of losing his job and that this may calm him down. Lisa uses the arrest studies[48] to suggest that this may work to stop the violence but only after Michelle has thoroughly explored her own assessment of the situation.

---

47. For a further discussion of the intersectional issues related to domestic violence and child welfare, *see* Linda G. Mills, "Intimate Abuse and the Violence of State Intervention in the Child Welfare Context." Presentation, Sixth National Child Welfare Conference, March 30, 2000, U.S. Department of Health and Human Services.

48. For a summary of the arrest studies, *see*, Linda G. Mills, *Mandatory Arrest and Prosecution Policies for Domestic Violence: A Critical Literature Review and the Case for More Research to Test Victim Empowerment Approaches*, 25 CRIM. L. & BEHAVIOR 306 (1998).

Emotional Subtext (LISA): *At one point in the interview, Michelle is undecided whether to get the restraining order. I remember my agonizing experience over this decision and decide not to tell Michelle about it. I feel that my decision not to get one may influence what Michelle is going to do. If I felt that Michelle needed permission not to get one, or if I felt it would enlighten Michelle's thinking, I would tell her, but neither seem true. What seems obvious to me is that Michelle is pretty much decided she wants to get one, she is fed up with Gary's shenanigans; she is just afraid that getting a restraining order will backfire and wants some reassurance it won't. I can't and don't promise, but rather help Michelle feel stronger in the ambiguity of the situation.*

Michelle: There's another problem. My parents really hate when I say anything bad about Gary and I am afraid that if I get a restraining order against him that they will get really mad. Anyways, I don't think you would understand.

Emotional Subtext (LISA): *I observe that Michelle really wants to factor her parents into her final decision. I am currently married to an African-American man and am trying to decide whether to tell Michelle that I do feel that I understand the cultural issues involved in this decision. I quickly weigh and balance the advantages and disadvantages. The advantage is that Michelle may feel more at ease sharing her story with me. On the other hand, Michelle might react to the fact that I am married to an African-American, and she might judge that negatively. I decide against disclosure. I think that it is adding something to Michelle's full emotional plate, which she does not need. I conclude that she will probably gain little from the disclosure, except maybe that she would be more forthcoming—something I have been concerned about throughout the interview. I need some personal story here to help Michelle through. I decide to share how my parents reacted to the abuse in my first marriage.*

Lisa: Actually, I might understand, but you tell me. I was in a bad marriage, and my ex-husband used to hit me. When I told my parents, they not only told me to "make it work," but they also told me that they would "disown me" if I divorced him.

Michelle: Gosh, what did you do?

Lisa: It was really difficult, but I told my parents that if I didn't leave him I was afraid they'd read about me dead one day in the newspaper. End of story. After two years they got used to the idea and they're okay now. It just took a while.

Michelle: Yeah. So, that's a good thing to say.

Lisa: The advantage you have is that you can say that your children
             are unsafe when your husband gets crazy. Sometimes that works
             with grandparents. Again, that's assuming you decide you want
             to leave Gary. You may decide that the good outweighs the bad.
             That's up to you, but what's really important is that you assess
             whether you feel that you or your children's lives are truly in
             danger.

Emotional Subtext (LISA): *I know how important it is to allow battered
women to own their feelings. Michelle should not feel that I would judge
her if she didn't leave Gary or if she did something different than what
I had done. The point is only to open up spaces, points of entry, new
ways of thinking about opportunities for Michelle to explore.*

Michelle proceeds to share her history of abuse with Lisa. She feels
that they have connected and that she isn't absolutely sure whether her life
is threatened. She'd like to lay it all out and maybe they could decide
together.

Transgressing to an Affective Practice

Meet the Client/Know Oneself

The method which I reveal in this brief interaction begins with meeting
the client. First impressions are always critical and you should be self aware
enough to know where your strength comes from (was it passed on, was
it the result of overcoming the adversity of your life's circumstances, etc.)
and where your weakness is situated. It is helpful to know what your prejudices and predilections are, and what your positive biases may be. What
makes you melt into tears? What makes you angry? If a client disapproves,
or asks many questions, or is needy—how do these responses affect you?
How do your responses reflect your childhood experiences? Who in your
family tends to be impatient? Who in your family takes a long time to tell
a story? How do you generally react when someone reminds you of that
person?

Ultimately, you should learn how to enter an interaction and to temper
your emotional responses to your clients. If your client needs you to be
strong, be strength. If your client needs to see you as vulnerable, reveal
your vulnerabilities. This is part of meeting your client where she is, of
seeing her non-judgmentally, and for who she is in the moment. It is to
meet her in a space where you know what you bring in terms of emotional

baggage, and you can detect what the client brings too. Remember that she is new and different to *you*. She is her own person and not the essentialized stereotypes you may unreflectively impose. It is not to deny our clients weaknesses, but rather to see them without negative judgment. To see them as our weaknesses, the weakness we all share. And similarly, to see her strengths, as you see your own—not to judge them as intrusive, in the way, or demanding, but rather, to respect clients for their emotional complexities.

In addition, it is to consciously recognize that you see a client as she is "a woman of color," "a woman with a disability," "a woman with a sexual preference." To see how cultural or difference history situates you both and to acknowledge that her biography poses sites or opportunities for connection, and even possibly for mutual growth. It is to tolerate the ambiguity of the difference and the newness of the interaction and to be sensitive to every little nuance. It is to sense every breath, to anticipate every feeling, and to respond as precisely to her needs as is humanly possible.

Know the Issue/Know Oneself

If the issue is domestic violence, acknowledge consciously or unconsciously, depending on the situation, your emotional and intellectual experience of intimate abuse. Know what the likelihood or chance of danger is to her or to her children, given a certain fact pattern. Read the literature, criticize the empirical studies. Have the skills to provide her with a safe place to explore the answers to the questions nobody can answer. The client in an intimate abuse case is in the best position to assess dangerousness, assuming she is given a safe space to judge it. Together you should reason through the likely scenarios. Solicit the history and help her weigh and balance each relevant factor. But to do this work you start from where she is, as was the case in the interaction between Lisa and Michelle. It was important first that Lisa help Michelle feel strong enough to share. Often, to be able to start from where she is, you must start from your own story.

If helpful or relevant, share with her your history. Use it only to cross bridges, to provide moments of connection; don't share because *you* need to share. Does it help to tell her you have lived a similar trauma? As in the Michelle/Lisa scenario, do not necessarily tell her how you resolved a given problem unless you feel she is ready enough to hear you, and that she will not feel judged for taking a different path. Or tell your story in such a way that you remain ambivalent about the outcome. Or quite simply, share with her your own predicament and how difficult it was to decide.

Understand the Context/Know Oneself

Be familiar with the psychological and political context of the work you do. If you are inclined to judge someone for their sexual orientation, deal with it by talking these issues through before you enter an interview with a gay or straight client. What is threatening about working with a gay man if you are straight, or a straight man if you are gay? What is scary about talking to people about problems you yourself may never share? Discuss this with friends, co-workers, or with people trained in the field to address your prejudices. And limit these interactions should your discomfort persistently interfere in your work together.

Using emotional subtexts and interpretations can be key to knowing the context, knowing oneself, because they provide sites or opportunities for political and personal growth. The only way lawyers can truly understand difference is if they engage themselves in their own and their client's lives, not as we are taught in law school, to remove ourselves from client interactions. The rewards in practicing law are beyond the few victories we have in court; they also lie in the dynamics between the similarities and differences of people, in the uniqueness of the opportunity to transgress boundaries where very few lawyers have ventured.

In summary, Affective Lawyering can provide lawyers with the emotional skills necessary for doing a more therapeutically-engaged and psychologically-oriented practice. These methods give lawyers the tools to dialogue, to open up spaces of conversations that traditional legal or formal discourse prevents. Affective Lawyering provides the impetus and the emotional desire to grow personally from our work with the clients we meet and to reflect on that growth as a method of mutual understanding. It is, in this regard, a fundamental shift in how we practice law.

I have argued that self-reflection, that living at the subtext, actually enables us to have the difficult conversations lawyers need to have in order to accomplish the tasks involved in developing a more effective practice. It gives us the tools to meet in cross-cultural or difference contexts and to appreciate how these seemingly impossible barriers might be met with love and appreciation. Affective Lawyering is an avenue for exploring the spaces that seem so marred by difference, and for penetrating them. It is in the shared suffering, in the transference and the countertransference, and in the emotional capacity to discern when and how to share, or not, that we can meet in ways that make for a comprehensive yet nuanced response. Toward this end, Affective Lawyering provides opportunities to meet clients' emotional needs, and in doing so, to better understand their legal and material needs. In this regard, Affective Lawyering accomplishes multiple goals, and overall, provides the possibility for a more rewarding and successful practice.

VI.

Therapeutic Jurisprudence
and Legal Culture

Chapter 15

Therapeutic Jurisprudence and the Culture of Critique

David B. Wexler

In *The Argument Culture: Moving from Debate to Dialogue*,[1] linguist Deborah Tannen explores how a culture of argument and critique severely limits creative problem solving. Tannen demonstrates how an argument culture or culture of critique pervades Western society and manifests itself in politics, journalism, academia, and, of course, law.

Tannen's argument is not with the value of argumentation itself; she has no qualms with argumentation and critique as legitimate and indeed crucial aspects of critical thinking. Her concern is rather with the *culture of critique* — the political, journalistic, academic and legal cultures that *privilege* argumentation and critique and *disparage* other approaches of intellectual inquiry.

I am struck by how developments in therapeutic jurisprudence have overwhelmingly been the product of just such alternative approaches of intellectual inquiry. This essay will summarize Tannen's main points and then trace the evolution of therapeutic jurisprudence in theory and practice, illustrating how, in the law and mental health area, an alternative approach has taken us along a different, and occasionally bumpy, but always stimulating, problem-solving path.

I. The Culture of Critique

Although argumentation and critique have, as methodologies, served us well,[2] "[o]ur spirits are corroded"[3] by a *culture* of critique that "urges us to approach the world — and the people in it — in an adversarial frame of mind."[4] In our culture of critique, opposition and debate are the preferred methods of resolving conflicts and of solving tough problems. We engage

---

1. DEBORAH TANNEN, THE ARGUMENT CULTURE: MOVING FROM DEBATE TO DIALOGUE (1998) [hereinafter ARGUMENT CULTURE].
2. *Id.* at 3.
3. *Id.* at 3.
4. *Id.*

in debate rather than dialogue, use war metaphors to describe disagreement over policy, and generally have come to enjoy a good fight and to regard politics as a spectator sport.

Despite its short-term entertainment value, the costs of a culture of critique are considerable. It leads us to focus on controversial matters. We ask questions such as "What is the most controversial thing about your book?,"[5] even when, as is often the case, "the most controversial thing is not the most important."[6] It prods us to be "provocative" rather than "thought- provoking," which "can open old wounds or create new ones that are hard to heal."[7]

By encouraging debate rather than dialogue, the culture of critique leads us to believe that every issue has "two sides — no more, no less,"[8] and ignores the fact that "often the truth is in the complex middle, not the oversimplified extremes."[9] When "the middle ground, the sensible center, is dismissed as too squishy, too dull,"[10] and when nuanced views are denigrated and the policy-makers who support nuanced, middle ground positions are regarded as two-faced,[11] compromise is often sacrificed in favor of polarized, rigid ideology.[12]

The argument culture revels in debate on inflammatory issues. It encourages us to take on the "big divisive issues" rather than to attempt to heal a hurtful divide.[13] A "big divisive issue," however, is often so categorized "not because it is very important but because it is very divisive."[14]

Relatedly, intellectual inquiry in a culture of critique focuses on criticism rather than on "integrating ideas from disparate fields...."[15] Moreover, "opposition does not lead to the whole truth when we ask only 'What's wrong with this?' and never 'What can we use from this...?'"[16] We tend to play what Peter Elbow calls "the doubting game,"[17] approaching "others' work by looking for what's wrong,"[18] and do not systemati-

---

5. *Id.* at 5.

6. *Id.*

7. *Id.* at 7.

8. *Id.* at 10.

9. *Id.*

10. *Id.* at 29 (quoting Washington Post media critic Howard Kurtz).

11. *Id.* at 42.

12. *Id.* at 99. *See also id.* at 97.

13. *Id.* at 117-18.

14. *Id.* at 119.

15. *Id.* at 19.

16. *Id.*

17. *Id.* at 273 (referring to Peter Elbow, Embracing Contraries: Explorations in Learning and Teaching (1986)).

18. *Id.* at 273.

cally approach new ideas with the different spirit of a "believing game,"[19] that would encourage us to look for new insights and do "integrative thinking."[20]

The believing game by no means requires uncritical acceptance of new ideas, theories, findings. As Tannen puts it:

> The believing game is still a game. It simply asks you to give it a whirl. Read *as if* you believed, and see where it takes you. Then you can go back and ask whether you want to accept or reject elements in the argument or the whole argument or idea.... We need a systematic and respected way to detect and expose strengths, just as we have a systematic and respected way of detecting faults.[21]

In addition to systematically playing the believing game, Tannen believes we can better our problem-solving skills by the use of other helpful approaches and techniques—several of them suggested by communitarian scholars. We might look at a specific problem and ask "What shall we do about this?"[22] In doing so, we might look at the problem from several angles, not simply from two polarized sides. In moving from debate to dialogue, it may also be useful to leave some issues out, to avoid talking exclusively about rights, which seem non-negotiable, and to focus more on "needs, wants, and interests."[23]

With such an expanded approach to problem solving, we may also increase the pool of problem-solving talent. In a culture of critique, those who do not thrive on a steady diet of criticism or confrontation may drop out of—or never choose to enter—the domains of academia,[24] politics, journalism, and law.[25]

Law seems to play a central role in the argument culture. First of all, "[t]he American legal system is a prime example of trying to solve problems by pitting two sides against each other and letting them slug it out in public."[26] Moreover, the legal system both "reflects and reinforces our assumption that truth emerges when two polarized, warring extremes are set against each other."[27]

---

19. *Id.*
20. *Id.*
21. *Id.*
22. *Id.* at 276.
23. *Id.* at 288.
24. *Id.* at 268.
25. *Id.* at 277.
26. *Id.* at 131.
27. *Id.*

The corrosive effect of an attitude that "[l]itigation is war,"[28] and of judging lawyers by such standards as whether they performed a tough or lackluster cross-examination,[29] may explain in part the well-documented phenomenon of lawyer distress and dissatisfaction.[30] The adversarial culture, therefore, needs also to be examined for its impact on "what it does to those who practice within the system, requiring them to put aside their consciences and natural inclination toward human compassion."[31]

And when the legal system and its lawyers put aside natural inclinations toward human compassion, we begin to take for granted certain behaviors and practices that we ought to find disturbing. For example, our legal system discourages a driver from apologizing after an automobile accident.[32] Our criminal law system similarly discourages people from admitting wrongdoing and accepting responsibility.[33] And our emphasis on litigation often does not allow people to get on with their lives until a lawsuit is resolved, thus exacting a high psychological cost.[34] "As so often happens with the argument culture," says Tannen, "the ultimate price is paid by human beings in personal suffering."[35]

Tannen notes with approval the ameliorative measures of mediation and other alternative dispute resolution and problem-solving approaches that are beginning to gain support both within the legal profession and among society at large.[36] It is within this alternative framework that therapeutic jurisprudence would fit—both in terms of its mission of scholarship/law reform and in its mission to infuse the human element into day-to-day lawyering and judging. Accordingly, it is time to turn our attention to therapeutic jurisprudence and its development.

II. Therapeutic Jurisprudence

Therapeutic jurisprudence, with its focus on the law's impact on emotional life and psychological well-being, is today a therapeutic perspective on the law in general, and is by no means substantively restricted to the

---

28. *Id.*
29. *Id.* at 144.
30. *Id.* at 159.
31. *Id.* at 146.
32. *Id.* at 148.
33. *Id.* at 149.
34. *Id.* at 155.
35. *Id.*
36. *Id.* at 163.

realm of mental health law.[37] Therapeutic jurisprudence originated, however, as a new look at mental health law.[38]

Traditional mental health law — and the scholarship that shaped it — was very much a product of the argument culture. Did we want a "therapeutic orgy"[39] or did we want patients to "rot with their rights on"?[40] Patients were "prisoners of psychiatry,"[41] and should accordingly be entitled to the panoply of constitutional rights recognized in the criminal arena.[42]

Moreover, traditional mental health law, although of professional interest both to legal and mental health professionals, was not a truly interdisciplinary endeavor.[43] When mental health information, rather than pure constitutional theory, was used at all by legal scholars, the scholarship underscored the *limitation* of the knowledge — the woefully inaccurate predictions of dangerousness[44] and the potent risks associated with various treatment modalities.[45]

Before this near revolution,[46] doctors and hospitals were accustomed to being treated by the courts with a hands off attitude[47] — leaving medical decisions unscrutinized by the outside world even when such decisions resulted in a deprivation of liberty. It is no wonder, then, that the initial legal activity and scholarship took the form of a war against those practices and practitioners. The rhetoric was of rights, and psychiatric insights were subjected to "the doubting-game," often coming up short.

---

37. *See* LAW IN A THERAPEUTIC KEY: DEVELOPMENTS IN THERAPEUTIC JURISPRUDENCE (David B. Wexler & Bruce J. Winick eds., 1996) [hereinafter KEY]. The book is a large anthology of relevant journal articles. For the convenience of citing to a single source, when those particular articles are referred to, the citations will be to KEY.

38. *Id.* at xix.

39. Robert Plotkin, *Limiting the Therapeutic Orgy: Mental Patients' Right to Refuse Treatment*, 72 NW. U. L. REV. 461, 461 (1978).

40. Thomas G. Gutheil, *In Search of True Freedom: Drug Refusal, Involuntary Medication, and "Rotting with Your Rights On,"* 137 AM. J. PSYCHIATRY 327, 327 (1980).

41. BRUCE J. ENNIS, PRISONERS OF PSYCHIATRY (1972).

42. Bruce J. Ennis, *Civil Liberties and Mental Illness*, 7 CRIM. L. BULL. 101, 102 (1971).

43. DAVID B. WEXLER, THERAPEUTIC JURISPRUDENCE: THE LAW AS A THERAPEUTIC AGENT 3 (1990).

44. Joseph J. Cocozza & Henry J. Steadman, *The Failure of Psychiatric Predictions of Dangerousness: Clear and Convincing Evidence*, 29 RUTGERS L. REV. 1084 (1976).

45. Plotkin, *supra* note 39.

46. *See* PAUL S. APPELBAUM, ALMOST A REVOLUTION: MENTAL HEALTH LAW AND THE LIMITS OF CHANGE (1994).

47. DAVID B. WEXLER, MENTAL HEALTH LAW: MAJOR ISSUES 219 (1981).

What traditional mental health law scholarship did *not* do was explore ways in which mental health developments might be used to *shape* the law.[48] Accordingly, a legal academy accustomed to playing the "doubting game" was somewhat taken aback—maybe even angered[49]—by initial efforts in therapeutic jurisprudence. Such efforts, after all, urged us to play the "believing game"—to take seriously work in the clinical behavioral sciences, and to consider how a legal system might look if such work were to be brought to bear on the formation of legal doctrine and procedures. In fact, when viewed from the perspective of Tannen's description of the culture of critique and possible antidotes to avoid the limitations of the argument culture, therapeutic jurisprudence scholarship has consistently followed Tannen's prescriptions—maybe giving new meaning to the "therapeutic" in therapeutic jurisprudence.[50]

Recall that Tannen does not have qualms with argumentation and critique as essential intellectual techniques. Her difficulty is with a *culture* of critique. Similarly, therapeutic jurisprudence scholarship recognizes the crucial importance of empirical inquiry to test the accuracy of its speculations. For example, in an article written several years ago, canvassing the then-existing therapeutic jurisprudence literature, I suggested that:

> The key task is, of course, to determine how the law can use mental health information to improve therapeutic functioning without impinging on justice concerns.

---

48. Because of its recent history and its antagonism toward psychiatry and related disciplines,...modern mental health law has not profited from truly interdisciplinary cooperation and interchange—from having the knowledge, theories, and insights of the mental health disciplines help *shape* the law, the legal system, and the behavior of legal actors, just as economic principles have been used to inform legal development in certain other areas of the law, such as antitrust. WEXLER, *supra* note 43, at 3.

49. John Petrila, *Paternalism and the Unrealized Promise of Essays in Therapeutic Jurisprudence, in* KEY, *supra* note 37, at 685. *Cf.* ARGUMENT CULTURE, *supra* note 1, at 97 ("The very fact that defending our nation's elected leader makes one suspect—an "apologist"—is itself evidence of the culture of critique by which only criticizing seems like worthy intellectual work.").

50. It is interesting after the fact to note that in an essay I wrote several years ago, the heading I used to introduce therapeutic jurisprudence as an alternative to traditional mental health law was "Therapeutic Jurisprudence as an Antidote." *David B. Wexler, Putting Mental Health into Mental Health Law, in* ESSAYS IN THERAPEUTIC JURISPRUDENCE 3, 7 (David B. Wexler & Bruce J. Winick eds., 1991) [hereinafter ESSAYS]. Furthermore, in a blurb placed on the book jacket of that work Paul Appelbaum wrote, "therapeutic jurisprudence is a tonic for what ails mental health law."

In digesting the therapeutic jurisprudence literature presented below, the reader should keep in mind the hypothesis-generating role of therapeutic jurisprudence. That is, the overall project of therapeutic jurisprudence should not stand or fall on the reader's assessment of the empirical accuracy of particular illustrations. Indeed, the illustrations themselves typically call for further empirical research.[51]

Thus, scrutiny and critique of mental health information was surely invited, and indeed was regarded as crucial, but the therapeutic jurisprudence enterprise was sufficiently new and unfamiliar that pains were taken in the preceding paragraph to urge readers to play the "believing game." Unlike much of traditional mental health law scholarship, then, therapeutic jurisprudence is not part of the "anti-psychiatry movement,"[52] and the "believing game" is basic to its mission. In fact, one major approach to "doing" therapeutic jurisprudence has been referred to as the "Psychology-Based Approach,"[53] where one "looks through the therapeutic jurisprudence lens at promising psychological/clinical literature, and contemplates how the particular psychological advance may be brought profitably into the law and the legal system."[54]

The search for promising psychological literature also contrasts sharply with the corrosive and dispiriting search for flaws that typifies a culture of critique. I tried to capture this spirit when, at a talk at the University of Virginia celebrating its Institute on Law & Psychiatry, I described therapeutic jurisprudence as "an optimistic perspective"[55] that "sees the can of Diet Pepsi as half-full rather than half-empty, as it searches for promising developments in the clinical behavioral sciences and tries to think creatively about how such work may be imported into the legal system."[56]

---

51. David B. Wexler, *Therapeutic Jurisprudence and Changing Conceptions of Legal Scholarship*, *in* KEY, *supra* note 37, at 597, 601.

52. ESSAYS, *supra* note 50, at 7.

53. David B. Wexler, *Therapeutic Jurisprudence in a Comparative Law Context*, 15 BEHAV. SCI. & L. 233, 234 (1997).

54. *Id.*

55. David B. Wexler, *The Development of Therapeutic Jurisprudence: From Theory to Practice* (paper delivered at University of Virginia School of Law, October, 1997). This paper will, in a revised form, constitute a chapter in LYNDA FROST CLAUSEL & RICHARD J. BONNIE, MENTAL HEALTH LAW IN EVOLUTION: A 25-YEAR RETROSPECTIVE 1972-1997 (forthcoming 2000).

56. *Id.* An optimistic explanatory style can apparently be taught, and such a style is associated with increased motivation, productivity, and satisfaction. *See* MARTIN E. SELIGMAN, LEARNED OPTIMISM (1991). This may have implications for therapeutic jurisprudence instruction in law school and continuing legal and judicial education settings.

Inspired by "the believing game," the therapeutic jurisprudence scholar is exhilarated when he or she comes across a title such as Meichenbaum and Turk's *Facilitating Treatment Adherence*.[57] The exhilaration comes from the hope that, in this book for health care professionals—(a book that does not deal with the legal system at all]—the therapeutic jurisprudence scholar might find some kernels and, through an exciting process of creative integration, [demonstrate how health care compliance principles might be used by the judiciary and the legal system to increase the medication and treatment compliance of a very worrisome group—conditionally released insanity acquitees."[58]

Similar excitement greeted the arrival of James McGuire's edited collection entitled *What Works: Reducing Reoffending*.[59] Noting that this book would help the field of corrections rise from the doldrums it has suffered since the 1974 publication of Martinson's assessment that nothing works in rehabilitation,[60] I wrote a review essay of McGuire, entitled *How the Law Can Use What Works: A Therapeutic Jurisprudence Look at Recent Research on Rehabilitation*.[61]

The use of relevant psychological principles to shape legal arrangements and legal doctrine is now standard fare in therapeutic jurisprudence. Moreover, the approach has been rejuvenating "core" mental health law scholarship. Recent illustrations include Bruce Winick's book, *Therapeutic Jurisprudence Applied: Essays on Mental Health Law*,[62] Kirk Heilbrun's work on risk management and prediction,[63] and Stephen Behnke and Elyn Saks' *Therapeutic Jurisprudence: Informed Consent as a Clinical Indica-*

---

57. DONALD MEICHENBAUM & DENNIS C. TURK, FACILITATING TREATMENT ADHERENCE: A PRACTITIONER'S GUIDEBOOK (1987).

58. David B. Wexler, *Health Care Compliance Principles and the Insanity Acquittee Conditional Release Process, in* ESSAYS, *supra* note 50, at 199. A later effort expanded the application of the principles to criminal law probation decisions. *See* David B. Wexler, *Therapeutic Jurisprudence and the Criminal Courts, in* KEY, *supra* note 37, at 157, 165-70.

59. WHAT WORKS: REDUCING REOFFENDING (James McGuire ed., 1995).

60. *See* Robert Martinson, *What Works? Questions and Answers About Prison Reform,* 20 PUB. INTEREST 22 (1974).

61. *See* David B. Wexler, *How the Law Can Use What Works: A Therapeutic Jurisprudence Look at Recent Research in Rehabilitation,* 15 BEHAV. SCI. & L. 365 (1997).

62. *See* BRUCE J. WINICK, THERAPEUTIC JURISPRUDENCE APPLIED: ESSAYS ON MENTAL HEALTH LAW (1997).

63. Kirk Heilbrun, *Prediction Versus Management Models Relevant to Risk Assessment: The Importance of Legal Decision-Making Context,* 21 LAW & HUM. BEHAV. 347 (1997).

tion for the Chronically Suicidal Patient with Borderline Personality Disorder.[64]

Behnke and Saks' fascinating analysis demonstrates just the type of integrative thinking and intellectual activity that Tannen finds in short supply. Their approach is so relevant to our discussion that their introductory remarks are worth quoting in some detail:

> Identifying areas of the law ripe for a therapeutic jurisprudence analysis requires a reasonable degree of psychological sophistication. For example, an analysis must be able to determine which sector of the population a given law is most likely to affect; to explore the psychological dynamics of that sector; and given these dynamics, to examine what effect the law is likely to have. Without all three components the analysis will be incomplete.[65]

They then continue by carving out their particular project:

> Winick demonstrates how obtaining informed consent may bring about clinical gains by making the patient an active participant in treatment decisions. Winick argues that when a patient consciously embraces a treatment goal she is more likely to achieve that goal, especially when the treater predicts success. In analyzing the benefits of informed consent, Winick looks to considerable empirical evidence that when people are self-determining, they function more effectively and with a higher degree of commitment and satisfaction. He points out that treating patients as competent adults enhances the therapeutic alliance.
>
> This Article takes Winick's discussion a step further by exploring how informed consent may be especially beneficial to a particular clinical population — namely, chronically suicidal individuals who meet the criteria for borderline personality disorder (BPD). The Article discusses how a new treatment modality, dialectical behavior therapy (DBT), makes obtaining informed consent an essential aspect of the treatment. The Article shows how patients appear to benefit as a result of incorporating informed consent into DBT, and will speculate about the reasons why doing so is helpful to patients.[66]

Note that Behnke and Saks play "the believing game," and they explore the psychological literature in an effort to find areas in which playing the

---

64. Stephen H. Behnke & Elyn R. Saks, *Therapeutic Jurisprudence: Informed Consent as a Clinical Indication for the Chronically Suicidal Patient with Borderline Personality Disorder*, 31 Loy. L.A. L. Rev. 945 (1998).

65. *Id.* at 945.

66. *Id.* at 946.

believing game seems particularly warranted. They integrate promising psychological work with relevant legal areas (here, the doctrine of informed consent), and seek to build on prior work.

That is not to say their article brushes over problematic areas. In fact, a second part of their article underscores the necessity of therapeutic jurisprudence scholars confronting difficult legal theory questions that to date have gone largely unaddressed. But that intellectual endeavor is clearly undertaken in the spirit of engaging in a dialogue, and not in a polarized, demonizing debate. Again, consider how the authors introduce the legal theory aspect of their project:

> This Article elaborates on the therapeutic jurisprudence literature in a second way by raising challenges to the concept of therapeutic jurisprudence. Our hope is that by providing an illustration of therapeutic jurisprudence at work and exploring problems as yet unaddressed by the doctrine of therapeutic jurisprudence, we will contribute to the therapeutic jurisprudence literature. Our ultimate goal is to provide concrete avenues by which the law can promote the mental health and well-being of individuals who struggle with significant psychological and behavioral difficulties.[67]

Besides playing the "believing game," the therapeutic jurisprudence literature also typically follows the other methodological suggestions made by Tannen. Certainly, the work tries to eschew doctrinal niceties and symmetries in favor of looking at a problem and trying to develop reasonably workable solutions. I once likened therapeutic jurisprudence to the "New Public Law" scholarship, giving recognition to primary lawmakers:

> Today's primary (non-judicial) lawmakers are not particularly interested in legal principles and meticulous reasoning processes. To them, the law is an instrumentality designed to deal with a particular problem; law is successful if its results satisfactorily tackle the problem. Incrementalism is not a necessary part of this lawmaking process. Reasoning by analogy is inappropriate. Prior legislation is looked to as "data"—it is looked to for its efficacy rather than for its precedential value. Increasingly, in other words, the referent of legal analysis is social problems, not the body of law itself.[68]

In approaching social problems, therapeutic jurisprudence scholarship most typically conforms to Tannen's interpretation of the "sensible cen-

---

67. *Id.*
68. Wexler, *supra* note 51, at 598-99.

ter"[69] and the "complex middle."[70] Clearly, as I wrote some years ago, "[i]t is accurate to categorize the great bulk of therapeutic jurisprudence writing to date as rather 'centrist'. . . ."[71] Instead of seeking controversy, the scholarship often does "leave some issues out,"[72] and it often strives creatively to seek compromise or, better yet, convergence of various interests. As Bruce Winick notes in *The Jurisprudence of Therapeutic Jurisprudence*:

> Scholars, of course, engage in an act of judgment when they select particular issues for examination with the lens of therapeutic jurisprudence. When constitutional or other strongly held normative values support a rule in a way that is morally or politically unchangeable, the value of conducting a therapeutic jurisprudence analysis of the consequences of the rule will be considerably reduced. Because therapeutic jurisprudence has a law reform as well as scholarly agenda, its practitioners presumably will wish to select issues for examination that can at least potentially lead to legal change in line with their own and the society's strongly held normative values. In this sense, a particularly appropriate focus for therapeutic jurisprudence scholarship would seem to be a seeking for convergence between therapeutic values and cherished constitutional, moral, or other normative values. Rather than choosing areas for therapeutic jurisprudence work in which there is likely to be conflict between therapeutic consequences and important normative values, the therapeutic jurisprudence scholar would be better off exploring areas in which such values appear likely to converge. Seeking such convergence . . . can be quite rewarding and can produce significant original proposals for law reform that are not politically implausible.[73]

Just as the integrative exercise of Behnke and Saks involved creative and rigorous thinking, so too the search for convergence of interests is typically a challenging intellectual exercise, and not at all the "squishy and dull" ho-hum endeavor that adherents to the culture of critique might anticipate. Often, the effort leads us to probe beneath a rhetoric of rights and to focus instead on needs and interests, all the while seeking a creative convergence or compromise.

---

69. ARGUMENT CULTURE, *supra* note 1, at 29.

70. *Id.* at 10.

71. David B. Wexler, *Reflections on the Scope of Therapeutic Jurisprudence, in* KEY, *supra* note 37, at 811, 822.

72. ARGUMENT CULTURE, *supra* note 1, at 288.

73. Bruce J. Winick, *The Jurisprudence of Therapeutic Jurisprudence, in* KEY, *supra* note 37, at 645, 662.

The result is a kind of Fisher and Ury *Getting to Yes*-type scholarship, in which the scholar goes through the process of carefully anticipating the various needs and interests (as opposed to rigid rights and positions), expanding the possible options through brainstorming, and finally mentally mediates (through a type of internal dialogue) a proposed solution.[74] One inquiry along these lines grew out of a student's proposal made in my therapeutic jurisprudence seminar. Natelsky proposed to reform the civil commitment hearing so that it would in some respects resemble the fact-finding process of the Continental criminal justice system. To me, the proposal raised a series of questions. Note that the questions begin with rights, but then take us into the real-world grimy application of those rights, ask what we are *really* hoping to accomplish (what are our needs and interests), and finally ask whether the proposal might accomplish those measures as well as our traditional civil commitment hearing.

Under Natelsky's scheme, some important fact-gathering by the investigative/judicial official will apparently take place outside the presence of respondent. Such a proposal therefore raises questions about a cluster of rights, including the right, in theory and practice, to face-to-face confrontation.

Does or should the right to face-to-face confrontation apply to a civil commitment hearing as well as to a criminal hearing? How important is face-to-face confrontation in a jurisdiction where respondent's presence at the hearing can be waived "by such person or by adversary counsel acting in her behalf and for good cause shown?" How important is the right in jurisdictions where counsel routinely waives respondent's presence or where patients overwhelmingly choose not to attend? How important is the right in jurisdictions where the respondent is required to appear at the hearing but where live medical testimony will not be offered unless the respondent, before the hearing, notifies the court that he or she wishes to cross-examine the examining physician? Is the purpose of face-to-face confrontation tied exclusively to promoting the integrity of the fact-finding process? If so, is Natelsky's proposal likely to yield at least as accurate a factual picture as would a traditional civil commitment hearing? Are there some other values protected by face-to-face confrontation? Are there ways of modifying the proposal to accommodate those values?

---

74. *See generally* ROGER FISHER & WILLIAM URY, GETTING TO YES: NEGOTIATING AGREEMENT WITHOUT GIVING IN (1981).

How should procedural law reform proposals be constitutionally assessed, given the massive difference between the theory and the reality of adversary commitment hearings? Those familiar with hearings know that the Supreme Court unfortunately understated the situation when it noted that "the supposed protections of an adversary proceeding to determine the appropriateness of medical decisions for the commitment of mental and emotional illness may well be more illusory than real."(When traditional "adversary" hearings typically take only a matter of minutes, can we really say the traditional due process right is meaningful?)Which proceeding would the typical respondent find fairer? A currently conducted hearing or the procedure proposed by Natelsky?... [I]f a state were genuinely interested in implementing the Natelsky adjudicative model, should we mechanically condemn the procedure as unconstitutional and insist upon continuing the sham that may well now exist in that state?[75]

Not only has therapeutic jurisprudence scholarship followed the methodological path proposed by Tannen, but it has also begun to address substantively Tannen's areas of concern regarding the legal system: how courts might influence a criminal defendant's acceptance of responsibility,[76] the role of apology in tort[77] and other settings,[78] the anti-therapeutic consequences of delaying the resolution of personal injury cases,[79] the therapeutic implications of mediation,[80] the therapeutic inappropriateness of the adversary

---

75. David B. Wexler, *Justice, Mental Health, and Therapeutic Jurisprudence, in* KEY, *supra* note 37, at 713, 718-19 (citations omitted).

76. *See generally* Peggy Fulton Hora & William G. Schma, *Therapeutic Jurisprudence,* 82 JUDICATURE 8 (1998); Thomas J. Scheff, *Community Conferences: Shame and Anger in Therapeutic Jurisprudence,* 67 REVISTA JURIDICA U.P.R. 97 (1998); David B. Wexler, *Therapeutic Jurisprudence and the Criminal Courts, in* KEY, *supra* note 37, at 157, 159-64.

77. Daniel W. Shuman, *The Psychology of Compensation in Tort Law, in* KEY, *supra* note 37, at 433, 457-60.

78. Bruce Feldthusen, *The Civil Action for Sexual Battery: Therapeutic Jurisprudence?, in* KEY, *supra* note 37, at 845, 871-72 (discussing the criminal context).

79. Daniel W. Shuman, *When Time Does Not Heal: Understanding the Importance of Avoiding Unnecessary Delay in the Resolution of Tort Cases,* 5 PSYCHOL. PUB. POL'Y & L. (forthcoming 1999).

80. Ellen Waldman, *The Evaluative-Facilitative Debate in Mediation: Applying the Lens of Therapeutic Jurisprudence,* 82 MARQ. L. REV. 155 (1998). Note that, on occasion, litigation itself may serve a therapeutic function. *See* Feldthusen, *supra* note 79, at 845.

system in at least certain settings,[81] and the contribution of the legal system to lawyer distress.[82]

Moreover, in a true integration of theory and practice, therapeutic jurisprudence is beginning to influence day-to-day judging[83] and lawyering.[84] Day-to-day lawyering, of course, is not ordinarily geared to law reform *per se*, and the contribution of therapeutic jurisprudence to day-to-day lawyering has accordingly come principally from that aspect of therapeutic jurisprudence scholarship concerned with *applying* existing law therapeutically.[85] That may be accomplished through a fusion of the therapeutic jurisprudence perspective with the perspective of preventive law—an approach that advocates careful client counseling, planning, legal audits, and checkups and the like.[86]

In another illustration of "integrative," rather than "critical," scholarship, Dennis Stolle first proposed the fusion of the two perspectives,[87] and the integrated perspective has rapidly led to additional writing and activity.[88] In contrast, critical legal scholarship has itself been criticized for not constructing an effective model of lawyering. Melanie Abbott, for example, who works in the area of homelessness, has written an interesting arti-

81. *See generally* Janet Weinstein, *And Never the Twain Shall Meet: The Best Interests of Children and the Adversary System*, 52 U. MIAMI L. REV. 79 (1997) (adversary system inappropriate mechanism for adjudication of "best interest of the child" issues).

82. *See* Amiram Elwork & G. Andrew H. Benjamin, *Lawyers in Distress, in* KEY, *supra* note 37, at 569. For a synthesis and interesting discussion of empirical literature on lawyer attributes, *see* Susan Daicoff, *Lawyer, Know Thyself: A Review of Empirical Research on Attorney Attributes Bearing on Professionalism*, 46 AM. U. L. REV. 1337 (1997).

83. *See* Peggy Fulton Hora et al., *Therapeutic Jurisprudence and the Drug Treatment Court Movement: Revolutionizing the Criminal Justice System's Response to Drug Abuse and Crime in America*, 74 NOTRE DAME L. REV. 439 (1999); Peggy Fulton Hora & William G. Schma, *Therapeutic Jurisprudence*, 82 JUDICATURE 8 (1998); William G. Schma, Book Review, 36 THE JUDGES' J. 81 (Summer 1997); Michael D. Zimmerman, *A New Approach to Court Reform*, 82 JUDICATURE 108 (1998).

84. *See* David B. Wexler, *Practicing Therapeutic Jurisprudence: Psycholegal Soft Spots and Strategies*, 67 REVISTA JURIDICA U.P.R. 317 (1998).

85. David B. Wexler, *Applying the Law Therapeutically, in* KEY, *supra* note 37, at 831.

86. ROBERT M. HARDAWAY, PREVENTIVE LAW: MATERIALS ON A NONADVERSARIAL LEGAL PROCESS (1997).

87. Dennis P. Stolle, *Professional Responsibility in Elder Law: A Synthesis of Preventive Law and Therapeutic Jurisprudence*, 14 BEHAV. SCI. & L. 459 (1996).

88. *See generally* Marc W. Patry et al., *Better Legal Counseling Through Empirical Research: Identifying Psycholegal Soft Spots and Strategies*, 34 CAL. W. L. REV. 439 (1998); Dennis P. Stolle et al., *Integrating Preventive Law and Therapeutic Jurisprudence: A Law and Psychology Based Approach to Lawyering*, 34 CAL. W. L. REV. 15 (1997).

cle with a revealing title: *Seeking Shelter Under a Deconstructed Roof:*
Homelessness and Critical Lawyering.[89]

Efforts are underway to introduce therapeutic jurisprudence— and other models that are alternatives to the argument culture[90]—into law schools, and judicial, and legal practice settings. The hope, of course, is that bringing an explicit ethic of care into law practice will better serve clients, humanize law practice for clients and lawyers, contribute to lawyer satisfaction and decrease lawyer distress, and begin to attract to the legal profession many who have opted out of practicing in a culture of critique.[91]

III. Conclusion

Tannen observes a growing dissatisfaction with the argument culture, manifested in law by the movement toward mediation and alternative dispute resolution (ADR). ADR is no doubt the strongest alternative force operating in practice, but others are emerging in the scholarly and professional literature, and increasingly in legal education, en route to gaining a foothold in practice. These include, for example, therapeutic jurisprudence, preventive law, restorative justice,[92] holistic lawyering,[93] and, as a possible canopy, creative problem solving.[94]

As James Cooper, Executive Director of the McGill Center for Creative Problem Solving at California Western School of Law, has recently written, these perspectives need to form symbiotic relationships and explore ways in which they may enrich and reform legal education, legal practice, and legal culture.[95] Beginning efforts are already underway.[96] As these perspectives mature, perhaps they will lead to an understanding, in the legal

---

89. Melanie B. Abbott, *Seeking Shelter Under a Deconstructed Roof: Homelessness and Critical Lawyering*, 64 TENN. L. REV. 269 (1997).

90. *See* James M. Cooper, *Towards a New Architecture: Creative Problem Solving and the Evolution of Law*, 34 CAL. W. L. REV. 297 (1998).

91. Daicoff, *supra* note 82, at 1398-1403 (discussing relative absence of ethic of care in law students).

92. *See* Daniel W. Van Ness, *New Wine and Old Wineskins: Four Challenges of Restorative Justice*, 4 CRIM. L.F. 251 (1993).

93. *See* Dennis P. Stolle & David B. Wexler, *Therapeutic Jurisprudence and Preventive Law: A Combined Concentration to Invigorate the Everyday Practice of Law*, 39 ARIZ. L. REV. 25, 28 n.9 (1997).

94. *See* Cooper, *supra* note 90.

95. *Id.* at 302.

96. *See* Stolle et al., *supra* note 88 (therapeutic jurisprudence and preventive law); Waldman, *supra* note 80 (therapeutic jurisprudence and mediation); Scheff, *supra* note 76 (therapeutic jurisprudence and restorative justice); Robert F. Schopp, *Integrating Restora-*

community and beyond, of the positive force of critique as a *technique* and of the extremely negative force of critique as a *culture*.

---

tive Justice and Therapeutic Jurisprudence, 67 REVISTA JURIDICA U.P.R. 665 (1998) (therapeutic jurisprudence and restorative justice).

Afterword

The Role of Therapeutic Jurisprudence within the Comprehensive Law Movement

Susan Daicoff

Introduction

The rapid rise of therapeutic jurisprudence in the last decade of the twentieth century heralds the emergence of a new era in the legal profession—one in which law and legal practice may be more humane, therapeutic, beneficial, humanistic, healing, restorative, curative, collaborative, and comprehensive.[1] This new era may be emerging in response to growing dissatisfaction in the legal profession and in society with law's traditional approach to law practice and to resolving legal matters.

It has become evident in the last fifteen years that the American legal system is not entirely satisfactory to clients, to society, or even to lawyers themselves.[2] Clients are unhappy with their lawyers,[3] with the system, and

---

1. These concepts, the vectors, the comprehensive law movement, and their relationship to lawyer personality are explored more fully in the final chapter of SUSAN DAICOFF, LAWYER, KNOW THYSELF (in press), being published by American Psychological Association Books.

2. See Susan Daicoff, *Lawyer, Know Thyself: A Review of Empirical Research on Attorney Attributes Bearing on Professionalism,* 46 AM. U. L. REV. 1337, 1342-48 (1997) (documenting the existence of a "tripartite crisis" in the legal profession: deprofessionalism; low public opinion of attorneys; and lawyer dissatisfaction and distress, and then reviewing and analyzing forty years' worth of empirical studies on the personality characteristics and preferences of lawyers as compared to the general population) [hereinafter Daicoff/Lawyer]; *see also* Susan Daicoff, *Asking Leopards to Change Their Spots: Should Lawyers Change? A Critique of Solutions to Problems With Professionalism by Reference to Empirically-Derived Attorney Personality Attributes,* 11 GEO. J. LEGAL ETHICS 547, 549-557 (exploring the tripartite crisis in more detail) [hereinafter Daicoff/Leopards].

3. *See* Gary A. Hengstler, *Vox Populi, The Public Perception of Lawyers: ABA Poll,* A.B.A. J., Sept. 1993, at 60, 62-63 (reporting the results of the well-known Peter D. Hart Research Associates survey, commissioned by the American Bar Association, in which the

with the outcomes of the process.[4] Lawyers are extraordinarily unhappy[5] or even psychologically impaired.[6] In fact, there is a "tripartite crisis" in the legal profession, consisting of deprofessionalism, low public opinion of attorneys, and lawyer dissatisfaction and distress.[7] In addition, traditional nonlegal dispute resolution mechanisms in society have failed[8] and society has become overly dependent on litigative processes to resolve conflict. As a result, society in general is suffering from the effects of adopting law's overly adversarial, other-blaming, position-taking, and hostile approach to conflict resolution. Anecdotes abound about minor interpersonal disputes that have erupted into full-blown litigation, rather than resolved via a simple apology or heartfelt interpersonal interaction.[9]

Fortunately, a number of alternative approaches to law and legal practice have developed to replace the current system's monolithic reliance on the adversarial, litigative model. These alternative approaches function as independent "vectors" of a growing movement in the law. They are characterized as "vectors" because they all move towards a common goal of a more comprehensive, humane, and psychologically optimal way of handling legal matters. Although there may be others, the vectors include: preventive law, therapeutic jurisprudence, therapeutic jurisprudence/preventive law, procedural justice, restorative justice, facilitative mediation, transformative mediation, holistic law, collaborative law, creative prob-

---

public expressed significant dissatisfaction with the American legal profession, including people who had used lawyers in the past).

4. *See* Tom R. Tyler, The Psychological Consequences of Judicial Procedures: Implications for Civil Commitment Hearings, in DAVID B. WEXLER & BRUCE J. WINICK, EDS., LAW IN A THERAPEUTIC KEY: DEVELOPMENTS IN THERAPEUTIC JURISPRUDENCE 3 (1996) (empirical research suggesting that litigants are more influenced by intangible, noneconomic factors in legal procedures—such as being treated with dignity and respect and being heard—than they are by the strict legal outcome of the matter).

5. *See* Daicoff/Leopards, *supra* note 2, at 553-555 (noting that recent American Bar Association studies and other studies agree that about 20-25% of lawyers are very or somewhat dissatisfied with their jobs).

6. *See* Daicoff/Leopards, *supra* note 2, at 555-557 (noting that the rate of depression and alcoholism among lawyers is 17-18%, which is at least twice that of the rate in the general population; incidences of other psychopathology—like anxiety, obsessive compulsiveness, and global distress—may be even higher).

7. *See* Daicoff/Leopards, *supra* note 2, at 547 (describing the "tripartite crisis").

8. Traditional nonlegal resolution of disputes occurred through one's church, community, neighborhood, friends, and family.

9. *See* Steven Keeva, *Does Law Mean Never Having to Say You're Sorry?*, A.B.A. J. (Dec. 1999) (on the value of apology).

lem solving, and specialized courts.[10] Bridges are being built between the "vectors" and hybrid versions of these vectors are evolving from the integration of two or more vectors. If this synthesis continues, ultimately the movement may result in a full-blown transformation of legal practice, legal education, and society in general. This chapter describes the vectors, the "comprehensive law" movement, and the place of therapeutic jurisprudence within this framework.

Historical Development of the Comprehensive Law Movement

The comprehensive law movement evidenced by the growth of these vectors is not entirely new. Certainly, a number of alternatives to the litigation model have existed for years, including preventive law[11] and alternative dispute resolution ("ADR"). The ADR movement, which has been

---

 10. Specialized courts such as domestic violence courts, drug treatment courts, and mental health courts are a judicial development that may constitute a separate, albeit therapeutic vector. These courts have been associated with therapeutic jurisprudence; *see* Peggy Fulton Hora, William G. Schma, & John T. A. Rosenthal, *Therapeutic Jurisprudence and the Drug Treatment Court Movement: Revolutionizing the Criminal Justice System's Response to Drug Abuse and Crime in America*, 74 NOTRE DAME L. REV. 439 (1999) (describing in detail the drug treatment court movement and linking it with therapeutic jurisprudence); and Peggy Fulton Hora & William G. Schma, *As Demonstrated By Drug Courts, Judges Can Improve the Psychological Well Being of People Subject to the Legal Process And, In Turn, Make Their Own Jobs More Rewarding*, 1 JUDICATURE 82 (July-August 1998) (discussing the therapeutic effects {on participants and judges alike} of drug treatment courts). Another important development is the law and socioeconomics movement, which has some links with therapeutic jurisprudence, *see* Jeffrey L. Harrison, *Law and Socioeconomics*, 49 J. LEGAL EDUC. 224 (1999) (a law and economics perspective that emphasizes social and psychological values and concerns (e.g., self-esteem)). The following "movements" may also be tangentially related to the vectors and to comprehensive law generally: the religious lawyering movement, which interjects religious values into law practice; the movement to resurrect secular humanist values in law; the politics of meaning; the efforts of the Contemplative Mind & Society Institute, including the Yale Law School meditation project sponsored by the Fetzer Institute; and affective lawyering and rebellious lawyering, both important approaches in the domestic violence context.

11. *See* ROBERT M. HARDAWAY, PREVENTIVE LAW: MATERIALS ON A NON ADVERSARIAL LEGAL PROCESS xl (1997) (documenting the emergence of preventive law as early as the 1930's and 1950's in the United States and generally providing a wealth of material on preventive law).

expanding since the late 1960s, was originally designed "to relieve court congestion (cost and delay; to enhance community involvement in the (resolution [of disputes]; to facilitate access to justice; and to provide more 'effective' dispute resolution."[12] Today, mediation has become an increasingly popular mode of resolving otherwise litigable disputes among parties. However, the newer, therapeutically oriented alternatives to litigation included in the comprehensive law movement differ from the ADR movement's traditional alternatives to litigation in several distinct ways. Therefore, they truly represent a philosophical shift in emphasis beyond simply providing more efficient, inexpensive, or fair alternatives to traditional means of resolving legal disputes.

The philosophical shift underpinning the comprehensive law movement is towards an appreciation for the psychological dynamics involved in legal matters, legal procedures, disputes, and dispute resolution processes. This emphasis on psychological effects includes a growing awareness that individuals' emotional wellbeing is often dependent on positive social support, meaning good relationships with family, friends, employers, neighborhoods, and various communities to which people "belong." The philosophical shift underlying this movement is thus consistent with several other philosophical shifts in society that have been observed in the late twentieth century. These other shifts include a decreased emphasis on individualism and individual rights and liberties and an increased emphasis on preserving relationships, connectedness, identity within a community or culture, and familial ties.[13]

Some of the events and developments within the last decade of the twentieth century also explain these philosophical shifts. For example, during this time, awareness of the Earth's global community and of the need for greater care and concern for human relationships and for the environment (on a large and small scale) has increased. Not surprisingly, this awareness coincided with the end of the Cold War, which may have ended a long period in the United States of a national adversarial posture or mind-

---

12. STEPHEN B. GOLDBERG, ERIC D. GREEN, & FRANK E. A. SANDER, DISPUTE RESOLUTION 5 (1985). ADR originally focused on resolving disputes in a cheap, quick, final, procedurally fair, efficient, and satisfying manner. *See id.* at 7.

13. *See* Thomas D. Barton, *Troublesome Connections: The Law and Post-Enlightenment Culture*, 47 EMORY L. J. 163-64 (1998) (noting the shift in society and law from an Enlightenment philosophy emphasizing individual will, liberty, and rights to a Post-Enlightenment philosophy acknowledging relationships, connectedness, and community); *see also* ROBERT A. BARUCH BUSH & JOSEPH P. FOLGER, THE PROMISE OF MEDIATION 229-59 (1994) (placing transformative mediation within a larger paradigm shift from an Individualist worldview to a Relational worldview).

set. At the same time, disillusionment with the American adversarial legal system became obvious, perhaps peaking in some ways with the O.J. Simpson trial, and commentators began to focus on dissatisfaction with the law. Finally, legal scholars began to document the problems in the profession and call for more care-oriented and morally responsible forms of lawyering.[14]

Although the vectors of the comprehensive law movement may not be consciously or explicitly related or responsive to these events, the theoretical underpinnings of the movement are entirely consistent with the philosophical shifts inherent in these precursor events. The convergence of the individual vectors is briefly described below.

---

14. Re: lawyering with an ethic of care, *see* Carrie Menkel-Meadow, *Is Altruism Possible In Lawyering?* 8 GA. ST. U. L. REV. 385 (1992) (arguing that lawyers should become more altruistic); Carrie Menkel-Meadow, *Culture Clash in the Quality of Life in the Law: Changes in the Economics, Diversification and Organization of Lawyering,* 44 CASE W. RES. L. REV. 621, 660 (1994) (arguing that diversity resulting from the influx of women and minorities into the bar will benefit the legal profession and associating some of the solutions to the tripartite crisis to gendered issues); Carrie Menkel-Meadow, *Review Essay: Moral Boundaries: A Political Argument for an Ethic of Care by Joan C. Tronto,* 22 N.Y.U. REV. L. & SOC. CHANGE 265 (1996) (also discussing lawyering with an ethic of care); and Theresa Glennon, *Lawyers and Caring: Building an Ethic of Care Into Professional Responsibility,* 43 HASTINGS L. J. 1175 (1992) (calling for lawyering that is consistent with an ethic of care). Re: lawyering with moral accountability, *see* Robert M. Bastress, *Client Centered Counseling and Moral Accountability For Lawyers,* 10 J. LEGAL PROF. 97-99 (1985) (arguing that lawyers need to become more client-centered in the Rogerian sense as well as morally accountable in their representation of clients and arguing for lawyering which requires the lawyer to discuss his or her personal morals and beliefs with the client and to refuse to take actions which are inconsistent with these morals and beliefs—"moral accountability"—as opposed to morally blind representation, e.g., the hired gun approach). Re: the distress in the legal profession, *see* ANTHONY KRONMAN, THE LOST LAWYER: FAILING IDEALS OF THE LEGAL PROFESSION (1993) (chronicling the distress of the profession), as explained by David B. Wilkins, *Practical Wisdom For Practicing Lawyers: Separating Ideals From Ideology in Legal Ethics,* 108 HARV. L. REV. 458, 460-61 (1994) and reviewed by Thomas L. Shaffer, *The Lost Lawyer: Failing Ideals of the Legal Profession, By Kronman,* 41 LOY. L. REV. 387 (1995); and MARY ANN GLENDON, A NATION UNDER LAWYERS: HOW THE CRISIS IN THE LEGAL PROFESSION IS TRANSFORMING AMERICAN SOCIETY (2d ed. 1995) (also exploring the problems in the legal profession). Re: lawyers as wise counselor or Aristotelian "friends," *see* Thomas L. Shaffer, *Inaugural Howard Lichtenstein Lecture in Legal Ethics: Lawyer Professionalism as a Moral Argument,* 26 GONZ. L. REV. 393 (1990/91) and Thomas L. Shaffer, *Human Nature and Moral Responsibility in Lawyer-Client Relationships,* 40 AM. J. JURIS. 1 (1995) (in both, Shaffer argues for the role of lawyer as wise friend in the Aristotelian sense, another form of morally responsible lawyering).

Intersection of the Vectors of the Comprehensive Law Movement

The vectors are characterized as components of a movement because they all seek to deal more comprehensively, humanely, positively (from a psychological viewpoint), and creatively with the individuals, relationships, communities, and effects presented by the particular legal matter at hand. Further, they all intersect at two points (although some of the vectors intersect in many more ways). First, all attempt to optimize the psychological wellbeing of the individuals, relationships, and communities touched by each legal matter. Second, all acknowledge the importance of concerns beyond simply the strict legal rights, duties, and obligations of the parties.

(1) First, all of the vectors attempt to *optimize human wellbeing*. They seek to achieve the most psychologically beneficial outcome for the particular legal matter by explicitly being nongladiatorial, noncontentious, at times collaborative, interdisciplinary, creative, respectful of others' feelings and needs, and nonbrutalizing. They are clearly focused on maximizing the emotional wellbeing of all parties involved, including the clients' families, employers or employees, and friends. They may even consider the emotional wellbeing of the lawyers and judges involved. This feature illustrates the psychological or humanistic nature common to all the vectors comprising this movement.

Interestingly, a 1993 article contained in a book on restorative justice describes this feature rather well, in its effort to explain how mediation can have a healing focus:

> We see ourselves as caring individuals who believe that clients have the inner capacity to find their own solutions. We activate the hope that life can be better, that solutions are possible. We value self-determination and empowerment. We are oriented toward the future, supporting clients in moving forward and in constructively coping with change. We help them work toward the higher good for themselves and their families.[15]

(2) Second, all of the vectors explicitly focus on extra-legal concerns, meaning factors other than the strict legal rights and obligations of the parties, in considering how best to resolve the legal matter presented. Such extra-legal concerns include the parties' emotions, relationships, feelings, needs, resources, goals, and psychological health, among other things. One com-

---

15. Lois Gold, *Influencing Unconscious Influences: The Healing Dimension of Mediation*, 11 MEDIATION QUARTERLY (1993), included as Appendix 3 to MARK UMBREIT, MEDIATING INTERPERSONAL CONFLICTS: A PATHWAY TO PEACE 251 (1995).

mentator calls this feature, "*rights plus.*"[16] This feature illustrates the comprehensive, holistic, and broad nature of these emerging approaches to law. The individual vectors are explored in more depth, below.

The Vectors of the Comprehensive Law Movement

There are about ten or eleven vectors of the comprehensive law movement. Preventive law, which developed in the 1930s to 1950s, may be the oldest vector; many of the others emerged in the late 1980s or early 1990s, such as therapeutic jurisprudence and holistic law. Several are even newer, such as transformative mediation and creative problem solving. Others are likely to continue to emerge. Some are more concrete, practical, and tangible while others are more theoretical and academic. Some focus on dispute resolution while others encompass nonconflictual legal matters such as estate planning. Some focus on criminal law, some on civil law, some on law in the courts, and others on law outside the courts, yet all share the two common features outlined above. Bruce Winick has aptly compared the vectors to a family and their common features to family resemblances—that is, some members are tall, some are short, some are brown-haired, and some are blonde, but all have similar noses and eye color. Each vector is a distinct, independent entity with its own individuality, yet all the vectors are clearly "related," that is, part of a larger family.

⭑ Therapeutic Jurisprudence

Therapeutic jurisprudence ("TJ") focuses on the therapeutic or countertherapeutic consequences of the law and legal procedures on people. Specifically, it focuses on the effect on the individuals or groups of people involved, including the clients and their families, friends, lawyers, judges, and communities. It attempts to reform law and legal processes in order to promote the psychological wellbeing of the people they affect. The website of the International Network on Therapeutic Jurisprudence explains:

> Therapeutic Jurisprudence concentrates on the law's impact on emotional life and psychological well-being. It is a perspective that regards the law (rules of law, legal procedures, and roles of legal actors) itself as a social force that often produces therapeutic or anti-therapeutic consequences. It does not suggest that therapeutic concerns are more important than other consequences or factors, but it does suggest

---

16. For this term (among other insights) I am indebted to Pauline Tesler, a collaborative divorce lawyer in the San Francisco area. Interview with Pauline H. Tesler, Esq., of Tesler, Sandmann and Fishman, Dublin, Ireland (July 8, 1999).

that the law's role as a potential therapeutic agent should be recog- ⌉
nized and systematically studied.[17]

Although TJ was originally applied mainly in the area of mental health law, it has been widely applied to a number of substantive law areas[18] as well as to legal processes. Its popularity and applications have quickly grown since its emergence around 1990. Its scope has broadened from proposing law reform to asking how existing law can be applied more therapeutically. For example, TJ proposes that the practicing lawyer identify, consider, and seek to improve the psychological effects any proposed legal action or process may have on the individuals and groups involved. More recently, TJ has been utilized in police work, judging, specialized courts,[19] and the appellate opinion process.[20]

Recent applications of TJ illustrate the optimal effect it can have on individuals' mental health. For example, drug treatment courts explicitly provide defendants with an option to convert a legal crisis into an opportunity for recovery from drug and alcohol addiction and for sustained life change. They do this by utilizing the substance abuse treatment knowl-

---

17. http://www.law.arizona.edu/upr-intj/.

18. *See generally* David B. Wexler & Bruce J. Winick, Eds., Law in a Therapeutic Key: Developments in Therapeutic Jurisprudence (1996) (applying therapeutic jurisprudence to mental health law, correctional law, criminal law and procedure, family and juvenile law, sexual orientation law, health law, personal injury and tort law, evidence law, labor arbitration law, and contracts and commercial law); *see also* Susan L. Brooks, *Therapeutic Jurisprudence and Preventive Law in Child Welfare Proceedings: A Family Systems Approach*; Pauline H. Tesler, *Collaborative Law: A New Paradigm for Divorce Lawyers*; Penelope Eileen Bryan, *"Collaborative Divorce:" Meaningful Reform or Another Quick-Fix?*; and Pauline H. Tesler *The Believing Game, The Doubting Game, and Collaborative Law: A Reply to Penelope Bryan* (all of the foregoing apply therapeutic jurisprudence to family law) all in 5 Psychology, Pub. Pol'y & L. __ (1999) (in press); *and see* David B. Wexler, *Relapse Prevention Planning Principles for Criminal Law Practice* and Bruce J. Winick, *Redefining the Role of the Criminal Defense Lawyer at Plea Bargaining and Sentencing: A Therapeutic Jurisprudence/Preventive Law Model* (both applying therapeutic jurisprudence to criminal law) both in 5 Psychology, Pub. Pol'y & L. (1999) (in press).

19. *See generally* Hora, Schma & Rosenthal, *supra* note 10 (linking TJ with drug treatment courts); and Randal B. Fritzler & Leonore M. J. Simon, *Creating a Domestic Violence Court: Combat in the Trenches*, 37 Court Rev. 28 (2000) (in press) (linking a therapeutic jurisprudence approach with domestic violence courts).

20. *See* Nathalie Des Rosiers, *From Telling to Listening: A Therapeutic Analysis of the Role of Courts in Majority-Minority Conflicts*, 37 Court Review 54 (2000) (in press) and Amy D. Ronner, *Therapeutic Jurisprudence On Appeal*, 37 Court Review 64 (2000) (in press) (both exploring the therapeutic consequences of appellate opinions by courts).

edge about what works, about the need for continued support from the court, and about relapse, etc. <u>Domestic violence courts</u> similarly provide an opportunity for offenders not simply to experience short-term punishment but actually to move into a transformational process encouraging positive and long-term change. Even the words used in a judge's opinion or interaction with the litigants can be nontherapeutic or therapeutic, if chosen with an appreciation for the psychology underlying the case. In some cases, <u>the judge may be the only person</u> with sufficient power, author- ✗ ity, or opportunity to persuade or support a troubled, defensive, or isolated individual to change.

✗ Therapeutic jurisprudence is a very inclusive field with a robust literature. It has made a real effort to explore the relationships between many of the vectors, thus illustrating the convergence of the movement.[21] For example, TJ and preventive law have been linked (see *infra*); specialized courts have often been linked philosophically to TJ;[22] and bridges have also been built between TJ and restorative justice,[23] TJ and collaborative law,[24] TJ and holistic justice,[25] TJ and procedural justice,[26] TJ and mediation,[27] and TJ and creative problem solving.[28]

---

21. *See* authorities cited in notes 22-28, *infra*.

22. *See* Note, *The Trend Toward Specialized Domestic Violence Courts: Improvements on an Effective Innovation*, 68 Fordham L. Rev. 1285 (2000) (discussing a TJ approach to dealing with domestic violence and comparing it to the traditional legal means of dealing with the problem); *see also* Fritzler & Simon, *supra* note 19 (also linking domestic violence courts with a TJ approach), and Hora, Schma, & Rosenthal, *supra* note 10 (linking drug treatment courts with TJ).

23. *See* Robert Schopp, *Integrating Restorative Justice and Therapeutic Jurisprudence*, 67 Rev. Jur. UPR 665 (1998) (exploring the integration of TJ and restorative justice); and Thomas J. Scheff, *Community Conferences: Shame and Anger In Therapeutic Jurisprudence*, 67 Rev. Jur. UPR 97, 97-98 (1998) ("In recent years, an alternative approach to law, a worldwide movement, has been building momentum. This movement has two vectors, restorative justice and therapeutic jurisprudence" and proposing a "welding" of the two).

24. *See generally* Tesler, *supra* note 18 (authoring two articles on collaborative law in a special journal issue devoted to TJ).

25. For example, the seventh annual conference of the International Alliance of Holistic Lawyers included a presentation on therapeutic jurisprudence by University of Miami School of Law Professor Bruce Winick, November 4-7, 1999, Marathon, Florida.

26. *See generally* Tyler, *supra* note 4 (procedural justice article appearing in a text devoted to therapeutic jurisprudence).

27. *See generally* Andrea Kupfer Schneider, *The Intersection of Therapeutic Jurisprudence, Preventive Law and Alternate Dispute Resolution;* and Ellen Waldman, *Substituting Needs for Rights in Mediation: Therapeutic or Disabling?*, both in 5 Psychol., Pub. Pol'y & L. ___ (1999) (in press) (both relating TJ to ADR and mediation).

28. *See generally* Thomas D. Barton, *Therapeutic Jurisprudence, Preventive Law, and*

Preventive Law

⨍ Preventive law is a long-standing, harm-averse movement within the legal profession that explicitly seeks to intervene in legal matters before disputes arise. It advocates proactive intervention to avoid litigation and other conflicts. It emphasizes the lawyer-client relationship, clients' relationships with others in general, and planning. While not explicitly therapeutic, preventive law certainly recognizes the enormous psychological and financial costs involved in litigation and seeks to avoid those negative outcomes. In many cases, its application would preserve ongoing relationships by intervening in potentially troublesome situations before they erupt into litigation.[29]

↝ Employment law is particularly appropriate for the practice of preventive law. There are often situations in which an employer knows that an employee is disgruntled and not performing optimally, but hesitates to deal effectively with the situation. The employee's performance continues to decline, the situation becomes embittered, the employer fires the employee for nonperformance, and the employee sues the employer with possibly a real grievance. The entire situation could have been prevented and the employment relationship salvaged, if the lawyer had practiced effective preventive law. However, resolution of the difficulty between the employer and employee may require that the lawyer be sensitive to and proficient with interpersonal dynamics, again emphasizing the potentially psychological aspects of this type of practice.

Therapeutic Jurisprudence/Preventive Law

Perhaps due to this need in preventive law sometimes for sensitivity to the psychological aspects of legal matters, it became clear that TJ and preventive law could benefit from each other. Therapeutic jurisprudence originated primarily as an academic discipline focused on theory, while preventive law focused on ways of practicing law. Preventive law therefore

---

Creative Problem Solving: An Essay on Harnessing Emotion and Human Connection, in 5 PSYCHOLOGY, PUB. POL'Y & L. ___ (1999) (in press) (relating TJ and preventive law to creative problem solving).

29. *See generally* HARDAWAY, *supra* note 11 (entire casebook devoted to preventive law). The Brown Program of Preventive Law, formerly of the University of Denver College of Law, is now affiliated with California Western School of Law in San Diego, California, potentially providing the opportunity for further links between creative problem solving and preventive law.

offered TJ a practical framework and a set of procedures that helped TJ lawyers actually apply the law therapeutically. Preventive law benefited from TJ's explicit focus on the psychology of law. Thus, in a series of articles, the two vectors were, for many purposes, joined as an integrated approach to law and lawyering.[30]

For example, an integrated, TJ/PL approach asks the lawyer to identify "psycholegal soft spots," or areas of psychological effect that a strict legal analysis would overlook or ignore. It then proposes that the lawyer raise these concerns with the client and, through the resulting dialogue, seek a course of action that takes these concerns into account. For example, an estate planner will discuss with the client the psychological effects a bequest will have on the testator's children. If the will leaves a bequest outright to one child and in trust for the other because the testator trusts the judgment of one child and not the other, then certain psychological consequences may result. The less trustworthy child may feel that his or her parent did not love him or her as much as he or she loved the other child, even though the lack of the parent's trust was justified. Or, the estate planner or divorce lawyer will be sensitive to the psychological dynamics of the grief process, when dealing with a client diagnosed with AIDS or one undergoing a divorce, respectively. The lawyer in these cases will be prepared for dealing with the client's resistance to cooperation with the lawyer, if the client is in denial about his or her medical or marital condition.[31]

30. *See* Edward A. Dauer: *Preventive Law Before and After Therapeutic Jurisprudence: A Foreword to the Special Issue*; in 5 Psychol., Pub. Pol'y & L. __ (1999) (in press); Dennis P. Stolle, David B. Wexler, Bruce J. Winick & Edward A. Dauer, *Integrating Preventive Law and Therapeutic Jurisprudence: A Law and Psychology Based Approach to Lawyering*, 34 Cal. W. L. Rev. 15, 16 (1997); Dennis P. Stolle & David B. Wexler, *Therapeutic Jurisprudence and Preventive Law: A Combined Concentration to Invigorate the Everyday Practice of Law*, 39 Ariz. L. Rev. 25 (1997); Dennis P. Stolle, *Professional Responsibility in Elder Law: A Synthesis of Preventive Law and Therapeutic Jurisprudence*, 14 Behav. Sci. & L. 459, 462 (1996); and Dennis P. Stolle & David B. Wexler, *Preventive Law and Therapeutic Jurisprudence: A Symbiotic Relationship*, 16 Preventive L. Rep. 4 (1996) (all discussing the integration of the two).

31. *See, e.g.*, Bruce J. Winick, *Client Denial and Resistance in the Advance Directive Context: Reflections on How Attorneys Can Identify and Deal with a Psycholegal Soft Spot*, 4 Psychol. Pub. Pol'y & L. 901 (1998) (examining how lawyers counseling clients about advance directive instruments can deal with clients' denial and resistance, explaining the psychological defense mechanism of denial and resistance, and offering suggestions about techniques lawyers can use for dealing with them and ways in which lawyers can develop their interpersonal skills, becoming more empathic and more sensitive to their clients' psychological needs) and Dennis P. Stolle, *Advance Directives, AIDS, and Mental Health: TJ Preventive Law for the HIV-Positive Client*, 4 Psychol. Pub. Pol'y & L. 854

The lawyer also will need to be patient with the client and may need to assist the client in moving through denial into the next phase of the grief process.[32]

Restorative Justice

Restorative justice refers to a movement in criminal law in which criminal justice and criminal sentencing are carried out by the community, the victim, and the offender in a collaborative process. In this process, all players are present and the process focuses on the relationships between the offender, the victim, and the community.[33] It is the antithesis of a top-down, hierarchical system where the judge, who is on top, imposes a sentence on the defendant, who is below the judge in the hierarchy. The web site of the Center for Restorative Justice and Peacemaking at the University of Minnesota explains:

> The Center for Restorative Justice & Peacemaking at the University of Minnesota School of Social Work on the University's St. Paul campus has been established to provide technical assistance, training, and research for those in the state of Minnesota, nationally, and internationally in support of restorative justice practice and principles. Through restorative justice, victims, communities, and offenders are

---

(1998) (arguing for the need for an explicit focus on psychological wellbeing in a lawyer's representation of an HIV-positive client and illustrating how a TJ/PL approach would fulfill that need).

32. Elisabeth Kübler-Ross' five stages of the grief process are incredibly relevant to lawyers dealing with any clients whose legal matters represent a loss, such as death, divorce, loss of a job, or a personal injury. The stages are: denial (no; this can't be happening to me); anger (I don't deserve this; it must be someone else's fault); bargaining (if only I or someone else had done x or y, this would not be happening to me; maybe there is some action I can take to avoid it); depression (this is happening and it hurts; I am sad and in pain); and acceptance (this happened, there is nothing I can do about it, and now I must move on). *See* BURL E. GILLILAND & RICHARD K. JAMES, CRISIS INTERVENTION STRATEGIES, 402-03 (1998) *citing* ELISABETH KÜBLER-ROSS, ON DEATH AND DYING (1969).

33. Mark S. Umbreit, *Restorative Justice: Implications for Organizational Change,* 59 FED. PROBATION 47 (1995) (discussing results of using restorative justice by the Dakota County Community Corrections Department in Minnesota and the steps an organization must go through in order to implement a restorative justice program); Mark S. Umbreit, *Victim Offender Mediation and Judicial Leadership,* 69 JUDICATURE 202 (1986) (encouraging judges to refer cases to restorative justice programs and describing two specific programs in Valparaiso, Indiana and Batavia, New York); and Mark S. Umbreit, *Mediation of Victim/Offender Conflict,* 31 MO. J. DISP. RESOL. 85 (1988) (concerning the ability of restorative justice programs to fulfill the emotional and informational needs of victims of crime which often outweigh the need for compensation).

placed in active roles to work together to...Empower victims in their search for closure; Impress upon offenders the real human impact of their behavior; Promote restitution to victims and communities. Dialogue and negotiation are central to restorative justice, and problem solving for the future is seen as more important than simply establishing blame for past behavior. Balance is sought between the legitimate needs of the victim, the community, and the offender that enhances community protection, competency development in the offender, and direct accountability of the offender to the victim and victimized community.[34]

Interestingly, its origins are associated with nonlawyers, unlike most of the other vectors. Due to its psychologically beneficial effects on offenders and victims, its integration with therapeutic jurisprudence has been proposed.[35] It appears to have been most enthusiastically employed in Australia, Canada, and the United Kingdom, although it is being used in a number of American jurisdictions. It bears a resemblance to traditional Native American and aboriginal justice in its emphasis on the community and on the therapeutic value of "normal, reintegrative shame" (which is acknowledged by the offender), rather than on privately imposed punishment.[36]

Procedural Justice

Procedural justice refers to empirical studies finding that, in judicial procedures, litigants' satisfaction sometimes depends nearly as much upon certain psychological factors as upon the actual outcome of the legal matter (e.g., winning vs. losing). These factors are: being treated with respect and dignity, being heard, having an opportunity to speak and participate, and how trustworthy the authorities appear and behave.[37] It does not advocate any particular way of administering the law other than recommending that, for optimal participant satisfaction and thus optimal dispute resolution, judges and attorneys must treat litigants and other individuals with respect and dignity, they must be authentic, honest, and trustworthy, and legal processes must provide participants with an oppor-

---

34. http://ssw.che.umn.edu/rjp/.

35. *See generally* Scheff, *supra* note 23 and Schopp, *supra* note 23 (both exploring the links between restorative justice and therapeutic jurisprudence).

36. *See* Scheff, *supra* note 23 at 104-09 (discussing the therapeutic and antitherapeutic effects of and forms of shame).

37. *See generally* Tyler, *supra* note 4 (explaining these primary, empirically-based insights of procedural justice).

tunity to speak freely. Psychologists have long been aware of the power inherent in speaking certain statements aloud in the presence of another person, but the law explicitly focuses neither on people's need to do so nor on the therapeutic effects of allowing individuals a forum for this.[38] Procedural justice thus nicely integrated the law with psychology in exploring litigants' satisfaction with judicial procedures.[39]

Facilitative Mediation

As mediation developed within the ADR movement, it began to split into two forms, evaluative and facilitative. In evaluative mediation, the mediator functions as a third-party evaluator of the parties' cases and can adopt an authoritative, adjudicatory posture. The evaluative mediator is likely to evaluate the merits of the parties' legal positions, discuss what they would probably obtain if they litigated the case, and use that information to move the parties towards agreement.[40] In contrast, facilitative mediation is a three-party process in which the mediator seeks to assist

---

38. *See* JAMES W. PENNEBAKER, OPENING UP: THE HEALING POWER OF CONFIDING IN OTHERS (1990) (on the healing power of writing and speaking about traumatic events), as discussed by David Wexler *in* David B. Wexler, *Some Thoughts and Observations on the Teaching of Therapeutic Jurisprudence,* 35 REV. DERECHO P.R. 273, 285 (1996). *See also* MICHAEL L. PERLIN, LAW AND MENTAL DISABILITY, Section 5.04 at 669-671 (1994) (discussing the negative effects of "pretextuality," meaning courts' willingness to tolerate "testimonial dishonesty," distorted expert testimony, and dishonest decision-making in dealing with mentally disabled litigants). While the First Amendment may well legally protect one's right to oral expression, it does not do so because of the human need to do so. Instead, it is couched as a "right." Certainly the law does not always provide opportunities in the litigation process for such expression nor does it believe those opportunities are indispensable.

39. Procedural justice has also been important to therapeutic jurisprudence. *See* DAVID B. WEXLER & BRUCE J. WINICK, EDS., LAW IN A THERAPEUTIC KEY: DEVELOPMENTS IN THERAPEUTIC JURISPRUDENCE 3 (1996) (containing Tyler's article on procedural justice, *supra* note 4); Bruce J. Winick, *Therapeutic Jurisprudence and the Civil Commitment Hearing,* 10 CONTEMP. L. ISSUES 37 (1999) (applying the psychology of procedural justice and therapeutic jurisprudence principles to restructure the civil commitment hearing and the role of the lawyer therein); and Bruce J. Winick, *Therapeutic Jurisprudence and the Role of Counsel in Litigation,* 5 BEHAV. SCI. & L. __ (forthcoming, 2000) (using procedural justice and therapeutic jurisprudence to suggest how lawyers can fulfill their professional roles in more psychologically sensitive and therapeutic ways).

40. *See* Ellen Waldman, *The Evaluative-Facilitative Debate in Mediation: Applying the Lens of Therapeutic Jurisprudence,* 82 MARQUETTE L. REV. 155 (1998) (comparing evaluative and facilitative mediation and discussing the therapeutic effects of facilitative mediation).

each party to express their needs and reach a solution acceptable to both parties. The therapeutic aspects of facilitative mediation have been noted.[41] It can empower the parties, give them a feeling of control and ownership over the process and its outcome, and lead to a greater sense of agreement and resolution between the parties. However, it is worth noting that there are times when evaluative mediation, albeit possibly less collaborative and party-centered, may actually be more therapeutic than facilitative mediation. For example, evaluative mediation might be therapeutic where there is a great power imbalance between the parties or where one party is unaware of what he or she might be entitled to in a litigated outcome and could subjugate himself or herself unnecessarily without such information.

Transformative Mediation

✗ Transformative mediation is a newer form of mediation that emerged around 1994. It sees mediation as an opportunity for the parties to learn how to resolve disputes more effectively. It explicitly seeks to change the parties in the mediation process to improve their conflict resolution abilities so that they can resolve future disputes themselves, without help. In this process, the procedure and the players are dynamic. The process is not viewed as a one-shot, static event accomplishing the resolution of simply one dispute. Instead, the parties are moved towards effective, continuing relationships with each other. It is obviously particularly appropriate in family law and employment law settings. Apparently, the United States post office is training mediators in this process and is using this approach to mediate employment disputes with its employees.[42]

Collaborative Law

✗ Collaborative law is a nonlitigative, collaborative process employed mainly in divorce law, where the spouses and their respective attorneys resolve the issues outside of court in a four-party process. It differs from mediation in that no third party is involved; it is a four-way process rather than a three-party process and it involves six, ongoing relationships between the four individuals involved (i.e., lawyer-client, client-client, and lawyer-lawyer). It differs from traditional settlement negotiations in that: (1) no formal court proceedings are usually instituted until settlement is reached;

---

41. *See id.*

42. *See generally* BUSH & FOLGER, *supra* note 13 (describing the theory and practice of transformative mediation in detail).

and (2) the attorneys are contractually forbidden from representing their clients in court should the agreement process break down. It accomplishes resolution of the parties' dispute by engaging the divorcing spouses and their respective attorneys in a series of collaborative, four-way discussions designed to reach settlement outside of litigation. Because the attorneys must withdraw if the process breaks down, the attorneys' financial interests are aligned with the clients'—all four people want to reach settlement. This contrasts with the usual process, in which the lawyers "win" whether the clients settle or not, since they simply litigate the case if settlement negotiations break down. This aspect is said to have a definite salutary effect on the lawyers' motivation to achieve resolution. Because of the personal investment of all four parties in achieving resolution, proponents maintain that more creative, altruistic, and harmonious solutions are proposed and implemented in collaborative law.[43]

Collaborative law also explicitly recognizes the psychological dynamics inherent in the process. It acknowledges that there are times that the clients are too angry or hurt to effectively collaborate and it provides a mechanism to suspend the process when these times occur. There is also a strong psychological component to the lawyer-client relationship. The clients' emotions, needs, transference, etc. are openly acknowledged and discussed by the attorneys in order to maximize results of the four-way conferences. Although currently being used only in the domestic area, collaborative law is appropriate for a number of other areas, such as employment law and probate law.

Holistic Law

Holistic law or holistic justice is a movement that arose among practicing lawyers around 1990. The web site for the International Alliance of Holistic Lawyers explains that holistic law:

> acknowledge[s] the need for a humane legal process with the highest level of satisfaction for all participants; honor[s] and respect[s] the dignity and integrity of each individual; promote[s] peaceful advocacy and holistic legal principles; value[s] responsibility, connection and inclusion; encourage[s] compassion, reconciliation, forgiveness and healing; practice[s] deep listening, understand[s] and recognize[s]

---

43. *See* Tesler, *supra* note 18 (describing collaborative law generally); and Bryan, *supra* note 18 (critiquing Tesler's article). *See also* Amy E. Bourne, *Some Lawyers Use What Sounds Like Psychotherapy, Others Simply Avoid Litigation and Embrace Mediation and Cooperation,* San Francisco Daily Journal, August 3, 1999 at 1 (profiling Pauline Tesler and describing the collaborative law approach generally).

the importance of voice; contributes[s] to peace building at all levels of society; recognize[s] the opportunity in conflict; draw[s] upon ancient intuitive wisdom of diverse cultures and traditions; and [encourages the lawyer to] enjoy the practice of law.[44]

It is explicitly interdisciplinary, allows the lawyer to incorporate his or her own morals and values into client representation, and seeks to "do the right thing" for the lawyer, clients, and others involved. Like holistic medicine, it uses a broad, holistic approach to solve legal problems and it deals with legal matters in a humane, often collaborative, and frequently healing fashion.[45] It originated perhaps because of dissatisfaction with the current modes of practicing law and because of an emerging awareness among certain attorneys that practicing law in a different way was necessary for the emotional wellbeing of themselves and their clients. Some of the philosophies of the individual lawyers involved may be rooted in humanistic principles, some in New Age principles, some in psychology, some in religion or spirituality, and others in universal moral principles. In recent years, holistic justice as a practitioner movement has increasingly explored therapeutic jurisprudence and collaborative law in an acknowledgement that they are related disciplines.[46]

Creative Problem Solving

Creative problem solving ("CPS") is a very broad discipline that is explicitly humanistic, interdisciplinary, creative, and preventive in its approach to legal problems. It seeks to find solutions to legal problems using a broader approach than is traditionally associated with legal work. It has been described as:

---

44. http://www.iahl.org/index.htm.

45. The International Alliance of Holistic Lawyers reports about 800 members nationally and in other countries; it will hold its eighth annual conference in 2000. Holistic lawyering is rather broadly defined, which is done intentionally in order to maximize its inclusiveness. President and founder William Van Zyverden explains that all legal conflicts are "emotionally based," that "settlement is not resolution, and resolution only happens when the person forgives and lets it go and releases any animosity," and that "[p]art of the holistic approach is to see everything positively" (describing resolution of a divorce case which came quickly once the issues were reframed positively), *quoted in* Barry E. Katz, *Putting the Counsel Back In Counselor*, 28 STUDENT LAWYER 32, 34 (2000).

46. For example, the agenda of the 1999 annual conference of the International Alliance for Holistic Lawyers included a presentation on therapeutic jurisprudence; the 2000 annual conference is expected to include presentations on most of the vectors of the comprehensive law movement.

...an evolving approach to law. It combines law, sociology, social anthropology, and the behavioral sciences (particularly cognitive psychology, group dynamics, and decision-making) in a holistic fashion. It also includes the assessment of the impact of business theory and economics [and]...sciences and applied sciences[']...diagnostic and planning skills...In Creative Problem Solving, problems are thought of as multidimensional, often requiring non legal or multidisciplinary solutions. Most conflicts have interconnected causes and their effects often impinge on competing jurisdictions and disciplines. In short, entrenchment of law and legal precepts can sometimes work against the solving of problems. In fact, Creative Problem Solving requires the parties to part with the linear understanding of history of the situation. By focusing on a problem's past, we are often stuck in entrenched positions, from which no collaborative solution can be found....We assume that problems may be prevented or solved more effectively by professionals from many disciplines joining together...Not all problems require a legal solution and not all legal problems should result in a lawsuit. The Creative Problem Solving lawyer does not litigate for the sake of litigation....Indeed, only occasionally do a client's problems call for the kind of legal solutions that attorneys are so used to providing. In fact, rarely does any situation require just a legal solution. Problems often call for an inquiry into the psychology of the parties involved and a thorough analysis of all the interests of the various constituents....The practice of Creative Problem Solving requires a certain flexibility of mind and a bent towards the interpersonal sensitivity that enables one to apply the most appropriate skill at the most appropriate time....Likewise, conflict, so often viewed as a zero-sum game, must be re-evaluated. With all the binary byproducts that come with conflict - rights and liabilities, winners and losers, victors and vanquished - a new multipolar, nonlinear approach must be embraced....Creative Problem Solving techniques [are]...interactive listening, consensus-building, and proactive dialoguing...[47]

The American Bar Association has been active in sponsoring discussion about the scope and efficacy of creative problem solving. Some of its pro-

---

47. James M. Cooper, *Towards a New Architecture: Creative Problem Solving and the Evolution of Law*, 34 CALIF. WEST. L. REV. 297, 312-13. (1998) (citations omitted). *See* Linda Morton, *Teaching Creative Problem Solving: A Paradigmatic Approach*, 34 CAL. WEST L. REV. 375, 376-78 (1998) (further describing creative problem solving and its use in legal education). The website for the McGill Center for Creative Problem Solving at California Western School of Law is found at http://www.cps.cwsl.edu.

ponents view CPS as an "umbrella" discipline incorporating all of the other vectors under its aegis. It has recently been associated in some ways with preventive law, illustrating yet another bridge between vectors.

Specialized Courts

Specialized courts, such as drug treatment courts, mental health courts, and domestic violence courts, take an explicitly therapeutic approach to their treatment of alcohol- and drug-addicted individuals, those with mental disabilities, and those involved in domestic violence.[48] They use psychological insights about human nature and the nature of the mental problems involved to achieve optimal results of the judicial interface with people's lives. In some cases, these courts' approach has dramatically reduced recidivism rates among offenders.[49] Their popularity in recent years and efficacy demands that they be included as a vector of this movement, albeit in the area of judging rather than in the area of lawyering. Not only have they had a salutary effect upon the troubled individuals brought to court, but the effects of their work have also rejuvenated the spirits of the lawyers and judges involved.[50]

Comparison of Traditional Law with Comprehensive Law

Several charts effectively illustrate the differences between some of these comprehensive law approaches and more traditional approaches to practicing law. The first compares traditional, adversarial law to collaborative law but was adapted from a comparison of holistic law and traditional

---

48. *See generally* the May, 2000 special issue of COURT REVIEW devoted to "Judging for the New Millennium," including Deborah J. Chase & Peggy Fulton Hora, *The Implications of Therapeutic Jurisprudence for Judicial Satisfaction* 37 COURT REVIEW 12 (2000) (in press) (on drug treatment courts and their demonstrated potential for increasing judges' job satisfaction); and Fritzler & Simon, *supra* note 19 (on domestic violence courts). *See also* Note, *supra* note 23 (on domestic violence special courts); and Hora, Schma & Rosenthal, *supra* note 10 (on drug treatment courts generally).

49. *See* Barry E. Katz, *Putting the Counsel Back In Counselor,* 28 STUDENT LAWYER 32, 36 (May, 2000) (more than half of all defendants convicted of drug possession generally recidivate with a similar offense in 2-3 years; but recidivism for drug treatment court participants ranges from 5-28% and is less than 4% for graduates of the programs).

50. *See* Chase & Hora, *supra* note 48 (reporting the results of an empirical study on the positive effects on judges of judging from a therapeutic jurisprudence perspective); *see also* Hora, Schma, & Rosenthal, *supra* note 10 (anecdotally discussing same).

law, so arguably reflects both; the second compares evaluative mediation to facilitative and transformational mediation; and the third compares traditional courts to more problem solving-oriented ones (such as the specialized courts described above).

✗ Comparison of Adversarial and Collaborative Lawyering[51]

Adversarial	Collaborative
Limited time for client; emphasis on getting the legal work done	Time with client central to process
Focus on legal analysis: facts, law, cases	Focus on client and other party
Aligns with client's view of the facts	Understands the client's inevitable coloring of the facts
Q&A of client for efficient retrieval of essential elements of case	Active listening for clear comprehension of situation: history, goals, priorities, fears
Asks close-ended questions to fit facts into legal framework	Asks open-ended questions to elicit full understanding
Views emotions and feelings as distractions from the "real work"	Views emotions and feelings as important elements of collaborative process that need to be acknowl edged and appropriately managed
Supports client in his/her beliefs about others—including negative beliefs	Encourages respect for all participants
Supports client's self-concept as victim	Aims to foster personal responsibility
Takes directions which may arise from client's anger, fear or grief	Separates client's true interests from emotion-based impulses and reactions
May foster or disregard client's unrealistic or illusory perceptions	Counsels and challenges client to transform understanding of what is real and what is not

---

51. Copyright 1999 Pauline H. Tesler. This table is reprinted with permission of Ms. Tesler. It was adapted by her with permission from a similar comparison of "adversarial vs. holistic" lawyering by William Van Zyverden, president and founder of the International Alliance of Holistic Lawyers.

May support client's desire for revenge and undue advantage

Encourages compassion and enlightened self-interest

May support client's shifting of responsibility for actions toward others

Educates client to accept personal responsibility for consequences that naturally follow actions

Insists on control over all contacts with client related to case

Values team approach, including mental health and financial neutrals

Tells client what game plan is

Presents options for strategy and tactics

The law is for lawyers

Invites client to understand the law

Fears that the other professionals will compromise the lawyer's ability to "win big"

Works collaboratively with all retained professionals to achieve the overall best outcome for the client

Tries to control advice and conclusions of other professionals involved with client

Values sound input from other disciplines as aid to providing high-quality legal assistance; respects potential contribution of other disciplines in problem-solving effort

Considers the work of other professionals in the divorce process ancillary to the main task, legal work

Considers the legal issues in a divorce only a subset of a larger, longer and more complex human transition

Mediation Styles[52]

	Controlling	Empowering
Direct victim/offender communication	Minimal	Maximum
Victim/offender facing each other	Sometimes	Always
Range of victim/offender discussion	Narrow	Broad
Importance of context/feelings	Minimal	Very
Presentation of choices	Infrequent	Frequent
Judgmental statements	Frequent	Infrequent

52. Mark S. Umbreit, *Mediation of Victim/Offender Conflict*, 31 Mo. J. Disp. Resol. 85, 95 (1988) (table reprinted with permission of the author).

✗ A Comparison of Transformed and Traditional Court Processes[53]

Traditional Process	*Transformed Process*
Dispute resolution	Problem-solving dispute avoidance
Legal outcome	Therapeutic outcome
Adversarial process	Collaborative process
Claim- or case-oriented	People-oriented
Rights-based	Interest- or needs-based
Emphasis placed on adjudication	Emphasis placed on post-adjudication and alternative dispute resolution
Interpretation and application of law	Interpretation and application of social science
Judge as arbiter	Judge as coach
Backward looking	Forward looking
Precedent-based	Planning-based
Few participants and stakeholders	Wide range of participants and stakeholders
Individualistic	Interdependent
Legalistic	Common-sensical
Formal	Informal
Efficient	Effective

Organizational Chart of the Vectors of the Movement

While the vectors might appear to be co-equal developments within the law, they are actually functionally different. These functional differences suggest an organizational chart of the comprehensive law movement. For example, some of the vectors are more practical, concrete, and tangible while others are more philosophical, theoretical, and broad. The more philosophical ones can be categorized as "lenses" through which the other, more concrete vectors can be evaluated by the therapeutic practitioner seeking the best approach to a particular legal matter. The more concrete vectors can be categorized as humane or therapeutic "processes" for resolv-

---

53. Roger K. Warren, *Reengineering the Court Process*, Madison, WI, Presentation to Great Lakes Court Summit, September 24-25, 1998.

ing legal matters—or tangible mechanisms for practicing law therapeutically. Finally, therapeutic jurisprudence may either be a lens for evaluating the various legal mechanisms or it may actually be an overarching theory underpinning the entire comprehensive law movement. These relationships are explored below.

Traditionally, dispute resolution experts suggest that dispute resolution occurs via three primary processes: adjudication (litigation, arbitration, or private adjudication, for example), negotiation (a two-party process), and mediation (a process involving a third party whose role is to assist the parties in arriving at their own solution). These three primary processes can be further combined to produce a variety of hybrid processes, such as private judging, neutral expert fact-finding, mini-trials, ombudsman, and summary jury trials.[54] Within this framework, specialized courts are an alternative form of litigation. Facilitative mediation and transformative mediation are two newer forms of mediation that fit within the comprehensive law movement and are consistent with therapeutic jurisprudence.[55] Collaborative law is clearly a new form of negotiation with a very specific therapeutically oriented agenda and procedure. Restorative justice is another form of dispute resolution, primarily used in criminal matters that might be seen as a form of negotiation.

If legal practice is expanded to include not only "dispute resolution" but also any legal procedures available for dealing with legal matters, then clearly client counseling, transaction planning, and document preparation (such as wills, trusts, and contracts) are other legal "processes" that lawyers utilize daily. Preventive law, TJ/PL, and TJ-oriented client counseling are therapeutic processes that fall into this larger group of lawyer tools. Therapeutic lawyers can choose from among this expanded set of tools or processes in determining which approach will work best for any particular client or matter,[56] as follows (comprehensive approaches in italics):

---

54. *See* GOLDBERG, ET AL., *supra* note 12, at 7-8. Note that in these authors' taxonomy, litigation is involuntary, binding, public, and formal and involves an imposed third-party decisionmaker who makes a principled decision. Arbitration is voluntary, binding, private, and less formal and involves a party-selected third-party decision-maker who makes a principled or compromise decision. Mediation is voluntary, can be contractually binding, private, and informal and involves a party-selected outside facilitator to reach a mutually acceptable agreement. Negotiation is voluntary, can be contractually binding, informal, and private and does not involve a third-party decision-maker; the parties reach a mutually acceptable agreement themselves. The hybrid processes combine these elements in other variations. *See id.* at 8.

55. *See* Waldman, *supra* note 40 (integrating and comparing TJ and facilitative mediation).

56. *See* Schneider, *supra* note 27 (regarding the importance of the lawyer and client discussing the various alternatives available in each matter).

Legal Processes or Tools[57]

Adjudication	Arbitration	Mediation	Negotiation	Hybrid Dispute Resolution	One-Client Counseling, Planning, or Document Preparation
Litigation		*Facilitative mediation*	Traditional adversarial	Neutral expert fact-finding	Traditional
Private judge		*Transform-ative mediation*	Collabora-tive law	Mini-trial	*Preventa-tive law*
Specialized Court		Evaluative mediation	*Restorative justice*	Ombudsman	*TJ/PL*
				Summary jury trial	*TJ*

The remaining vectors of the comprehensive law movement are broader, more theoretical, and less concrete. Therefore, they may function as "lenses" through which the attorney evaluates the above legal processes, tools, or options. They help the attorney evaluate the likely consequences, outcomes, viability, and desirability of each process for each legal matter handled by the attorney. For example, each of the foregoing legal processes can be evaluated from a therapeutic jurisprudence perspective, in which the attorney asks, "Is this process therapeutic or not? How could it be made so? Are the legal rules involved likely to have a therapeutic or countertherapeutic effect? Can those effects be enhanced or mitigated?", or a holistic perspective, in which the attorney asks, "How does this process take into account the healing of the client and lawyer? Does it encompass the whole person of the client (emotionally, spiritually, etc.) or simply the legal matters presented?" The processes can be evaluated from a procedural justice viewpoint, from which the attorney asks, "How will this process affect the participants psychologically? How satisfactory will they find it?", or a creative problem solving perspective, in which the attorney asks, "Does this process allow for the broadest, most creative approach to solving the problem?". A related lens may be religious lawyering, where the lawyer asks whether the process is consistent with the lawyer's and the client's religious beliefs.

All of the lenses are abstract, value-laden mechanisms for evaluating the desirability of the processes. All are more comprehensive and humane

---

57. Material in table represents an expansion and adaptation of a table found in GOLDBERG, ET AL., *supra* note 12, at 8.

than lawyers' traditional approach, which tends to focus primarily on legal rights and duties[60] and the economic "bottom-line" of the outcome.[61] One unanswered question is whether therapeutic jurisprudence is the overarching theory for all of the "lenses" comprising the comprehensive law movement. In other words, it is unclear whether all of the lenses (therapeutic jurisprudence, procedural justice, holistic law, creative problem solving) are similar in that they are all "therapeutic" in intent or whether they differ from each other in intent but not in function. Further development of the comprehensive law movement and of therapeutic jurisprudence is likely to reveal the answer.

Comprehensive Legal Education

As noted above, the comprehensive law movement originated among practicing lawyers (possibly those most dissatisfied with the traditional, gladiatorial practice of law), law professors primarily working in the field of law and psychology, and nonlawyers such as social work professors and other social scientists. Perhaps because of its many-headed origins, it has

---

58. Empirical studies on lawyer personality actually suggest that this focus is part of the typical personality traits favored by lawyers, see Daicoff/Lawyer, *supra* note 2, at 1403-1410 (discussing empirical studies on lawyers' moral decision-making styles). *See also* Lawrence R. Richard, *How Personality Affects Your Practice*, A.B.A. J. (July 1993) (lawyers preferred Thinking to Feeling on the Myers-Briggs Type Indicator); Vernellia R. Randall, *The Myers-Briggs Type Indicator, First Year Law Studies and Performance*, 26 CUMB. L. REV. 63, 80-81, 86-87, 91-92, 96-97 (1995-6) (replicating Richard's findings and exploring links between preferences and law school grades); Kurt M. Saunders & Linda Levine, *Learning to Think Like a Lawyer*, 29 U.S.F. L. REV. 121 (1994) (echoing an emphasis on a rights-based focus in law school); Erica Weissman, Gender-Role Issues in Attorney Career Satisfaction (unpublished Ph.D. dissertation, Yeshiva University, 1994) at 74-76 (determining that a minority of both women and men attorneys were exclusively care-oriented); Sandra Janoff, *The Influence of Legal Education on Moral Reasoning*, 76 MINN. L. REV. 193, 218-30 (1991) (verifying that law school tended to silence an ethic of care; women law students more often demonstrated an ethic of care while men law students demonstrated a rights orientation, but care-oriented students had shifted to a rights orientation by the end of the first year); and Janet Taber et al., *Project Gender, Legal Education & the Legal Profession: An Empirical Study of Stanford Law Students & Graduates*, 40 STAN. L. REV. 1209 (1988) (demonstrating that female law students found contextual factors more important while male law students focused on abstract factors).

59. Russell Korobkin & Chris Guthrie, *Psychology, Economics & Settlement: A New Look at the Role of the Lawyer*, 76 TEX. L. REV. 77 (1997) (empirical study finding that lawyers — but not nonlawyers — tended to focus on the economic bottom-line of various settlement options in legal disputes; nonlawyers were more persuaded or influenced by noneconomic, psychological factors).

neither fully coalesced nor revolutionized legal education, yet. However, several therapeutic jurisprudence scholars have either integrated therapeutic jurisprudence into their existing law school courses or, in some cases, actually created entirely new courses designed to teach law students how to practice law with a therapeutic or comprehensive orientation.[60] Courses are springing up in law schools across the country that encourage students to examine the psychological, moral, ethical, and human aspects of legal matters, cases, and practice. Many of these courses or emphases have occurred in clinical legal education, somewhat naturally.[61] Greater emphasis on the vectors and their underlying theories are likely to appear in law schools, however, only when the comprehensive law movement becomes more cohesive and the demands of lawyers and law students for comprehensive law approaches force institutional change.

Conclusion

The beginning of the twenty-first century is an exciting time in the law. Despite the discouragement and disillusionment of many lawyers (and clients) expressed in the last fifteen years or so, the malaise is beginning to produce positive change. Numerous developments within legal scholarship, law practice, judging and courts, and legal education reflect a growing, hopeful movement. In this movement, law is a more comprehensive, psychologically sophisticated, interdisciplinary, holistic, and at times harmonious and collaborative discipline. It functions as a more positive, humane, humanistic, transformative, therapeutic, salutary, healing, restorative, and creative agent in people's lives. At least ten "vectors" of this movement have emerged. Most of these have appeared within the last decade of the twentieth century. As the movement coalesces, certain vectors are developing as legal processes for dealing concretely and humane-

---

60. Professor David B. Wexler at the University of Arizona and University of Puerto Rico law schools; Professor Bruce Winick at the University of Miami law school; Professor Michael L. Perlin at New York Law School; various professors at California Western School of Law (who have integrated creative problem solving into their courses); the author at Capital University and Florida Coastal law schools.

61. For example, a new list serve of law professors dedicated to "Humanizing Legal Education" was established in 1999 by clinical law professor Lawrence Krieger of Florida State University College of Law. *See also* the following three articles in 5 PSYCHOL. PUB. POL'Y & L. __ (1999) (in press) on using therapeutic jurisprudence and preventive law in law teaching: Pearl Goldman & Leslie Larkin Cooney, *Beyond Core Skills and Values: Intergrating Therapeutic Jurisprudence and Preventative Law into the Law School Curriculum*; Mary Berkheiser, *Frasier Meets CLEA: Therapeutic Jurisprudence and Law School Clinics*; and Marjorie A. Silver, *Emotional Intelligence and Legal Education*.

ly with legal matters, while other vectors are developing as nontradition-
al philosophies by which the other processes are evaluated and chosen.
Therapeutic jurisprudence stands as one of the most fully developed, theoretical vectors of this "comprehensive law movement." It remains to be
seen whether therapeutic jurisprudence is an organizing principle around
which the vectors coalesce or simply one of several philosophies underpinning and guiding other, more tangible parts of the movement. Certainly
its development over the last ten years has been a driving, organizing, synthesizing force for the entire movement as a whole. Without TJ and its
relationships to the other vectors, the movement probably would not be
developing with the energy, synthesis, and visibility that it currently possesses.

Despite the appeal of the vectors of the comprehensive law movement,
they are not always appropriate in all matters or for all clients. Further, not
every attorney can effectively practice law in this way.[62] There are clients and
legal matters for whom a comprehensive approach is inappropriate (perhaps
even countertherapeutic), such as situations in which the client is entirely
unwilling to discuss any psychological concerns inherent in the case or is
closed to any possibility of cooperative collaboration with the other parties
involved. There may be times when the lawyer cannot seek to optimize human
wellbeing or consider concerns beyond legal rights. For example, it may be
unclear in the situation what measures would improve the client's psychological state or condition, there may be conflicting psychological demands, or
the client may be simply unwilling to optimize human wellbeing or consider extralegal concerns. Finally, there may be times that gladiatorial, adversarial, hostile lawyering is actually the most therapeutic and empowering
approach for the individuals involved in the dispute—for example, in situations where a plaintiff finds himself or herself forced to sue an intractable,
resistant, defensive, and other-blaming defendant who minimizes or deni-
grates the plaintiff's concerns unless the threat of judicial action is present.

---

62. Indeed, the author's review of almost forty years' worth of empirical studies comparing lawyers to the general population suggests that a large percentage of lawyers have
personality traits and preferences which might make it difficult for them to practice comprehensive law easily or effortlessly. These lawyers' personality styles are likely to cause
them to deemphasize or even ignore the human, relational, and emotional aspects of legal
matters. However, there is a significant percentage of lawyers whose personality traits are
extraordinarily well-suited to a more comprehensive, transformative, therapeutic, restorative, and humanistic way of dealing with clients and legal matters. For a full discussion of
these ideas, *see generally* SUSAN DAICOFF, LAWYER, KNOW THYSELF, *supra* note 1, and *see*
Susan Daicoff, Making Law Therapeutic For Lawyers: Therapeutic Jurisprudence, Preventive Law, and the Psychology of Lawyers, 5 PSYCHOL. PUB. POL'Y & L. __ (1999) (in press)
(discussing the appropriateness of a TJ/PL practice for lawyers with certain traits).

However, a few years or decades ago, the comprehensive law approach was not an explicit option. Clients and lawyers were relegated to a gladiatorial, psychologically-blind style of law that often wreaked emotional damage upon all who were involved with or touched by the process. Happily, today clients and lawyers have a choice. As the holistic lawyers say, "There is another way." These "other ways" are likely to continue to grow and develop in years to come. TJ is likely to continue to be a rallying point for many of the vectors of the movement. At the very least, it is one of the most vibrant, well-developed, and respected disciplines within the comprehensive law movement.

Appendix

Identification of Psycholegal Soft Spots and Strategies

This project has been approved by the University of Nebraska Institutional Review Board, IRB # 98-04-328EP. Confidentiality of responses will be protected by the investigators. For questions, contact the UNL IRB at (402) 472-6965.

Please indicate whether you are a (check one):

Judge: _____ Attorney: _____ Law Student: _____

Other (please specify): _____

Contact information (optional):

    Name: _____

    Telephone: _____

    Fax: _____

    E-mail: _____

Would you object to follow-up contact if it was necessary or advantageous for research purposes?:

No _____ Yes _____

Please remember to protect the identity of individuals involved in the cases you discuss.

1) Identify the area of law that this problem relates to:

2) Provide a brief description of the legal situation as it was at the time you initially became involved:

3)   Describe the potential or actual nonlegal motivations or consequences to the parties involved:

4)   In your experience, how often does this type of situation occur?

5) Provide a description of the action taken and the legal and nonlegal outcomes:

6) Explain whether or not you believe this approach resulted in success-ful legal and nonlegal outcomes and why:

7)   Describe alternate approaches that could have been taken and how the legal and nonlegal outcomes may have been more or less successful than the actual outcomes:

8)   Using the "rewind" technique (e.g., "rewinding" the case to an earlier point in time), describe how this situation may have been prevented or diminished in severity by other attorneys or other judges at earlier points in time:

9) General comments:

Please photocopy, complete, and return the completed form to:

THERAPEUTIC JURISPRUDENCE &
PREVENTIVE LAW PROJECT
Law/Psychology Program
University of Nebraska-Lincoln
238 Burnett Hall
Lincoln, NE 68588-0308

You may also fax a completed version of the form to
(402) 472-4637 or complete the form electronically by accessing it
on the University of Nebraska Psychology and Law web page:
http://www.unl.edu/psylaw/index.html

About the Contributors

Stephen J. Anderer is a member of the Family Law Department and the Health Law Group at Schnader Harrison Segal & Lewis LLP in Philadelphia, Pennsylvania. His practice includes domestic relations as well as psychological issues that arise in other matters. Particular areas of concentration include civil competency, child custody, and mental health matters. Dr. Anderer received his Ph.D. in Clinical Psychology from MCP Hahnemann University. He received his B.A. degree from Yale University, and his J.D. from Villanova University School of Law. His writings include a monograph entitled Determining Competency in Guardianship Proceedings that he wrote for the American Bar Association and a book he co-authored for the American Psychological Association entitled LAW FOR MENTAL HEALTH PROFESSIONALS—Pennsylvania.

Susan Daicoff is an Associate Professor of Law at Florida Coastal School of Law in Jacksonville, Florida. She has taught contracts, jurisprudence, law and psychology, corporate taxation, partnership taxation, the taxation of mergers and acquisitions, and commercial law. She received her J.D. from the University of Florida, her LL.M. from New York University, and her M.S. in clinical psychology from the University of Central Florida. Since 1995, she has been researching and writing in the areas of the psychology of lawyers, lawyer personality, lawyer distress and dissatisfaction, the legal profession, professionalism, and ethical decision-making by lawyers. She is also the immediate past chair of the Law and Mental Disability Section of the Association of American Law Schools.

Edward A. Dauer is Dean Emeritus and Professor of law at the University of Denver, where his teaching and research concentrate on questions of legal risk management-principally, alternative dispute resolution and preventive law. He was a co-founder and for ten years the President of the National Center for Preventive Law. Dauer holds degrees from Brown University and the Yale Law School, where he served as Associate Professor and Associate Dean for a decade before becoming Dean at Denver.

David J. Glass is a member of the Family Law Department and the Health Law Group at Schnader Harrison Segal & Lewis LLP in Philadelphia, Pennsylvania. His practice includes all aspects of domestic relations litigation and appeals. Particular areas of concentration include child custody, the mental health aspects of divorce, and the use of psychological expert testimony in general litigation. Dr. Glass received his Ph.D. in Clinical Psychology from MCP Hahnenmann University. He received his B.A. in psychology from the University of Pennsylvania and his law degree from Villanova University School of Law. His dissertation on the effectiveness of legal coercion to drug treatment won first place in the 1997 National Dissertation Competition sponsored by the American Psychology-Law Society (APA Division 41).

Monica Kirkpatrick Johnson is a Post-Doctoral Fellow in the Carolina Population Center at the University of North Carolina-Chapel Hill. She received her Ph.D. in Sociology at the University of Minnesota in 1999. Her recent publications appear in WORK AND FAMILY: RESEARCH INFORMING POLICY (edited by Toby Parcel and Daniel B. Cornfield), *Social Psychology Quarterly*, and in the *Journal of Research on Adolescence*.

Kathryn E. Maxwell received her B.A. from Christopher Newport University in 1984, her M.Ed. from the University of Arizona in 1986, and her J.D. from the University of Arizona College of Law in 1998. She is currently engaged in the practice of law, including general litigation and family law, in Arizona.

Linda G. Mills is an Associate Professor at the New York University Ehrenkranz School of Social Work and Affiliated Professor at the New York University School of Law. Dr. Mills holds a J.D. from the University of California, Hastings College of the Law and a Ph.D. in Social Welfare from Brandeis University. Dr. Mills founded The Hawkins Center of Law and Services for People with Disabilities in 1986 located in Richmond, California. She currently serves on the Board of Directors. Recent publications include, *The Heart of Intimate Abuse: New Interventions in Child Welfare, Criminal Justice and Health Settings* (Springer Publishing, 1998); *A Penchant for Prejudice: Unraveling Bias in Judicial Decision Making* (Michigan University Press, 1999); and "Killing Her Softly: Intimate Abuse and the Violence of State Interventions" (*Harvard Law Review*, 1999).

Marc W. Patry is a graduate student in the Law/Psychology Program at the University of Nebraska-Lincoln. His program of study will culminate in a doctoral degree in Social Psychology and a Master of Legal Studies degree. He received his undergraduate degree in Psychology, Concentration in Forensic Psychology, from Castleton State College, Castleton, Vermont, in 1997.

Jennifer K. Robbennolt is an Associate Professor of Law at the University of Missouri School of Law. She received both her J.D. and her Ph.D. in Social Psychology from the University of Nebraska-Lincoln. She has served as a law clerk to the Honorable John M. Gerrard of the Nebraska Supreme Court and as a post-doctoral research associate and lecturer at the Woodrow Wilson School of Public and International Affairs and Department of Psychology at Princeton University. Her recent publications appear in *Law and Human Behavior, Behavioral Sciences and the Law*, the *Journal of Social Issues*, and THE HANDBOOK OF FORENSIC PSYCHOLOGY (edited by Allen K. Hess and Irving B. Weiner).

Marjorie A. Silver is Professor of Law at Touro College Law Center in Huntington, New York, where she regularly teaches Civil Procedure and Professional Responsibility. In recent years her research and writing interests have focused on the importance of emotional competence for lawyering and legal education. She is an active member of the Association of the Bar of the City of New York, and former chair of its Committee on Sex and Law. Professor Silver served as the Chief Regional Civil Rights Attorney for the United States Department of Education before entering law teaching in 1983. She holds degrees from Brandeis University and the University of Pennsylvania Law School.

Pauline H. Tesler is a partner in the San Francisco/Marin County law firm of Tesler, Sandmann and Fishman, certified as a specialist in family law by the California State Bar Board of Legal Specialization since 1984, and a fellow of the American Academy of Matrimonial Lawyers. After a vigorous career as a litigator and appellate advocate, in the mid-1990s Ms. Tesler became a pioneer in developing and extending the practice of collaborative law. Since 1996 she has limited her practice to collaborative representation. In addition to speaking widely and writing about collaborative law, Ms. Tesler trains lawyers (as well as mental health and financial professionals) in how to become skilled collaborative practitioners, and provides mentoring, coaching, and case consultation to lawyers who are learning how to practice collaboratively. She is presently completing a training manual for collaborative lawyers to be published by the American Bar Association in 2001. Ms. Tesler received her B.A. degree from Harvard University, her M.A. from the Victoria University of Manchester, England, and her J.D. from the University of Wisconsin Law School.

Alan J. Tomkins serves as Director of the University of Nebraska Public Policy Center, professor in the University of Nebraska-Lincoln's Law/Psychology Program, and Editor of the journal, *Behavioral Sciences and the Law*. He received his J.D. in 1984 from Washington University and his Ph.D. in social psychology the same year from the same institution. Since July 1996, Professor Tomkins has administered a training grant ("Training in Mental Health And Justice Systems Research") that encourages the use of therapeutic jurisprudence to guide research and analyses of mental health/justice systems interactions. Professor Tomkins is a fellow of the American Psychology-Law Society, Division 41 of the American Psychological Association.

About The Editors

Dennis P. Stolle is an attorney with the Litigation Department of Barnes & Thornburg in Indianapolis, Indiana. His practice is concentrated on commercial litigation, contractual disputes, and trade secrets litigation, with a special concentration on empirical issues related to jury decision-making. He received his law degree from the University of Nebraska, where he served as Research Editor of the *Nebraska Law Review* and where he became a member of the Order of the Coif. He currently serves on the board of directors of the Indianapolis Art Center and is a member of the Indiana State Bar Association, the American Psychology-Law Society, and the American Society of Trial Consultants. He is admitted to practice law in the states of Nebraska and Indiana and in the U.S. District Courts for the Northern and Southern Districts of Indiana. Following law school, he served as an instructor of legal research and writing at the University of Nebraska College of Law. He received his Ph.D. in Social Psychology from the University of Nebraska. His doctoral dissertation research was supported by a grant from the National Science Foundation, was supervised by Dr. Steven Penrod, and focused on the effects and effectiveness of plain language contract drafting. He has been a recipient of the Franklin & Orinda M. Johnson Fellowship, the Frank & Marie Wheeler Fellowship, and a National Institute of Mental Health Traineeship. He received his B.S. in psychology *summa cum laude* from Saint Louis University. His other writings include numerous articles published in law reviews and peer-reviewed interdisciplinary journals.

David B. Wexler is Professor of Law and Director of the International Network on Therapeutic Jurisprudence at the University of Puerto Rico in San Juan, Puerto Rico and John D. Lyons Professor of Law and Professor of Psychology at the University of Arizona in Tucson, Arizona. His other books include LAW IN A THERAPEUTIC KEY: DEVELOPMENTS IN THERAPEUTIC JURISPRUDENCE (with Bruce J. Winick, Carolina Academic Press, 1996), ESSAYS IN THERAPEUTIC JURISPRUDENCE (with Bruce J. Winick, Carolina Academic Press, 1991), THERAPEUTIC JURISPRUDENCE: THE LAW AS A THERAPEUTIC AGENT (Carolina Academic Press, 1990), and MENTAL HEALTH LAW: MAJOR ISSUES (Plenum Press, 1981). He received the American Psychiatric Association's Manfred S. Guttmacher Forensic Psychiatry Award; received the National Center for State Courts Distinguished

Service Award; chaired the American Bar Association's Commission on Mental Disability and the Law; chaired the Association of American Law Schools Section on Law and Mental Disability; chaired the Advisory Board of the National Center for State Courts' Institute on Mental Disability and Law; was a member of the Panel on Legal Issues of the President's Commission on Mental Health; was a member of the National Commission on the Insanity Defense; served as Vice President of the International Academy of Law and Mental Health; received the New York University School of Law Distinguished Alumnus Legal Scholarship/Teaching Award; and served as a member of the MacArthur Foundation Research Network on Mental Health and the Law.

Bruce J. Winick is Professor of Law at the University of Miami School of Law in Coral Gables, FL, where he has taught since 1974. He is the author, co- author, and co-editor of numerous books, including THE ESSENTIALS OF FLORIDA MENTAL HEALTH LAW (WWNorton, 2000) (with Stephen Behnke and Alina Perez), THE RIGHT TO REFUSE MENTAL HEALTH TREATMENT (American Psychological Association Books, 1997), THERAPEUTIC JURISPRUDENCE APPLIED: ESSAYS ON MENTAL HEALTH LAW (Carolina Academic Press, 1997), LAW IN A THERAPEUTIC KEY: DEVELOPMENTS IN THERAPEUTIC JURISPRUDENCE (Carolina Academic Press, 1996) (with David Wexler), and ESSAYS IN THERAPEUTIC JURISPRUDENCE (Carolina Academic Press, 1991) (with David Wexler). He also is a frequent contributor to law reviews and interdisciplinary law journals. Winick is co-editor of the American Psychological Association Press book series, *Law, and Public Policy: Psychology, and the Social Sciences*. He is legal advisor and member of the board of editors of *Psychology, Public Policy & Law*, serves on the editorial board of *Law & Human Behavior*, and is a reviewer for numerous interdisciplinary law journals. He has served as legal consultant to the American Psychiatric Association Task Force on Consent to Voluntary Hospitalization, and has chaired the Association of American Law Schools Section on Law and Medicine. Winick has received numerous awards, including the Thurgood Marshall Award of the Association of the Bar of the City of New York and the Human Rights Award of the American Immigration Lawyers Association. Prior to joining the faculty of the University of Miami, he served as New York City's Director of Court Mental Health Services and as General Counsel of the New York City Department of Mental Health and Mental Retardation Services. He received his law degree from the New York University School of Law.

Index

Active Listening Response, 340-341
ADA, Confidentiality, 34, 55, 58, 72-73, 78-79, 130, 295, 319
Advance Directive, 16, 19-20, 51-52, 57, 95, 97-98, 101-102, 104-112, 125, 250, 285, 311, 327-330, 333-336, 342-345, 347-348, 370, 475
Affective Lawyering, 30, 252, 319, 336-337, 353, 362, 395, 397, 419-423, 425-427, 429, 431-435, 437, 439, 441, 443, 445-446, 467
AIDS Dementia Complex, 87, 91, 98, 100
Alternative Dispute Resolution, 60, 62, 213, 219-220, 224, 227, 230, 252, 317, 337, 398, 452, 463, 467, 486
American Academy of Matrimonial Lawyers, 174, 176, 199
American Bar Association, 176, 199, 352, 378, 392, 412, 465-466, 482
American Institute of Collaborative Professionals, 199
American Psychological Association, 199, 355, 365, 465
Association of Family and Conciliation Courts, 199
Appeals, 178, 194, 212-213, 232, 260-262, 412, 424
Arbitration, 8, 174, 185, 193, 213, 224, 317, 472, 486-488

Bankruptcy, 48, 52, 59-61
Behavioral Contracting, 280-281
Behavioral Patterns, 242
Believing Game, 189, 451, 454-458, 472
Best Interest of the Child Standard, 168-169

Boundary Violations, 366, 373-374, 376, 409, 411
Business Planning Law, 10, 21-22, 28, 30-31, 33, 85, 92-93, 132
Bypassing, 335, 427

Central Route Persuasion, 290, 292, 343
Checklist, 22, 40-42, 180, 182-184
Children, 9, 11, 15-16, 21-22, 24, 35, 50-51, 53, 61, 67, 72, 75-77, 93, 95, 99, 120-121, 133, 135, 138-139, 145, 155, 161-174, 176-184, 188-194, 198, 208, 210-211, 213, 215, 219, 221, 224-230, 232, 234, 264, 285, 396, 403, 437-439, 442, 444-445, 462, 475
Client-Centered Approach, 6, 20, 23, 41, 52, 60, 70, 90, 94, 110, 179, 286-287, 302-304, 346, 350, 370, 420
Client-Centered Counseling, 469
Coaching, 289, 314
Coercion, 226, 278, 285, 287-289, 291, 304, 320-321, 346, 350-353, 355, 368
Cognitive Behavioral, 242, 247, 291, 482
Cognitive Self Change, 238-239, 242
Collaborative Divorce, 192, 196, 199, 205, 230, 317, 471-472, 479
Collaborative Law, 187, 189, 191, 193, 195, 197, 199, 201-205, 317, 466, 472-473, 479-481, 483, 487
Committed Partners, 113-135, 137, 139, 141, 143-153, 155, 157, 159
Community Conference, 240
Compliance Audit, 281-282
Compliance Program, 275-281

Conditional Release, 89, 240-242, 280, 456

Confrontation, 60, 191, 335-336, 451, 460

Consultation, 11, 15, 20, 26, 50, 58, 89, 111, 148-149, 209, 212, 219-221, 233, 322, 375, 401, 416

Contingency Management, 280

Continuing Legal Education, 36, 110, 276, 283, 298, 324, 339, 348, 411, 415-416, 455

Corporate, 22-24, 28, 33, 85, 93, 113, 127, 132, 271-273, 277-279, 292, 422

Corporations, 42, 126, 249, 251, 271-275, 281, 283-284, 291

Counseling, 11, 20, 23-26, 30-33, 36-48, 62, 69-71, 73, 75, 77, 79, 87-89, 91-95, 110-111, 125, 127, 131-132, 150, 153, 179, 185, 193, 210, 214-216, 218-220, 225-226, 230, 232, 237, 247, 252-253, 260, 269, 271, 280, 283-286, 288, 291-294, 296-298, 302-303, 305, 311-312, 328, 336, 339-340, 345-351, 353, 358, 362, 366, 370, 373, 375-377, 382, 386-390, 393, 395-399, 401, 409-411, 414, 416, 462, 469, 475, 487-488

Counter-transference, 192, 294-296, 363-365, 371-372

Counseling, 11, 20, 23-26, 30-33, 36-48, 62, 69-71, 73, 75, 77, 79, 87-89, 91-95, 110-111, 125, 127, 131-132, 150, 153, 179, 185, 193, 210, 214-216, 218-220, 225-226, 230, 232, 237, 247, 252-253, 260, 269, 271, 280, 283-286, 288, 291-294, 296-298, 302-303, 305, 311-312, 328, 336, 339-340, 345-351, 353, 358, 362, 366, 370, 373, 375-377, 382, 386-390, 393, 395-399, 401, 409-411, 414, 416, 462, 469, 475, 487-488

Creative Hyperspace, 202

Creative Problem Solving, 396-397, 449, 463, 471, 473-474, 481-482, 488-490

Credibility Heuristic Principles, 292, 344

Critique, 8, 190, 194, 201, 358, 383, 411, 449-451, 453-455, 457, 459, 461, 463-465

Cross-cultural, 419, 432, 446

Custody Evaluation, 212, 227

Death, 12-13, 15, 19, 51, 57, 60, 75, 87, 95-96, 100, 107, 120-121, 128, 133, 138-141, 144-148, 152, 155, 190, 194, 312, 328-329, 332-334, 340-345, 350, 352-354, 403-404, 435, 476

Deferred Sentencing, 240, 251, 266-267, 284, 291

Denial, 84, 87, 250, 282-283, 285-286, 296, 311, 318-319, 327, 329-337, 339-343, 345, 347-351, 353-355, 370, 379, 398, 475-476

Detachment, 167-168, 421, 426, 428, 437

Developmental Model, 209, 212, 214

Diagnosis, 27, 91, 98-99, 331, 394

Dignity, 193, 222, 289, 320, 346, 466, 477, 480

Distraction, 177, 314, 335

Divorce, 21-22, 35, 38-39, 53, 61, 67, 93, 114-116, 126, 146-147, 161-184, 188, 190-194, 196-200, 203, 205, 209, 211-212, 216-219, 222, 224, 226-227, 230-231, 317-318, 336, 363, 367-368, 376, 389, 403, 416, 471-472, 475-476, 479, 481, 485

Domestic Partner, 19, 124, 126-127, 143, 160

Domestic Violence Courts, 467, 472-473, 483

Don't Ask, Don't Tell, 54, 58-59, 62-63

Drug Court, 237, 259, 297, 299, 303-304, 462, 467, 483

Ecology of Human Development, 177

Effective Parenting, 164, 166, 179, 181

Elder Law, 5, 9-11, 18, 20-21, 30-31, 35, 46, 70, 85-86, 92, 130, 132, 250, 354, 403, 462, 475

Empathy, 32, 221, 266, 283, 294-295, 319, 337-342, 350-354, 358, 363,

370-371, 381, 402-404, 409, 427, 436-437

Empirical, 26, 31, 34, 37-41, 44, 62-63, 66, 69, 85-89, 92, 108, 110-114, 122, 133, 162, 189, 226-227, 232-233, 238, 252, 296-297, 312, 320, 349, 353, 380, 395, 445, 454-455, 457, 462, 465-466, 477, 483, 489, 491

Employment Benefits, 113, 126-127

Emotional Subtext, 426, 434, 439-441, 443-444

Enforcement, 209, 211-212, 214, 230, 232, 273, 363

Estate Planning, 11, 18, 28, 43, 83, 85, 123, 133, 135, 141, 147, 149-153, 345, 348, 359, 471

Ethics, 125, 176, 178, 190, 195, 199, 266, 304, 345, 354, 363, 365, 367, 369, 378, 382-383, 412, 414-416, 424, 438, 465, 469

Express Agreements, 117, 119

Facilitative Mediation, 466, 478-479, 484, 487-488

Family Breakdown, 191

Family Law, 8, 10, 21-22, 43, 61, 122, 132, 146-147, 162-164, 166-167, 170-171, 176-177, 187-188, 190, 193-200, 204, 207-211, 213-215, 217, 219, 221-223, 225, 227-234, 317, 368, 466, 472, 479

Family Reconciliation, 19-20, 52, 61, 110

Formalist Tradition, 426, 428

Future Disability, 13-14, 51, 57

Gladiator Model, 189

Health Care, 11, 13, 16, 18-19, 35, 38-39, 83, 89, 91, 97, 101-107, 109, 112-114, 116, 123-126, 128, 132-133, 138, 142-144, 146, 148, 150-153, 158-159, 197, 241, 279-280, 285, 327, 329, 343, 347, 393, 456

Heuristic Principles, 292, 344

HIV/AIDS law, 10, 18, 20-21, 30-31, 51, 61, 70, 72, 75, 83-84, 91, 101, 125, 132, 151, 354, 475

Holistic Law, 397, 463, 466, 471, 473, 480, 483-484, 489-490

Human Relations, 297, 347, 385-387, 389, 409-410, 412, 414, 416

Hybrid Directives, 95, 97, 102

Imbalance of Power, 161, 359-360, 364, 402, 479

Implied Contracts, 117-118

Impulsivity, 238

Incarceration, 243, 247, 264-265, 268, 359

Incompetence Labeling, 53, 57

Incompetency, 29, 53-54, 57-58, 288, 304, 329-330, 354

Instability, 163-164, 167, 179, 181-182, 218

Integration, 5, 9-10, 24, 28, 30-32, 43-44, 46, 55, 70, 131-132, 208, 283, 349, 414, 456, 462, 467, 473, 475, 477

Integrity, 193, 203-204, 210, 228, 246, 460, 480

Interdisciplinary, 7-9, 22, 32, 36, 39, 41, 45, 48, 65, 85, 92, 129, 132, 177, 191, 199, 251, 297, 311, 324, 349, 420, 423, 453-454, 470, 481, 490

Interest-based Bargaining, 200

Interparental Conflict, 164-166, 173, 179, 181, 183

Interpretation, 37, 57, 335-336, 358, 372, 405, 427-428, 437, 458, 486

Intestate Succession, 120-121, 140

Interventions, 47-48, 99, 125, 210-211, 213, 215-218, 227, 238-239, 252, 330, 342, 391, 421

Interviewing, 42, 62, 70-71, 151, 253, 286, 293-294, 299, 311, 336, 339, 348, 350, 358, 362, 370, 373, 375-377, 382, 386-387, 389-390, 399-401, 409-411, 413-414

Issues, 5, 13-14, 17-20, 30-31, 34-35, 38-39, 47, 49, 56-57, 60, 67, 69-70, 79, 83-85, 95, 97-98, 104, 110-111, 113-116, 132-133, 138, 144-146, 151-152, 163, 177, 182-183, 188, 190, 192-193, 195-196, 200-202, 211, 214, 216, 219-225, 230, 232-

234, 237, 247, 252-254, 268, 270, 278-279, 282, 285, 288, 296, 301, 303, 310, 313, 318-320, 324, 329-330, 332, 334, 336, 342-343, 345, 347-348, 360, 364, 366-367, 371, 374, 388, 391-392, 394, 398, 403-404, 410, 413-414, 416, 420, 427, 430-432, 435, 438-439, 441-443, 446, 450-451, 453, 459, 462, 469, 478-479, 481, 485, 489

Joint Custody, 139, 163, 168-174, 179, 182, 184, 221

Law Reform, 8, 24, 37, 45, 70, 132, 251, 311, 452, 459, 461-462, 471-472
Law School, 9, 33, 40-43, 62-63, 65-66, 71, 95, 189, 191, 195, 251, 324, 336, 339, 348, 377, 380-386, 388, 395-396, 398, 408-415, 417, 423, 430-432, 436, 446, 455, 463, 467, 473-474, 482, 489-490
Legal Check-ups, 6, 17, 23, 131-132, 149, 153, 233, 328
Legal Realists, 385
Legal Registration, 126-127, 130, 132, 143, 149
Legal Therapy Counseling, 230, 382
Life Insurance, 18, 83, 123, 127, 132-133, 141, 157, 185
Like-minded Clients, 21-22, 53, 67, 178
Liking Heuristic Principles, 292, 344
Living Will, 96-97, 125, 139, 179

Marriage Counseling, 210, 214, 218-219
Mediation, 95, 146, 161-162, 168, 172-174, 179, 182, 185, 191, 194, 201, 203, 213, 218, 224-225, 243, 317, 398, 411, 452, 461, 463, 466, 468, 470-471, 473, 476, 478-480, 484-485, 487-488
Mental Health, 7-8, 11-12, 19, 24-25, 29-30, 33, 38, 44-45, 49, 53, 62, 70, 83, 85-87, 89, 91-93, 95, 97-99, 101-109, 111-112, 125, 129, 168, 190, 195, 199, 201, 210-211, 214, 216-217, 220, 223, 225-227, 233-234,

240, 245, 250-252, 278, 285, 288, 299, 302, 304, 316, 320-321, 327-328, 334, 337, 346-347, 349, 353-355, 360, 376, 386, 391-394, 398, 409, 449, 453-456, 458, 461, 467, 472, 475, 483, 485
Mental Health Care Directives, 101, 112, 125
Mental Health Court, 214, 225, 299
Mental Health Law, 8, 24-25, 29-30, 45, 53, 70, 83, 85-86, 95, 101, 109, 125, 129, 190, 195, 210-211, 251-252, 288, 302, 304, 316, 320-321, 346, 353-355, 376, 386, 398, 449, 453-456, 458, 472, 475
Minimization, 276, 281, 318
Modification, 49, 55, 62, 209, 211-212, 214, 230, 232
Moral, 92, 193, 195-196, 360, 383, 385, 392, 396, 420, 459, 469, 481, 489-490

Negative Emotion, 197
Negotiation, 10, 41, 146, 172-175, 179, 200, 203, 212, 316-317, 342, 374, 377, 390-391, 398, 410-411, 413, 415, 477, 486-488

Oppression, 419, 432, 435
Organizational Sentencing Guidelines, 273, 276, 280-281
Over-litigate, 189

Participate, 25, 43, 124, 128, 171, 173, 182, 184, 203, 213, 215, 310, 322, 409, 477
Passive Listening Response, 340
Paternalistic, 8, 234, 285, 287, 295, 305
Persuasion Theory, 290, 323, 343, 353
Plea-bargaining, 316
Positional Bargaining, 200
Post-offense Rehabilitation, 247-248, 251, 254, 258, 260-263, 267, 269, 271, 284, 290
Power of Attorney, 34, 97, 107, 125-127, 139, 148
Preventive Interventions, 210-211, 213, 215-217, 227

Problem-solving, 202-204, 208, 220-221, 238-239, 247, 299, 397-398, 449, 451-452, 485
Problem-solving Approach, 220-221
Procedural Justice, 108, 173, 231-232, 241, 320-322, 466, 473, 477-478, 488-489
Preventive Medicine, 6, 52, 67, 252, 279, 328, 351
Prison, 238-239, 243, 245, 247, 265, 267, 432, 456
Probation, 226, 237, 239-243, 245, 247, 249, 255, 259, 264-265, 268, 274-275, 280, 284, 292, 297, 299, 302, 456, 476
Problem-solving Skills, 204, 238-239, 398, 451
Property Division, 116-118, 138, 147, 155, 177, 209, 211-212
Proxy Directives, 95-97, 106
Psychojudicial Soft Spots, 64-66
Psycholegal Soft Spot, 35, 37, 48-49, 59-61, 66, 72, 93, 222, 250, 253, 311, 327, 330, 347, 475
Psychology of Choice, 38, 346

Rationality, 223, 380
Rationalization, 318, 400
Reassurance, 226, 322, 335, 443
Reciprocal Beneficiaries, 127-128, 132-133
Rehabilitation, 64, 237-240, 243, 245-251, 253-254, 258-271, 280, 283-284, 287, 289-292, 294-295, 297-298, 300-302, 305, 456
Relapse Prevention, 237-243, 246-247, 249, 253, 278, 280, 284, 291-292, 300-301, 472
Relational Lawyering, 252, 336, 354, 434
Relational Structure, 434
Restorative Justice, 65, 240, 397, 463-464, 466, 470, 473, 476-477, 487-488
Retooling, 201
Rewind Technique, 65, 71, 73, 75, 77, 79, 292
Role-play, 41, 314

Self-actualization, 287, 346, 375
Self-awareness, 358, 375, 379, 389, 398, 406, 408-409
Sentencing, 46, 164, 240, 245, 247-251, 253-260, 262-271, 273, 275-276, 280-284, 288-292, 296-302, 304-305, 472, 476
Sentencing Guidelines, 248-251, 254-260, 263-264, 268-271, 273, 276, 280-284, 292, 299
Sentencing Reform Act 1984, 255
Settlement, 35, 90, 146, 172, 174, 179, 194, 199-201, 203-204, 212-213, 225, 227-228, 230, 316-320, 322, 413, 479-481, 489
Sexual Relationships, 163, 360, 364-369, 372, 402
Specialized Courts, 299, 467, 472-473, 483-484, 487
Stipulation, 202-203, 229
STOP (Straight Thinking on Probation), 199, 239, 285, 296, 335, 340, 420, 439-440, 442
Stress, 16, 24, 30, 35, 51-52, 59-61, 145, 163, 166, 169, 172, 183, 189, 204, 298, 311-316, 322, 324, 329-331, 334, 347, 381, 383, 394, 416
Surrogate Decision Maker, 52, 97, 106-107, 110, 123-125, 142-143
Synthesis, 5, 9, 46, 70, 86, 92, 114, 130-131, 246, 250, 354, 462, 467, 475, 491

Tax Preparation, 52, 58-59
Teaching, 26, 31, 40-41, 57, 63, 65, 71, 189, 192, 208, 215, 218, 280, 339, 348, 381, 386-387, 390, 395, 409, 414, 423, 428, 431, 450, 478, 482, 490
Termination of Relationship, 116, 138, 144-146, 363
Therapeutic Concerns, 11-14, 28, 33, 49, 93-94, 426, 454, 471, 491
Therapeutic Moment, 66
Therapy, 18, 20, 52, 83, 99-100, 103-104, 107, 111, 208, 214-216, 220, 226, 230, 233, 238, 242, 258-259, 269, 287, 301, 331, 336, 338, 346,

353, 358, 372-373, 382, 393-394, 401-402, 407-409, 419, 439, 457
Transference, 192, 196, 294-295, 339, 349, 351, 360-364, 366, 370-374, 376-377, 386-390, 399, 402-403, 409, 413, 415-416, 431-432, 435, 437-438, 446, 480
Transformative Mediation, 466, 468, 471, 479, 487
Tripartite Crisis, 465-466, 469

Uniform Laws Annotated Health Care Decisions Act of 1993, 97, 102
United States Sentencing Guidelines, 248-251, 255, 258, 264, 268, 273

University of California, Judith Wallerstein Center for the Family In Transition, 194, 199

Venn Diagram, 9, 94

White Collar Crime, 271
Will Contest, 64-66, 72-74, 179
Wills, 16, 19, 43, 49, 74, 83, 91, 95-97, 105, 120, 122-123, 132-133, 136, 139-141, 144, 147-152, 156, 327, 347, 487
Written Agreements, 135-138, 144, 146-147, 150, 154-155